CLOSE OF PLAY
President, Prince, and Cricket

CLOSE OF PLAY
President, Prince, and Cricket

WILLIAM H. WALCOTT

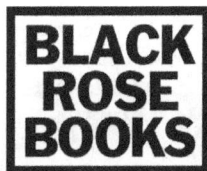

BLACK ROSE BOOKS

Montréal/Chicago/London

Black Rose Books No. TT403

Library and Archives Canada Cataloguing in Publication

Title: Close of play : president, prince, and cricket / William H. Walcott.
Names: Walcott, William Henry, author.
Identifiers: Canadiana (print) 20190080450 | Canadiana (ebook) 20190081481 | ISBN 9781551647142 (hardcover) | ISBN 9781551647166 (softcover) | ISBN 9781551647180 (PDF)
Subjects: LCSH: Obama, Barack—Language. | LCSH: Lara, Brian, 1969-—Language. | LCSH: Cricket—Terminology. | LCSH: Cricket—Social aspects. | LCSH: World politics—Terminology. | LCSH: Cricket—Political aspects. | LCSH: English language—Idioms.
Classification: LCC E891.5.O332 W35 2019 | DDC 973.932—dc23

Cover design: Rodolfo Borello, Associés libres Design

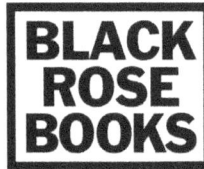

**BLACK
ROSE
BOOKS**

C.P.35788 Succ. Léo-Pariseau
Montréal, QC, H2X 0A4

Explore our books and subscribe to our newsletter:
www.blackrosebooks.com

Ordering Information

USA/INTERNATIONAL	CANADA	UK/IRELAND
University of Chicago Press Chicago Distribution Center 11030 South Langley Avenue Chicago, IL 60628	University of Toronto Press 5201 Dufferin Street Toronto, ON M3H 5T8	Central Books 50 Freshwater Road Chadwell Heath, London RM8 1RX
(800) 621-2736 (USA) (773) 702-7000 (International) orders@press.uchicago.edu	1-800-565-9523 utpbooks@utpress.utoronto.ca	+44 (0) 20 8525 8800 contactus@centralbooks.com

TABLE OF CONTENTS

President and Prince: That John Arlott glory of batsmanship
(Photo courtesy of the White House Press Office, President Obama's tenure.)

ACKNOWLEDGEMENTS

My thanks to Mr. Gregory Armstrong (Barbados Tourism Authority), who made it possible for me to converse with Sir Gary Sobers. Mr. Mark de Sousa, who took time to cover crucial Caribbean Test Matches. Mr. Guy Yearwood, who put me and Mr. de Sousa at centre stage in Antigua for some of that coverage. While Dr. Perry Mars, Professor of Political Science, Wayne State University, was lost to academia far too early, I shall forever cherish his very incisive exploration of the writing. I thank, also, Mr. Wesrick Stephen, the scientist with a cricketing intellect, as well as Mr. Isseiah Berhane and Mr. Freddie Chen, "Sir Freddie" (Humber College), for the sound advice they offered when I was wrestling with the writing in its first stages. Gratitude to Mrs. Maisie Walcott, my mother, who told me that reading textbooks is of greater value than playing cricket. Thanks, also, to THE BOYS OF VERSAILLES, whose excellence I used to give some of my first efforts at cricketing talk improvisational flare. For authoritative and inspirational leadership on a cricket field I must include captain "Blades," Mr. Birchnell Paul, a player with a very noticeable swagger well before emergence of someone known as Isaac Vivian Alexander Richards. For pristine cricketing editorial elegance befitting that Arlott ascendancy pride of place must go to Clara-Swan Kennedy of Black Rose Books.

THE BOYS OF VERSAILLES

The boys of Versailles, Basil the boldest, and Norman, the notable! They laid their pitches in yards and inches and moved their feet with jointed sticks. They played with strength of stillness and flows of flourish. These boys of Versailles, Harold, the helmsman, and Phillip, the purist. They soaked in torrents and stroked with rigour. They baked in fury and paced with power. The boys of Versailles, Joban, the guardian, Granville, the genius, and a Kentish crafty in Dover, the decisive! They paid for work in windowless frames. They priced their goods in abundant green. The boys of Versailles, Kenneth, the curler, and Churu, the candid. They lived with bat to ball and guava and coconut to boot. They soared on highs. The boys of Versailles, Ivan, the eagle, Inder, the emperor, and Michael, the master! They loved to hear this game, these boys of Versailles.

PREMATCH
FOREWORD
Dr. Perry Mars

The central theme of the book relates to the very important notion of communal identity, which is one of the major intellectual challenges of a generation of Caribbean academics since Caribbean states gained political independence in the 1960s. The crafting, nurturing, and cultivation of West Indian identity is critical to the development of a self-understanding that is so necessary for the realization of national advancement and crucial social change. Much of this self understanding must take our colonial past into consideration. Thus much controversy surrounds whether West Indian postcolonial identity is necessarily and at the same time an anti-colonial identity. In this book William Walcott boldly confronts this controversy by declaring West Indian assertiveness and improvisation as exemplified in the premier game of test match cricket as being a weapon against colonialism.

I agree with his logic that what unites the middle and lower classes in the Caribbean, which together become equalized in their enthusiasm, even fanaticism for West Indian cricket, is the very nationalist spirit that defiantly fought the colonial powers in the decolonization struggles since the 1950s.

Walcott is even more daringly specific than that in his perspective that cricket is usually internalized as an instrument of social formation among an oppressed people, particularly among West Indians. He recalls Frank Worrell's brilliant captaincy performance in Australia in 1960-61 as a source of togetherness and pride for West Indians across the region lasting for a long time beyond the 1960s. His question is: to what extent can his favourite subject, Brian Lara, match that level of performance to evoke similar types of identity fermentations among West Indians? Put another way: how far away is Lara from approximating that quintessential Worrellian attainment in the 1960s to make him worthy of comparison with the great Frank Worrell himself? These are important provocative questions which will undoubtedly be debated for a long time, and this book will undoubtedly give important stimulus and relevant insights to feed that exciting debate.

The author further raises questions about the disjunction between Lara's excellent/brilliant batting performances (some say "genius") and his abject failures in the captaincy dimension as bases for understanding the ebb and flow of West Indian identity development patterns over distinct periods of time. The analysis of this disjunction can inform future generations of Caribbean leaders about creative leadership styles in every field beyond cricket itself.

Generally, the real strength of the book resides in its academic as well as its social/entertainment potentialities. The author's writing style is both lucid and colourful. It projects theoretical promise in its allusions to globalization and the political-economic environment as important to the success and/or failure of WI cricket—with attendant ramifications on West Indian identity patterns. The work is comprehensive, analytical, and interdisciplinary at the same time, compared to the more descriptive, anecdotal, and literary works before it in this field. Very imaginatively, also, the author uses cricket to enhance our understanding of the relationship between talent, genius, and greatness in individual leadership qualities in contexts of social disadvantage and struggles against serious or overwhelming odds. Political leaders can learn a lot from cricket in this respect. His insights into the relationship between leadership and community are equally profound, particularly in explaining failed leadership and community disappointment.

One must also commend the uniqueness of the book's potential contribution to social science, particularly its multidisciplinary dimension. The analogy the author makes of the dexterity of cricket with the improvisation of jazz music is very intriguing, to say the least. Based also on a peculiar but interesting ethno-methodological approach, a skilful attempt is made here to weave Caribbean folk wisdom with individual commentary gleaned from personal interviews with the most accomplished of test cricketers. And William Walcott possesses the background qualifications and capabilities to successfully accomplish the task at hand. His recommendation for the establishment of an Institute of Caribbean Cricket as necessary for the development of West Indian togetherness and identity is very forward looking and relevant, since sport and cultural development are most appropriate sources for the development of wider group loyalties and identities.

The work is comprehensive enough to appeal to a wide-ranging audience, both academic and popular. Sports enthusiasts in particular will find this book fascinating. Cricket itself has a ready-made audience throughout the British Commonwealth of nations, inclusive of England, Australia, India, Pakistan, Zimbabwe, South Africa, Sri Lanka, New Zealand, and other places. Additionally, the book compares well with some of the best before it. Of course, C.L.R. James' *Beyond a Boundary* is a classic which all contenders to such excellence can only hope to emulate or approximate, and Walcott's is among those in close approximation to this level of excellence. It is, indeed, a worthy and entertaining contribution to the field and theme.

Dr. Perry Mars
Professor, Political Science
Wayne State University

1st INNINGS
INTRODUCTION:
BEYOND THE
MESOPOTAMIAN MIRAGE

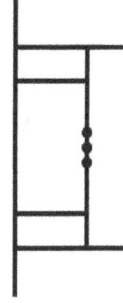

In this piece of work about the game, the sporting life, cricket, and the fiercely competitive field, American politics, which I juxtapose, I want to focus on the leadership of two figures of enormous prominence within the United States and West Indies, two figures I locate squarely upon sticky wickets. The figures are Caribbean cricket captain, Brian Charles Lara, and United States President, Barack Hussein Obama, the politician who once resorted to fulsome figurative foray for the purpose of alluding to the claim that consistency is the hobgoblin of narrow minds. The second is universally acknowledged to be a great orator, while the first is addressed adoringly and cynically, sometimes, as the "Prince of Port-of-Spain," Trinidad. While the bulk and core of the writing will be centred on Brian Lara, I shall not lose sight of the Obama significance, as well as the great importance of situating the two luminaries within the breadth of cricketing, socio-economic, and socio-political contexts.

For all who wonder about placing Brian Charles Lara alongside Barack Hussein Obama, let me meet a significant requirement to justify doing so. Through a juxtaposing of the Lara presence with that of Obama's, I can do three things: (a) build a platform on which some readers—tangentially familiar with cricket, but profoundly knowledgeable about economics, politics, and sociology—can stand to build on tangential awareness by looking at how socio-political issues are interwoven with Brian Lara's links to the game; (b) construct a foundation on which those deeply knowledgeable about cricket but only peripherally aware of economic, sociological, and political issues are given opportunities for enhancing their understanding of these matters through a focus on Brian Lara's connections to the game; (c) set up a link between platform and foundation which is, centrally, made up of leadership issues for Brian Lara. There are, of course, those who are profoundly knowledgeable about sociology, economics, politics, and cricket. Their possession should enable them to connect platform and foundation with enormous advantage. I am afraid, however, that I am not in a position to make any contribution to those who are deeply unfamiliar with either cricket, sociology, politics, and economic issues.

Be that as it may, I would be the very first person to wrestle with the question: while it is, in principle, reasonable to erect platforms and foundations for the purpose of addressing oneself to significant issues, why use the West Indian, Brian Lara, as my platform? Before replying it is important for me to provide some meaningful sense about the idea, leadership. I do so by inviting readers to examine the presence of: President Nelson Mandela, Dr. Martin Luther King, Ms. Rosa Parks, the Christian martyr Blandina, the Roman general Gnaeus Pompeius Magnus Africanus, and Roman political figure, Dictator Perpetuo, and military strategist Gaius Julius Caesar. The goal here is not to express preference for any particular individuals but to offer a set of contexts which could serve as templates for assessing the leadership of President Obama and Captain Lara. I start with Dr. King and Ms. Parks, both of whom are central to the non-violent civil rights movement in the USA.

Their story is simple, moving, and powerful. Both were engaged in the battle to remove the injustice of race discrimination from their society. Both were steadfast in their assertiveness, and self-sacrifice. Both were honoured by their followers with charismatic leadership. At a much later stage in the writing I shall refer to Dr. King's impact. At this point, I want to continue with two members of the first Roman triumvirate, Gaius Julius Caesar and Gnaeus Pompeius Magnus Africanus, the second of whom Berry (2006, p. 105) assesses as the greatest Roman general of the period in which he lived, who became an enemy of Caesar's and was defeated by him at Pharsalus.

It is Caesar to whom I turn first via a focus from Marcus Tullius Cicero, an eques[1] member of the Roman equestrian order that became a senator and extraordinarily superb orator. In an invective written as philippic against fraudster and thief, Marcus Antonius, after Caesar's assassination, Cicero, despite his opposition to the Dictator and support of the assassins who murdered him, offers a comparison between Antonius and Caesar only to draw some sharp contrasts. Of Caesar the orator notes his innate capabilities, strategic acumen, fine memory, literary talent, methodical disposition, as well as capacity for hard work. He added that his military attainments, although catastrophic to Rome, were significant. Caesar concentrated also upon monarchy for a lengthy period; with tremendous and risky effort he reached his objective. Through theatre, construction projects, banquets, as well as largesse, he gained the confidence of the uninformed masses, extended clemency to opponents, and rewarded his followers. In his myriad efforts, claims Cicero, he was successful in making Rome accept servitude, partly because of its passivity. Even though Caesar imposed evil upon the republic, one good emerged: Roman people learned the extent of the trust to be invested among themselves, those upon whom they can depend, and of whom they should be watchful. For Cicero, Antonius is similar only in the category of lust for power—certainly in no other category.

While assessing Caesar, British historian Fisher (1949, pp. 73-75) writes that nobody would have predicted that he, the youngest in that triumvirate, would outrange Gnaeus Pompeius Magnus Africanus in military renown and alter the face of Europe. Except for a year of military duty in Spain, well past forty, Caesar lacked experience in handling troops. Educated as an intellectual at the feet of the most capable Greek Masters[2] to become an eloquent advocate in the forum, and a judicious manager of democratic intrigues, Caesar was prominent in the Capital.

His gallantries, his lavish spectacles and entertainments, his debts were famous, and since he was the nephew of Marius and son-in-law of Cinna rumour was prompt to associate him with every dark plot to upset the Republic (Fisher, 1949, p. 74).

Adding that indicators of the realistic measure of Caesar emerged during his consulship year, Fisher notes he passed a decree to remove extortion, abolished constitutional impediments, and served notice that he would have his way in Rome. Those accomplishments could not match what Fisher describes as eight wonderful Gallic campaigns that showed for the first occasion his full range as statesman and soldier. He accomplished everything he had intended to.

Caesar, the political and military tactician, knew how to exploit every weakness. He could cajole, threaten, conciliate, as well as coerce. No one, claims Fisher, can apprehend the sober narrative in which Caesar himself renders his Gallic campaigns without realising the scope and audacity of his conceptions, personal courage, extraordinary combination of patience and velocity, as well as the fidelity and skill with which he dispensed his duties.

> *At every extremity of Gaul he gave evidence of Roman power. He crossed the Rhine to impress the Germans, the Channel twice to overawe the Britons, and built a fleet on the lower waters of the Rhine to help the Celtic mariners of the channel to realise that Rome was mistress of the seas. Three great barbarian leaders, Ariovistus, the German, Cassivelaunus, the Briton, and Vercingetorix, the Arvenian noble who headed the last and most formidable of the Gauls, went down before him (Fisher, 1949, p. 74).*

At the time of Caesar's European success, all seemed well between him and Gnaeus Pompeius Magnus Africanus. It is the latter, according to Berry, that defeated Mithridates Eupator VI, king of Pontus, a very prickly thorn in the side of the Romans. Fisher believes that Mithridates posed a serious danger in the East to the Romans. Just who was Mithridates? According to Fisher, a Philhellenic barbarian, he was an oriental of remarkable force and huge ambition that saw himself as leader and patron of the Hellenic world, passionate to liberate itself from Roman oppression. His territory was attacked by Nicomedes of Bithynia, a client of Rome's. Since no justice came his way, he declared war against Rome. Although defeated by a very experienced campaigner, Lucius Cornelius Sulla, Mithridates was undaunted. The Romans decided to deal with him once and for all, and this is a task that seemed suitable to none other than Gnaeus Pompeius Magnus Africanus.

Berry provides his readers with an entire English translation of the panegyric/epideictic/deliberative oratory, *De Imperio Cn. Pompei (On the Command Of Gnaeus Pompeius)*, delivered on the general's behalf to the Roman Senate by Marcus Tullius Cicero, the greatest orator of the ancient world (Berry 2006, p. xi). Cicero states that there are four qualities a great commander must possess: military know-how, luck, authority, and ability. Waxing eloquent about ability, the orator asks rhetorically: what speech could do justice to it?

Adding that the qualities of a great general are made up not merely of dedication to duty, courage in danger, thoroughness in undertaking tasks, speed in accomplishment, foresight in planning, but these very features are more evident also in Pompeius Magnus Africanus than all other commanders put together. For Cicero, Pompeius Magnus Africanus's excellence is to be located in non-military contexts such as great integrity, good faith, universal moderation, graciousness, humanity, and intellectual capability—all to the highest degree. What does Cicero state in regard to luck? Luck, heaven sent good fortune, under control of, and bestowed by the Gods, helps men of distinction such as Pompeius Magnus Africanus accomplish honour, glory, and huge success.

I have absolutely no doubt that in addressing himself to luck, Cicero is alluding to the huge significance of the spiritual, a matter about which he writes at great length in his work *The Nature Of The Gods*. Readers are, of course, free to examine this work. Here, I draw their attention to the ideas of Mr. Mandela (2012, pp. 148-149). It is his view that the impact of spiritual weapons, which can be dynamic, is not easy to apprehend. Spiritual weapons, nevertheless, make prisoners free persons, convert commoners into monarchs, and dirt into pure gold. These are ideas with a profoundly figurative ring, the sound of which is unmistakable in:

In judging our progress as individuals we tend to concentrate on external factors such as one's social position, influence and popularity, wealth and standard of education. These are, of course, important in measuring one's success in material matters and it is perfectly understandable if many people exert themselves mainly to achieve all these. But internal factors may be even more crucial in assessing our development as a human being. Honesty, sincerity, simplicity, humility, pure generosity, absence of vanity, readiness to serve others—qualities which are within easy reach of every soul—are the foundation of everyone's spiritual life (Mandela 2012, p. 149).

I take my position in this ring to offer MADIBA.

MADIBA

Shuttered scales and teething thunder break the granite gales of fitful fathoms while breathless broods on cubic quests sedate all servile soles with musket moans. Leavened loam and dripping debt seclude the chiming quarters on frigid favours while woeful wells on rustic rites caress all earthen emblems. Weighted walls and guarded gullies crave the shackled cores on martyrs' mane while talon tidings span the iron isthmus on chanting colours. Trusted tales of tiring troopers singe the Orange odes below a sunlit sky while dancer deities on gaping greed reflect each chromium charm in primal pleasure. Sinking shoals with coral clusters mark the trader tolls on tardy traffic while sabre scans from poacher purses hoard the panting plumes in charring chests. This haze on howling hues, this Cape with captor sales, this quilt in choral charm, this buoyant bliss, this band of crossing circles, must shield its trove of chieftain shamans and breed its game in verdant veldt. This stalk of sibling stripes, this silting seam, this sheltered splinter, must recharge its tidal truce. This haul of hellish hate, this pool of potent peace, this core of captive currents must refresh its freedom fabrics.

For such—Madiba—is the legacy of cruel castes on leaden lumber with timber tapers. For such—Madiba—is the legacy of bulging boots in putrid passes on severed shapes. For such—Madiba—is the legacy of syllabic séances in risky routines for fertile freedom. For such—Madiba—is the legacy of bonded boundaries from scripted sands on ghastly groans. For such—Madiba—is the legacy from blighted beacons with frontal faces in scorching states. For such—Madiba—is the legacy of Sharpville sisters from Kaffir curses on trekker tribes for Pretorius pulses. For such—Madiba—is the legacy of hefty heaping from that roving Richards on a languid legion. For such—Madiba—is the legacy of a leaping Lloyd with feline flourish who reclaimed those wholesome heights atop the Sydney stumpers. For such—Madiba—is the legacy from that Bradman broker who survived the steamy tempest of a lightning Larwood. For such—Madiba is the legacy from his surging stock, you learned through Malcolm's message, that it sheared the scorching eighties. For such—Madiba—is the legacy you have crafted that your ageless assets shall beam beyond the Rivonia ramparts and bathe the bloodless banks for soulful spirits beyond the Etosha Pan.

One of the most moving accounts of courage, steadfastness, assertiveness, and sacrifice through faith in spirituality is offered by Omrani (2017, p. 296) about a woman martyr named Blandina victimised by some of the most unspeakable cruelty by Roman conquerors in France at a Lyons amphitheatre. Describing her as the most courageous of the Christian martyrs, Omrani states that during the early phases of her horrific torture she was whipped and her body was all but torn to pieces, but with great resolve in nobility she refused to submit to the pain she was enduring. Later bound to an amphitheatre stake along with other Christians and left to be devoured by wild animals, the beasts spared her. She was taken out of the amphitheatre, but brought back to see the deadly destruction of other Christians, so that her resolve might be broken. This eventuality did not unfold, and she was, once more, removed and returned with a fifteen year old male, Ponticus, whom she told to be resolute. Ponticus did not survive his torture. Whipped yet again, she was fed once more to the animals and placed in a hot iron chair, but could not be killed. Removed from the chair, she was placed in a net and thrown to a bull that trampled, tossed, and gored her until death.

I return now to the query about using West Indies cricket captain, Brian Lara, as a platform from which observers can understand the Obama-Lara connection. I begin replying by making reference to statements from none other than Mr. Nelson Mandela (2012, pp. 112-113), who writes that sport, a crucial window for propagating fair play and justice, has the power to surmount old schisms and create bonds for common aspirations. Sport, he adds, can unite people in ways that other pursuits cannot. More powerful than governments, sport engenders hope in place of despair. It breaks down race barriers and laughs in the face of myriad forms of discrimination. Anyone who has doubts about the Mandela statements is free to examine the excellent speech Garfield St. Aubrun Sobers delivered at the Lord's Cricket Ground in summer 1970, when he captained, with extraordinary success, a multicultural world team made up of fellow West Indians, Australians Indians, Pakistanis, and South Africans against an England team. That England meeting with the world side had replaced a scheduled tour by an all-white South Africa team. It is with Mr. Mandela that I continue by noting a strong precedent for addressing myself to exploring the Obama-Lara significance.

That precedent can be found in what President Mandela did in using Rugby Union and cricket as two extremely solid foundations for working assiduously with Black, Coloured, and White South Africans, especially the Afrikaner/Boer segments of South Africa, to prevent that society from imploding. What many around the world know dramatically about setting up such a foundation is known through the film INVICTUS.

What is less well known is that, in addition to Rugby Union, cricket and everyday Afrikaner everyday life have been linked inextricably. Thus when the international sporting ban against South Africa was lifted and that society readmitted to the Commonwealth, the very first Test Cricket Match in which South Africa participated was not an encounter with Australia, New Zealand, England, or Zimbabwe. It was with the West Indies in Barbados. Just as importantly, apart from ex-West Indies Test Match opening batsman, Mr. Conrad Hunte, having been granted a long term coaching contract in post-apartheid South Africa, none other than former West Indies luminaries such as Clive Lloyd and Gary Sobers were invited to the country for the purpose of helping to resuscitate high level South African cricket. They had not travelled such distances to be on the veldt or to enjoy the ocean breezes.

They were highly reputable cricket ambassadors requested to aid in preventing what some pessimists, cynics, racists, and their sympathisers thought would be the demise of a new South Africa. Let me add that one of my principal concerns in placing captain Lara alongside President Obama is leadership, the lack thereof, and failure. I want to get also to the core of what many deem greatness, the lack thereof, and elusiveness. Just as importantly, I must deal with the obvious. That is the appearance of the President and captain Lara—cricket bats in hands—in Port-of-Spain, Trinidad (2010), when Lara demonstrated to the President how the forward defensive and cover drive playing styles in cricket should be executed.

By no means insignificant is the fact that the very first large scale, well organised, and hugely successful protest against apartheid was launched in the United Kingdom, where an all- white South Africa cricket team was supposed to tour England in the summer of 1970. All Commonwealth societies where the populace was solidly people of colour stood resolutely behind the anti-apartheid campaign spearheaded by a youthful white South African exile, Mr. Peter Hain, under a banner STOP THE SEVENTY TOUR. Among the former Dominion territories of Great Britain, Canada, Australia, and New Zealand, it was New Zealand, under a Prime Minister, Mr. David Lange, who later took explicit action banning any sporting contacts between New Zealand and apartheid South Africa.

The New Zealand decision was a major blow to Afrikaner nationalism, because all-white South Africa Rugby Union teams were always extremely eager to mount challenges to New Zealand sides, noted globally for their sporting dominance. On the heels of the impact from THE STOP THE SEVENTY TOUR also came sporting bans against South Africa by the International Olympic Committee (IOC), the All England Lawn Tennis Club for matches at Wimbledon, and the International Cricket Council (ICC). The relevance of the South Africa matters should be seen in the indubitable fact that sport, especially at the very highest of levels, is eminently a huge socio-economic issue deeply enmeshed within questions of injustice, status degradation, status ascription, domination, economic oppression, and opposites, justice, status elevation, status achievement, freedom, and economic progress.

In contemporary socio-economic life within the USA, these matters were clearly evident via highly abusive language from US President Donald Trump against American sportsmen who, rather than stand for their country's national anthem, chose to kneel on one knee, something described as 'giving the knee' or 'kneeing.' To be sure, giving the knee, a version of civil disobedience once used by Dr. Martin Luther King, is their way of drawing attention to white police brutality against young black men murdered by white police officers all across the Union. For his part, in late September 2017, Trump issued his public derogation of the action by describing the sportsmen as people disrespecting the US flag, as "sons of bitches" whom he billowed emphatically should be fired. The protest against injustice was well and truly joined across not merely American football teams, but also by some eminent basketball players such as Mr. Lebron James and Stephen Curry, the latter, a member of the 2017 and 2018 National Basketball Association (NBA) championship teams, declined an invitation from Trump to visit the White House.

Readers may well ask what is the link between 'kneeing' and former US President, Mr. Obama? My reply is not simply that in US contemporary sports circles the action was initiated by football player, Mr. Colin Kaepernick, in 2016, a time when Mr. Obama was still President. Mr. Kaepernick's action was not directed against his country's flag. It was against police brutality, an egregious act just as despicable and revulsive as civilian murders of policemen and fellow citizens in mass killings, all of which have been condemned by Mr. Obama. What I think is even more compellingly significant here is that while Mr. Kaepernick did not make an explicit statement against failure within the US to implement the 1776 *Declaration Of Independence*, something Mr. Obama has done, it is not out of order to conclude: the Kaepernick 'kneeing,' like the Obama statement, is an act against failure to implement.

So, what did Mr. Obama state? On the occasion of his second inauguration speech, January 2013, Mr. Obama stated that the self-evident truths in *The Declaration* have never been self-actualised. The police brutality against black men all across America is, unquestionably, implementation and self-actualisation failure. Described superficially, his statement is one against self-actualisation failure. Assessed profoundly, it is an indictment against injustice and the other opposites to which I alluded. Described superficially the Kaepernick 'kneeing' is action against brutality. Assessed profoundly, it is an indictment also against injustice and other opposites. Thus, Messrs. Obama, Kaepernick, and all other American sportsmen, including Mr. Curry and Mr. James, are on the same page. Should President Obama have turned to other pages? Should he have gone further, not necessarily during the course of that second inauguration speech, than noting implementation and self-actualisation failure? Were there grounds for having gone further?

I take the position that there were, and still are, such grounds, which Trump, of course, will never tread, but which President Obama did not tread, because to have done so would have meant challenging capitalism, one of the sturdiest foundations to the injustice opposites. For him to have mounted any effective challenge to capitalism, prior forms central to European racism and imperialist expansion, as well as contemporary versions in corporate free market guises which emanate directly from the racism and expansion, he would have had to reject free market capitalism, something he has supported ardently. By contrast, not only is Trump an ardent supporter of free market capitalism, he is also the racist who wasted no time in extending his full support to National Football League (NFL) team owners and the Commissioner, who issued a decision in late May 2018 that all players on the field must stand and cannot give the knee when the American national anthem is being sung.

It is noteworthy to me that the May 2018 decision was made without any consultation with players' representatives. One historical context of such decision-making is ownership for huge profit-making, a pernicious principle, of course, not alien to slavery. American football, baseball, and basketball teams are owned. Thus, Trump's support for the NFL decision is support integral to ownership, huge profit-making, as well as racism, capitalism, and imperialism. I will address myself later to the absence of rejection from President Obama of capitalism when I deal with cultures of violence. Here, I will use the very *Declaration of Independence* to which the President alluded in his inauguration speech for purposes of highlighting the imperialist expansion via wars and racism linked to it.

While referring to that very *Declaration*, Olusoga (2016, p. 146) notes: without embarrassment, proponents of the *Declaration*, rebels and patriots, employed the term, 'slavery', for describing their exposure to British taxation. Observing that well before those patriots had issued their *Declaration* cries to which they professed that all men are equal, they revealed their hypocrisy which was noted and ridiculed by none other than Dr. Samuel Johnson, whose companion was an African, Francis Barber. With help from the pen of Bundock (Bundock 2015), Olusoga states Dr. Johnson asked "how is it we hear the loudest yelps for liberty among the drivers of Negroes?" Apart from Dr. Johnson, there were words from someone I regard as pre-eminent among the global abolitionists and civil rights campaigners, someone who used the letter of the law to make his convincing case against slavery in Britain.

I am referring to none other than Granville Sharp, who issued a warning that: "American liberty cannot be firmly established without some scheme of general Enfranchisement." Why? "The toleration of domestic slavery in the colonies greatly weakens the claim or natural right of our American brethren to Liberty. Let them put away the accursed thing (that horrid Oppression) from among them, before they presume to implore the interposition of divine justice."[3] Pointing one finger at a Virginia politician, Richard Henry Lee, and another at George Washington, Olusoga emphasises the hypocrisy while stating that the Virginian moved a resolution in the Second Continental Congress claiming independence. Using a public parade against British imposition of the Stamp Tax upon the colonies, Lee unveiled banners that served as denunciation of that most hated of taxes which placed CHAINS OF SLAVERY around the necks of white American colonists. He experienced no embarrassment in making his slaves carry the banners. Nor, for that matter, did any of Lee's Virginian brethren feel any dis-ease at the spectacle.

Another notable slaveholder with whom I associate no embarrassment, someone to whom President Obama was fond of alluding, is George Washington, PATRIOT-IN-CHIEF. Around the very time the Treaty of Versailles to end hostilities between the victorious patriots and the British was to be ratified, George Washington sent to his New York City representatives a list of his escaped slaves thought to be there and whom he hoped would be recaptured. This he did after he had been successful in recapturing many of his former slaves in places such as Philadelphia and other locations in the horrible wake of the Battle of Yorktown. Drawing from the work of Hirschfeld (1997), Olusoga refers to these Washington words: Some of my own slaves... may probably be in N York... I will be much obliged by your securing them, so that I may obtain them again. The Washington probability was the Washington reality. Some of his former slaves, escapees from his Mount Vernon plantation, were, indeed, hiding in New York.

By no means peripheral to *The Declaration* and its aftermath is European expansion, expansion in which Britain is audaciously present. I shall look at such expansion and British presence, examine Frederick Douglass' stinging critique of *The Declaration*, and offer my own interpretation of *The Declaration*, as well as of the argument that the American seaboard colonists had with the British Crown and Parliament. I begin with some of the significant wars among the imperialist rivals and the Treaties signed after their conclusion. Further, when treaties were signed, they were not signed in the names or on behalf of the non-white sub-persons, slaves, on whose broken backs much of America's and Great Britain's wealth accumulated. Here, the wars of Spanish Succession (1702-1713), Jenkins' Ear (1738-1749), and the Seven Years' War (1756-1763) all come to mind. Thus, when I observe exploration of the Seven Years' War and War of Jenkins' Ear, I see battles within European capitalism and the brutality of oppression in slavery. While recording his ideas about these conflicts, Fisher (1949, p. 748) views the prelude to them as controversies fraught with issues among England and its maritime rivals, France and Spain.

He adds that wherever an Englishman encountered a Spaniard or Frenchman on the high seas, he espied a rival and an enemy.

It was a struggle not of courts and cabinets, but of men on the spot, of sailors and merchants, smugglers and privateers, of lumbermen, settlers, and free traders, of rival mercantile companies, brawling and quarrelling either along the Spanish main or in Acadia and Newfoundland, or along the banks of the Ohio or the St. Lawrence, or under a burning Indian sky among the rice fields of the Carnatic, or the canes and mango trees of Bengal. Inevitably, the unregulated competition for trade, colonies and dominion in Asia and America provoked innumerable collisions between the Anglo-Saxons and their Latin rivals (Fisher 1949, p. 748).

Fisher's assessment is a most apposite one, a matter I shall exemplify by referring to the War of Jenkins' Ear. Fisher (1949, p. 748) writes it was sufficient that English ships trading on the Spanish Main should have been searched for contraband by Spanish guard vessels and chained English sailors should have been consigned to unsanitary Spanish prisons. Noting that complaints of English sailors and merchants always elicited ready hearing, he states that the story that a wicked Spaniard had lopped off Captain Jenkins' ear sent Britain into convulsions of fury, which only declaration of war, as impolitic as it was unjust, was able to assuage. This was a war associated with the Spanish right of search, which the British Prime Minister, Robert Walpole, did everything to avoid, but according to Fisher, because of popular clamour, echoed and solidified by opposition in Parliament, he was compelled to initiate.

What Fisher excludes from the War of Jenkins' Ear is direct connection to Africa, the West Indies, and slavery. This is a link provided, and provided in most persuasively fluent fashion, by Olusoga (2016, p. 24). This eighteenth century battle, given the oddest of titles by the British, emerged from an incident in which the Rebecca, an English brig, was intercepted by a Spanish vessel, La Isabella, off the Cuba coast. Jenkins, an English smuggler and captain of the Rebecca, was accused of piracy by Leon Fandino, Isabella's skipper, who cut off Jenkins' left ear. Noting what he assesses as the British addition of Fandino's unrehearsed auriculectomy to a questionable dossier of excuses and pretexts justifying war with Spain, Olusoga states that it was only a century later that the battle was named by Victorian writer and apologist for African slavery, Thomas Carlyle. Further, Spain titles the war La Guerra del Asiento, The War of the Asiento, fought not to avenge Jenkins for loss of an ear, but in regard to contracts pertaining to selling African slaves to Spanish colonies. These contracts emerged from one of the imperialist peace treaties, the Treaty of Utrecht.

The day before the British declaration of war, Jenkins appeared in Parliament, where he narrated the lopping off. Jenkins stands immortalised in an engraving of his parliamentary presence revealing removal of his wig to show absence of the left ear. The person removing the wig as depicted in the engraving is a black man attired in liveried coat, uniform of enslaved black British servants during the mid-eighteenth century. Racist, Thomas Carlyle, is also the individual who described economics as 'Dismal Science,' a term Olusoga states is used with obvious relish by correspondents and celebrity economists at times of economic upheaval. There is more. The Carlyle terminology is part of his 1849 essay *Occasional Discourse on the Negro Question*, writing Olusoga describes as a virtually hysterical condemnation by the racist of black humanity, which served also as a powerful attack against British anti-slavery politics.

The phrase ['Dismal Science'] is often reused without remembering the essay from which it came. So complete was the decoupling of the phrase from Carlyle's toxic writing on race that over time an alternative genesis myth emerged. This suggested that the phrase arose from Carlyle's essays on the great eighteenth-century political demographer Thomas Malthus. This alternative origin story, being conveniently free from any association with the history of slavery and racism, has often been favoured (Olusoga 2016, pp. 24-25).

Given what I know about interpretive sociology, specifically, conversational analytic sociology, as well as linguistics, especially Firthian linguistics, I must state that I am tempted to search the nether reaches of his racist ruminating with an interest in the contextual significance of 'Dismal Science.' Such is, however, a pursuit for another time. Hence, I continue with the imperialist wars.

In specific reference to the 1763 peace treaty after the Seven Years' War, Fisher (1949, p. 765) points not merely to the imperialist principals locked in battle, he enables the observer to consider—though not with the same forcefulness as Olusoga—also the dehumanisation in slavery to which Africans bound for the New and Old World were subjected. At the end of the Seven Years' War, France was evicted from India. Canada and Senegal were ceded to England, while Spain relinquished Florida. England also acquired St. Vincent, Tobago, Dominica, and the Grenadines.

I certainly do not miss the fact that fifty years earlier, when the Treaty of Utrecht was signed to end the war of Spanish Succession, maritime superiority, once shared by the Dutch and English, had been passed to England (Fisher 1949, p. 687). England, of course, solidified its power of imperialisation by gaining Gibraltar, Port Mahon, Newfoundland, and Nova Scotia. Most significantly, it reclaimed from the French the Asiento, a treasured right of trading African slaves and other property to the Spanish Indies.[4]

All the West Indian possessions were locations of slavery. Senegal was also a place from which slaves left for the New World. Alexander Hamilton, whose photograph appears on US currency, was not born in any of the Caribbean territories noted above but is undoubtedly British, born in the Anglo-Caribbean. He and several other Europeans of Caribbean birth left the tropics for an America where they were integral to the growth of American capitalism.

Let me not forget that during the course of one of his rousing speeches of exhortation (Second World War), Mr. Churchill stated that if the British Empire should last a thousand years, men would speak of the war effort as one of their finest hours. Mr. Churchill was not making reference to African American fighting men who did fight on behalf of the USA and alongside British soldiers. Those African Americans had to swallow the unpalatable pill of segregation, while fighting for the very freedom enshrined in their own democracy and, most ironically, extolled by Britain's racist philosophers such as John Locke whose British and American presence I must examine before turning to Don Christobal Colon.

John Locke is the great-great-great grandson of John Lok, leading member of an English Merchant family, who made trips to Africa in the sixteenth century when he returned to Britain with commoditised Africans as slaves (Olusoga 2016, pp. 44-45). It is the Locke philosophy which was expounded in the theorising that civil government is based upon consent of the governed, the right to private property is based on labour, as well as the doctrine of religious toleration, and rational education of the young. These are all honourable pronouncements which cannot, however, be separated from a context of English eighteenth century superiority actualised and relished among European residents of the thirteen seaboard colonies, but lewdly inapplicable to African slaves and their descendants, unwilling providers of labour in the unspeakable brutality of dehumanisation:

> In the eighteenth century the rivalry of England and France continued, but tended to be fought across the ocean, in Canada and India, rather than upon the continent of Europe. Colonies and commerce became more important as motives of public policy

than religious affiliations and dynastic alliances. The Puritan of the second generation was apt to be a shrewd, money-making man of business. Conservatism—or, as it was then called, Whiggism—in politics, rationalism in philosophy, an easy-going comfort in social life, were the mottoes of the Hanoverian age (Fisher 1949, pp. 443-444).

One of the most potent instantiations of consideration I can give to oppression in American socio-economic formation takes the shape of what constitutes activities of the pressure group, The Tea Party. Here, I do not miss the retrospective relevance to what took place in Boston Harbour, part of the prelude to *The Declaration*. I am also attuned to an invocation teeming with disrespect to Mohawk persons.

Further, the Tea Party, in its strident opposition to what its members have seen as President Obama's big spending, big government, and hugely peeved about the President's healthcare legislation, has targeted him as a massive threat to what I term their selfish pretence to democracy, which they shamelessly adorn with appeals to rugged frontier reliance. This is not just a nasty disposition wholly antithetical to the reshaping of America Mr. Obama strongly believed he was elected to orchestrate, it is also a blatantly vulgar strategy aimed at discrediting the being of a black visionary whose values of renewal and redemption are dissonant with the pretence.

That pretence, I emphasise, reared its ugly head only two days after Mr. Romney was supposed to have run amok all over the reliable rhetorician, Barack Obama, in the first presidential debate (October 2012). None other than Mr. Jack Welch, former CEO of General Electric, a capitalist transnational behemoth responsible for producing some of the most deadly weapons available to the captains of free market fundamentalism and rugged frontier reliance, used the miracle of the internet to challenge the validity of less than gloomy job numbers for September 2012, which he implied should be questioned. In all of my teenage and adult life I have never heard any CEO question job numbers—favourable or unfavourable—during the tenure of European American Presidents seeking a second term. Subjecting the Welch disrespect to discourse is to dignify the grotesque nature of European essentialism linked to perverse exceptionalism aimed at demeaning the hard work of a chief executive, something with which his white predecessors were never linked.

I am saying that even Mr. Obama, in the twenty-first century, despite his elevated presidential presence in contemporary America, was not immune to, or insulated from, degradation. He is, after all, an African American bedevilled by an identity dilemma. Allow me to deal with four instances of just such bedevilling. I want to begin with the Republican Party convention in August 2012, when veteran actor, Mr. Clint Eastwood, addressed Tea Party faithful and kindred spirits. One spirit with which he communicated—if I can resort to the notion of connection—was that of President Barack Obama. To the gushing delight of a rapturous audience, Eastwood constructed a frame within which he imagined himself in discourse with an invisible chief executive. Importantly, the actor standing tall before a podium was not conversing with a spirit in front of him or one seated beside him, Eastwood's choices clearly indicative of subordinating Mr. Obama. He merely glanced diagonally to his left, presumably a position which his listeners could have imagined the President occupying.

He also proceeded to construct in his own devious utterances, what he deemed or dreamed to be Mr. Obama's turns in talking. Eastwood was not merely mischievously and absurdly misrepresentative in his stagecraft of erasure, he was, unquestionably, demeaning the President and the high office Mr. Obama held also.

By no means insignificant to me is that "Dirty Harry," the man who epitomises more than any other actor the presence of rugged frontier individualism residing within the insistently intoxicating and irremediable recesses of American gun culture, could not have separated himself from that culture and individualism. At all times in the existence of America both entities have been consistent with degrading black people.

It is just such degrading as it is linked integrally to John Locke which occupies me now. John Locke was a principal shareholder in the Royal Africa Company, a joint stock company to supply England and American colonists with African captives. Charles II, his brother, King James, Duke of York and their cousin, Prince Rupert, saw such a company as the ideal arrangement from which to create a profitable slave trade (Olusoga 201, p. 73-74). To be sure, two other companies, The Company of the Royal Africa Adventurers Trading, and the Company of Gambia Adventurers, preceded the Royal Africa Company. Under its charter the first was mandated to have the "whole, entire and only trade for the buying and selling bartering and exchanging of Negroes, slaves, goods, wares and merchandise" to be located within Africa. In business for seven years, it delivered to British planters sixteen thousand African slaves. The Gambia Adventurers was granted rights in 1668 to trade North of Benin, and the Royal Africa Company was established in 1672 by Charles II.

Readers will learn that when challenges were being made to the monopoly power of the Royal Africa Company, such challenges, early indicators of desire for free trade, as well as principles of freedom, there was absolutely no consideration given to the freedom of Africans. Olusoga (2016, pp. 72-74) observes that the Royal Africa Company was responsible for the transporting and enslaving of more Africans than any other company in British history. Establishing Britain as a crucial participant in Atlantic slavery, the company launched the UK on an upward movement enabling the Union to become the dominant slave trading European power. Its most prosperous period, between 1672 and the 1720s, was linked to no fewer than well over five hundred forays into Africa. Within a single ten year span since its creation, the British share of the slave trade rose from 33% to 74%.

Under the terms of its creation the company was granted broad operational scope inclusive of total power to make and declare war and peace with any societies deemed heathen within its area of operation. It was authorised with the right also to secure services of the Royal Navy for the purpose of searching and seizing vessels manned by those regarded as interlopers, independent slave traders who made efforts to trade from Morocco to the Cape of Good Hope. Interestingly, during the course of the late seventeenth century, Englishmen, "the separate traders to Africa," independent merchants, set out to enter the African trade and challenge the power of the Stuart kings to be sole profiteers from slavery. Drawing from insights of historian William Pettigrew, Olusoga (2016, p. 74) observes that the separate traders committed themselves to a political campaign through which they battled with what they deemed the 'African Monster.' With their own conceptualising of natural freedoms and demanding that access to the trade be made a right of all Englishmen to trade anywhere, in any commodity, and with anyone, they claimed that the right was bestowed upon all Englishmen.

With obstinate blindness they stated, in boldly frontal and strident fashion, that enslaving Africans was a defining quality of English freedom. Further, in their attempts to influence public opinion via lobbying and pamphlets, they argued that the trade in enslaved humans ought to be pursued, not merely for the advantage of the monarchy and the groups within its sphere, but also for the benefit of the entire UK.

From time to time, the voices of the West Indian plantation owners and tobacco farmers of Virginia and Maryland were raised in support of these contentions and in opposition to the monopoly of the Royal Africa Company. For England to thrive, for her balance of trade to be healthy and for her power to be extended into the Atlantic world, the slave trade had to be deregulated and privatised, they reasoned. Without such a move, the sugar and tobacco plantations of the Americas had no viable future, and England would no longer be able to supply the nation with those highly desirable commodities. Few people disagreed with the economic case, and fewer still concerned themselves with the plight of the enslaved Africans whose commoditised bodies were placed at the centre of a debate about the nature of English freedom (Olusoga 2016, p. 74).

Well over two hundred years prior to signing any of the treaties emergent from imperialist rivalry, Don Christobal Colon, Christopher Columbus, so-called founder of America, had sat courtside with the King of Portugal, Don Juan, who informed the Genoese sailor that he wanted a line drawn across the map of the world from Pole to Pole, North to South. The exact position of the line was to be 370 leagues west to the westernmost islands of Cape Verde. The goal of demarcation was division between two Catholic Kingdoms. Positions west of the line were to be designated Spanish and those east were to be Portuguese. One year after the discussion, Spain and Portugal signed the treaty of Tordesiallas, on 7 June, 1494 (Van Sertima 1976, pp. 8-9).

In dealing with the Frederick Douglass critique, I cannot ignore my own reference, and what Mills (1998) conveys as the orator's lambasting the hypocrisy of divided independence and the speaker's demystification of celebrating Independence Day as fraudulent. Demystification and lambasting come respectively:

What, to the American slave, is your 4th July? I answer; a day that reveals to him, more than all other days in the year, the gross injustice and cruelty to which he is the constant victim. To him, your celebration is a sham; your boasted liberty, an unholy license; your national greatness, swelling vanity; your sounds of rejoicing are empty and heartless; your denunciations of tyrants, brass fronted impudence; your shouts of liberty and equality, hollow mockery; your prayers and hymns, your sermons and thanksgivings, with all your religious parade and solemnity, are, to him, mere bombast, fraud, deception, impiety, and hypocrisy—a thin veil to cover up crimes which would disgrace a nation of savages. There is not a nation on the earth guilty of practices, more shocking and bloody, than are the people of these United States, at this very hour. Go where you may, search where you will, roam through all the monarchies and despotisms of the old world, travel through South America, search out every abuse, and when you have found the last, lay your facts by the side of the everyday practices of this nation, and you will say with me, that for revolting barbarity and shameless hypocrisy, America reigns without a rival (Douglass 1852/2004, p. 132).

Asserting that he was not included within what he assessed as the pale of a glorious anniversary, he insisted that the high independence celebrated on the 4th of July was a revelation of massive distance between him and white European celebrants. He added that the sunlight which brought light and healing to white America had delivered stripes and death to him, and he mourned rather than rejoiced. Hauling him, a man in fetters into the grand illuminated temple of liberty, and requesting that he participate in joyous anthems, was tantamount to inhuman mockery and sacrilegious irony. In a challenge to listeners that they ponder whether he was being mocked by being asked to speak, he noted there was a parallel to their conduct. And in issuing a warning that danger lay in copying the example of a nation whose crimes, towering up to heaven, were thrown down by the breath of the Almighty, burying that nation in irrecoverable ruin, he was explicit that he stood with the cause of plaintive lament from a peeled and woe-smitten people (Douglass 1852/2004, p. 128).

Douglass did much more than mourn. He made it absolutely clear that there was massive distance between the platform on which he was speaking and the slave plantation from which he had escaped. Resorting to depth and breadth in contrast, he acknowledged, through reciting, a resolution from the Continental Congress on 2nd July, 1776,[5] and added that the 4th of July was the first great fact in America's history, a matter he assessed as the very ringbolt in the chain of an undeveloped destiny."

It is with illocutionary force equal to his declaration above that he stated: when European Americans celebrate with tumultuous joy he hears the doleful cries of millions, the bleeding children, with heavy and grievous chains, fettered humanity, on the way to slave markets where victims are sold like *horse, sheep,* and *swine,* claimed by the highest bidders. Describing the slave trade as murderous traffic, an active operation of a vaunted republic, he points to the most tender links ruthlessly severed to gratify lust, caprice, and rapaciousness of sellers and buyers. These are some of the sickening sights and scenes amidst which he was born. Recalling his own childhood, he states:

To me the American slave-trade is a terrible reality. When a child, my soul was often pierced with a sense of its horrors. I lived on Philpot Street, Fell's Point, Baltimore, and have watched from the wharves, the slave ships in the basin, anchored from the shore, with their cargoes of human flesh, waiting for favourable winds to waft them down the Chesapeake. There was, at that time, a grand slave mart kept at the head of Pratt Street, by Austin Woldfolk. His agents were sent into every town and country in Maryland, announcing their arrival, through the papers, and on flaming "hand-bills," headed CASH FOR NEGROES. These men were generally well dressed men, and very captivating in their manners. Ever ready to drink, to treat, and to gamble. The fate of many a slave has depended upon the turn of a single card; and many a child has been snatched from the arms of its mother, by bargains arranged in a state of brutal drunkenness (Douglass 1852/2004, p. 134).

Ideas very similar to these Douglass descriptions and assessment can be located in the ground breaking and painstaking exploration from Olusoga (2016, pp. 82-83) about slavery in Britain, a crime against humanity, I emphasise, by no means peripheral to Atlantic slavery, to which the West Indies and the thirteen American seaboard colonies were central.

I offer, via the Olusoga eyes, part of a 13th December, 1744 notice in the *London Daily Advertiser*[6] about the sale of an African child from a London pub: "TO BE SOLD. A PRETTY LITTLE NEGRO BOY, ABOUT NINE YEARS OLD, AND WELL LIMB'D. IF NOT DISPOS'D OF, IS TO BE SENT TO THE WEST INDIES IN SIX DAYS TIME. HE IS TO BE SEEN AT THE DOLPHIN TAVERN IN TOWER STREET." The notice was sandwiched between a listing for Scottish linen 'of the best Fabrick and Colour,' and an employment offer for Two Journeymen Taylors who might be desirous of working in the Caribbean. Adding that the appearance of the notice was not unique, Olusoga points to as many as forty listings similar to it in English newspapers and eight Scottish periodicals during the period 1790-1792. In 1709, *The Tattler* ran an advertisement for "a black boy, twelve years of age, fit to wait on a gentleman." Prospective buyers could find the child in "DENNIS' COFFEE-HOUSE IN FINCH LANE." From the George Coffee House in Chancery Lane (1759), interested buyers could find a Negro boy about fourteen years old free from any distemper and who had become accustomed to doing all forms of household chores, and waiting on tables. His price: twenty-five pounds.

The Coffee Houses were parts of broad loci in British cities such as Bristol, Liverpool, and, of course, London. In addition, Africans were auctioned by art dealers whose paintings and human commodities were typically offered to those newly enriched by wealth gained from sugar in the West Indies.

> *Black people were passed on in British wills and inherited alongside real estate and livestock. In 1701 Thomas Papillon of London left his son an enslaved man, 'whom I take to be in the nature of my goods and chattels.' That Papillon felt the need to assert his claim to the enslaved man as chattel hints at some understanding on his part that the laws of England were unclear on the exact status of slaves, as they were to remain for at least another seventy years. In October 1718 the Bristol merchant Beecher Flemming evidently felt more confident about his right to leave 'my negro boy, named Tallow' to Mrs. Mary Beecher, presumably his widow (Olusoga 2016, p. 83).*

Chiding European Americans for the flagrant inconsistency to their politics and republic, Douglass notes their boast about love of liberty, superior civilisation, and purity in Christianity, alongside their political power embodied within political parties beholden to support and perpetuate enslavement of millions of blacks. He offers, explicitly, instances of the incongruence by alluding to white America's nominal pride in democratic institutions and directing anathemas to European monarchical tyranny but consenting simultaneously to be instruments and gate keepers of Virginia and Carolina tyrants.

Incompatibility is evidenced also in an obvious double standard exemplified via stark contrast between invitation and honouring granted foreign fugitives of oppression, on the one hand, but on the other, hunting, arresting, shooting, and killing of fugitives in America. European- Americans glory in boast of refinement and universal education, yet maintain a dreadful and barbarous political and economic system initiated in avarice, buttressed by pride, and maintained in cruelty.

Frederick Douglass delivered his oratory a very very long time ago. If anyone who cares deeply about the African American dilemma harbours any doubt that his 1852 speech is relevant to present time, s/he should take extremely careful note of the emphasis he places upon incongruence by declaring that existence of slavery stains republicanism as a sham, white American humanity as mere base pretence, and Christianity a lie. Such existence destroys American moral power abroad, corrupts politicians in the USA, saps religious foundations, and makes the name America just a hissing and notable instantiation for mockery. Slavery fetters societal advancement. A curse to earth, a deadly enemy of improvement, it advances pride but breeds insolence, promotes vice, and shelters crime. With acute insight he issues this challenge:

Oh! Be warned! be warned! be warned! a horrible reptile is coiled up in your nation's bosom; the venomous creature is nursing at the tender breast of your youthful republic; for the love of God, tear away, and fling from you this hideous monster, and let the weight of twenty millions, crush, and destroy it, forever!(Douglass 1852/2014, pp. 142-143).

Today, there are well over 300,000,000 people in the USA. How many of this number among the adult populace are willing to crush the massive impact of slavery with its tons of literal and figurative deadweight on the backs of those who call themselves African American!

The point I am making is that the content of Douglass' stinging critique, *The Declaration of Independence*, is of very great significance to my case for the African American dilemma, a matter to which Mr. Kaepernick referred and of which President Obama made note. This is the dilemma deeply encrusted in free market capitalism to which the President subscribes and which emanated from *The Declaration* and expansionist accomplishment prior to and after it. Appropriately, I address myself to this Declaration by examining its basis not in a yearning for fairness, freedom, rights, and justice, but as a major battle between two quarters of capitalism camped on both sides of the Atlantic. Let me begin by noting that sugar and cotton, two of the main profitable commodities integrally connected to the fight for independence brought untold wealth to the pockets of British citizens in the thirteen seaboard colonies and the United Kingdom. That wealth emerged mainly from the repression of African slaves who, despite the apparent justice in *The Declaration* statements were not, by any means, free.

Which Africans and their descendants participated in the Revolutionary War either on the British or American side from 1776-1783? Is their participation located centrally or peripherally within knowledge about American history at all educational levels about links between metamorphosing capitalism and European imperialist expansion? Was slavery not in full operation during the course of the independence struggle? In what ways are African Americans—Mr. Obama included—apprised today about any juxtapositions of slavery and the African participation in *The Declaration* battles? How are they applying their awareness today as one important means of liberating themselves from the clutches of contemporary free market corporate capitalism? These queries are queries partially, but very significantly, about history.

It is a delving into historical significance through the insight of Fisher that enables me to strengthen my position about links between capitalism and the Revolutionary War. Fisher takes the view that one prominent basis to the Revolutionary War was constituted by the very English victory over France and Spain to which I alluded. Thus, the eviction of the French from Canada and the Spanish from Florida weakened American reliance on the mother country and rid the American colonists of two dangerous neighbours. With reduced need of English assistance, the colonists were not tardy in their challenge of English mother country pretensions.

When George Grenville proposed a stamp tax to defray part of the cost of an army for the protection of the colonies, motives niggardly and narrow were combined with others which belonged to the best political inheritance of the Anglo-Saxon race to frustrate the imposition (Fisher 1949, p. 767).

The English, so states Fisher, have always quarrelled over money, and the colonists in America—showing great faithfulness to the habits of their ancestors—resisted the Stamp Tax on grounds of no taxation without representation. Grenville withdrew the Stamp Tax, but George III took the view that mutinous colonists should be dealt with by force. In place of withdrawal there was a parliamentary declaration that Britain had the complete right to tax the colonists, and it imposed duties on such commodities as glass, lead, and paper.

In addition, the colonies were prevented from starting factories which could compete with those of the mother country and were compelled to ship their exports in British or colonial vessels manned by two-thirds of British or colonial crews. Colonists were also forbidden to smoke tobacco grown in places other than Bermuda and America. The greatest irritant to the American colonists, however, was the Molasses Act prohibiting importation of French produced sugar, molasses, and rum. According to Fisher, this directive dealt a blow to New England distilleries.

The atmosphere of acrimony did not abate until some colonists disguised as Mohawk people vented their disdain for the actions of England by boarding three ships in Boston Harbour and dumping their entire cargo of tea into the water. The response of the British Cabinet was closure of Boston Harbour and changes to the Charter of Massachusetts, so that prisoners indicted on capital charges there might be sent for trial to some other colonial possession or to Britain. Other seaboard colonies closed ranks with Massachusetts to resist English punishment. Resistance took the form of a solemn League and Covenant through which subscribers were bound to abstain from commercial arrangement with Britain, until all imposition from the imperial power had been repealed.

Protagonists on both sides made ready for war, which did occur, but in the words of Fisher, had both France and Spain, as well as Holland, of course enemies of Britain, not intervened on the side of America, the colonists might have been defeated. The entire world knows that the colonists were victorious, but the Fisher insightfulness shall remain with me, for despite the fact that in the eyes of Europe an empire had been lost, he writes about what I regard as the continuing triumph of capitalism against which Douglass waxed eloquent—a triumph which I see as placing African Americans outside the space-time continuum of American cultures. The insight is contained in the view that the defeated country was fast becoming through a series of unprecedented economic changes the workshop of the world and the principal centre of its finance. Thus, I am aware that independence did not prevent victor and vanquished from engaging in massive trade—among other goods—in that slave commodity, cotton, which went to the North of England for processing.

Nor does it elude me that when the British abolished slavery officially on 1st August 1834, in her West Indies possessions massive economic and political power of the slave owners bore down on abolitionist fighters such as William Wilberforce, Thomas Clarkson, and Thomas Fowell Buxton. The abolitionists were compelled to accede to the slave owners' demand that there could be no abolition without substantial monetary compensation to the owners.[7] Thus, via an Act of the British Parliament, the sum of twenty million pounds had to be paid to the owners. The slave owner that was paid the largest compensation sum was a man called John Gladstone, father of the parliamentarian, William Gladstone, who went on to become one of Britain's successful Prime Ministers, and whose ideas have had impact on the course of North American politics, a context from which the long serving Canadian Prime Minister, Jean Chretien, once told media correspondents about William

Gladstone's lengthy tenure in the UK. John Gladstone, owner of the most slaves at two locations, the Wales and Vreed-en-Hoop plantations on the most fertile agricultural land in the nineteenth century on the West Bank of the Demerara river in British Guiana, later invested his windfall from the compensation and other slavery profits in British industrial development such as railways. It is the British railways which powered that workshop to which Fisher refers and formed a major basis to trade between Britain and the USA.

It is profits from British slave holding and the compensation that were used also in creating some of the most important institutions such as the very prestigious Royal Society, highly respected in British and American intellectual circles. While the Vreed-en-Hoop plantation went out of business long before the beginning of the twentieth century, Wales continued and became a major capitalist triumph under ownership of a modern British transnational behemoth, Booker Bros., later, Booker, McConnell and Company, under the Chairmanship of a British Labour Party socialist, Lord Campbell of Eskan, known formerly as Sir Jock Campbell to all who gave their labour on British Guiana sugar plantations, the most extensive and most profitable within the Anglo-Caribbean. It is those profits mainly from British Guiana sugar and rum manufactured on the broken backs of people of colour toiling under the hottest suns and worst thunderstorms well known to the capitalist world as Demerara Sugar and Demerara Rum that were used to create the highly prestigious literary Booker Prize. There is no Booker Prize for any field or factory worker

What plantations did Booker McConnell own in British Guiana? Here is part of the list: Wales, Utivlugt, (West Demerara), La Bonne Intention, Lusignan, Enmore (East Demerara), Rose Hall, Blairmont (West Berbice), Albion, Skeldon (East Berbice). Other highly profitable plantations not owned by Booker McConnell were: Leonora and Diamond, (West and East Demerara, owned by British rival Jessel Securities), Versailles and Schoon Ord, Houston (West and East Demerara), associated for a long time with the highest yield of sugar per hectare in the entire country, managed by Booker McConnell but owned by a local capitalist family, the Vieiras, who had amassed much more than a small fortune from the early trade in diamonds harvested from the depths of Amazonia by many a person of colour known locally as "porkknockers." These plantations, though not associated with slavery during the late nineteenth and twentieth centuries, constituted continuation of sugar cultivation and manufacture, which made Britain unimaginably wealthy and prosperous.

The significance of such wealth creation and prosperity to my work here lies in recognising that both were accomplished and sustained on the double consciousness of people of colour, the type of double consciousness that has existed among people of colour such as Mr. Kaepernick, his colleagues on the field, as well as their countless spectators, within the United States. Let me, therefore, offer a brief exposition of double consciousness, and address myself to it on the sugar plantations within British Guiana.

While writing about double-consciousness among African Americans, Du Bois (1903) states that the American Negro is a type of seventh sibling, born with a veil, yet endowed with second sight within the USA from which he derives no true self-consciousness, for he is allowed to see himself via revelation from the world of other. This peculiar experience, one of double consciousness, is a sense of always looking at one's self via the lenses of others, of assessing his "soul" with gazes from a world that looks on in amused contempt and pity. I regard double-consciousness as not only indicative of what some sociologists term role strain, I see it as also strongly reflective of that which I call role ambiguity hovering precariously over a site saturated with flirtations from distrust of selfhood.

When I delve into the issue, double consciousness, how can I ignore the matters: (1) If the Negro is a type of seventh sibling, what is the space-time distance overlain with socio-economic complexity between this sibling and other siblings? (2) Veils do enable and impede sight—both of wearers and those who gaze upon them. (3) Veils are placed voluntarily by wearers, or are worn as a result of actions from those who have power over wearers. (4) Given the socio-economic trauma continually experienced by those who designate themselves African American, how should any reasonable observer grant validity to the claim that such trauma has been emanating from inseparable links between gazers from ranks of the powerful and wearers belonging to the category, oppressed? (5) If the Negro sense of self is a formation shaped along avenues of contempt and pity from gazers, what value has the Negro been assigning to his/her identity?

I submit that all five of these matters are very pertinent to the way in which West (1994, p. 139) explores double consciousness through the eyes of Malcolm X, whom he conceptualises as delivering an implicit critique of Du Bois. The critique takes the form of Malcolm X viewing duality as referable more to African Americans who exist "betwixt and between" black and white worlds where they traverse the borders of both contexts but are settled in neither. Thus, African Americans yearn for peer acceptance in both settings, are not validated in either, but nevertheless persevere in looking at themselves via the lenses of dominant European-American society. Crucially, West opines, for Malcolm X, the description, double-consciousness, is less applicable to "a necessary black mode of being in America than a particular kind of colourised mind-set of a special group in black America" (West 1994, p. 139).

Double consciousness has always been alive on the British Guiana sugar plantations and locations associated with their operation where rigid socio-economic divisions, status differences, power, privilege, and prestige existed. Those at the very senior executive levels, typically white, lived in opulence and grandeur. Apart from being provided with basic necessities, such as free medical care of the very highest standards, free electricity, running water, indoor plumbing, of course they resided within gated enclaves in suburbia. They had access to the best recreational facilities, such as swimming pools and tennis courts on their properties, as well as paid servants and other domestic help, enjoyed paid leave for a three month period, which they usually spent in some part of Europe, and had the cost of their trips paid for by the company. On the plantations the person of the highest status, typically a European, was the administrative manager, who occupied a grand expansive house set behind a huge expanse of land ringed by giant trees standing guard around a billiard table like enchanting green space. It was on one such space, I recall distinctly, that a certain Mr. Powell, who had succeeded Lord Campbell, met the senior staff of the Versailles and Schoon Ord plantation. The administrative manager at the time, by then a mulatto, a light skinned person of colour, like his colleagues had access to the same power, and privilege enjoyed by the senior executives.

Just below him was his deputy, designated the field manager, and under him were the overseers, personnel managers, chemists, and resident engineers, whose lifestyles, though not so opulent as the managers and senior executives, were nevertheless grand. Every white plantation resident was a member of the senior staff, evidenced not merely in living conditions, but also exclusive access to a staff clubhouse associated with indoor and outdoor sports. The outdoor areas were almost always used for tennis, the balls from which were fielded by boys of colour paid a mere pittance for an afternoon of work. These ball boys had no access to the clubhouse. The only persons that were not plantation employees who had clubhouse membership and access were the District Commissioner, effectively a local government Czar with extensive reach into a vast range of rural life, the District Engineer, and the District Government Medical Officer, white for many a year and educated only in British academic higher education institutions. Next to the outdoor playing fields for senior staff was a playground, exclusively for use by their children.

Well away from the senior staff residences were homes for those designated junior staff, people of colour, individuals such as clerical workers, high level artisans, nurses, and dispensers. Although the junior staff had access to indoor plumbing, free electricity, free medical care, and enjoyed free housing, the standard of their medical care was considerably lower than that enjoyed by the senior staff. Further, it was not until the early 1960s when those junior staff considered important to the goal of sugar manufacture were given three months paid leave and paid passages of far lower cost that those enjoyed by the senior staff. The junior staff had access to a clubhouse, by no means equal to the one for senior staff. The children of junior staff were, of course, allowed access to a playground. There was, however, no playground for children of the vast armies of low paid factory and field workers, overwhelmingly people of colour who lived in villages and what were termed housing schemes by the company. Village and housing scheme occupants had no access to indoor plumbing and electricity. They enjoyed no leave of absence, and although they had access to free medical care, it was well below the standard of even the junior staff. While their children had no access to the types of playgrounds for children of junior and senior staff, these children were free to use excellent indoor and outdoor sports facilities provided by the company at what were called community centres always located within the core of housing schemes where the majority of field workers resided.

There was another side to the hierarchical organisation in plantation life. Some would describe it as benevolence. I adopt a different position. I assess the other side as pacification. Capitalists are fond of describing certain decisions of communist governments as efforts to pacify the masses. Capitalists have used pacification also within their imperialist possessions, but much of that pacification was very unsuccessful: before the French imperialists were defeated in a humiliating battle against the Vietnamese people at Dien Bien Phu in 1954, pacification alongside their horrific brutality against the locals failed ignominiously. So did pacification measures adopted by the Americans, not merely in Vietnam, but right across South East Asia, to which the theory about one place falling like a domino having an impact all across the region was applied as well. The domino theory was enunciated by Presidents Eisenhower, Truman, Kennedy, and Johnson, all of whom poured billions into the continent to no avail.

I am not aware of any of these leaders enunciating the theory in regard to Latin America. This, I do know from my teenage years growing up in the region: both Presidents Kennedy and Johnson were very concerned about communism spreading from Cuba across Latin America. The entire world knows about the disastrous Bay of Pigs debacle under Kennedy. Less well known is the Johnson military intervention in the Dominican Republic in 1965. So is the Kennedy Alliance for Progress, ostensibly, a programme of peaceful links between the US and the region to combat communism. I am aware—and very acutely so—during those teenage years that while the US was spending millions in military support to puppet regimes across the region in the battle with communism, American pacification took the form of major financial, media, and educational assistance under the umbrella of the United States Information Service (USIS), United States International Agency For International Development (USAID), as well as the Peace Corps volunteer effort.

Of course, Dr. Castro and his revolutionary comrades such as the Argentine born physician Dr. Ernesto "Che" Guevara, dubbed the American presence Yankee imperialism, against which Dr. Guevara died fighting alongside guerrillas in the Amazon jungle, where he was assassinated by a Bolivian army officer after having been wounded but captured alive. Long after this horror, when a democratically elected Bolivian government under President Evo Morales, who has maintained very good relations with the Cubans, was receiving much needed medical assistance from the Castro administration, the very murderer of Dr. Guevara had his eyesight restored by Cuban physicians who, by that time, were well established across the region in their provision of medical care to their Latin American brothers and sisters.

At the same time American pacification was failing across much of Latin America, British pacification was a huge success in one place there, not in association with any government efforts, but via the work of Booker, McConnell, and Company in British Guiana. Juxtaposed with the injustice to power, privilege, and prestige founded upon assumptions about racial superiority and inferiority was a programme to develop company loyalty on behalf of the mistreated masses. What do I mean? The vast armies of working people of colour within the villages and housing schemes were able to apply for, and use, company loans for home building. Many a worker sang the praises of the Sugar Industry Labour Welfare Fund, by means of which countless were able to have their own houses. It was also sport within which cricket was always paramount at community centre grounds through which extraordinarily great loyalty from the working class was developed. Next to every community centre were homes for junior staff employees, all persons of colour, the social welfare officers, answerable to someone who occupied a senior executive post, the Chief Social Welfare Adviser.

As far as I am aware the first and only person in this post was Sir Clyde Walcott, a Barbadian person of colour revered by his welfare officers as 'Chief.' Walcott, a member of the hugely famous trio of West Indies Test Match cricketers designated endearingly as the 'Three W's,' Everton Weekes, Frank Worrell, and himself, had reached some of the greatest heights on international cricketing arenas. When he began his job in British Guiana he had a few more years before retiring from the highest levels of the sport. He was not merely a revered person. Using rare diplomatic graciousness and judiciousness as his mainstays, he quickly became a charismatic authority figure within a British Guiana under the imperialistic yoke. The field and factory working class from the plantations who trekked and flocked to community centres saw him as one of them and treated him like a God. Cricket was their balm, and it was the Walcott soothing that had a magically curative impact. Thus, the working masses who knew injustice, and knew every day of their lives that they had to bear the huge burdens of such injustice, were so enmeshed in the game of cricket, via their community centre experiences, that there was never a hint of any meaningful challenge to the burdens or the socio-economic structures from which those burdens emanated.

It is out of community centre cricket cultural formation touched and moulded by the Walcott hands in Berbice that five of the most outstanding of West Indies players emerged: Alvin Kallicharran, Basil Butcher, Rohan Kanhai, Joe Solomon (Port Mourant Plantation), Roy Fredericks (Blairmont Plantation). These are only five of the working class men who were very instrumental in laying strong foundations to the unparalleled assertiveness and excellence of West Indies cricket handed to Brian Lara as a legacy which he squandered. These are just five of the working class persons who made West Indies cricket into a heroic song that Brian Lara turned into an unimaginable tragedy.[8] These are men who could narrate, in vivid detail, the contradictions under which they strained as working people under that imperialistic yoke. These are the same men who could talk, just as vividly, about avoiding a hint of challenge and opting to tell stories about what cricket did for them, cricket that came from the community centres Walcott inspired his social welfare officers to supervise efficiently. These are the same men who could talk about singing the British national anthem and showing respect to the Union Flag.

Are the Kallicharran, Butcher, Kanhai, Solomon, and Fredericks stories—I ask rhetorically—not also the Kaepernick, James, and Curry stories? Are these latter three not the children of working class Americans of colour burdened by socio-economic inequity and attendant racism, but who know they have been schooled in loyalty to their American flag, *The Declaration Of Independence*, as well as the inestimable virtues of democracy, who can narrate vividly what pick-up games in their neighbourhood and high level sport did for them?

Moving from a significant socio-economic matter overlain with double consciousness to parallelism in politics and cricket, I must note quite strikingly as well that like Mr. Obama's immediate predecessor, a West Indies captain named Richie Richardson, Lara's predecessor, was much maligned domestically for not maintaining West Indies leadership at the highest levels of international cricket Test Matches. To massive domestic acclaim and with great international respect that leadership established by two West Indies captains immediately prior to Richardson, Clive Lloyd and Vivian Richards, has been the longest in cricket history—almost sixteen continuous years. Political analysts will recall that when President G.W. Bush, Mr. Obama's immediate predecessor, left office, his approval rating was very low, the US economy was teetering on the brink of collapse, and there was huge discomfort over the Afghanistan and second Iraq war, the last of which was launched—at least, officially—on the basis of strident claims from the Bush administration that Iraq under a volatile dictator, President Saddam Hussein, was in possession of weapons of mass destruction.

Very much like captains Clive Lloyd and Vivian Richards, immediate predecessors of a vilified successor, captain Richie Richardson, Presidents George Herbert Walker Bush and Bill Clinton had performed well on the international and domestic theatres. Significantly, it was during the course of President G.H.W. Bush's tenure (1989-1993) that the dreaded American nemesis, communism, came to an end. That was no small foreign policy feat for the USA. The senior Bush—unlike his son—had demonstrated in a successful war against Iraq the enormous value of strategic leadership. While Mr. Bush did not win a second term, it is very reasonable to state that his immediate successor, President Clinton, had distinguished himself within the domestic theatre. Fondly known as "the comeback kid," Mr. Clinton is respected, not merely for his rhetorical splendour, he has been hailed as spectacularly successful also in managing the US economy during two terms of prosperity (1993-2001). To reinforce my point, let me say Lloyd and Richards (pinnacles of success) and Richardson (bringer of humiliation) are to Lara who George Herbert Walker Bush and Bill Clinton (pinnacles of success) and George Walker Bush (bringer of humiliation) are to Barack Obama.

Well outside the realms of cricketing contests, Mr. Obama, who loves basketball, has formed and nurtured his character by immersing himself in attainments of American heroes such as activist Dr. Martin Luther King, as well as Presidents Abraham Lincoln and John Kennedy. Today, the presence of Dr. King and Mr. Obama's predecessors stands as a matter of compelling history to several across the world who affix their individual and collective gazes upon thorny political and economic questions. While I cannot help wondering whether Mr. Obama's success—or otherwise—in having negotiated these questions may well become matters of compelling history, I am also moved to ask myself: what were the circumstances under which the "Michael Jordan of cricket," Brian Charles Lara, was led to demonstrate techniques of playing two very contrasting cricketing strokes at the Trinidad Hilton Hotel to President Barack Hussein Obama in 2010?

It is highly unlikely that I shall know the answer. This much I do know. Many a keen follower of the game is well aware that the forward defensive is employed by batsmen as a matter of caution, protection, care, or precaution against loss. It is, also, an admirable stroke of great resolve, in the face of hostility. The cover drive is, quite simply, a delightfully assertive move overflowing with grace and glory. Its execution on numerous occasions has, however, spelt doom for performers. Playing of the forward defensive is no guarantee against loss, and batsman, Brian Lara, himself, has met peril squarely while playing defensively.

Not unlike Brian Lara's work in his Test Match playing days, the President's work is to be understood via its grounding in teamwork. In Mr. Obama's case, his teams in the United States Congress have not been fully supportive of his efforts. He has had to face tough battles with significant numbers of legislators from his own Democratic Party over passage of his much heralded healthcare bill, of which his intensely loyal and politically eminent Vice President, Joseph Biden, is reported to have whispered: "big f—deal," but which predecessor, Bill Clinton, campaigning for his wife Hilary in 2016, deemed totally crazy. When he made the early December 2009 decision to send 30,000 troops to Afghanistan, Mr. Obama was openly criticised on Capitol Hill by members of his own party. The themes in Mr. Lara's on and off field strategies for Test Match cricket have not always been supported by his player colleagues, who have had to contend with great peril and loss emergent from strategies employed by him.

It may thus not be out of place for me to ask: how much of President Obama's immersion in basketball and peripheral association with cricket gained from within and beyond playing fields has been used by the leader to grapple with perils of American healthcare reform, economic catastrophe, and the war effort which confronted him on the sticky wickets where he has had to do far more than performing at bat? It is improbable that I would be able to deal with my interest in a satisfactory manner.

I do, however, feel that I can set the stage or lay the exploratory foundation for grappling with a query of parallel significance by turning my attention specifically to cricket, whose association with politics, economics, and above all, leadership issues, have saturated the lives of sporting luminaries. Here names such as Donald George Bradman, Sachin Ramesh Tendulkar, Garfield St. Aubrun Sobers, Isaac Vivian Richards, and of course, Brian Charles Lara spring to mind immediately.

ENDNOTES

1 *Equites (plural) originally members of the cavalry, although not senators, were from the Roman upper class. To enter this group persons needed to possess the equivalent of 400,000 sesterces—one sesterce equivalent to four asses. A sesterce was a silver coin. Equites, unlike senators, could embark upon such things as tax-farming and trade. The term, eques, is frequently translated to mean KNIGHT. The term, EQUESTRIAN, is, however, a preferred term to connote EQUESTRIAN ORDER. When Cicero assumed the title of senator he wanted to minimise conflicts between the order and senators. SOURCE: D, H. Berry. Cicero: Political Speeches (Oxford University Press,: 2011) pp. 341-342.*

2 *One of whom, we know, was Apollonius Molon.*

3 *The remarks attributed to Sharp were provided by Olusoga.*

4 *Writing under the title,"The English get The Asiento,," F. Augier and S.C. Gordon, note: "To procure a mutual and reciprocal advantage to the sovereigns and subjects of both Crowns, her British Majesty does offer and undertake for the persons whom she shall name and appoint that they shall oblige and charge themselves with the bringing into the West Indies of America, belonging to His Catholic Majesty, in the space of the said thirty years, to commence on the first day of May 1713, and determine on the like day which will be in the year 1743, viz., 144, 000 negroes, Piezas de India, of both sexes and of all ages, at the rate of 4,800 negroes, Piezas de India, in each of the said thirty years, with this condition, that the persons who shall go to the West Indies to take care of the concerns of the asiento shall avoid giving any offence, for in such a case they shall be prosecuted and punished in the same manner as they would have been in Spain, if the like misdemeanours had been committed there.*

That for each negro, Pieza de India, of the regular standard of seven quarters, not being old or defective, according to what has been practised and established hitherto in the Indies, the Asientists shall pay 33 pieces of eight and one-third of a piece of eight...

His Catholic Majesty, considering the losses which former Asientists have sustained, and upon this express condition, that the said company shall not carry on nor attempt any lawful trade, directly or indirectly... has been pleased... to allow the company of this asiento a ship of five hundred tons yearly during the thirty years of its continuance, to trade therewith to the Indies, in which His Catholic Majesty is to partake a fourth part of the gain, as in the asiento; besides which fourth His Catholic Majesty is to receive five per cent of the net gain of the other three parts which belong to England, upon this express condition, that they may not sell the goods and merchandises which each of these ships shall carry but only at the time of the fair; and if any of these ships shall arrive in the Indies before the flotas and galleons, the factors of the asiento shall be obliged to land the goods and merchandise with which they shall be laden, and put them into warehouses that shall be locked with two keys, one of which is to remain with the Royal officers and the other with the factors of the company, to the end the said goods and merchandise may be sold during the continuance of the said fair only; and they are to be free of all duties in the Indies."

Source: Augier, F.R. and S.C. Gordon. "The English get The Asiento.," In Sources Of West Indian History. Longmans, 1962).

5 *That resolution is: "Resolved, That these united colonies are, and of right, ought to be free and Independent States; that they are absolved from all allegiance to the British Crown; and that all political connection between them and the State of Great Britain, is, and ought to be, dissolved.*

6 *Olusoga notes that the advertisement was reprinted in the work, Black Settlers In Britain, by Nigel File and Chris Power (1981): p. 9.*

7 *My reference here to compensation comes from a British Broadcasting Corporation (BBC) World Service Television presentation, summer, 2017, when I saw the programme, Britain's Forgotten Slave Owners. According to the programme host, and author, David Olusoga, the basis of the programme was research done by London University about the very profitable ownership of human slave property in the Caribbean, the greatest profiteers from compensation, as a result of such property ownership, as well as, the fabulous wealth transferred from slavery and compensation to the core of capitalism within Britain.*

8 *My reference to the difference between a heroic song and unimaginable tragedy is an adaptation from statements by Vietnamese patriot, Mr. Nguyen Ngoc, who appeared in the Public Broadcasting Systems (PBS) documentary, The Vietnam War, made by distinguished American filmmakers, Lyn Novick and Ken Burns.*

Awaiting the Hubert Hour: Clive Lloyd, the greatest cover point fieldsman in Test Match cricket, and William H. Walcott

2nd INNINGS
EXPLORATORY
SOCIOLOGICAL
FOUNDATION

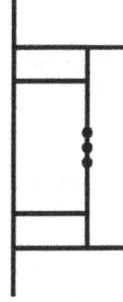

It is very important for me to point out that in laying an exploratory foundation for my work I am not attempting to offer what can be regarded as a theoretically correct or methodologically sacrosanct analysis. Nor for that matter, do I assume, think, or imply that what I present is more valid than other positions. From my sociological standpoint I acknowledge, very readily, the importance of approaches such as symbolic interactionism, conflict theory, Marxism, and structural functionalism. I understand, also, the major differences between quantitative and interpretive work. I chose the interpretive path exemplified by links among a Marcusean Marxian-Freudian synthesis, C. Wright Mills' sociological imagination, which embodies the sociologist's distinction between issues and troubles, Schutzian phenomenological sociology, with its links to ethnomethodology, conversation analytic and dramaturgical sociology, as well as speech act analysis, quite simply because this is just one exploratory path among others. The substantive glue binding connections along the route I traverse is revealed, quite explicitly, by links between the personal and the social evidenced in language use.

Further, I am mindful that whatever exploratory method(s) I employ must be appropriate to the subjects/social actors/phenomena I examine. As such, I know that the technical terms I, the analyst, use must have ordinary application. In other words, I must satisfy the Schutzian postulate of adequacy. Thus, my analytic constructs must be meaningful in common sense ways to the subjects/actors studied. Satisfying the postulate does mean, as well: I must be acutely aware that understanding held by these very subjects/social actors can, and sometimes does, make a difference for the description, assessment, and conclusions I, the analyst, provide. Consequently, there are, I emphasise, limits[1] to the certainty of my description, assessment, and conclusion.

It is obvious that race and racism feature in my work. Hence, I do have an obligation to address myself to it in a systematic way. What I wish to do is lay a conceptual template or set a sociological foreground on which three matters can be apprehended. They are: the Obama claim about non-actualisation of self-evident truths in *The Declaration Of Independence*, the Kaepernick kneeing, and West Indies cricket captain Brian Lara's squandering of a legacy left by his illustrious predecessors who battled racism. Appropriately, I begin with Holt (2000, pp. 41-43), who makes some important points about Don Christobal Colon, the navigator that named Lara's birthplace Trinidad because he thought he had seen the Christian Trinity. Holt notes that Don Christobal Colon penned a congratulatory missive to the Spanish sovereigns, Isabella and Ferdinand, before he had sailed towards the West Indies. In that document, he wrote favourably about Spain having routed the Moors and expelled the Jews from Spanish soil. To him, the initial significance of triumph was the emergence of the Spanish nation.

Holt reasons that the Columbus message served to connect race with discovery, nation building, imperialist expansion, as well as exclusion founded on race difference. He rejects the notion that the interpretive link embodying race and exclusion is anachronistic, because early modern Spain was by no means a prototypical nation state and the Jewish expulsion was religiously rather than racially motivated. The year of Columbus initially sailing to the West Indies, 1492, he emphasises, was a protean movement in the evolution of race and nation. Holt supports his argument by drawing from the observations of Elliot (1963, p. 110) that the triumph Columbus wanted the sovereigns to savour formed the basis of a unitary state in the only sense possible during the late fifteenth century.

It was purity of the Christian faith (Roman Catholicism) which did the job of nationalism. Religion did the work of race later used as the conduit for religion. Importantly, when the Spanish Inquisition targeted Jews, purity of faith was altered to mythic purity of blood. Though valid establishment of such purity would not have been possible for Imperial Spain or Imperial Britain, the use of blood droppings (one drop rule in the US, for instance), such droppings are imprinted within deeper venous tracts constitutive of what Holt identifies as a network linking the modern nation state, fashioning of national consciousness, and varied racial identities.

Race and nation, which therefore emanated from European expansion and development of modern political economies, have been two principal instruments for setting boundaries, while other signals of identity and difference either weakened or ceased to exist (Holt 2000, p. 55). This is a point eloquently captured in Williams (1964), who would find favour with the view that race and nation served as balms for socially dangerous anxieties of persons meeting the challenges of rapidly changing social environments. I continue with Holt, who exemplifies the perversity of race by looking at his own biography, which he links to the inadequacy of using biology as a foundation to generating claims about race.

Using the experience in university classes where he posed the question 'What is race?' to American students, he states that what typified responses was a reliance in different forms upon biology or physical difference. Upon hearing such answering he gave himself the job of deconstructing the replies by explaining that though biological attributes, assessed phenotypically or genetically, may well be race markers, they do not do actual work of race distinction and differentiation. He points to just such inadequacy by describing his own physical presence: he is classified as black because of dark skin, but only after location in sunny regions does his skin become dark brown. For the greater part of any year, however, especially within Chicago where he teaches, his skin tone is ashy brown. He adds that among extended family, specifically on his paternal grandmother's side—thanks to the lustful ways of a Virginia slave master—there are many relatives whose presence is not distinguishable from what is typically defined as white. According to what measures, he asks, did these relatives come to be classified as black in America? His reply: using colour alone cannot be applied as the sole referent to account for one family branch, even if he conceded that colour places him within a phenotypic order.

The invocation of genetics is inadequate also. He observes that genetics has been used to define races as sharing a common gene pool, something which predisposes them to particular physical tendencies such as body type, hair, and eye coloration. This use, which seems congruent with much of common knowledge persons possess about their bodies, carries a veneer of scientific solidity and objectivity. It seems to make good sense also because people can point to predisposing circumstances for ailments like sickle cell anaemia, Tay-Sachs disease, or the condition lactose intolerance, all traceable racially. Even in the face of all this information, biology fails to perform its task within race language construction. Biological race cannot be accommodated within its boundaries.

> *Common gene pools arise and are sustained in the first place because of the endogamous mating practices of a given population, which are in turn the consequence of geographic isolation, social or political restrictions on mating outside the group, and so forth. In short, gene pools don't decide by themselves that they "share" something (Holt 2000, p. 11).*

One upshot of the foregoing state of affairs is that biological, essentialised race categorisation frequently constructed as given, is dependent upon several other factors which are social rather than biological. Further, when the inoperability of these factors becomes exemplified via developments such as population migration, interracial social contacts, as well as modification to socio-legal practices, biological foundations, the pillars and cornerstones to race, become untenable.

It is with an eye upon social factors that Jackson (1971, pp. 160-161) notes racism is a matter of ingrained traditional dispositions shaped by institutions. Some racists, for whom the evil is as natural as the reflex of breathing, can be identified in three categories. The overt, self-satisfied racist does not conceal his hatred, while the self-interdicting racist adopts and develops racism regardless of his/her studious attempts at hiding hate. In addition, there is the unconscious racist, whose dispositions emerge from preconceived ideas owed to historical circumstances. What Jackson does in addressing himself to racism is identify exactly the type of feature some interpretive sociologists deem the social construction of reality.

My point is that racism can be viewed as a form of social construction whose important aspects include, but are not restricted to, the negotiated emergent use of language through which persons balance their organisational roles with the discursive movement of talk, interpretive practices of such use, along with the inter-subjectivity of meaning. The notion that race and racism are socially constructed is clearly not lost to Holt (2000, pp. 21-22), who states that social construction varies according to different historical moments and social contexts. Further, what emerges from apprehending different historicity is an appreciation that there is no particular or single ahistorical racism. Racisms are historically specific. Thus, analysts ought to explore ways in which racial issues intersect with other social phenomena. Doing so signifies an understanding that the meaning of race and racism can be located at the junctures it creates with social formations of particular historical periods. Holt is clear that when he refers to social formations, he points to all interconnected structures of economic, political, and social power, as well as systems of meaning emergent from, and reflective of, the structures. Importantly, his focus is upon social relations which are neither totally determined nor completely voluntarist.

Holt's assessment of race and racism can be solidified by examining views of other analysts such as Espinosa and Haney Lopez.

> *Race is like a riddle. The answers seem obvious, yet with each one we find that race becomes even more puzzling, almost mysterious. We think we know race, yet none of the definitions seem to work. It is no accident that race is clear-cut and unknowable at the same time. Race works as an effective system of oppression because it is there*

and not there—is both a reality and a social construction. Race is quite like the "Tar baby." You punch the "tar baby," you think you have got him, but instead you become stuck. The more you try to exercise dominion, the more you are dominated. It may well be impossible to know what race is. Nevertheless, by critically examining that which we call race, we may move closer to an operational understanding of that which is experienced as real oppression (Espinoza 2000, p. 445).

Espinoza continues to problematise her very insightful efforts at understanding the paradox of race by assessing it as comprehensible and illusory: It is certainly indicative of matters of colour, ancestry, bloodlines, cultural histories, language, and rationality but also not about these matters. Race is elusive, despite efforts at systematic explanation, naming and category refinement.

Prominent among those who grapple with this sense of elusiveness in its dehumanising oppression are Mills (1998, pp. 76-77) and West (1999, p. 262). West states that racism, a social practice, is explained not by situating it primarily or solely within modes of production, but by locating it within cultural traditions of civilisations. It is just such locating he does while alluding to what he terms the brutal atrocities of white supremacy in the American past and present that loudly expose the harsh limits of American democracy against professed democratic ideals.

Race is the crucial intersecting point where democratic energies clash with American imperial realities in the very making of the grand American experiment of democracy. The voices and viewpoints of reviled and disempowered Amerindians, Asians, Mexicans, Africans, and immigrant Europeans reveal and remind us of the profoundly racist roots of the first American empire—the old America of expansionist Manifest Destiny. How ironic that the New World outpost of the British empire, which rested upon Amerindian lands and was greatly aided by predominantly African enslaved labourers, would institute a grand anti-imperial revolution and embark on a rich democratic experiment? (West 2004, p. 14)

Mills sees race as a politically constructed category forming the background for division between privileged whites and disadvantaged non-whites. It is against this background that he poses the query, who gets to be white?

Nine features make up the background. Here are the first five: (1) Race is relational, rather than autonomous. At least two groups must exist for the purpose of categorisation. (2) Race is dynamic and not static. Connections among races are altered with time. So are rules of racial membership and belonging. (3) The link between race and phenotype is conditional. That is to say, a given appearance is neither necessary nor sufficient for inclusion in the privileged group. Thus, in apartheid South Africa, Mills points out, quite correctly, that Japanese were classified as honorary white for trade purposes. Hence, phenotypical whiteness was not a requirement for being white. Similarly, in the USA where genealogical criteria were vital to racial assignment, phenotypically white persons who could pass as whites would count as black, because of the rule 'one drop of black blood.' (4) Race is typically designated in vertical terms of hierarchy and subordination. (5) For persons of a particular phenotype, race can vary temporarily while rules change within time, as well as geographically as a consequence of entry to other loci. Hence, persons of mixed black and white heritage passing as brown, mulattoes, or whites by Caribbean and Latin American rules can, and do, become black within the USA.

The latter four categorisations take the forms: (6) Race is an unreal categorisation. From biological and anthropological standpoints, race is non-existent. Thus, although persons make use of different race categories, Mills asserts most scientists deem such use to be on par with the category of phlogiston. (7) Race, in socio-historical and socio-political dispositions, however, is a reality with huge impact on persons' chances within the variation of everyday life. (8) Race is preserved via boundary maintenance against protests from subordinated races whose members seek inclusion among the privileged and against others who aim to abolish the categorisation. (9) Race is a global feature of white domination structured upon a white/non-white axis.

Mills (1998, pp. 50-53) points also to criteria that are used for racial identification in the world of everyday life: bodily appearance, ancestry, culture, and experience. Bodily appearance, or the eyeball test, is regularly applied for making summary assessments about race. Historically, this has been so for scientific and lay judgments of race. Further, appearance is generally—but not always—a valid visible manifestation of a deeper essence located in ancestry. According to Mills, the rule for ancestral adjudication is relative to specific socio-historical, socio-economic, and socio-political settings.

Culture is employed by persons committed to racial realism as an emanation of biological race. Mills stresses, however, that a crucial presupposition to invocation of culture as a criterion of race difference is the existence of clear demarcating features. Clarity in demarcating is not easily attainable and what Mills terms constancy of intermingling of people indicates: patterns originally connected to a particular group can be adopted by another group. It is, of course, adopting which Painter (2010, p. ix) explores with compelling intellectual insight that she offers from the standpoint that race is not a fact but an idea, the questioning of which requires replies from the conceptual rather than factual realm.

An important part of the Mills questioning takes the form of exposing the erroneous connections made between colour and space—connections with historical precedents or backgrounds deeply rooted within the white European imperialist experience of conquest and arrogated superiority in judgment over persons of darker skins. This is the experience, I submit, which has become foundational to European intellectual dispositions geared towards discourse formation used for distorting or erasing achievements of Africans—including those who came to America involuntarily. Mills (1997, pp. 41-42) is therefore correct in alluding to European norming of people via the act of spacing, representing some individuals as imprinted with particular features of persons (Europeans) and sub-persons (non-Europeans in other parts of the world) according to the spaces they occupy.

The matter of norming and a connection to space can, of course, be identified in the very popular Francis Ford Coppola Hollywood film *Apocalypse Now*, based on the novel *Heart Of Darkness* by Joseph Conrad. For Mills, the upriver journey in the screen portrayal of the book is an interior journey, a passage from the outposts of European civilisation to savage territory. Such passage, consisting of a correlation between evil within and evil without, is meant to signify expedition into a geographic and personal heart of darkness.

Thus in Apocalypse Now, Francis Ford Coppola's 1979 rewriting of Conrad in the context of Vietnam, Willard's (Martin Sheen) journey upriver to find Kurtz (Marlon Brando), whose stages are sartorially marked through the gradual stripping away of the (civilized) uniform of the US army, the final mud-caked, machete-carrying figure indistinguishable from the Cambodian villagers ceremonially killing the buffalo, is both a normative descent into moral corruption and moral ascent to the realization that the war could have been won only by abandoning the restraints of Euro-American civilization (as demonstrated in My Lai presumably) and embracing the "savagery" of the North Vietnamese army (Mills 1997, p. 47).

Mills is, unquestionably, correct in his claims. After having read the book I drew some remarkable conclusions: (a) Conrad was an unapologetic racist (b) He demonstrated an extraordinary interest in contrasting enlightenment, which he linked to Europe, and darkness, which he linked to Africa (c) He used the contrast as a powerful way to evoke horrific imagery about Africa. Allow me to begin making my case by referring to an analysis from the African writer Achebe (1975) about the Conrad contrast between the Thames and the River Congo.

In Achebe's view, Conrad projects an image of Africa as the antithesis of Europe, a locus of civilisation. Africa in its triumphant bestiality mocks human intelligence and refinement. What Conrad does is point to a need in Western psychology to use Africa as a foil to Europe. Africa, unquestionably remote and hardly familiar, is a place of negations. It is unlike Europe, a place in which spiritual grace is manifest. One way in which this difference between Africa and Europe is brought into very sharp focus by Conrad can be seen in accounts of the rivers Congo and Thames. For Conrad the River Congo is decidedly not like the Thames, a River Emeritus, a waterway that has rendered its service and is deserving of what Achebe calls 'old-age pension.' Through eyes of the seemingly ubiquitous Marlow travelling on the Congo, it is like travelling back to the earliest beginning of the world. This, according to Marlow, "wanderer" and follower of the sea, is Africa, a locus that has been one of the dark places of the earth.

This is clearly not the Conrad experience of the Thames:

We looked at the venerable stream not in the vivid flush of a short day that comes and departs forever, but in the august light of abiding memories. And indeed nothing is easier for a man who has, as the phrase goes, "followed the sea" with reverence and affection, than to evoke the great spirit of the past upon the lower reaches of the Thames. The tidal current runs to and fro in its unceasing service, crowded with memories of men and ships it has borne to the rest of home or to the battles of the sea. It had known and served all the men of whom the nation is proud, from Sir Francis Drake to Sir John Franklin, knights all, titled and untitled—the great knights—errant of the sea. It had borne all the ships whose names are like jewels flashing in the night of time, from the Golden Hind returning with her round flanks full of treasure, to be visited by the Queen's Highness and thus pass out of the gigantic tale, to the Erebus and Terror, bound on other conquests—and that never returned. It had known the ships and the men. They had sailed from Deptford, from Greenwich, from Reith—the adventurers and the settlers; kings' ships and the ships of men on 'Change; captains, admirals, the dark "interlopers" of the Eastern trade, and the commissioned "generals" of East India fleets. Hunters of gold or pursuers of fame, they all had gone out on that stream, bearing the sword, and often the torch, messengers of the might within the land, bearers of the spark from the sacred fire. What greatness had not floated on the ebb of that river into the mystery of an unknown earth! The dreams of men, the seed of the commonwealths, the germs of empires (Conrad 1984/2002, p. 446).

Reverence for the River Thames in the foregoing passage is unquestionable. What is indubitably obvious in those words is the horror in imperialism which doomed Africans whose lands were parcelled, pillaged, and plundered by the European invaders. One such interloper was Mr. Kurtz, a central figure in *The Heart Of Darkness*. It is to his presence that I turn with the very specific aim of revealing some aspects of the Conrad racism.

Born to English and French parents, Mr. Kurtz, one of the most successful ivory dealers, a man whose sympathies—according to Conrad—were in the right place, was once asked by the International Society for the Suppression of Savage Customs to provide it with a report for its future guidance. The report, seventeen pages long, which vibrated with eloquence and ended with the imperative, 'Exterminate all the brutes', began with the argument that because of the advancement among whites they must appear to savages as supernatural beings. Such beings, through sheer exercise of their will, can exert power for infinite good. Whites, members of an august benevolence, are rulers of an exotic Immensity. Although Conrad makes no effort to provide the complete report, it should be obvious that he is alluding to the superiority of whiteness.

Anyone who has doubts about his allusion should be persuaded by noting the great frequency with which he uses the words 'nigger' and 'niggers' with unmistakeable derogation. Achebe is clear that the writer has an inordinate love of such terms, something that could be of interest to psychoanalysts. Let me add that it is not just psychoanalysts who could express their interests. I think experts such as speech act analysts, sociologists in the fields of ethnomethodology, dramaturgy, and conversation analysis, linguistic scientists, all of whom make language use a central investigative concern, could take a profound interest. All the people to whom Conrad applies the N word, his savages, are of course black Africans. These are beings immersed in darkness, a preoccupation with which he begins and ends his writing.

Thus, in a description and assessment of one embodiment of this darkness he refers to "a wild and gorgeous apparition of a woman" whom Achebe regards as, perhaps, a mistress to Mr. Kurtz, who lay dying in what Conrad described as the heart of an immense darkness:

> She walked with measured steps draped in striped and fringe cloths, treading the earth proudly, with a slight jingle and flash of barbarous ornaments. She carried her head high; her hair was done in the shape of a helmet; she had brass leggings to the knee, brass wire gauntlets to the elbow, a crimson spot on her tawny cheek, innumerable necklaces of glass beads on her neck; bizarre things, charms, gifts of witch-men, that hung about her, glittered and trembled at every step. She must have had the value of several elephant tusks upon her. She was savage and superb, wild-eyed and magnificent; there was something ominous and stately in her deliberate progress. And in the hush that had fallen suddenly upon the whole sorrowful land, the immense wilderness, the colossal body of the fecund and mysterious life seemed to look at her, pensive, as though it had been looking at the image of its own tenebrous and passionate soul (Conrad 1984/2002, pp. 487-488)

For Achebe, this woman's location in the *Heart Of Darkness* serves to fulfil a structural requirement to Conrad's tale. She is a savage counterpart—I would claim a savage antithesis—to the elegant European female who completes the story. Who is this counterpart? She is a mourner who visits the massive dark expanse and eulogises Kurtz in an effusively charming manner. With her fair hair, a pale visage, mature capacity for fidelity, she speaks to Marlow of Kurtz's noble confidence, his generosity, his goodness, and his greatness.

I think the distinction between the two women is significant for other reasons. In speaking about Kurtz, whose death was reported by an insolent black head in a doorway, the European female retrieves and restores his character. She resurrects it. She overlays it with reverence; in doing all of these things she venerates Europe, all of which contributed to making him who he had become. There is no such veneration of Africa from the presence of the black woman whom, I emphasise, has just a physical presence. Conrad denies her language. Without speech he condemns her to silence: she is present and yet absent. Clarity in the verbal and non-verbal presence from her European counterpart sets her apart, for she has a mere physical presence which reeks of a stark ambiguity.

The Conrad denial of language is also rather odd—perhaps both piercing and paralytic: he was enormously proficient in at least two European languages, Polish and English, and quite probably French. It is his extraordinary literary skill in English, neither his first language nor mother tongue—not Polish—which gave him world prominence. He however denies the African woman language. Given her closeness to Kurtz, another European language user, she has no hint of a facility in language from that continent. Such absence is especially compulsive, for through Conrad's eyes European imperialists, givers of benevolence—whatever that means to him—would have wasted no time imposing their cultures upon Africa. Even worse is the Conrad denial of a first language facility to the African woman whose application he could not have lost in translation. Without extending the heights to my imagination I must add that there is no hint of her proficiency in a lingua franca within a setting where followers of the sea had been interacting.

The Conrad denial of language to Africans is part of a large context within which denial has long existed. Achebe reports, very validly, that none other than Hugh Trevor Roper, an Oxford professor, claimed that African history was non-existent. Roper is in the very good company of other notable British intellectuals such as H.A.L. Fisher, who makes it clear (Fisher 1949, p. 1219) that Africa, like South America where countless have dwelt, left no memorial, and contributed nothing to the future. To the conquest of nature via use of knowledge contributions by Africans (Egyptians excluded), introduced to the world as an economic convenience, lies within the non-existent category. In emphasising the grand world significance of European civilisation, Fisher declares that Europeans, children of Hellas, have marked their civilisation with a stamp which is distinct from other great civilisations within the human family: Semites, Chinese, Persians, Hindus. He adds that European civilisation, all-pervading and preponderant, is indicated in operation of the European mind. I presume it is with this mind that Conrad was operating when he made Marlow the central character, principal narrator, and participant observer in *The Heart of Darkness.* It is to Marlow that I direct my attention now.

Those who are unaware of Conrad's portrayal of Marlow's socio-geographical and socio-economic insights, as well as imagery in figurative language use, should ponder these Marlow ideas.

"Now when I was a little chap I had a passion for maps. I would look for hours at South America, or Africa, or Australia, and lose myself in all the glories of exploration. At that time there were many blank spaces on earth, and when I saw

one that looked particularly inviting on a map (but they all look like that) I would put my finger on it and say, 'When I grow up I will go there.' The North Pole was one of these places, I remember. Well, I haven't been there yet, and shall not try now. The glamour's off. Other places were scattered about the Equator, and in every sort of latitude all over the two hemispheres. I have been in some of them, and...well, we won't talk about that. But there was one yet—the biggest, the most blank, so to speak—that I had a hankering after. True, by this time it was not a blank space any more. It had got filled with rivers and lakes and names. It had ceased to be a blank space of delightful mystery—a white patch for a boy to dream gloriously over. It had become a place of darkness. But there was in it one river especially, a mighty big river, that you could see on the map, resembling an immediate and immense snake uncoiled, with its head in the sea, its body at rest curving afar over a vast country, and its tail lost in the depths of the land. And as I looked at the map of it in a shop-window, it fascinated me as a snake would a bird—a silly little bird. Then, I remembered there was a big concern, a Company for trade on that river. Dash it all! I thought to myself, they can's trade without using some kind of craft on that lot of fresh water—steamboats! Why shouldn't I try to get charge of one. I went on along Fleet Street, but could not shake off the idea. The snake had charmed me."[2]

My exploration of the Marlow fascination—figurative and literal—laced with contradiction in imagery not unfamiliar to hard hearted imperialists—conveyed through the Conrad experience of *TheHeart of Darkness* would be of little use if I did not add that novels of the imperialist period explored connections between whiteness in colonising societies and non-white others abroad in colonial territories (Bhattacharyya, Gabriel, and Small 2002, p. 11).

While examining what Bhattacharyya et al. regard as development of white male settler ideology in relation to non-white others, Morrison (1992, p. 44) proposes that concerns of autonomy, authority, newness, difference, and absolute power become principal themes and presumptions within American literature. These concerns are shaped also by a complex awareness and application of social formation about Africanism. Morrison solidifies her proposition with the view that whiteness served as both the synonym for self-realisation via conquest, civilisation, and enlightenment, and antonym for boundless nature, savagery, and darkness.

It would by no means be trivial of me to emphasise that Joseph Conrad was Jozef Teodor Konrad Nalecz Korzeniowski, born in 1857. It was his great love of the sea that propelled him to make voyages during the latter half of the nineteenth century to Australia, South America, the West Indies, Pacific Islands, and Africa. Interestingly, it was while he served in the Belgian Imperial Service, what I have no reservation in characterising as a blatantly illegal organisation, that he navigated the Congo River. It was that African experience which formed the basis to his *Heart of Darkness*. This extraordinarily impressive literary genius, greatly revered in European circles for his command of the English language, had no trouble writing about "dusty niggers with splay feet" and "sulky niggers," as well as the European organisation "Society For The Suppression Of Savage Customs and Niggers" in varied circumstances.

Long after Korzeniowski had died (1960), powerful echoes of his racism in popular writing, I add by no means coincidentally, could be found in none other than a lurid assessment of the first black African leader of an independent Congo where he was brutally assassinated to satisfy European and United States imperialists. His name: Patrice Lumumba, assessed by a Belgian mouthpiece of imperialism, the paper *La Libre Belgique*. According to de Witte (2001, p. 147), Lumumba was portrayed as a man of unstable character, propelled at best by infantile impulses, at worst by a form of psychosis specific to blacks noted in *Conrad's Heart of Darkness*.

> *He was a man of prodigious vitality. He was said to be paranoid, and probably was. He had the physical signs of it, slim hands with long fingers, an eager and animated expression, a feline mask, extreme agitation. His ambition was boundless, his hatred merciless. He would have sacrificed the whole world for his thirst for power... Charming, an immensely talented orator, he could stir crowds. He was by far the most talented of the Congo's politicians... He was a cruel man, incapable of governing... He lived only for political struggles, showing exceptional stamina and physical courage, never hesitating to enter his adversaries' bastions, loving the challenge of it, and sowing fire and blood in his wake... On thirtieth June [1960] he read his speech insulting the King whom only the day before he had greeted full of smiles... After the mutiny, he had words of consolation for the rebels' victims... A few days later, he was spitting out the venom he had so far held in check... He had a plan: to seize and hold power. All the rest was improvisation. And this in the end was his undoing. For him, politics was merely a terribly exciting game which he played with successive displays of audacity. The game turned out badly for him, and for the Congo, victim of his insanity. It will continue to pay the price with his blood, for killing will continue in his name. We must not forget this.*

It was in this very newspaper that a former Belgian Ambassador to the Congo described Patrice Lumumba as someone personifying a new kind of Lucifer in the silence of the African night (de Witte 2001, p. 149). That silence and, I add, darkness, was not unknown to Belgian King Leopold II, who used the dehumanisation in work from his International Association for the Civilisation of Central Africa made up of explorers, geographers, and scientists for subjecting Africans to machinations of Fisher's European mind.

It is that very European mind which was churning in January 1863, the very month when *The Emancipation Proclamation* was put into legal effect within the American South (Olusoga 2016, pp. 374-375). What was churning? Olusoga writes that a faction of the London Ethnological Society seceded and created the Anthropological Society of London. The founders, all eminent men, included the Africa explorer Richard Burton, poet, A.C. Swinburne, anthropologist, James Hunt, and arguably the principal propagandist for the American Southern cause within Britain, editor of the pro-slavery Confederate newspaper *The Index*. The secessionists were mainly men subscribing to polygenism, an idea that the various races are so hugely anatomically and intellectually different that they make up different and distinct species associated with no common ancestor. Several members advocated the pseudoscience phrenology, an erroneous but fashionable set of views that measurements of various features of the human skull indicated intellectual capabilities of individuals and races.

During the course of an 1863 meeting of the British Association for the Advancement of Science in Newcastle upon Tyne, Hunt delivered a paper titled *On The Physical And Mental Character Of The Negro*, in which he offered the view that Africans, members of a separate species, were closer to apes than Europeans. Just prior to the Hunt delivery, John Crawfurd, an ex-colonial governor, convert to polygenism, presented his paper titled *The Comixture Of The Races Of Man As Affecting The Progress Of Civilisation*. In a frontal denunciation of the capabilities of Africans,

Crawfurd claimed that although African children displayed intellectual potential during early years, they were overcome later by intellectual lethargy. Thus, in the West Indies all Africans in positions of trust requiring intellectual ability possess European features. In the Hunt terminology, full-blooded woolly-haired typical Africans were in every instance devoid of intellectual gifts. Civilised Africans, those possessing skills, capacities, and aptitudes, are not pure blacks: in almost all cases European blood flows through their veins. Further, African children there, though precocious, do not benefit from any progress in education once they attain puberty. They simply remain children mentally.

Overtly and emphatically hostile towards abolition of slavery, the Anthropological Society mocked and derided Christian missionaries for doing work among Africans, whom the Society claimed could neither progress nor be civilised. The hostility reached a high point when scorn was heaped upon the Christian Union in a front window display made up of an articulated skeleton of a 'savage.' Away from public scrutiny their intense racism was not concealed: Burton became central to formation of The Cannibal Club, entirely a male only dining club whose members met in the private banquet room of Bartolini's Dining Rooms close to Fleet Street. The club's official symbol, a mace carved to look like the head of an African male, served to show the man's jaws gnawing at a human thigh bone. Swinburne even entertained fellow diners with his composition of a Cannibal Catechism meant to deride Christian rites. While accepting that The Cannibal Club proceedings did become subjects of lurid speculating and academic exploration, Olusoga is clear in linking the club with what he assesses as its bacchanalian, fanatical antipathy to Christianity, fixation with sex, male sexuality, and pornography.

Patrice Lumumba was eliminated in horrific form. While his African brother, Kamau Ngengi, Dr. Jomo Kenyatta, did not suffer such a fate at the hands of the British he—deemed by them to be leader of the Mau Mau, which they branded as cruel blood drinkers—was incarcerated by them. A British governor to Kenya, Sir Patrick Renison, a governor in British Guiana also, once described Dr. Kenyatta as a leader unto darkness and death. The British, so stated the Courts in London—albeit only at the beginning of the twenty-first century—did torture Kenyans during the time of the independence struggle. I am certain other instances of British torture against Africans across the continent at the time of independence struggles can be found.

In his efforts to apprehend the analytical complexity linked to assessing race, inextricably bound up with the despicable brutality I have noted, Haney Lopez (2000, p. 165-166) states that race is not essence or illusion. It is a continuous, self-reinforcing, but contradictory and plastic process influenced by macro forces of social and political struggles and micro forces of everyday life. He explains race as constituting a group of persons loosely connected by historically contingent, socially significant aspects of their morphology and/or ancestry. Race, he adds, should be regarded as a social reality within which contested systems of meaning form the links among physical features, faces, and personal features. It is social meanings that link physical presence to our souls. Hence, terms such as black and white and yellow are social groupings, rather than genetically distinct branches of humanity resting on science. Further, race designation such as Caucasoid, Negroid, and Mongoloid emanates from European imagination of the Middle Ages referable only to Europe, Africa, and the Near East. This restrictive construction did not account for people of the American continents, India, East Asia, South East Asia, and Oceania.

Confusion of the social with restrictive science can be seen in efforts to construct racial typologies on the basis of skin colour.

On the basis of white skin, for example, one can define a race that includes most of the people of Western Europe. However, this grouping is threatened by the subtle gradations of skin colour as one moves south or east, and becomes untenable when the fair skinned peoples of Northern China and Japan are considered (Haney Lopez 2000, p. 167).

Thus, in 1922, when Japanese born Takao Ozawa made an application for US citizenship, on grounds that he was white under the United States Naturalisation Act, his application was rejected. So was his claim to the United States Supreme Court. The Court reasoned that racial divisions do not accord with skin colour. Accepting Ozawa's petition would also have been tantamount to including persons who were clearly non-white in the white category and excluding others who were white. The Court's reasoning rested on its consideration of an inconsistency between common knowledge and science, but used both to render its ruling: Ozawa was not of the type popularly known (common knowledge) as a member of the Caucasian race (science) (Haney Lopez 2000, p. 629). That year, Bhagat Singh Thind, an Indian, petitioned the Court and, like Ozawa, did not succeed.

Thind would not have been successful in the very early twentieth century either because pressure from organisations such as the Asiatic Exclusion League had a major impact on laws surrounding naturalisation. Among the principal claims advanced by the League was the position in 1910 that Asian Indians belonged to an effeminate, caste ridden race whose members were ineligible for citizenship (Haney Lopez 2000, p. 627). Indians, like Syrians, were sometimes, however, designated as white and non-white for naturalisation purposes, while applicants from Hawaii (US statehood in 1960), China, Japan, Burma, and the Philippines were deemed non-white.

In Thind's case, Haney Lopez reasoned that because the Court had equated Caucasian with white, he should have been granted citizenship on grounds of being Caucasian, thus white. The Court, on common sense, condemned what it deemed scientific manipulation which removed racial difference by classifying far more individuals as Caucasian than were necessitated in what was suggested by the unscientific mind. Importantly, the average well informed white American would express dismay upon learning that his race consists of varied membership. In part of his assessment of the Thind case, Haney Lopez argues that application of common knowledge to justify racial designation shows that racial typology is nullified by social demarcation and race is a socially mediated idea.

Given the precedence he attaches to the social, Haney Lopez (2000, p. 167) is explicit in his view that the rejection of race in science is almost complete. What were once deemed objective race categories are empty relics, enduring shadows of social beliefs that dominated early scientific thinking. Biological race is just illusion (Haney Lopez 2000, p. 172). He calls for acceptance of a position from historian Barbara Fields: "Anyone who continues to believe in race as a physical attribute of individuals, despite the now commonplace disclaimers of biologists and geneticists, might as well also believe in Santa Claus, the Easter Bunny and the tooth fairy are real, and that the earth stands still while the sun moves." The Fields and Haney Lopez stances are quite consistent with those of Johnson (2006, p. 23) who states that racial differences are superficial rather than fundamental, and phenomena such as pure black or pure white races do not exist.

If biological race is to be rejected in favour of social meaning, what would be an appropriate way of conceptualising race? Haney Lopez (2000, p. 168) opts for the derivation of something from racial formation. He calls it racial fabrication, which suggests the intention to deceive. His goal—not unlike that of Holt's—is emphasising the social construction of race through which humans (not abstract social forces) produce races which make up a social configuration that also covers gender and class connections.

There is, obviously, no single sociological view of race and racism. One thing is clear to me about the accounts I use. They are all indicative of differential treatment and encompass elements of power exercised on the part of those who are racist. Farley (1988, p. 8) regards racism as any attitude, belief, behaviour, or institutional arrangement favouring one race or ethnic group over another. For Eliot and Fleras (1992, p. 52), racism is a doctrine which unjustifiably advances the supremacy of one group over another on grounds of arbitrarily chosen features relevant to appearance, intelligence, and temperament. Fleras and Kunz (2001, p. 33) regard racism as a set of ideas, ideals, and ideology used for asserting or suggesting the superiority of one social group over another on grounds of biological or cultural features linked to institutionalised power. Further, the connection is applied to actualise racialised beliefs in a manner aimed at denying or excluding minority persons. The reference to biology and power can be understood also as a reference to: (1) application of judgmental and moral features aimed at ranking persons into different categories (2) the manner in which some individuals and groups create ideas about what constitute normality, desirability, and acceptability, which serve to solidify super-ordination (3) Ways in which aspects of super-ordination and domination are used for invoking racial and cultural differences geared to enforcing control over others designated as subordinate in the battle for scarce resources.

In doing further exploration of matters of super-ordination and its opposite, inferiorisation, as well as justification—albeit perverse—for these two features I turn to West (1999, pp. 70-71), who examines racism from a genealogical perspective. He claims, pointedly, that the African American engagement with the modern world has been shaped primarily by the doctrine of white superiority, which is integral to institutionalised practices and actualised in everyday folkways. His principal concern is with the discursive possibilities under which ideas of white supremacy are legitimised and made intelligible. He wants to uncover the complex configuration of metaphors, notions, categories, and norms that foster and produce white super-ordination as an object of discourse. This is configuration born of a logic from which specific conceptions of knowledge, truth, character, and beauty are applied with exclusionary purposes. Thus, black equality in beauty, culture, and intellectual ability are not subjects of the logic. They are relegated to silence that reflects powerlessness of black people and point to discourse mechanisms within late seventeenth and eighteenth century Europe.

He lists three moments in his genealogical approach, all of which are pertinent to the dilemma highlighted by West Indies cricket captain Brian Lara, President Obama, and Mr. Kaepernick. They are: (1) A radical inquiry into the emergence, growth, and support of white supremacist logic within modern western civilisation (2) A micro-institutional examination of strategies which foster and oppose the logic in persons' everyday lives. Included here are modes in which self-images and identities are formed, as well as consequences for persons of colour of degrading cultural styles, aesthetic ideals, psychosexual sensibilities, and linguistic gestures. (3) A macro-structural approach in which emphasis is given to strategies persons of colour employ for resisting overdetermined class exploitation, state oppression, and bureaucratic domination (West, 1999, p. 263).

No exploration of race and racism would be adequate without reference to the term, nation. It is to this matter that I grant my attention, now with particular focus upon the USA in 2016, a time when the Donald Trump gambits integral to shameless racism and sexism were paraded under the guise of making America great again! Trump, former Reagan aide, Jeffrey Lord, Sheriff Joe Arpaio, Governors Jan Brewer, Chris Christie, Sarah Palin, as well as New York Mayor Rudy Giuliani, who claims that President Obama does not know about Western civilisation, and supporters, one of whom stated he might have to kill a protester the next time such a protester appeared at Trump rallies, and his throngs of 2016 Confederates, have been steadfastly beholden to creating what could be described as the US cultural nation, a community constitutive of distinct people, their own language, ways of life, homeland, and history.

> When a state claims to constitute such a cultural nation it is seeking to arrogate to itself the power of the kinship myth by portraying the whole society as an ethnic community. The claim to cultural nationhood allows the state to demand the allegiance of its people in ways that echo the imperative of ethnic loyalty. The nation is depicted as offering identity, security and authority to its members such as the family offers the child, and in return the nation demands the loyalty and allegiance the child owes to the family. The more that the state can point to, or itself generate, the common cultural attributes which define the cultural nation, the more claim it has to allegiance of its members. Similarly, the more clearly an individual possesses the cultural attributes which define the national community, the more fully does that individual deserve the citizenship rights accruing to membership of the nation (Brown 1996, p. 307).

This is the exclusive Trump nation which gives no dignified spaces and statuses to people of colour. This is the Trump nation, the nation of Hannity, Limbaugh, Coulter, and base supporters scowling furiously about absence of that border wall over which THE MAAFA MUZUNGU MONSTROSITY shut down government and barked brazenly about associating his billion dollar wall construction with a state of emergency. This is the very Trump nation in which those base supporters take comfort from what Baldwin (1971, p. 22) assesses as refuge in their whiteness, one of the monstrous traps where they are placed at a sinister distance between their own experience and the experience of others.

Baldwin is emphatic that they can never see themselves as sufficiently human, adequately worthwhile to take responsibility for themselves, their leaders, country and fate.

> They will perish (as we once put it in our Black church) in their sins—that is, in their delusions. And this is happening, needless to say, already, all around us (Baldwin 1971, p. 22).

Refuge, unquestionably a delusion, according to Baldwin, comes in an exclusivist disposition that their brothers are all white, but also that whites are all their brothers.

The election year, 2016, followed also the murders of young black males on city street corners where the blood of American citizens such as Mr. Freddie Gray, Mr. Trayvon Martin, and Mr. Mike Brown still marks terror trails from racist white policemen and civilians. 2016 is the year which immediately follows the time when there was racist elimination by a young Mr. Dylan Roof of black congregants in a

Southern church, which had become more than a citadel, sanctuary, and bedrock in battles within the Deep South. I will never forget that in the wake of the brutality, state legislators, rather than remove the apartheid Confederate Flag from its building, made it clear that the matter of removal had to be debated by lawmakers who would have to vote in regard to such removal. A dismayed and horrified Dr. Cornel West wasted no time on television in issuing an explicit challenge to white America by asking his interviewer to imagine whether a debate would have been held in America to remove the Nazi flag.

The West reference to the Nazi flag should in no way be taken as an oblique reference: Van Den Berghe (1980, p. 80) does make the point that the closest historical parallel to the South African apartheid political system is to be found in the deep South of the United States. He notes, also, that Nazism and Afrikaner nationalism in apartheid South Africa are unquestionably similar in their heightened nationalism and racism. In accepting the good sense to the Van Den Berghe statements I wish to draw from ideas of Connor (1996, pp. 72-73) for specifying one despicable aspect to the parallel, an aspect still alive across the deep South. Connor uses what he describes as the German maxim 'Blut will zu Blut!' which when translated to English expresses the sentiment, 'People of the same blood attract!' He adds that a German writer, Adolph Stocker, broadened the sentiment in claiming: "German blood flows in every German body, and the soul is in the blood."

When one meets a German brother and not merely a brother from common humanity, there is a certain reaction that does not take place if the brother is not German."[3] The term, 'German,' so adds Connor, could be replaced by terms such as Russian, Lithuanian, and English without affecting the validity in the passage. Knowing what I know specifically about the city where Roof committed his acts, and generally the deep South, I take the view that among the large numbers of racists there, the terms 'American' or 'white American' could be used as replacements.

With the foregoing matters very much at the forefront of my mind I turn, initially, to 'issues.' In using the term 'issues,' I am guided by a Marxian Freudian synthesis offered by philosopher Herbert Marcuse, one of the leading proponents of what has become known as critical theory from the Frankfurt School, and the sociological imagination enunciated by sociologist Charles Wright Mills. Thus, when Marcuse (1982, p.52) claims that art, a rupture with the established repressive reality principle, invokes images of liberation, I am in total agreement and, rather importantly, view Test Match cricket, especially West Indies Test Match cricket prior to Brian Lara, in the way Marcuse views art. Further, the links to which I allude make sense, not merely because epistemological grounding to them all can be located within interpretive sociology, a centrepiece to my writing overlain with dramaturgical sociology and conversation analysis, but all elements to the links are also not antithetical to each other. While a project elucidating the connections is well-nigh outside the scope of my work here and could be handled effectively by interpretive experts, especially those with affinities to sociological theory, the very least I think I should do is lay some groundwork to the Marxian-Freudian synthesis, point to some significant ideas within the sociological imagination, explain the importance of dramaturgical and conversation analytic sociology, speech act analysis, and Marcuse's philosophical inquiry of Freud. Let me begin with dramaturgy, speech act analysis, and conversation analysis, all of which are connected with exploring the importance of language.

It would be reasonable to claim that the most prominent spokesperson for dramaturgical sociology is the Canadian sociologist, Erving Goffman, who—according to Hochschild (2003, p. 56)—sees everyone as an actor. It would not be out of order for me to add that the concept of 'impression management' which Goffman (1959) takes from Ichheiter (1949, pp. 6-7) lies at the core of dramaturgical sociology. I understand 'impression management' to be constitutive of: (a) In everyday life persons act as if they are on stage or performing (b) In their presence to each other they perform intentionally or unintentionally to express themselves (c) They aim to impress others (d) In expressing themselves, offering impressions, they give, as well as give off, signs (e) While giving off, they convey to others that their actions are done for purposes other than those stated in verbal symbols (f) In their presence to others, they also make use of information they already have about those others (g) They use the information to help define situations[4] in which they are (h) They use their subjective experiences, but it is not possible to determine all the factors that make up situations (i) They employ their definitions to control performance of others (j) They influence others by giving others the types of impression which lead those others to act in accordance with plans.

While considering impression management I am drawn to another matter of exploratory interest to Goffman (1967, p. 5). That matter is 'face,' someone's public self-image which is invested emotionally, can be protected, damaged, and lost. According to experts on politeness Brown and Levinson (1978, pp. 63-214), whenever persons use politeness strategies in their talk they risk threatening and damaging what these experts describe as positive and negative face. Dare I say that persons' use of politeness strategies constitutes very fertile exploratory ground, not just for conversation analytic sociologists, but also speech act analysts who would be very familiar with Searle's exemplification of indirect speech acts, some of which are, unquestionably, forms of politeness. When I look at Brian Lara's leadership flaws later, and consider what a predecessor stated about his leadedrship, I shall address myself to damage and loss of face within the Caribbean damage and loss that cannot be separated from such leadership. Let me turn now to speech act analysis.

Speech act analysis, owing to the pioneering work of Austin (1956, 1962) and Searle (1969, 1971, 1974, 1979a, 1979b, 1980, 1982, 1999), based upon viewing language as action, a matter of major direct interest to conversation analytic sociologists, has become prominent, partly but significantly, because of a categorisation of such action into five classes: assertives, commissives, directives, declaratives, and expressives. The significance of the classification rests not merely on links among speaker/hearers' intentionality, performance of action, and what Searle deems background assumptions to performance, but also the rule bound nature to performance. These rules, named by Searle constitutive rules emanating from speaker/hearers' knowledge about conventions in language, are not linguistic ones. Speech act analysts, I must emphasise, are not linguists either with a neo-Kantian, continental Cartesian, and neo-Platonist Chomskyan bent stemming from a focus upon universal transformational grammar rules (Chomsky 1982, p. 190), a focus the anarchist socialist psycholinguist/philosopher states is not separable from his work about the theory of mind, liberty, and human rights. Speech act analysts are philosophers of language who reject positivist sociological practice evidenced in preference for quantitative work by the social scientists, as well as the positivist turn in philosophy which reached its apogee in the work of the Vienna Circle.[5]

This very rejection is evidenced in the work of conversation analytic sociologists whose subject of study is what Hutchby and Woffitt (2002, p. 14) regard as the interactional organisation of social activities. For these experts, conversation analytic sociology, a radical shift from other linguistically oriented exploration, constitutes a primary focus upon what they deem practical social accomplishment. Thus, utterances in naturally occurring conversation are not examined as semantic units, but as constructs designed and used for negotiating activities. The reference to practical accomplishment is a deafening echo of what Garfinkel and Sacks (1970), respectively founders of ethnomethodology and conversation analytic sociology, regard as members' practices. What are members' practices? This term is used in reference to speaker/hearers' mastery of natural language use.

> The fact that natural language serves persons doing sociology—whether they are laymen or professionals—as circumstances, as topics, and as resources of their inquiries furnishes to the technology of their inquiries and to their practical sociological reasoning its circumstances, its topics, and its resources (Garfinkel and Sacks 1970, p. 338).

In an effort to exemplify just such mastery, Churchill (1978), who credits Garfinkel and Sacks for their pioneering work, explores criteria for identifying utterances as questions, question forms used for requesting information, and differing degrees of belief or certainty speaker/hearers use in proposals they make while posing questions. I take the view that such work is extremely significant. I add, however, that this significance can be embodied within a distinction I will use later. Here is the distinction: (a) forms of speech in which lexico-grammatical and phonological constraints on how hearers should speak is intended to give them the freedom to construct their own meaning (b) forms of speech in which lexico-grammatical and phonological constraints on how hearers should speak is not intended to give them the freedom to construct their own meaning. I refer to (a) as type 1 forms and (b) as type 2 forms.

Let me thus address myself to examining the Churchill position. In accepting claims from Bolinger (1957) about criteria for identifying utterances as questions, Churchill states that utterances must have interrogative distribution. In other words, the fact that a reply follows an utterance is evidence for inferring that a question elicited that response. An utterance must have interrogative syntax also. Examples of such construction are word order inverted from declarative form, question tags, and use of what I deem interrogative pronouns and adjectives at word initial positions in utterances. The third criterion for identifying an utterance as a question is use of interrogative intonation at the end of the utterance. Lastly, a question is uttered if production is associated with gestures indicating the utterance is a question.

Churchill points out that queries used for requesting information can be categorised into two groups, general questions and specific proposal questions. A general question can be exemplified in the form, WHAT IS SINGH'S OCCUPATION? This question, initiated with use of an interrogative pronoun, is aimed at wanting a hearer to select an element from an answer set for the question in the absence of any proposal to the hearer for a specific response. A specific proposal question can be exemplified as IS SINGH A LAWYER? This question is used for proposing as correct one of the elements from an answer set to the question. According to Churchill, elements in the answer set, Yes, No, can be used to confirm or disconfirm the proposal in the query. Further, specific proposal queries are of two types: intensive and non-intensive questions.

An example will make the distinction between non-intensive and intensive clear. The non-intensive form of the specific proposal question for the time is "Is it four o'clock?" The intensive form of that question that I have in mind is "Isn't it four o'clock?" The negative "not" carries the appearance that S [the speaker] has more belief in his proposal than in the non-intensive case. Hence, it is not a genuine negative in this usage (Churchill 1978, p. 51).

There are two other ways in which speakers can heighten appearance of belief in specific proposal queries. They can place what Churchill deems the question part after the proposal instead of prior to it. Thus, an utterance of the form, "It's five o'clock, isn't it?" suggests that a speaker has a higher degree of belief in her proposal than she does in "Isn't it four o'clock?" Speakers can use inflection, also with a purpose to heighten degree of belief. The query "It's four o'clock, isn't it?" with greater inflection upon *isn't* than upon *it* in utterance final position, is produced with greater certainty than the utterance with greater inflection upon *it*.

I must state that while I can, on a principled basis, accept the Churchill distinction between general and specific queries, as well as intensive and non-intensive questions, I can find no evidentiary basis to differing degrees of belief or certainty. In my view, making claims about speaker degree of belief or certainty is tantamount to making attributions about speakers' states of mind. To me this is not something that can be done with validity while using lexico-grammatical and phonological organisation for exploring the intricacies of speaker/hearers' conversations. It makes good sense to me, if someone claims that in uttering questions, general and specific, intensive and non-intensive specific, speakers use different strategies to restrict how hearers should respond. In other words, conventions to lexico-grammatical and phonological organisation, conventions used by speaker/questioners furnish me with hearable evidence that these speaker/questioners can, and do, set, particularise, and specify limits or boundaries within which responses should be offered. It is the idea of limiting, specifying, or particularising that I do not find alien to my type 1 and type 2 distinction.

It is Garfinkel (1967, p.11) who describes ethnomethodology as inquiry into the rational properties of indexical expressions and other practical actions as contingent ongoing accomplishments of organised artful practices of everyday life. In so doing he is indicating not merely that indexical expressions are meaningful as a consequence of their placement in contexts, but meaningfulness results also from what is negotiated in orderly and methodical ways of which speaker/hearers' naturally occurring talk is one instantiation. Further, with unmistakeable allusion to the pioneering phenomenological work from Alfred Schutz in elucidating the everyday world, Garfinkel (1967, p. 37) rightly credits his predecessor for having explored the seen but unnoticed background expectancies in everyday life, exploration linked to clarifying what Garfinkel describes as concerted actions. It is of course Schutz—via his clarification—who regards as fruitful exploring language construction in the world of everyday life.

It is thus without question to members' practices in everyday life that Hutchby and Woffitt (2002, p. 23) allude when they summarise the significance of conversation analytic sociology in four points: (a) talk-in-interaction is very ordered and organised systematically (b) the construction of talk-in-interaction is methodic (c) examination of talk-in-interaction should have a foundation in naturally occurring discourse (d) examination should not be constrained by prior theoretical assumptions. Adherence to these four ideas—principles—lies at the core of foundational work done by conversation analytic experts such as Heap (1979), Sacks and Schegloff (1975), Sacks, Schegloff, and Jefferson (1974, 1977), Schegloff (1972), Turner (1976), Atkinson (1984a, 1984b), Atkinson and Drew (1979). The basic building blocks for such work can be located in action that can be described as:

Action is social insofar as, by virtue of the subjective meaning attached to it by the acting individual (or individuals) it takes account of the behaviour of others and is thereby oriented in its course (Weber1964, p.88).[6]

The significance of the Weberian view to conversation analytic sociology lies not merely in the subjective meaning attached to action by social actors; that significance should be seen also in the reality that the subjective is a matter negotiated methodically and systematically in the practical accomplishment of naturally constructed talk.

Laying the groundwork to a Marcusean Marxian-Freudian synthesis and ideas of Mills consists in noting: (a) Both Marcuse and Mills demonstrated how movement can and should be made between the psychological and social (b) As such, they created important bridges between what has come to be known as social structure and social practice (c) Mills' work prefigured dramaturgical sociology partly well-known because of Erving Goffman's focus upon impression management. It is, of course, to dramaturgical sociology that conversation analysis, once deemed merely peripheral to sociology in general and orthodox interpretive sociology but now central to both, partly owes its emergence (d) Marcuse's work prefigured a move from what Prime Minister Mr. Michael Manley, cricketing expert, regards as doctrinaire Marxism to a Marxism within which there is ample room for a focus upon cultural issues to which discourses about several forms, including discourse about domination, are now central.

It is, thus, not out of place for me to note Marcuse's own words in regard to a question about marriage between Marxism and Freudianism. I invite readers to examine his claims and ask: Are these claims not applicable to the twenty-first century dominated by oligopoly capitalism?

I think they can easily be married, and it may well be a happy marriage. I think these are two interpretations of two different levels of the same whole, of the same totality. The primary drives, the unconscious primary drives which Freud stipulated—namely erotic energy and destructive energy, Eros and Thanatos, the Life Instincts and the Death Instinct—develop within a specific given social framework which in one way or the other regulates their manifestations. The social impact goes even further than that. According to Freud, the more intense the repression in society, the more sweeping the activation of surplus repression. Now, since, again according to Freud, repression is bound to increase with the progress of civilisation, then at the same time, and parallel to it, surplus aggressiveness will be released on an ever larger scale. In other words, with the progress of civilisation, we will have a progress in destructiveness, self-destruction as well as destruction of others—subjects and objects. It seems to me that this hypothesis well elucidates what happens today (Marcuse 1982, p. 48).

Before the reader replies, s/he should look at two other important points I offer about Marcuse's disposition, after which I shall begin looking at ideas from C.W.

Wright Mills. Marcuse (1966, pp. xxvii-xxviii) writes about the twentieth century human condition, especially within affluent capitalist societies such as the United States. Under this condition which in my view exists today, totalitarianism exists, although such totalitarianism has not produced totalitarian states.

This is the very condition, adds Marcuse, which has made the boundary between psychology and political and social philosophy obsolete. He states also that previously autonomous and identifiable psychical practices have been absorbed by functions of the individual in the state. Thus, psychological issues have been turned into political issues, private disorder reflects very directly societal disorder, and "the cure" of personal disorder rests very directly upon the cure for societal disorder. Further, such circumstances mean that using psychology to explore social and political occurrences is vitiated by links between private and societal disorder. What is needed for dealing with the connections is giving sociological substance to psychological notions.

Mills (1959, pp. 11-13) eschews what he skilfully examines as two of the dominant, but misleading intellectual forces in sociology, grand theory and abstracted empiricism. He is insistent that studies which do not encompass the problems of biography and history and of their intersections within society have not completed their intellectual journeys. He applies the sociological imagination as a means of locating ways in which persons become falsely conscious of everyday life. The sociological imagination facilitates apprehending connections between history and biographies within societies.

Its pursuit encompasses a tripartite inquiry: (a) What is the structure of a particular society? What are its essential components, how are they related and how do they differ from other versions of social order? (b) What is the place of society in history? What are its mechanisms of change? Where is the society positioned within humanity and what meaning does it have for humanity? (c) In what ways does the specific aspect of the society under examination affect, and is affected by, the historical period where it moves? What types of persons are dominant in that society currently, and what kinds of individuals are emerging as dominant? How are both groups of humans "selected and formed, liberated and repressed, made sensitive and blunted?"

> *Whether the point of interest is a great power state or a minor literary mood, a family, a prison, a creed—these are the kinds of questions the best social analysts have asked. They are the intellectual pivots of classic studies of man in society—and they are the questions inevitably raised by any mind possessing the sociological imagination. For that imagination is the capacity to shift from one perspective to another—from the political to the psychological; from examination of the single family to comparative assessment of the national budgets of the world; from the theological school to the military establishment; from considerations of an oil industry to studies of contemporary poetry (Mills 1959, p. 15).*

He adds that the sociological imagination embodies movement from the most impersonal and remote transformations to the most intimate features of selfhood, as well as the capacity to apprehend links between the two. What is foundational to this imagination is, invariably, an urge to become familiar with the social and historical meaning of persons in societies and the periods in which they have their qualities and their being.

What we experience in various specific milieu... is often caused by structural changes. Accordingly, to understand the changes of many personal milieu we are required to look beyond them. And the number and variety of such structural changes increases as the institutions within which we live become more embracing and more intricately connected with one another. To be aware of the idea of social structure and use it with sensibility is to be capable of tracing such linkages among a great variety of milieu. To be able to do that is to possess the sociological imagination (Mills 1959, p.17)

In using this sociological imagination to assess twentieth century American capitalism, assessment I think is applicable today to an America in the grip of oligopolistic corporate capitalism lauded by that MAAFA MUZUNGU MONSTROSITY, the misogynist-fascist Donald Trump, Mills (1959, pp. 276-287) writes that American capitalism is largely what he assesses as military capitalism.

It consists of a structure in which the most significant relations of giant corporations to the state, relations defined by the corporate wealthy and warlords, power elite relations, rest upon coincidence of interests between corporate and military needs. Within the entire power elite configuration coincidence strengthens not only the corporate and military sectors, it subordinates the roles of men in the political sector. While noting that effective units of power in the USA are giant corporations, what he also describes as inaccessible government, and the grim military establishment, he points to absence of a sense of security and authority within intermediate organisations among such units, on the one hand, and families and small communities, on the other.

The top of modern American society is increasingly unified, and often seems wilfully co-ordinated: at the top there has emerged an elite of power. The middle levels are a drifting set of stalemated, balancing forces: the middle does not link the bottom with the top. The bottom of this society is politically fragmented, and even as a passive pact, increasingly powerless: at the bottom there is emerging a mass society (Mills 1956, p. 324).

During the time of President Obama's tenure mass society was not just emerging, it had emerged already. It is the depth of the Mills insight I must continue using for the purpose of looking at this society in the twenty-first century. With his exploratory eyes cast away from grand theory, Mills rejects using the simple Marxian and liberal views for dealing with American capitalism, a phenomenon from both standpoints in which "the big political man" and "the big economic man" constitute the centrepieces of power.

For Mills both views, reflective of political and economic determinism, are oversimplified. In avoiding them by repudiating an assessment of capitalist power as something in the hands of a ruling class, Mills' choice to use the idea, 'power elite,' clearly not a choice to examine an aristocracy, is an analytical choice to examine organisational configuration often involving what he terms an uneasy coincidence of economic, military, and political power. Mills adds that power elite members are able to adopt one another's viewpoints, quite readily, feel responsibility to one another, define themselves as persons who count and must be taken into account. In addition, they incorporate into their personal integrity, honour, and conscience, the standpoints, expectations, and values of each other. This is the power elite, he adds, whose rise rests upon transformation of American publics into a mass society. A genuine public, which suggests a liberal tradition, in a society of publics is sovereign. It needs no master. Mass society is sovereign only on some plebiscitarian moment of adulation to an elite as authoritative celebrity.[7] Public opinion in publics exists when citizens, persons who are not members of government, claim rights to express their ideas freely and publicly, as well as, the right that such ideas should impact or determine personnel, policies, and actions of government.

The Mills notion of public opinion is a parallel to what he regards as the economic idea of a free economy. Let me be explicit that he is not, in any way, beholden to what is offered today as the benefits of free market capitalism. His notion of a free economy is of a market consisting of freely competing entrepreneurs. The parallel to this market is a public constitutive of discussion circles with opinion peers. Just as price is a reality resultant from anonymous, equally weighted bargaining individuals, public opinion emanates from each citizen having analysed socio-economic matters for herself and contributing her voice to what she deems the great chorus, I presume, known as public opinion.

What does Mills mean, when he writes about a liberal tradition? He specifies his stance by stating that in a milieu of liberal education, such education prevents publics from being overwhelmed. This is a context in which persons develop to become bold and sensible citizens who cannot be sunk under the deadweight of mass life. Yet, twentieth century America, he adds—and I state clearly, twenty-first century USA—is a locus in which educational practice has neither made knowledge directly available to citizens, so that they might be able to discern the foundations to their own biases and frustrations, nor conceptualise clearly about themselves.

A huge part of the deadweight to mass life in early twenty-first century United States was laid by the power elite. The twenty-first century—including the time of Mr. Obama's tenure, (2009-2017)—is a time when the globalisation imperative solidified: with powerful instruments such as the North American Free Trade Agreement (NAFTA), the Trans-Pacific Partnership (TPP), regular G-20 and Pacific Rim Partnership meetings within a foreground of a United States dominated World Bank and IMF America's power elite is well and truly entrenched. The time of Mr. Obama's tenure is a time also when the US is dominated and being destroyed by oligopoly capitalism from transnationals whose captains use the lure and lore from insatiable consumerism for priming their pockets. Such is the case, despite the catastrophic ecological consequences of priming, not just for the WRETCHED OF THE EARTH[8] eking out an existence within global cities[9] in the USA, but the WRETCHED OF THE EARTH also spread across the extremely poor developing societies—including the Anglo-Caribbean. Domination and destruction make up a context in which five features of transnational capitalism conducive to the flourishing of the power elite exist. I turn to Hill (2004), a reference I use in Walcott (2007) for identification of these features.

The features are: (a) sectoral and international spread of capitalism, (b) deepening of capitalist social relations and commodification of everyday life, (c) increasing employment of repressive economic, legal, military, state, and multistate mechanisms, globally and locally, (d) increasing use of ideological and state apparatuses within media and education systems, (e) increasing concentration of wealth and power in possession of capitalist classes. The first encompasses privatisation, deregulation of controls on profit, and labour intensification. The second, aimed at reconstituting personhood, is implemented via the media and educational institutions. The third is attained locally via police action, imprisonment, surveillance, threats of, and actual job dismissals. Its main goal is to accomplish subordination to international capital and its state agents. The fourth is meant to advance capitalist social and economic links and justify punitive measures towards anti-capitalist actions and activists. The last is geared to enhancing hierarchical social relations via augmenting racialised and gendered class inequalities. It covers strategies such as stringent fiscal policy, reduced expenditure on welfare benefits, and unleashing market forces on pensions, healthcare, primary, secondary, and tertiary education.

The views propounded by Hill constitute deafening echoes of the Marcusean stance on developments of capitalism offered well over two decades before: (a) concentration of economic power (b) fusion of economic and political power (c) increasing state intervention in capitalist economies (d) decline in rates of profit (e) the need to implement neo-imperialist policies for the purpose of ensuring market expansion and capital accumulation (Marcuse 1982, pp. 53-54). Further, while justifying the significance of his Marxian-Freudian approach, he points to huge insoluble crises for capitalism constitutive of contradiction between accumulation of wealth and its destructive application, ecological degradation, and the widening global gap between rich and poor. These very contradictions created, partially but significantly, by US transnational behemoths, exist within Latin America and the Caribbean. Let me, therefore, turn my exploratory attention specifically to the Anglo-Caribbean.

At the time of Brian Lara's accession to the captain's job, and during the course of his leadership tenures in West Indies Test Match cricket (1998-2007), the region lay trapped by the international spread of capitalism. Nowhere was such a state of affairs more prominent than in the sport-tourism-entertainment fusion in the hands of overseas oligopolies that turned international cricket into a multibillion commnodified entity overflowing with vulgar dramaturgy in the form of one day cricket. Currently, all media control and presentation of such a spectacle is in the hands of three oligopolistic behemoths: Rupert Murdoch's News Corp through Sky television, The International Management Group through Trans World International, and ESPN. Cricket, especially one day cricket, is packaged by these organisations as a commodity overflowing with spectacularly colourful imagery quite like the deliberately presented impression management stage craft imagery integral to occasions on which National Basketball (NBA) and American football games are played.

Just as significantly, while the fortunate few gain access to venues where they can watch these cricket matches, the entry fees are prohibitive to the majority among the Caribbean WRETCHED OF THE EARTH who eke out a dreadful everyday socio-economic existence of toiling in a region where unemployment levels are chronically high within settings of hopelessness, despair, and fatalism. Much later, when it is appropriate for me to emphasise my focus upon the dread, commodification, and high level administrative paralysis—if not ineptitude—across the region, I shall address myself to two matters: the 2007 cricket world cup in the West Indies, and glaring abdication of responsibility by the West Indies Cricket Board, the administrative body for West Indies cricket. I shall explore both of these by combining a Marxian-Freudian approach with dramaturgical sociology. For now I must not lose sight of the sociological imagination. Lack of access to venues for the masses is by no means so burdensome to the Caribbean WRETCHED OF THE EARTH as the infinite struggle to put literal and figurative bread on their tables. From Mills's standpoint, reality of such struggle is not personal trouble. The fact that it is widespread is clear indication of hugely burdensome regional issues: like countless human beings elsewhere the Caribbean WRETCHED OF THE EARTH cherish the basic right to put bread on tables, as well as, the values connected to such a right. Like countless others within ranks of the WRETCHED OF THE EARTH, they know collectively, also, the burdens posed by threats to life, and are aware that their everyday socio-economic experience of such burdens is massively incongruent with messages from governments in the region.

This region, the Anglo-Caribbean, is one in which many territories—including Jamaica, Trinidad and Tobago, Barbados, Guyana, and Antigua—are independent of Great Britain. The places named are also locations from which West Indies cricket captains Frank Worrell, Gary Sobers, Rohan Kanhai, Clive Lloyd, Alvin Kallicharran, Vivian Richards, Richie Richardson, Courtney Walsh, Brian Lara, Jimmy Adams, Shivnarine Chanderpaul, and Carl Hooper were selected by the governing body of cricket in the region, the West Indies Cricket Board. Independence, however, is neither political nor economic, for what Mills regards as the national one or two crop economies[10] are based on industrial and agricultural products such as sugar cane, rice, bananas, oil, natural gas, bauxite, timber, gold, and diamonds.

Prices of these products are determined in established centres of transnational corporate control such as the USA and Britain where the power elite exists.[11] In the island territories where tourism provides seasonal subsistence to armies of local service workers, some of the greatest financial benefits from this operation accrue to owners of hotel chains. Persons who make up the largest proportions of the Caribbean population, people of colour, are very poor, suffer under the deadweight of colourised racial and class divisions which were systematically instituted in the days of sugar plantation slavery and indenture under imperialism. Many of these individuals crave routes of emigration with false expectation that movement to the metropolis shall bring them economic salvation. At the same time, others all across the region enmesh themselves in the illicit drug trade and use, both of which they assume will provide them with socio-economic deliverance, assumption—if not, phantasy—associated with a regional scourge.

At the political level, all of the independent societies named operate with the Westminster parliamentary model. In addition, ranks of the politically dominant have not been filled by the Caribbean masses. While I have no access to the inner lives of the masses of Caribbean people, I do know that the observable external careers of political leaders in government are neither geared to mounting effective challenges, nor offering alternatives to Eurocentric socio-economic arrangements. In this type of setting, the links between biographies of leaders and historical circumstances from which they claim to be emancipating persons could not be more asymmetrical. The meaning of their biographies to the lives of persons they claim to serve has not been one in which reciprocal identification exists.

The opposite has, however, prevailed in regard to links between many West Indies Test Match cricketers and adoring masses. The sporting life, Test Match cricket, has filled a huge socio-political vacuum in the experiences of excellent West Indies cricketers and the massive ranks embracing them. Herein lies the legitimacy to authority created by these cricket loving masses for their collective benefit which gained potent reciprocation via cricketing excellence of players, some of whom have been granted heroic status.

The discrepancies to which I refer above are derived from a neat conceptualisation offered by Mills (1959, pp. 14-18). He notes that the most productive difference with which the sociological imagination operates is that which exists between personal troubles and public issues of social structure. Troubles take place within individuals and the range of their direct links to others. They are relevant to ourselves and the restricted contexts of social life of which we are personally familiar. Thus, articulation and solution of troubles reside within persons as biographical entities and their immediate settings. Troubles are private. They are indicative of values appreciated by individuals who sense threats to the values.

Issues, on the other hand, lie beyond the localities of settings within inner lives of persons. Issues are public matters over which there is debate about what values really are and what pose threats to them. Issues, continues Mills, exemplify crises within organisational arrangements articulated frequently as Marxian "contradictions" or "antagonisms." If ever there was a continual issue for the Caribbean masses, towards the end of the twentieth and beginning of the twenty-first century, its existence was constituted in a contradiction between the rhetoric and reality about (a) economic emancipation touted by leaders in Caribbean governments, (b) resurgence of West Indies Test Match cricket under Brian Lara's leadership.

Mills adds that in order to conceptualise issues and troubles, specific queries must be posed: what values are appreciated but threatened? What values are appreciated and supported by defining trends of particular periods? Further, inquiries of threats and support should be framed in terms of salient contradictions of structure. When persons appreciate a group of values and do not experience threats, they enjoy well-being. They experience crises, however, when they appreciate values, but sense threats. People also experience indifference when they are neither aware of any values, nor sense any threats. Anxiety, which can become "a deadly unspecified malaise," emerges under circumstances in which persons are not cognisant of values but sense threats.

Men in masses are gripped by personal troubles, but they are not aware of their true meaning and source. Men in public confront issues, and they are aware of their terms. It is the task of the liberal institution, as of the liberally educated man, continually to translate troubles into issues and issues into the terms of their human meaning for the individual (Mills 1956, pp. 318-319).

Clearly, making connections among liberal institutions, the liberal tradition from which they emanate, mass, publics, issues, as well as troubles lie at the core of Mills' work. To the extent that such work is not alien to Marcuse's on links between Marx and Freud, and the very reality of everyday existence can be apprehended and comprehended via exploring all the connections in the myriad ways language use is accomplished, a very meaningful basis for focusing on captain, Brian Lara, and President, Obama, exists.

I shall show that Brian Lara, the superb West Indies Test Match batsman, did not create debate about the identity of West Indies values and threats to them. From this position, he did not create issues which exemplified crises. He brought well-being to the Caribbean. It is my mission, also, to indicate that from the leadership issues of Brian Lara, the West Indies Test Match captain, came significant crises and great uneasiness for the region, uneasiness and crises whose opacity is removed by juxtaposing Prince and President at close of play.[12]

I refer to close of play, a term very familiar to many a cricketing connoisseur, for the purpose of bringing attention to the end of play for a day when a Test Match is being played. According to the cricket laws today—there are laws in cricket, rather than rules—a Test Match lasts for five consecutive days, each of which is made up of three two hour sessions within which there is a forty minute recess for lunch and a twenty minute recess for tea. Close of play is a time when a media expert who has been watching a Test Match for the entire six hour day provides a summary that includes assessment of team advantages and disadvantages that may be connected to what unfold on forthcoming days. In a very important sense, the summary at close of play constitutes a report about THE STATE OF PLAY, something that has been borrowed from Test Match cricket by academic and media experts on political matters within Britain, Canada, and the USA, where reference to the STATE OF PLAY is made with the aim of summarising and assessing the fortunes of leading political figures.

With the juxtaposition I will show that Brian Charles Lara, the Prince, has been a captivating and superb world class Test Match batsman elevated to his own lofty perch by hugely adoring followers in the tens of millions within Britain, Australia, South and East Africa, Canada, USA, India, Pakistan, Bangladesh, Zimbabwe, and of course, the Anglo-Caribbean. His presence on the perch, doubtless, emanates partly but significantly from having been the sole Test Match player to have scored a triple and quadruple century at the same Antigua venue, once a profitable slavers' cauldron in the crushingly cruel clutch of European imperialism. While it is obvious that President Barack Obama has had a significant following, that following was, by no means, so large as Brian Lara's. Be such as it may, what is obvious to me, also, is: from Prince and President well before close of play much was promised, magnificence was expected, but somewhat more than minutiae was mustered by both players on their respective stages.

ENDNOTES

1 *The idea, limits to certainty, is derived from one of my university Professors, James L. Heap, one of the leading experts in conversation analytic sociology.*

2 *I took this excerpt attributed to Marlow from The Heart Of Darkness.*

3 *The idea attributed to Adolph Stocker comes from the work of Carlton Hayes. A Generation of Materialism, (1871-1900). New York, (1941) p. 258.*

4 *The notion, 'defining situations' or to be exact—the 'definition of the situation,' ante- dates Goffman's work on impression management. According to R.E.L. Faris, author of the publication, Chicago Sociology, it is W.I. Thomas, a founder of symbolic interactionist sociology, who coined the term, 'definition of the situation,' and stated, also: If men define situations as real, they are real in their consequences.*

5 *Modern philosophy can be said to have begun in 1903 with the breakaway of G.E. Moore and Bertrand Russell, followed by that of Wittgenstein, who was a pupil of Russell's—here developed in the 1920's, in Austria, the first fully-fledged school devoted to the new philosophy. This school was known as the Vienna Circle. To the philosophy which they developed they gave the name 'Logical Positivism'. For a long time afterwards that label was attached to modern philosophy generally in the minds of many laymen, and indeed one still encounters people who imagine that all contemporary academic*

philosophy is more or less like Logical Positivism." See Men Of Ideas by Bryan Magee. Oxford University Press, (1982,) p. 95. British philosopher, A.J. Ayer, the sole English speaking member of the Circle, names Otto Neurath, (official leader of the Circle), Moritz Schlick, Rudolf Carnap, and Kurt Godel as important to the Circle. It is, nevertheless, in order for me to make reference to information about a Cambridge University quarrel between Ludwig Wittgenstein and Karl Popper—never a Circle member. While writing about that duel in their book Wittgenstein's Poker (Harper Collins, 2001, p. 149),) authors, John Eidinow and David Edmonds, state about the Circle: "The members included economists, social scientists, mathematicians, logicians, and scientists, as well as philosophers—thinkers of the calibre of Otto Neurath, Herbert Feigl, Rudolf Carnap, Kurt Godel, Viktor Kraft, Felix Kaufmann, Phillip Frank, Hans Hahn, and Hahn's blind, cigar-smoking sister, Olga, an expert on Boolean algebra. There was also Friedrich Waismann, the man whose livelihood would become prey to the rise of Nazism and later to Wittgenstein's brutality."

6 *May I note that this Weberian account of action is an account accepted by another sociological luminary, the structural functionalist, Talcott Parsons, P.h.D dissertation supervisor for Garfinkel's Harvard University work, Perception Of The Other. In his ground breaking ethnomethodological exposition, Studies In Ethnomethodology, Harold Garfinkel heaps effusive deserving praise upon Parsons in much the same was as he does on Alfred Shutz. From my own vantage point I have concluded that Garfinkel's ethnomethodology was influenced by the Chicago School of Symbolic Interactionism, some of whose notable exponents were: William Isaac Thomas, Charles Horton Cooley, and George Herbert Mead.*

7 *Here I think of the so- called anger from the white American working class during the 2015-2016 election cycle, which ended with the Donald Trump victory, despite his strident racist and misogynist ranting.*

8 *This term, title of a best selling book by Caribbean psychiatrist, Frantz Fanon, about burdens of European imperialism upon people of colour globally, is used both literally and figuratively.*

9 *Those wanting to know about global cities where the massive power of ever-changing technology, oligopolistic capitalist solidification, groups of the privileged wealthy, and the poor are linked inextricably can read: Sassen, S.,"Locating Global Cities On Global Circuits,"in Social Networks, Inked Cities. New York: Routledge (2000).*

10 *I am using the term, 'one or two crop economies', in the way Mills uses it in another of his remarkably insightful accomplishments, his book Listen Yankee, about the Cuban revolution.*

11 *Britain is not, of course, the United States. To the extent that US transnational oligopolistic domination exists within all three economic sectors in Britain, production, distribution, and exchange, Britain is not spared the clutch of power elite configuration.*

12 *CLOSE OF PLAY at the end of each day of Test Match cricket is, by no means, a trivial matter to any avid follower of the game and, for that matter, the millions globally who follow it closely.*

Staring beyond the Slip Cordon: Clive Lloyd and Brian Lara.

3rd INNINGS
BOWLING BEYOND THE
MESOPOTAMIAN MIRAGE

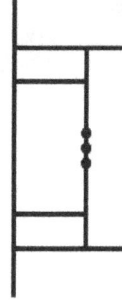

I continue my exploration by posing a question: did Brian Charles Lara give cricketing life splendour? I reply in an explicitly affirmative way, but must state that he did so only as a top class Test Match batsman. Was President Barack Obama able to combine his rhetoric with a redrawing of the socio-economic and cultural boundaries across the United States? I reply in an explicitly negative manner. Allow me the liberty of stretching my own imagination and asking that you, readers, do the same as a basis for exemplifying my disposition to the two luminaries. I begin by locating the President and captain on international cricket and political arenas. My first pointer is to figurative dramaturgy or grand stage performance in cricket as a way of locating the problem Mr. Obama faced in regard to the Islamic State (ISIS). in late spring 2015, not quite one full year after the President had made an announcement to his fellow Americans about degrading and defeating ISIS.

What I find rather striking is that I am able, immediately, to find analogies between the leadership of Brian Lara and Barack Obama: Brian Lara, a batting behemoth, a Caribbean cricketing colossus, was unable to bring much needed victory to the Caribbean. Barack Obama, President to a society possessing monumental militaristic might, was far from a position of comfort in regard to the anti-ISIS campaign. By way of contrast I note, as well, it is President Obama who stated shortly after the November, 2015 ISIS terror in Paris that the Climate Change Summit in the European city was an act of defiance on the part of those opposed to terror. It was he—in the wake of that brutality—who claimed, also, that no credible ISIS threat to the American homeland existed. It was he who used the White House Oval Office on the evening of 6th December, only a few days after an ISIS connected act of brutality on US soil, to reassure his fellow Americans that the "medieval monsters"[1] would be defeated, an accomplishment marred by later devastating ISIS attacks within NATO member countries.

In turning specifically to using imaginary cricket commentary on radio I place President Obama within realms of that grand international stage, a placement many an avid student of politics and the game would not deem fanciful. If, however, there are those inclined to query my use, I ask that they note part of a speech delivered by Mrs. Margaret Thatcher in 1990 to those in attendance for the annual Lord Mayor's banquet in London. In that delivery they will find much more to ponder than the imaginary, something I shall do when I repeat and examine her statements later. At this point, I simply wish to offer what she said, then proceed to that imaginary commentary:

Since I first went to bat eleven years ago, the score at your end [the Lord Mayor's end] has ticked over nicely. You are now the 663rd Lord Mayor. At the Prime

Minister's end we are stuck on 49. I am still at the crease, though the bowling has been pretty hostile of late. And in case anyone doubted it, can I assure you there will be no ducking of bouncers, no stonewalling, no playing for time. The bowling's going to get hit all around the ground. That's my style.

Here is pure assertiveness from someone who saw herself in full command of her craft, a politician who meant what she said and said what she meant.[2] Readers can, of course, decide after attending to my commentary if Mr. Obama was overflowing with assertiveness and in full command of his craft.

One hot August week in 2014 Barack Hussein Obama began giving himself the task of responsibility for a performance of unparalleled excellence. His job: securing enormous success well beyond a Mesopotamian mirage playing "nasty, brutish, and short" in dauntingly devilish ways from every conceivable cricketing crevice.[3]

Barack Hussein Obama—no new ball yet—with a stiff breeze behind him at the Northern end—left arm fast medium over the wicket immediately after tea to Abu Bakr Al Baghdadi. Obama with that habitual tug on the right trouser leg coming in—he may soil the seam. That does not matter: the cleaners will do their job. The wicket he wants is Al Bagdhadi's. Here he is running away from us, bowling flat out in a manner very reminiscent of the great left arm fast medium experts Alan Davidson (Australia), Wasim Akram, Imran Khan (Pakistan), and, of course, the incomparable Garfield St. Aubrun Sobers (West Indies). Long after this game in these very hot, dry, and humid conditions is over and the stories are written, his performance may well be compared to those men. It is the story this afternoon that matters. Al Bagdhadi—wrapped on the pad. The bowler and everybody behind the stumps in a loud appeal for L.B.W. The umpire unmoved. Al Baghdadi—a long way forward and offering a stroke. Obama—full of resolve and bowling flat out—extracting life from the wicket. Uncoached, he is, undoubtedly, a keen student of the game. He enmeshes himself within the intricacies of the game, particularly the extraordinary feats of great players before him.

A very shrewd and unhurried strategist, he knows a thing or two about dislodging menacingly aggressive batsmen, just when they appear to be well set. He is a unique fast-medium left armer: operating at quickish pace around the wicket to right handers, he pitches a few just short of a good length on about middle and off stump, forcing batsmen onto the back foot where they get the faintest of outside edges to away swingers. Remarkably, the wicket keeper has to move only fractionally in the direction of slip and take what turns into a simple catch. In spring, 2011, contrary to conventional wisdom, he, himself, took the new ball just before lunch and made that very crucial dismissal with a quickish delivery which moved through the air and off the pitch, quite late—double deception. Al Baghdadi, just as resolute—on 92 and moving towards what would obviously be a big hundred. He is, by no means, intent on going on the defensive. He is always looking to score. A VERY VERY KEEN tussle unfolding.

Obama polishing the ball vigorously, presumably only on one side and, no doubt, letting teammates know polishing should be done only on that side. Wasim Akram, the left armer, was quite expert at that and so was his charismatic skipper Imran Khan, who is now a Parliamentarian in the Pakistan Legislature where he opposes Mr. Nawaz Sharif and campaigns ardently against US drone strikes. The American skipper still polishing the ball vigorously. This matter of polishing only on one side I remember was a topic of interest to some physicists and mathematicians a few years ago who offered their own theories about the merits of so doing in newspaper articles—not something demanding the attention of the experts on swing, both on the field and in the commentary box. All that matters to them is that the ball does swing and I suppose that is what matters to Obama now.

Is he going to try that away swing to Al Baghdadi? In he comes and there's the away swinger. Al Baghdadi shuffles across and misses. What noise there is around this ground! The crowd abuzz and sensing something big. Wicketkeeper, Durbin, moving adroitly to his right pouches the ball and, in an instant, relays it to his skipper via one of the slips and the person at point. Yes, the batsman did everything right—I suppose from his standpoint—but makes no contact. His wicket still intact he prepares to face Obama once more.

Obama—he asks for the new ball. The umpire removes that brand new dark beet red ball from his pocket, holds it up for the scorers, and hands it to Obama, who wants a field change. He is moving mid-wicket to silly mid-off and bringing cover into a silly mid-on position. A very very attacking field—not quite an umbrella field—but an attacking field, nevertheless. What will he do? Obama again to Al Baghdadi. A bouncer and—contemptuous clobbering. Al Baghdadi hooks imperiously, the stroke of a conductor signalling a flashing overture—one bounce over the boundary board backward of square. No one ever said he is afraid, even against the best bowling, to drive off both front and back foot, pull, hook, and cut in a ferociously aggressive manner. He moves to 96. Obama would certainly want to get HIS wicket tonight. No one will forget that dramatic turn of events in the American first innings of the previous match, early July, when batsman, Obama, walked to the crease and Al Baghdadi took the ball.

He sent Obama four deliveries, all of which deceived the US captain. The first was a doorsa.[4] Then came the leg break and two consecutive flippers, the second of which, just short of a good length, really hurried on to the batsman. Obama—well out of his ground and searching in a rather confused state on the front foot—never got a touch. The wicket keeper, in a flash—not unlike Langley, Marsh, Healy, Evans, Grout, Bari, Alexander, Walcott, Engineer, Knott, Hendriks, and Dujon, whipped the bails off. Up went that index finger. Obama, beaten in the air and off the wicket, was truly and comprehensively stumped—one of the spectacular pieces of superb stumping. It was perhaps just as spectacular, given the colourful Valentine description, as the Walcott stumping of Hutton (first innings, 2nd Test Match, Lord's, 1950) .

It was that very July—in fact, 4th of July—when team USA took an unforgettable hammering from the hands of Al Baghdadi some describe as an Abu Musab Al Zarqawi zealot and successor. Obama was in charge of team USA then, chose not to lead the opening pace attack—opting instead to be first change agent—pardon me—change bowler operating with the ball still relatively new and, of course, the benefit from a stiff breeze. He did not prevail—fodder to his critics and, perhaps, detractors who claimed well before he had earned, decisively, the much coveted captaincy, that he lacked the capability needed for success on tough wickets and, generally, very high level campaigns abroad. Could there have been greater embarrassment for team USA than on the 4th of July, when the entire world watched that Al Bagdadi hammering! Perhaps, history will decide. Let me return to current events and the flipper, that dreadful delivery even for the best of batsmen.

The flipper—first or any other—is the type of delivery that comes only from the arms of those whom Trevor Bailey[5] calls "class" spin bowlers: Alfred Valentine, Lance Gibbs, Sonny Ramadhin, Gary Sobers (West Indies), Jim Laker, Tony Lock (England), Abdul Qadir, Saqlain Mushtaq, originator of the doorsa (Pakistan), Subhash Gupte, Anantharao Prasanna, Srinivasaraghavan Venkataraghavan, Bishan Singh Bedi, Anil

Kumble (India), Clarence Grimmett, inventor of the flipper, Richie Benaud, and of course Shane Warne, (Australia), as well as that man whom Martin-Jenkins (1996, p. 695) states sometimes turned his off spinners almost square, Muttiah Muralitharan (Sri Lanka). Obama was out without scoring, a duck, of course, and should he get to the batting crease for a second knock he would, doubtless, be on a pair[6]—not to use a Tony Greig term—"a king pair." A pair is a pair, nevertheless.

In he comes again to Al Baghdadi. He's bowled him. NO BALL signals the umpire. Al Baghdadi survives. A polite inquiry from the American skipper about the call. The umpire shows him where he overstepped. He walks back to his mark with that characteristic pursing of his lips and bustles in over the wicket. Al Baghdadi drives superbly between the second of the two gullies and cover. FOUR RUNS: That is the hundred—a huge roar from Al Baghdadi's supporters around the ground. He removes his white floppy hat—no helmet—mops his brow, turns to the pavilion, and hoists his bat.

Not surprisingly, no one on the American team applauds the hundred. They have other things on their minds. They must win this game. A loss or a draw does mean they cannot win the series. Two more deliveries left in the Obama over. He comes in and A CHANCE. Al Baghdadi driving again off the front foot—deceived by Obama. The ball flying away between third slip and the first of the gullies who got some fingers on it but grassed the catch. It is Rice whom many will recall certain senior members of the US selection team stated openly was not the right choice for a frontline position on the American team. They were also going to block her selection for such a position. Obama defended her by stating, among other things, that if they wanted to attack someone for the team they should not do so to her. They should direct their salvos to him. He did find a way to get her in the side and in this match she has dropped the ball, catch, and should I say, possibly, the match. While I have not heard statements that catches lose matches I have heard statements that catches win matches.

A really difficult chance but a chance. At this level, regardless of the time of day, close catchers must hold on to their chances. It is not unknown for excellent catchers—even late in the day—to hold on to the most difficult of chances. Lance Gibbs—fielding in the gully—comes to mind immediately. Late in the afternoon, on the very first day of an inter-territorial game (Guyana-Barbados), during the late nineteen-sixties Guyana—batting first on an excellent batting wicket at the Bourda ground—declared well beyond a score of 400. Before close of play, the prized wicket of an elegant Seymour Nurse, a Barbados frontline batsman, was claimed as a result of a miraculous left handed catch by Lance Gibbs at leg gully. Apart from Lance Gibbs, other exceptionally good catchers were: Colin Cowdrey, Gary Sobers, Rohan Kanhai, Clive Lloyd, Bob Simpson, and that Yorkshireman, Phil Sharpe, who presumably, according to BBC cricketing telecaster Mr. Peter West, took difficult slip catches with the same ease as he solved the crossword puzzles in the London newspapers. Obama throwing his hands in the air—not in admonition—more in astonishment—then locking his fingers in a clasp and placing the clasp behind his head.

I suppose the one notable occasion on which he admonished a member of his team was that on which he made a public disclosure about a generalist/all-rounder and prominent on- field tactician, Stanley David McChrystal, to whom he gave the sack. From a West Indies cricketing standpoint, the very open criticism from Gordon Greenidge of winning leader, Clive Lloyd, comes to mind. In a book publication Greenidge spared no effort while playing under Lloyd's captaincy to hurl criticism at his boss. Clive Lloyd has never admonished Greenidge publicly. Nor for that matter, requested that the batsman be given the sack.[7]

In 1954-'55 West Indies spectators and supporters did much more than throw their hands in the air when West Indies fielder Glendon Gibbs—no relation to Lance Gibbs—dropped an easy catch from Neil Harvey when the Australian batsman was not well set. The story I heard is: Harvey was dropped when he had not yet scored. Part of the embellishment to the tale is that under the white floppy hat he used to wear his face turned red when he was dropped by Gibbs. He went on to make a brilliant hundred. The very morning after the missed opportunity one of the Caribbean dailies ran a headline: SAVE HYLTON AND HANG GIBBS. Leslie George Hylton, in the company of Manny Martindale, and Learie Constantine, comprised the most fearful fast bowling trio when MCC toured the Caribbean (1934-'35) (Martin-Jenkins 1996, p.746). At the time of Gibbs' blunder he was on death row for the murder of his wife. He was eventually executed—the only Test Match cricketer to have been on death row and executed. Mercifully, Glendon Gibbs was spared the hangman's noose, but he never played regularly for the West Indies after his costly error. In that 1954-'55 series Harvey's scores were: 133, 133, 38, 41, 74, 27, 204.

A lengthy line of some of the most talented of superb batsmen can be drawn to illustrate the chances they got either when they had not scored or were close to a big hundred. Notably present on that line are: Neil Harvey, of course, Sunil Gavaskar, Stephen Waugh, Colin Cowdrey, Garfield Sobers, Rohan Kanhai, Clive Lloyd, and of course one Donald George Bradman. Chances, however, are not in the record books or on score cards. It is old "hard knuckled" men who tell good stories of dropped catches at slip or elsewhere.

Obama comes in, once more, to Al Baghdadi. Outside the off stump. The batsman lets it go through to the wicket keeper. It is the end of the over. And the umpires are walking to the centre, probably, to confer about the light. They turn towards the batsmen and offer them the light. They accept. The bails come off. It is close of play. The full scorecard, in a moment. What an absorbing day! Al Baghdadi unbeaten on a hundred approaches the pavilion steps, removes his white floppy hat, mops his brows, and lifts that custom made bat of his. Even in the fading sunlight there is an obvious glint from the full face. Alongside him is someone, notoriously known by the initials J.J., moving towards his hundred too. J.J.—British educated, but quite unmindful either about coaching manuals and the fundamentalism in batting—is quite adventurous in his stroke making.

He is a tremendous hooker and puller and does cut rather liberally. He bats with a very upright stance, wears no helmet, and possesses his custom made bat as well. Of course, his back lift is quite pronounced—very little forearm in the stroke—relies a great deal on precision in placement. Many batting styles have always been notable. One of the oddest to emerge in the West Indies was the stance of Tony Greig in the early nineteen-seventies when used to adopt what looked like a baseball batter stance—bat aloft—from which I saw him post a well-crafted hundred in the Guyana Test Match during that series. In 1990, touring England captain Graham Gooch batted against the Caribbean side in much the same way. The point of the stance, according to information reliably offered, was using a technique in India to counter the mysteries from Indian spin bowling. Test Match cricket today is, of course, dominated by the baseball batting stance for what reasons I do not know. Both Gooch and Greig have departed from Test Match cricket and it is J.J. very much in focus poised for a probable hundred. Unlike his skipper, he does not remove his floppy hat and even through the binoculars and with the TV image his visage is unrecognisable. His captain is, at this stage, not a displeased contender; in all likelihood, he is not either.

Rather contrastively, Obama—head bowed—leads his team up the pavilion steps. He must be asking himself: WHAT NEXT? There will be no shortage of views later in the evening when much conversation unfolds about producing what many a West Indian calls a "ball dadee" or what Michael Holding calls the master ball. He could have got that information well before his 2015 hop to the island either from one or other or both of Jamaica's heroic legendary fast bowlers, Mr. Courtney Walsh, the man with the "Heart of a Lion," and Mr. Michael Holding, "Whispering Death," who always reminded himself that prior to bowling in a Test Match, especially on the Kensington Oval wicket in Barbados, he needed to pitch up his deliveries.

While visiting Cuba's Caribbean neighbour, the American President did not pay courtesy calls on either of the two players. Five years earlier he met Brian Lara, got some expert advice about stroke making and praised the former captain. In Jamaica the President met Mr. Usain Bolt, that man who attained what has come to be known as the triple-triple (Beijing 2008, London 2012, Rio De Janeiro 2016), and even positioned himself with the sprinter for that lightning pose but did not meet Walsh and Holding. IS THAT CRICKET! In so called "cricket speak," did a huge chance go a begging!

Away from Jamaica—Sabina Park and other environs—clearly, an inspirational surge from President Obama is what is sorely required. He can get some of that from Winston Churchill, whom he praised effusively in Westminster. It should be noted that although Churchill was an Harrovian, there is no record of him having played in the annual Eaton-Harrow Match or in any of the Public School games. He might well have been taught the rudiments of the game or played for his Form or House but I know of no record of Winston Churchill, the prominent English cricketer.

Be that as it may, it is by no means fanciful to think of the ardent British imperialist, Churchill, exuding unbridled admiration for Sir Henry Newbolt's poem, *Vitai Lampada*, in which there is an obvious connection among cricket, the socio-economic expanse beyond the game, and playing fields of Clifton, Newbolt's alma mater. Ardent imperialist Barack Obama certainly is not. He may well find inspiration in Newbolt's words. Better still, given his erudition about the tactical acumen, perseverance, and heroism of George Washington, he could ruminate over what Fisher (1949, p. 771) regards as black days in the military annals of the Sons of Liberty, Long Island, Trenton, and Brandywine. With his rumination complete he could juxtapose it with:

> It was Washington, and he alone, who in the camp of Valley Forge, amid the dire hardships of a bitter winter, brought back a severely shaken and ill-provisioned army to a sense of disciplined efficiency and once more made of it an instrument of victory. So little was the revolution the work of a convinced and united people that at no time in the war did the army of Washington exceed twenty thousand men (Fisher, 1949, p. 771).

Obama is, of course, President to a highly fractious Congress, both houses of which reverted to Republican hands in early November 2014,[8] and a society deeply split along racial, class, and regional fault lines. He knows he has to lead, but at the same time play an innings in Kilburn's heroic mould, and must never ever forget that war is the parent of illusions (Fisher 1949, p. 772).

Leading and playing in heroic mould, he informed his fellow Americans, shall not be easy. He has likened team Al Baghdadi to a malignancy that will take time to root out. If the implication from him is about Americans meeting the requirement of patience, he is not outside the boundaries of many a cricket field within which, more than anything else, tons of patience is required. President Obama's problem is that he could not be sure his fellow Americans would grant him the space and time needed for using his versions of patience, versions he might well have discovered were antithetical to the idea about war and illusions.

In fact, his departure in January 2017 means he will not have had the time. It was time and lots of it which three American skippers had in the nineteen-sixties and early seventies while engaged in a tussle within Asia where the United States did not emerge victorious. Those leaders are, of course, Kennedy, Johnson, and Nixon. All three had massive firepower at their disposal, but the much sought after victory did not eventuate. Many a year from now the historians will know much more than how many American skippers were needed to degrade and defeat ISIS. In the US skippers cannot lead for more than eight years, but in other societies, such as Britain, leaders can remain in office for as long as they choose, if they continue winning. The names William Gladstone and Stanley Baldwin come to mind immediately. British skippers have been known to depart unexpectedly, in very ignominious circumstances. One recent case is that of Mr. David Cameron, to whom reference will be made later; prior to him Harold MacMillan resigned over what came to be associated in some political circles with the Profumo Affair.

Politics, not unlike cricket, can be for some a matter of glorious certainty and uncertainty; for others it can be a matter of inglorious certainty, as well as uncertainty. It is the uncertainty, albeit the inglorious form, that has pervaded selection committee rooms, Test Match cricket grounds, and wider society in Britain on those occasions when England cricket captains, to great dismay from the rest of the world, were given the sack, or those expected to be appointed skippers were ignored. Standing prominently among the notables in both categories are: Colin Cowdrey, Brian Close, Geoff Boycott, Michael Smith, and Freddie Brown. While Barack Obama does not have to give one iota of concern to being sacked, like every American skipper before him, he has to have a concern with his legacy. While he, a skipper with quite a favourable rating among the American public towards the end of his eight year tenure, does have control over shaping his legacy, he cannot be too confident that his departure would be clothed by glorious certainty. An Al Baghdadi dismissal by him or anyone else would be a great confidence booster which, doubtless will have to be balanced with how the American batsmen negotiate the ISIS bowling, both medium fast and mainly wrist spin.

So, everything to play for in the next two days. It is a fair bet that when play resumes Al Baghdadi will use the heavy roller in a major effort to break up the wicket further. Batting for the US team could, thus, become nightmarish. That is a daunting prospect: cracks on the wicket are already wide open, there are boot marks all over it—not to mention the rough just outside the batting creases. Rough spots there have been for President Obama. Just about a month into the degrading and destroying bombing campaign against ISIS led by the USA, CNN claimed that although a majority of Americans supported that campaign, there was "no bounce" in polling numbers for the President. From a cricketing standpoint, bounce from a wicket is what bowlers—both spinners and those who propel the quick stuff—relish. A bowler getting no bounce is in for some very definite toiling. So, it is good night while members of this large capacity crowd glued to every delivery and locked onto every stroke in a day of very absorbing cricket depart. Several of them will, no doubt, return tomorrow, even well before eleven o'clock, express no inclination to drift away from the stands before close of play but remain until six o'clock or beyond, should the light be good enough for bowling some remaining fraction to the mandatory ninety overs.[9]

Here we are—day four of the Test Match. So far, Al Baghdadi and his men have built a score of 589 for 4. One of those wickets is, of course, that of the vice-captain and leading tactician, Taha Subhi Falah, otherwise known as Abu Muhammad-Al-Adnani. No question about that dismissal, a clear and comprehensive blow struck by Obama himself going over the wicket with an unplayable yorker. At the moment, the second innings lead is 380 and I suppose when the declaration comes later today, Al Baghdadi will want to set a target of well over 400 and throw everything he's got at the Americans in at least one and a half sessions today, as well as all day tomorrow. Should he and his men attain their intended target—whatever that is—they might put the Americans in at about forty five minutes after lunch, thus planting in the batsmen's minds ideas about how difficult survival can be before and after tea. Al Baghdadi did, of course, use the heavy roller this morning. Thus, the declaration will definitely come before close of play.

When that happens it would be quite interesting to note who is chosen to be the night watchman and, more significantly, if Obama changes the top half in the batting order, a move geared not so much towards winning the match but saving face, maintaining dignity and stature. There are some experts who do not favour batting order change, regardless of the circumstances. The most explicit expression of such a posture I heard came from Learie Constantine in 1968 in the aftermath of West Indies defeat by England (fourth Test Match, Trinidad). During play in the fifth Test Match analyst/commentator, a censorious Constantine, let his listeners know that the decision by West Indies skipper, Gary Sobers, to change the top half of his batting order for the first innings was wholly unjustified. Sobers might well have been concerned that with the loss of three frontline batsmen, Nurse, Camacho, Butcher, in quick succession, his side could have been facing another defeat. Constantine could find no sound reason for a decision he thought was unwarranted. Twenty years later, after Pakistan under Imran Khan had defeated West Indies—without ailing skipper, Viv Richards—in the first Test Match at Bourda in Guyana, the decorously diplomatic senior statesman in West Indies cricket, Clyde Walcott, stated publicly that his opening batsmen for that lost Test Match would have been regulars, Gordon Greenidge and Desmond Haynes, highly dependable duo for the Caribbean team. That loss to Pakistan was, of course, not just face threatening, it was face damaging also, and told a tale of stature depletion for West Indies: Imran had come out of retirement to remove West Indies supremacy at the Test Match level and was most ably assisted in his quest by none other than the very mysterious leg spinner, Abdul Qadir, and Wasim Akram who, like Imran, could move the new ball in the air and off the wicket with devastating impact.

So, with a lot more than dignity, face, stature, and, I imagine, pride on their minds, the American fielders take centre stage in front of a crowd considerably larger than those at Lord's, the Sydney Cricket Ground, or Gaddafi Stadium. Obama is, of course, in front and almost immediately behind the Americans appear Al Baghdadi and J.J., the second of whom will be at the striker's end to face—it looks like—Joe Biden still with the new ball. The field is a typically attacking one: three slips, two gullies, a silly mid-on, someone at very short backward square. I shall complete the field in a moment. Biden comes bustling in over the wicket. J.J. lets this one outside off stump go through to the keeper. Biden, once more, off a shortish run, and this time well up to the batsman on middle and leg; J.J. is right forward—almost a dead bat stroke. The ball trickles to the left of silly mid-on who picks up and returns to the bowler. Once more, it is Biden to J.J. An explosive shot, a towering six. One step forward, a huge cloud of dust, and the ball sails way way above long on—six runs. J.J. on 98. This huge crowd utterly vocal—perhaps in anticipation of another hundred.

Meanwhile the ball has yet to be retrieved. In baseball the umpire would certainly have made a new ball available. This is cricket, however, and unlike baseball, no new ball is provided. It is the old one which, hopefully, will be retrieved momentarily, and will continue to be used. And the ball has been found. The umpire at the non-striker's end rightfully asks to inspect it. All is well. Play resumes. It is Biden, again. This time that ferocious square cut sending the ball rocketing to the left of point—futile to chase—four runs. That's the hundred. J.J. one hundred and two, his fifth century. What a hundred! And it looks, today, as if these Americans are in for another very tough day of leather hunting. It appears as if their toiling in these hot, dry, very humid conditions is not coming to an end soon. We are just into the beginning of day four.

Will Obama himself take the ball for this second over? He has the ball in his right hand and appears rather business-like in setting the field which is still an attacking one: three slips, a gulley, someone at silly point, mid-off, mid-on, cover, and mid-wicket, quite short. It will, indeed, be Obama off a longish run to bowl his quick stuff and he is coming around the wicket this morning. In he comes. Al Baghdadi steers this one between first and second slip to third man. An easy single which brings J.J. to the striker's end. Obama makes a field change immediately: he is moving mid-off into a second gulley position—quite wide. So, now there is a wide gap on the off side between cover and the stumps at the bowler's end. In comes Obama, once more to J.J. and he's OUT. He IS OUT—he's CAUGHT by the second of the two gullies attempting an extravagant cover drive which Obama—clever bowler that he is—invited by removing mid-off. This is a major wicket, A PRIME wicket. The catch, a superb one by Biden diving full stretch to his right and making absolutely no mistake. A huge grassy green stamp now adorns part of the cream flannel on his right trouser leg—a bit of work for the cleaners but work well done.

A clutch of American players now surrounding Biden, unswervingly loyal teammate to Obama and a highly experienced campaigner himself. This is the man many an American political pandit thought would be a candidate to replace Obama, but despite their assumptions, opted not to be considered. Here, he and those watchers must now find other words of wisdom to assess an event to which he was central, an event he and they will long remember. With J.J. dutifully dispatched Obama opts to keep the pressure on the incoming batsman and maintains his two gullies. Biden just trotting back next to Rice who must be relieved about the fall of J.J.'s wicket. His is clearly not Al Baghdadi's, but a vital wicket, nonetheless.

Such has not been lost to this sizeable American crowd leaping with uncontrollable delight at the demise of J.J. and being joined by others in the members' stand where David Cameron, Angela Merkel, and Francois Hollande are very visible. In rather polite fashion they rise and cheer, I suppose, in acknowledgement of Obama's quite shrewd and insightful leadership. Seated in the members' stand also, one row immediately behind the other three dignitaries, is Mr. Stephen Harper, Canadian Prime Minister, whom some political pandits claim will be locked in a tough election battle with challenger, Mr. Justin Trudeau, son of the famous Pierre. Rather sedately, Harper, an avid follower of National Hockey League (NHL) contests, remains poised, conveying a ponderous presence, perhaps because of his unfamiliarity with cricket or wondering about the new strategy Trudeau plans to adopt in combating ISIS, if he becomes the Canadian Prime Minister. This is a strategy which—ostensibly—entails discontinuing Canada's bombing missions against ISIS and initiating what Trudeau deems a humanitarian focus. Time will, of course, tell.

So will this wicket that, belonging to J.J., "one of those deadly, dangerous batsmen," to borrow a term from the inimitable A.W. Greig, change the course of proceedings and signal, yet again, why this is a game of glorious uncertainty. The fall of two more wickets in quick succession can tilt the balance significantly. Obama knows this and will do all he can to harry the opposition. He is, of course, the sole American bowler possessing the ability to propel the medium fast stuff and move the ball all too deceptively in the air. It does appear as that is what he did to remove J.J.—not much movement off the seam or what Michael Holding terms "lateral movement." Some describe this aspect of the Obama offensive as his secret weapon or his secret war, the great success from a "covert," rather than "overt" strategy. Whatever it is, he will be quite pleased about its application and impact, on this particular fourth day of the Match, a day on which he also got the wicket of a big regional player, Mansour, once a sore point for the Americans.

He has not, however, been able to rattle Al Bagdhadi's cage and get his wicket. He has not been able to beat the bat and secure that vital wicket. It is rattling to which captain Obama referred in the presence of Susan Rice, while taking just a little breather: in front of another skipper to what was once a dreaded nemesis he stated that one of the leading contenders to succeed him in January 2017 had "rattled" other skippers. This is a contender who has believed, very strongly, that the once mighty team America had lost tremendous status globally and vowed to restore just such might by implementing a very muscular set of stratagems on overseas tours.

Clearly, Al Bagdhadi—covert or overt strategy—is no one's—most of all Obama's—rabbit. Rabbits and tall tales about rabbits there have been in high level international cricket: in Caribbean inter-colonial cricket regardless of how many runs the hugely attacking Barbados and West Indies opener, Cammie Smith, scored against the menace, Roy Gilchrist, from Jamaica, Smith was utterly clueless against the British Guiana quick bowler, Pat Legall. In Test Match cricket the frontline Australian batsman, Arthur Morris, seemed to be just as ineffective against England medium pacer, Alec Bedser. By no means a rabbit, another prominent Australian batsman, Doug Walters, who showed enormous promise in his first home series against England in 1965, did quite well on Australian and West Indies wickets but was never at ease on the green wickets in England. Whose rabbit he was I do not know.

I do know that when England under Ray Illingworth toured Australia in 1970-1971, Keith Stackpole seemed to be the opposing fast bowlers' rabbit: ducking against bouncers he kept exposing an obvious weakness, holding his bat aloft in what some commentators claimed was a periscope like position, a position from which he, literally, was giving away his wicket. Although it is highly unlikely that he was doing just that on a subsequent tour to the Caribbean, many a spectator/expert claimed that he was prone to being dismissed easily while dealing with the quickish swing from Bernard Julien. Only an official scorecard can reveal the truth. There is no truth to the story that during the course of the first West Indies tour to Australia (1930-1931), the great Don Bradman was Herman Griffith's rabbit. While it is true that the Don was out for four low scores in the Test Match series (caught Grant bowled Griffith, 4, 1st innings, 1st Test, caught Barrow bowled Francis, 25, 1st innings, 2nd Test, caught Francis bowled Martin, 43, 1st innings, 5th Test, and bowled Griffith, caught Martin, 0, 2nd innings, 5th Test), he was nobody's rabbit.

Obama leaves in early January 2017, a time when he will have had some very notable achievements—with or without Al Bagdhadi's wicket—both at home and abroad. Critics and detractors there will be. Some of them, even towards the end of his captaincy tenure, cannot help stating that he has been weak on tours abroad. In late May 2016, for instance, I heard one notable strategist in the G.W. Bush team state publicly that there is a huge difference between strategising within hotel lobbies and strategising once a captain walks onto the Oval and has to lead officially. This expert might not have heard statements from a former British ambassador to the United Nations, Lord Caradon, one of the famous Foot brothers and a former Governor to Jamaica, where he might well have seen a Test Match or two and heard radio commentary. The ex-Governor claimed that a lot of good and productive work done by him and ambassadorial colleagues did not take place within the Security Council chambers. Such work was done in the lobbies.

Come autumn 2016, Mr. Obama—albeit with a different team—will have traversed some of those very lobbies for the last time. He will, in all probability, take one more opportunity to make his case, not merely to a home crowd but to a very diverse spectator group—not something unusual to high level cricket—on behalf of his team and the strategies for which he has been taking responsibility. While utilising the opportunity, he would do well to familiarise himself with the phrase 'glorious uncertainty,' and ponder the implications emergent from: 'inglorious uncertainty.'

ENDNOTES

1 A term used by British Prime Minister, Mr. David Cameronto describe ISIS when he was speaking in regard to a British Parliamentary mandate for bombing ISIS by British aircraft over Syrian territory.

2 The statement about meaning and saying was coined by Mr. Tony Benn, veteran left wing British Labour Party politician, when he wrote an assessment about Mrs. Thatcher shortly after her passing.

3 Those who possess a keen cricketing interest will, of course, recognise the figurative and literal significance in the term, 'cricketing crevice.' In a literal sense, this term conveys ideas about cracks on the pitch/wicket surface, that 22 yard strip in the middle of a cricket field on which bowling and batting take place. Cracks are conditions that bowlers have used, and relish using against—even the best of batsmen. The term, 'cricketing crevice, is very different to 'sticky wicket,' words that are used, quite often, figuratively, by Americans. Among other things, I shall offer a profound explanation of the term, 'sticky wicket.' May I add: the cricketer-readers should experience no difficulty in situating the President's international political headache within a cricketing context. They will know, immediately, that my assessment about Brian Lara is, eminently, a cricketing matter. While those possessing mainly political knowledge are not likely to appreciate the cricketing detail I associate with the President, they should, nevertheless, see that I point to a major political headache for Mr. Obama. Absence of knowledge about cricketing detail should also not preclude an appreciation about Brian Lara's inadequacy.

4 The utterance, 'doorsa,' is a reference to an Urdu term that means 'second one.' The doorsa, different to the off spinner's arm ball, spins off the wicket from leg to off side and is a rather subtle deceptive tool. Some Test Match umpires have questioned the legitimacy of the delivery and at least one user from the Pakistan side has been deemed to be in contravention in accordance with the Laws. Nevertheless, Saqlain, who is credited with inventing the delivery, does not regard it as illegitimate. I would certainly like to hear what Gibbs, Sobers, Bedi, Illingworth, Venkataraghavan, Gupte, Prasana, Qadir, and Ramadhin think about this delivery.

5 Trevor Bailey, once a very prominent member of England Test Match cricket teams and very shrewd judge of the game, became a greatly respected analyst whose observations and conclusions about subtlety in the sport was valued enormously by cricket commentators.

6 Anyone possessing rudimentary understanding and appreciation for cricket would know that the term, 'duck', is a figurative signification for (0) or no score. I assume, not unlike several with a keen interest in the sport, that the figurative turn represents, partially but significantly, the shape of a duck egg. Further, the idea that someone sits on a pair is used to convey, not simply, considerable mental discomfort for the player, but also,imagery of a duck sitting on a nest with eggs.

7 Clive Lloyd and Gordon Greenidge have been working together for many years in the roles of senior administrators to West Indies cricket.

8 In the aftermath of the re-conquest, Mr. Obama, made it clear that he was ready and willing to work with Congress but was just as clear in asserting that the instrument of presidential EXECUTIVE POWER was not something he would be afraid to use in regard to issues such as immigration reform. Not surprisingly, the emboldened and battle ready, house speaker stated, rather forcefully, that the American people voted to reject "Obamacare," the legislation that some of his fellow republicans reasserted they would repeal. What I did not miss, also, was the dismissively racist verbiage from the speaker who tarred President Obama with a thick coat of irresponsibility in stating that the President was playing "with matches." The claim is not merely indicative of gross disrespect shown to the President and his office, it is a highly toxic blast of racism: the speaker's remark belongs to the category of assertives those in great authority and power use in reference to others obliged to obey their ascendant statuses. This is the type of remark parents uses to children in many cases—following their remarks with disciplinary action.

9 With the assumption that analogy can be made between this imaginary game and the highest level of international cricket, Test Match cricket, I can make reference to what is mandatory. With limits imposed on the duration over which any Test Match lasts, as a result of a Test Match in England between England and Australia (1938) that went beyond five days, Test Matches are now played over only five days, each of which, consists of three two hour sessions. Further, as a result of other changes to cricket laws, ninety overs must be bowled in a six hour day. Failure to satisfy this mandate means that the fielding side is penalised financially.

4th INNINGS
BRIAN LARA AND THE
PERIPHERY OF POLITICS

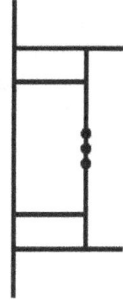

B rian Charles Lara could hardly have been pleased about the application and impact of his leadership tactics within and beyond hotel lobbies in summer 2014. It was horrific toiling which the West Indies captain and his men experienced more than four years prior to 2014—to be exact—July 2004, at the Cathedral of Cricket, Lord's, St. John's Wood, where a Lara led West Indies lost heavily to England under Michael Vaughn. It is to that toiling I give my attention mainly through the eyes and ears of Tony Cozier, prominent Caribbean cricket commentator/historian. Defeat at the St. John's Wood location was, probably, the most vulgar of features in a huge failure under leader Lara. My description shall be centred on the first three days of the game which, in its entirety, lasted from the twenty-second to twenty-sixth of July.

On day three, twenty-fourth of July, England, in their second innings, had amassed a (223) run advantage. The home side (568 all out) was put in to bat by captain Lara. It is assessment from Tony Cozier about unfolding of events at Lord's that I find remarkably interesting, for it is used to formulate Lara as someone who was peripheral to the devastating depression into which his team had been plunged by the end of the third day. Despite the Cozier effort to distance the captain, my view is that Brian Lara stood firmly at the centre of his team's troubles.

Writing in the Friday 23rd July edition of *The Barbados Daily Nation*, Cozier began by stating:

> *Even given the standards that have become depressingly commonplace, West Indies plumbed new depths of mediocrity before a full house at the game's most prestigious ground yesterday. The plot began to unravel from the moment Brian Lara informed Michael Vaughan at the toss that the West Indies would bowl on the opening day of the Power Test series.*

He continued by claiming it was clear that Andrew Strauss and Robert Key, two England front line batsmen, had scored at a run a minute and raced to a partnership of (291) at a rate of more than five runs an over. Not only did they accomplish their goal by mid-afternoon, but they also re-established "the psychological advantage" England had secured in the (3-0) defeat of Lara's men only a few months earlier. The Cozier reference here is to England victory over West Indies in the Caribbean. The correspondent noted that boundaries flowed in all directions. By the time bad light "mercifully ended the carnage with six and a half overs still available, England had reached 391 for two."

A day later, 24th July, he invoked the highly reputable scientific authority of renowned physicist, Stephen Hawking, to claim:

Hawking's field is advanced physics unintelligible to ordinary mortals. But had he followed West Indies cricket in recent times, he would have come to appreciate that, in this particular sphere of human endeavour, at least, it is quite possible to fall into a black hole, break out of it, drop right back in and start to climb out again, all in the space of a couple afternoons.

He added that West Indies could not have been in a deeper hole than they were at the end of the first day, which began when Lara "chose to bowl on winning the toss and watched helpless as his bowlers offered up such inviting fare that England rattled up 51 fours amassing 391 for 2 off 84.1 overs."

Anyone who is interested in the theoretical complexity surrounding the physics of black holes should ponder these views from Hawking (1988): black holes are hypothetical regions of space emanating from gravitational collapse of stars. This eventuality, supposedly occurs, because of exhaustion of the stars' nuclear fuel. Further, the gravitational fields around the regions would be so heightened that matter and radiation would not escape from them. What a dismal picture offered by Cozier! The imagery I get about West Indies Test Match cricket under leader, Brian Lara, in the splendour of a July afternoon at St. John's Wood, is one of sheer destructiveness in horrific confinement. Here is a canvas of even darker colouring than that, perhaps, spreading from the Black Hole of Calcutta.

It is to Hawking that I turn, once more, for the purpose of conjuring an imagery of darkness. The distinguished scientist defines a black hole as a set of events from which it is impossible to escape for a substantial distance. The central idea behind this definition is:

It means that the boundary of the black hole, the event horizon, is formed by the paths in space-time of rays of light that just fail to get away from the black hole, hovering forever just on the edge... It is a bit like running away from the police and just managing to keep one step ahead but not being able to get clear away (Hawking 1988, p. 99).

Further, the event horizon, the boundary of a black hole, is similar to the edge of a shadow of forthcoming doom. Thus, should an astronaut fall into a black hole, s/he would, in Hawking's terms, be recycled, a poor version of immortality. Such would eventuate because the astronaut would not be able to have any personal grasp of time on account of having been ripped apart within the black hole. All that would remain of the traveller in outer space is his/her energy mass.

Cozier clearly opened a door to the crushingly destructive fate of Caribbean Test Match cricket. As one way of highlighting opposites in parallels between his reference to a black hole and the Hawking allusion to what would befall a hapless astronaut there, I want to dwell on what is implied, from a cricketing standpoint, by the scientific view about the astronaut.

Astronauts are high flying scientific experts elevated way beyond the earthen surface and curvature by forces far more powerful than any phenomenon comparable to the express pace attacks which defined the Lloyd, Richards, and Richardson resort to the sociology of group domination, physics of particle motion, and psychology of fear. Importantly, at St. John's Wood, in summer 2004, whom could captain, Brian Lara, choose to soar like "Big Bird" Joel Garner? Could he have called for someone such as that resourceful raider, Andy Roberts, Sunil Gavaskar, one of India's greatest batsmen, told me was a quick bowler against whom it was a mistake to relax? Was the two tenured skipper, Brian Lara, able to depend on any breath taking spells of quick bowling displayed from Holding heights well above that figurative soft snow where Brian Johnston states the West Indies paceman could run but leave no prints? Was he able to depend on devastating spells of quick bowling such as those unleashed by Curtly Ambrose for his skippers, Viv Richards and Richie Richardson, in Barbados (1990) and Trinidad (1994)?

It is, doubtless, the case that captain Brian Lara in summer 2004 called upon quick bowler, Curtly Ambrose. Anyone with a cricketing brain would have known that Ambrose was, however, well past his best bowling days when he struck great fear in the minds of several frontline opposing batsmen. I witnessed, first- hand, such decline in the Caribbean, during the course of the successful tour by Australia under the resolute and focused, Mark Taylor. One of those days when Ambrose was at his most brilliant best, I shall long remember, was 30th March, 1994, the fourth and penultimate day of the third Test Match between England and West Indies at Port-of-Spain, Trinidad. On that day England under Michael Atherton were all out for (46) in their second innings, a dreadful display, the worst in one hundred years—only one run better than an (1887) performance. Final scores in the game were: England three hundred and twenty eight and forty six, West Indies two hundred and fifty two and two hundred and sixty nine.

In seven overs and five balls after the tea interval, on day four, Curtly Ambrose roared like the raging Caribbean sea and marshalled a fearsome West Indies fast bowling fraternity with massive force and fury to overrun the England barricades. At stumps, he had launched his side to an unassailable position by taking six second innings wickets for twenty two runs, thereby making it impossible for their batsmen to have saved the game.

In their second innings the tourists were precariously poised—forty runs for the loss of eight wickets, a hundred and fifty four from the remote landmark of victory—with only two wickets in hand and one day to go. From Ambrose England got neither a baptism of fire nor a crucifixion from hell. He struck HMS Disaster, the listing vessel, like a hurricane, long before its skipper, had time to find his sea legs. Indeed, when captain Atherton strode to the centre in Alec Stewart's company, his feats at the crease never anchored, heavily.

Ambrose trapped him—first ball—Leg Before Wicket (L.B.W.). His duck (0) and two others from frontline batsmen in the innings were some of the strongest signs of fragility against bowling excellence of the highest class. During one sensational spell, Ambrose forced Graeme Hick, Jack Russell, Robin Smith, Alec Stewart, and Graham Thorpe to follow their captain. England managers, Keith Fletcher and Michael Smith, watched with sheer bewilderment as their players returned to the dressing room, after having responded, in utterly clueless fashion, to the West Indies surge.

Only a massive downpour on day five could have prevented England from escaping huge embarrassment. I assume that Ambrose, who got more than ten wickets in the Test Match, would not have minded, if the skies opened long after he and teammates had made their final moves. Those moves were initiated by Courtney Walsh, who took the last two England second innings wickets only after six runs had been added to the overnight total.

When West Indies skipper Richie Richardson and his side triumphed in a previous one day encounter, he said he wanted England "suppressed." I doubt if he could have predicted that the Port-of-Spain venue was going to be the place where West Indies baffled and burdened their opponents beyond belief.

The point of the foregoing opposition between fearsome fast bowling in the hands of Brian Lara's leadership predecessors and its absence in his hands is this: West Indies have long ceased to ascend those terrestrial contours from which awe struck admirers visualised the blazing comet like glory with which they demolished opponents. Was Brian Lara unaware of this restrictive reality? How could he not have been! Asking an opposing side to bat without subjecting its batsmen to a penetrative pace attack would be based on vacuity of imagination, sheer phantasising, invalid counselling odoriferous with "the ideology of fast bowling" or just plain foolhardiness.

What a catastrophic application from Brian Lara of sociology, physics, and psychology, the strategic application of which, is essential to success in contemporary Test Match cricket! If England captain, Michael Vaughan, was as insightful a cricket analyst as Tony Cozier about black holes, then the skipper and teammates—vividly aware of that thirty six year darkness under suffocatingly thick fog like blankets of Caribbean blackwashes—would have been utterly gleeful about their opponents' self-inflicted pain. Anyone who, therefore, wishes to unpack or unravel meaning in Cozier's use of the term, 'psychological advantage,' should not lose sight of the massive emotional burdens that were being borne by West Indies players and their throngs of supporters within and beyond tropical shores hoping or dreaming of Test Match series victories under Brian Lara. Dare I state: reversal of fortune never runs sweetly on the minds of former tormentors and dominators! Let me add that life—including cricketing life—has a cruel way of returning to players the gifts they have chosen for others.

Those individuals wishing to conduct additional exploration of black holes from a technical standpoint are, of course, free to explore the work of John Wheeler, John Mitchell, Marquis de Laplace, Roger Penrose, Subrahmanyan Chandrasekhar—neither the Indian spinner Bhagwat Subrahmanya Chandrasekhar who toured West Indies in 1975-'76 under Bishan Singh Bedi's captaincy, nor the batsman Vakkadurai Bikshewaran Chandrasekhar—but the extraordinarily insightful Nobel prize winning physicist in whose name the Chandrasekhar limit is well known to astronomers. With both eyes on history, they can do more than unpack significance of lyrics from notable Caribbean calypsonian Mr. Francisco Slinger—stage name "The Mighty Sparrow." Sparrow's question in song is: "Who is the greatest cricketer on earth or Mars?" His reply: "HE IS THE GREAT GARFIELD SOBERS." Insofar as I am aware, humans have not yet been able to set foot on this hostile planet. Perhaps I am dreaming, but can I say that under Brian Lara's leadership it was just as difficult for West Indies to win Test Matches as it continues to be problematic for humans to land on Mars? Humans may well land on Mars, but West Indies teams may still be incapable at landing time of winning Test Match series on a consistent basis.

May I add that theoretical physics may be very complicated to ordinary cricketing mortals. The science is not, however, thoroughly inexplicable. In the words of radical British psychiatrist, Aaron Esterson, an observer can analyse events as owed to movement of atoms and molecules or to the intentionality of people, major features of which, are directions and relations created by thinkers. That black hole into which the collective West Indies cricket, had fallen was, thus, not a peril separable from the questionable directions and relations captain, Brian Lara had established.

Great Test Match batsman that Lara was, he repeatedly failed to appreciate the fact that he was merely one of the travellers along the cricketing causeway. As such, he continually jeopardised the comfort of the passengers whose well-being he had been entrusted to secure. Some of those passengers were the very bowlers whose suffering at the hands of the England batsmen Cozier avoided attributing to Lara.

West Indies, under Brian Lara's captaincy in the summer of 2004, lost (4-0) to England in a humiliating "whitewash." That was testament to yet another huge blemish on his tarnished tenures, the ruins of which, stood in sharp contrast to his dreams of stellar service. Not surprisingly, in the wake of the shame, ex-West Indies fast bowler, Colin Croft, called for his resignation. Writing on the BBC World Service website on 24th August, 2004, the former express bowler stated: "Yes, West Indian cricket is played with a certain flair, but for a team to win the basics of the game must be learned, understood and implemented."

Let me put the matter in figurative language used by Jeremy Coney. It was the insightful New Zealander who states that cricket is about bread and butter, not champagne. If you are musically inclined, you might be able to locate the Croft verdict as an unmistakable echo of these statements from renowned violinist, Yehudi Menuhin: "I have nothing against virtuosity. There comes a time when virtuosity becomes destructive. It must be fed by musicianship." Here is a juncture at which I invite observers to think reflectively about the prosaic and poetic. I invite them to ponder the words of former New York governor, Mario Cuomo: politicians campaign in poetry and govern in prose. President Barack Obama clearly grasped this difference during his first term as President. How much he is assessed to have maintained this posture to the end of his second term remains to be seen. Brian Lara, who clearly wanted the job of West Indies captain, failed to grasp the difference.

Observers can also determine whether Cozier recognised that time, albeit too late, when he wrote in the 30th August, 2004 edition of the *Stabroek News* in Guyana about the dreadful mess that West Indies cricket had become under Brian Lara's leadership. He was prudent enough to lay partial but significant blame at the feet of the West Indies Cricket Board. I could not help locating attribution of major responsibility to Mr. Lara, as well. Here are relevant excerpts from what I deem the Cozier conversion. After having noted that the West Indies experienced the most agonising ten months in its history, he added that if the woe expressed itself in a forthcoming April, 2005 South African tour of the Caribbean, the repercussions would be too awful to contemplate.

West Indies lost that four game series against South Africa (2-0). Despite artistically excellent batting displays from player Brian Lara, which brought him unforgettable centuries, he could not save his team from humiliation, although it was shepherded by a much sought after coach, Australian Bennet King. And though hard hitting Caribbean Test Match batsman, Chris Gayle, treated faithful followers at the Antigua Recreation Ground to a breath taking blast of belligerence which earned him a memorable triple hundred in the fourth and final Antigua game, Ramnaresh Sarwan, another St. John's centurion, and other senior West Indies lieutenants, were among a hapless collective that had succumbed to one more clever challenger.

If I focus on Cozier's repercussions, I can state, quite simply, that elementary rules of that rather old enterprise, interaction, are still applicable to this game, cricket, which West Indies captain, Brian Lara, erroneously assumed he could enhance with trappings of his selfhood. An assertion from Michael Holding is instructive, here. Soon after Pakistan had inflicted a huge defeat on transitional West Indies captain, Courtney Walsh, leading batsman, Brian Lara, and teammates, in late 1997, Holding was moved to claim that all the hard work he and his contemporaries had done was forfeited. This was, clearly, a call to vindicate a serious search for the importance of the Caribbean collective to the playing of Test Match cricket.

In early May, 2005, the end of the South African Test Match campaign, West Indies cricket was, however, West Indies cricket in name only. Holding was alluding to almost sixteen years of unquestioned excellence dictated by sheer skill in descendants of the downtrodden who never doubted the validity of their own self-education and that of their predecessors. What passed for Caribbean Test Match cricket under Brian Lara's leadership, was being delivered by those I deem aliens' apostles as a result of truncation of that education.

Let me grant additional consideration to the Cozier repercussions and state that skipper, Brian Lara, bore significant responsibility for truncation. I ground my claim by referring to other comments of the writer's. He pointed out, rather importantly, that in Brian Lara's second chance as leader, West Indies decline clearly intensified. Cozier continued by claiming:

> As exceptional a batsman as he is, Lara's motivational influence and tactical awareness are certainly open to the censure it has received from former players and others who have closely followed the team's trials and tribulations under him and care passionately about West Indies cricket. It would reflect worrying indifference if they didn't show their concern.

Readers would notice that I have framed the quote in terms of claims. A technical interpretation of the statements is that they can be classified as assertives which are either true or false. Keen observers can judge the nature of their credibility. They can, however, give themselves greater latitude than that resting in the Cozier gloss by exploring views of Stabroek News correspondent Orin Davidson, who penned his thoughts on the same day as the Cozier piece appeared. Davidson was explicit in his assessment of Lara.

Of the West Indies team in 2004, he writes that its Test Match players are poor in almost all facets of the game. Their leadership in Test Matches, for which they are under- prepared, is inadequate. "It is an open secret that Lara as captain is wholly and solely in control of the team, notwithstanding the presence of coach, Gus Logie. He has the final say in all the cricketing decisions, but as great a batsman he may be, his leadership is well below par and the players continue to make the same fielding, batting and bowling errors day in day out. His strategic decisions on field are no less impressive and have given commentators easy fodder to malign the team wherever they go. His belief that the players are young and must not be harshly dealt with, is an open admission of his shortcomings." Davidson adds that Lara's personal success should not constitute reward for inadequacy in a leadership role.

Regardless of whatever disposition I or others adopt to the Davidson's claims, no reasonable observer should miss the massive dilemma Cozier creates for Lara led West Indies, which the commentator/historian embeds in figurative links among imagery and repercussions, collapse, exhaustion, and inability to escape. It is, however, quite possible that these connections may not be pondered. Should the observers choose not to, they may see the literal significance in the Davidson, Holding, Croft, and Coney claims: these are all people with direct and specific interests in cricket. Observers may also find some merit to reflecting upon the Lara and Obama presence by pondering the significance to links between British politics and cricket.

Well over two decades ago I found myself focusing on an article by Craig Whitney in the New York Times Magazine (29th, 1992) I was—among other matters—giving my very rapt attention to a full colour photograph of British Prime Minister, John Major, executing, rather elegantly, what—in cricketing jargon—appears to be a square cut.

With clear interest in the demonstration, I began examining the caption, "JOHN MAJOR AT BAT," accompanying its rare presentation in the American publication. I could not help noticing that the story which followed was about whether, Mr. Major, "an avid cricket player in his youth," and whose favourite sport is cricket, could have won the April 1992 British general election, despite massive economic recession in his country.

Mr. Major, according to Whitney, a man possessed of a largeness of spirit unusual among politicians, did emerge triumphant at the 1992 polls, despite a very lengthy recession, an unemployment rate of 9.4%, and although his opponent, Mr. Neil Kinnock, a debating champion at the University of Wales, stated boldly prior to the '92 election that the Prime Minister was a fool not to have called a general election just after the Gulf War when he was highly popular. According to Whitney, Mr. Major opted for a different date, because of a simple reason: "he [Mr. Major] didn't think it was cricket, since the opposition parties had stood behind the government."

While recognising that the caption about Mr. Major bore a striking resemblance to baseball terminology, I could not fail to see that *The Times* was using that very English of games, cricket, as compelling imagery in its efforts to inform Americans about electoral battles in the U.K—contests which are never boring. Part of the imagery I also drew from the presentation was a powerful sense of the Prime Minister with that largeness of SPIRIT on a sticky wicket where he needed all the deftness, guile, and curiosity (Lee, 1996, p. xiv) associates with cricket, if he was going to succeed at the April event. Dare I state that this is the very SPIRIT which has served to define, so admirably, the presence of some of the greatest cricketers the world over whom Mr. Major would never hesitate to recognise as excellent exemplars, Sir Len Hutton, Mr. Alec Bedser, Mr. Herbert Sutcliffe, Sir John Berry Hobbs (England), Sir Frank Worrell, Sir Gary Sobers, Mr. Conrad Hunte, (West Indies), Sir Donald Bradman, Mr. Ray Lindwall, Mr. Neil Harvey, and Mr. Lindsay Hassett (Australia) come to mind readily.

Mr. Major, notes Whitney, is unlike his Conservative predecessors. He is not an Oxbridge graduate or "some upper class twit with four names who went to a posh private school." Different from Mrs. Thatcher—certainly not, I add, upper class, but a grammar school product that went to Oxford and brought up by a green grocer father and alderman—Mr. Major did not accept that it is poor people's fault that they are poor. From personal experience, so states Whitney, he carried an awareness that "poverty is sometimes plain bad luck." This is not an awareness—I emphasise—which is alien to the Obama thinking.

I emphasise, that unlike Mr. Obama, however, Mr. Major, is quintessentially British with a cricketing thrust clearly linked to fast thinking on his feet. Always the gentleman-cricketer and gentleman-politician, he has stated he thinks his opponent, Mr. Kinnock, "is a man of many fine qualities"—something of which one can't imagine Thatcher ever admitting. But then, Whitney emphasises "cricket is Major's favourite sport." Obama may well be a gentleman-politician. Although his favourite sport is clearly not cricket, and after the bruising 2012 election he did invite Mr. Romney to the White House, no one should ever be lulled into assuming that his Democratic Party colleagues such as Harry Reid and Dick Durbin in the American legislature were slow thinkers on their feet and were unaware of the toughness needed to fight republican rivals such as House Speaker, John Boehner.[1] It is the Speaker who was, after all, front and centre in a lawsuit against Mr. Obama over the President's handling of the US border debacle and associated stalemate in regard to US immigration reform.

The Whitney pointer to fast thinking on his feet is evocative of my vivid memory about Roy Clifton Fredericks, that diminutive but destructively domineering left hand West Indies opening batsman, assessed, rather appropriately by one writer as someone quick on his feet and a wristy cutter of deadly certainty. Later, I shall write, most deservingly, about Roy Fredericks, whose batting style Brian Lara admired intensely. My immediate focus is, of course, on John Major, politician, avid cricketer, and fan, who has found time to appear at the Kennington Oval where he watches Test Matches. On one occasion, David Gower, the high scoring ex-England skipper-turned-commentator, pointed to the Prime Minister seated with former England master of medium fast swing bowling, Sir Alec Bedser. Although Mr. Clement Atlee and Lord Douglas-Home were great lovers of cricket, I do not know of Mr. Major's predecessors—Labour or Conservative—who watched Test Matches regularly either at Lord's or the Oval. That I emphasise may well not be cricket.

The Major cricketing thrust, I add, is admirably captured by Whitney, when he asserts not just that Mrs. Thatcher's successor is fundamentally a decent man, but exemplifies the decency, also, while noting: soon after he succeeded Mrs. Thatcher, he walked across the Commons floor to extend a warm greeting to a very ill Labour back bencher, Mr. Eric Heffer.[2] Heffer, to those familiar with the British political scene, was a staunch socialist always ready to storm the palaces of capitalist plunder. This is a point which should not be missed. In cricketing terms, Mr. Heffer was not unlike a figurative representation of that "old enemy" of England in Ashes series, Australia, in keen sporting tussles within and outside the British Isles. It would not, of course, be cricket, if Mr. Major did not cross the Commons floor—not unlike the warmth extended by England cricket captain, Sir. Len Hutton, to competitor, the incomparable and legendary Australian, Sir Donald Bradman, whom Hutton well knew was one of England's most formidable foes.

The Whitney imagery of a square driving John Major at bat serves as a powerful reminder to leading political figures in contemporary English speaking democracies that he must have used that cricketing SPIRIT to play extremely well on the sticky election wicket where he and teammates found themselves. More significantly, I wonder how much of the SPIRIT had come from his immersion in the sport he had known both from his experience within and beyond fields of play where both political and—I add—economic matters can, and do, burden statesmen. My wondering well after the year of his performance is hardly a restrictive posture. These very matters in their crushingly destructive versions did exercise the constructive minds and spirits of one of Mr. Major's successors, Prime Minister Gordon Brown, an avid follower of rugby.

Economic and political deadweight did also burden the 2009 winner of the Nobel Peace Prize, President Barack Obama, who has presented himself as more passionate about basketball than baseball. To many a keen observer Obama was clearly standing at the crossroads just over a year before the crucial 2012 elections. This was part of a thorny prelude for him during which I heard Emily Rooney, the host of a reputable American TV programme, "GREATER BOSTON", assert to one of her distinguished guests, African-American academic, Randall Kennedy, that the American President was elusive about "the old sticky wicket," affirmative action.

There was nothing elusive in the President's conduct about race, a matter integral to the affirmative action controversy, about a week after the Florida jury in the George Zimmerman trial returned a unanimous not-guilty verdict, and on the day 12th July 2016, he, along with former President G.W. Bush and Dallas Police Chief, spoke at a memorial for five police officers murdered by bullets from an automatic weapon used by a black man, Mr. Micah Johnson. Mr. Zimmerman had been charged in the murder of African-American teenager, Trayvon Martin. The defendant admitted to having shot young Martin but claimed he did so in keeping with a Florida law widely described as a stand-your-ground law. Race, always a sticky wicket for leading American political figures—Mr. Obama included—was apprehended in a forthright fashion when the President held a press briefing shortly before massive demonstrations were scheduled to be staged across America in protest against the court verdict. Significantly, that apprehending was part of a very judicious—if not nuanced—set of moves on what was clearly another occasion when Mr. Obama found himself on a sticky wicket where he used guile, deftness, and curiosity.

The President noted that the jury conducted itself professionally and added that is "how the system works." Nevertheless, in what was, indubitably, an empathetic mode he asserted that African-American men—including him prior to the time when he had become a senator—know all too well the feeling of being followed in a department store or hearing the sound of car door locks operated by European-Americans, when they spot African-American males in car parks or stepping on to elevators where European--American females clutch their purses.

Quite apart from having used the term 'African American' on numerous occasions at the briefing, two of his most direct pronouncements came: "When Trayvon Martin was first shot, I said that this could have been my son. Another way of saying that is Trayvon Martin could have been me thirty-five years ago." In clear reference to the Florida law, he asked: "Do we actually think that he [Trayvon Martin] could have been justified in shooting Mr. Zimmerman instead of the other way around? Do we actually think that he [Trayvon Martin] would have been justified in shooting Mr. Zimmerman, who had followed him in a car, because he felt threatened. And if the answer to that question is, at least ambiguous, it seems to me that we might want to examine those kinds of laws."

I wonder how many more laws the erudite legal scholar could have asked his fellow Americans to examine in regard to the shooting death (early August, 2014) of an unarmed black teenager in the heart of Ferguson, Missouri, part of the racist American south. Brown's death was followed, almost immediately by an almost week- long set of pitched battles between the Ferguson police, whose chief was European-American[3] and white, and largely African-American groups of demonstrators who claimed stridently that young defenceless Brown was gunned down brutally by a white police officer, Mr. Darren Wilson, despite what Brown is widely believed by several blacks to have uttered to the officer: "HANDS UP. DON'T SHOOT." In the immediate aftermath of the tragedy, the golfing President on the green with Michael Jordan—vacationing on Martha's Vineyard—appealed to Americans for calm and requested a societal wide conversation—presumably about RACE IN AMERICA.

It is that very conversation for which he asked when he stood up at the infamous Edmund Pettus Bridge early in 2015 and spoke to an approving group of onlookers—including his Attorney General, Mr. Eric Holder; civil rights icon, Congressman Mr. John Lewis; and former President, George Walker Bush. Not too long after, early April 2015, all of America saw the horrific and fatal shooting of Mr. Walter Scott, a fleeing unarmed African-American civilian, in the back by Mr. Michael Slager, a police officer from Charleston, South Carolina, another cesspool for black dehumanisation. Wither goest the conversation! Soon after the Charleston shooting the officer was charged with murder, and thankfully no violence erupted in the wake of the shooting. The world knows that Brown's shooter was never charged, and even before the District Attorney had made the announcement the shooter would have no court date, Ferguson erupted.

On the morning following one of the worst confrontational evenings there, 13th August, 2014, the President condemned violence from both the police and certain elements among the demonstrators. Regardless of what the President had to say about the shooting matter itself and, or, the contexts that were associated with it, one thing is certain to me. The President's placement on the sticky wicket, race, is not one from which he could have played productive innings: to the extent that the imprint on the Obama presidency of the Lyndon Johnson legacy of wrestling with poverty, race, and civil rights is not immediately obvious in the everyday lives of countless African-Americans—especially those in the south—Mr. Obama would have been on the back foot while dealing with race. This is not the only claim I wish to offer. Later, when I address myself to the implications of the horrific child murders in Newtown, Connecticut, I shall offer other arguments. At this point, I want to state a little more about being on the back foot, from a sporting standpoint.

From a strictly Test Match cricketing standpoint, when someone finds herself/himself on a sticky wicket, s/he has to remain there for as long as possible. There is no opportunity of eluding what has to be served by the opposing side. Clearly, survival does depend heavily upon guile, deftness, and curiosity, all of which were very evident in batsman/batter Obama's presentation about the case.

It is also purely from a Test Match cricketing standpoint that I state: cricketing experts—experienced commentators included—do not speak of sticky wickets/pitches. They speak about damp wickets/pitches or wickets/pitches laden with moisture. How does a wicket become moisture laden? That does happen, as a result of rainfall—heavy or light. If during the course of play, umpires notice very overcast skies and worry about the imminent threat of rain, they will suspend play and order that the wicket and immediate surrounding areas be covered very securely with tarpaulin. If the rain does pour, especially on a hot and humid day, although a wicket is covered, there will be condensation on that wicket, or to use a rather ordinary term, the wicket will "sweat." Play may also be over for a particular day, and as far as I am aware right up to the end of the nineteen seventies wickets were covered securely overnight. Again, heavy overnight rain in hot and humid conditions would mean condensation. Such could eventuate even before the very first day of a Test Match or other first class games lasting four days. Regardless of the circumstances, it is a nightmare for batsmen—even the very greatest—having to perform on a wicket which has "sweated."

Why do I use the term 'nightmare'? Deliveries served by quick bowlers who have mastered the art and science of lateral movement off the wicket make it very problematic for even the very best of leading batsmen to negotiate their deliveries, which can rise rather awkwardly off the wicket and in the demanding presence of awkward lift find the edges of their bats and land in the safe catching hands of fielders who stand in attacking positions known as slips or gullies. Wicket keepers/catchers on fielding sides have also been known to catch balls flying off the bat edges of leading batsmen on moisture laden wickets.

Such wickets are ideal for some other types of bowlers known as spin bowlers. Their deliveries are slow, but as a result of delicate finger and wrist movements these bowlers have deceived some of the most accomplished batsmen, who misjudge the line of flight of the ball or fail to make contact with the ball, after it is made to deviate prodigiously when it bounces unpredictably off the wicket. Readers can determine for themselves whether batter/batsman, Obama, was negotiating spin bowling or quick bowling when he dealt with the Zimmerman verdict, a move I heard more than a few American political analysts claim he was obliged to make.

History may well decide if the President was on back or front foot on 12th July 2016, when a highly expectant America awaited his delivery at the Dallas Memorial. After he had got well into his oratorical stride, many a European-American television commentator/pandit/expert claimed he had done a marvellous job, despite the obvious pain on his facial expression while telling the world he had been in attendance for too many a funeral. In stating that he knows America much too well to accept that his society was so divided that it might not be able to deal with the race divide and economic disparity exposed, as a consequence of the Dallas murders, the Baton Rouge and St. Paul police shooting antecedent to the murders, the President resorted to St. John's gospel and exhorted fellow Americans to seek truth and move well beyond language to actions other than language use. In that very Dallas delivery—not deliverance—I emphasise, he acknowledged that his own words have not been adequate in dealing with the gun violence across an America about which he had spoken so optimistically at the Democratic Party convention in July 2004, when he asserted to very rapturous applause that there is no black and white America but The United States of America. I shall return to the matter, gun violence. Let me focus upon the cricket, specifically the Brian Lara-Barack Obama pair.

It is, of course, the politician—not batsman/batter—Barack Obama who paid a visit to Brian Lara's country in April, 2009, when he attended the summit of the Americas. British Prime Minister, Mr. Brown—somewhat later—in November of that very year, was, also in Trinidad to attend for the Commonwealth Heads of Government Conference. While Dr. Manmohan Singh and Mr. Kevin Rudd, Indian and Australian Prime Ministers, had audiences with the Port-of-Spain Prince, I have no idea whether the British leader found time for the illustrious company of Mr. Lara. President Obama could hardly have had the advice of CNN presenter, Mr. Piers Morgan, that he knows no West Indian who cannot play cricket. Mr. Obama did meet Prince Lara at the Trinidad Hilton—hardly a sticky political or economic wicket.

Did Barack Hussein Obama deserve a first appearance in Trinidad with Brian Charles Lara? From a purely cricketing standpoint, my reply is definitely affirmative; I support it with, perhaps, the most elegant prose I have read about the batsman:

In the space of a few weeks in 1994 Brian Lara broke the two most romantic and significant of all batting records and thereby achieved a pre-eminence amongst his contemporaries equalled only by W.G. Grace and Sir Donald Bradman. A left-hander of innate genius, he was only 24 when he made the highest individual score in 117 years of Test cricket, 375 against England in the fifth Test in Antigua in 1994, surpassing Sir Gary Sobers' previous record of 365 not out. Exactly seven weeks later he recorded the biggest score ever in first class cricket, an undefeated 501 for Warwickshire against Durham at Edgbaston. This was run-feasting of gargantuan proportions, when seemingly unattainable landmarks in cricket history were bypassed, the unthinkable became almost commonplace, and memories of Bradman's appetite for long innings were rekindled. Like Bradman, Lara was hailed as a cricketing God, his batting invested with a style and panache that his contemporaries could never hope to match. Short in stature at 5 ft. 5 in., with a school boyish demeanour, Lara's sublime skills are underpinned by steely wrists and excellent footwork and have established him as an icon to all those who appreciate the aesthetics of batsmanship. A master of technique, his placement all around the wicket is unerring, his attacking shots are unfurled from a flamboyant high backlift, and his trademark whip stroke is played with ease and elan off the back foot or front foot (Martin-Jenkins 1996, p. 753).

There was more to come from Lara in the Test Match realm, to which I refer later. Let me get back to the Hilton.

It was at the Hilton where Lara gave the President a few pointers on cricket, among which were how to play the cover drive and forward defensive stroke. Lara also gave the American President a gift, one of the batsman's own autographed bats. What a meeting! My exclamation is meant to convey the inextricable delicacy coursing through the pathways formed from the intersection of politics and cricket which—in circumstances of the Lara-Obama connection—warrant close scrutiny. Why do I state that scrutiny is warranted, when there is ample room for comparing Mr. Obama to predecessor Presidents?

Here, the names, Lyndon Baines Johnson and William Jefferson Clinton,, spring to mind immediately. President Clinton—never mind his sexual escapades in the White House—is the late twentieth century leader who personified enormous economic success for America, the man who used the words of Mr. James Carville, an adviser, at the time of his second presidential campaign to state that it was "the economy stupid" which was the central issue to the 1996 race he won. It is President Clinton who—in the eyes of many a shrewd political commentator—electrified the Democratic Party convention in Charlotte, North Carolina in September 2012. It is also President Clinton—hoarse and obviously physically exhausted from hectic campaigning on behalf of President Obama in 2012—that many of those same observers credit with playing no small role in Mr. Obama's November 2012 success. These are the very observers who note that Mr. Obama admires President Clinton, would have loved to emulate his economic success, but unlike President Clinton is not at ease in everyday discourse with ordinary American citizens.

The Johnson name was invoked by one of the partisan American television networks, MSNBC, at the height of the thorny fiscal cliff tangle, late December, 2012, between the republican dominated Congress and a newly elected President Obama. During the course of a regular late afternoon show one week before the festive holidays, a news analyst posed the question: what could President Obama learn from President Johnson while dealing with the looming fiscal cliff? The ready reply from a keeper of the Johnson presidential library was that Mr. Obama could learn a great deal from his Democratic predecessor, despite the huge rigidity—if not inflexibility—to congressional party loyalty with which the US legislature has been seized. In the eyes of the respondent, Mr. Johnson was a "master psychologist" who possessed the great ability to persuade people on the other side to say yes to his legislative proposals. Such was, unquestionably, the case in regard to the Civil Rights (1964) and Voting Rights Acts (1965) Acts. Let me add that I find the views expressed by the Johnson library spokesperson fully consistent with a position taken by the great West Indian/American activist and talented artist, Belafonte, (2012, p. 292), who writes: no one was a shrewder strategist than L.B.J.

President Johnson was, above all else, supposed to be the ambitious grand reformer aiming to build the "great society." It was he who initiated such programmes as Head Start, aimed at uplifting the poor and dispossessed in America. This was a man who—according to his Secretary of State, Dean Rusk—knew in his heart that racial discrimination in America was wrong. It was he who piloted the Voting and Civil Rights Bills through the American legislature. It was, however, a bitter and defeated Johnson—largely because of a war he had not initiated—who announced publicly that he would neither seek nor accept the Democratic Party nomination for the 1968 presidential race.

Barack Obama, who did not initiate any of the two wars in which he was deeply enmeshed, knows about the American poor and dispossessed, wanted to be an ambitious grand reformer, and must have known in his heart that racial discrimination is wrong, had to wonder whether he could have had more than one term in office. It is, thus, not difficult for me to avoid the temptation to wonder: (a) How far down the Johnson road he travelled? (b) Could he equal the communicative and economic success of President Clinton? Another way of giving room to my speculative and imaginative pursuits would be to consider a number of other queries: (c) What efforts were being made by Mr. Obama to avoid pitfalls of the Johnson presidency? (d) Will a major aspect of the Obama legacy encompass favourable comparison to President Clinton? These are, undoubtedly, leadership questions which are central to writing about presidential history.

Given the leadership similarities between Messrs. Obama and Lara I shall explore, I can also ask: (a) If Mr. Obama failed as President, in what ways could Caribbean people use his lack of success as a basis for learning anything about Brian Lara's failures and addressing themselves to any harmful implications such learning has for Caribbean life outside cricket? (b) If Mr. Obama succeeded in his presidency, how could Caribbean people use his success for the purpose of elevating their region within and beyond cricket fields? Both of these questions become highly relevant to the Caribbean in the twenty-first century, not just because the region continues to be a zone of socio-economic exploitation, but also because of the unfulfilled expectations associated with Brian Lara's leadership performance. I want to continue the Lara-Obama exploration by paying attention to what I deem a significant similarity, failure to challenge a destructive tradition, cultures of violence, and a major difference in 'ground game.'

The first is related to that horrific shooting in Newtown, Connecticut, in December, 2012 which moved the President to tears, as well as, police terrorism against two young black men, Mr. Alton Sterling, in Baton Rouge, Louisiana, and Mr. Philando Castile in St. Paul, Minnesota, and, of course, murder of the Dallas police officers by Mr. Micah Johnson, whose conduct the President asserted was "an act not just of demented violence, but also, racial hatred." While addressing a large gathering at a memorial service for the Newtown victims, a stone- faced chief parent-in-grief poured out his deep feelings over the massacre. Towards the end of his delivery, at times probing and poignant, the President said: "I am very mindful that mere words cannot match the depth of your sorrow, nor can they heal your wounded hearts." In what could be seen as a direct and explicit presentation to all his fellow Americans, he challenged them to ponder the relevance of what he considered to be the value of their freedom and asked: can we say that we're truly doing enough to give all the children of this country the chance they deserve to live out their lives in happiness and with purpose? I've been reflecting on this the last few days. If we're honest with ourselves, the answer is no."

Living in happiness is not just part of the American materialistic dream, it is a very significant component many Americans also regard as part of their constitutional right secured after the successful revolt against their British imperial rulers during the course of the eighteenth century. Mr. Obama's December 2012 Newtown address was, thus, not an oblique reference to how contemporary America should handle its traditions. When I ponder this matter of traditions, I am compelled to tell myself that Mr. Obama, who set up a Task Force on gun violence led by his Vice-President, Mr. Joseph Biden, might not have been on the right road to challenging traditions in cultures of violence, insofar as those traditions relate to the Newtown slaughter. I make this claim despite passionate pronouncements from Georgia Congressman Mr. John Lewis, who shed tears over the horror.

Mr. Lewis, Democrat, staunch civil rights advocate, noted publicly: too many guns, the Russians are not coming, and the British are not coming. America does not need weapons of mass destruction. He insisted the President, who revealed that what was seen as his inaction and silence on guns during the course of the 2012 campaign could be accounted for by his focus on a monumental economic crisis, needed to lead on the gun problem. Mr. Lewis reminded Americans that guns killed civil rights activist, Mr. Medgar Evers, his friend, Dr. Martin Luther King, Attorney General/Senator, Robert Kennedy, and brother, President, John Kennedy. May I add it was a gun that killed four unarmed students at Kent State University, Ohio, in 1970? It was guns, also, that killed three New York, and two Mississippi policemen in 2015.

Not unlike Mr. Lewis and other politicians from the Democratic Party, the President called for tougher gun control and a ban on assault weapons; at the time he gave the Vice- President the job of heading the Task Force. In the Newtown speech, he expressed a clear commitment to using whatever power his presidential office confers for the purpose of engaging law enforcement officials, mental health experts, parents, and educators to prevent more tragedies such as that in Newtown. Can such a move be a reasonable approach to wrestling with, and halting, a harmful tradition? I say no. Contemporary United States is a society hewn from cultures of violence: even in the wake of the Newtown horror, the National Rifle Association (NRA) was advancing claims about teachers carrying guns and expressing regret that the Sandy Hook School Principal was not carrying a gun she could have used to blow Adam Lanza's head off. Further, tougher gun control or tackling a gun culture is not workable in a foreground where cultures of violence loom large.

Allow me to make a simple, yet powerful observation. Sandy Hook is not just a suburb on the East Coast of the United States. It is, also, one of those locations Cornel West would describe as a vanilla suburb, very distinct to what he calls chocolate cities. Vanilla suburbs are settings to which several whites flee in the belief they can avoid—among other burdens and dangers—interpersonal violence. One immediate response to the gun horror visited on Sandy Hook was very similar to that of Columbine and Aurora: in such quiet, pleasant, middle and high income areas, how could that type of horror have taken place? The dismay is clearly—albeit by implicature—about setting chocolate cities apart from vanilla suburbs.

The point here is that paradoxically in a democracy where individualism—distinct from the sharing, togetherness, and the United States of America about which Senator, Barack Obama, spoke publicly (summer 2004, autumn 2012)—is supreme, cultures—including cultures of violence—are bound neither by social distance nor physical distance. Such is especially painfully true in the digital age. What I see as productive is dealing with the thorny issue, tackling cultures of violence strongly and integrally connected to—among other events—slavery, two world wars, the Vietnam War, the War Of Independence, three Iraq wars, one Afghanistan war, and the Civil War.

Americans—President Obama included—cannot be unaware of the immense sacrificial work done by Mr. Malcolm X, who eventually embraced Dr. King's message of non-violence, and had an American dream which was distinctly different to the vulgar materialism of the American dream. Americans are aware of Mr. Mohandas Karamchand Gandhi, whom Dr. King revered, and Mr. Nelson Mandela. Well before Mr. Obama's two term tenure began, his predecessors, Mr Lyndon Johnson, Mr. Jimmy Carter, and Mr. Bill Clinton, openly embraced the ideas of Dr. King, Mr. Gandhi, and Mr. Mandela. Yet, President Johnson was trapped within the Vietnam debacle, Mr. Carter, Sunday School teacher and devout Christian, built the neutron bomb, Mr. Clinton—I remember very well—did not flinch to use cruise missiles and other ordinance, and bombed the daylight out of Yugoslavia. I am fully aware that well after the conclusion of his single term tenure, President Carter (2012) issued public criticism of US drone strikes which—along with what some in the Washington and New York media circles deem Obama's secret war—intensified. Mr. Obama has offered no public reaction to his Democratic predecessor. Nor, for that matter, has he offered any public reaction to regular activist criticism from Mr. Imran Khan, former Pakistan charismatic Test Match hero, of drone strikes. It is Mr. Obama—to use his own term—who ramped up the bombing campaign in Iraq against ISIS forces and offered no explanation to either the world at large about violating the territorial sovereignty of Syria, another member state of the UN, in efforts to "hunt down" terrorists.[4]

While none of the American leaders has offered any public acknowledgement of Mr. Malcolm X, he is, doubtless, part of the American tradition of US citizens living in a world of non-violence and happiness. They would also never disagree with the idea that Mr. Mandela, an important initiator and user of peace, harmony, and happiness via the Truth and Reconciliation Commission, in the aftermath of the official end of apartheid, eventually spurned cultures of violence. So, if in 2012 and onwards President Obama, Nobel Prize recipient and *Time Magazine* Person of the Year (2008, 2012) wanted to use a challenge to tradition for the purpose of creating a climate of peace, harmony, and happiness, did he not have to make the tough choice of beginning to take the lead in amending the American tradition hewn from cultures of violence? My reply is explicitly affirmative.

Did he give any signals about moving in such a direction? My reply is explicitly negative. Just as importantly, with an eye to making such a move, President Obama, who loves to reflect, President Obama, the insightfully shrewd politician, the devout Christian who embraces Dr. King's work, reveres Mr. Mandela and Mr. Gandhi, must have wrestled with the thorny issue: given the cultures of violence with which America is riveted, were there any differences, on the one hand, between (a) actions from Kevin Paddock, Jared Loughner, James Holmes, Adam Lanza, Operation Greystone, and police kill lists, and (b) on the other, presidential drone kill lists? Were there any differences between air strikes in Iraq and Syria, US enhanced interrogation techniques, on the one hand, and Al Qaeda torture techniques, on the other!

Kevin Paddock murdered well over fifty people in Las Vegas early in October 2017. The same time when millions of Americans were glued to their television sets watching the Lynn Novick and Ken Burns highly acclaimed film *The Vietnam War*, Paddock had numerous very destructive guns in his hotel room from where he rained his terror on fellow citizens. Was there not massive terror rained by US soldiers upon Vietnamese citizens with thousands of guns, very huge and mightily destructive to humanity, dubbed disdainfully, via rabid racism from the US soldiers, as gooks and dinks! Was such not despicable dehumanisation by the US soldiers! Was Kevin Paddock's dehumanisation not despicable also! How can someone such as President Obama be invested, or invest himself with the moral mandate to claim, both validly and justifiably, as he has, that the United States needs strict gun control! An expert idea is not out of order at this juncture.

It comes from, Howard Becker, one of America's best known pioneering sociologists, who explicates the labelling perspective of deviance. It is he who writes that social groups create deviance via constructing rules, the infraction of which, counts as deviance. Further, the rules are applied to specific persons labelled as outsiders.

From this point of view, [the labelling perspective] deviance is not a quality of the act the person commits, but rather a consequence of the application by others of rules and sanctions to an "offender." The deviant is one to whom that label has successfully been applied; deviant behaviour is behaviour that people so label (Becker 1963, p. 9).

The label on Paddock shall remain affixed to him well after disposal of his remains. Will the label against the US citizens at the highest levels of government, as well as the men in uniform on the ground, in the air, and on water in Vietnam, remain affixed to them as deviants long after they leave planet earth!

The exclamation after my queries is not misplaced: violence of every sort is, unquestionably, loudly, stridently, violence, even when committed in the name of democracy against others such as Vietnamese citizens, Osama bin Laden, Mohammed Emwazi, and Anwar El Awlaki. Rather remarkably, the Nobel Peace Prize recipient, who intensified the secret war beyond America's shores against terrorist enemies of democracy, received cheers and strident repetitive chants of 'USA, USA,' from fellow Americans at the time he informed the nation about Mr. bin Laden's demise. Is it not remarkable, also, that vicious interpersonal violence perpetrated by people—civilian and uniformed—bearing arms intensified, during the course of the recipient's presidential tenures! Is it not remarkable, as well, that arms bearing is linked indelibly and inextricably to metamorphosing capitalism to which the President is beholden!

I must state that I have heard two residents of Sandy Hook, a Vietnam veteran, and a Reuter's correspondent who received his early education in the suburb, speak about tackling a "culture of violence" or "the violence of the [American] society." None of these two citizens was the President. Further, I have grave doubts Mr. Obama could have tackled cultures of violence: evolution in American cultures of violence has taken place in conjunction with the metamorphosis of capitalism, of which the President remained a strong supporter. Was it, therefore, possible for him to tackle cultures of violence without tackling structures of contemporary capitalism and appear to be dismantling such structures? I say no.I shall say no, also, when I consider the 2014-'16 police shootings and juxtapose them with that secret war. I do so by resorting to what I call SOVEREIGN LANGUAGE common all across the Anglo-Caribbean, language with which the President should experience NO PRABLEM MAHN.

Wah gwan baas? Yoh does use high high technalagy fu kill people outside Merica. Merican Babylan does use high high technalagy fuh kill people toh. Yoh en ga fu ansah to nobady but wen di Babylan kill de gah fu ansah. Some does ga fuh goh to court, even wen de mek mistake. Yoh en ga fu goh to none court—mistake ar nat. Wen you an yoh bayz tek out some mahn in Janwery, 2015, ahyoh seh ahyoh mek mistake an yoh apalahgise monts aftah: fuh monts ayoh "soh bloomin qwyat." When di Babylan tek out people in America you an wan ah yoh bayz—wid nutun bettah foh doh—look up di law book—ayoh "mekin BIG riyat." Iz you get Nobel prize! fuh wah baas! Yoh get Nobel prize fuh kill people! Mi nevah know NONE Babylan in America get Nobel prize an ah kill people. How dah kyan be, bass! Wah gwan bass? Lang lang time bifoh al Qaeda nuf nuf Rasta mahn taak bo wah kina bad bad mahn Babylan mahn is. Yoh kyan do like di Babylan an ton rung an bad taak dem. Iy nah mek sens baas. Ah gon tell yoh someting ah hear in a rum shap in a place nah far from weh a barn. Ah hear a mahn seh someting ah tink come frum dem ole ole black peepl in Guyana. Di mahn seh: JACKASS AZE LAANG. E know e matty stohrey but e en know e own. Tink bu duh baas.

It is at this juncture that I must return to the Obama assertive about Mr. Micah Johnson, whom the President claimed committed an "act not just of demented violence, but also racial hatred." Like Mr. Obama, who states he knows America very well, I know the West Indies very well, and know about slavery there very well. I know as well from the exceptionally scholarly work of perhaps the foremost West Indies intellectual, Dr. Eric Williams, that slavery in the West Indies began as an economic—not a racial—question. Williams points out that racism was one of the later justifications offered on behalf of what was an economic matter. I am well aware, too, about the slave assertiveness against dehumanisation dubbed uprising by the imperialists right across the West Indies. This assertiveness was not infrequently connected to taking up of arms by the Africans who believed that their actions were honourable and being committed in very good faith. Today, evidence of the assertiveness can be found in the lives of the Maroons in Jamaica and Suriname, some of whom were invited to the US in 1976 on the occasion of the bicentenary. It is indubitably the case that slavery does not exist in the West Indies and, for that matter, the United States.

Is it not the case that capitalism, the economic matter, that bedrock upon which slavery originated and continued for so long, has not just metamorphosed, but is inseparable from what I have heard described as "weaponised blackness" in the USA! Thus, when conduct by a young black American is assessed as an act of demented violence and racial hatred, is the assessment not assessment that serves to besmirch the memory of martyrs who believed, and believed, very strongly, that they were doing battle against the tyranny from brutal weaponised blackness in dehumanisation from slavery and the cruel capitalism from which they emanated! Hawaii born, Barack Hussein Obama, lived for quite some time in Chicago, where he lost a crucial political battle against Mr. Bobby Rush, a former member of the Black Panther organisation.

Many in this organisation were engaged in physical battle for their honour and humanity with agents of cruel capitalism. Mr. Obama must know about Bobby Seale, Huey Newton, George and Jonathan Jackson, James McClain, William Christmas, Bunchy Carter, Bobby Hutton, and Fred Hampton. They were Panther people whose courageous acts helped lay foundations for the emergence of Mr. Obama. Can he state, validly, that actions of those Panther people against racism and cruel capitalism, actions by people who believed, and believed very strongly, that their calling was just and honourable, were actions of demented violence and racial hatred! I will not reply in the affirmative. I will not reply in the affirmative also to: can the President state, validly, that actions of the police officers who brutalised and killed Mr. Sterling in Baton Rouge and Mr. Castile in St. Paul were not actions of demented violence and racial hatred! If I assume that he cannot, I would have to view him as someone devoid of the moral authority in the posture: he has sanctioned, and justified his sanctioning, of weaponised violence beyond American shores.

I do also have an explicitly negative reply to the query: was West Indies cricket captain, Mr. Brian Lara, able to tackle a Caribbean culture of violence and use a West

Indies tradition in his leadership? Not unlike the tradition from the United States, the West Indies tradition has been hewn from cultures of violence. Those cultures can, undoubtedly, be identified in the horror of slavery and indenture, as well as, the European Empire imperial wars waged over invaluable sugar growing territories. During the course of his three term leadership tenure, Mr. Lara spoke effortlessly and effusively about using an alternative tradition to that he had inherited.

That tradition is, of course, strongly associated with astute leadership of predecessor leaders such as Vivian Richards, Frank Worrell, Gary Sobers, Clyde Walcott, Everton Weekes, Clive Lloyd, Lance Gibbs, and Rohan Kanhai. Each of these leaders, especially Richards—publicly explicit about the horrors of slavery and apartheid, acknowledgement of Rastafarian culture, and love of Bob Marley's reggae music—clearly amended, via their innovative and productive leadership, the dominant European imperial cultures out of which the Caribbean had been hewn. Brian Lara's abysmal leadership record offers some of the strongest evidence about his great inability to have amended such cultures.

When the matter of ground strokes/ground game is looked at, there is obvious difference between President Obama and captain Lara. In earning decisive victory over his presidential challenger, Governor, Willard Romney, Mr. Obama—not unlike his success four years earlier—depended upon what his Democratic Party organisers termed a "superior ground game." When I hear that term, I think about what experienced telecasters for Wimbledon tennis contests used to say in regard to player success at the All England Club Matches. They attributed many victories to excellence of "ground strokes." What interests me very much about strokes in the Obama ground game is that team Obama possessed and used its craft to persuade numerous constituents and did so in stunningly successful ways: at the time of the first Obama victory, the American voting public had just crossed the threshold of ethnic and cultural transition. Team Obama understood the crucial significance of that development. Team McCain did not. Four years after the crossing, Team Obama—hugely confident that the crossing meant no turning back—clasped its propulsion and left Team Romney and television network pandits non-plussed about a loss, the magnitude of which, in popular and Electoral College votes, was not predicted. Florida, Pennsylvania, Virginia, Wisconsin, Ohio, all states about which Team Obama had spoken confidently in regard to its ground game, but which the pandits claimed were either "too close to call" or crucial "battleground states," did not go to Team Romney.

Just as significantly, those very states which many in the media polling panditry had predicted Mrs. Hilary Clinton should win in the 2016 presidential election did not give her victory. Reference to the matter of Mrs. Clinton's loss enables me to make another significant comparison between Mr. Obama and Mr. Lara. During the course of the 2016 campaign, Mr. Obama and his wife campaigned assiduously across America on behalf of Mrs. Clinton, I would add, partly—but in no small measure—because the President and his wife wanted to bequeath that legacy to Mrs. Clinton. I suppose from his standpoint he had ample justification for so doing: he was, quite unlike his immediate predecessor, President G.W. Bush, not at all unpopular, and although burdened in 2008 with horrific economic performance—including high unemployment and interpersonal misery among the lower middle and working class socio-economic strata—he had brought unemployment to the 4% level. Nevertheless, most voters in the states to which I alluded denied him the grand opportunity to bequeath his legacy.

Unlike President, Obama, however, Lara with one of the worst—if not, the worst—leadership records, never made any effort to bequeath his legacy to any probable successors. I presume he opted not to do so in full knowledge that he had left his post without any success comparable to that of the President's. There was, thus, no legacy for him to bequeath. In a manner partially similar to the manner of captain Lara's imminent departure, the departure of President, G.W. Bush, who had to have known about his huge unpopularity, was not associated with any effort on his part to bequeath a legacy to his probable successor, Mr. Willard Romney. Here, following Brown and Levinson (1978) and, of course, Goffman (1959), I state boldly, as well, that in 2008 President Obama had to have been acutely aware that in America his public self-image, the face he had invested in his fellow Americans with much more than emotion, was always going to be under threat, could be damaged, and lost, and he could experience embarrassment, as well as, humiliation. Towards the end of his tenure, however, Mr. Obama would have been well justified in reasoning that he evaded any significant threats to face, endured no significant damage, was not embarrassed or humiliated, as a consequence of his actions, and did not lose face among his fellow Americans. None of this could be stated about his immediate predecessor, President, G.W. Bush, who like captain Lara, had lost face massively among his fellow West Indians.

One other reason Lara could have chosen not to bequeath a legacy to his probable successor can be found in the area, ground game. With enormous emphasis I assert that captain, Brian Lara, can in no way be associated with a ground game that brought success to his teams. Quite like the arena of the political game across the United States of America, the huge world expanse of the game, Test Match cricket, was past the state of transition when Lara began to lead West Indies. His decisive task was to inspire and energise his players via strategic moves aimed at apprehending the impact of change. Insofar as the Caribbean region is concerned, apprehending the change, though a cricketing matter, was, and always has been, rather significantly a matter of profound sociological and political consciousness on leader Lara's part also. Unlike Frank Worrell, Gary Sobers, and especially Viv Richards, as well as Clive Lloyd before him, Brian Lara lacked such consciousness.

The point about transition, its link to ground game, success and absence of a connection can be stressed further in regard to captain Lara. I choose to do so by focusing upon that huge expanse in international cricket. Frank Worrell was THE TRANSITION in WORLD TEST MATCH cricket. His tour in the post of West Indies captain to Australia (1960-1961) changed Test Match cricket forever. Overflowing with elegance, grace, dignity, and style, Worrell elevated the game to great heights, giving the term, 'gentleman's game', new meaning. To this very day, Gary Sobers, the man who succeeded Worrell, speaks about the manner in which very high level sporting competition can be pursued without selfishness, disrespect, and with civility. Such talk from Sobers is an unmistakably loud echo of the Worrell impact. On that tour Worrell did not just breathe new life into cricket. In becoming the very first West Indian of colour to lead a Test Match team for an entire series, he showed the European overlords/administrators of Caribbean cricket at the time that he was correct in attributing West Indies losses to Australia during the 1953 tour Down Under to what John Arlott describes as splits and dissent within the West Indies team.

The Worrell impact on West Indies Test Match cricket continued to be experienced—perhaps, most fittingly—in 1963, 1965, and 1966, when the team led by him, then Gary Sobers, beat England, won a series for the very first time against Australia, and defeated England decisively yet again, although the England selectors used three captains for a five Test Match series. It should be noted that even though Sobers had acceded to the leadership post and was the victorious skipper in 1965 and 1966, his elevation emanated chiefly from a Worrell recommendation to the West Indies Cricket Board. Conrad Hunte was vice-captain to Worrell who, upon departure from the Test Match arena, did not opt for Hunte.

The Lara-Obama juxtaposition deserves additional exploration from cricketing and non-cricketing stances. Let me, therefore, restate that one of my prime concerns here is with leadership, the lack, thereof, and elusiveness. Just as importantly, I note the obvious. That is the appearance of the President and captain Lara—cricket bat in hands—in Port-of-Spain, which Mr. Obama visited to deal with complex hemispheric affairs, affairs to which American foreign policy, leadership of Latin America and the Caribbean, as well as, economic progress are highly pertinent.

During the course of the President's first and second terms, US foreign policy has not been bereft of vicissitudes that served as more than irritants to the executive branch. On the economic front—especially domestically—even during Mr. Obama's second term—American economic growth, though steady and encouraging to the White House, was not very robust. Like Mr. Obama's, captain Lara's foreign policy, if such a term is applicable, cannot be linked to great success against opponents abroad whose teams trounced his in catastrophically humiliating fashion. Correspondingly, such losses were not linked only to diminution in West Indies status internationally, they meant also financial woe for cricket in the Caribbean. Defeats went hand in hand with significant waning of regional support for Caribbean teams.

ENDNOTES

1 *In early autumn, 2015, Speaker Boehner stepped down from his post.*

2 *When Baroness Thatcher passed away, Mr. Tony Benn, veteran left leaning Labour Party Member of Parliament, Cabinet Minister and orator, wrote a piece in which he made reference to having seen the Baroness at a funeral for Mr. Heffer. Mr. Benn notes that when he heard someone coughing behind him, he turned around and saw her. He states that he asked her why she had come, whereupon she burst into tears. He adds that he assumes she made an appearance out of respect.*

3 *That Police Chief who had refused to resign in the face of strident calls from African-American civil society groups eventually left office in the wake of a very damning US Justice Department Report about systemic racism in his department.*

4 *Shortly after the Obama address to his fellow Americans in early September, 2014, about enhancement, Russia made it clear that any US Military presence in Syria via air strikes would violate territorial sovereignty. According to my reading of the UN charter, Russia is correct. Did the President have any inkling that an American presence in Syrian air space fuelled the sentiments and preferences of gun-toting loyalists within the USA and satisfied the inclinations of heirs and heiresses to the glory of European imperialism?*

5th INNINGS
STRENGTHENING
THE LARA-OBAMA
SIMILARITIES

I continue the Lara-Obama exploration by boldly assessing the strikingly obvious pictorial link between them at the Port-of-Spain Hilton as signifying a less than elegant, glorious or, perhaps, graceful pointer to oppression in which both men located themselves while thrusting their imagery on what was more than a figurative sticky wicket. Dare I state that hotel lobbies, especially those owned by well-known barons of contemporary capitalism, should hardly be locations where Brian Lara and Barack Obama, descendants of subordinated ancestors, show the world the charm of liberation and steadfastness to resolve in a West Indies cover drive or forward defensive stroke?

Given the existence of the Queen's Park Oval, a famous West Indies Test Match venue where many a cover drive and forward defensive stroke has been executed, might it not have been suitable for Mr. Lara and President Obama—both clad as cricketers—in the presence of a Lara mentor, Sir Gary Sobers, to grace the global arena with their strokes? Was it not Sir Gary visiting Toronto in autumn 1994 to be honoured at an important ceremony? Did he not find time to appear on one of the morning shows of a well a known telecasting network, CITY TV? In part of his appearance meant to spread the gospel of cricket, did someone not send down a few deliveries to him which he played on the front foot—not clad in a jacket and necktie within a studio—but on a real open space?

Canadians sipping their coffee may, thus, have savoured, also, one fleeting sequence of the man's majesty which made him the world's greatest cricketer. Here, I remind observers, especially Caribbean observers, that C.L.R. James, who sees Sobers as a living embodiment of centuries of a tortured history, describes one of the batsman's most elegant drives off the front foot as the "not-a-man-move" shot, many of which the Caribbean intellectual would have seen at the very Queen's Park Oval.

In addition, when Mr. Obama visited Trinidad and Tobago, he was on an international team, many of whose players were acutely aware about the continuing gnawing unjustified absence of one important player, Cuba, from the Summit of the Americas. From geographical, cultural, and economic standpoints, it is well known that Cuba is not merely Caribbean, it is, also, importantly, Latin American. Somewhat similarly to Mr. Lara when he assumed the West Indies Test Match captaincy, President Obama was regarded as a new and dynamic hemispheric team captain. In 2009, team captain, Obama, had not, however, made any moves to include Cuba in the Organisation of American States (OAS). Yet he stood on Caribbean soil, Trinidad, a place not too distant from Cuba, which, like his own country and neighbour, were once invaded and oppressed by imperialists from Spain.

I cannot miss the fact that he stood as Commander-in-Chief of a society which Dr. Fidel Castro and many of his compatriots have said maintained a spitefully punitive trade embargo and continued an illegal occupation in Guantanamo.[1] It is precisely that illegal occupation, as well as "the bandits" behind the Bahia de Cochinos invasion, to which a very emotional Cuban President, Raul Castro, referred at the plenary session (11th April 2015) Panama Summit of the Americas six years later. Although Mr. Obama rightly noted that he was not even born when the cold war in which Cuba was enmeshed started, one of those "bandits" has to be President John F. Kennedy, whom Mr. Obama reveres. Here are my questions for President Obama. Could you be respected simultaneously as a liberator and occupier in 2009 when the people on whose soil you stood were displeased about your imposed presence? Could you be respected simultaneously as a liberator and occupier when your society has been instrumental in obstructing an association between the societies (Anglo-Caribbean and Latin American) of those who view you as a liberator and a society whose occupation you were yet to end?

Years later, early April, 2015, the second query carried just as much force as that at the time of the Trinidad Summit, although Mr. Obama—according to leading Western media outlets—had an historic meeting with Dr. Fidel Castro's successor, President Raul Castro, at the Summit of the Americas in Panama, and the US President removed Cuba from a list of societies associated with terrorism. It is well known that removal resulted from a series of undisclosed meetings between high ranking Cuban and American officials over a two year period. Significantly, when Mr. Obama issued a public announcement about the US and Cuba normalising relations, he did not do so as a result of having followed a principled pathway, but as a consequence of hard-nosed strategic foreign policy practicality[2] stemming from his view that the lengthy US economic embargo against Cuba has been a failure.

Further, while nearing the completion of a two term presidential tenure (2015), Mr. Obama was certainly in no reasonable position to claim that the economic core in United States foreign policy towards Panama and the rest of Latin America brought economic well-being to the "Wretched Of The Earth" labouring ceaselessly to eke out an everyday existence: the poignant C. Wright Mills' cry "LISTEN YANKEE" to fellow Americans well ensconced in their capitalist quarters, the sociologist's ground breaking publication shortly after the successful Cuban revolution against the very imperialism, still echoed in 2015 in Panama and beyond, places still exploited by US oligopolistic transnationals. These are the very oligopolistic behemoths that featured rather prominently in Mr. Obama's last remarks before leaving Panama for Washington: the core of his initiatives aimed at helping Latin America and the Caribbean elevate themselves economically rested on the foundations of free market capitalism, an abject failure within Latin America and the Caribbean.

So, while a well-dressed Barack Hussein Obama was greeting Jamaican Prime Minister, Simpson-Miller, on his way to the 2015 Summit, it is very unlikely that he would have known: at the same time as he was observing the loch gate movement on that contemporary marvel, the widened Panama Canal, countless thousands of Colon residents had no idea of where their next meals were coming from and could not look forward to any meaningful financial benefits from Canal revenues. This dreadful type of experience is not alien to the existence of many a Caribbean cousin of the Colon citizens whose forebears worked and suffered to construct the Canal. While exchanging greetings with the Jamaican Prime Minister, it is quite likely that Mr. Obama knew about the Jamaica-Panama connection via Canal construction. It is very unlikely he would have known that the highly revered George Alphonso Headley, the Caribbean cricketer with the highest Test Match batting average (60.83) was born in Panama, where his father helped to build the famous waterway. What he does need to know is that today in Colon and other regions in Panama there are numerous descendants of builders from the Anglo-Caribbean. They are also among the very "Wretched Of The Earth" who continue to live without economic hope and continue being doomed by "Yankee Imperialism" of which he is no staunch critic.

There are also several "Wretched Of The Earth" located in the Anglo-Caribbean. They could not look forward to any regional economic liberation from captain Lara's leadership, but had very great expectations in regard to a cricketing liberation. Without necessarily acting on their behalf, I could pose an appropriate query to Lara. Have you been respected simultaneously as a liberator at, and occupier of, batting creases and other cricketing posts when people on whose soil you sat and were nurtured lived with the continuing humiliation of the Test Match teams you led? Here is a poem which I think is applicable to the captain, as well as the President.

Mr. President

Mr. President: we, united speakers from our stuttering states, ask what heaving hours lie on placid pales of our facial fury? We know not what drumming debtors defy our panes in Lucy's lofts. What soulless severance parades amidst the curling circles of our wretched waves. We ask what lustful labours betray the porous plumes caressing our charming cadence? How do your stately centuries who scale the chimes of dreamy daze on our hilly hovels scold your servile sages and read their raider rites? Mr. President: we, united speakers from our stuttering states, ask which screaming sergeants on their tethered treasure await the Trojan torments rank with rumour from Afar? We know not when the contour charters on our colour claimants forsake their rental rides to praise our tangled towns. How can the darkest drift from leafy labour on summer shadows bless our snowy smiles on blameless bays? How can the sharpest seals on creaking crevices below the crumbling changes recede in seismic solace to charm our bookish bards? How do we evade those restless reefs below the harbour hail from battle bruises in every stable sailing past our jarring gales?

Mr. President: we, united speakers from our stuttering states, ask how we hoist our racing rivers above the rancid ruins and tumble not our trusted masses amidst the tyrants' treasures? When do we price our victors' virtues in freedom's tallest tails and trumpet our finest floes in praise of fortune's favours? How do we champion our tranquil tufts above all sovereign sects of flightless fate? Where do we ascend the clusters of our bloated burdens along those shimmering soles of slender seasons? How do we begin to savour that soothing splendour of life's timeless aging by sounding spirits of our shrouded survival? Mr. President: we, united speakers from our stuttering states ask: how do you read the breathless beads of damning dungeons selling their debtor daze on snoring stables? When do you hear the crowded coasts of pouting pleasures raid their taunting tides on lifeless lore? How do you dare the swollen spirits of sightless swarms to confuse their heaving hosts on truthful tales? Where do you rest the fictive fares of moneyed mischief claiming their gloated gaze on childless contracts? When do you hear the gulping ghosts of poison pills steer their cluster clues on panting panes? Mr. President: we, united speakers from our stuttering states ask: how do you read the listless love caressing all pistol pools? When do you hear the butted barons aping every anxious arsenal? How do you dare the remnant rituals clutching every shimmering sole? Where do you rest the blemished bridges scolding every famished future? How do you hear the hunted hordes renting every pavement passion?

President Obama and Mr. Lara share certain commonalities. There was enormous hope surrounding the victory of Democratic Party candidate Barack Hussein Obama at the 2008 election. On the evening of his historic victory, Senator Obama boldly proclaimed to crowds a plenty in Grant Park, Chicago and around the world: "CHANGE HAS COME TO AMERICA." When promising Trinidadian star batsman, Brian Charles Lara acceded to the West Indies Test Match captaincy, vocal Caribbean crowds a plenty around the globe saturated themselves and the West Indies team with great expectation for a resurgence of their region. American voters and avid supporters of West Indies cricket filled themselves with buckets of hope for the leadership of Messrs. Obama and Lara, at the times of their leadership accession.

Both men seemed, however, to be woefully stuck on sticky wickets. With barely a year of his term of office completed, President Obama's huge popularity that apparently helped sweep him to the top post in grand dramaturgical style dipped substantially. It is, thus, with an interest in cricket, as well as, politics, that I do not miss the deeper significance of part of an article written by the editor of the *Pittsburgh Post Gazette*, Shribman, in the wake of the British Petroleum disaster (Spring, 2010). Among other things, the editor claimed that the once fluvial, fluent, unruffled, and unflappable, Barack Obama was on "the defensive."

Let me add that this cricketing term in no way signalled that Mr. Obama was in a position of comfort: in cricketing terms, the President was on his back foot, an uncomfortable posture of retreat. To several, Mr. Obama was firmly on the defensive and the back foot in regard to the matter of gay marriage, just over a year before elections in 2012. While she may hold no brief for America's gay community, well known media analyst, Maureen Dowd (Op-Ed Piece for *The New York Times*, 26th June, 2011) characterised the President's position on such marriage, Afghanistan, Libya, the budget, and politics as littered with ambivalence. She assesses him unflatteringly as the young, hip, black President that was swept in on a gust of change, audacity, and hope, but, also, someone lagging behind a couple of old white conservatives, Dick Cheney and Ted Olson.

On Afghanistan, for instance, she asserts that he wants to leave, but wants to remain. On the budget, he wants to cut spending, but increase it. On politics, he likes to be friends with the other side, "but bash 'em at the same time." Dowd adds that Obama, who beat the Clintons in 2008 because America needed a break from Clintonian euphemism and casuistry, is clearly not separable from the two features. She adds that his reluctance to be on the side of gay marriage appears hugely and willfully incongruent with what is known about his progressive worldview.

It is odd, she continues, that he, the first black President, is allowing New York Governor Andrew Cuomo, who piloted a gay marriage bill into law, to be remembered as a leader on the front lines of the civil rights issue of current times. In what I deem a stinging rebuke she states: "As a community organiser, Obama developed impressive empathetic gifts. But now he is misusing them. It's not enough to understand how everybody in the room thinks. You have to decide which ones in the room are right and stand with them. A leader is not a mediator or an umpire or a convener or a facilitator." Apparently, Obama still had to learn the profound significance of what *TIME Magazine* described as Richard Nixon's words to Bill Clinton when the latter began his first four year term in 1992. Those words were: "America must lead." I wonder how much he could have learnt from the comment of the Afghanistan cricket coach who said in September 2012, when his team was participating in the T-Twenty competition (Sri Lanka 2012): cricket is the only thing to give Afghanistan hope.

On 9th May, 2012, he did state publicly that he was in support of gay marriage. In the eyes of many a media analyst, he had no choice: his garrulous Vice-President, Joe Biden—only a few days earlier, 7th May, 2012—made an explicit declaration that gay and lesbian couples should enjoy the same civil rights as heterosexual couples. For his part, Obama sought to justify his early May stance by claiming that he, a Christian whose thoughts on same sex marriage had been evolving, was struggling with the matter. He also claimed that he felt his earlier support given to the idea of civil union had been an adequate way of addressing himself to the matter. I doubt if Barack Obama led decisively from 2008-2012, when, in my view, he lost his way, a position similar to that of Brian Lara's which I shall explore, much later.

Let me add that gusts of change, audacity, hope, progress, on the one hand, ambivalence and massive lag, on the other, are huge unfulfilled expectations and major indiscretions strongly connected to Brian Lara's three leadership tenures. Further, Brian Lara was once adored as the hip, fluvial, fluent, unruffled, and unflappable cricketer. All the opposites, however, surrounded him in his post as West Indies captain, where he stood "Engulfed"—not unlike the oil-splattered Barack Obama—in a front cover image created by *Bloomberg Business Week Magazine* (June 2010). Mr. Lara, who held the top cricketing post of captaincy between 1998 and 2007, became a close companion of unimaginable leadership failure.

Well before Brian Lara had become West Indies captain, his candidature was aggressively promoted by none other than the inimitable West Indies batting luminary, Isaac Vivian Alexander Richards. In retirement from the game, Richards was given an important on-field supervisory role over captain Lara and teammates. The manner of the official Richards departure from high level West Indies cricket has, however, left me wondering about the close association between him and Brian Lara. No such wondering is connected to my understanding of a severing of ties between Mr. Obama and his long time spiritual advisor, mentor, and friend, Reverend Wright. Many will recall that an important basis to the separation was a forthright public condemnation from the Reverend about the white American capitalist power structure of which the Reverend boldly asserted his protégé was fully aware.

In quite remarkably similar fashion, Barack Obama and Brian Lara have hurled public criticism at the roles played by significant members of their teams only to regret the courses of action they had taken. Such has been the case in regard to the Lara criticism and public apology directed to Mr. Andy Roberts, a former leading West Indies cricketer, over supervision by the latter of pitch preparation in the Caribbean. I hope many Americans have not forgotten the prematurely harsh and unreasonable commentary about stupid police conduct delivered by their President during the course of a summer 2009 press conference when he was asked about the incident surrounding treatment from the lawmen given to renowned African-American scholar, Henry Louis Gates, whom Obama stated publicly is a friend of his. While there was no explicit apology from the President, he did seek to salve a self-inflicted wound by inviting the police and Dr. Gates to sip beer with him on the White House grounds.

Stinging criticism a plenty pointed at the American intelligence services emanated from Mr. Obama, in response to clear breaches of United States security by hostile enemies at Christmas, 2009, when a United States airliner could have been blown up over Detroit, Michigan. Dare I state that Commander-in-Chief, Barack Hussein Obama, is—and should be seen—at all times the leader of his teams. His stinging criticism about "systemic failure" was, however, devoid of any reference to him, team captain, on whose watch the breach took place. He was the main man on the bridge at the time.

Reference to systemic failure is, at best, just a veiled and inelegant attachment of culpability to persons playing roles of boatswains, first mates, and deckhands. At worst, the sense of separation in the President's distancing smacks of preference for self-imposed alienation. His public conduct over the security breach serves to create the impression that when things turn out right for his team he includes himself in its collective success or triumph. When they turn out badly, he seeks the routes of negativity and separation.

In making my case against Mr. Obama I am fully aware major television networks claimed that he accepted responsibility for the debacle. Their pronouncement came only when the President made such statements as "ultimately, the buck stops with me." These were his words on 7th January, 2010, close to a two week period after the Detroit incident. For me not only did the statement come too late, it was a tardy reaction to what BBC World Service Television consultant, Mr. Ted Koppel, deemed an absolute triumph for Al-Qaeda terrorists. How much the idea, systemic failure, is clouded or overshadowed by the dramatic, daring, and heroic moments surrounding the end of "Geronimo," Osama bin Laden (Pakistan, May, 2011) remains to be seen.

Victory does, of course, come with rewards. While holding his very first press conference soon after electoral success in early November 2012, President Obama—obviously emboldened—wasted no time in placing himself right at the forefront in regard to the tragic events in Benghazi, Libya, where four Americans—including an ambassador—was killed. Clearly realising that Senator, John McCain and his legislative colleague, Senator Graham, were attempting what could be described as a pre-emptive move against the erudite Susan Rice, US ambassador to the UN, over remarks she had made about the Libya attack as spontaneous rather than a terrorist act, the President was quite explicit in his assessment about the Senators. He pointed out, most emphatically, that for them to be attacking the UN Ambassador is outrageous. Rice was expected to—but did not—replace Hilary Clinton as United States Secretary of State: the UN ambassador, who became Mr. Obama's National Security Chief, made it clear that she did not wish to be considered for the top post at the State Department because of probable great controversy to which her nomination might have led.

Test Match cricket team captain, Brian Lara, did resort to a strategy of sparing himself criticism, when hostile opponents from Australia, South Africa, and England did not just breach West Indies batting security with explosive bursts of quick bowling and clever spin. They also followed intrusion by humiliating their Caribbean opponent that had once revelled in unprecedented lengthy dominance on the international cricket scene. Unlike President Obama, captain Lara could not, and did not, use a popular constituency to strengthen his leadership position.

Mr. Obama and Mr. Lara have adorned their onstage presence with their soulful dramaturgy. One is well known for his soaring rhetoric. When he is not addressing crowds, the President is an arduous worker for consensus. He champions, and is enmeshed in, collaborative conversation, rather than divisive discourse. This much I have gathered from his talk over the economic meltdown plaguing his society and lengthy engagement that preceded the decision to send 30,000 troops to Afghanistan. Given my interest in the interactive strategies of talk, I would say that while constructing his conversations he is extremely artful in his verbal delivery of the two speech forms I delimit: (a) forms of speech in which use of linguistic constraints is intended to grant hearers the freedom to construct their own meaning (b) forms of speech in which use of linguistic constraints is not intended to grant hearers the freedom to construct their own meaning. Versions of the first are presented often as Churchill's general questions, while versions of the second are presented as the intensive forms of his specific proposal questions.

If you are interested in delving further, you may want to consider: (a) how the President manages strategic delivery of these speech forms while he converses with others, (b) how the President's use of one or the other form exemplifies a skilful presentation of authority that is not obviously overbearing. I can offer a demonstration of just such a presentation by looking at a brief segment of Mr. Obama's interaction, when he made a surprise telephone call to a radio show. A few days before Christmas 2009, a caller, "Barry," was introduced to the guest of a monthly Washington D. C. radio programme.

The guest was Virginia Governor, Tim Kaine, a close colleague of Mr. Obama's and running mate to Hilary Clinton in the 2016 presidential contest. Barry was none other than the American President, who began his conversation with the Governor by stating, "Governor Kaine, this is actually the President of the United States calling." After the surprised Governor had reacted by uttering, "No. Oh, my gosh," the President proceeded to state: (a) "I want to complain about traffic in Northern Virginia" (b) "Rather than go there, I just wanted to say how proud we are of your service."

The President's initiation of his conversation with the Governor and his statement of pride can be assessed as a greeting and a congratulation, respectively. Both of these utterances are used by persons to create a two part structure of talk in which the purpose of the first speaker is obliging his/her hearer to talk. Examples of obligation are evident in questions and forms of greeting. The talk expected and preferred from a hearer is a return greeting and reply. I thus see the President's greeting and congratulation as forms of speech whose use of linguistic constraints is not intended to give his hearer, the Governor, freedom to construct his own meaning.

What is equally significant about the greeting is it is stamped conversationally with the highest authority in the land. In addition the authority is laced and sealed with the force of a demonstrative "this is actually..." Further, although the purpose of the President's congratulation is that which sets the stage for discourse obligation on the Governor's part, his exaggerated expression of pride offered with an inclusive "we" serves to reduce the width and soften the impact of his hearer's obligation.

The President's expression of an intention to complain is conversationally masterful. Use of this type of presentation is clearly aimed at securing, not merely the right to speak, but also, the opportunity to place oneself in the position of being able to use a question and thus the chance to set the stage for obligatory speech. Interestingly, the President kept his speaking posture, did not utilise any chance to specify his complaint, and opted not to pause, for the purpose of enabling the Governor to ask about his complaint. The exchange between Governor and President was, doubtless, brief and apparently of no substantive significance.

Having done a close exploration of it, I am able to get a glimpse of how the President combines conversational skill with his authority to gain and hold the attention of those with whom he interacts. Another occasion on which President Obama demonstrated his conversational acumen with great mastery was during the time he appeared on the CBS programme *Sixty Minutes* a week after his country's success against Osama bin Laden. He did a very excellent job of negotiating questions from television correspondent Steve Kroft. In a lengthy interview close to forty-five minutes, Kroft peppered his interlocutor with what I counted to be no fewer than thirty five utterances of the type: forms of speech whose use of constraints is not intended to give a hearer the freedom to construct his own meaning (intensive forms of specific proposal questions). These are the very types of speech forms that emanated from correspondent Major Garrett at the time of the President's press conference on Saturday, 11th April, 2015, when the Summit of the Americas in Panama ended. When the President used his turn to speak, he began by stating: "That is a well-crafted question."

In expressing my understanding of the Garrett and Kroft strategies differently, I can draw on the work of critical discourse analysts such as Thornborrow (2002: pp. 4-8) who emphasise the application of "power" in face-to-face conversation. In her view, questioners, Garrett and Kroft, use their discursive identities (they are the TV interrogators/managers of talk) and resources, talk, strategically for the purpose of strengthening those identities and weakening the President's identity. Kroft's and Garrett's main goal is to restrict the discursive paths or spaces available to the President.

Those who prefer not to focus on discourse—critical or otherwise—but maintain a keen eye on image and imagery can situate interviewer Kroft and the President within this assessment:

> For politicians, indeed, publicity has become essential. This means subjecting themselves to a series of newspaper and television interviews by men who have become professional questioners. The new technique assumes that a man is accountable not only to the public, but publicly for the trust he bears, and must not only answer for his political conduct but reply to more personal questions; that he must answer not only face to face but in the face of television cameras trained to detect shades of meaning or embarrassment which words can hide. Such ordeal by interview calls for qualities not necessarily associated with statesmanship or integrity. The showman's art is equally important. Yet so anxious is every public figure to promote a favourable 'public image' of himself that he dare not refuse to be interviewed—and lucky the man whose temperament and training enables him lightly to turn the embarrassing and impertinent question (Gregg 1965, pp. 574-575).

There is absolutely no doubt in my mind that President Obama handles the new technique masterfully in the presence of the professional questioner. His immense skill in doing so goes well beyond statesmanship and integrity. I cannot say whether any luck is associated with that skill.

For those wanting to experience a far more powerful instance of the President's artfulness, I say consider his speech to the American public, shortly after he had given the sack to General Stanley David McChrystal, Commander of Special Forces in Afghanistan for what one reliable media organisation in the US, Public Broadcasting System, (PBS), described as egregious conduct in derisive talk about Mr. Obama and his top aides. In that speech, from the Oval Office of the White House on 23rd June, 2010, Mr. Obama chided the General.

Most interesting to me about the entire speech is that Mr. Obama also wasted no time in using that rhetorical device of contrast well known to some conversation analytic sociologists who explore the technique as evocative, not merely of attention from a large audience, but also a tactic which often results in rapturous applause from that audience. The Oval Office delivery was, of course, not part of campaign rhetoric intended to draw rapturous cheering. It did elicit a great deal of attention from media experts who kept emphasising it as one of the most significant segments of admonition from the President.

I offer the segment in full:

I don't make this decision [the sacking] based on any difference in policy with General McChrystal, as we are in FULL agreement about our strategy. Nor do I make this decision out of any personal insult. <u>Stan McChrystal has always shown great COURTesy and carried out my orders faithfully. I've got great admiration for him and for his long record of service in uniform over the last nine years—America fighting wars in IRAQ and Afghanistan. He has earned a reputation as one of our nation's FInest soldiers. That reputation is founded upon his extraordinary dedication, his deep intelligence, and his love of country. I've relied on his service particularly in helping to design and lead our new strategy in Afghanistan</u> [underlining mine]. So, ALL Americans should be grateful for General McChrystal's remarkable career in uniform. But war is bigger than any ONE man or woman—whether a private, a General or President. As difficult as it is to LOSE General McChrystal, I believe that it is the right decision for our nation, for our national security. The conduct represented in the recently published article does not meet the standard that should be set by a commanding General. It undermines the civilian control of the military that is at the core of our Democratic system. And it erodes the trust that is necessary for our TEAM to work together to achieve our objectives in Afghanistan.

The President did not simply employ contrast, he also—extremely importantly—combined his contrast with what conversation analysts call lists, which I underline. While preparing the very expectant audience for the powerful force of contrast, he summarises the rhetorical value of his list by offering what appears to me to be an interim conversational closing in which he exhorts Americans to express gratitude to the General: "So, ALL Americans should be grateful for General McChrystal's remarkable career in uniform."

That inference is followed immediately by the authoritative force from the Commander-in-Chief who flows assertively with the verifiable or unverifiable claim about war being bigger than any ONE man or woman. The claim is then followed by a belief—not a fact—about rightness of his action for which he offers dual justification. How could I miss the President's deliberate use of what descriptive linguists regard as extra loud stress to do his speaking work: "TEAM," "CORE," "LOSE," "ALL"! In each case, the stress is designed to grab listeners' attention.

I cannot resist the temptation to refer to part of President Obama's speech to his fellow Americans late on the evening (Sunday, 1st May, 2011) when he announced that Osama bin Laden was killed. Not unlike the manner in which Brian Lara has played some of his great Test Match innings, Mr. Obama wasted no time in ascending his customary oratorical heights. Shortly after he had issued his routine greeting, he launched into setting up his lists and contrasts:

It was nearly ten years ago that a bright September was darkened by the worst attack on the American people in our history. The images of 9/11 are seared into our national memory: hijacked planes cutting through a cloudless September sky, the Twin Towers collapsing to the ground, black smoke billowing up from the Pentagon, the wreckage of flight 93 in Shanksville, Pennsylvania, where the actions of heroic citizens saved even more heartbreak and destruction.And yet we know that the worst images are those that were unseen to the world: the empty seat at the dinner table, children who were forced to grow up without their mother or their father, parents who would never know the feeling of their child's embrace, nearly 3,000 citizens taken from us, leaving a gaping hole in our hearts *[underlining mine].*

There was much more to come from the President on 6th September 2012, the night when he delivered his acceptance speech for nomination by his party in Charlotte, North Carolina. To me he was extraordinarily brilliant and superbly magnificent in his presentation of self that evening. Unlike virtually all members of the established British and American televisual media, I did not see him as "defiant." I saw Barack Obama, the eminent barrister, the lead defence attorney-at-large, take on the Romney-Ryan-Perry-Rubio-Christie-Santorum-Gingrich prosecution team. What a job from Obama! Let me state what I deem the obvious.

On that night, I was watching the BBC World Service television coverage. At about the halfway point in the President's delivery, programme host, Mr. Mike Embley, interrupted for station identification which he did: "Very briefly, if you've just joined us, you're with BBC News—LIVE, of course—at the Democratic Convention, in Charlotte, North Carolina. Barack Obama in FULL flight making his pitch for a SE cond term in the White House—a second go at the most powerful job in the world. We're staying with this. DO stay WITH us." My focus in this writing is on what he stated after identification: "Barack Obama in FULL flight making his pitch..." Let me emphasise that from anyone else I see no cricket. From British citizen, Mike Embley, seated not far from those hallowed cricketing headquarters, Lord's, I see pure cricket in "FULL flight," "pitch," "a second go" with a ring not dissimilar to the term, 'second spell.' He invoked the presence of Statham, Trueman, "typhoon" Tyson, Lee, Lillee, Lindwall, Gibbs, Griffith, of course, "Big Bird," Joel Garner, Hall, and Holding—yes, "Whispering Death"—in full flight at the St. John's Wood location. In the Embley remarks I could hear, against a background of spectator roar, echoes in the cadences from commentators, E.W. "Jim" Swanton, John Arlott, Christopher Martin Jenkins, Neil Durden Smith, Trevor Bailey, Brian Johnston, Alan McGilvray, and Henry Blofeld. Like Embley, I shall return to the cricket later. At this point, I want to concentrate on the work of preacher and barrister, Barack, whose assertives (verifiable or unverifiable speech), expressives (carriers of emotion), declaratives (indicative of authority), directives (giving orders), and justification, matters of major interest to speech act theorists, as well as, his lists, contrasts, extra loud stress, also of interest to conversation analytic sociologists, drew rapturous applause.

A major segment in the core of the President's delivery was reminiscent of that forceful summation rendered by attorney Mr. Johnny Cochran in the O.J. Simpson murder trial. I do not recall how many times the President used the term, 'you,' in appealing to voters, so that they might reject the message of the Romney-Ryan ticket propelled in hefty charges against Mr. Obama's economic record. Consider: (a) [DIRECTIVE, INDICATIVE OF COMMANDS, ORDERS, REQUESTS] "You can choose a future where we reduce our deficit without sticking it to the middle class" (b)

[ASSERTIVES, VERIFIABLE OR UNVERIFIABLE ACTIONS THAT, IN ADDITION, CONSTITUTE A CONVERSATIONAL LIST] "So you SEE, the election four years ago wasn't about ME. It was about YOU. My fellow citizens, YOU were the change [pause and applause]. YOU'RE the reason there's a little girl with a heart disorder in Phoenix who gets the surgery because an insurance company can't limit her coverage. YOU did that [pause and applause]. YOU'RE the reason a young man in Colorado who never thought he'd be able to afford his dream of earning a medical degree is about to get that chance. YOU made that possible [pause and applause]. YOU'RE the reason a young immigrant who grew up here and went to school here and pledged allegiance to our FLAG will no longer be deported from the only country she's ever called home, why selfless soldiers won't be kicked out of the military, because of who they are or who they love, why thousands of families have finally been able to say to the loved ones who served us so bravely, welcome home [pause and applause], welcome home [pause and applause]. YOU did that. YOU did that [pause and applause]. YOU did that [pause and applause]. If you turn away now, if you turn away now, if you buy into the cynicism that the change we fought for is impossible, well, change WILL NOT happen. If you give up on the idea that your voice can make a difference, then other voices will fill the void: the lobbyists and special interests, the people with the ten million dollar cheques who are trying to buy this election, and those who are trying to make it harder for you to vote, Washington politicians who want to decide who you can marry or control healthcare choices that women should be making for themselves [pause and applause]. [ASSERTIVES] Only YOU can make sure that doesn't happen [pause and applause]. Only YOU have the power to move us forward."

Not unlike events in the O.J. Simpson case, the Romney-Ryan charges had been offered as part of that mountain of evidence against Mr. Obama. What did the Cochran team do? Members of that team responded meticulously and methodically to discredit the prosecution. Remember Drs. Baden, Uelmen, and Lee, the last of whom said while speaking dubiously about blood evidence against Mr. Simpson in what must now be part of a famous line, AN ASSERTIVE, "All I can say... something wrong." Remember Drs. Neufeld and Scheck interrogating criminalist, Fong, and his assistant, Mazzola. What did these two men expose? My answer: glaring flaws in the evidence collection practices. What did barrister, Obama, expose?

Using only assertives, I repeat, matters speech act theorists consider verifiable or unverifiable, he exposed a glaring flaw in the Romney-Ryan foreign policy credentials after he had stated that both men are short on foreign policy experience, the very thing the President's opponents thought they could have used to weaken Obama. Consider this excerpt from the President on the night of 6th September:

Now we have a choice. My opponent and his running mate are [significant pause] NEW to foreign policy but from all that we've seen and HEARD they want to take us back to an era of blustering and blundering that cost America so dearly. After all, you don't call Russia our number one enemy—not Al Qaeda, Russia—unless you're still stuck in a cold war mind warp. You might not be ready for diplomacy with Beijing if you can't visit the Olympics without insulting our closest ally [Great Britain].

Mr. Obama did much more than exposure. Those who followed the Simpson trial will recall the "dream team." Barrister Obama's team for the entire period of the convention was notable in the persons of two frontline governors from

Massachusetts and Montana, a wife, a former President, and a vice-President who delivered a frontal blow to the Romney-Ryan prosecutorial team. Mr. Biden stated—not once, but on many occasions—Osama bin Laden is dead and General Motors is alive." My focus here is not just on the contrast of economics and foreign policy, it is also on the fact that the Vice President had cleverly issued an assertive, a speech form which is either true or untrue. The whole world knows the truth.

Equally significant for comparative purposes or analogy is the comment from Mr. Cochran about the bloody glove detective Mark Fuhrman claimed to have found on Mr. Simpson's property. Mr. Simpson was obliged to try on the glove, which the world knows did not fit. Remember Mr. Cochran's words to the Jury: "If it [the glove] doesn't fit, you must acquit." That was one of Mr. Cochran's directives to the jury. In quite a significant way Mr. Biden had delivered a double barrelled volley stoked with compelling countervailing evidence against the Romney prosecutorial group. Further, while the Cochran team needed to expose reasonable doubt against the Clark prosecution team, the Obama team focus was on reasonable certainty. That certainty came, among other matters, in the Biden assertive.

My reference to the Simpson case would not be complete if I did not deal with the absence of a murder weapon widely believed—if the Clark prosecution team was credible—to have been a knife. According to the Romney-Ryan prosecutorial team, the weapon in the hands of a misguided President Obama was gross mismanagement of the United States economy. Given the Biden assertive and the hugely destructive impact of the Bush years that followed what several commentators deem massive economic prosperity during the Clinton tenure, the argument that a weapon of mismanagement in the Obama hands which slew rather than rescued the US from certain doom is rather hollow to me. Immediately before and after the Democratic convention—if public opinion polling was still valid and reliable—the Romney-Ryan ticket had not been bought lock, stock, and barrel.

Perhaps, the most riveting segment from barrister Barack came when he spoke about changing times. Here was a clever insertion lacing the boot and booth of authority bathed in contrasts with lists, and offered with compassion, feeling, fervency, as well as, persuasion nestled in the bedrock of humanism with humility. Remarkably, it was a segment bubbling with assertives and justification that were tied to the exhortation from the President that voters should reject the hefty charges from the Romney-Ryan ticket.

You know I recognise that times have changed since I first spoke to this convention. Times have changed and so have I. I'm no longer just a candidate. I'm the President [pause and rapturous applause]. And [pause and rapturous applause] and that—and that means I know what it means to send young Americans into battle, for I've held in my arms mothers and fathers of those who didn't return. I've shared the pain of families who've lost their homes and the frustration of workers who've lost their jobs. If the critics are right that I've made all my decisions based on polls, then I must not be very good at reading them. And while I'm very proud of what we've achieved together, I'm far more mindful of my own failings knowing exACTly what Lincoln MEANT when he said 'I've been driven to my knees many times by the overwhelming conviction that I have no place else to go.' [pause and applause]. But as I stand here tonight, I have never been more hopeful about America not because I think I have all the answers, not because I'm naive about the magnitude of our challenges. I'm hopeful because of YOU, the young woman I met at a science fair who won national recognition because of her biology research while living with her family at a homeless shelter. She gives me HOPE [pause and applause], the auto worker who won the lottery after his plant almost closed but kept coming to work every day and bought flags for his WHOLE town and when the cars that he built [interruption from Mike Embley for station identification] even when their competitors shut down dozens of plants, even when it meant the owner gave up some perks and some pay, because they understood that their biggest asset was the community and the workers who had helped build that business. THEY give me hope [pause and applause].

Barrister Barack was preacher Barack also. Which preacher? I state, without hesitation, a preacher who revived the memory of none other than Dr. Martin Luther King, who had been to the mountain top and seen the Promised Land. In Dr. King's offering there was the obvious call to sacrifice and rebirth which came from the President at the very beginning of his presentation. Such sacrifice and rebirth, I contend, are not just strivings for the depth of Protestant Christian spirituality, a rejection of conservative Christianity, it is also a loud echo of the African roots within the black church overflowing with oratory.

All of America heard that oratory on the early morning of 7th November, 2012 when President Obama won a second term by beating rival, Willard Romney, in most convincing fashion. From his campaign headquarters in Chicago he spoke emotionally about America moving from colonial status to a progressive independent society. In what I now regard as typical of his oratorical splendour he drew from the solidity of a legacy crafted by his favourite political predecessor, President Abraham Lincoln. That was not all. He alluded to America's great diversity and reiterated a position he had enunciated eight years earlier while electrifying the Democratic party Democratic Party convention about unity in that diversity. What was also significant about the 7th November address is the fact that whether he appreciated it or not Mr. Obama—not unlike captain Brian Lara at the time of his first leadership appointment to the West Indies—was leading a team in decline. One year earlier, America's Triple A credit rating had been downgraded and the country's trillion dollar overspending, by no means, divorced from what came to be known as the fiscal cliff, stared the President and a divided legislature squarely in their faces. In November 2012, the People's Republic of China, where there was a regular ten year leadership change, was still on course to overtake the USA as the most economically prosperous society.

Nevertheless, when the President made his 17th December 2014 statement about Cuba-US relations, described by two television networks as " a political global warming of sorts" and "a stunning move," not only did he lay some very solid groundwork for his legacy to be regarded in a very favourable manner, but in my view, he had begun to place himself also not alongside, but above President Richard Nixon, who despite the Watergate smudge, will never be forgotten for his China policy. In addition, although he could not be a candidate for the 2016 election, Mr. Obama had begun setting the tone for that contest. Let me, therefore, point out that many of those who could not understand the significance of the Raul Castro-Barack Obama handshake when the two were among world leaders in South Africa for President Mandela's funeral should have been able to cast away their ignorance. Those who did not see the great value in Mr. Obama's eulogising President Mandela as the last great liberator of the twentieth century should have been able to get a clear sighting on 17th December 2014. Cuba-United States talks facilitated by Canada about normalising relations began in 2013, the first year in President Obama's second term. Messrs. Obama and Castro met—albeit very fleetingly—in South Africa after the talks had begun. On the occasion of the encounter both were fully aware of the talks. Just as significantly the Obama eulogising was delivered, not merely in the presence of President Raul Castro, but also millions of blacks right across Africa who knew about the struggles against imperialism in Angola, Mozambique, Guinea Bissau, Namibia, Zimbabwe, and South Africa.

Those persons, as well as, Chicago activist, Barack Obama, Chicago Senator, Barack Obama, and President, Barack Obama, knew very well, the decisive role Cuba played in breaking the imperialist stranglehold. The liberator all the way from the Caribbean whom Mr. Obama and his black African viewers knew was crucial to such breaking was none other than Dr. Fidel Alejandro Castro Ruz, someone who had clear precedence over liberator, Nelson Mandela.

Why is Barack Hussein Obama not in the same category of foreign policy success as Richard Nixon? My response is explicitly simple: several political aficionados who make claims about presidential greatness use America's relations with communist societies as yardsticks for issuing such claims. Ronald Reagan was deemed great for playing a huge role in defeating communism. Richard Nixon is remembered fondly for ending the American fight with "RED" China. Some say Nixon was being pragmatic. Others take the view that Reagan had history behind him. I say in making his 17th December 2014 declaration President Obama was both pragmatic and an excellent student of history.

So, why, in my view, is he not simply alongside but above Richard Nixon? I do not make this claim simply because President Obama has not been smeared. I make it because I am able to see, also, one strategic core in his foreign policy craft. I am able to do so as a result of locating that strategy within a global geographical, political, and sociolinguistic context where the 2015 Cuba-United States choreography was some of the most artfully elegant performance ever accomplished. Allow me to explain by focusing on the Obama Jamaica trip immediately prior to the 2015 Summit of the Americas. President Obama followed President Reagan after a thirty three year gap. If symbols mean a great deal in politics, then the N.R.A. supporter, President Reagan's gift of a rifle to staunch conservative ally from Jamaica, Prime Minister Edward Seaga, was not insignificant in 1982, a time when the American President had accused Grenada, Cuba, and Nicaragua under Prime Minister, Maurice Bishop, Presidents, Dr. Fidel Castro, and Mr. Daniel Ortega, of undermining democracy in Latin America and the Caribbean by threatening the regions with communism. It was only one year later, October, 1983, that Mr. Seaga and Miss Eugenia Charles, Prime Minister of Dominica, another staunch Caribbean conservative ally, stood shoulder to shoulder with President Reagan in Washington, when he announced what he called a rescue mission, that which many dubbed an American invasion of Grenada, a clear challenge to Cuba and Nicaragua.

While I know not what gift President Obama brought to the Jamaican people and their Prime Minister Portia Simpson-Miller, the whole world knows that Mr. Obama, certainly not an NRA supporter, enraptured a huge crowd of millennials on the Caribbean island when he greeted them by intoning "WA GWAN JAMAICA?"[3] Just as—or even more significantly—I note that Mr. Obama appeared in Jamaica, which is geographically close to both Cuba and the United States. There is a long history of very amicable relations between Jamaica and Cuba, and when the entire Caribbean, South and Central America are looked at, what emerges is a clear pattern in acceptance of Cuba as an equal partner, friend, and provider. It was none other than Mr. Obama himself who acknowledged publicly something no American President before him had ever done about Cuba's international efforts, that the Cuban presence in West Africa made a difference in the fight against Ebola. He pointed out, as well, that the Cuban presence in Haiti, in the aftermath of the devastating 2005 earthquake, made a difference.

Further, the Cuban presence in the Caribbean and across Latin America is significantly different to the China presence across Asia. Geographically, the China presence in Asia is restricted to a single continent, while the Cuban presence extends beyond a single continent. Socio-linguistically, and thus, culturally, the one language that brings most of the Latin American societies close to Cuba is Spanish. No such reality exists in regard to China and the rest of Asia. From an American foreign policy standpoint, all the Obama-Raul Castro conversations—including those at the 2015 Summit of the Americas—as well as their direct references to each other's societies at the Summit Plenary session, can be located quite reasonably as parts of a significant sociolinguistic, geographical, and political context. I note the political aspect, not merely because foreign policy is always linked to it, but also, because of President Obama's statement that the Cold War began before he was born and he was also looking to the future. I note, as well, President Castro's view that Mr. Obama is an honest man who does not have a socio-economically privileged background, and a direct apology from President Castro to Mr. Obama at the same time as he, President Castro, could not help expressing deep emotion in addressing himself to US injustice against Cuba. The implicature behind these statements does indicate that strong, productive, viable foundations to cooperation between Cuba and the United States exist, and that such foundations should be used to the mutual benefit of their societies.

Another way of situating President Obama well above the Richard Nixon China achievement would be to recognise the former as a very important player in an accomplishment owed to Cuban choreography that can be described by using a part of Rastafari wisdom: SMALL AXE DOES CUT DUNG BIG CHREE / SMALL AXES CUT DOWN BIG TREES. Cuba is the small axe used to gain respect from the very big tree, the United States. At the time of the Richard Nixon deal with China, both the United States and China were very big trees. Such is not just clearly the case today, but none of these two very big trees can cut down the other. In 2015 very big trees, China and the United States, are fully aware that the United States economy cannot survive in viable ways without a China presence within America domestically and the wider global setting.

Quite notably, very expectant and expected candidates for the 2016 presidential race were very ready to criticise the December 2014 Obama decision. Notable among them were former Florida Governor, Jeb Bush, and Senator Marco Rubio, the second of whose parents fled from Cuba under Dr. Castro. Were these men still living with historical fiction? Pope Francis, a leading Latin American citizen, was deeply involved in negotiations related to the December decision. Canada—along with Britain—two of the staunchest American allies, have had long- standing diplomatic and economic ties with Cuba. How could the United States continue with an unworkable embargo against a foreground of economic and diplomatic links with Cuba from Canada and Britain!

Regardless of the response/reaction observers wish to offer, one thing is obvious. With the Affordable Care and Patient Protection Acts, acceptance of gay and lesbian marriages, an executive order to regularise the status of illegal aliens, and quite encouraging signals of economic recovery, the December 2014 announcement, historic progress at the 2015 Summit of the Americas, the spring 2015 "framework" agreement with Iran, and a clear reference to enhanced interrogation techniques

(E.I.T.) as "torture," there streamed no shortage of unofficial censure along President Obama's path. Be such as it may, he set the tone, well and truly, for the 2016 contest. This is one hallmark of shrewdness in presidency, especially during a "lame duck session." It is just such tone-setting that did more than echo only just about three weeks prior to crucial midterm elections in early November 2018, when the Party led by whom I dub THAT MAAFA MUZUNGU MONSTROSITY lost massively in congress. Trump kept gloating about his victory in regard to the Kavanaugh US Supreme Court ascension, with thumping fists and authoritarian trash about angry Democratic Party mobs wanting to rule America that would be overrun by streaming caravans of illegal aliens. If the "fake news media" are to be believed, his conduct could not, however, prevent more than a few Republican congressional incumbents, worried about losing from claiming disingenuously that they embrace health care coverage inclusive of what has come to be known as pre-existing conditions. Pre-existing conditions feature prominently in the Affordable Care Act, something Trump and his raucous "base supporters" within and outside congress have always known they regarded as anathema.

What hallmarks are to be found in the Brian Lara leadership tenures? I must say that when he became West Indies captain, Brian Lara wasted no time in alluding to unity in diversity within the Caribbean, touted the value of the legacy he had inherited from previous captains, and reminded supporters that he was at the helm of a team representative of a move from colonial status to independence. What is now known explicitly about captain Brian Lara's three term leadership tenure from 1998-2007, roughly the same as President Obama's two term presidency, is that Lara failed to use the West Indies leadership legacy for the purpose of elevating the teams he led. While President Obama's second election victory is widely regarded by many American experts as a stroke of genius in securing votes from a spectrum spanning a pluralistic belt of ethnic and sexual hues, his greatest challenge in a second term was undoubtedly whether he could use the tradition he so has so passionately espoused to create a band around an economically fit and rejuvenated America. History will be the best judge of that for which he hoped.

It is the same history which will be the best judge of the manner in which he had been showering the English language with his sentential sparkles of rhetorical richness and Brian Lara had enhanced his batting elegance with stroke-making splendour of staggering stylishness. It is no exaggeration to state that artful West Indies Test Match cricketer Brian Lara, has left many an enthralled spectator indescribably stunned at the magisterial command of his batting craft.

This is performance he constructed brilliantly along routes designed from blends of attacking and cautious stroke play strongly and indelibly etched in such displays as cuts, flicks, pulls, hooks, cover and extra cover drives, as well as, defence on the front and back foot. Let me refer to one of his command performances against Australia at that most picturesque of Caribbean Test Match grounds, Sabina Park, Jamaica. My source is part of a British Broadcasting Corporation (BBC) World Service programme, "*Sports Roundup*", (Spring, 2000) in which there was a headline, "BRIAN LARA RETURNS TO FORM IN DRAMATIC STYLE IN A JAMAICA CRICKET TEST."

Immediately after the headline announcement, I listened, spellbound, while Australian radio commentator Jim Maxwell described Lara's "majestic double hundred," an answer to his critics that began when he walked to the crease on day two with the West Indies in dire trouble at thirty seven runs for the loss of four front line wickets. At the end of play on that memorable second day, he had scored an unbeaten double century and steered his side to a massive three hundred and seventy seven runs for the loss of four wickets.

Here is the Maxwell description: Lara's masterly double hundred is one of the most important of his distinguished and turbulent career. Universally criticised for a lack of discipline, Lara batted with the conviction of a man determined to re-establish his reputation. In the process, he defied, plundered, and then battered Australia's expectant bowlers ably supported by Jimmy Adams. They added an undefeated record three hundred and twenty one for the fifth wicket—Lara hammering thirty two fours and three sixes. He gave one chance at forty-four to Mark Waugh at second slip from McGrath, who was the most likely Australian bowler on a rare barren day for their attack. He was particularly severe on the leg spinners. He hit McGill for two sixes. At stumps, the West Indies having a lead of one hundred and twenty-one at four for three hundred and seventy-seven—Brian Lara inspiring the West Indies.

Later, I shall retrace similar routes taken by Lara, when I assess what he did in scoring other memorable single and double Test Match centuries, as well as a rare quadruple Test Match century and quintuple century in an English county game. Another way of placing the President and Mr. Lara side by side would be for me to think about basketball, the very game Mr. Obama loves. I regard basketball, at its highest professional level, the NBA, as a game in which the superlative abilities of players such as Steve Nash, Allan Iverson, Gao Ming, Jeremy Lin, Kobe Bryant, Larry Bird, Michael Jordan, and Lebron James emanate from a complex of conjunctures in which highly judicious choices to make specific plays are determined by sophisticated intellectual skill, time requirements, challenges from opponents, and ways in which motivation for success springs from teammates.

Beyond the arenas of sporting competition, President Obama and Mr. Lara, whose fathers had direct experience of the harsh reality of British imperialism, did not live with such horror. Both men are, nevertheless, heirs to the populist activism used to battle the oppression. They have also had to buckle under weighty loads thrust from the impact of that very oppression. Well before he had ascended to the heights of the presidency, Barack Hussein Obama was an assertive activist working on behalf of the dispossessed in the Chicago inner city area. While there are no official records of Mr. Lara having worked on behalf of the hordes of dispossessed in the Caribbean, he was, surely, aware of the efforts of activists in the West Indies who advocated for the dispossessed in the region. In addition, while both President Obama and captain Lara have spoken effusively about grand visions and traditions of their respective citizenship, neither of them has been able to translate such visions into sustained benefits for their fellow citizens. Lara has been a very unsuccessful leader, and the President, though buoyed by economic recovery which began in earnest during year two of his second term, could not have been comfortable about the financial cruelties heaped upon the American working class, especially his fellow African-Americans.

Here, I do not think it unimportant for me to note: both men have had to consider the value of leadership tradition when executing their moves. In President Obama's case, the tradition can be seen in the work of predecessors Clinton, Kennedy, Truman, and Roosevelt. In captain Lara's case, tradition lies in the work of predecessors Kanhai, Richards, Sobers, Lloyd, and Worrell. While I am certain that the President has a profound grasp of tradition and was using that grasp to enliven and energise his Democratic base, I am not sure he was able to apply his grasp for the purpose of successfully energising and enlivening the wider American citizenry. What is unquestionable about Lara is that his brilliant batting served to enliven and energise throngs of supporters in the West Indies. I am not, however, certain that captain Lara had any meaningful grasp of leadership tradition within West Indies cricket and was thus able to use that grasp for the purpose of energising and enlivening his cricket team.

Mr. Obama is, also, quintessentially American, in the sense that he does support the tenets of "free" market global capitalism—even when such support entails bailing out some of the most greedy carnivores at the heights of the predatory corporate capitalist food chain. Mr. Obama cannot be unaware that some at the top of the chain are, today, successors of those which featured prominently in imperialist exploitation of people of colour. Some of these very successors are, themselves exploiters of underdeveloped and developing societies, within Africa, Asia, and Latin America.

It is, therefore, without passing interest that I, a Caribbean person, note a characterisation by the Cuban foreign Minister of the President's conduct at the December 2009 Climate Change Summit (Copenhagen, Denmark). In a 22nd December report that same year by the *New York Times*, the foreign Minister, Mr. Bruno Rodriguez, is reported as having described Mr. Obama as: imperial and arrogant, someone who refuses to listen, imposes his positions, and one who threatens developing societies. The Minister deemed the summit a farce and a fallacy. He also saw Washington as having employed back room arguments and strong arm strategies to foist a deal on the world which urges but does not oblige major polluters to implement deep emission cuts.

Mr.Lara is, very much a western essentialist in his dispositions to, and immersion in, the battle against socio-economic derogation. Insofar as both leaders have endured the pain and suffering of intentional action at dehumanising, I find it quite intriguing that neither has demonstrated any significant ability to transform the burdens of socio-economic domination into tools of liberation. It is with a keen eye on the Obama first tenure that I note the cogency of remarks from Professor Paneil Joseph of Tufts University in the United States about the presidency.

While conversing on the Public Broadcasting (PBS) Television programme *Basic Black*, Professor Joseph observed that during the course of his campaign, Mr. Obama invoked the name of Dr. Martin Luther King as a basis for promoting the suitability of his candidature for executive office. From his presidential position, he ordered massive troop movement to Afghanistan at a time when some of the highest unemployment rates were burdening young African Americans. Dr. Joseph asserts, with equal force, that Mr. Obama profiled people of colour, including Nigerians, over the Detroit air incident. He, however, wonders whether the President would have taken the same course of action if a citizen from France or Italy had been alleged to have attempted destruction of an American plane.

President Obama, in 2010, 2011, 2012, heavily burdened with the very weighty figures of high unemployment, (just over 8% in August, 2012),[4] an agonisingly bitter battle over raising the level of that gargantuan trillion dollar debt ceiling, the enormous pain of delivering what many of his staunch opponents still deem that bulging pregnancy in patient management otherwise known as health care/Obamacare, and gnawing public impatience over wars in Iraq and Afghanistan, premised upon an insatiable urge to destroy domestic and international terrorism, doubtless - needed more than the bat he received from Brian Lara, whom he called the Michael Jordan of cricket. Playing the cover drive and forward defensive stroke, both literally and figuratively, to defeat the enemy requires immense skill, especially in the face of great hostility.

If he delves deeply into the history of West Indies cricket, he would soon realise the enormous value in the Caribbean tradition behind the foregoing stroke play. This tradition can be located in the performances of batting geniuses such as Everton de Courcy Weekes, Roy Fredericks, Rohan Kanhai, Garfield Sobers, Alvin Kallicharran, Vivian Richards, and Lawrence Rowe, whose [302] against England at the Kensington Oval in Barbados still stands as a monument to the charm of batting elegance.

Apart from tradition, there is a host of other matters to be pondered about the Obama-Lara stroke play, at the Trinidad Hilton. To those interested in clues or meaning about reading character behind the matter, pictorial presentation of stances adopted by the two men, some words from cricket commentator, Mr. Henry Blofeld, one of the wise counsels in cricketing circles, would be most relevant.

In October 1996, while participating in a British Broadcasting Corporation World Service programme with Lara compatriot Sir Trevor McDonald, and Dr. Ali Bacher, former Test Match captain of South Africa, Mr. Blofeld had this to say, when he responded to a question about what is so special about cricket:

> I think I am in a position of some authority—being married to a Swedish lady—who knew absolutely nothing about cricket, until we got married and has become rather taken with it. She was saying... there are three great things about cricket. She loves the idea of white flannelled fools on green grass. She loves the beauty of the game and she made rather an interesting remark. She said when you watch a cover drive, played really well, it's got something of the grace of going to Covent Garden Opera House, in the old days and watching Margot Fonteyn and Rudolph Nureyev dancing Swan Lake. There's movement. She said it's very interesting meeting cricketers who bat, bowl, and whatever according to their character. I mean she was making the point—I think—that if you watch someone play cricket for the first time, and you watch him bat for half an hour, you can probably go away and write a hundred words about his character and find most of them are right.

I add that the cover drive, described as the glory of batsmanship by John Arlott, is a stroke played by the greatest with all the decency, deftness, dignity, and grandeur that Test Match cricket deserves. Watching Rohan Kanhai sail majestically to one of his splendid hundreds, in 1968 commentator Brian Johnston was moved to assess the Kanhai surge as full of square cover drives. Anyone who knows fielding positions in cricket well will not deny me this imaginative extravagance: everyone watching that surge unfold was bearing witness to nothing less than mathematical munificence within mystifyingly melodic moments. This is the same description I would offer in regard to the Roy Fredericks (150) and the Gary Sobers (150) against England in 1973, the Fredericks (138) and (109) in 1976 against England, his (73) and (169) against Australia in 1973 and 1975, as well as the Kanhai (92) and (77) against England in 1963.

I suppose what mattered greatly to Mrs. Blofeld can reasonably be described as the meaning behind body language. Americans, including Mr. Obama, to whom baseball does matter, might also be interested to learn how an understanding of character through observing body language could have been gleaned by either looking at, or imagining forward defensive and cover driving postures of batsmen to the bowling action of Mr. Barton King. According to Woodcock (1998, p. xi), King was the American bowler who took English cricket by storm while touring with the Philadelphians in 1897, 1903, and 1908. Not only had he studied the theory and practice of swing, he was extraordinarily innovative in its use.

ENDNOTES

1 *These matters are still relevant, despite the fact that the American President made a very significant public announcement on 17th December, 2014 about Cuba-US relations. During the course of his delivery, he stated that Cuba and the US would restore full diplomatic ties and declared the long running US economic embargo against Cuba had been a failure. I shall be referring later to the wider importance of the President's announcement.*

2 *Cuba, though geographically small, is a fount of advanced education in areas such as pure and applied science. Cuba's healthcare system is one of the best in the world. In addition, Cuba's great prominence in the arts and sports is something from which the United States can benefit. Of course, Cuba's physical closeness to the United States makes it very appropriate to the US tourism business.*

3 *I do not view language as a symbol system.*

4 *To his credit, something his acerbic critics in the Republican controlled Congress refused to recognise, the official US unemployment rate was 4.9 % in October, 2016. In Canada, where international observers claim there has been efficient fiscal management and monetary policy, the unemployment rate at the same time was above 7%.*

The Lara solitude

6th INNINGS
SIMPLY CRICKET, LOVELY CRICKET, FOR LORDS, KNIGHTS, LADIES, GENTLEMEN, AND MORE

Before I embark on performing tasks relevant to the iconic figure Lara became through his innovative negotiation of swing and spin on international arenas, I think it is prudent to give my readers explanatory accounts about the game, the sporting life, cricket. I want to use the stylistic—if not dramaturgical—breadth and imaginative depth on a contrastive sporting canvas saturated with intricacies, which I invite readers to explore while considering socio-economic dimensions of the game, cricket.

It is none other than ex-Labour British Prime Mister, Sir Harold Wilson, who is widely credited by several media circles in Britain and North America for having coined the term, A WEEK IS A LONG TIME IN POLITICS. Wilson, a Yorkshireman, whose electoral constituency was Huyton, declared, also, that Frederick Sewards Trueman, who told Geoffrey Boycott he bowled for five sessions, almost two days in a Barbados Test Match against Frank Worrell and Gary Sobers without having taken a wicket, was the greatest living Yorkshireman. Those seeking to dispute, verify, or put THEIR OWN FLIGHT, SPIN OR SHINE—borrowing an elegant derivative from cricketing circles befitting the best of bowling excellence—on the Wilson claim about politics would have had plenty over which to ruminate, during the period, 9th to 13th July, 2018, and later that month, as well. In so doing, they would have found more than very ample room for accommodating links between politics and sport, links to which cricket is central.

Like some scholars in the Classics, many there are who know that ancient Roman aristocratic males immersed in religion and ritual were supposedly guided by DIGNITAS, PIETAS, and VIRTUS. Many there are who know about aristocratic acceptance of deities such as CASTOR, POLLUX, VENUS, and JUPITER—acceptance integrated centrally with unshakeable belief in portents, all of which were inseparable from omens, oracles, Geniuses, Augurs, and Haruspecies (forget about Aediles, Consuls, Equites, Praetors, and Lictors with fasces). If, like these ancient Romans, you believe in portents too, there are certain events you will not miss. They are: (1) English defeat in the 2018 football World Cup came two days before 13th July, birthdate, so some experts claim, of Flamen Dialis, Father of the Fatherland, Corona Civica recipient, Pontifex Maximus, Dictator Perpetuo, Gaius Julius Caesar in 100 B.C. (2) 13th July is just one day before Bastille Day; it is also two days before the July Ides, four months after the March Ides when Caesar was assassinated, as a result of a conspiracy associated with more than sixty plotters led by the Servilli brothers, the Bruti, Marcus Junius and Decimus, Gaius Cassius, Tillius Cimber, and supported by equites, Marcus Tullius Cicero, faithful friend of Marcus Junius (3) Not so long after his murder a comet blazed for seven days.

(4) According to notable Roman rhetorician, Gaius Suetonius Tranquillus, while Caesar was making a sacrifice, seer Spurinna warned him to look for danger that

would befall him at a time no later than the March Ides (5) It is Suetonius Tranquillus who claims, also, that despite sacrificing victims Caesar was unable to obtain favourable omens; upon his entry to the Senate Chamber on that DAY OF PARRICIDE he was dismissive of religious scruples and mocked Spurinna for having rendered false predictions, because the Ides had come and he was not harmed (6) Spurinna, nevertheless, informed him that although the Ides had come, they had not yet gone (7) 11th July, 2018 came just two days after the "windblown" racist, Boris Johnson, ex-London mayor who used the services of fellow racist, Toby Lancaster, as campaign manager in an unsuccessful bid against Mr. Sadiq Khan for the top city post, departed from the May cabinet. (8) He did so over her handling of BREXIT negotiations with the EU, negotiations he claims serves to reduce Britain to the status of a "colony."

July 2018 is that month also when a most extraordinary—if not unique—event occurred. Imran Khan, protester against drone strikes, that charismatic former Pakistan cricket captain, IMMY, to his faithful cricketer friends of yesteryear, became the first ever superb Test Match pantheon to step into the role of Head-of-State. Even more noteworthy about what I assume those friends would hope is his auspicious ascending on the 27th is that he became leader of one of the most populous societies thrust at the centre of simultaneous global strife where the USA inserted itself, even well before the terror tragedies of 11th September served to change the course of world history. Many may recall that the American presence antedates convulsions over Afghanistan, geographically contiguous to the Soviet Union, what was once a very close ally of Indira Gandhi's, Nehru's, and Shastri's India at a time when American Presidents were not shy of publicising their massive concerns over communism, despite the vitriolic verbiage fuelling the Sino-Soviet quarrel. IMMY, deemed the Pathan Prince by some, has used his strategic elegance to charm countless clusters globally with his shine, swing, swerve, and scorcher seamers. He will, of course, have to be dealing with Donald Trump, that "serial exaggerator" whose gross ignorance of both the cricketing literal and figurative renders him hugely vulnerable against the all-rounder's virtually unplayable movement through the air: how could a WHARTON WEASEL match that Oxonian anchorage!

Shortly before the IMMY victory, 26th July, there was BREAKING NEWS from CNN that Mr. Michael Cohen, once Trump's priestly purveyor, dubbed the President's "long time fixer," would be prepared to state in a New York courtroom that the man for whom he would take a bullet knew about a summer 2016 meeting at the Manhattan Tower; while pleading guilty in a New York Federal courtroom, late November, Mr. Cohen fingered THE MAAFA MUZUNGU MONSTROSITY as INDIVIDUAL 1 who had such knowledge. The "New York White House" is, of course, not too far from that East River location of the thirty-nine storey UN building where many a diplomatic stalwart, including the current Secretary General and his immediate predecessor, gave his blessing to the Iran nuclear deal, an arrangement Trump and his arrogantly jingoistic national security adviser, Mr. John Bolton, have been only too happy to rescind. That summer 2016 meeting over which Trump has agonised constantly—if the "FAKE NEWS MEDIA" are to be believed—a meeting at which his son, Donald Jr., was present, was supposed to be about delivery of "DIRT" by Russian operatives about rival, Mrs. Hilary Clinton.

IMMY, someone who has trampled many a dirt covered surface in his day and knows more than most- friends and foes- on cricket pitches about sordid scandals within and beyond the field, can use that grand cricketing SPIRIT in which he was once immersed to soar above the tawdry tide pools swirling so dangerously inside Trumpian cesspits. If stench emergent from the President's orbit is too potent a probability to ponder, consider this: just one day after 26th July more than one US television news channel presented viewers with an image of Donald Jr., clad in baseball cap and jeans standing on a queue waiting at Gate 35 (Reagan Airport). Seated not too far—somewhat in front of that queue—was Mr. Robert Mueller, seemingly engrossed in reading a newspaper.

Nicolle Wallace, someone—I hasten to add—with unmistakable connections to Scotland, and long-serving, insightful, as well as hugely adept ex-official in both President G.W. and Governor J.E.B. (John Elliot Bush) Bush's administration, someone in the role of MSNBC hostess of the hour-long 4:00 PM programme *DEADLINE WHITE HOUSE*, even invited her listeners to "test their faith in coincidence" while looking at the image in which Trump son and Mr. Mueller appeared. I dare state that FAITH, HOPE, AND CHARITY somewhere in Inverness not too far from peaks of the Scottish Highlands are perched a long distance from the blistering Washington Beltway close to where one, Mr. Paul Manafort, was feeling intense courtside heat since the very last day in July. Nevertheless, with the Mueller probe having moved into high gear at top pace Trump father and son needed much more than their headgear to negotiate what I would describe as "short examination papers" from that "avalanche" known as John Snow to deal with Imran like bouncer barrages pitched at them just short of a good length by the Special Counsel. After all, it is most unlikely that Trump Sr., that blundering buffoon, who told the British Prime Minister, May, she should SUE—so she stated emphatically and repeatedly—the European Union over BREXIT negotiations was blessed by the grand cricketing SPIRIT while he occupied Churchill's chair at Blenheim. Churchill, unlike the "ISLAMIC PALADIN," has never taken the field at Fenners and beyond. Nor has he ever been in a position to score a century while savouring glory in the best of batsmanship.

The "human rights nightmare," brusque, abrasive, tactless, undiplomatic, and inelegant Trump, who landed in Britain only a day after the England loss, and expecting to meet Britain "in turmoil," expressed a desire to see "friend" Boris, once welcomed by self-destructive David Cameron, as a good partner on the cricket pitch. Shortly after Trump had returned to the United States from the NATO Helsinki summit, he found himself at the centre of a continuing massive firestorm over Russia's intervention in the 2016 presidential election. Many there are in and from Guyana who remember strident and justified claims within certain local political circles about US involvement in destabilising Guyana during 1962, 1963, and 1964, which reached one of its highest points when Dr. Jagan was ousted from office. They may also not forget US involvement in elections across Latin America. The names, Bolivia, Brazil, Chile, Paraguay, and Uruguay come to mind immediately. My! My! My! Election chickens do come home to roost. Given the depth of his education in the Classics, friend Boris, who became British Prime Minister in June, 2019, shortly after Trump had completed a state visit to the Kingdom, would readily apprehend the figurative significance about chickens.

This is the same Boris Johnson who, very shortly after having left the May cabinet, 16th July 2018, returned to one of his previous occupations, penning columns for the very conservative *Daily Telegraph*. To me the Johnson piece titled "THE REST OF THE WORLD BELIEVES IN BRITAIN. IT'S TIME THAT WE DO" was as much a revelation about Trump, "one of the most image conscious men" posing on Churchill's Blenheim Castle chair, as it was about Johnson, whom I deem among the most unrestrained racist/imperialists in the twenty-first century. Trump may, of course, be wholly ignorant of the fact that Churchill, assessed correctly as "an unapologetic imperialist" by Mr. J.R.S. Luck, my high school headmaster, warned in

1945 of AN IRON CURTAIN descending from Szczecin, Poland, to Trieste, Italy: the President once spoke of the great Frederick Douglass as if the icon was well and truly alive in the twenty-first century. While reminiscing in his columns about his first day in the Atrium of the British Foreign Office in the Durbar Court, adorned, he notes, with busts of British explorers, Johnson pointed to his vision for a "GLOBAL BRITAIN" that he enunciated before an attentive gathering. This is a vision consisting of a more open, outward looking, engaged United Kingdom than any time previously, a Britain using the BREXIT referendum as a chance to rediscover dynamism of the "bearded Victorians" (presumably, some of the explorers) for returning to a world forgotten for more than four decades and a half. Here is the Johnson world of open markets rekindling old friendships in the fifty-two member Commonwealth, as well as promotion of British culture and values.

Claiming that people around the world believe passionately in Britain and exhorting British citizens to share such confidence, he asserted that world elites accord his country the highest compliment by wanting to give their children a British University education and reside in the Union.

> *They see a first rate military power, one of the few capable of projecting force 8,000 miles. They see by far the most innovative economy in Europe; the tech capital of the hemisphere; the greatest financial centre: a place where one Oxbridge college boasts more Nobel prizes than France; that exports six times more television shows than any other European country and produces most of the world's top-selling artists. They see a country whose royal weddings transfix the globe; a country with 0.7 percent of the world population, whose sportsmen and women in the past five years have come second in the Olympics, won Wimbledon, and whose fancied side has come fourth in the football World Cup under leadership of a man whose very waistcoat incarnates—in the eyes of our friends—the charm and eccentricity of the U.K. This is the soft superpower.*

I have absolutely no doubt Johnson would accept wholeheartedly a view from fellow imperialists that the superpower status he claims for Britain emanated from strong foundations set by forbears such as Robert Clive—albeit not a bearded Victorian, but integral to the power of the British Raj in the jewel of that crown Queen Victoria wore during the course of her lengthy reign. More than acceptance, he would, most certainly bask in the glow from this panegyric:

> *The career of Robert Clive, the son of an impoverished squire, who started as a merchant's clerk in the employment of the East India Company and founded an empire, is one of the romances of the world. Clive died by his own hand at the age of forty-nine. His whole period of Indian service, which was broken by two visits to England, did not exceed twelve years. In his first spell he made England supreme in the Carnatic; in his second he re-conquered Calcutta from Suraj-ud Dowlah, defeated his army at Plassey, defeated the Dutch, cleared the French out of Bengal and the northern Circars, destroyed their influence in Hyderabad, and established British power in the valley of the Ganges. In the third and not the least honourable period of his public service he organised and purified the civil administration of Bengal. Extraordinary daring characterised his military enterprises. At the age of twenty-six he led five hundred men to Arcot, the capital of the Carnatic, and there held a crumbling fortress against ten thousand Indians with a stiffening of French troops*

for fifty days. On the decisive field of Plassey he brought three thousand men into action, of whom nine hundred were Europeans, against a force of forty thousand infantry and fifteen thousand cavalry, and with a loss of less than a hundred men routed his opponents (Fisher 1949, pp. 763-764).

Let me hasten to add that the reference to Wimbledon, obviously a reference to sport, is devoid of links between slavery and tennis at the ALL ENGLAND CLUB: the men's singles champion hoists the two kilogram CHALLENGE CUP priced originally in 1887 for one hundred guineas, currency largely out of circulation today but minted in gold looted by British thievery in the name of Victoria on the broken backs and branded chests with the letters D.Y. (DUKE OF YORK) of Africans on the continent and Anglo-Caribbean.

From Olusoga (2016) I learn that this is the very gold linked integrally not just to the centuries old prestigious 10,000 guineas, a British horserace connected to the Tattersall family whose members still deal in guineas, but also to both the South Sea and Royal Africa Companies (RAC), principal profiteers from Atlantic slavery. Among the major beneficiaries from the RAC were the prominent philosopher John Locke, central to *The Declaration of Independence* and the Carolina slave constitution, Locke's thieving seafarer great-great-great grandfather John Lok, Charles II, as well as the Duke of York who became James II, and after whom New York derives its name (Olusoga, 2016).

In my view, and rather remarkably so, the very terms DURBAR COURT and ALL ENGLAND CLUB evoke far more than powerful imagery about the misogyny, racism, and exclusivist trappings integral to lives of the British Raj, as well as some of the landed aristocracy and business tycoons spread all across Britain, where another prominent view was revealed by that perversely charismatic classical scholar, Mr. Enoch Powell. His ideal about Britain's GREEN AND PLEASANT LAND was associated with repatriating British citizens of colour to their countries of birth during the nineteen-sixties to prevent a flow of RIVERS OF BLOOD across the land. The contrast between images of rivers of blood and a green and pleasant land will clearly not look like those emergent from a juxtaposing of different origins to the terms Durbar Court and All England Club. May I suggest: part of the juxtaposing can be conducted to find out how a very young Harold Adrian Russell Philby, under blistering heat of an Indian sun commingled with Indian boys his age group, became fluent in their languages, and above all, his deeply tanned skin came to be associated with the name, KIM, that of a principal character in one book of racist Rudyard Kipling, who writes about the White Man's burden.

I have no ready replies, but this much I shall add. Did Philby, the young boy in India, begin gaining awareness of pernicious socio-economic stratification wrapped in blatant British racism? Did the ESTABLISHMENT youth Philby—while a Cambridge undergraduate, presumably, very anti- imperialist—use his Indian immersion experience as a strong basis for opposing the rising tide of fascism? Did he use his immersion and Cambridge experience to help shape an affinity with Soviet communism? Was he, despite his defection to the Soviet Union, unable to make a clean break with the ESTABLISHMENT, to the extent that of all matters British, he continued to read ESTABLISHMENT mouthpieces such as *THE TIMES* newspapers where he, supposedly, took careful note of events within the first class cricket world? While I harbour no pretensions that IMMY is an ardent anti-imperialist, I state, with considerable validity, that his forebears grew up in British imperialist India, where the introduction of cricket by the Raj, not dissimilar to what was done in Lara's

Trinidad and other West Indian locations, was followed by use of the sport as a vile and destructive mechanism. If IMMY is able to surmount or bypass the impact of divisiveness, he might well emerge to become a statesman genius. Why?

Allow me to begin replying by using expertise in a conclusion emanating from some profoundly insightful exploration:

> The object of the analysis set out in this chapter has been to demonstrate the importance of sport in Indian socio-political and economic life, at the same time trying to highlight that the history of the game was always subject to influence beyond the sporting arena. A history of Indian cricket, I have tried to argue, only makes sense when we take into account its social and commercial context read in terms of power equations governing the day-to-day administration of public life in the country (Majumdar 2002, p. 184).

It is because I accept, fully, the Majumdar claim about intersection between context and power equations that I give none other than Bapu, Mohandas Karamchand Gandhi, a central place from which he opposed and sought to nullify the impact of such intersecting positioned directly on cricket pitches where the British perversion Boris Johnson shrouds in his panegyric to imperialism was at play.

To be specific, I am referring to the Bombay Pentangular competition Majumdar states was controlled by the Bombay gymkhanas in the city. Adding that the Pentangular originated in Presidency games of the 1890s initially involving competition between Parsees and Europeans, it grew to include Hindus in 1907, Muslims in 1912, and others, largely Anglo-Indians, as well as Christians collectively called the "Rest" in 1937. The tournament was prolonged until 1946, although there was considerable opposition to, and agitation against, the communal organisation integral to its staging. Emphatic about just such organisation, he provides a reference from the publication THE INDIAN SOCIAL REFORMER (1906), where this description appeared: The Hindu boys played in dhotis without shoes or boots, bowled under-hand and made all the mistakes of novices. Parsee players, far more advanced by then, ridiculed the Hindus for their dress and style of play. Further, according to THE REFORMER, what I would describe as an obvious difference led to the generation of "bad blood" between the competitors.

While I knew, via information from a BBC World Service radio programme on cricket sometime in the nineteen-nineties, that Bapu Gandhi opposed communal matches because of their divisiveness, it was only after having read the piece by Majumdar (2002, pp. 169-170) that I derived a very clear sense of the activist's massive disfavour. The anti-Pentangular movement, so writes Majumdar, reached its zenith with a Gandhi assertive on 7th December 1940, I note, just one year after the Second World War had begun. Conveying an excerpt he took from the Bombay Chronicle, which the publication attributes to Gandhi, Majumdar reports: Numerous inquiries have been made as to my opinion on the proposed Pentangular cricket match in Bombay advertised to be played on the 14th December 1940. I have just been made aware of the movement to stop the match. I understand this as a mark of grief over the arrests and imprisonments of the satyagrahis more especially the recent arrest of leaders.

Here was the work of Gandhi, the shrewdly insightful activist steward who, in the most radical of senses, was seeking truth via his implementation of SATYAGRAHA, morally persuasive civil disobedience of injustice. All who are very familiar with his activism know he stood fearlessly at the helm of a movement consisting, all across India, of hundreds of thousands that combined their search for, and revelation of truth, with AHINSA, HARTALS (strikes), as well as DHANDI marches (salt marches). Gandhi, from whom Dr. Martin Luther King derived ideas about civil disobedience and who died revering the icon from India, like King understood the huge value to press publicity of his views. Thus, he would have been quite satisfied that another pronouncement of his appeared on the front page of the *Bombay Chronicle*. What did he state? According to Majumdar he expressed discountenance of what he termed 14th December amusements at a time when the entire thinking world should be mourning in regard to war threatening European civilisation and stability, war that bid to overwhelm Asia.

It would be hard for anyone aware of the Gandhi shrewdness and insight not to know that his opposition to the communal matches was anti-imperialist opposition at its best. This is opposition I am sure he grounded partly, but very significantly, in his knowledge of insidious attempts from Trinidadian born racist, Lord Harris, and another vile jingoist, Cecil Headlam, someone who can be put into the Johnson category at the Durbar Court. Here, I make the observation that Majumdar relegates his reference to Harris in a footnote where he states: By the 1890s the Parsees of Bombay had acquired considerable cricketing prowess and had no difficulty defeating the Europeans of the city. This led to a proposal that they should henceforth play a combined European team in the Presidency. With encouragement from Lord Harris, Governor of Bombay between 1890 and 1895, these matches were started in 1895.

The casual observer reading (Martin Jenkins 1996, p. 225) might be lulled into accepting that George Robert Canning, fourth Lord Harris, Oxford University, Kent, England, and Under-Secretary of State for India, Under-Secretary of State for War serving the Marquess of Salisbury, was the greatest administrator and missionary in the history of cricket to which he was connected all his life, promoting the honour and skill of the game, at all levels. Hugely impressive! Never mind the Martin Jenkins observation that he was autocratic and unable to suffer fools gladly.

The Martin Jenkins view is not one which Mohandas Karamchand Gandhi would have accepted, given what I know of assessment—albeit not wholly glowing—about the activist Fisher (1949, pp. 1026-1027) offers. Writing that Gandhi, someone he describes as "this little Hindu lawyer who has given so much trouble to the British Raj," was an acclaimed hero among Indians, the historian states that he possessed several qualities which, if his lot had been cast in a Western land, would have served to position him at the head of political life. What are those qualities? They are great personal charm, ardent patriotism, exceptional dialectical ability, a keen sense for publicity, subtlety in attack and defence, as well as distinguished command of the English language. Adding, rather condescendingly—if not begrudgingly with racist overtones—that the qualities which pertain to the Western category of political virtues and are appreciated easily by Englishmen marked Gandhi as an epitome of picturesque and baffling contrasts that made for a remarkable and exciting challenge to patience and prudence of the West. For Fisher, those contrasts, both elusive and perplexing, emanate from an indubitable saint. Yet, through his membership of the money-lending caste he was a friend to usury. Ardent patriot, he doubtless was, but as a politician, benefited from some of the worst slum properties in India; though an avowed opponent to Western modernism, he was not averse to availing himself of the convenience of a Ford automobile.

IMMY is no little lawyer in battle with the British Raj that have long since left a partitioned India. Unlike Fisher, I have no valid basis for elevating his humanity to that of sainthood. I will state that like Gandhi he is a shrewdly insightful and very charismatic person who has wrestled successfully with divisiveness on many a Test Match team he led. Like Gandhi he is very concerned with Asia being enveloped in twenty-first century turmoil that can have hugely devastating consequences far more horrific that those emanating from the second World War. Like Gandhi his association with high level politics is grounded in a passionate and moral cause for peace and justice. With his charm, patriotism, dialectical acumen, acute sense of publicity, subtlety in his practices, and several other attributes he would, in my view, have been vaulted to the summit of political life in any of the so-called democracies. If in his twenty-first century world he can use these attributes to help wrestle successfully with that daunting Kashmir conundrum, secure assistance from counterparts in India, Sri Lanka, and Bangladesh, to keep big power manipulators at a very safe distance from South Asian affairs, and can work ardently to unleash that huge reserve of intellectual capability in the region, with the purpose of blunting impact from regional divisiveness, he could well surpass the standards Fisher so condescendingly associates with Gandhi. Given the glorious uncertainty in cricket which he knows only too well, attaining such heights is clearly within his grasp.

Donald Trump can never aspire to such ascending. He lacks three very significant attributes, all conveyed quintessentially in the words DIGNITAS, PIETAS, and VIRTUS, indicative of what Goldsworthy (2006, pp. 44-45) assesses as carrying a far more forceful resonance than the English derivatives, dignity, piety, and virtue. Dignitas, the sober bearing explicitly expressive of significance and obligation of men, commanded respect. Such respect, not trivial to any citizen of ancient Rome, grander to an aristocrat, was even more significant to a man in the role of magistrate. Pietas encompassed respect for Gods, tradition, the law, family, and parents, while virtus, with clear military indication, embodied confidence, physical audacity, moral courage, as well as capabilities integral to the roles of soldier and commanding officer.

> For Romans, Rome was great because earlier generations had displayed just these qualities to a degree unmatched by any other nation. The stern faces carved on funerary monuments of the first century BC, depicting in detail all the idiosyncrasies and flaws of the man in life and so unlike the idealised portraiture of Classical Greece, radiate massive pride and self-assurance. The Romans took themselves very seriously and raised their children not simply to believe, but to know that they were special. Their pride in themselves and in belonging to the Republic was very strong amongst even the poorest citizens, and even more pronounced in those of greater wealth and more privileged birth (Goldsworthy 2007, p. 45).

Readers are free to use their own judicious comparative assessment of IMMY'S and Trump's links to dignitas, pietas, as well as virtus. I ask that three standards for such use should be the strident Trump claim about making America great again, something based upon his use of a Reagan campaign slogan, the mess in which he embroiled himself over what he terms "THIS RUSSIA THING," doubtless, a major matter, by no means peripheral to the noxious foot dragging from him and his lawyers over meeting special counsel Robert Mueller, and last—but not least—what some would deem his manipulation by Vladimir Putin, as well as his shameless disregard of ethics.

In retaining their freedom, these readers can use their own senses of dignitas, pietas, and virtus; at the same time, they can let their imaginative insights soar to the furthest reaches of their own figurative summits and picture IMMY on Test

Match cricket fields spread across the West Indies, Europe, Asia, and Australia. According to what I know about some of the most superb Test Match cricketers the world over where they have been immersed in selfless service, dignitas, pietas, and virtus have saturated their performances. So, standing firmly on the field of Test Match cricket, the profundity to which has been misapprehended, most flippantly and vulgarly, by the careless, I do not, at this juncture, ask that readers suspend or abolish their freedom. Hence, they can make, literally and figuratively, what they will of that bitter, unpalatable, anti-climactic soccer humiliation in Vladimir Putin's Russia. I state boldly that soccer is not—and will never be—like Test Match cricket.

So, when the telecaster on British Independent Television (ITV) resorted to using the cricketing figurative by proclaiming "England are on the front foot," after the team had scored a goal only five minutes into the semi-final, he failed to plumb the depths of the cricketing SPIRIT permeated by what every superb international cricketer knows is glorious uncertainty. That glorious uncertainty came Croatia's way in extra time when the team scored a second goal and booked an historic place in the final played in Russia.

It was there that ex-KGB spymaster Vladimir Putin, unswerving admirer of comrade Yuri Andropov, who must have known about Soviet honouring British double agent, H.A.R. Philby—otherwise known as "Kim" Philby—as a KGB colonel, would have savoured England's loss. I am absolutely certain that all the superb cricketers to whom I shall refer would reason that speculating about their craft is a very precarious pastime. I wonder if they would ponder the probability that while comrade Vladimir watched the France-Croatia final on Sunday, 15th July, he sought guidance from that Andropov SPIRIT, in all likelihood, not entombed within the Moscow Hall of Columns while he, Putin, was considering those Trump tantrums at the July NATO Summit. If the comrade President did seek guidance, he would, most certainly, have fancied himself—to use another cricketing term—to be well and truly off the mark and scoring runs off both front and back foot. May I add: consonant with the intrigue he knows only too well, the comrade would never have revealed his accomplishment during the course of the Helsinki summit with decorous Donald, about whom many an astute American political pundit claims he possesses damaging information. Who says this game, Test Match cricket, is boring, especially in these paradoxically turbulent times of almost instantaneous electronic transmission!

The Helsinki summit took place just a few days after the very first night of the BBC Promenade Concert (13th July) at a point almost simultaneous with the arrival of Trump, the world's foremost bigot and misogynist, at Prestwick airport in Scotland. Trump, who twice sought the counsel of Microsoft billionaire, Bill Gates, to educate himself about distinctions between HPV and HIV would not have a clue about the grandeur to FIRST NIGHT AT THE PROMS in 2018, a centenary year, let alone appreciate any significance to choice of music for that first night, "mesmeric" music by Gustav Holst, Raith Vaughn Williams, and Anna Meredith. Nor, for that matter, would he have any clue about what conductor Zachary Oramo stated in regard to Holst: composing of THE PLANETS was not done to offer exposition about the science of physics, but to evoke the psychological within people, specifically, their emotions towards the scientific reality of THE PLANETS.

If my memory serves me well, it was Johannes Kepler who wrote *Harmonices Mundi, Harmony Of The World*, around 1619. The *Harmonices Mundi* emanated from methods he devised in another published work, *Mysterium Cosmographicum, The Secret Of The Universe*. In the *Harmonices* he devised his third law of planetary motion: the ratio of the cube of the average radius of the planet's orbit to the square of its periodic time is equal to a constant for all planets. Experts regard *The Harmonices* as his synthesis of epistemology, astronomy, geometry, and music. I do not know whether, like Holst, his music was used to express emotion, or whether Holst was in any way inspired by his work.

If conductor Oramo is reasonable about Holst, then I do not think it would be out of order for me to claim that when Sparrow offered his rendition of Mars in song by enunciating that Garfield St. Aubrun Sobers is the greatest cricketer on Earth or Mars, he was evoking his unique emotions to the planets, and without being explicit he was offering his own synthesising of music, epistemology, geometry, and astronomy. Here was synthesising not unlike that done by compatriot, C.L.R. James, who assesses the Sobers close fielding, batting, and bowling as a living embodiment of centuries of a tortured history. James was no physicist or astronomer. He was, unquestionably, an epistemologist with profound knowledge of the music Sparrow created, as well as what he assesses as the NOT-A-MAN-MOVE stroke from Sobers. It is certainly not too late for me to ask cricketing aficionados possessing profound knowledge of physics to ponder how both Kepler and James would have used their imagining and synthesising to assess the Rohan Kanhai stroke for six runs scored with the batsman almost flat on his back. Without much pondering I hasten to state that the Sparrow accomplishment had to have emanated from enormous depth to his imaginative insights about links between the cricketing literal and figurative. I add, rhetorically: is such Sparrow linking not partially but significantly similar to the linking ex-President G.H.W. Bush, made when he delivered his January 1989 inauguration speech, a speech in which he alluded to the huge importance to countless points of light? Yet, that MAAFA MUZUNGU MONSTROSITY sought to ridicule his predecessor by heaping scorn on President Bush's linking. This is ridicule of someone whose long unselfish service to country is unmatched by many a distinguished contemporary.

In rendering his link, President Bush, like predecessor John Kennedy, twenty-eight years earlier, was issuing a call to selfless service. He was doing something no different to what Garfield St. Aubrun Sobers, fully deserving of a NOBEL PRIZE, Rohan Kanhai, and Clive Lloyd, all global leaders in their own right, were doing in selfless service to Test Match cricket the world over for many a glorious year when their extraordinary achievements were mesmeric to all who experienced them. In this regard, it would not be out of order for me to suggest that the cricketing aficionados would take great interest in assessment of two experts, Arlott (1986) and Martin Jenkins (1996), who possess depth of knowledge about integral links between emotion, on the one hand, and synthesising of music, geometry, and physics, on the other. Of Kanhai, Martin Jenkins writes that this small, elegant right hander, who possessed every cricket stroke and a notable inventive one, that full-blooded sweep which swung him off his footing while the ball soared out of the ground, displayed a wondrous gift of timing enabling him to be consistently productive all over the world.

Arlott, who would experience no difficulty in regarding the Martin Jenkins assessment as valid, assesses Kanhai as someone that demonstrated a remarkable blend of consistency and improvisational excellence. No less eloquently, he regards Sobers as a cricketer who set and broke records, but added that those who watched him experienced his transcendence of records. That is the transcendence I locate in:

Blessed with every necessary attribute for greatness as a cricketer, he had rare natural genius, determination, stamina, and a remarkable capacity to continue to produce high-quality performances, despite an exceptionally heavy workload, intense pressure from publicity, and the burden of always being the player whom the crowd most wanted to see and the opposition feared most (Martin Jenkins 1996, p. 781).

Writing about transcendence of a different sort, Martin Jenkins describes Lloyd as a cricketer who revealed rather a phenomenal speed and reach in the covers during his early Test Match tenure, sterling performance throughout a distinguished career, associated also with his sheer presence and batting which thrilled spectators all over the world.

Instantly recognisable with his heavy spectacles, lean gangling figure, and loping walk with head bowed, he would explode into sudden action—whether swooping to cut off an apparent four and throw down the wicket, diving to take a slip catch, or hitting the ball with murderous power, using a heavy bat to bludgeon fours and sixes with basically orthodox drives, hooks, and cuts (Martin Jenkins 1996, p. 756).

Unlike the cricketers whose achievements I note, Trump has become notorious for his prolifically persistent lying, something that can hardly be deemed a productive pastime in Test Match cricket. One of "the world's two disruptors-in-chief," also a "most image conscious" person "well below par," he knows nothing about selfless service, a principal necessity to Test Match cricketing glory. He may well be critical of Sparrow in a manner not dissimilar to that in which he sought to ridicule President Bush. Why not! Is he not the authoritarian aspirate bulging boisterous bigotry! How he would assess Kepler's *Harmonices Mundi* is an altogether massively different matter, perhaps deserving of writing on far more than many a quire.

Before I urge others to pick up their parchment allow me to observe that the England loss to Croatia even sparked animated television conversation on the programme *NEWS NIGHT*, 11th July, about whether the racial colour mix on the team and spirited performance from players reflect "ENGLISHNESS." Herein lies what I regard as a good example of: when significant sporting events are juxtaposed with or—perhaps, laid in the foreground of international politics—both appear to illuminate each other, sometimes pleasantly or unpleasantly. Thus, with Croatia well and truly ahead during extra time (2-1) and elation from the soccer telecaster collapsing fast, surely he had to have searched the depths to contrast, and rendered: The country needs something from somebody. England are on the back foot here. England are throwing caution to the wind. How long? Not long. You feel the sands slipping away between the feet. This is defeat with honour, with hope.

The very next day after defeat, 12th July, *The Guardian* and *The Telegraph*, two dailies, perhaps at opposite ends of the political spectrum, posted headlines: END OF THE DREAM, PRIDE OF LIONS. These phrasal offerings, in their connotative ambiguity, serve to evoke much that goes beyond football, rugby union, Test Match cricket, British imperialism, as well as contemporary international and domestic British politics. With my eyes fixed firmly on the domestic and international, I note one of the last pronouncements from that soccer telecaster. He stated: "After all that effort the ghost of '66 lives on." These are words uttered in the foreground of despondent England players sprawled across a field partially wet with their rivulets of tears. What a contrast to the fulsome flora on weeping willow whose timber still stands for elegant figurative flair to the best of batsmanship which England witnessed in 1966 when Rohan Kanhai, Basil Butcher, Garfield Sobers, Lance Gibbs, Wes Hall, Charlie Griffith, David Holford, and others blazed comet-like for well over seven days and brought glory not too far from that Foreign Office Durbar Court location and elsewhere! It is courts and turf—albeit of a different sort—with which I continue.

Garfield St. Aubrun Sobers: "The greatest cricketer on earth." - The Mighty Sparrow

7th INNINGS
CRICKET, COURTS, AND CLIMATE CHANGE

I start with that game which the Tudor terror, Henry VIII, did much to popularise, although in his reign the game was played very differently to the way it is today. Tennis at the All England Club (Wimbledon) has become associated with a Ladies Final and Gentlemen Final Matches. Horse racing has been known as the sport of Kings. Soccer, so named as a consequence of a phonological quirk in repetitious pronunciation of the abbreviation, ASSOC—A SOCK, SOCK A[1]—well before the advent of the 2006 World Cup in France, is being called via elegant phonological rendition the "Beautiful Game." Soccer continues to be called the "Beautiful Game." Never mind the plethora of very physically harmful fouls in all World Cup Matches since 1966, especially that committed against Brazilian striker Neymar da Silva Santos by a Colombian opponent (4th July, 2014), as well as the hugely unfair play from Uruguay striker Suarez, who bit an opponent during the course of the 2014 Brazil World Cup, from which Suarez was expelled and fined $120,000, although he admitted, in rather untimely fashion, of his indiscretion and apologised.

I am very mindful, also, that in May and October, 2015, the game was given a very very black eye that resulted from what appeared to be the sudden arrests and indictments of top FIFA officials in Switzerland, as well as, the Caribbean, as a result of a United States Justice Department probe into claims about bribery, racketeering, and corruption among very senior FIFA officials, one of whom was the garrulous Trinidadian, Jack Warner, who made some very uncomplimentary remarks about Test Match cricket. In the face of international press reports that the Justice Department investigation would include the once defiant FIFA President, Mr. Joseph Blatter—re-elected in late May, but stating by early June he would relinquish his post, and learning at the beginning of October that he and Michel Platini had been suspended for ninety days—it seemed as if there was "a darker side to the beautiful game."[2] With Mr. Blatter going, the last studs and spikes might well not have been thrust into more than the soccer ground game. If it does recover from the thumping, thudding, and trickery about which several have done more than whisper, then the sporting elegance and administrative acumen with which it once gilded the memory may well serve to remove the sordid spectacles of power that emanated from Baron Blatter's bluster. That is a matter for the future, however.

It is that very recovery that was hugely jeopardised in March 2018, when an ex-KGB spy and his daughter living in the picturesque cathedral city, Wiltshire, had to fight for their literal and figurative lives after having been poisoned, if British authorities—including Prime Minister May—are to be believed, by a nerve agent whose sole origin was the Russian government under Vladimir Putin. Amidst retaliatory rumbles on diplomatic fronts between North Atlantic Treaty Organisation (NATO) members and Russia, the May government announced, well before it had expelled dozens of Russian embassy officials, that the British Royal Family would not be in attendance for the 2018 World Cup in Russia, nor would any British politicians appear. The world held its breath and waited to find out if the boycott would grow to the proportions reached in summer 1980, when the US and some other societies did not appear for the Moscow Olympic Games, because of the presence of Soviet troops in Afghanistan. No such ascendancy emerged, but not too long before the 2018 final took place, one of two more people, British citizens, poisoned by the same nerve agent died.

Once more, the finger from official British government sources was pointed at comrade Vladimir in an impending foreground of what turned out to be yet another Trump tantrum aimed at America's NATO partners, as well as, that Helsinki summit, proceedings of which, none of the top brass in US intelligence circles knew: none of them was beside Trump when he met Putin. The intrigue swirling around the American President intensified when MSNBC veteran correspondent, Andrea Mitchell, learned in full public view from the hugely surprised, Mr. Dan Coats, a very high ranking member in that top brass, that he knew nothing about an invitation from Trump to Putin for a meeting at the White House. Who keeps stating that politics and sport are separate! Certainly not Donald Trump hurling an early August insult at NBA superstar, Mr. Lebron James, and CNN presenter, Mr. Don Lemon. After having watched James being interviewed, Trump tweeted that the player had been interviewed by the dumbest man on television, interaction that made James look smart, not something done with ease, in regard to James. Given the James acumen and insight on, and well away from the court, the iconic genius from whom dignitas, pietas, and virtus are inseparable would be well aware that early August, doubtless a time for profound reflection, can be used for focusing on the future and past when the very best of sporting elegance literally on fields, turf, tracks, and courts other than basketball has been displayed.

With an obvious reference to that past I can think about lovely autumn and summer days for athletics, boxing, tennis, Rugby Union, horse racing and soccer too, at where else but Madison Square Garden, The All England Club, Cardiff Arms Park, Epsom, Newmarket, Haydock Park, Aintree, Sandown, Wembley, Bella Horizonte, Recife, Stamford Bridge, The Baseball Ground, Old Trafford, Maracaibo, Churchill Downs, and Aqueduct. Who would not have been thrilled to have watched Gabriela Sabatini, Zena Garrison, Hana Mandlikova, Ken Rosewall, John Newcombe, Tony Roach, Stan Smith, Margaret Court, Ann Jones, Virginia Wade, Billie Jean King, Pete Sampras, John McEnroe, Jimmy Connors, and Arthur Ashe!

Which spectators would not have been enthralled at the sights of Lester Piggot, Steve Cauthen, Edson Arantes do Nascimento [Pele], Ferreira Da Silva Eusebio, Lev Yashin, Neymar da Silva Santos, Christian Ronaldo, Luigi Riva, John Barnes, Theo Walcott, Jimmy Greaves, Carlos Alberto, Geoff Hurst, Paulo Rossi, George Best, Dennis Law, Billy Bremner, Gordon Banks, Martin Peters, Allan Clarke, Bobby Moore, Sir Bobby Charlton, Lionel Messi, elegant, sophisticated Messi, winner of the 2014 World Cup golden ball award, "the class player,"—to use a phrase from cricket expert Trevor Bailey—as well as, Barry "King" John, Delme Thomas, and Gareth Edwards, "arguably the greatest player ever to don a Welsh [Rugby Union] jersey!"

Cricket, that "meadow game with the beautiful name" that can soothe the mind (Kilburn 1960,: p. 44) has always been known as the gentleman's game. What finer tribute could there have been than that accorded to the unique GENTLEMAN COMMENTATOR, Mr. Leslie John Arlott, on the occasion of his last commentary, during the course of the centenary Test Match between England and Australia in

England (1980) at—where else—but Lord's! According to biographer, Ravern Allen (1996, p. 328), when Arlott began his last twenty minute stint on the final afternoon of the Match, there were some who wondered how he would conclude the stint. It is the beginning of the conclusion I offer to convey that inimitably captivating Arlott talking style: "The sun bright, the wind still, and just fluttering the flag—the MCC flag on the works office... and Lillee turns, six feet tall and wide shoulders, he comes up, a little stammer in the middle of his run, but then he gets it straight again, bowls short and—Boycott hooks that. That looks like being four..." In the midst of the commentary, broadcasting colleagues, Trevor Bailey and Christopher Martin-Jenkins, broke into spontaneous applause and, in quite unprecedented fashion for a Test Match, Lillee and his Australian fielding teammates broke into applause, too. So did Boycott and spectators in attendance for the game.

Rather poignantly, perhaps, in anti-climactic fashion, but exemplifying a supreme measure of his modesty, Arlott ended his stint by saying, simply: "and after Trevor Bailey it'll be Christopher Martin-Jenkins." Moments later, that modesty was illuminated in a cordial exchange with ex-England captain, Tony Lewis, about Arlott's last words. Tony Lewis: I thought you'd say something more romantic than that. Arlott: There's nothing more romantic than a clean break.

Beyond the commentary box, on the field of play, some will argue that cricket has, indeed, produced its gentlemen—notably, the unique, Donald George Bradman of Australia, the genius, Garfield St. Aubrun Sobers of the West Indies, the serene, John Berry Hobbs of England, and, of course, Herbert Sutcliffe, a man of "imperturbable temperament," whose Test Match batting average against Australia is (66.85) and overall average in Test Matches is (60.73) (Woodcock, 1998: p. 42). Of course, there is, also, Keith Ross Miller, the Australian opening batsman and bowler whose cricketing capability Kilburn (1960, pp. 54-55) states was to be appreciated on sight. Miller, so adds Kilburn, burst onto the big cricket scene like sunshine through a cloud to emerge dramatically from promise to power. Always the fascinating, fieldsman, bowler, and batsman, Miller was invariably the first to applaud an elegant stroke off of his own bowling; if beaten by good deliveries while batting, especially by fellow pacemen like himself, would acknowledge his opponents' accomplishment. Though temperamental he was never aloof, and if a disapproving crowd roared after he had delivered a fierce and purposeful bouncer, he would hoist his arms in mock submission and bowl another bumper.

Quite apart from the gendered euphemism inevitably linked to massive expansion of the British Empire and its attendant stratification via sport, one of the most intriguing aspects about cricket at all levels is that it is far more than a game. The breadth of this reality—doubtless at high level international competition against England—encompasses, quite often, anti-imperialist assertiveness, searches for new societal identities, genius in improvisation, as well as, fluency in sporting elegance.

There is absolutely no doubt that such fluency and its absence are linked intimately to what has come to be known as the glorious uncertainty of cricket. I shall focus now on: this glorious uncertainty, as well as cricket and weather conditions, cricket in film and verse. While I cannot offer a comprehensive presentation I hope I can, at least, reduce the incomprehensibility—if not mystery—which surrounds it. My point is—without claiming any special status—exalted or otherwise for cricket—quite simply that cricket is a part of life well outside the ambit of the game, and life outside of cricket is, very much, a part of the game. This is a point more than amply borne out in what I term the tragedy surrounding one of the greatest of West Indies fast bowlers, Mr. Roy Gilchrist, someone, in the words of his fast bowling partner Mr. Wes Hall, whom his Jamaican compatriots wanted to be a "REAL HERO."

I do know of a time, 1959, and many a keen Caribbean cricketing enthusiast there must have known then, the year when Roy Gilchrist, the best West Indies Test Match fast bowler for a long time, who took hundreds of Lancashire League wickets and got several hat tricks (Martin Jenkins, 1996,: p. 732), was sent home from India. Roy Gilchrist, despite notable public pleas for his readmission, never played for West Indies again. In my mind he was, unquestionably, a genius and a West Indies working class hero. His story is a compelling presentation of links between life and cricket. Here, I simply ask for readers' permission to pen some verse about him within which I situate the connection.

PLEBEIAN PURSE

God's arcane appreciation, no gifts of greatness granted, this hapless hunter, this toil of tribe which seduced the slaves. His fronds of fear fragment all fretted fortunes. This maroon menace in sight supreme to raid all trusted tales.

God's seclude serf, a plebeian purse he lured in thirteen throes with tutored tables beside those dangers of the damned. A homeless hero, no soles to muse the mite. His centuries soiled by stifled surges in shrieks of stateless sanity.

God's majestic marauder, no bulges of that brutish bravery to bathe the victor's vaults. The people's profit, colonial charge with race on runs. This fated fury with tilting trails to still the drumming daze.

God's patrician plight, no plaintiff plume presides the poll. This captive curse, his tempered thrusts desert the drones to raze all regal routes. His distal dreams denude the dance to claim a champion's chorus. God's predictable pique, this conscience crowding craven cauldrons. No frontal folds in cultured craft. This thread of tumult cramped with crazed contempt.

To continue making my case about cricket and life, I note that socio-political and sporting talk outside the realms of cricket on both sides of the Atlantic overflows with figurative language hoisted right out of cricketing realms. Here, I ask readers to think of terms such as "take the shine off the ball," the closest link between bat and ball of which I am aware. I saw this remark in The Daily Telegraph early October 2015 obituary for former British cabinet Minister, Mr. Denis Healey. The words were supposed to have been uttered by British politician Mr. James Callaghan, who succeeded Mr. Harold Wilson as Prime Minister when the latter left office in the mid nineteen-seventies. Callaghan had resigned as Labour Party leader in the wake of electoral defeat by Conservative Party leader, Mrs. Margaret Thatcher.

Upon Callaghan's departure a new leader of the Labour Party had to be chosen. Given the leadership candidature of two prominent Labour left wingers, Mr. Tony Benn and Mr. Michael Foot, Callaghan's words should be taken to signify not merely support for Healey, but also, a dulling of the sharpness from the two contenders against whom Healy stood. Despite the Callaghan disposition, Healey lost to Foot, who was comprehensively demolished by Thatcher in a later general election. I must note that I have never heard of Callaghan, the cricketer, and the strongest connection I can make between him and cricket is that which took place in summer 1970, a time when he, the current British Home Secretary, and his Prime Minister refused resolutely to cancel the upcoming tour by a South African Test Match team. Bowing to enormous public pressure, the MCC did cancel the tour. Later, I shall examine that tour cancellation and focus upon direct cricketing contexts where much more than shine was removed from the ball.

Apart from removing 'shine,' other cricket terms used by politicians, media experts, and sports people outside the game are back-stop, a matter to which I shall refer in detail later when I address myself to Theresa May's dilemma in regard to BREXIT, gathers, good spell, good ball, state of the game, state of play, everything to play for,[3] dismissed/dismissal, spin, stumped, sticky wicket, in swing, on the defensive, on the front foot, and on the back foot. While focusing with rapt attention on the telecasting of the 2014 football World Cup in Brazil, I did not miss the use of just such figurative reference during the closing stages of a one-sided contest between Croatia and Mexico: "Croatia went suicidally onto the front foot and left the back door open." The telecaster, who described Mexico as fluid and effervescent, was rendering his account of what began to take place during the course of the last twenty minutes of the match. In those final moments that very telecaster noted that a Croatia player, Rebic, was shown the dreaded red card, a sure signal that he was to be "rightfully dismissed."

In moving to the obvious, I observe that life is full of uncertainty. One of the terms I learned very early in my childhood playing days is that cricket is a game of glorious uncertainty. I was able to enhance my knowing when Sir Gary Sobers exemplified the quality by telling me that batsmen stroke some difficult deliveries through the air, but some fielders dive in extraordinary ways to take catches. In quite an opposite way, other batsmen hit the ball straight to a fielder who drops it. Such is, he notes, the misfortune of the game. All players do not handle the misfortune in glorious uncertainty the same way.

Here are other events linked to glorious uncertainty. Allow me to focus on Yohan Blake, competitor and compatriot of Usain Bolt's, featured in the Canadian newspaper, *The Globe And Mail* (22nd September, 2012, p. S2) under the caption, "IT'S BEEN A GOOD WEEK FOR...": "He may be the beast on the track but he's hardly shabby on the wicket either. The triple Olympic medallist returned to his favourite sport last Saturday (15th September, 2012), inspiring his cricket team, Bartley's XI, to a 36 run win over the Correctional Services. Of his 21 runs, one six certainly left an impression on the crowd in attendance, in particular one unlucky car owner, who found a rather large hole in the back windshield. Still, no doubt accepting that he'd been touched by greatness, the owner simply shook Blake by the hand, telling him "it's part of the game." Clive Hubert Lloyd, "The Disciplined Calypso", knew, all too often, albeit with regular certainty, that leaving several large holes in windows of homes and windshields when batting against opposing sides was part of the ill luck/uncertainty/misfortune associated with the glorious uncertainty of cricket when he unleashed the crushing force of his very heavy bat with what Learie Constantine assessed as the free swing and hoisted deliveries to make the ball soar well above and beyond boundary confines.

It is part of the ill luck and great uncertainty for players, as well as ardent spectators—perhaps inglorious uncertainty for them all—when rain falls excessively and ruins a game at any level—Test Match cricket included. One location which I know from personal experience linked to this uncertainty is Guyana, where the Bourda Ground has been the oldest of Test Match playing arenas within the

Caribbean. Guyana, many will know, is close to the equator, and ruinous rain is a constant enemy. In 1990, the entire second Test Match between England and the West Indies was cancelled: RAIN, NO PLAY. Not a single delivery was bowled. Allow me to offer some views about a tall tale connected to the inglorious uncertainty. The story emanates from West Indies telecaster/radio commentator Tony Cozier.

While conversing with a telecaster colleague during the course of a shortened England-West Indies limited over game at Bourda, a few days after the Test Match was supposed to have ended, Cozier offered a jocular explanation for the excessive rainfall. He said that at the height of the local Hindu Holi Festival, a superintendent responsible for the operation of sluice/loch gates outside Georgetown had forgotten to lower one of them, because of an enforced sleep that followed his excessive drinking. As a result of the indulgence, a large section of suburban Georgetown was flooded at high tide. Cozier concluded his story by claiming that many a studious Guyanese cricket spectator fatalistically attributed the disruptively ruinous torrential downpour at a time when they should have been watching the Test Match proceedings to the superintendent's intoxication and resultant flooding.

I am no expert on the significance of storytelling in Guyana, even when the author is a very notable West Indies sports telecaster. And although I am not fatalistically inclined, I can see connections between water and cricket in that society. What I therefore wish to do is make reference—albeit superficially—to relations between cricket in what was once affectionately described as the Garden City, Georgetown, and tourism in the land of many waters. When Cozier spoke about the sluice gate, he alluded to what Guyanese describe as a koker. Any image of a koker from where I reside, Ontario, Canada, is a picture of canals and empoldering/polderisation used for essential purposes of draining and irrigating valuable lowland coastal space. Kokers, empoldering, and canals are typically associated with the excellent civil engineering activities of Dutch imperialists.

Some of these very activities led, not only to the canal network within Stabroek (later renamed Georgetown), but also the existence of locations within the city such as Vlissingen Road. Vlissingen is, in fact, another name for Flushing. I am aware of two places which bear the name, Flushing. One is a port in South West Netherlands in Zeeland Province. The other is Flushing Meadows in New York City, a major centre where the US Open Tennis championships are usually staged. New York is also the name the British imperialists gave to New Amsterdam after they had taken it from the Dutch.

Guyanese are well aware that the capital of Berbice County in their society is called New Amsterdam too. They know, as well, that the Dutch imperialists have been highly skilful navigators. With their outstanding engineering talent, the Dutch have been largely responsible for good harbour facilities in Schiphol and Amsterdam. What else do Guyanese know about Dutch ingenuity? They know that many of the canals which the Dutch constructed in Georgetown have been filled or are maintained poorly. The canal, for instance, which almost surrounds the famous Bourda Cricket Ground—regrettably, no longer a Test Match venue—is typically clogged with silt and stagnant water.

My point here is that European imperialism in Guyana might have been destructive, precisely because of the way it was used to inferiorise people of colour. Did Guyanese not, however, discard baby with bath water when they opted to reject European imperialism at the time of independence, 1966? Have they not been perpetuating their own subordination at very basic levels by failing to ensure that the canal systems in their Garden City have been all but destroyed? City folk and several rural denizens have not been traversing Georgetown streets with a post-imperial consciousness emergent from the ecological comforts in various blends of local "socialist" governance ostensibly linked to much vaunted claims about promoting a sport-tourism fusion within which Test Match cricket and Amazonian nature feature prominently. Many Guyanese use the everyday terms, jetty and groyne, with unchecked frequency, and never lose sight of that imposing structure, the Stabroek Market Clock, once a sure guidepost for many a rural cricketing pilgrim trekking straight for the Bourda Ground where they have been mesmerised, frequently by the glorious uncertainty of Test Match cricket.

I dare state that if Guyanese—administrators and cricketing pilgrims included—want to enjoy the foregoing comforts and would like tourists to participate in the enjoyment, they should be acutely aware of the fact that: there are Caribbean islands which several tourists prefer to visit—never mind the attractive mainland Amazonian ecology. Is it, thus, likely that when Test Match teams visit the West Indies, their arrival will be preceded by the descent of tourist hordes on cities such as St. John's, Kingston, Bridgetown, Port-of-Spain, rather than Georgetown? Is it not likely that tourists may not venture past the blue Caribbean Sea into the muddy brown Guyanese waters from the Orinoco? Such will not be matters of glorious uncertainty for Guyanese citizens.

There are, however, substantial numbers of Guyanese cricket pilgrims resident in Britain who are intimately familiar with the lands upon, and through which, these muddy waters flow. In 1990, when some of them glimpsed the beauty of Georgetown flora on television, they could not restrain themselves from reporting that they felt homesick. Should these people not be persuaded by means of informative advertising to leave the fog and damp of London, Leeds, Manchester or Birmingham temporarily for the warmth and brightness of Georgetown, suburbs, as well as, rural retreats? While departure could be linked to Test Match cricket, should it not be linked to occasions such as Eid, Holi, Easter, and Christmas? If Guyanese can leave dreary London, they can leave the extreme cold in Calgary, Edmonton, Ottawa, Toronto, Winnipeg, Saskatoon, Regina, Montreal, Minneapolis, New York, and Boston to be among palm trees, crotons, and ferns.

Lest I be accused of trivialising the value of cricket tourism to Guyana, geographically, the largest of the Caribbean Test Match locations, which has yet to learn valuable lessons for the twenty-first century, let me say: efforts to entice tourists should be a concerted one. It ought to involve artists, writers, educators, social, and environmental scientists, as well as cricketers who work cooperatively with governance agencies responsible for matters such as education, economic development, culture, and agriculture. A central theme of cooperation could be fostering social well-being inclusive of leisure and ecological balance via meaningful socio-economic progress.

The lure and lore of Guyana cannot be understood completely through temporary visits from overseas. Should Guyanese in large numbers travel to their homeland regularly and frequently, they may still continue to hear tall stories from others—telecasters included—with rings of inglorious uncertainty clasped around Test Match cricket. In addition, they and countless others can benefit from realistic accounts of everyday life in Georgetown, suburbs, as well as, settings quite distant from stellings, groynes, jetties, and kokers. Should such learning take place, Guyanese shall have started creating one basis to a very meaningful sport-tourism-ecology fusion its Caribbean island cricketing neighbours wish—but are nowhere near—to accomplishing.

To anyone thinking that I have just provided a basis to idle chatter, she should think again: on 14th July, 2014, only over two weeks into the official Canadian summer, I listened to three reports about wicked weather during the course of the busy evening news cycle on American and Canadian television. From National Broadcasting Corporation (NBC) correspondent Tom Costello—umbrella aloft under a torrential downpour—came statements about temperatures in the US being ten to twenty degrees below normal and "a blast of cold air from Canada." From CTV in Canada I heard meteorologist, Anwar Knight, say that Tuesday, 15th July, 2014 will "feel like a raw autumn day." In very stark contrast, Johanna Wagstaffe, fellow meteorologist from the Canadian Broadcasting Corporation (CBC), referred to eight days of frequent lightning strikes, intense wild fires, and stifling heat in the Canadian North West Territories, where the government was spending close to $100,000 daily to fight the fires, and British Columbia, Western Canada. In the Northwest, she added, for good measure, that Yellowknife was hotter than Toronto and Memphis. At the same time, Prairie Canada was experiencing unusually cold weather.

Memphis, Yellowknife, Regina, New York, and Ottawa are not world cricket centres. None of them is immune to GLOBAL WARMING. The same goes for many places in Guyana, a major locus for Test Match and other high level forms of cricket. Guyana—with extremely low coastal locations—is particularly susceptible. Here are some of the countless Guyana regions with links to a Dutch imperialist presence that are exposed, rather acutely, to susceptibility: Stabroek, New Amsterdam, Blegezeight, Blankenberge/Blankenburg, Sosetdijk, Den Amstel, Utivlugt, Tuvlugt, Huis T'Dieren, Canje, Tyd en Vlyt, Nog Eens, Onverwagt, Onderneeming, Goedverwagting, Supenaam, Meter-Meer-Zorg, Hoff Van Aurich, Sparendaam, Vryheid's Lust, Zeeburg, deWillem, Haarlem, Orange Walk, Hague, De Kendren, Ruimveldt, Vergenoegen, Vreed en Vriendschap, Vriesland, Schoonoord, Tuschen. GLOBAL WARMING is not coming, it is among us, already, so claims, most authoritatively, the expert group of international social and natural scientists who tabled more than one of their long awaited Inter-Governmental Panel on Climate Change (IPCC) Reports. With their expertise, these scientists inform us of perils from what are with us: raging wild fires, very intense winter and tropical storms, acidic oceans, excessive flooding, prolonged drought periods, devastating food shortage, and great socio-economic unrest. None of this bodes well for cricket in Guyana and, for that matter, the rest of the Caribbean. With the destructive impact of global warming, Guyanese and other West Indies cricket lovers may be in such dire straits as they could well see worse than in the three words: RAIN. NO PLAY—hardly a matter of welcome glorious uncertainty.

Guyana is a tropical region close to the equator from which Canada is quite distant. Nevertheless, the climate change that is a primary concern for the IPCC is a massive threat, not just to world Test Match cricket, but also one of Canada's most alluring sports, ice hockey/the NHL (National Hockey League), associated with many more billions of dollars than claimed on behalf of contemporary Test Match cricket. Before I get to this matter, let me note that in 2017, because of intensely suffocating pollution, Test Match cricket in India was interrupted at the time. Such has not happened yet in Australia, but it will one day in the not too distant future. Ian Hanington and Canadian television notable, world ecological activist, and intellectual, Suzuki (2017) write that while Arctic ice melts, Australia burns. Such cannot be good news for Test Match cricket on the island continent, especially those whom E.W. Swanton deems the hoboes on the Sydney Hill. Suzuki and Hanington point out that like Europeans and Japanese, Australians, who constitute a fifth of the world population, gobble up more than four fifths of the world's resources. Australia, in their view, ranks among the principal planetary predators and despoilers. Suzuki and Hanington are explicit in naming these destroyers, corporate capitalists propelled by profit-making.

Only nine years earlier, Suzuki made this observation and assessment within which he locates Australian and Canadian culpability:

> Australians elected four consecutive Conservative governments that denied the reality of human-induced climate change and refused to ratify Kyoto even though the country suffered severe drought for years. Australia is an island continent with most of its population living along the edges where sea level rise will have its greatest impact. My own country, Canada, is extremely vulnerable. We are a northern country and warming, we know, is going on more than twice as rapidly in the north as it is in temperate and equatorial areas. For decades Inuit people of the Arctic have begged for action to reduce greenhouse gas emissions because they can see the changes, but they have been ignored. Canada has the longest marine coastline of any country in the world and simple sea level rise through thermal expansion will impact Canada more than any other nation on earth. And Canada's economy continues to depend on climate sensitive activities like agriculture, forestry, fisheries, tourism, and winter sports (Suzuki 2008, p. 5).

I know that two of those conservative governments have been led by Malcolm Turnbull and Tony Abbot, the second of whom made a trip to Canada during which he thanked fellow conservative, Canadian Prime Minister Stephen Harper, for exemplifying staunch adherence to conservatism, adherence, if *Globe And Mail* feature writer, Geoffrey Simpson is to be believed, was used by Abbot for ascending his office. Anyone who assumes that Turnbull and Abbot have not ignored Australian aboriginal peoples is living in a phantasy land.

I am very cognisant that starkness in the foregoing exposition may not stir cricketing imaginative insights quite readily. For those who remain unmoved and have their own cricketing linguistic sense of the term, glorious uncertainty, I ask for consideration of this profound explanation:

> The phrase about 'the glorious uncertainty of cricket' applies to the individual as much as to the fortunes of struggle [in the game]. For there is no second chance: the batsman who is out first ball must retire to the pavilion and brood on his ill-luck until it is time to field and forget it—when, as likely as not, he will miss a catch and enter purgatory again. The lawn-tennis player, no matter how badly he is playing, completes the set; the footballer, [soccer player] no matter how inept, kicks again; the polo player and the hockey player, though covered with shame, are assured of their full afternoon's sport. But it may easily be the best batsman's fate to have nothing to do but watch more fortunate batsmen receiving easier bowling than he did. This constant risk of making no runs would, you would think, deflect boys and men from the game. But no. The cricketing temperament, always slightly sardonic, accepts it. The uncertainty spells also glory (Lucas 1933, p. 2).

It is precisely that link among uncertainty, glory, and its opposite which I heard presented during the course of a British Broadcasting Corporation (BBC) World Service radio programme, *TALES FROM THE CREASE*, in 1991. At the time, narrator,

Michael Diamond, offered a powerful contrast between two England cricketers, Harold Gimblett and Denis Compton, who played at the highest level, Test Match cricket, for their country.

What did Michael Diamond say? Gimblett, a very excellent cricketer, he observed, was a very shy person, an insecure man who kept away from the fame linked to success. He played only a few games for England and committed suicide in his sixties but Compton blossomed splendidly. Many years after Gimblett's death, Diamond noted that the cricketer-analyst, Peter Roebuck, reflected on a biography of him written by David Foot. From Roebuck came these words:

> This game [cricket] preys on doubt. It's a precarious game—form, luck, confidence are transitory things. It's never easy to work out why they have so inexplicably deserted you. Inevitably, you analyse, you fret, you try to understand what's happened. Why was the game so easy yesterday? Why is it so impossible today? Sometimes, you tense yourself to try harder. Sometimes, you decide to relax and to go for your shots. Probably, neither works. As Foot says, cricket is played very much with the mind. Only the unimaginative player escapes the tension. Many, whatever their seeming unconcern, retreat into caverns of introspection. Gimblett must have torn himself with worry. He must have twisted himself into rejection, not only of his own personality, but of people around him, too. He must have sensed envy and plots. Suspicions of others must have burdened him as he sought some explanation for his failures. Usually, the good times return. Gimblett had a magnificent career but there's no guarantee. That's the worst of it. Why should runs ever return? You're trying hard, the pitches are good, the bowling only fair. There's no rational reason for failure nor any rational reason why fortune's wind should change. Maybe, cricketers shouldn't take it so personal but most of us do, all the same. In this light, it's strange that cricket attracts so many insecure men. It's surely the very worst game for an intense character yet it continues to find many obtuse sensitivities amongst its players: men of imagination, men of ideals risk its harsh exposures. There must be some fascinating stimulation in the game to make so many of us so ill-prepared for turmoil risk its ugly changes. Otherwise, we'd never tolerate its bounce of failure. And it is mostly failure, even for the best.

Allow me to use an assessment from Kilburn (1960), an assessment I think intersects very clearly with the Roebuck view about preying on doubt and precariousness. Writing about one of the many keen Australia-England tussles, Kilburn claims: it is an axiom of cricketing wisdom that if the batsman thinks the ball is turning it is turning.

It is no wonder that the Roebuck words moved narrator, Diamond, to pose a rhetorical query, who can doubt that cricket mirrors life?

With the largest possible mirror in front of me I continue with some information outside of playing cricket which lovers of film, literature, and politics should find interesting. Almost three decades ago, 29th November, 1990, *The Manchester Guardian* carried a story about preserving a cricketing tradition by British Prime Ministers. In specific reference to the "IRON LADY," the *Guardian* writer claimed:

> Mrs. Thatcher, of course, tried to carry it [the cricketing tradition] on by her disastrous resort to cricketing metaphor at the Lord Mayor's Banquet two weeks ago when she promised not to duck any bouncers and then suffered the inevitable fate of being smacked in the mouth.

November 1990, was, of course, a time associated closely with Mrs. Thatcher's inglorious exit, a departure which followed bitter struggles within her ruling conservative party over leadership and the Prime Minister's job for which some of her most vocal opponents, including her cabinet colleague, Mr. Michael Heseltine, nicknamed "TARZAN," felt she had become unsuitable and should relinquish. I, therefore, see the *Guardian* reference to her being smacked in the mouth as figurative assessment via a cricketing route of her ultimate humiliation, a distasteful relegation which many in the cricketing and political world could readily understand as part of the glorious, as well as inglorious uncertainty to cricket from which Mrs. Thatcher borrowed but suffered.

This was borrowing by someone who had no intention of going on the defensive: if I assign Mrs. Thatcher the batsman's/batter's role, a logical assignment consequent on her resort to the figurative, I would have to take the additional step of recognising that any batsman opting not to duck bouncers from opposing quick bowlers is playing the game in a very aggressive mode or style, posture and practice not alien to the Prime Minister. In literal terms, while it may be an altogether different and strange matter for a batsman to be negotiating bouncers from her own team, in Mrs. Thatcher's case, and figuratively so, as well, she was facing bouncers from within her own team, the governing Conservative Party. 1990 was a time when persons in her own party had unsheathed their long knives and wanted her gone from the top job. Her approach, of course, was to unsheathe her own cutting instruments along with a barrage of cannon fire. Anyone with basic knowledge of cricket will note that aggressive postures and practices against bouncers, though hugely enlivening to appreciative crowds, are fraught with very big risks, not the least of which, is being literally and figuratively shattered after a smacking in the mouth. I make my point with the greatest of respect owed to the finest of batsmen at the highest level of the game, Test Match cricket, all over the world.

If, by analogy, Mrs. Thatcher at the highest levels of politics, perches from which she delivered the 1990 Guildhall speech, can be equated with such batsmen, the distasteful relegation she experienced was not dissimilar to the type literally imposed upon these batsmen on cricket fields. Thus, the significance of the *Guardian* assessment lies not within the cricketing or political realm. It resides at the confluence of the two, a point where immense depth to the intersecting awakens the imagination and triggers a quest to unravel conundra at the foundation of our very existence. With more than a generous helping from Margaret Thatcher, those interested in a re-plumbing or gauging could not have asked for a heartier serving than that offered in the Guildhall speech, prelude to the inglorious certainty which felled her. For emphasis I re-present:

> Since I first went to bat eleven years ago, the score at your end [the Lord Mayor's end] has ticked over nicely. You are now the 663rd Lord Mayor. At the Prime Minister's end we are stuck on 49. I am still at the crease, though the bowling has been pretty hostile of late. And in case anyone doubted it, can I assure you there will be no ducking of bouncers, no stonewalling, no playing for time. The bowling's going to get hit all around the ground. That's my style.

I have no idea how keen a student of the game skipper/Prime Minister, Thatcher, was in 1990. Any of the leading radio commentators and telecasters of Test Match cricket would have been immensely proud of her. These are some of the very people who would have been able to remind her about an event some distance away,

Manchester,[4] just over fourteen years prior to 1990, when West Indies imposed massive defeat on an England Test Match team led by South African born Tony Greig, who declared boldly before that Manchester game that he would make his opponents grovel. Part of the imposition was a continual barrage of bouncers to the England batsmen—including skipper Greig—who could neither have played for time nor stonewalled, but were forced to stand at their creases wondering whether bouncers would smack them in the mouth.

Mrs. Thatcher might well not have apprised herself about life on a literal sticky wicket after rain, which makes for both the glorious and inglorious uncertainty to subsequent play. Had she been so aware, she might well have tempered her adventurism with some very sound common sense, which I detect in wise words about what were clearly conditions on a sticky wicket, as well as, well as assessment in regard to the meaning behind other vicissitudes on cricket fields, meaning that could, in principle, be extended to political life. Writing about an afternoon of rainstorms during the course of the Brisbane Test Match between Australia and England (1946-'47), Kilburn (1960, pp. 10-11) reports that although two inches of rain saturated the ground within just a few hours, the power of the Queensland sun on an unprotected pitch ensured that play was possible the next day without any loss of time.

> It was of course astonishing play; cricket of breathless fascination with batsmen trapped on a pitch where the ball did everything except deliver itself. The only semblance of rationality in it was the assurance that a good length ball would rise shoulder-high. Pads were a formality and when there was no need to play at the ball hands and bat had to be lifted above the head to be out of harm's way. Breastplate and helmet would have been sensible protection and this without any malicious intent on the part of the bowlers (Kilburn 1960, p. 11).

While I do not—and shall never—know whether any malicious intent was integral to the hostile bowling Mrs. Thatcher identified, I fail to see how she, an aggressive batsman bent on hitting the bowling all around the ground, could have been unaware of a very basic fact. Cricket, the living game, has to experience cycles of change indicative of decay/decline, renaissance/resurgence, rejection and development of techniques, as well as ideas (Kilburn 1960, p.1). Until all players and resources of play have been expended, continues Kilburn, the balance of bat against ball shall waver to and fro with dominance rising and falling.

Away from cricket fields and politics I waited more than ten years before I got some measure of the glorious uncertainty to the game when I stumbled upon a very captivating film, "A Wondrous Oblivion," (2003), which I watched twice. The leading actors are Sam Smith (David), and Delroy Lindo (African-Caribbean father). This is a tasteful piece of British screen artistry about fantasy, ethnic and colour bigotry, tolerance, traditional orthodox Jewish and Anglo-Christian family values, as well as, cricket. Set against a compelling foreground of West Indies Test Match cricketing assertiveness over England during the nineteen-sixties and the Notting Hill race riots of the nineteen-fifties, the film is a portrayal of an obsessed eleven year old English born boy, David, of Polish background. David, who loves cricket, is not a good player, whom his school cricket coach dubs "wondrously oblivious" about his lack of skill. His school coach wastes no time in relegating him to the task of "official scorer."

Well outside the realm of cricket, his orthodox family is targeted in their working class neighbourhood with ethnic bigotry. David and his family observe that their new neighbours are members of an African-Caribbean Jamaican family whose presence in the area is also disturbing to intolerant Anglo-Saxons. David soon learns that the male head of the Caribbean family is an adept cricketer, from whom he learns the game and himself becomes rather adept. The youngster, who develops a friendship with his neighbours' daughter of about his age, and learns the game from her too, appears for his school team in a crucial game with an opposing school eleven. Encouraged by cheers from his teammates, the boy bats with effortless brilliance and guides his team to victory.

Another film with which I am familiar is the Stevan Riley production "*Fire In Babylon* (2010)"about the unprecedented and hugely successful West Indies assertiveness over England in Test Match cricket, from around the middle of the nineteen seventies to the mid-eighties under the astute captaincy of Clive Lloyd, who unleashed crushingly ferocious quick bowling terror in the awesome speed of Joel Garner, Colin Croft, Michael Holding, and Andy Roberts on England batsmen. In marvellously balanced imaging, Riley does not exclude the aggressively domineering batting of leading West Indies players, especially Lloyd himself, Roy Fredericks, Gordon Greenidge, Desmond Haynes, and Viv Richards.

Interestingly, this is not just a film about cricket, it is also a clever depiction of a conjuncture of social forces in assertiveness from people of colour, assertiveness juxtaposed with racism within climates of inequity, particularly in a Britain under Thatcherism. To me the title is evocative of the type of imagery the American writer James Baldwin creates in his reference to fire, water, and the rainbow, terms he uses towards the end of one of his widely read books, *The Fire Next Time*. The very imagery is evoked also in the manner in which Rastafarians, one of whose most prominent spokespersons was Bob Marley, use the word Babylon. In this very piece of writing I examine, in my own ways, Baldwin's ideas. I hope readers do not miss my accounts.

I continue with the interplay between cricket and life outside it by looking at ideas of Eastaway (1992), whose lists of quotes on cricket, literary fanatics of the sport, screen actors who loved the game, films about it well before 2003 and 2010, and cricket-loving Prime Ministers can be useful to those who do not know much about cricket. I start with five quotes: (a) "Cricket is organised loafing."—William Temple, Archbishop of Canterbury. (b) Cricket is baseball on Valium."—Robin Williams. (c) "Basically it's just a whole bunch of blokes standing around scratching themselves."—Kathy Lette. (d) "Cricket is not so much a game as a substitute religion. It certainly gives one a very clear idea of eternity"—Lord St. John of Fawsley. (e) "If there is cricket in heaven, let us all pray that there will be rain."—Arthur Marshall. (f) "Cricket is the greatest thing that God ever created on earth."—Harold Pinter.[5]

The literary-minded and film-watching public can add to their depth of knowledge in becoming aware: Hampshire born, Charles Dickens, bowler and scorer in eighteenth century cricketing events, described the game as bringing enormous joyfulness to those who find everyday life monotonous. It is he, writes Martin Jenkins (1996, p. 215), who was instrumental in making the very first England tour to Australia a reality. Many West Indians, Sri Lankans, Bangladeshis, Englishmen, Indians, Pakistanis, South Africans, New Zealanders, and Australians who are literary-minded and also love cricket would, of course, know that in part of the ode to British imperialism in Barbados—always British up to the year of independence—one of the well-known locations for watching Test Match cricket at the Kensington Oval was the PICKWICK PAVILION.

Cricket poetry titled "*The Cricket Match*," by William Goldwin, has been written in Latin. Sir Arthur Conan Doyle, P. G. Wodehouse, Harold Pinter, Stephen Fry, and

Samuel Beckett, the only first class cricketer to be awarded the Nobel Prize, were all literary cricket fanatics. So were the poets, John Arlott, Edmund Blunden, John Betjeman, Thomas Moult, Lord Byron, and Lewis Carroll. Lee (1996, pp. viii - xiv) writes, quite correctly, that what separates cricket from all other sports—save boxing—is the passion and poetry of verse and prose occurring at every level of the game.

If lament is a song of grief or a form of passionate grief, then it comes out, most poignantly in cricket verse, *O MY HORNBY AND MY BARLOW LONG AGO*, from Francis Thompson, whom Frith (1978/1996) describes as a wretched Lancastrian that was retrieved by a prostitute, Wilfrid Meynell, from his pestilent, drug-ridden twilight existence on the Thames Embankment. To be fair, Thompson, who had studied medicine but never practised, because he became a writer, was an opium addict. To me, that unfortunate turn in his life is hugely overshadowed by his poetry, not the least of which is the one I noted. This is a poem about Thompson's memories of two cricketing heroes participating in a match between rivals, Lancashire whose emblem is the red rose, and Gloucestershire, the second of which gained an immense reputation largely as a result of the most notable among a cricketing brotherhood of five, Dr.William Gilbert Grace, regarded by everyone who knows her/his cricket as one of the greatest batsman ever.

To hear Thompson's verse read in one of the Lancashire dialects is a movingly enthralling experience of the imaginary. While I cannot present the imagery and reminiscence evoked in the voice, I would be doing somewhat of a disservice to my readers, if I did not offer those captivating words in writing. Here they are:

O MY HORNBY AND MY BARLOW LONG AGO

It is little I repair to the matches of the Southron folk,

Though my own red roses there may blow;

It is little I repair to the matches of the Southron folk,

Though the red roses crest the caps, I know.

For the field is full of shades as I near a shadowy coast,

And a ghostly batsman plays to the bowling of a ghost,

And I look through my tears on a soundless-clapping host

As the run stealers flicker to and fro,

To and fro:

O my Hornby and my Barlow long ago!

It's Glo'ster coming North, the irresistible,

The Shire of the Graces, long ago!

It's Gloucestershire up North, the irresistible,

And new-risen Lancashire the foe!

A Shire so young that has scarce impressed its traces,

Ah, how shall it stand before all resistless Graces?

O, little red rose, their bats are as maces

To beat thee down, this summer long ago!

This day of seventy-eight they are come up North against thee

This day of seventy-eight long ago!

The champion of the centuries, he cometh up against thee,

With his brethren, every one a famous foe!

The long-whiskered Doctor, that laugheth the rules to scorn,

While the bowler, pitched against him, bans the day he was born;

And G.F. with his science makes the fairest length forlorn;

They are come from the West to work thee woe!

It is little I repair to the matches of the Southron folk,

Though my own red roses there may blow;

It is little I repair to the matches of the Southron folk,

Though the red roses crest the caps, I know.

For the field is full of shades as I near a shadowy coast,

And a ghostly batsman plays to the bowling of a ghost,

And I look through my tears on a soundless-clapping host

As the run stealers flicker to and fro,

To and fro:

O my Hornby and my Barlow long ago.

In shifting from lament to the overwhelmingly amusingI discover that the Scottish poet interested in folklore and mythology, Andrew Lang (1844-1912), wrote a cricketing parody of BRAHMA, a poem by one of America's most famous literary figures and transcendentalists, Ralph Waldo Emerson (1803- 1882) In the authoritative voice of none other than that of John Arlott from the English Channel island of Alderney, a location fit for the poetic, Emerson is assessed as someone who had strange mystic interests and urges. The appearance of Emersonian uncertainty, so adds Arlott, is clearly overshadowed by the unquestionable grounds of his probing and searching. To Arlott, the sincerity and mystic feature of BRAHAMA prompt much thought.

BRAHMA by Andrew Lang

If the wild bowler thinks he bowls,

Or if the batsman thinks he's bowled,

They know not, poor misguided souls,

They too shall perish unconsoled.

I am the batsman and the bat,

I am the bowler and the ball,

The umpire, the pavilion cat,

The roller, pitch, and stumps, and all.

The "BRAHMA," Supreme God of Vedic mythology about whom Emerson wrote, is described by the American thinker:

BRAHMA by Ralph Waldo Emerson
If the red slayer think he slays,
Or if the slain think he is slain,
They know not well the subtle ways
I keep, and pass, and turn again
Far or forgot to me is near;
Shadow and sunlight are the same;
The vanish'd gods to me appear;
And one to me are shame and fame.
They reckon ill who leave me out;
When me they fly, I am the wings;
I am the doubter and the doubt,
And I the hymn the Brahmin sings.
The strong gods pine for my abode,
And pine in vain the sacred Seven;
But thou, meek lover of the good!
Find me, and turn thy back to heaven.

Dare I state that I am not in unsafe hands if I leave it to readers to ascertain how and why Andrew Lang, someone with an interest in folklore and mythology, would parody the work of Emerson, who had deep roots in transcendentalism? Should the readers look long and hard, they may well discover that between what Lang terms Border cricket, on which he was nurtured in Scottish locations close to England, and Test Match cricket, lies a lengthy stretch on which can be found not merely the ritual of the game, but also its deeply rooted SPIRIT.

Be that as it may, Lee is clearly on the mark when he claims that cricket is, in many ways, a game of rhyme, stanza, and beautifully crafted moments which—though inspirational for the gifted few—must conform to strict rules that prose, oddly, need not. Though I am not one of the inspired gifted few, I have made efforts to craft the beauty of the game. Here, I offer two such efforts in the forms of verse titled: "*CRICKET*" and "*THE TEST.*"

THE TEST

Oh! To see the toss with coin of spin is to steal a walk with the boss to win.

Oh! To go to all five and hold them live is a delight in every year. Oh! To see the white in light and catch the red in flight is a dream to care. Oh! To stand and cheer and watch the throes is to hear the ebb and floes. Oh! To take the blows and match the din is to catch the ball with every roar. Oh! To count the score with every four is the Test of cricket.

CRICKET

Cricket! With hitches on pitches, take your stride and turn it from the herd.

Tell the pride in gleaming white to let the knight stay still.

Show the team that verdant splendour.

Clear the course in route red candour.

Sight the floes and line the drives.

Tell your force the innings well over.

Hoist the gold to seams of old.

Oh! Pay the yield.

Savour the fruits of your field.

Take good aim.

Peel the seal and watch the name.

This is the game!

Runs and byes.

In tons of highs for skippers with flippers that cut the drives

Which slip to cover.

Cricket, Lee adds, is a game that is watched by old large-knuckled men who sit in the last of the sun and dream of days gone by, for it is a game of memories. May I, in passing, note that I cannot state whether V.S. Naipaul, Derek Walcott, and Arthur Lewis, also Nobel Prize winners, who were raised in cricket crazy Caribbean societies, can be associated with the term 'literary fanatics of cricket.'

Five screen acting lovers of cricket, notes Eastaway (1992), are David Niven, Boris Karloff, Basil Rathbone, Errol Flynn, and Dame Peggy Ashcroft. I must add Ralph Richardson. Five older films in which cricket features are: (a) *Hope and Glory* (1987)—depicting life in suburban Britain during the second World War in which a boy is taught to bowl a googly; (b) *The Go-Between* (1970)—featuring Farmer Ted played by Alan Bates, who is caught by a boy, Leo, on the boundary; (c) *The Final Test*(1953)—featuring Jack Warner, who plays a cricketer looking forward to his final game,(d) *A Yank at Oxford* (1938)—featuring Vivien Leigh and Robert Taylor, who portray cricket as one of the eccentricities with which Americans must come to terms. (e) *The Lady Vanishes* (1938)—a thriller by Alfred Hitchcock in which two people are obsessed about wanting to know a Test Match score. While dealing with the arts, allow me to add that two leading British vocalists, Mr. Mick Jagger and Sir Elton John, are lovers of cricket. I do recall, also, a batsman at the crease taking his stance on the Jacket covers of a Sir Elton John record.

On the political front of cricket loving statesmen, Eastaway names Sir Robert Menzies,[6] who described cricket as the most delightfully illogical game on earth, Robert Hawke [Australia], Clement Atlee, Lord Alec Douglas-Home [United Kingdom], and Michael Manley [Jamaica]. To this list I add Stanley Baldwin and the old Harrovian, Henry John Temple, third Viscount Palmerston of Palmerston, Baron Temple of Mount Temple [United Kingdom], Jawaharlal Nehru [India], Forbes Burnham [Guyana], Erskine Sandiford [Barbados], Keith Mitchell [Grenada], V.C. Bird [Antigua], John Major [United Kingdom], Nawaz Sharif [Pakistan] and John Howard

[Australia]. Perhaps, the most distinguished of the lot is Lord Alec Douglas-Home, also known as Lord Dunglass or Lord Home of Hirsel. He played for Eton, Oxford University, Middlesex County, whose iconic cricket ground is Lord's, Free Foresters, and Harlequins, as well as I ZINGARI, a club formed in 1845 by ex-Harrovians.

While Dr. Eric Williams, Prime Minister of Trinidad and Tobago, admired and appeared in photographs with Sir Gary Sobers, the great West Indies cricketer, I cannot say whether he loved the game. Nor can I state that Sir Harold Macmillan, Prime Minister of Britain—later Lord Stockton—who appeared in photographs alongside Sir Frank Worrell, and Mr. Ted Dexter, West Indies and England captains, loved cricket. I should not, however, miss the fact that while Nobel Prize winning South African President, Nelson Mandela, was in gaol on Robben Island, he did maintain a keen interest in Test Match cricket. Thus, when he first met Australian Prime Minister, Malcolm Fraser, on the island, one of the initial questions he posed to the Prime Minister was whether the legendary Australian batsman, Sir Donald Bradman, was still alive. The Don was, very much, alive, at the time of his query.

What more can I state about the game? I accept, without hesitation, a rather shrewd assessment from Kilburn (1960, p. 5) that cricket never was, and never can be, a game of continuous excitement or of great accomplishments on a daily basis. The cricket lover cannot live endlessly on superlatives without a diminution of appetite and a jading of the palate. Kilburn is most reasonable in acknowledging that the quiet hours, the simple strivings, are as much features of its attraction as its high drama. Cricket, which he rightly adds, cannot be made excellent by so naming it and assuming a virtue that is not present, is a composite joy, a blending of the modest and magical.

A good deal of that composite joy, that blending, would have emanated from the fluvial batting presence of "one of the game's immortals" (Martin-Jenkins, 1996,: p. 372), Yorkshire and England opening batsman, Herbert Sutcliffe (1894-1978). Herbert Sutcliffe was a player of immense concentration, unflinching courage, and consistent success (Arlott, 1986,: p. 252), who scored a staggering (149) first class centuries, some of which, he made in the company of Sir John Berry Hobbs. It is with overwhelming respect for cricket and life outside the game that Woodcock (1988, p. 42) states: when an England innings was in the hands of opening batting partners, Hobbs and Sutcliffe, everything seemed well with the world. What finer tribute could there be to Yorkshiremen than for Woodcock to emphasise it is Herbert Sutcliffe—not Geoffrey Boycott or Len Hutton—who monopolises Yorkshire batting records!

I, therefore, do not believe—like Mr. Ted Koppel, the former American Broadcasting Company (ABC) host of the program NIGHTLINE—that the only virtue to baseball is that it makes cricket look more boring. In my view, he has smeared both games. He may not know of the sporting excellence from performers such as Roger Maris, Ron Guidry, Rodney Richard, Tom Glavin, Eddie Murray, Don Mattingly, and Roberto Clemente. I do not support, also, the claim from Grant (1991, p. 7) that followers of cricket possess a greater sense of the history of their favourite game than the partisans of any other sport. Not unlike cricket lovers, I know that many lovers of baseball, basketball, and ice hockey do very readily provide lists of great moments in their sports.

I do believe—to use a cricketing term which has been borrowed by politicians and media analysts, at least in Britain—that cricket is a profound experience in which there is everything to play for. The profundity in playing for everything is something to which British Prime Minister, David Cameron, had to give his every consideration while tawdry detail of the phone hacking scandal linked to Rupert

Murdoch's News Corp was unfolding in summer 2011. This is a story that can be explored by using the figurative significance of cricket. I would not hesitate to state that the scandal has very close parallels to high level international cricket, not merely because Mr. Paul McMullan, once employed by the defunct NEWS OF THE WORLD claimed that Mr. Cameron is either an idiot or a liar or that he, McMullan, hid in Rebekah Brooks's garden and watched Mr. Cameron riding horses with her and other media tycoons. Rebekah Brooks is, of course, none other than the former NEWS INTERNATIONAL chief executive who quit her job in the heat of the scandal, was charged by London police, and found not-guilty of all charges, at the end of her trial.

The close parallels exist partly because the scandal involves two societies, England and Australia, that have literally been at each other's throats[7] during their battles for the much coveted Ashes at the Test Match level. They also exist because McMullan did make a direct comparative reference to the game while singing the praises of British scandal sheets, "red tops," when he uttered this statement to Canadian Broadcasting Corporation (CBC) correspondent, Susan Ormiston: "It's harder to get a story on a corrupt politician than it is to write for The Daily Telegraph some boring old gof [nonsense] about cricket." What an offence from McMullan who does not come close to befitting the persona of any leading cricketer—Brian Lara included!

In the words of New Yorker correspondent, Lane (2011, p. 28), McMullan, the man with a fuddled melancholy, former deputy features editor at NEWS OF THE WORLD, whistle—then trumpet—blower on phone-hacking, informed the British Broadcasting Corporation (BBC) that the hacking of messages on the phone of murdered British teenager, Milly Dowler, was "not such a big deal." His presence, that of a dishevelled character dressed in a stained white suit with tie askew below a despairing beard, is of someone wearing tufts of hair no comb would dare to engage. He is the one player in a drama, so adds Lane, acting without a trace of caution and confessing cheerfully to what he senses as wrongs while struggling to apprehend moments when he might have exceeded his brief.

The venerable cricketing connoisseurs, Messrs. John Arlott, Brian Johnston, Trevor Bailey, and especially the unique E.W. Swanton, long-serving distinguished cricket correspondent for the Telegraph, must have turned in their graves when McMullan issued his salvo against cricket. Goodness knows what Brian Johnston would have said about McMullan. He might well have plumbed the treasured depths of hilarity and treated the slight with one of his "leg-over" gems.

Be that as it may, it is parallelism—not gardening, gamesmanship, or rumpled resonance—which drew me like a magnet as soon as I had learnt that Rebekah Brooks was assessed by BBC News correspondent, Edward Stourton, on 15th July, 2011, as someone who was put on the back foot in the public eye. Stourton was, without question, making use of a cricketing term employed for describing the forced defensive play of batsmen.

Placed within a wider context of actual participation in a game of cricket at the Test Match level, the Stourton usage could not have been lost to acutely keen England followers of the sport in a compelling foreground at a time, mid July 2011, when India began a tour of the scepter'd isle. India, those followers would have known, was ranked the leading team in Test Match cricket, where they forced Australia—soundly beaten in consecutive Ashes series by England—on the figurative back foot. I shall deal with the cricketing and non-cricketing significance of the Brooks back foot position as a batsman once I have addressed myself to the agonising plight of other leading players such as that of the British Prime Minister placed in the role of a batsman and Mr. Rupert Murdoch, both batsman and fielder.

My initial pointer is to events that unfolded on 13th July, 2011, the day when there was a rare show of unity between the ruling Conservatives led by Mr. Cameron and the Labour opposition led by Mr. Ed Miliband. On that very day, BBC television alluded to an unprecedented collision of public opinion, politics, high finance, and the media. I should note that one such day did occur in the late nineteen-seventies at the very highest level of international cricket when another Australian media mogul, the flamboyant Mr. Kerry Packer, rocked the staid environs of Test Match cricket by luring some of the best cricketers from Australia, England, the West Indies, and South Africa to play cricket his way for huge sums of money.

To this day, some of those very Packer cricketers credit his move with allowing them to demand more money and getting it for playing Test Match cricket. Further, although they were absent from the Test Match scene for a brief period, some observers were afraid that form of the game would cease to exist. Test Match cricket did not die, but white balls, and coloured clothing introduced to cricket by Packer, are used in the short and very short forms of the game, the one day or fifty over game, the highest levels of which are, respectively, the immensely popular and hugely profitable cricket World Cup staged every four years and Twenty cricket or T-20.

What became known as the Packer circus is of far less significance than events of the 13th. On that day, I saw, among other things, a headline from BBC television, "EMPIRE UNDER FIRE." The reference was not to the British Empire but to the media conglomerate, News Corp, led by the "buccaneering" and "ruthless" Rupert, the former Oxford undergraduate who once displayed a bust of Karl Marx in his university lodging. This is the Australian who dominated the British media landscape in a manner not dissimilar to that in which domineering touring Australian Test Match teams demolished England.

What is not lost to me is the imagery evoked on that very day when Murdoch withdrew his bid for total ownership of the British satellite media organisation, British Sky Broadcasting (B Sky B), a highly lucrative and prosperous business which made a profit of one billion pounds in 2010. B Sky B generates huge sums of cash from its sports coverage, of which cricket is an integral part. Moreover, to the extent that he withdrew his bid, what does not escape me is that such a move triggers a picture of once highly aggressive leading Australian Test Match batsmen withdrawing towards the direction of the square leg umpire, rather than getting behind the line of the ball, in the face of menacingly hostile quick bowling from the likes of pacemen such as Harold Larwood and Frank "Typhoon" Tyson of England, Charlie Griffith, and Wes Hall of the West Indies.

Mr. Murdoch—unquestionably standing in searing heat and certainly not playing for team Britain—was also forced to keep fielding questions from a baying pack of Fleet Street interrogators. In addition, he issued an apology to the grieving relatives of the murdered teenager, Milly Dowler, one of countless alleged telephone hacking victims. The Dowler family solicitor, Mark Lewis, obviously echoing more than a Rupert Murdoch contrition, said: "He [Mr. Murdoch] was humbled to give a full and sincere apology to the Dowler family. We told him—the Dowler family told him—that his papers should lead the way, to set the standard of honesty and decency in the field and not what had gone on before." Mr. Murdoch also issued an additional apology in all the major national British newspapers.

While the ageing tycoon languished on the boundary ropes, a zestful Ed Miliband—keenly cognisant that every run he scored for team Britain counted—continued notching up boundaries past the very ropes alongside the veteran Australian who had to appear for a special Parliamentary inquiry. Late on the very day he had been subjected to a grilling, 19th July, 2011, Mr. Nicholas Wapshott, a senior editor of the *London Times*, literally once a broadsheet, one of the Murdoch papers, claimed: "He [Mr. Murdoch] looks as if someone has come across him with a cricket bat or baseball bat. He comes from Australia." The last occasion on which I thought a Test Match cricketer would come across another with a cricket bat was that on which I saw Pakistan star batsman, Javed Miandad, square off with leading Australian quick bowler, Dennis Lillee. Be that as it may, the Wapshott claim is a remarkably powerful echo of the deep enmity between England and Australia over the Ashes. When Wapshott also stated that Rupert Murdoch turned his back on the old British establishment from which his father, Sir Keith Murdoch, came he had mounted a very sturdy frame within which the profundity of that enmity can be encapsulated.

The most powerful of cricketing parallels emerged for me when I heard a remark on 13th July, 2011 from a BBC television correspondent who said that Mr. Cameron's fellow legislators (Members of Parliament, MP) in his Conservative Party feel he is "on the back foot while Ed Miliband is doing all the running." This, I have to state, is quite a claim from the correspondent. For me, it is like the fulcrum on which all other powerful facets of that July day stand: stinging rebuke of News Corp from former Prime Minister, Gordon Brown, who stated publicly that NEWS OF THE WORLD had hacked some of the most private forms of information about his family, words from an embattled Prime Minister, clever politicking from Mr. Miliband. Let me say that the connection between the back foot and running is an unmistakable cricketing link. Batsmen play both defensively and aggressively from the back foot. It is—I remind readers—not always productive, however. In another chapter, I shall be exploring the matter of back foot play in detail. Prime Minister Cameron on the back foot is not just an allusion to defensive play, in the context of the telephone hacking scandal, it is indicative, also, of what West Indians term "back-to-the-wall cricket." being played by a batsman who is back in his shell.

When a leading batsman in the position of a captain on a Test Match team, a position akin to that held by Mr. Cameron, is playing "back-to-the-wall" cricket," he is forced by dominant bowlers and excellent fielders on the opposing team to defend tenaciously and not score any runs or score very few runs. Interestingly, to the extent that Mr. Miliband was seen as doing all the running, he is a batsman who, unlike the captain, was not dominated by his fielding opponents, and he scored off both his front and back foot. While scoring in this manner he played assertively. It should not be difficult to reason that Mr. Miliband and Mr. Cameron, both leading political players, were batting for the same team, the British public, especially families of the deceased who passed away in horrific circumstances and whose telephones were allegedly hacked. Interestingly, Mr. Gordon Brown, whom Mr. Cameron replaced after the 2010 general election, speaking in the House of Commons on 13th July was addressing team British public not merely in the role of a former player, he was doing so to, in the role of a former captain rebuking News Corp.

The Miliband ploy coupled with the Brown rebuke is both embarrassing and damning to the Prime Minister, whom one seasoned British political observer, Peter Osborne, of The Daily Telegraph, a Conservative supporting quality broadsheet, assessed as being in deep trouble of his own making, "a sewer."

Cameron was, and remains, under fire not just for his naivete in that appointment [Andy Coulson] but for the ease with which he had mingled with members of News International; lips were pursued at his personal amity with Brooks, who was a neighbour of Cameron's, in Oxfordshire. (Her husband, a racehorse trainer, was educated at Eton, as was the Prime Minister. Nothing suspicious about that, but it does oil the wheels) (Lane 2011, p. 26).

Outside Westminster immediately after the parliamentary debate on the 13th, Mr. Miliband told team British public: "This [the Murdoch withdrawal of a bid for B Sky B] is a victory for people up and down the country who have been appalled by the revelations about phone hacking. I would have thought it beyond belief that Mr. Murdoch could—when this criminal investigation was going on—expand his stake in the British media." For his part, Mr. Cameron, who deemed allegations about hacking disgusting, said that the decision to hire—as his communications director - Andy Coulson, a decision for which he took full responsibility, was his and his alone. He added that he had made a conscious choice to give someone "who had screwed up a second chance." Coulson was, of course, charged by Scotland Yard over the phone hacking.

That chance, the Prime Minister noted, was not working. With much more than echoes of his embattled posture, Mr. Cameron claimed: "The truth is we have all been in this together. Yes, including me." He announced the launching of two far-reaching inquiries into the affair and underlined the enormous seriousness of his disposition by reacting to the Murdoch withdrawal in stating publicly he thought it was the right decision for News Corp and the country. Takeovers, he continued, must not constitute the priority at News Corp. The priority had to be one of sorting out its problems. In some of his boldest and most courageous declaratives he told a packed—sometimes raucous—House of Commons that what it and all Britain has to confront frankly was a disgraceful episode, a firestorm engulfing parts of the British media, sectors of the police, and, unquestionably, sectors of the political system's ability to deal with the storm. He stressed that however high or low the perpetrators at News Corp may be, they must not merely be brought to justice, they must, also, "have no future role in running a media company in our country." Root and branch at News International, the British arm of News Corp, in its entirety, he insisted, must be changed.

So, on a wicket very unfriendly to batsmen forced on to the back foot, one big question was whether skipper David Cameron would survive. Mr. Cameron, who cut short a foreign trip in the heat of the crisis, would have known that representatives of what a Labour predecessor of his, Harold Wilson, once dubbed the Tory Press had called for his resignation. David Cameron—not unlike past England Test Match captains—must be an avid student of history. He could not have been unaware that the call girl and Vassal spy scandal of the early nineteen-sixties forced Sir Harold Macmillan—later Lord Stockton—to quit his Prime Ministerial post. Mr. Cameron could not have been unaware of the Westland helicopter issue which engulfed and weakened the inflexible "Iron Lady," Baroness Thatcher. Lane was thus quite in order when he posed the query whether the scandal could not just have corroded, but also brought down a government.

Let me add that when a British Prime Minister truncates a foreign trip in circumstances such as the telephone hacking mess, one of the matters he has to ponder is: does the sand beneath my feet keep shifting constantly while I must walk horizontally beyond the shoreline of an ocean where uncontrollable waves keep moving against me? This is the very matter which England Test Match captains who were on the verge of suffering humiliating losses during the summers of 1950, 1966,

1976, 1980, 1984, 1988, and 1989 had to ponder. This same matter—albeit in different playing conditions—will be central to my exploration of the leadership from West Indies Test Match captain, Brian Charles Lara.

It would not be unreasonable to state that player Murdoch had to consider the foregoing query. Further, what was the disposition to the state of play from Australian/American batsman, Murdoch, dubbed by a competitor as "just a bloke with a printing press" and no longer citizen Kane? What was the posture of the man who once said: "Everything has to... end sometime. We just can't leave the clock standing still any longer." From which foot and for which team was he batting? Was he doing any running? What was the placement of the Aussie player/interloper who had moved high tech computer printing devices into Wapping, London, in daring night time stroke making off his front foot, part of a bold and successful move against Fleet Street trade union titans which left them in a stupor from which they never recovered?

To members of a Parliamentary committee examining the intricacies of the hacking affair, a deeply shaken Mr. Murdoch stated: "I would just like to say in just one sentence. This is the most humble day of my life." I have no doubt that he was put firmly on the back foot. I am convinced that he had his back to the wall. Clearly, he was doing no batting for team British public whose voracious appetite—rather paradoxically—for the constancy of salacious detail in his NEWS OF THE WORLD and SUN publications swelled his bulging financial sacks. This is the very kind of spectator devouring of spoils from "bull dog journalism" that is not dissimilar to what some cricketing observers dub, 'new cricket,' the colourful spectacle of that cavalier slogging which overwhelms wildly cheering fans supping on the shortened versions of the sport, the limited over one day game which reaches its most wildly intoxicating phase every four years in the cricket world cup last staged in Australia and New Zealand (early 2015).[8] He was doing no running and was on a highly beleaguered team.

Like Mr. Murdoch, the humbled team Britain captain, Prime Minister, David Cameron, issued an unqualified apology to the British public. With the apology rendered he seemed well prepared to play another crucial game when he had to face principal opponent, Ed Miliband, during the course of the May 2015 general election in Britain. The News Corp scandal clearly did not dog him then, 7th May, Election Day, and although the British economy did not see robust growth under his initial stewardship in a minority British Government with Nick Clegg as his deputy, Ed Miliband still lost the election to him. So, Mr. Cameron continued to be a high level participant on the pitch—literally and figuratively—and knew that the "windblown" mildly eccentric London Mayor, Mr. Boris Johnson, who won his seat on 7th, would be a good pitch participant and partner to him. Was Boris Johnson really such a participant!

Both Johnson and Cameron know that cricket, the game of glorious uncertainty, is a remarkably absorbing exercise; when paired with politics the political game does become a game of inglorious cruelty. An ashen face, Ed Miliband got to know that all too well during the early morning hours on 8th May, immediately after it had become obvious to him that Scottish nationalism had overwhelmed his Labour Party in the far north and the expected gains for Labour within England did not materialise. Such was part of the business-like public account he offered for the Labour trouncing. Rightfully, it was David Cameron—presumably on the back foot—who called the election.

In cricketing terms, it was his call. Ed Miliband—assumed to be doing all the running—wasted no time in setting off, but was stranded in the middle of the pitch, way out of his ground, and was out, run out. It is David Cameron who got the crucial support from team Britain on 7th May—not Ed Miliband, whom some political pandits claimed could not maintain his position of Labour Party leader. The beneficial impact from cricketing glorious uncertainty did not pass his way. He was overwhelmed by inglorious cruelty. He did relinquish his leadership post, a decision which stood in stark contrast to what seemed like the achievement from David Cameron who claimed the morning after that Britain was on the brink of something special and can be made greater still.

That very bold prediction in his declarative came under very close scrutiny barely into a year of his second tenure. It was early April 2016 when a startling worldwide revelation through what became widely known as the Panama Papers was made about secretive financial arrangements involving very rich people and political leaders. One of those rich individuals was Mr. Cameron's late father, a stupendously wealthy British citizen. It took David Cameron more than four days to admit that he did benefit from financial transactions made by his father, transactions concealed for years by a Panamanian law firm named in the Panama Papers.

He was, of course, questioned in Parliament under the very watchful eyes and keen ears of Mr. Miliband's replacement, Mr. Jeremy Corbyn, a so-called far left of centre labourite whose ideals and polices are very close to those of Mr. Miliband's late father, Dr. Ralph Miliband, the hugely insightful leading sociologist with a clear Marxist bent. David Cameron was questioned outside Parliament where he denied, initially, that he was a beneficiary from his father's dealings kept secret by the law firm. It was not until Friday, 8th April, 2016, he stated explicitly that he had been just such a beneficiary and claimed outside Parliament that the week was not a good week for him. The following day, 9th April, 2016, there was a massive London protest from which came a chorus of chants that he resign. Whether he did so was, of course, his choice.

In my view, from a cricketing standpoint, there was a big appeal for a Leg Before Wicket (L.B.W.) dismissal. He, like Ms. Brooks, was out plumb L.B.W. He may well not have foreseen the delivery onto which he failed to get his bat. Nevertheless, the man looking for good partners on the pitch, in the SPIRIT, not merely of fair play, but very fair play, also, of which he had to have known in his Eton days, had a huge obligation to walk, even if the ruling umpire did not raise an index finger: he has known the written and unwritten Laws in the game, cricket, for a very long time. Remaining at the literal and figurative batting crease, in my view, constituted a besmirching of the game not dissimilar to the besmirching which emanated from England player, Stuart Broad, during the course of a Test Match between England and Australia. This is an appropriate juncture at which I can offer readers, via implicature, an opportunity to see some of the beauty in cricket.

None of that beauty flowed the Cameron way, more than just two months later. On 26th June, 2016, skipper, captain, David Cameron made a public announcement outside Downing street, presumably after he had spoken with the most senior sovereign and selector, that he was leaving his Prime Ministerial post, as soon as a replacement could be found. From a cricketing standpoint he was not bowled, caught, L.B.W., or stumped. He had not handled the ball deliberately or trod accidentally onto the stumps. He was out comprehensively going for a run that was never there. Most painfully, while only a few centimetres from the batting crease at the bowler's end, but without a grounded bat, he was run out to a robustly riveting, as well as forcefully flat, arousingly artful and amazingly accurate return[9] to the bowler's end from whom: that windblown fieldsman deep on the extra cover boundary, one Boris Johnson, to a certain Sir Ian Botham, a seasoned old salt of an apprentice cricketer at Lord's!

This time Cameron did not wait for the ruling umpire well positioned to admire Johnson's return right over the bails and adjudicate in regard to the batsman's posture. He turned straight in the direction of the pavilion, tucked his bat under his right arm, simply wrenched his gloves off, and up the pavilion steps he ambled. There were no cheers from the members for a long and glorious innings while he began to make his way through the long room. He, of course, knew he had lost a very crucial game. This was a match in which he must have assumed there was everything to play for, a battle which he said he approached in the only way he knew. He had fought with passion, heart and soul, to keep Britain in the European Union, but when the state of play was examined he lost and made a decision that another skipper was needed for the task of helping MAGNA BRITANNIA write itself into another chapter within the historical record.

In political terms, Boris Johnson was not on David Cameron's side, during the deeply divisive campaign leading up to a referendum on whether Britain should leave the European Union. Ex-cricketer, Sir John Major, had held up one end on Cameron's behalf, but to no avail. When the votes had been counted, a slim majority of British citizens sided with Botham and Johnson to leave the Union. Clearly, David Cameron, who had lost face, felt he had no option other than resigning. His was an inglorious exit from a contest full of cruel and harsh uncertainties. This type of departure is not alien to England Test Match cricket, surely something about which Cameron had to have been well aware. In the age of televisual glare, passion might be good for politics but cricket, that craft which Thomas Lord bequeathed to more than a few quarters of what is now a confused world, is both a tremendous torment and torrid trial for the temperamental.

Cameron's official departure on 13th July, 2016, took place earlier than the time he had announced publicly: he had stated he wanted to leave in October, 2016; within an oddly unexpected unfolding of events a certain conservative, Mr. Michael Gove, close anti-E.U. ally of Mr. Johnson's, abandoned his partner, rather shamelessly, in an effort to replace Cameron. In the immediate aftermath of the fracture, Mr. Johnson announced he would not seek to replace David Cameron. It is Johnson who ultimately secured some solace out of the ashes, for he became a senior cabinet figure in a new administration where there was no immediate place for a somewhat pompous Gove, a Cameron cabinet colleague. On the very afternoon when Cameron left Downing Street, where he was replaced by former Home Secretary, Mrs. Theresa May, the new Prime Minister appointed Johnson to the much coveted post of Foreign Secretary.

Thus, Boris Johnson, in that sordid spring of 2016, joined a sorority and fraternity line of Foreign Office luminaries, among whom Anthony Eden, Lord Douglas-Home, Michael Stewart, Francis Pym, the colourful and hugely eccentric George Brown, James Callaghan, Margaret Beckett, David Miliband, the youthfully zestful brother of Ed Miliband, and unquestionably the lordly banker, Peter Carrington, stand prominently. Quite similarly to Test Match cricket, Boris Johnson, politician, and Ian Botham, Test Match cricketer, can lay claim to an eminent tradition of players from India, England, Australia, New Zealand, South Africa, Pakistan, West Indies, and Sri Lanka, with which some of the deified can be associated: Donald George Bradman, Garfield St. Aubrun Sobers, John Berry Hobbs, Sydney Francis Barnes, Walter Reginald Hammond, Isaac Vivian Alexander Richards, Leonard Hutton, Barry Anderson Richards, Victor Thomas Trumper, George Alphonso Headley, Raymond Russell Lindwall, Sunil Manohar Gavaskar, Everton de Courcy Weekes, Clyde Leopold Walcott, Frank Mortimer Maglinne Worrell, Richard John Hadlee, Herbert Sutcliffe, Hugh Joseph Tayfield, Rohan "Babulal" Kanhai, Javed

Miandad, Ian Michael Chappell, Wasim Akram, Michael Anthony Holding, Learie Nicholas Constantine, Clive Hubert Lloyd, Clarence Victor Grimmett, Curtly Elconn Lynwall Ambrose, William Harold Ponsford, Lancelot Richard Gibbs, Stanley Joseph McCabe, Pinnaduwage Aravinda de Silva, and Alan Falconer Kippax, of course.

May, a Prime Minister seen as "batting for Britain" in the tough 2018 Brexit negotiations, like her husband, a cricket lover, has the same last name as an England Test Match notable, Peter Barker Howard May for whom cricketing experts the world over have very high regard, mainly because of his batting ability and leadership skill. Many a West Indian shall long remember the tremendous fourth wicket stand between Peter May and Colin Cowdrey, in 1957, during the course of the first Test Match at Edgbaston, Birmingham, where the England pair scored a mammoth 411 runs. The May contribution was an unbeaten 285.

> He was an effortless timer of the ball and his approach to batting, as indeed to all his affairs, was disciplined and fastidious. Gentle, good-mannered, and self-effacing in character, he always had a hard, almost ruthless streak as a cricketer—very much an amateur with a professional approach (Martin Jenkins 1996, p. 309).

Theresa May, who fits the assessment in the first Martin-Jenkins statement, might well not have needed to be self-effacing or, for that matter, ruthless. She needed far more than discipline and fastidiousness in dealing with the rest of Europe over Britain's exit from the European Union, where she was required to play an innings of far greater length that the one at Edgbaston in which Peter May featured.

While the placid Edgbaston wicket was very unresponsive to the spinning complexities of that very tricky West Indies pair, Sonny Ramadhin and Alfred Valentine, performing on European turf for a home crowd very concerned about Britain's sovereignty was never going to be easy. Peter May, who followed the very astute Len Hutton in the role of England Test Match captain, was a prime beneficiary of his predecessor's great skill in removing the literal and figurative shine off the new ball delivered by fearsome opponents. Captain Cameron could not even give himself the opportunity to take the shine off any new ball. Some players on his team worked diligently to deny him any such opportunity. It is Theresa May and Theresa May alone in the presence of a concerned home crowd who had the unenviable task of taking the shine off the new ball Europe was delivering.

By mid-December 2018, it was all too obvious that she was failing and failing fast in such a role: both Donald Tusk, Jean Claude Junker, as well as, Angela Merkel, that E.U. powerhouse from the Chancellor's desk, were emphatic that the departure deal which May had accepted would not be changed. Having discovered that several in her own conservative party were unhappy with the arrangement, she appealed, to no avail, to her European partners for amendment. Worse was to come. Perhaps sensing that she could not prevail in a House of Commons confidence vote in regard to the deal, she postponed the vote but could not prevent a move from her party's 1922 committee to trigger a confidence vote among her conservative colleagues. That vote did take place; even though she survived (200 conservatives voted in her favour, but 117 were against) she stated that she would not lead the party into the next general election.

Clearly bruised and battered by hostile bowling from many a quarter, despite what came to be known as a BACK-STOP provision in the deal pertaining to migration from the Republic of Ireland to Britain, she would, of course, have been expected by her conservative parliamentary colleagues to time her exit in a manner least damaging to the party's chances of winning the next election. That exit came in early June, 2019, shortly after the Trump state visit during which the braggart bigot expressed a wish to meet friend, Boris, who could find no time to talk in person, presumably, because friend was busy campaigning to replace May and, perhaps, understood that a meeting with Trump would be impolitic. Surely, friend had to have known that such a meeting would have constituted a breach of political etiquette, a breach Trump was too uneducated to comprehend: the visiting racist had already launched a tirade against the London Mayor. If cricket is a useful guide—perhaps important reminder—to what has unfolded around her, let me point out that a BACK-STOP is far more useless than the crumpled paper from which information about it has been circulated: at the very lowest levels of cricket among school boy teams with, and against which, I played, BACK-STOPS or BYES-KEEPERS were placed behind wicket keepers to prevent extras, chiefly byes, from accruing to batting teams, as a result of the wicket keepers' failure to gather deliveries behind the wicket. At higher levels, even in school boy cricket, wicket keepers are usually excellent enough to prevent extras in the form of byes from making up noticeable parts of total runs scored. BACK-STOPS in cricket are some of the clearest indications of team weakness, as well as strategic acumen.

Having pondered the parallels and perils of passion, politicking, and telephone hacking, I accept, without any reservation the words of former cricket loving Australian Prime Minister Sir Robert Menzies: cricket is a reflective game that, above all, lends itself to writing in beautiful flexible English. While I lay no claim to producing beautiful, flexible language, I hope that I have pointed to what is reflective about the sport, this game that has been played for over a quarter of a millennium and began with curved bats, two stump wickets, and scorers notching up runs on their tally of sticks (Green 2003, p. 17).

Those who want more than the reflective can turn to Arlott (1976, p. 169-187), who describes cricket as an 11-a- side bat-and-ball game played mostly in English speaking societies. He adds, quite correctly, that the main centres of the first-class game are England, Australia, South Africa, the Anglo-Caribbean—I include Guyana—New Zealand, India, and Pakistan. Today, of course, Afghanistan, Bangladesh, Zimbabwe, and Sri Lanka must be included, for these places and the others play the game at very high levels. Arlott also states that at a lower level cricket is established in Scotland, Ireland, Wales, Bermuda, Fiji, Argentina, Hong Kong, Singapore, Denmark, Holland, Kenya, Tanzania, Uganda, Nigeria, Ghana, Liberia, Gambia, and Sierra Leone. I am aware, also, that the game is played in Swaziland, the USA, and Canada.

No one should take the references I have made so far as attempts to render accounts which bring readers great familiarity. I would not even be one of the last to accept that such a goal is unattainable. It is with such awareness uppermost in my mind that I offer:

Cricket, which has evolved over several centuries, is a complicated game, and those who are not familiar with it as part of their environment often find it difficult to follow. It has been described as 'casting a ball at three straight sticks and defending the same with a fourth,' but in addition to defending the 'sticks' (stumps which form the wicket), the batsman attempts to score a run (the unit of scoring) or runs. The winning team is that with the greater aggregate of runs in a completed match, which may last from a few hours to as much as six days in some Test (international) matches (Arlott 1976, p. 169).

According to Eastaway (1992, p. 114), followers of cricket view it as a recreation and a religion. They do not merely watch it, they use it also as a basis of incorporating it into their conduct. Cricket lovers appreciate the artistry, as well as physical and intellectual challenges linked to playing it. It is a metaphor for life. I suppose a good effort to offer the figurative can be located in a remark from the cricketing aficionado Kilburn (1960, p. viii), who alludes to a link between the game and the Welfare State. Writing about what he assesses as presenting the privileges of watching a great deal of cricket across the globe, sharing historic occasions, as well as establishing friendships and asking for honest evaluation of the presentation in return, he states that the reciprocity will contribute enormously towards accomplishment of the Welfare State.

One of the best known cricket lovers the world over who understood the link between literal and figurative senses of the game, as well as the necessity of the Welfare State in his war-ravaged society, and indeed all of western Europe virtually destroyed via conflict, is, doubtless, the "voice of cricket," English poet, and wine connoisseur. I am referring, of course, to that very expert writer/analyst, none other than the uniquely authoritative Arlott himself, whom compatriot Johnston (1988, p. 165) rightly assesses as the person that did more than anyone else to spread the gospel of cricket—taking it to mansions, cottages, crofts, mud huts, and, perhaps, igloos.

A very strong effort to spread the gospel and, of course, reduce unfamiliarity took place in September 1996 (Toronto, Canada) when Messrs. Ravi Shastri (India), Geoff Boycott (England), and Ian Chappell (Australia), three former cricketers at the highest level of the game, Test Match cricket, used the backdrop of a baseball stadium, cricket clubhouse, and Hockey Hall of Fame to inform, mainly their North American audience, about cricket. I offer their remarks in full:

Chappell: *The Sky Dome here in Toronto is one of the most famous roof stadiums in the world. It's the home of the Toronto Blue Jays who were the first non-American baseball team to win the World Series. That was back in 1992. Well, with the roof on, obviously no problems with rain. Baseball and cricket: well, there's a lot of similarities. The balls, for instance: they're about the same size and, roughly, the same weight. But in baseball there is no spot for the blocker. So, I am very sorry Geoffrey Boycott. There's no place for you as a bunt specialist.*

Boycott: *Thanks Ian. Well, whether it's blocking at cricket or bunting at baseball, I don't think I really need this [a baseball bat] here. Will I? I'm here for the cricket, because we think baseball is a bit of a girl's game in England. We call it rounders. And cricket in Toronto: what a place! India versus Pakistan—great emotion and passion, great rivalries. I've seen both teams in England, this year. I thought India disappointed. They didn't play up to their best but they've always got Tendulkar and Ganguly with Prasad and Srinath—great bowlers. But Pakistan—what a team! They outplayed England. They're playing well together. They're well marshalled and captained under Wasim Akram. I think I've got to put my finger on them to do well and, possibly, just pip India. Now, here's my colleague, Ravi Shastri. He's in a dressing room.*

Shastri: *Funnily enough, Geoffrey, I'm in a changing room but it's not a cricketing one. It's an ice hockey changing room and I'm here at the Hall of Fame in Toronto. And as everybody knows here, it's one of the biggest sports played in this part of the world. But like you, I'm here for the cricket between India and Pakistan and having* *played against the Pakistanis on numerous occasions, let me tell you one thing. There's always a contest, when you play Pakistan and these five matches are going to be no different. Pakistan and India have played a lot against each other over the last couple of months. India won the big one in Bangalore, the World Cup quarter final. Pakistan got one back in Singapore and, now, the two teams are at full strength. Pakistan have a fully fit Wasim Akram as captain and the Indians have a new captain at the helm, Sachin Tendulkar. And he seems to be improving by the day. So, we are in for a cracking contest over the next few days.*

A cracking five game contest there was, indeed, between India and Pakistan from which Pakistan emerged victorious (late summer and early autumn 1996). Before I get to a description of matters directly relevant to the five games in that 1996 contest, it would not be out of place for me to let my readers in Japan, Canada, and especially, the USA know that the Boycott reference to rounders does have both a literary and historical grounding.

Americans can, of course, ruminate over this observation which I am certain has a strong basis in profound exploratory work:

Baseball, long regarded as the American national game, evolved directly from the old English game of ROUNDERS. The myth that baseball was spontaneously invented by Abner Doubleday in 1839 at Cooperstown, New York, has no basis in fact. The game was played in simple form under the name 'base ball' in England and America as early as the eighteenth century (Arlott 1976, p. 50).

Rounders, which has features in common with baseball, is an outdoor bat-and-ball game best known as an impromptu leisure activity in which two teams of nine players participate. It is played widely in British schools and some adult and youth club leagues (Arlott 1976, pp. 752-753). May I add that some American students of baseball may be well aware that the term, home run, was used in cricket well before it had entered the baseball realm?

Arlott notes that the earliest known literary reference to base-ball is a (1744) account rendered in the publication, *A LITTLE PRETTY POCKET BOOK*, by John Newbery, which contains a woodcut of the game and a verse under the name, 'Base-ball.' Later, (1829), a description of the rules was contained in the once immensely popular *THE BOY'S OWN BOOK* by W. Clarke. Newbery's verse for "base ball" is:

The Ball once struck off,

Away flies the Boy

To the next destin'd Post,

And then Home with Joy.

This verse is associated with his example of a moral lesson:

Thus Britons for Lucre

Fly over the Main;

But with Pleasure transported,

Return back again.

While writing about something that has become so commonplace in North America, "A Sticky Wicket," the well-known British literary figure, P.G. Wodehouse, provides an account of part of an exchange between Mr. Bingley Crocker, an American new to London, and his English butler Bayliss, who had never seen a baseball game. After having reacted to Bayliss's lack of knowledge by telling the butler, 'Then Bill, you haven't lived,' Mr. Crocker proceeded to explain the American game with the aid of cutlery, breakfast ware, and bread rolls.

When the Crocker explanation was over, P.G. Wodehouse offered the turn of events:

'Quite an interesting game,' said Bayliss. 'But I find, now, that you have explained it, sir, that it is familiar to me, though I have always known it under another name. It is played a great deal in this country.'

Mr. Crocker started to his feet.

'Is it? And I've been five years without finding it out! When's the next game scheduled?'

'It is known in England as rounders, sir. Children play it with a soft ball and a racket, and derive considerable enjoyment from it. I have never heard of it before as a pastime for adults.'

Two shocked eyes stared into the butler's face.

'Children?' The word came in a whisper. 'A racket?'

'Yes, sir'

'You-you didn't say a soft ball?'

'Yes, sir'

A sort of spasm seemed to convulse Mr. Crocker. He had lived five years in England, but not till this moment had he realised to the full how utterly alone he was in an alien land.

Americans can take very great pride in the fact that their imprint is marked solidly at the unique Lord's cricket ground, where refurbishment of the Mound Stand is owed to substantial financial contribution from Mr. John Paul Getty. It is Mr. Getty who also bought the great and weighty Bible of cricket statistics, *The Wisden Almanac*. It is he, as well, whose name and huge investment sit behind the exquisitely crafted cricket ground at Wormsley.[10]

Great interest, pride, tremendous enjoyment, profound shock, and deafening loudness—not whispers—were some of the many significant features in the 1996 TORONTO SAHARA SERIES, cricket matches between India and Pakistan. Ardent followers of international cricket may well remember that in those games, staged away from the sub-continent because of continual political tension between the South Asian neighbours, the two teams (each with two wins in the previous four games) seemed evenly matched when they played the fifth game in that 1996 series, which Pakistan clinched in the fifth encounter. All matches were beamed live via satellite to a few million in Britain. Significantly, they were seen live by hundreds of millions of cricket crazy fans in India, Pakistan, Sri Lanka, and Bangladesh.

Further, of no small significance to ardent followers of high level international cricket are these facts: the games were not played at the Sky Dome. They took place at a ground well over two hundred years old, the Toronto Cricket Club Ground, the best with natural playing conditions in Canada. This is a place steeped in cricket history. According to Brown (1988, pp. 17-18), a New York Club, St. George's, appeared unexpectedly at the Toronto Cricket Club to play a game in (1844) against Canada. Five thousand spectators were on hand for the game in which they placed side bets amounting to $100,000. Canada was victorious. In (1846) spectators witnessed another contest between the two teams, which had to be abandoned.

In those days, it was legitimate under the Laws of cricket for a batsman to physically charge an opposing bowler waiting for a catch. In that (1846) game, a United States bowler was waiting to take a catch off a ball struck by a Canadian batsman who charged the bowler to the ground. A major argument between the teams ensued, the American threw the ball at the batsman, and the game ended without a result. Could a cricketing contest be more cracking!

Perhaps. During the course of another SAHARA SERIES staged in the nineteen nineties at the very Toronto venue, I and others who were covering the games watched spellbound while frontline Pakistan Test Match star batsman Inzamam-ul-Haq left his batting crease at the end of one over and proceeded—bat in hand—rather briskly to the terrace just behind the cover point position, where he dealt several blows with that bat to a spectator. The game stopped for some time, but unlike the events which unfolded in 1846 it was not abandoned.

Once the contest had been completed and the regularly scheduled post-game press conference took place, the Pakistan captain, Wasim Akram, stated that his player had been provoked and taunted repeatedly by the spectator. Subsequently, I asked an official of Trans World International (TWI), the British media organisation beaming proceedings to the sub-continent, for details of the incident. It is he who gave me a description of what I saw as some of the most provocatively vile forms of abuse hurled by the spectator at Inzamam, whom he added found it impossible to suppress his disgust. A few years before Inzamam had wielded the willow, (August, 1996), Canada and the United States met at the same ground for the (151st) Anniversary of the Canada-USA international series, which Canada won without any incident on or off the field.

The manners and Laws of cricket have long since changed and, I emphasise, changed. International cricketers, not always dressed in white, can now challenge certain decisions of umpires; in Test Matches substitutes can bat. In 1996, however, when India and Pakistan met for the first time on Canadian soil, the games were not played by men dressed in gaudy coloured clothing. Unlike what currently occurs in high level international cricket, the umpires' decisions were final. Batsmen could not challenge their decisions, and there were no such things as television replays, the accuracy of which was judged by a third umpire who could use his interpretation to overrule umpires on the field of play. A match referee with full view of television camera images strategically positioned off the field could be called upon to examine and mete out penalties to players whose on-field conduct was damaging to the SPIRIT and Laws of cricket.

Three highly experienced former Test Match cricketers were on hand, also, to name a player for the Man-Of-The-Match Award, after each contest. The judges were Sir Garfield Sobers (West Indies), Mr. Ian Chappell (Australia), and Mr. Geoffrey Boycott (England). After the completion of the series, they chose—in the presence of Sir Clyde Walcott—Chairman of the world governing body for cricket, the International Cricket Council (ICC), Indian leg spinner, Anil Kumble, as the Man Of The Series.

ENDNOTES

1 *I became aware of this quirk while conversing with Dr. John Mallea, Professor of Sociology in Education (Ontario Institute for Studies in Education).*

2 *I heard these words while watching a PBS Newshour telecast.*

3 *With my eyes and ears affixed to television coverage while watching the experts convey results for the British general election in early May, 2015, I heard more than one polling analyst use the term, EVERYTHING TO PLAY FOR. These were British Broadcasting Corporation experts who would have - of course - grown up with more than a cursory awareness about cricket. Well away from Britain, in what was once a far flung former Dominion territory, Canada, I read a caption, "STATES OF PLAY," in a respectable publication, The Globe And Mail (16th May, 2015) about the autumn general election in Canada that same year when the incumbent Conservatives led by Mr. Harper were roundly routed by a re-energised Liberal Party headed by Mr. Justin Trudeau.*

4 *The Manchester encounter was recalled by Sky Sports telecaster, Mr. Tony Greig, in early 1990 while he was watching an England team wince and wilt in the face of more bouncers from West Indies on Caribbean soil.*

5 *The statement attributed to Harlold Pinter comes from Martin-Jenkins (1996, p. 328).*

6 *I have taken the description attributed to Sir Robert Menzies from Martin-Jenkins (1996, p. 94).*

7 *This is not an exaggeration or fanciful reference: for many decades England and Australian quick bowlers have resorted to using bouncers, quite dangerous deliveries, which fly past the heads of opposing batsmen, some of whom have been intimidated. Whether Australian batsmen were intimidated in the summer 2019 Ashes series by England quick bowler, Jofra Archer, the man "with genuine pace", is a matter the experts will be eager to reveal.*

8 *At the time of writing I was well aware that 2019 was another world cup year. The venue: England.*

9 *My exaggeration here is, unquestionably, adapted from John Arlott, who offers his own unique assessment of returns from Clive Hubert Lloyd, the greatest among the few excellent cover point fieldsman in modern Test Match cricket.*

10 *My reference to Getty is derived from the writing of Martin-Jenkins (1996).*

8th INNINGS
BRIAN LARA ON THE
BOUNDARY OF CRICKETING
RESPECTABILITY

B
rian Charles Lara has participated in many a cracking contest, not just against India, Pakistan, and Australia, he has been involved also in such contests against England at the "Cathedral of Cricket," Lord's cricket ground, home of the Marylebone Cricket Club (MCC). Any profound exploration of the Brian Lara international cricket presence would be incomplete if such examination did not include a very significant gaze at the imposing stature that is Lord's. Appropriately, it is to the St. John's Wood location that I turn before providing some of the best exemplars within and beyond cricket fields, exemplars in whose company I can find no place for Lara.

The MCC and Lord's have been linked to high level cricket for over two-and-a-quarter centuries. Lord's was founded by an entrepreneur, Thomas Lord. Born on 23rd November, 1755 in the market town, Thirsk, Yorkshire, he was believed to have come from a family which enjoyed considerable prosperity but fell on difficult times (Green 2003, p. 21). Green adds that romantic legend portrays some members of the Lord family as Roman Catholics that had been deprived of their land holdings for having given backing to the Jacobite Rebellion (1745-1746) led by Charles Edward Stuart, the Young Pretender. The Rebellion was, of course, crushed at Culloden. While it is certain that Bonnie Prince Charlie came through the North of England as far south as Derby in 1745, there is, alas, no firm evidence to support any involvement on the part of the Lord family in the Jacobite cause (Green 2003, p. 21). I have, nevertheless, heard BBC cricket correspondent, Christopher Martin-Jenkins describe Thomas Lord as the son of a Roman Catholic yeoman who lost most of his wealth owing to the backing he gave to the Stuart rising of 1745. Lord grew up in a Norfolk town, Diss, and settled in the St. Marylebone area of London, where he became a highly successful wine merchant and joined the Church of England. He got to know such English patrician cricket enthusiasts as Lord Winchilsea and the Duke of Richmond, and joined a cricket club, the White Conduit Cricket Club, made up of other English patricians that employed him to bowl.

Acting on advice from the Duke of Richmond and Lord Winchilsea, so states Martin-Jenkins, he opened a ground where the White Conduit Club merged with another in (1787) to form the Marylebone Cricket Club (MCC). At the time he took up residence in a house on the Marylebone Road and with his entrepreneurial spirit leased a nearby property consisting of seven acres of ground. He set up a pub through which those who wanted to watch cricket had to pass and pay him a club fee, a break with the English tradition of people watching cricket on a village green at no cost. One year later (1788), Lord was compelled by building developers to move the MCC to St. John's Wood, another London location, where nobleman and gentleman of the club would continue playing. Only three years later, however, the

British Parliament ordered that a canal, the Regent's canal, should pass through the new location. It was not until [1814] that Thomas Lord rented a new ground for the sum of one hundred pounds annually.

Lord's is, doubtless, overflowing with history and tradition, among which is the annual cricket match between two of Britain's oldest and most famous public schools, Eton and Harrow. Green writes that the first such meeting (1805) is the oldest contest in the Lord's fixture list. Batting at number nine in this match was none other than the Harrow pupil that went on to become one of the world's finest poets, Lord Byron. While recording his memory of the match in what must now be a highly treasured missive kept in the Harrow archives, Byron, whom Green reasons was inspired more by poetic licence than any desire for factual accuracy, wrote: "We have played the Eton and were most confoundedly beat, however it was some comfort to me that I got 11 notches the 1st innings and 7 the 2nd." The scorebook, an Eton possession, "does not seem to support the version of events which Lord Byron gave" (Green 2003, p. 30). Another part of the Lord's tradition which began in 1806 and ended in 1962 was made up of annual matches between Gentlemen and Players. Green notes that the discontinuation of what he terms "this great and historic fixture" was unavoidable, as a result of abolition from first class cricket of amateur status for cricketers.

In dealing with the Lord's tradition, it would be a cardinal sin to omit reference to something which has to be a majestically moving experience for every cricketer at the very highest level of the game, Test Match cricket. That experience is walking through what is famously known as the LONG ROOM, especially if a player has scored a splendid hundred or completed a superb bowling spell. Batsmen, particularly some of those who score hundreds on their first appearance at Lord's, George Headley, Allan Rae, Clyde Walcott, Charlie Davis, Bernard Julien [West Indies], Saurav Ganguly, Dilip Vengsarkar [India], know the experience all too well. The LONG ROOM is the place players must go through in full view of club members sedately seated before walking onto the ground. It is a part of Lord's former Australian captain, Richie Benaud, says makes an indelible impression on the memory of most cricketers. Test Match cricketers at Lord's, Benaud adds, are aware that all the great players have already been there and the current ones do get the sense that despite any great excellence from them, such display might not be classified in so sparkling a manner as that of predecessors.

While hosting a special edition of the BBC World Service programme *SPORTS INTERNATIONAL* to commemorate the bicentenary of Lord's (1988), the Corporation correspondent, and President of the MCC in 2012, Christopher Martin-Jenkins, had this to say:

MCC is unique with eighteen thousand members and many more waiting years and even decades to be accepted as members. A private club which once administered first class cricket in the United Kingdom still makes and guards the laws of the game and provides the chairman and secretary of the International Cricket Conference [ICC][1]—standing almost above the commercial hurly burly of modern Test cricket to watch over the spirit of the game, to foster it in as many countries as possible, and to encourage the young, especially in Britain, to learn the pleasures and traditions of the best loved of all the sporting past times which remain one of Britain's greatest legacies of the days when Britannia ruled the waves. MCC was the second highly influential cricket club of England, almost immediately, taking on, from Hambledon in Hampshire, the position of the premier club and retaining it to this day.

In those days of British rule it was not out of place for notables such as Sir Pelham 'Plum' Warner, England Test Match captain, the very "revered dean of Cricket's Cathedral [Lord's] and Cricket's gentil knight" (Martin-Jenkins 1996, p. 393) to use his favourite description of cricket as a factor which cemented the bond of the British Empire/Commonwealth (Swanton, 1975). With one eye on the Caribbean and the other on Empire, British author, Cutteridge (1957, p. 139), writes that the achievements of West Indians on the savannahs of their territories and playing fields in England "have made our colonies well known in the world of cricket throughout the Empire."

Britannia has stopped ruling the waves around far-flung Caribbean islands such as Trinidad and Tobago, from which Brian Charles Lara hails. Brian Lara, Sachin Tendulkar, Wasim Akram, Mohammed Azharuddin, Aamir Sohail, and Saurav Ganguly, just some of many whose grandparents experienced the huge impact of British rule, have changed cricket massively. Their presence in cricket is the subject of profound exploration by correspondents such as Martin-Jenkins. I wish to make my own contribution to this gaze and will do so by looking at Brian Lara, the superb West Indies Test Match batsman and very unsuccessful captain.

My aim is simple. It is to examine the Brian Lara impact within and beyond cricket fields. He was, of course, born and raised on the twin island, Trinidad and Tobago, birthplace of Sir Pelham Warner, and for his unparalleled batting genius became revered by loyal and adoring West Indies followers as the "Prince" of Port-of-Spain. Although my focus is on cricket at the highest level, Test Match cricket, I shall not lose sight of past and current intersections between the game and socio-economic conditions in the Anglo-Caribbean, as well as the rest of the world.

For those who know of the Anglo-Caribbean through far more than its sun, sand, and fun, a gaze—both telescopically and microscopically—on the region via the compelling figure that is Brian Charles Lara is a very worthwhile exercise. For those who are well aware and have delighted in the tropical enchantment of island flavour, following run chases and glaring leadership lapses of batsman and three tenured West Indies Test Match captain, Brian Lara, is another mode through which they can blend their imaginative insights and emotional flows with exploratory surges. In choosing to deal with the magnitude of a presence such as Brian Charles Lara's, I am assuming, with both considerable reason and personal interest that I am wrestling with some intricate complexities of a cricketing personality. I state, quite hastily, that I am also attempting to unravel some of the paradoxes within a game, cricket, whose attributes can be both simultaneously liberating and suffocating.

Although this is a game whose growth through the centuries has been, doubtless, connected to the oppressive spread of British imperialism, many of those burdened by the evil have never been able to extricate their souls from the enthralling grip that is Test Match cricket. Such is no disposition towards mere toleration, co-existence, or blind immersion. It is a willingness to be enraptured by collective performance that has enlivened and continues to enliven the urges of millions across the globe who cherish the glorification of all humanity.

Prominent among those who—for much of their adult lives—have enlivened their urges and have not been able to free themselves from the thrall of Test Match cricket are the West Indian calypsonians (stage names, Lord Beginner and Lord Kitchener). In 1950, when the West Indies defeated England for the first time on English soil, Beginner sang a Kitchener composed calypso titled "Cricket, Lovely Cricket." I provide a segment of the lyrics well known to West Indians and English people:

CRICKET LOVELY CRICKET

Cricket lovely Cricket,
At Lord's where I saw it;
Cricket lovely Cricket,
At Lord's where I saw it;
Yardley tried his best
But Goddard won the Test.
They gave the crowd plenty fun;
Second Test and West Indies won
With those little pals of mine,
Ramadhin and Valentine

If there is any significance in the foregoing claims about thrall, rapture, glorification, enlivening, and collective performance, such significance can be located within the dramaturgy of superlative cricketing presence. Without question, it can be found, also in the looming presence of links between C. Wright Mills' biography and history, as well as the psychological and social. I would be the very first to state, however, that this very significance, a deeply sociological significance, I add, has eluded me for close to half a century. It is only out of a reflective gaze on work from that very insightful philosopher, Lord Bertrand Russell—to my knowledge, not a cricketing student— that I was able to grasp what should not have bypassed my focus. I happened to be re-reading Professor Noam Chomsky's *Problems of Knowledge And Freedom: The Russell Memorial Lectures* (Fontana, 1972, p. 9). There, I noticed that Lord Russell had written about the task of a liberal education, which Professor Chomsky reiterated is to give a sense of value to matters other than domination, to aid in the creation of wise citizenry within a free community. Further, through the combination of citizenry with liberty in individual creativeness, persons would be enabled to give human life a splendour few have demonstrated it can attain.

While alluding to an irresistible temptation to quote some of Lord Russell's own words, the psycholinguistic/anarchist scholar writes:

Those whose lives are fruitful to themselves, their friends, or to the world are inspired by hope and sustained by joy: they see in imagination the things that might be and the way in which they are to be brought into existence. In their private relations they are not preoccupied with anxiety lest they should lose such affection and respect as they receive: they are engaged in giving affection and respect freely, and the reward comes of itself without their seeking. In their work[2] they are not haunted by jealousy of competitors, but are concerned with the actual matter that has to be done. In politics, they do not spend time and passion defending unjust privileges of their class or nation, but they aim at making the world as a whole happier, less cruel, less full of conflict between rival greeds, and more full of human beings whose growth has not been dwarfed and stunted by oppression (Chomsky 1972, p. 9).

I can think of several cricketers whose work has been fruitful, defined by respect, and free of jealousy. Their performances, motivated by sheer dedication to the game, cricket, have inspired millions. Among the names that come to mind, immediately I recognise: Donald Bradman, Ian Chappell, George Headley, Garfield Sobers, Clive Lloyd, Michael Holding, Curtly Ambrose, Lancelot Gibbs, Conrad Hunte, Sachin Tendulkar, Basil Butcher, Riche Richardson, Rohan Kanhai, Colin Cowdrey, Graeme Pollock, Alan Davidson, Neil Harvey, Steve Waugh, Ray Lindwall, Clyde Walcott, Clarence Grimmett, Frank Worrell, Everton Weekes, Barry Richards, Viv Richards, John Berry Hobbs, Denis Compton, and Sunil Gavaskar.

It is Don Bradman, Gary Sobers, John Berry Hobbs, and Viv Richards whose names appear in the list of five cricketers of the twentieth century, a list created as a result of votes from one hundred judges secured by the producers of the authoritative *Wisden Cricket Almanac*. Not surprisingly, Bradman garnered one hundred votes, Sobers got ninety, Hobbs thirty, and Richards gained twenty five. Ray Lindwall and Don Bradman appear in a list of eleven Australians selected by former Australian captain Benaud (2005, p. 107) as his Australian team of the twentieth century, while Bradman, Sobers, Gavaskar, Hobbs, and Richards feature in his Greatest XI. Where does Frank Worrell fit in Benaud's scheme? Worrell is put in the post of paramount importance of team manager—not coach, a position I reject for Test Match cricket.

Although I have seen the performances of some of the cricketers named and can offer my own assessment with eagerness, I prefer to use the insightful accounts of Arlott (1986), Martin-Jenkins (1996), Woodcock (1998), and Benaud (2005). Here is my choice of twenty-two persons who have left indelible imprints on the game—a good enough number to make up two Test Match teams of players with extraordinary talent. My two teams would be: [TEAM 1 captained by Donald Bradman of Australia, managed by Richie Benaud of Australia]. This side would be made up of Garfield Sobers, Conrad Hunte, Lance Gibbs, O'Neil Gordon (Collie) Smith, Everton Weekes, [West Indies], Clarence Grimmett, Victor Trumper, William Ponsford, Ray Lindwall [Australia], Graeme Pollock [South Africa]. [TEAM 2 captained by Frank Worrell of the West Indies, managed by Learie Constantine of the West Indies] would consist of Rohan Kanhai, Roy Fredericks, Wes Hall, George Headley [West Indies], Alan Davidson [Australia], Colin Cowdrey [England], Ian Chappell [Australia], Fazal Mahmood [Pakistan], Barry Richards [South Africa], Sachin Tendulkar [India]. While I shall not explore performances of the twenty-two, I hope that readers can use my choices of three players as a guide to stretching their imaginative insights about the other nineteen.. While doing so they are free to use DIGNITAS, PIETAS, AND VIRTUS as important guides. The three, all leaders in their captain roles, are: Donald George Bradman, Garfield St. Aubrun Sobers, and Frank Mortimer Maglinne Worrell.

The President of the International Cricket Council (ICC), the governing body for world cricket, would be Sir Clyde Walcott of West Indies. The umpires would be: John Sydney Buller, Harold Dennis Bird of England, Douglas Sang Hue of West Indies, and Srinivasaraghavan Venkataraghavan of India. There would be no officials playing roles of third umpires or match referees. The radio commentators would be: Leslie Thomas John Arlott, Brian Johnston, Alan Christopher Martin-Jenkins, Alan Gibson, Neil Durden-Smith of England, Herbert Peter Bayley, Harry Cressall of West Indies, Alban George Moyes, Alan David McGilvray, Ray Barber of Australia. Experts delivering commentary between overs would be: Bijoy Chandra "Berry" Sarbadhikari of India, Trevor Edward Bailey, Frederick Sewards Trueman of England, Clive Hubert Lloyd, Gerald Ethridge Gomez of West Indies, Sunil Manohar Gavaskar of India, and

Jeremy Vernon Coney of New Zealand. The experts delivering the summary for each day would be Ernest William Swanton, Norman Walter Dransfield Yardley of England, and who else but a cricketer in the heroic mould, I.L. Bula, the finest batsman produced by the Fijian people (Snow 1960, p. 73-75).

The first class international cricketing world knows much about the other two gentlemen I have suggested for roles of providing summaries. They may know very little about Bula, whose cricketing skill is that of prodigious quality with more than a tinge of the romantic from a man comfortable with his enormous modesty. His last name, pronounced BOO-LAH by New Zealanders, according to Snow, which means HELLO, HOW DO YOU DO, or GREETINGS, is taken from TALEBULAMAINEIILIKENAMAINAVALENIVEIVAKABULAIMAINAKULALAKEBALAU.

> When he was seen in New Zealand in 1948, in the first overseas tour ventured on by the All-Fiji team for fifty years, the experts judged him to be of the very highest class in that country, which was stronger then, with Wallace, Donnely, Sutcliffe (at his best, which was magnificent), Hadlee, Cowie, Burtt and Rabone, than it is now. So highly was he thought of that, when New Zealand was beginning to bring its thoughts seriously to bear on forming its team for what proved to be its most successful visit to England a year later, Walter Hadlee asked me whether Bula might feasibly be a candidate for the New Zealand side (Snow 1960, p. 73).

This man, an admirable blend of orthodoxy and unorthodoxy, who had once participated in a Fiji game in which fifty-three players on each side took the field and has a place alongside legends such as Gilbert Jessop, David Sheppard, Ewart Astill, Walter Hammond, Trevor Bailey (England), and Learie Constantine (West Indies), emerged from very little coaching. It came from fellow Fijians, Ratu Edward Cakobau, once an Auckland player, and the uncoached Vilame Tuinaceva Logavatu, who passed 200 twice in a first class innings.

This is the blend I am assuming he put to good use in 1956 at Suva where he came up against some of the best from a West Indies Test Match touring side en route to New Zealand. Against Tom Dewdney, Sonny Ramadhin, Alfred Valentine, Tom Goddard, Denis Atkinson, as well as the geniuses, O'Neil Gordon Smith and Garfield St. Aubrun Sobers, he was not only top scorer in a low scoring game where no side reached 100, he was on the winning team also (Snow 1960, p. 82). At age thirty-seven, it appeared as if England crowds might have been able to get ample measure of that heroic mould from which he could make slow left armers aware they were unable to use the audacity to bowl without a fieldsman in the deep and offer more than figurative brilliance to an overcast Manchester day at Old Trafford or startle the St. Johns Wood pigeons on a Lord's boundary with what Snow reports was his literal barefooted approach.

With the chance to play on English soil increasing, Mr. Harry King, a Sussex cricketing official and former secretary of the Fiji Cricket Association, wrote to inform Snow that Bula told him: "he could think of nothing more than visiting England where 'he could learn to play real cricket'" (Snow 1960, p. 82). To his surprise, Snow adds that King wanted him to know Englishmen thought real cricket was played the Bula way. That tour inclusive of Bula never did take place for reasons about which observers are free to ruminate by situating its lack of realisation within a context overflowing with power, privilege, and prestige founded upon colour hierarchy deeply set within British imperialism. There is provision of more than a hint of this context in the Snow assessment that unfortunately the reasons could not have been further from what Bula, in his essential Fijianism of the finest order, stood for.

Without trivialising the foregoing Snow allusion, let me state that those who live according to the gospel of cricket and have attended for mass at Lord's, and ponder hugely the miraculous deeds of cricketing Gods in Test Match cricket, are free to stretch additional boundaries of their imaginary movements while considering my choices of players and officials on and off the field. They can extend the limits even further by doing the opposite of what Mr. Henry Blofeld states his wife has been doing, observing the craftsmanship of bowlers, fieldsmen, and batsmen and using that craftsmanship as a major foundation to writing about their character. The opposite would entail creating exquisite pictures and very verdant fields framed and matted around the literary journeys I take while writing about the players.

To many, especially Americans not so familiar with cricket, I ask that they consider parts of a speech[3] delivered by United States Attorney General, Robert H. Jackson, to the annual conference of American attorneys in April 1940. I ask, as well, that part of the consideration should consist of comparing the Kilburn cricket ideals, unimpeachable honesty of purpose, as well as, unfailing rejection of the meretricious and unprincipled, to the swirl of illegality and unethical conduct within the Donald Trump presidency. While addressing himself to the features prosecutors ought to possess, the Attorney General had this to say: "The qualities of a good prosecutor are as elusive and as impossible to define as those which mark a good gentleman. And those who need to be told would not understand it anyway. A sensitiveness to fair play and sportsmanship is perhaps the best protection against the abuse of power, and the citizen's safety lies in the prosecutor who tempers zeal with human kindness, who seeks truth not victims, who serves the law and not factional purposes, and who approaches his task with humility." He asserted, also, that nothing better could emanate from the gathering before which he stood than rededication to the spirit of fair play and decency that ought to animate the federal prosecutor. For good measure, he insisted that while prosecutors are being diligent, strict, and vigorous in law enforcement, they can afford also to be just. To the Jackson's remarks I add: sporting behaviour involves generosity of outlook founded upon self-respect and correspondingly great respect for others.

Attorney General Jackson later served as a United States Supreme Court Justice and as United States Chief Counsel to the International Military Tribunal at Nuremberg subsequent to the end of the Second World War. I invite all readers, not merely those who are not profoundly familiar with cricket, but also those who are, to look for the Jackson adherence to sportsmanship, fair play, humility, kindness, and justice when he rendered the Supreme Court Opinion in January 1942 in regard to the case: The Merion Cricket Club vs. The United States, as well as judgment against the Nazi war criminals. Allow me to focus upon the Nuremberg trial, for it is certainly not out of order for me to note that the qualities to which Jackson alluded in that 1940 address were under very severe threat in the Trumpian world where Mr. Rudolph Giuliani, one of Trump's personal lawyers, a man who served as a prosecutor in the Southern District, New York, described a legally authorised search by that very office of premises associated with another Trump attorney, Mr. Michael Cohen, as a raid by "STORM TROOPERS."

The Jackson judgment at Nuremberg in regard to the Nazi criminals was, indeed, judgment against men on whose disgracefully illegal orders STORM TROOPERS acted during the Second World War when, in the opinion of the American jurist, these criminals could not be separated from: (a) THE SEIZURE OF POWER AND SUBJUGATION OF GERMANY TO A POLICE STATE (b) THE PREPARATION AND WAGING OF WARS OF AGGRESSION (c) WARFARE IN DISREGARD OF INTERNATIONAL LAW (d) ENSLAVEMENT AND PLUNDER OF POPULATIONS IN OCCUPIED COUNTRIES (e) PERSECUTION AND EXTERMINATION OF JEWS AND CHRISTIANS. Yet, Mr. Giuliani, well known for his unbridled promotion and support of hard policing when he served two acrimonious terms in the role of New York Mayor, tenures which many a shrewd observer would not associate with the prosecutor qualities offered by legal scholar Attorney General and Supreme Court Justice Jackson, has the pernicious audacity to link his former prosecutorial district with STORM TROOPING.

Let me, therefore, pose some queries and ponder probable replies: (1) Is it not true that some of the foregoing five matters can- in principle - be linked to a certain political figure who is alleged to have intervened directly in the 2016 US presidential election for the purpose of enabling a Trump victory? (2) Is it not true that the very Donald Trump, the MAAFA MUZUNGU MONSTROSITY, prepared his own sticky wicket shortly after he had become US President by accusing his immediate predecessor, the very "evil" President Obama (Trump terminology) of having wire-tapped Trump Tower? (3) Is it not true that Trump personal attorney, Giuliani, prepared his own sticky wicket when he claimed that the President, who is alleged to have had an extramarital tryst with a woman known as Stormy Daniels, orchestrated payment of $130,000 by another attorney, Mr. Michael Cohen, to Ms. Daniels, for the purpose of preventing her from making the tryst public? Is it not true that Trump repaid the sum above to Mr. Cohen? (4) Is it not true that personal attorney, Giuliani, prepared a very sticky wicket for himself and the President by making a statement about repayment, a matter which ties Trump very directly to Stormy Daniels, a connection Trump has denied repeatedly? (5) Is it not true that Trump created his own very sticky wicket when he stated on an Air Force One flight that he had no knowledge of a $130,000 payment to Stormy Daniels?

If, as I am inclined to think, replies to all five queries can reasonably be offered in the affirmative, neither should Donald Trump nor Rudolph Giuliani be linked to being a gentleman, sportsmanship, humility, fair play, kindness, decency, and credibility, the last of which Counsel Jackson at the Nuremberg trial stated was at the core of the proceedings against the men on whose orders STORM TROOPERS acted. Absence of such a link with a basis in all types of sticky wickets is not CRICKET. To me it is very noteworthy that all of the Jackson qualities can be connected to Harvard educated lawyer and scholar, Barack Hussein Obama, whose eight year tenure, very unlike not even a full two year period in the Trump presidency, was scandal free. Yet it is scandal after scandal which have plagued infancy of the Trump presidency, swirling scourge upon some sticky wickets, where absurdity and catastrophe to the Giuliani craftsmanship have earned the ex-New York Mayor the title "Anthony Scaramucci" among the Trump attorneys.

He may well know that among the many points advanced by the Nuremberg Counsel, there is a direct reference to the war criminals: "They stand before the record of this trial as blood-stained Gloucester stood by the body of his slain King. He begged of the widow, as they beg of you: 'Say I slew them not.' And the Queen replied, 'Then say they were not slain. But dead they are...' If you were to say of these men (war criminals) that they are not guilty, it would be as true to say there has been *no war,* there are *no slain,* there has been *no crime.*" What I do not think Mr. Giuliani knows is that he has never been a man who, like former British Prime Minister John Major, a fellow Knight Commander of St. Michael and St. George (K.C.M.G.), could have ever developed that distinct cricketing thrust of a gentleman cricketer and politician. He also does not know what covering up or a cover up in cricket is. Hence, I offer him a valuable lesson.

In Test Match cricket, whenever a batsman (batter in baseball) covers up, he presents a straight bat—not a crooked bat. He is right behind the line of the ball bowled (pitched in baseball) to him. He shows the figurative full and broad face of his bat to the bowler (pitcher in baseball). When a cover is up crafted by Test Match batsmen who are—to use a cricket term—well set, who have established their assertiveness over bowlers, but who recognise also the merit to deliveries eliciting the cover up, a remarkable sequence of events unfolds. In the SPIRIT of the game, something constitutive of the highly desirable and greatly admired non-legal[4] features to cricket, those very features identified by chief counsel Jackson, many batsmen, gentlemen in the Jacksonian sense, tell bowlers, their opponents, these opponents have bowled exceptionally well. I add this much, especially for American readers: in the Caribbean, some of the MAAFA MUZUNGU MONSTROSITY'S "SHITHOLE" societies, whose Test Match teams were led by three captains, Richie Richardson, Vivian Richards, Clive Lloyd, as well as two shrewd administrators, Allan Rae and Clyde Walcott, just a few of the men who had made Caribbean Test Match cricket the best in the world for more than a decade and a half, when batsmen from the region covered up their strident supporters have mouthed deafening NO.

That was, of course, cricket about which I was moved to pen verse:

ALIEN'S APOSTLE

Why come to see all champions of the soil invoke that glossy silence of earthen treasures? A pilot's plague defiles our fading forests and raids all solar spirits of our game. The cricketer's inferno has betrayed its winter treat. No: vaunt the bidders from Garrison, the seasoned square.

No: haunt the scribes from Bayland, the measure incomparable. No: taunt the yellers from Kensington, the venue preferred.

Why purge the charge of humid hides above all howling hues with wisdom's wealth? A princely pride anoints our jaunted juries in their fallow fields.

The century's tempest has bared a tale of wicket dreams.

No: crave the heroes from Kaieteur, the mystic fore.

No: brave the scions from Canje, the vision supreme.

No: rave the mentors from Bourda, the fortune favoured.

Why bridge life's annals with the barter's blessing to braid all brawny gusts of flaxen fragrance? A builder's blight adorns the stable shadows across our bloated boundaries. A skipper's shaman preens the salty passions of oceans past.

No: deign the sceptics from Arima, the noonday raver.

No: reign the pandits from Caroni, the wisdom forsaken.

No: feign the royals from Queen's Park, the Antillean ruse.

Why weave those crumpled credits of the chirping quire on Isaac's anthem where an alien's apostle treads all furrowed fathoms?

A mariner's mist befriends those lunatic labours of our meagre mandarins.

A dreadful drone of island cricketers defrocks the craft of wayward deliveries. No: wail the herd from Carib, the flavoured sound. No: hail the bayers from Ras, the hallowed yard. No: bail the chorus from Sabina, the distant North. No: rail the sages from St. John's, Alexander's arousal.

Readers can substitute their own locations and persons, should they see illegality in any actions associated with the Trump-Giuliani cover up.

Someone who is very acutely aware of the cover up in Test Match cricket is Mr. Tony Lewis. In the words of this ex-England Test Match skipper and MCC, President, it is the slow surges of the Test Match form of the game that are fascinating to watch. The Test Match game is a game of chess as opposed to draughts, it is symphonic as opposed to the quick-flashing overture, it is a game overflowing with all sorts of subtleties. From Geoffrey Boycott, ex-England Test Match opening batsman, this view: the great beauty in Test Match cricket is bearing witness to the ebb and flow in amazing advantages within the game

In a foreground of such poignancy from Jackson, Kilburn, Lewis, and Boycott, it is fitting that the first of the three with whom I start is Donald George Bradman, the greatest Test Match run getter of all cricket history (Kilburn 1960, p. 52), who was bowled for a duck [0] with a googly by the England wrist spinner, Eric Hollies, in his final Test Match at the Kensington Oval (1948). Some observers put forth their own claims about Bradman being denied an average of an even 100, that mythical landmark. They reason that he was overcome with emotion on playing his final game in England, where the Oval spectators gave him rapturous cheers when he walked to the crease. Be that as it may, his batting is, to this day, the standard according to which every other Test Match batsman designated great is judged. So should that standard be! James (1963, p. 141) is explicit that there were 10 to 1 odds that in any Test Match Donald Bradman would reach a score of one hundred and fifty or two hundred runs, and the more his team needed runs the greater the certainty he would get those runs.

Get them he most assuredly did, especially at Headingley, Leeds, where he, the victorious Test Match captain against England in summer 1948, appeared for the last game with bat in hand on the evening of Friday, 23rd July, the day when Kilburn states one of the most memorable public tributes was paid to him.

The Australians were batting by half-past five and had scarcely adjusted themselves to the idea before [Arthur] Morris mistimed [Alec] Bedser, to be caught at mid-wicket. The crowds broke from the boundary edge and raced to the pavilion entrance, making a lane half-way to the pitch. There was a silence of suspense; a murmur of "He's here," swelling to a roar of welcome to greet the greatest cricketing figure of his time. Bradman waved his hand, touched his cap and pushed the first ball through the leg trap in acknowledgment of compliment appreciated and as indication of 'business as usual' (Kilburn 1960, pp. 45-46).).

The Bradman business-as-usual was embracing that Headingley venue which offered him glorious beginning, continuity, and finale (Kilburn 1960, pp. 49-50). In six Test Match innings at the Yorkshire ground, his scores were: 334, 304, 103, 16, 33, and an unbeaten 173. Yorkshire County Cricket club awarded him honorary life membership and was prepared, so writes Kilburn, to make him Don Bradman, Lord of Headingley, for he had taken his feudal dues already.

Donald Bradman, (Australia, 1908-2001), so states Woodcock, the most revered Australian sportsman, is more than a legend. He became a demigod because of his extraordinary achievement with the bat. How good was Donald George Bradman? Although that genius of a batsman, Sunil Manohar Gavaskar from India, got thirty-four Test Match centuries—five more than the Australian—and amassed [10,122] runs, he had played many more games [a total of 125 Test Matches] than the Don and averaged [51.12].

I write in similar vein about Sachin Ramesh Tendulkar [53.78 average of runs from 200 Test Matches], who followed Gavaskar and broke numerous batting records. At the start of the Indian tour to England in summer 2011, Tendulkar, the "undisputed God" of India, needed just one more hundred in international matches to bring his total to one hundred centuries, which he got against Bangladesh in spring 2012. He has, however, played many more than thrice the number of Test Matches Bradman played. Tendulkar's Test Match batting average, when he departed from the cricket scene, was not anywhere close to the Australian's. Nor is the average of Brian Lara [52.89 from one hundred and thirty-one Test Matches] who—like Bradman—got more than three hundred runs twice in a Test Match at the same venues. Dare I continue by adding that Donald George Bradman, so claims at least one English cricket writer, was better than "Tiger" Woods at Woods' best. He was as good as classical music conductors, Simon Rattle, Daniel Barenboim, and Eugene Ormandy. Arlott (1986, pp. 33) writes that Bradman, at all levels, was the most efficient and prolific batsman the game has ever known.

The only batsman to have scored a thousand runs before the end of June in England twice, and three hundred runs in a Test Match in one day, he ended his career with the incredible batting average of 99.94 runs from 52 Test Matches. According to Arlott, even what some deem a failure by his own high standards, an Australian Test Match series average of [65.57] runs in the infamous "Bodyline" matches against England (1932-1933) placed him at the top of his country's batting against Douglas Jardine's England side. He possessed a rare ability to see and assess bowling early. An excellent timer of the ball and player off the back and front foot, he had every stroke and also improvised.

He used his wiry wrists to put great power into his shots which, doubtless, made him a major "draw card" at Test Match grounds, which would be almost empty when he was out. Is it any wonder that Donald George Bradman, with a Test Match batting average for Australia on the island continent against England [97.14], was above such Australian stalwarts as Norman O'Neil, Neil Harvey, Lindsay Hassett, Doug Walters, Greg Chappell, Keith Stackpole, Arthur Morris, Bob Simpson, Bill Lawry, Sid Barnes, and Bob Cowper!

I want to begin with Garfield St. Aubrun Sobers by focusing upon the solemnity in his sojourn to the centre in the roles of Test Match batsman and captain descending pavilion steps, and add that none other than C.L.R. James regards his performance in cricket arenas as a living embodiment of centuries of a tortured history. James is, of course, alluding to the Atlantic slave trade and the slavery in the West Indies integrally connected to the evil. My goal here is to explore the implications stemming from linking solemnity to the tortured history.

Let me state that on every occasion when I have seen Sobers take the field, he is always wearing a solemn visage—not a sense of aloofness—but a presence that can be likened to being alone. In pondering what that visage means to me, I have drawn from the exploration of Baldwin (1971), who penned a gut-wrenching missive to Angela Davis, at the time she was imprisoned and awaiting trial on capital charges. Addressing himself to his "dear sister," the novelist and insightful critic of racism writes about his hope that the sight of chains on a black body, hers, of course, would be so intolerable and unbearable to Americans that they would rise up and remove the shackles. Instead, they seem to glory in their own chains and gauge their safety in bondage and corpses:

> And so, Newsweek, civilized defender of the indefensible, attempts to drown you in a sea of crocodile tears ("it remained to be seen what sort of personal liberation she had achieved") and puts you on its cover, chained (Baldwin 1971, p. 19).

Noting that she appeared to be exceedingly alone, he exemplifies her oppressed presentation as similar to the Jewish housewife in a boxcar on the way to Dachau, or any one of the black ancestors chained together in the name of Jesus and bound for a Christian land. A keen observer does not have to stretch imagination to the realms of phantasy in concluding that the Sobers solemnity bordering on being alone can be reasonably juxtaposed with the presence of a chained Angela Davis, given that both of them have emerged from, and are living embodiments of, centuries of a tortured history.

Thus, if the Sobers on-field performance reminds James of that tortured history, I think I would be in order to state: the Sobers slave ancestors from Africa in the West Indies had hopes, fears, and dreams about their descendants in AFRICAN SOVEREIGN LANGUAGE AND CULTURE wrenched from them on Caribbean soil brutally stolen and claimed summarily as Christian land. Further, those hopes, fears, and dreams cannot be separated from their African Gods and spirits, among whom the river spirits were hugely significant. That the Sobers link via James to tortured history is a link to Africa is indubitable. In figurative cricketing terms, Test Match captain, Garfield St. Aubrun Sobers, IS the Moses of West Indies cricket: he was the very first West Indies captain to defeat mighty Australia, and did so in 1965 on soil where his African ancestors felt more that the pain from whips and chains on their black flesh; for more than good measure, one year later he defeated what was once the most cruelly successful slave owning society, England, whose use of three Test Match captains could not save the union flag.

In asking myself how captain Sobers attained such heights, I cannot merely seek refuge in the African ancestral spirit world and analogise that, to the Africans in Egypt, he was, like Moses, saved by water. What I can do—and with very good reason—is claim that like Moses in Egypt, who was a Hierogrammat,[5] Sobers is a cricketing Hierogrammat—albeit untutored. Although the Moses intellectual capability included profound familiarity with the Egyptian Mystery System, the intellectual capability of Sobers, the West Indies leader, was not founded upon any Caribbean Mystery System, but when demonstrated on cricket fields its extraordinary facticity appeared a mystery to many.

Where do I continue with this West Indies hero, whose unbeaten (365) at Sabina Park, Jamaica in 1958 is a unique achievement! That his accomplishment is unique can be seen in the indubitable fact that no other Test Match cricket all-rounder has ever made such a high score in that form of the game. Garfield St. Aubrun Sobers is unique in another very significant way. Five of his twenty-six Test Match hundreds were made at the Bourda Cricket Ground, Georgetown, Guyana: (125, 109 second Test

Match against Pakistan, 1957-1958), (145 against England, 1959-1960), (152 against England, 1967-1968), (108 against India, 1970-1971). No other batsman but great admirer Donald George Bradman comes close, with four hundreds at Headingley. I add that the closeness is clearly not out of order. Among West Indies Test Match batsmen who played before his time, during and after his time no one matches or exceeds, with the same or higher proportion, this record.[6] I make a similar claim about batsmen from Australia, England, India, Pakistan, Sri Lanka, and South Africa at Test Match venues in their own countries. Included here are Kippax, McCabe, the Chappell brothers, Harvey, Walters, Lawry, Simpson, Ponting, O'Neil, Cowper, Boycott, Hammond, Hutton, Hobbs, Sutcliffe, May, Cowdrey, Vaughan, Compton, Turner, Pollock, Tendulkar, Gavaskar, Ganguly, Dravid, and countless others. There is much more to be stated about this man.

Against all odds, one hot and humid afternoon, in February 1968, Garfield St. Aubrun Sobers scored also an unbeaten second innings (113) on a very horrific Sabina Park pitch playing "nasty, brutish, and short"[7] in a dauntingly devilish way from every conceivable cricketing crevice. To this day I still ask myself: who else but Garfield St. Aubrun Sobers! Yet, some who have sought to tarnish the Sobers cricketing acumen—and there are a few beholden to the imperialist union flag—civilised defenders of the indefensible, try to drown the West Indies hero in seas of crocodile tears more ruddy than the Red Sea by pronouncing that captain Sobers did not have a cricketing brain. There are men of minute muster deemed cricketing experts who have hurled criticism at Garfield St. Aubrun Sobers. Some of them, I add, have never won a Test Match series against the West Indies and Australia, but have found time to deem Sobers wanting. Let me follow the path of a gentleman philosopher Gilbert Ryle (1949, p. 17) and lift my finger—umpire style—against them who have committed a "category mistake." They have, most obviously, seen bowlers, batsmen, fielders, and scorers on the field of play, but fail to grasp, despite their presumed outstanding intellectual prowess, the concept of the Sobers abiding loyalty to cricketing team SPIRIT.[8]

There is also absolutely no question in my mind that when any illustrious category of Test Match cricketers is created, Garfield St. Aubrun Sobers stands out. Three times he captained a Rest-of-the World team and was successful on each occasion. Yet his critics take issue with his leadership. Had he not been an excellent leader overflowing with inspiration, he could neither have been successful with world teams nor with West Indies against Australia in 1965 and England in 1966. Who could have been more inspirational than him in the 1967-'68 series against England? On the very last afternoon of the first Test Match in Trinidad, West Indies were facing certain defeat with him and Wes Hall, the last pair at the wicket. Sobers was unbeaten on [33] and Hall—clearly not a batsman—was unbeaten too, on [26]. One story about that last Trinidad stand is that when Hall walked in, Sobers walked down the pitch and told him: "you just stay there." In 1966 at Lord's he did something similar when he batted with David Holford, both centuries who rescued their team and earned West Indies a very honourable draw. Six years later, 1972, at Bridgetown, Barbados, where West Indies were facing the possibility of another humiliating loss, Sobers [142 and Charlie Davis 183 second innings] denied New Zealand victory. Mike Brearley, however, finds the Sobers leadership wanting. Brearley may not know that after Sobers had relinquished the West Indies Test Match leadership post and was a senior player under Rohan Kanhai's leadership, Kanhai still addressed him as CAPTAIN. Such, I insist, is not blind respect, but notable honour given to the inspirational Sobers even outside the leadership role.

What about Sobers, the illustrious batsman? I state, without a hint of reservation, that although he did not enter Test Match cricket as a batsman, he towers head and shoulders in the batting averages [57.78] above almost all those—save Walter Hammond [58.45], Barry Richards [72.57], Herbert Sutcliffe [60.73], George Headley [60.83], Graeme Pollock [60.97], Donald Bradman [99.94]—assessed as great. With Everton Weekes and Clyde Walcott [West Indies—58.61 and 56.68] he is above Bob Simpson, Doug Walters, Neil Harvey, Greg Chappell, William Ponsford, Jim Woodfull [Australia], Sachin Tendulkar, Sunil Gavaskar, Surav Ganguly, Rahul Dravid [India], Javed Miandad Khan, Majid Jahangir Khan [Pakistan], Colin Cowdrey, Geoffrey Boycott, Elias Hendren, Peter May, Tom Graveney, Ted Dexter [England]. Purely from a batting standpoint, he is in the same class as: Ken Barrington, Walter Hammond, John Berry Hobbs, Len Hutton, Herbert Sutcliffe [England], Graeme Pollock, Barry Richards [South Africa].

Observers are free to challenge me. I ask that should they so choose they need to ruminate over:

Bloody hell, I wish I'd seen Sobers play. He sounds like an outstanding batsman. In the last year or so I've had dinner with Dennis Lillee and Ian Chappell and on each occasion I asked them who was the best batsman they ever saw. Not the best all-rounder, just the best batsman. They both said, without a second's thought, Sobers. The thing that set him apart, they said, was that when he was in the mood he could hit the best ball for four, never mind the bad ones (Smith, 2019: p. 97).

When I consider Kapil Dev [India—434 wickets—131 Test Matches—batting average—31.05], Ian Botham [England—383 wickets—102 Test Matches—batting average—33.54], Imran Khan Niazi [Pakistan—362 wickets—88 Test Matches—batting average—37.69], and Jacques Kallis [South Africa], those deemed notably outstanding all-rounders, Garfield St. Auburn Sobers has, perhaps, two equals. They are Jacques Kallis from South Africa. Kallis, with 292 wickets to his credit, also has a batting average of [55.73 from 166 Test Matches]. There is Walter Hammond of England whose batting average is [58.54 from 85 Test Matches]; his highest score was 336. Kallis and every other all-rounder of note, unlike Sobers, has scored triple centuries below the Sobers accomplishment, a Sobers record which still stands today.[9] Interestingly, every all-rounder I compare to Sobers—save Imran Khan Niazi—has played Test Matches with far greater frequency than Sobers.

Sobers [West Indies, 1936-present] [57.78 Test Match batting average] [26 centuries] and [235 Test Match wickets from 93 Test Matches] is the most complete cricketer the world has ever known (Walcott 1996, p. vi). Greatly admired by Bradman, he was all that could be required of a cricketer. It was Bradman—explicit in his astute assessment—that Sobers is, unquestionably, the best figure he ever saw. A delightfully modest human being, Garfield Sobers was a supreme sportsman and complete all-rounder. For Arlott (1986, p: 242), there has hardly been a more absorbing or exciting experience in modern cricket than observing the progress of Garfield St. Aubrun Sobers, to whom the cricket world was an oyster he relished in a princely manner. (1986, p: 242).

He perceived the value of wrist spin—in his case the 'Chinaman' and its associated googly, especially on plumb wickets; mastered the technique and exploited it most effectively. Later, to balance his team's bowling economy, he bowled fast-medium left arm with a born-perfect action which gave him swing, movement off the seam, and nip of the natural pace bowler. In the field, he was spectacular in the outfield or the covers as a young man, became a fine slip and, ultimately, a quite phenomenal short-leg (Arlott 1986, p. 242).

The Arlott assessment above is, aptly, about Sobers, the fine bowler. What about Sobers, the batting genius? Against Pakistan, at Sabina Park, Jamaica (1958), he surpassed Len Hutton's [364] at the Kennington Oval (1938, England vs. Australia). Thirty six years elapsed before his [365] was surpassed by Brian Lara at St. John's, Antigua.

If you ask me about the Sobers batting brilliance, I will not hesitate to tell you that a major part of it was as great as the dazzling footwork of Muhammad Ali, and as splendid as the fluvial cadence in the poetry of Nobel Laureate Derek Walcott. He did emerge to succeed his mentor, Frank Worrell, to become West Indies Test Match captain. Such was the case, crucially, on the basis of Worrell's recommendation, and when he first led West Indies against England in 1966, his extraordinary all-round achievement in that five game series earned him, most deservedly, the title "King Cricket." In another five game encounter against England (summer, 1970), he led a team for the Rest of the World,[10] and among illustrious company—including Farokh Engineer of India, compatriots Lance Gibbs, Rohan Kanhai, Clive Lloyd, Deryck Murray, as well as the South Africans, Graeme Pollock, Eddie Barlow, Barry Richards, and Peter Pollock—the cricket world became pleasantly aware of the good reasons he earned the assessment "incomparable" from great admirer, former England all-rounder, Trevor Bailey.

Many there are who have admired his fielding brilliance in attacking positions behind and close to the wicket. I want to convey part of just such brilliance that took place in the Australian first innings on day three of a crucial third Test Match (Australia vs. West Indies, Bourda Ground, Georgetown, Guyana, 1965). On that day, an overcast Easter weekend Saturday in dull light, skipper Sobers is fielding at leg slip to the devastatingly quick Charlie Griffith. Facing Griffith is Norman O'Neil, the man some Australians claim is the new Bradman. Gary Sobers knows, all too well, that if O'Neil is not removed early there is a lot of trouble for him and his side. Griffith steams in and sends a good length delivery on middle and leg stump. O'Neil plays, gets a thin inside edge. Like a bullet, the ball is flying past Gary Sobers. He dives only to discover than the ball eludes his grasp. In an instant, he knocks the ball upwards, rolls over, and takes the catch. O'Neil is dismissed for [27].

It was, where else but the Bourda Ground in 1968, on day one, during the course of the West Indies first innings [fifth Test Match, England and West Indies], when captain Sobers—having promoted himself in the batting order—as a result of a crisis in the face of that "avalanche of Snow,"[11] tumbling past the Bourda breezes joined the improvising genius Kanhai. Opening batsmen Seymour Nurse [17], Stephen Camacho [14], as well as number four Basil Butcher [18] are back in the pavilion. West Indies have not reached a hundred; Colin Cowdrey and his men are sensing a rout. At the end of the day, Sobers—on his way to another century at the Bourda ground where he ultimately gets the highest number of hundreds for any West Indies Test Match batsman—is still batting with Kanhai. At 9:10 that night, the time for the regular Guyana radio programme *SPORTS ROUNDUP*, notable commentator, B. L. Crombie, headlines with news that the incomparable Sobers has once more steered the West Indies out of danger and put them on "easy street." Had he not run out of batting partners in the West Indies second innings, he would, most certainly, have got another century. Lance Gibbs, by no means a batsman, was the last man out and captain Sobers was not out on [95].

There are, of course, others apart from the self-appointed sages who have levelled criticism against Sobers, the West Indies captain (1965-1972). Here, I recall a claim from Henry Blofeld that Sobers was a "laissez-faire" captain who "let things ride," and someone who lacked tactical leadership skill. Let me state explicitly that I see no validity to those views. If Sobers was, indeed, a laissez-faire captain, then I see nothing wrong with that, provided he had, at his disposal, the benefit of what Scottish intellectual, Adam Smith, advocated as the free movement of labour. Captain, Gary Sobers, did have the benefit of free movement of field labour in the persons of bowlers, Wes Hall, Charlie Griffith, Lance Gibbs, Joe Solomon, and of course himself, when he beat Australia, India, and England and used such benefit with immense tactical skill.

In my view, he was unsuccessful when such labour was unavailable to him. While reminiscing in 1994 about the Sobers greatness, none other than Wes Hall gave me the chance to ruminate over what West Indies Test Match cricket could have looked like if Sobers had at his disposal the menacingly destructive quick bowling attack of Joel Garner, Colin Croft, Malcolm Marshall, Michael Holding, Curtly Ambrose, Andy Roberts, and Wayne Daniel, which Clive Lloyd and Viv Richards used so effectively against the batting best on opposing sides. Blofeld himself does not find it easy to decide whether Lloyd, the second most successful Test Match skipper, was "a great captain," for he "had such a wonderful side." What did the highly animated Hall tell me?

He stated:

"Sobers was a captain that would give you a chance. I tell you what. He was unfortunate. Had Sobers been a captain of the West Indies when we had this four pronged attack and a team that he could gamble with, he would have been the most successful captain of all time. The fact of the matter is that by 1967, '68, and '69, Sobers had an ageing team."

It is also important for me to emphasise that when the views of experts such as Richie Benaud, Trevor Bailey, Ian Chappell, John Arlott, and E. W. "Jim" Swanton are considered, there is no validity to the ideas of the critics. Let me convey just one view about captain Sobers at a time, 1970, when brickbats were hurled his way:

For a few months of 1969, out of sheer weariness, Garfield Sobers ceased to produce the figures of the finest cricketer of modern times. Like all such lapses, his failure prompted little men to berate the great. His lack of success is unquestionable, but it no more detracts from the historic fact of his eminence than some indifferent verses make Coleridge less than a great poet. The only remarkable fact about Sobers' bad spell was that it did not occur sooner under the heaviest sustained strain any cricketer has ever known (Arlott 1970/1996, p. 237).

It is, thus, not out of place for me to recall that in the spring of 1969, just prior to the start of an unsuccessful West Indies tour of England under his leadership, he complained about being mentally tired, a cry that went unheeded.

During the course of that very 1969 tour, captain Sobers—set fair for a splendid hundred at Lord's, was run-out by batsman Charlie Davis, one of the worst runners between the wickets.[12] Realising that he had no chance of saving his wicket, the captain headed straight for the pavilion. I watched the proceedings and also listened to radio commentary simultaneously. Upon Sobers' dismissal, I heard Trevor Bailey state that when a batsman runs-out his captain he has to score a hundred, a feat Davis did achieve. The skipper, most certainly, knew that his player ran him out. This type of misdeed is, unquestionably, solid ground for a chiding—if not a verbal hiding—from the leader.

Not so from Sobers, whom England umpire, Dickie Bird, describes as a gentleman and a wonderful cricketer. I had an exchange with him about the run out twenty six years later:

W.W: *You were run-out—some people say—by Charlie Davis. I heard Mr. Peter Short [West Indies Cricket Board President] speak about your great generosity after you came into the pavilion. You passed through the long room. You turned to Charlie Davis and said: 'Never mind. Go out there and do your best.' Today, it would probably be difficult to hear a captain make such a statement. You have said that the game is always bigger than the players. You have said that the game is above players. Can you now say a little bit about what you think today in regard to this large question called discipline in Test Match cricket?*

G. S: *Well. That incident with Charlie and me was—really—just another part of the game of cricket. I don't think any player goes out there to deliberately run out another player—particularly if he is playing for the same team. And Charlie was a youngster. He called. I took off and he turned back. He thought that I probably could get back and it [the run-out] happened. I didn't see any reason I should have any malice or resentment or anything against Charlie, because it was one of those things. And that's what cricket is all about, a game of glorious uncertainty; it comes in more than one fashion.*

Another prominent gentleman cricketer and wonderful batsman was Frank Worrell [West Indies 1924-1967—Test Match batting average of 49.48 from 51 games] noted for his stylish and effortless performance both within and beyond cricket fields, where he, the first regular African-Caribbean West Indies skipper, exuded effortless authority and was a superb Test Match captain who elevated the quality and stature of West Indies and world cricket. When Frank Worrell became West Indies skipper (1960-'61, Australia), he removed team breaches and disputations several state were owed to territorial rivalry. Any West Indian who states that the Worrell accession would not have been possible had it not been for the constancy and persistence of a public campaign launched by C.L.R. James would be absolutely correct. My immediate concern at this juncture is not to justify the view about the James position.

What I want to do is offer a glimpse of that campaign, in the campaigner's own words:

An individual easily gets over the fact that he is disappointed in his desire to be captain. It is the constant vigilant, bold and shameless manipulation of players to exclude black captains that has so demoralised West Indian teams and exasperated the people—a people, it is to be remembered, in the full tide of the transition from colonialism to independence (James, 1963: p. 232).

The foregoing was part of what James characterised as his unsparingly energetic weekly move on behalf of the Worrell captaincy. Writing in the Caribbean publication *The Nation*, on 4th March, 1960, James notes that Frank Worrell is not simply at the acme of his reputation as a cricketer, but as a master of the game. Worrell, he adds, commands intense respect in a brilliant career. There is more from James' pen. West Indies player, Frank Worrell, a study in grace and dignity, drew tremendous admiration from the world of English cricket in 1957, I add, when the team under John Goddard, deficient captain, a member of the highly privileged Anglo-Saxon Barbadian aristocracy, lost heavily.

In that very Nation piece James declares boldly:

AUSTRALIA WANTS HIM AS CAPTAIN. This is the authentic fact. When Australian critics talk of [Victor] Trumper, Kippax and the few half dozen batsmen who have batted as if they were born to it they include Worrell. As a man he made a tremendous impression in Australia.[13] Thousands will come out on every ground to see an old friend leading the West Indies. In fact, I am able to say that if Worrell were captain and [Learie] Constantine or George Headley manager or co-manager, the coming tour [1960-1961] would be one of the greatest ever.

Readers will be able to see that the James words about leadership came to fruition. It is equally important to know about Worrell, the batsman.

At the batting crease, Arlott saw him as a cool, unhurried stylist possessed of all the purist stroke play: he never played across the line of the ball, never hooked but simply evaded the line of the ball with calm self-possession, even against the quickest of deliveries—all this from a man who was uncoached. Worrell, patterned what dramaturgical sociologist Erving Goffman, assesses as presentation of self on the "impression management" of school teacher Derek Sealey. What a patterning! Batting for home side, Barbados, in an inter-territorial series (1945-1946), he and Clyde Walcott amassed 574 for the fourth wicket against Trinidad. The Worrell contribution: an unbeaten 255.

Such was the shape of things to come. Batting for the very first time in a Test Match series against England (1947-1948), he made 97 at Port-of-Spain and followed this feat with an unbeaten 131 in Georgetown. His batting average for that series was 147 runs. On the 1950 successful tour—England again—he amassed 539 Test Match runs with another very high series average, 89.93. Part of that statistic came from a superb 261 in the third Test Match [Trent Bridge, Nottingham] made in five hours and thirty-five minutes during which he contributed to seven batting records. Seven years later, at the same ground, he showed England and the rest of the cricket world the elegance of batting beauty in a wondrously unbeaten 191. One of the many things I shall never forget about that 1950 tour is watching a photograph of the outstandingly brilliant Everton de Courcy Weekes and Frank Worrell walking out to resume an innings against Cambridge University (Fenners). Their partnership was worth 350 runs for the third wicket. West Indian and Indian raconteurs will also not forget his exquisitely crafted 237 in the fifth Test Match at Kingston (1952-1953), when he batted in the company of who else but Everton Weekes and Clyde Walcott.

Ask me how great a cricketer Frank Worrell was and I will tell you I find it difficult to express a preference for him over his two Barbadian colleagues, Everton de Courcy Weekes, and Clyde Leopold Walcott. Ask me how great Frank Worrell was. I will not hesitate to place him alongside two other great human beings overflowing with charisma, Mr. Nelson Mandela and Dr. Martin Luther King.

ENDNOTES

1 Today, the ICC is known as the International Cricket Council, the chairman of which, over many years, has come from places such as India and the West Indies.

2 It is, of course, not likely that Professor Chomsky knows about the intricacies connected to Test Match cricket. Further, when Professor Chomsky uses Lord Russell's ideas in referring to a liberal education, he is conveying a very specific sense about being liberal: he uses ideas from the European thinker Von Humboldt to indicate that being liberal means being concerned about granting persons human rights, freedom, and equality. Very importantly, Professor Chomsky also calls for dissolution of (a) what he deems to be massive state power that threatens individual liberties (b) authoritarian control over production and resources which he states imposes drastic limits upon human freedom.

Readers would have noted that in my exploration of C. Wright's Mills' ideas, I allude to his views about a liberal education. I am not aware that Mills' work contains arguments for dissolution of the state, although—not unlike Chomsky—he explores the heavy burdens placed upon persons by state and corporate capitalism. Thus, while I find great favour with all that Mills offers about liberalism, and I accept Chomsky's ideas about inequities and threats to human freedom, I do not advocate dissolution of the state.

3 My interest in this speech emerged after I had heard a reference to it on an MSNBC programme, THE RACHAEL MADDOW SHOW. Upon examining the complete speech via the internet I discovered that some links between it and the Kilburn sense of cricket can be made.

4 Cricket, unlike many other games, is governed not by rules, but by laws.

5 Later in the writing I shall provide an explanation of the term, Hierogrammat, and the Egyptian Mystery System.

6 Before his time, Clyde Walcott had scored five Test Match hundreds in a single series against Australia. The feat was accomplished in the 1954-'55 series against an attack that included the legendary Lindwall and Miller, the second of whom, partnered opening batsman, Arthur Morris.

7 These words are, of course, those of British philosopher, Thomas Hobbes.

8 Ryle points out that ' category-mistakes' are made by persons quite capable of applying concepts in contexts with which they are familiar. They are, however, in their abstract thinking, unable to allocate the concepts to logical types where the concepts do not belong.

9 While it is indubitably the case that Walter Hammond, a brilliant slip fielder and useful medium pacer, scored a Test Match triple century, unbeaten against New Zealand in 1932-33, any reference to him as an all-rounder cannot lie with the Sobers class. Walter Hammond's Test Match wicket tally was 83 from 85 Test Matches, an average of 37.80. He held 110 catches. Sobers held 109 catches and took 235 wickets. His average is 34.03.

10 I note that the games associated with teams named the Rest of the World were not Test Matches, although when the first such event took place as a result of a cancellation of the 1970 South Africa tour to England players on both teams had been informed by the cricket authorities that the games would be given the status of Test Match games. This promise was not kept, however.

11 A term used by West Indies manager, Everton Weekes, while assessing the surprising England victory under Colin Cowdrey's captaincy from which excellent use was made of fine attacking fast bowling from John Snow.

12 I was at the Bourda Ground in the early nineteen-seventies and saw an obviously hugely disappointed Clive Lloyd head straight for the pavilion after having powered a straight drive right past the bowler for what should, at least, have been an easy run. Even today I wonder what the grimace on Lloyd's face looked like, when he found himself almost at the non-striker's end close to a Charlie Davis still resting on his immobile bat. Lloyd's involuntary hasty return trip to the dressing room was followed immediately by bottle throwing on to the playing area at the boundary behind the striker's end. With order restored and an uneasy calm, play resumed, came to an end without further incident, and favourite local son, Clive Lloyd, took the opportunity that very evening to issue a public statement on radio where he appealed for good sense from spectators to prevail for the rest of the Test Match.

13 James is referring to another disastrous West Indies outing (1951-1952) under Goddard, and another member of the Caribbean aristocracy, Jeffrey Stollmeyer. It is, doubtless, the case that the Caribbean players were competing against a group of legendary Australians led, most ably by skipper, Lindsay Hassett. History does, however, teach West Indians that colour privilege trumped leadership ability on that tour.

Another imponderable?

9th INNINGS
BRIAN LARA ON
A STICKY WICKET

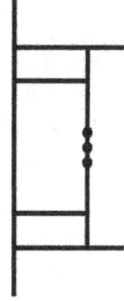

The names, Brian Charles Lara, have, of course, been omitted from my recognition. Such is not accidental. It is intentional. This is so, because in my view, Lara has certainly not shown he has been the beneficiary of a liberal education. Nor, for that matter, did he give himself the task of endowing himself with such education—at least, in the sense I derive from Lord Russell. I am by no means suggesting that he was unwise. I leave readers to be the best judges of his endowment with wisdom and how he used it. I am contending, also, that West Indies leader Brian Lara, who found himself—not unexpectedly—on many a figurative sticky wicket, a locus not unknown to most modern statesmen, has shown great incapability in negotiating the tricky territory which I invite readers to traverse.

For well over a decade (1995-2007), I have been grappling with the task of balancing my understanding of the commanding batting genius, and great leadership indiscretion, of Brian Charles Lara during three tenures as West Indies Test Match cricket captain (1998-2000, 2003-2005, 2006-2007). He is the illustrious Caribbean cricketer, someone whose sporting presence can reasonably be assessed as far more than a spectacle on a sticky wicket.

To those with deep interest in origins of the term sticky wicket,[1] reference can be made to one of several exchanges that American gentleman, Mr. Bingley Crocker, had with his English butler, Bayliss, about rounders, baseball, and cricket in London:

'It was a sticky wicket yesterday, sir, owing to the rain.'

'Eh?'

'The wicket was sticky, sir.'

'Come again.'

'I mean that the reason why the game struck you as slow was that the wicket—I should say the turf—was sticky—that is to say, wet. Sticky is the technical term, sir. When the wicket is sticky the batsmen are obliged to exercise a great deal of caution, as the stickiness of the wicket enables the bowlers to make the ball turn more sharply in either direction as it strikes the turf when the wicket is not sticky.'

'That's it, is it?'

'Yes, sir.'

'Thanks for telling me.'

'Not at all, sir.'

Regardless of whatever the term and explanation from butler Baylis mean to its many users who are familiar and unfamiliar with contemporary high level international cricket, I do not think I would be woefully out of order if I state that its figurative—if not broader—significance extends to settings well beyond cricket fields. Thus, although Brian Lara has literally roamed the reaches of many different types of wickets—grassy, flat, damp, moisture laden, hard, dry, bouncy, quick or lifeless—he would, by no means, be unaware of what such broader significance has had to his controversial presence within and beyond several cricket fields. It is this controversial presence that I find intriguing and deserving of incisive scrutiny. I want to know if major knocks from leader Brian Lara at bat have come from sticky wickets.

Appropriately, I note that from late 1992 to early 2007, no Caribbean cricketing persona loomed larger than the illustrious Test Match batsman, Brian Charles Lara, who was raised as a poor working class boy in a village of Trinidad, an island so named by the racist mariner, Don Christobal Colon (Christopher Columbus), because he thought he had seen a place of deep symbolism to his Catholic faith. I have a twofold aim in examining the Brian Lara persona. I want to explore his achievements as the world's best batsman on an intensely competitive international stage. I want—much more importantly—to place his accomplishments alongside his abysmal failure (his sticky wicket) as a three tenured leader/captain of a hapless team, West Indies.

One striking revelation of the juxtaposition was Lara's failure to incorporate and energise his leadership strategies with much needed post-imperialist assertiveness, a quality that defined the success of his predecessors who gave the Caribbean a new identity. In addition, his inability was a glaring parallel of high level political incompetence and economic mismanagement overwhelming the Anglo-Caribbean against a robustly destructive foreground of globalisation largely driven by the USA which has—itself—been destroying Caribbean cricket.

I am revealing the Anglo-Caribbean via the route of high level sport whose biographical attributes are embodied by sociological features which do demonstrate the meaninglessness of self-determination and socio-economic independence. This is not a point that will be lost to all those who are greatly concerned with how underdeveloped societies have been struggling against power from advanced capitalist interests whose singularly successful perversity has been its beguiling metamorphosis.

I am well aware that the psychological lens constitutes a valid measure of a persona of such greatness as the cricketer Brian Lara. I am, nevertheless, fully committed to laying bare ways in which one sport in the Anglo-Caribbean has become an instrument of neo-imperialism. Thus, I hope to make a contribution to debates about how this instrument, via cricket, has been crucial in destroying aspirations of an oppressed region where the blatancy of Eurocentric dominance emasculates productive values of Caribbean cultural forms.

I continue this contribution by observing that in 1998 John Woodcock offered this assessment of Brian Lara: "If Brian Lara does come to be regarded as one of the greatest batsmen of all time, it will not be for want of natural talent. No one has ever had more than that. But he has yet to show that he has the mind and the modesty to accommodate it... His problem has been in coming to terms with his fame and not being deflected by fortune... Chiefly, perhaps, it is a question of humility—for without that no batsman ever quite fulfils his potential." Woodcock also claims that Lara's progress towards what he terms absolute greatness has been slowed by instability.

One year earlier, in the *Sunday Times Magazine*, Woodcock provoked his readers with the contents of an exchange he had had with Sir Garfield Sobers. When Woodcock asked him what he thought of Brian Lara, the West Indian who had relieved him of his record Test Match score, Sir Garfield had this to say: "The word great is used too often. You can't call Don Bradman great and David Gower great too. If Gower was great you have to invent a different word for Bradman, who was an all-time great, like Everton Weekes. Greatness is something which comes with time and consistency of performance. There are exceptions. Ted Dexter [an England batsman/captain] wasn't around long, but I thought he was a great player because he was never in trouble and was always attacking and dominating the best bowlers in the world. I am certain Brian will be a great player, but he's not there yet. He's a potential genius, but they said that of Lawrence Rowe."

Woodcock readily credits Sir Garfield with correctness in his assessment that the word 'great' is not used "discerningly enough." Woodcock also registers a disagreement. He, Woodcock, viewed Lara as a "potential genius," a genius who is potentially great. Importantly, he adds that all geniuses do not become great cricketers any more than great cricketers are endowed with genius. It is problematic for even a genius to become great without singularity of aim and the humility to do the best with his talent. Cricketing greatness is to be found, not merely in statistics, it lies in manner, style, and impact of performance, as well.

Regardless of whatever dispositions observers hold towards Woodcock and Sobers, I am sure they can all agree about one thing. It is Brian Lara's unparalleled batting excellence during the period 1992-2007. I want to give my attention to much more than batting excellence. I want, among other matters, to conduct an exploration of Lara's massive presence in West Indies cricket by focusing shortly on the third occasion, 2006, when he was appointed skipper. My main aim in so doing is to initiate an assessment of the unprecedented three tenured leadership associated with the man deemed the world's best Test Match batsman, at the beginning of the twenty-first century.

This is, of course, the leadership that began late in 1998 and ended early in 2007. While I am fully aware that the assessment will not be regarded by Lara's adoring supporters as a favourable one, I must emphasise that my exploration, in its entirety, is used to strive for balance and fairness. Here, I am mindful of the principle that even greatness—potential or otherwise—is not completely insulated from, or can be galvanised against, criticism. It is thus with this cognisance that I adopt a position (albeit controversial) about Lara's third tenure as West Indies Test Match captain (2006-2007).

Brian Charles Lara, a skipper with whom abysmal leadership failure has been no strange bedfellow, was appointed in the spring of 2006 as West Indies captain for a third time. I dare say oddities have bedevilled West Indies cricket, since the loss to Mark Taylor's Australians in 1995, but the third Lara elevation stood well beyond the odd.

So, in a foreground of what I term one of the shameful Caribbean circus parades of the early twenty-first century, I began to vent my curiosity by pondering some issues: I began to think it might be a major contravention of good entrepreneurial principles to assess the Gordon Group[2] at the West Indies Board as an efficient waste management team. Be that as it may, I wondered if its members had too much of an affinity for reusing and recycling but were unaware of the links between refusing and renewing. Further, was the Anglo-Caribbean region so bereft of that cherished standard, self-criticism or self-censorship, that a crippling disease had invaded one of the highest levels of its sports administration? Was there any profound appreciation of the figurative futility of pouring new wine into old wineskins? Or was it possible that at the leadership levels, both within and beyond the field in West Indies cricket, there was no wine? When I, therefore, looked at whatever brew or concoction was being lowered onto Caribbean vessels, I wondered if a new generation of narcotised deck hands, Test Match cricketers led by Brian Lara, would be left to stagger aimlessly and drift amidst some of the roughest of world cricketing seas.

It is with equal significance that I did not discount the enormity of the adulation heaped upon Mr. Lara by his multitudes of disciples who have always served him as a Messiah. The Messiah, I note, was revered for his unbridled displays of selflessness and self-sacrifice, matters sorely needed in West Indies cricket but lewdly absent from Lara's two earlier and last leadership tenures. There were, however, both the possibilities and opportunities of reform or—even more desirable and humbling—chances of conversion, reminiscent of one which took place on the road to Damascus.

Frequent flashes of brilliance with a bat and the occasional flash of brilliance from blinding light, though subject to interpretation of science, art, as well as unshakeable senses of faith, meant different things to various categories of Lara supporters on and off the field. In those very lengthy shadows cast by ex-leaders, Frank Worrell, Garfield Sobers, Rohan Kanhai, Clive Lloyd, Alvin Kallicharran, Vivian Richards, and Richie Richardson, Lara might hardly have experienced visions of his own overwhelming twilight. Herein lay a huge impediment to any conversion along routes teeming with marauding foreign field forces eager to crush successive bands of beleaguered Caribbean opponents under him.

For the purpose of profound reflection, which I suspect was not alien to the Lara disposition at the beginning of the current century, I juxtaposed statements about the West Indies team the skipper had made, during the course of a tour to New Zealand, in early 2000, part of his first leadership tenure, with what took place in England (summer,2005) the year of unexpected Australian loss to England in an Ashes Test Match series. Immediately after a fourth consecutive one day loss to New Zealand by eight wickets in a five Match series (early, 2000) Lara wanted his charges to address themselves to very serious issues. Some of the main ones were the fact that West Indies cricket was always going to be around, a reality of which he and teammates wanted to be an integral part. He also noted that they were trying to "salvage" not merely a match, but also, "our [Caribbean] legacy." "I think it is important for us to realise that we've had great years. We've had disappointing times, and I think...the legacy will always live on and I think we need to play with a little bit more pride, a little bit more determination. And I think that's what missing in our game."

West Indies, under Lara, lost the fifth and final one day encounter which was preceded by total loss in the Test Match series. The BBC World Service programming is, once again, my resource for offering readers a sense of the depth to which Caribbean Test Match cricket had sunk under Lara's leadership. In his report, correspondent, Matt Davis, stated: "West Indies were once the Kings of international cricket and New Zealand the whipping boys. Now, it seems those roles have been reversed. The Kiwis' success comes off the back of series wins at home to India and away to England in the last twelve months. They also reached the semi-finals of the World Cup. West Indies, by contrast, went out in the first round of that competition and while they drew a Test series at home to Australia [under Lara] last year they've now lost their last ten matches on their travels. With fast bowlers, Courtney Walsh and Curtly Ambrose, in the twilight of their careers and few batsmen showing any consistency the future for cricket in the Caribbean looks bleak."

Lara relinquished the captaincy after the drubbing in New Zealand but, in most unprecedented fashion, was given the leadership role two more times, none of which was successful. Bleak is the world that engulfed and dogged all three of his tenures. At the start of his third tenure in 2006, Lara, the West Indies captain with the worst leadership record, needed to wonder how much of the "legacy" had remained in summer 2005, or was even more tarnished, when England defeated Australia, in astounding fashion, for the Ashes. For his consideration, I wanted to place the "legacy" alongside my own reasoning about that England success, which should not have been distant from his mind in 2006.

I reasoned that if Caribbean fans needed to remind themselves about who the geniuses in this great and glorious world of contemporary cricket are (not heirs to West Indians, Constantine, the three W's, Sobers, Lloyd, Holding, Kanhai, Richards, Kallicharran, Ram and Val, Gibbs, Butcher, Fredericks, Hall, Haynes, Greenidge, and the Griffiths, Herman and Charlie), they should immerse themselves beyond the wake of the 2005 England Ashes arousal. When that event came to an end, there was a parade in London. Queen Elizabeth 2 was moved to send a congratulatory message to captains, Ricky Ponting and Michael Vaughan. Part of the significant content was: "This has been a truly memorable series and both sides can take credit for giving us all such a wonderfully exciting and entertaining summer of cricket at its best."

Magnetised by the attractiveness of England's answer to Australian "arrogance," pommeland[3] to many Australian supporters, where soccer once soared to unimaginable dizzying heights, became a playground of pure pleasure. Against a foreground of demise of "the old enemy,"[4] I must stress that 2005 (like 1966, when England soccer captain, Bobby Moore and manager Alf Ramsey elevated compatriots above the rim of the Jules Rimet World Cup) might not have been "annus horribilis" for British Royalty. Nevertheless, I do recall that Garfield Sobers defeated England in 1966. So did his predecessor, Frank Worrell, three years earlier.

Worrell and his team were in Australia, too, in 1960-'61. What a farewell from throngs of thousands on Melbourne street parades they got as tribute for having helped resuscitate cricket and much more! Was the tribute not partly relevant to what he did for cricket in the tied first Test Match of that very series and far more! Was this not the same modest Frank Worrell who led an engaging side, secured affection and respect for cricket, from a society operable as a Commonwealth member in a setting known for its white Australia policy (Pullan 2001, p, 11)! Pullan adds, quite correctly, it was a Worrell led West Indies, in 1960-61, that restored excitement and pleasure to a game, but rescued Test Match cricket from the forbidding reputation it had acquired. I wonder what he did for cricket in the summer of 1963. I remember that Sobers, with that wonderful Worrell collaboration, beat Australian skipper, Bobby Simpson, Bill Lawry, Bob Cowper and the rest of the crew from down under in 1965. Was the defeat not part of an achievement of resuscitating cricket?

I am unaware of any message from Royalty to either West Indies captain for his service to cricket, during the periods I noted (1960-'61, 1963, 1965, and 1966). I should be reasonable (if not resourceful) and recognise that the years I have noted were times when Anglo-Caribbean assertiveness in a culture of resistance had just begun to challenge cultures of acceptance which flowed with British imperialism. When the assertiveness began to solidify in association with Clive Lloyd's leadership and reached its apogee as an important feature of Viv Richards', Test Match cricket, for which West Indies became the undisputed artists over more than a decade and a half, gained massive recognition outside the British Isles and its former dominion possession. No message from Royalty came to those captains.

In the summer of 2005, while Australia, "the old enemy," seemed to age, it received a message. So did England, its awakened challenger. Let us in the Anglo-Caribbean, therefore, not forget an important feature of the presentation. It emerged at a time when the ethnic nationalism significantly embedded in globalisation which defined ex-Australian Prime Minister, John Howard's Australia and Tony Blair's Britain replaced the blatant imperialism and settler sentiments noticeable in times of English and Australian cricketing superiority.

Painful as the realisation might have been, I had to locate it alongside that context of contradiction where no cleavage existed between Brian Lara's subtle and fully matured alienation from Caribbean cricket and the regional adulation showered on a shining star who could not elude the shame visited on a team smeared contemptuously with some of the thickest "whitewashes" from gleeful opponents. I submit that West Indies captain, Lara, was much more than a principal entangled within that monstrosity[5] of a player schism attributed to separate alignment with corporate information technology giants, Digicel and Cable and Wireless, over player contracts and sponsorship.

How could he and other close combatants who loved West Indies cricket and proclaimed their passion about its progress have been enmeshed in a contest fuelled by concerns over what two major players in the game, transcontinental profitability, meant to the regional sport at its highest level! One of those combatants was Mr. Teddy Griffith, the man succeeded by Mr. Ken Gordon as President of the West Indies Cricket Board. Mr. Griffith's collaboration with luminaries such as Dr. Keith Mitchell, Prime Minister of Grenada at the time, fell woefully short of promoting values of a culture of assertiveness, in Caribbean cricket. Coarsely textured blankets of inadequacy also burdened past Presidents, Peter Short, and Pat Rousseau, only two others who departed somewhat mysteriously after Sir Clyde Walcott.

I am not prone to indicting personalities. All those named (save Sir Clyde Walcott) were, however, some of the most public faces within institutions which continued failing to appreciate the crucial significance of "little people" participation to the sport. I was unshaken, as well, in my belief that: West Indies cricket in 2007, the year when its participation in the cricket World Cup was a horrible nightmare, had descended to disreputable depths. Thus, the Royal reprieve of 2005 granted to all new things good and great about that Anglo-Australian game crafted by imperialists, but uniquely redesigned within inventive field forces of "little people" of the Caribbean, was an immensely powerful force to England and Australia. West Indies creativity, which assigned new meaning to struggling Test Match cricket, and was deeply grounded in styles of those 2005 summer battles, became as useful a blur to the two societies credited by royalty with giving much needed domestic and international prestige to a quaint and boring indulgence.

The presence of this blur was heightened in mid-December 2006 and 2013-2014, when Australia avenged defeat by winning all ten Test Matches against England on the island continent and thus proudly regained the much coveted Ashes. Although some former leading England cricketers, most notably, Mike Gatting, Geoffrey Boycott, and Ian Botham, lamented the 2006 loss and criticised England severely, West Indians who followed the entire series should have been very aware that England did not surrender to opponents either in 2006 or 2013-2014. The first three games of the 2006 encounter were very keenly contested. Clearly, the much better side, in which Australian leg spinner, Shane Warne, ultimately secured seven hundred Test Match wickets, won the series. In part, the achievement was owed to what BBC radio commentator, Jonathan Agnew, assessed as an Australian side intensely focused on victory. When the teams met in 2013-2014, England was annihilated, chiefly as a result of some devastatingly lightning quick fast bowling from Australia which telecaster, Michael Holding, assessed with overwhelming approval.

What was far more significant about Australian intensity of focus was that it pointed to the depth of feeling, passion, and competitiveness in Test Match cricket which emanate from fundamental social tension between the imperial power (the pommes), and their discarded but inventive distant cousins ("the old enemy"). What the 2005, 2006, and 2013-2014 encounters made obvious to me was that there can be no sharper high level cricketing battle than that for the Ashes. England went to Australia with a strong and distinct interest in winning, and Australia—dependent on the perseverance, force, and drive of settler solidarity—was bent on crushing the invader.

Thus, regardless of the Boycott prediction in the wake of the third Test Match (2006) that England shall have been humiliated with an Aussie whitewash, one thing was certain to me and still is. In Test Match cricket, four superior teams, Australia, South Africa, India, and England stand out. Superiority was strongly evident in an England victory over Australia (2005), Australian victories over England (2006, 2013-2014), and South Africa (2014), Indian victory over Sri Lanka (2009) and West Indies (2011), when the sub-continental heroes crushed the Caribbean side like a steam roller on burnt earth useful for fair weather road surfaces, South African victory over Australia and Pakistan (2018, 2019), as well as Indian victory over Australia (2019). The four teams are several acres away from two other groups, the first of which is made up of Pakistan, Sri Lanka, and New Zealand. Below this second cluster is a third, constituted by Zimbabwe, Bangladesh, and West Indies. Dare I state that if Brian Lara had been selected for the West Indies captaincy against England in summer, 2007, an opportunity he very much wanted but did not get, his leadership burden would have been excessively heavy?

He did not shoulder such a burden, for the cricketing world knew, against a foreground of ignominious West Indies performance in the 2007 World Cup, he chose to announce he was relinquishing his leadership post. The announcement came on 19th April, 2007, merely two days before he had played his twenty-ninth one day international, a game against England, a team also eliminated from the 2007 World Cup.

On the very day of that loss, Lara did reveal that he wanted to tour England, in summer 2007: "I [Lara] know I sat with the selectors in Antigua to pick the team for England. Of course, I picked myself. That's all I know, at this present time." This England interest on his part does make me ponder. His participation in the selection process occurred quite some time after he had stated, publicly, that he was not going to play one day cricket anymore. Once he had taken such a course of action, the West Indies Cricket Board needed to make a significant decision: would its members maintain him for the England Test Match captaincy alongside a new West Indies captain for the one day games there? He has not revealed.

Although he mentioned that he helped in the selection process and did so, of course, as the Test Match and one day skipper, he has made no direct reference to any doubts or questions in Antigua from Board bosses about what his role in West Indies cricket following the 2007 World Cup would have been. Let me say that those bosses could not—in their grand wisdom—well before Antigua, have been unaware of doubts and queries over his leadership. He, also, well before Antigua, could not have been ignorant about doubts and queries surrounding his leadership.

Despite the absence of his direct reference to those doubts and queries, I submit that his good judgment, prior to Antigua, could not have been so fogged by naivety that he was unaware his leadership was questionable: on 21st April, he told the international cricketing press he had informed the West Indies Cricket Board President, Mr. Ken Gordon, that he wanted to move on with his life, added he felt he did the right thing, and offered the Board a chance to move ahead with West Indies cricket. These were utterances from a man possessed with unconditional love of West Indies cricket who knew no need for him to be physically on fields of play for the region existed. Here was a man convinced there was no reason for him "to carry on, at this stage"—a man wanting to play his part in enabling necessary team alteration against a foreground of his unfulfilled expectations.

When the Lara decision to leave all forms of international cricket came, most—if not all—of his adoring supporters knew of his illustrious record, at the crease and beyond: the leading run getter in Test Match cricket, at the time [11, 953 runs in one hundred and thirty one games],[6] a three tenured captaincy in forty-seven Test Matches of which his leadership brought him and teammates ten victories. Before I explore more of his leadership and extraordinary batting prowess in detail, I am compelled to address myself to what I see as the significance of his third and last departure. In order to do so, effectively, I want to begin by using some more of Brian Lara's own words and those of former Caribbean cricketers.

During the course of his April 2007 announcement, Lara, who stated that he held West Indies cricket dear to his heart, noted that he had had a good run in the game and enjoyed every single day of play. He wanted the cricketing world to remember him as a batsman who offered entertainment to fans and endeavoured, in adversity, to perform at his best. Lara also acknowledged that he had played with great West Indians and held the hope that once it was time for him to give back to Caribbean cricket he would be in a position to do so.

Thus, it came to pass that on Saturday, 21st April, 2007, at Bridgetown, Barbados, thirteen years after he had dazzled the cricketing world with a scintillating record breaking triple century [375], Brian Charles Lara played his last one day international and captained West Indies for the last time. His team narrowly lost to England and his own contribution with the bat was [18 run out]. Lara, proud of the West Indies team, told a crowd full of strong supporters that he had a tremendous time as a West Indies player whose happiness depended upon fans recognising that he entertained. The heights of that pride came in three batting accomplishments, [277] against Australia (1992-1993), [375] and [400] against England (1994 and 2004), as well as captaining his side to victory in the Champions Trophy (2004).

Lara added that when he began playing cricket in the Caribbean, West Indies were dominant in international cricket, a position he always wanted for the region. He however, admitted, that decline, which burdened West Indies cricket for the previous ten or twelve years, had been most disappointing to him. He declared that he is a "team player" desirous of seeing West Indies regain its top position within international cricket.

It is unlikely that the cricketing world shall see such a grand batsman of his stature in the short or medium term. I offer my claim in full knowledge about the enchanting presence of the two batsmen luminaries from India, Pujara and 'KING

KOHLI.' I say, boldly, that he ended his career as one of the greatest of all batting geniuses for West Indies. I offer this claim in full knowledge about George Alphonso Headley, the three W's, Clyde Walcott, Everton Weekes, Frank Worrell, Gary Sobers, (four with higher Test Match batting averages that him), Rohan Kanhai, Clive Lloyd, Roy Fredericks, Desmond Haynes, Gordon Greenidge, Alvin Kallicharran, and Vivian Richards. I add that some may claim he rivals Donald George Bradman as the world's best Test Match batsman, despite the Don's [99.94] batting average, [6,996] runs in only [52] Test Matches, and two Test Match triple centuries.

The cricketing world does, of course, know that well before Lara had made his very first triple Test Match century, the Don had compiled [309] in a single day. Brian Charles Lara of Cantaro, Santa Cruz, Trinidad, does stand well above the three G's, Sunil Manohar Gavaskar [India], David Ivon Gower [England], and the more famous or infamous of the Gloucestershire Graces, Dr. William Gilbert [England], as well as the four H's, John Berry Hobbs, Walter Reginald Hammond, Len Hutton [England], and Australian, Matthew Hayden, the last of whom, had overtaken his [375], briefly. How could I exclude Sachin Ramesh Tendulkar [India], over whom Australian paceman, Glenn McGrath, gives Lara the edge as the single best batsman he challenged! I include Tendulkar, although the batting genius from India scored more hundreds than Lara and has a slightly higher batting average, one that is not statistically valid inferentially, than the West Indian: throughout his long career Tendulkar, "the undisputed God of India," was never a member of either the [300] or [400] Test Match batting class. In the time away from the field, Lara's presence could, thus, become hugely attractive as an after-dinner speaker, broadcaster, telecaster or author.

Among former West Indies cricketers who offered their assessment of the April, 2007 announcement were West Indians Gary Sobers, Wes Hall, Charlie Griffith, Philo Wallace, Jimmy Adams, Joel Garner, and Michael Holding, the last of whom asserted that captain Lara remained longer than he should have. Holding stated that he should be thanked, but his departure marked the beginning of time for West Indies cricket to look forward. From Gary Sobers, one of Brian Lara's grandest admirers, came these comments: during the previous two and a half year period (I suppose, from late 2004), West Indies cricket experienced massive problems. Specifically, the West Indies Cricket Board had inadequate funds for training facilities, it was unable to field strong teams, and it was bedevilled by strikes. In a resort to the figurative, "King Cricket" added that a solid foundation is necessary to construction of a house which will be problem bound in the absence of such a basis.

Wes Hall, who had a sparkle in his eyes when he told me about Brian Lara, more than twenty years ago, but was at a loss for words, asserted that Lara, the great batsman, had left a fantastic legacy. Hall's bowling partner, Charlie Griffith, claimed that filling Lara's shoes will demand extremely hard work from numerous West Indies players. Philo Wallace lamented the departure as a big loss to world cricket. Jimmy Adams, Lara's former skipper and also Test Match player under Lara, deemed his former skipper a genius whose value to West Indies cricket was enormous. In Adams's words, Lara, the virtually single handed standard bearer for a decade who shouldered a huge burden, was still able to produce phenomenal statistics. Perhaps the most elegantly placed—if not artfully constructed—of discreet comments came from former West Indies quick bowler "Big Bird" Joel Garner. He said Lara made a choice to retire, a move he, Garner, could not say was the wrong one. Garner added: "A captain can only be judged by his success record and that's not good in his case. Now we have to take drastic steps to carry West Indies cricket forward."

Let me say that no West Indian lover of Caribbean cricket—friend, foe, or adversary of Lara's—critic or supporter—could have avoided assessing additional implications of the man's departure. In this regard, I do want to state that the West Indies citizenry have to live with the immeasurable depth of that leave-taking. They must live with the certainty of its debt and death, all of which bear scrutiny.

When Lara was given the leadership role, initially his mentor Gary Sobers, was so pleased that he issued a public statement about his protégé's elevation. Sobers told the cricketing world he would be extremely happy to serve as Lara's manager. He was discreet enough not to have mentioned the term 'coach' or 'cricket manager.' I am certain principals at the West Indies Cricket Board heard the former captain, Sobers. Sobers, despite his links to Lara, was, however, confined to the margins of service for the skipper. Sobers, despite much more than the figurative weighty tonnage of cricketing expertise formed and shaped by the three W's, was spurned by a West Indies Board. Sobers, despite his obvious validation within the anti-imperialist assertiveness of such expertise, was never integral, in any official capacity, to Lara's leadership attempts at re-establishing West Indies Test Match artistry, inventiveness, and insightfulness.

His—and I must state—Lara's designification through spurning constituted one of the worst forms of disrespect for the Frank Worrell wisdom and the Sobers efforts, within and outside the ambit of captaincy. Neither were the wisdom nor the efforts given the appropriate placement required at the close of the twentieth century and beginning of the twenty-first. Where I ask, rhetorically, was the Worrell continuity, via Sobers, in the Lara three tenured captaincy, even as it was foundering in the desolate chasms of sporting doldrums! Where was the fusion of the Sobers creative imagination with the Lara creative imagination through the confidence Worrell kept in Sobers! This is, I emphasise, the Gary Sobers whom that calypso King of the Caribbean, Francisco Slinger, "The Mighty Sparrow" ", assessed as the greatest cricketer on Earth or Mars, shortly after Australia was beaten by West Indies for the first time. This is the Sobers Sparrow invited West Indians to observe in his soaring, well beyond lyrical delights of artistic imagination that has been authentically Caribbean.

While continuing to live with death, debt, and depth, I think of C.L.R. James, about whom the insightful West Indian intellectual Norman Girvan, states: "I feel strongly that no Caribbean person can regard himself as being truly educated without having at least some familiarity with the life and work of C.L.R. James. Moreover, the work of James becomes a door through which one can enter an appreciation of all the great issues of the twentieth century."[7]

My thinking leads me to analogise about the Lara captaincy: (a) In Girvan's words, James would not have been successful in leading a government, for he was too much of an iconoclast and an uncompromising person (b) Though he was a grand thinker, teacher, inspirer, and organiser, he might well not have been a good administrator. Girvan found it difficult to imagine James being a Caribbean Prime Minister. (c) He would, most certainly, not have maintained good relations with political allies in the short term.

I will certainly use James' work as a strong basis to my own exploration later, but here I want readers to know that I do not view the Brian Lara three tenured Test Match captaincy as good administration in leadership. I readily credit him for having been a fine thinker in the batting department. I cannot grant him credit as an administrative organiser, inspirer, thinker, or teacher. Insofar as Lara having been iconoclastic is concerned, all I can state is that despite his bold assertion that West Indies cricket has been dear to his heart, he was never able to develop formulae out of Caribbean traditions for helping to create that bond of collective significance the Caribbean region sorely needed. Allow me to continue with James and the importance of analogising.

James has become well known for very sharp contrasts he provides about a youth, Matthew Bondman, in Trinidad. Bondman—unkempt, crude, barefooted, vulgar, impoverished—was a genius as a boyhood batsman, but greatly disliked by James' puritanical grandmother and teacher aunt. James, however, adored what he termed the saving grace in Matthew, his batting, which attracted crowds agog at the youngster's sterling stroke play. This was the same Matthew who befuddled another keen observer because of the great distinction between his batting excellence and waste of talent. One of the things I ponder when I think of Brian Lara, arguably the world's greatest Test Match batsman of the late twentieth and early twenty-first centuries, is how could a man of such extraordinary batsmanship fail—against grand Caribbean expectation—to liberate his team and region! I am saying that the Lara saving grace lay in his batting and it was the batting that left many an adoring admirer agog, at a time when he, a leader, needed to, at least, salvage the fortunes of a region. Herein lies a massive contradiction which will occupy me throughout my writing.

What more can I state about the Lara presentation in April 2007? The announcement served to devastate hordes of his loyal supporters, whose adoration of his mesmerising batting persona—albeit unidimensional—satisfied massive yearning within a socio-economically stagnant region, the Anglo-Caribbean, for much sought after heroism. Further, the pain of devastation would have been quite profound in view of: several of those supporters were unshaken in their conviction that Brian Lara would be the West Indies liberator capable of using the 2007 World Cup for resuscitating the sagging fortunes of Caribbean cricket. Given the massive attractiveness of his superb batting displays, which, clearly, were unique, there arose the obvious danger his departure would serve to quicken the demise of West Indies cricket already damaged heavily by powerfully uncontrollable forces such as globalisation.

I make this last point, because none of his batting contemporaries, at the beginning of the twenty-first century—including Ramnaresh Sarwan, the man chosen in 2007 to replace him—demonstrated consistency of excellence at the crease. Further, if the fans attach themselves to his idea of entertainment, it would be very reasonable to say that the quality of entertainment he gave cannot be matched by those contemporaries. Lack of fit would pose a huge problem for a West Indies Cricket Board which—despite the grand entertainment spectacle of the 2007 World Cup—was unable to fill stadia. I find it noteworthy to report an observation from Woodcock (1998), who states that Don Bradman's presence wherever he played served to double attendance. I do not know of figures for crowd sizes at Caribbean locations where Brian Lara played. His absence from those locations after 2007 cannot be very helpful to future crowd sizes.

The Lara decision to leave international cricket came rather soon after he had stated publicly that he was going to play Test Match cricket into his forties. I observe that his intention came before the beginning of the Super Eight stage of the World Cup. Once the Super Eight stage had unfolded and his side tottered to elimination, he let the cricketing world know he was leaving. For a man who had come to rely strongly on the validity of his own judgment to elevating team fortunes, his less than stellar batting performance at the Super Eight stage could have served as a strong basis to serious reconsideration of the intention. It is quite plausible that part of his reconsideration emerged out of contrasting his own experience with the fact that he, the three tenured skipper, albeit via the route of contradiction, did not select—that much he claimed—teammates whom he led onto the field. Non-participation in selection tasks is something to which he alluded when the team had lost a vital Super Eight game.

Brian Lara began his third tenure at a time, 2006, when he, the most experienced cricketer on his team, had to work with a coach whose big cricketing experience was no match for that which he, Lara, had amassed. When a team is winning, differences become designified, but are magnified in a foreground of losses. In the role of captain who had three chances to aid revival of West Indies cricket but became associated with the worst leadership record, he had to have known that in the blame game he would attract more criticism than his coach.

A lot of that criticism—stinging in its presentation—came from Michael Atherton, former England Test Match captain, who covered the 2007 World Cup for the British newspaper *The Daily Telegraph*. In an article for the paper, on 10th April, 2007, Atherton reported that the decision to have Lara lead West Indies for the big one day event was a personal one adopted by Ken Gordon, West Indies Board President who, from Atherton's standpoint, would have become cognisant of his mistake. The ex-England skipper continued: "It [the mistake] is an easy one to make, for it comes from assuming that Lara's gifts are not confined to batsmanship. Only someone with no cricket in his soul could fail to appreciate Lara's exquisite batting. But many of the qualities that have made him the great batsman of the past 15 years—the self-obsession, the ego, the individualism, the outrageous talent—are qualities that often do not transfer to captaincy. This World Cup has not told us much we did not already know about the Prince of Port-of-Spain: he is a great batsman who is singularly ill-equipped for leadership."

The very first thing I notice about the Atherton indictment is a grand contradiction posed in assessment. I am not an avid student of Marxism, in its various intellectual twists and turns dialecticians have created from their interpretation of it. Nor for that matter do I still delve into depths to which some eminent scholars of the twentieth century had taken their followers in trying to unravel complexities to that grand and "irremediable antagonism between the demands of instinct and the restrictions of civilisation" (Strachey, 1961, p. 4), which the psychoanalyst Sigmund Freud, identified in some of his earliest writing.

Quite apart from his work on dream analysis and neurasthenia, which Strachey claims Freud attributed to civilisation, the psychoanalyst regarded in some quarters as the greatest psycho-pathologist (Laing 1965) is well known as a theorist and practitioner who studied the self/personality, partially but significantly, by exploring the constant struggles humans wage against forces of power and authority. It would be reasonable to state that he advanced a theory of the individual psyche rooted in the social which determined the vicissitudes of persons' instincts. He was, in his time, certainly, one of the foremost archaeologists of the mind who delved into those painful inter and intra-personal battles that burdened some individuals. He searched by using psychoanalysis as a means of bringing to consciousness what persons had repressed in their unconscious.

One of the main goals in searching was to locate what he deemed various defence mechanisms, such as denial, projection, regression, and displacement. To several English speaking experts, a very important foundation to his work lay in his argument that all individuals strive to attain balance between two instinctual forces, the pleasure seeking, hateful, envious, violence prone id, and the controlling, authoritative, inflexible, morally restrictive superego. Both of these, in his view, had to be balanced by ego, a conscious, mediating force of reason.

Those with additional interest in psychoanalytic matters can examine the work of thinkers such as Marcuse (1955, 1969), whose brilliant exploration during the early twentieth century, still stands as testament to situating self-obsession, ego, and individualism within wider social contexts. I lay no claim to being a psychoanalyst. Nor, for that matter, can I claim to be using psychoanalysis as a basis to exploring Brian Lara's "ego." This much I do know. Once Michael Atherton uses the term, ego, in relation to the ex-West Indies skipper, he has stepped onto psychoanalytic terrain.

I am, thus, in a legitimate position to pose certain queries about Lara, despite Atherton's explicitly non-technical reference to ego: is Atherton suggesting that Lara's failed Test Match captaincy strongly reflected an imbalance between his id and superego? How much conscious control has the Lara ego been able to exercise over the forces of id and superego? To what extent was Lara's captaincy indicative of what he had been repressing? What defence mechanisms had been deeply harboured within the Brian Lara psyche? In what ways can Lara's defence mechanisms—if they do exist—be connected to the manner in which his psyche was rooted within Caribbean social circumstances? These are not questions to which I shall provide replies. I regard them as probative stances readers should feel free to explore. In so doing, they would enable themselves to sharpen their focus on that beguiling Lara problematic, cricketing leadership.

Further, the minute Brian Lara chose to tell the cricketing world about his unconditional love of West Indies cricket, he stepped onto territory covered by psychologists and psychiatrists who follow ideas of the psychotherapist, Carl Rogers. The Lara use of the term 'unconditional love' can be associated with the ideas of client-centred therapy and unconditional positive regard, ideas attributed to the American psychotherapist, Carl Rogers, who credits Standal (1954) for having developed the second concept.

I will also step into this territory, first, with statements from the therapist himself. Then I shall ask, via Atherton, about the authenticity of that Brian Lara unconditional love of West Indies cricket. Rogers (1986) derives a set of conditions he deems necessary for initiating what he assesses as constructive personality change, conditions when understood collectively appear to be sufficient for starting such change. This is a claim he offers not with assurance about its correctness, but with the disposition that it contributes value to theorising amenable to proof or disproof associated with extending knowledge to the psychotherapy field.

He lists six conditions required for personality change in clients: (a) two persons are in psychological contact (b) the client, the first, exists in a state of incongruence, rendering him anxious or vulnerable (c) the therapist, the second, a person who is congruent, is integrated in the relationship (d) the therapist experiences unconditional positive regard for the client (e) the therapist experiences empathetic understanding for the client's internal frame of reference and aims for communicating her experience to the client (f) communicating the empathetic understanding and unconditional positive regard is attained. In addressing himself to explicating the term 'client-centred' or 'person-centred' approach, he writes:

> The central hypothesis of this approach can be briefly stated. It is that the individual has within himself or herself vast resources for self-understanding, for altering his or her self-concept, attitudes, and self-directed behaviour—and that these resources can be tapped if only a definable climate of facilitative psychological attitudes can be provided. There are three conditions that constitute this growth-promoting climate whether we are speaking of the relationship between therapist and client, parent and

child, leader and group, teacher and student, or administrator and staff. The conditions apply, in fact, in any situation in which the development of the person is the goal (Rogers 1986, p. 197).

Further, the therapist's immersion within the person-centred approach, becoming a companion to the client on a journey to the core of the self, contributes to the client's self-exploration and self-discovery and, ultimately, constructive changes in client personality as well as conduct.

Three elements needed from the therapist for completion of the journey are what Rogers terms (a) congruence, realness, or genuineness (b) caring, prizing, or unconditional positive regard, (c) empathetic understanding. The first indicates that a therapist, through being open about feelings and attitudes flowing in the relation, contributes to close matching or congruence between what is experienced at "the gut level," present in awareness, and what is conveyed to the client. The second element exists when the therapist experiences a positive, non-judgmental, accepting attitude towards what the client experiences. The therapist, via "non-possessive caring," should be willing to accept whatever immediate client feelings are expressed. These include resentment, fear, anger, courage, love, and pride. Hence, when the therapist prizes the client in a total, instead of a conditional manner, conditions for forward movement are created. One requirement for empathetic understanding, the third element, is accurate awareness from the therapist about the client's personal meanings and feelings, as well as the therapist conveying "this acceptant understanding" to the client.

Unconditional positive regard is not a situation in which some client feelings are accepted and others are rejected by the therapist. There is as much an acceptance of presentation of painful, hostile, defensive, or abnormal feelings as presentation of good, positive, mature feelings. The therapist expresses unconditional positive regard for clients as persons. Communication of unconditional positive regard from a therapist offers a non-threatening context in which clients can explore their most profoundly shrouded aspects of inner selves. The therapist is not paternalistic and sentimental; he is not superficially social and agreeable. His profound caring is a necessary ingredient of the "safe" context in which the client can take the role of exploring himself and sharing deeply with another person.

Let me say that captain Brian Lara was never in the official position of a therapist. Nor was he mandated to deal officially with players who were his clients. Group leader and staff administrator, Lara, the West Indies captain, I submit—like all other captains for the region—did have to play the role of therapist, but failed to come anywhere near to showing unconditional positive regard for players and the mass of people in the region. The captain who did show this quality was Frank Worrell, whom Sobers, Kanhai, Lloyd, Richards, and Richardson made great efforts to emulate.

Through Michael Atherton I must, therefore, ask how much did Brian Lara care for or prize West Indies cricket? I have to ask where was his non-possessive caring, empathy for realness and congruence to, as well as unconditional love or unconditional positive regard of West Indies cricket in early 2007? Atherton notes that when Andy Roberts offered criticism about the World Cup team composition for a game against New Zealand, Lara readily reminded listeners that he, the skipper, played no part in team selection. Atherton always thought, however, that Lara had been a selector. "He is a selector. More than that, he ought to have been present at the selection meeting to choose the squad. In fact, he asked the selectors if he could be excused to attend to something in Trinidad. It is not clear what could have been more important. Given his self-inflicted absence, his subsequent berating of the selectors is remarkable, and he was forced to issue an apology to Roberts."

Though remarkable, this turn of events is not astounding to Michael Atherton. A similar situation unfolded in 2006, in the aftermath of the Indian tour to the West Indies. Then, Lara vented culpability against every factor other than his own leadership. Apart from having criticised pitch preparation for the Sabina Park Test Match against the Indians, Lara did not spare West Indies selectors in stating he did not get the side he had wanted to, but later apologised.

When he later stated publicly that he might relinquish the post of captain, because of devaluation to his reputation, rather than his own lack of leadership success, he had, according to student of British history Michael Atherton, been responsible for abdication of responsibility of which King Edward VIII would have been proud. Those who cannot picture the relevance to the English King should, at least, appreciate the significance of Atherton's point. Edward VIII, who has long since passed away, gave up the throne at a time when British citizens were badly in need of leadership—moral and sovereign. At the time Britain knew of winds of war blowing far beyond the German Reichstag.

Yet, King Edward, harshly criticised—even today—made a deeply personal choice to give up the throne, of very great importance to the collective soul of England, in preference for marriage to the American divorcee, Wallis Warfield Simpson. Apparently, King Edward was not cognisant of the fact that England always expects. Apparently, Brian Lara was not cognisant of the fact that West Indies always expects from its captains, who must spurn individualism and choose the collective soul of the Caribbean region.

It is at this juncture that I must refer to what I deem three emphatic assertives from Lara which contradict, very loudly, his claim about not being a selector: (a) "I [Lara] know I sat with the selectors in Antigua to pick the team for England." (b) "Of course, I picked myself" (c) "That's all I know, at the present time." I cannot, also, resist invoking the interest of that wisely inquisitive interrogator at the Watergate investigation of President Richard Nixon. Some do recall a question about the President being posed by the Harvard educated legal scholar that dubbed himself just "a country lawyer": what did he know and when did he know it? For Brian Lara, I reserve: what did I, Brian Lara, "know" about not having been a selector? When did I, Brian Lara, "know" that? How should I, Brian Lara, balance my replies with the unmistakable intentional force conveyed in the meaning of the three assertives?

The matter of individualism in Brian Lara's case is so important that I cannot allow it to exclude my exploratory gaze. I make reference to it in (Walcott,2007) when I report ideas of Cornel West who addresses himself to the dialectical links between individuality and community. Individuality, which should be intertwined with community, should never be absorbed in its distinctiveness and singularity by community. At the same time, individuality should not descend into a selfish, rugged, and ragged individualism.

Here is reference to delicacy of intersecting between individuality and what West terms democratic community which facilitates the flowering of someone's identity, who and what someone is as an individual but aids formation of community where ordinary persons are able to engage themselves in order to take steps which shape progress in their lives. What do I mean when I use the terms identity and community? Here, I observe that there is no single meaning for them. I borrow from West (1999, pp. 501-502), who states that identity, which has to be dealt with by exploring credible options for people, is connected to matters of protection, association, and recognition. What are persons protecting? It is their bodies, labour, and communities they use as means of forming links to those who value and respect them.

Community, which partly encompasses tradition, is used as a glue to identity what persons claim proudly as their own. Further, according to sociologist, Nisbet (1966, pp. 47-48), community encompasses all forms of relations characterised by high degrees of personal intimacy, emotional depth, moral commitment, social cohesion, and continuity in time.

> Community is a fashion of feeling and thought, of tradition, of commitment, of membership and volition. It may be found in, or be given symbolic expression by, locality, religion, nation, race, occupation, or crusade. Its archetype, both historically and symbolically, is the family, and in almost every type of genuine community the nomenclature of family is prominent. Fundamental to the strength of the bond of community is the real or imagined antithesis formed in the same social setting by the non-communal relations of competition or conflict, utility or contractual assent. These, by their relative impersonality and anonymity, highlight the close personal ties of community (Nisbet 1966, p. 48).

I add that if there was a major leadership challenge for captain Lara in what I noted about community, it lay in his ability to recognise that the throngs of West Indians on whose behalf he boldly paraded ideas of tradition needed to experience the benefits of his presentation. All too disappointingly, humiliatingly, and disastrously, the presentation was lewdly absent.

There is another very significant sense of community which was clearly absent from the Lara tenures. That sense comes from hooks (2003, p. 163), who acknowledges that community is an idea encompassing thoughts about being in the company of persons like ourselves, members of the same class, race, social standing, and ethnicity. She adds that all humans evoke senses of links between such thoughts of community and passion. She does, however want to know how many of us extend ourselves compassionately to locate an intimate other for the purpose of moving beyond the exclusivity featured in likeness. She sees community as emanating from people being wary of the danger of evoking experiences they do not challenge themselves to actually practice.

Wariness is, unquestionably, tied to matters of sacrificial love and preserving integrity of being in profound battles to transform society exemplified via the query, "What are the actions I will concretely do today, in order to bring myself into greater community? With that which is not here?" The hooks reply to her own query can be located in part of a letter she wrote to fellow intellectual, West:

> We bear witness not just to our intellectual work but with ourselves, our lives. Surely the crisis of these times demands that we give our all. Remember the song which asked "is your altar of sacrifice too late?" To me, this "all" includes our habits of being, the way we live. It is both political practice and spiritual sacrament, a life of resistance. How can we speak of change, of hope, and love if we court death? All of the work we do, no matter how brilliant or revolutionary in thought or action loses power and meaning if we lack the integrity of being (hooks 2003, p. 164).

Readers are, of course, free to substitute their own terms for those which fit the Brian Lara occupational spaces, spiritual thought, and practices and can certainly do their own inquiry about his integrity of being.

I want to say that beauty in joyfulness of that Lara unparalleled batting individuality descended to a Brian Lara individualism which overwhelmed his role as captain, he methodically stripped of links with West Indies community through promoting the nurturing and blooming of leadership found in people such as Worrell, Sobers, Kanhai, Lloyd, Richards, and Richardson.

No less pertinent than Brian Lara's individualism were what I term two destructive features of any traces in his claim to unconditional love or unconditional positive regard of West Indies cricket. Any expert on unconditional love or unconditional positive regard will state, very readily, that they are vacuous and insignificant if they are not underpinned by authenticity and respect. Michael Atherton's writing is again the substantive source for exploring these features.

Atherton recalls what he deems the verbal dexterity of Brian Lara associated with the abandoned 1998 Test Match encounter between England and West Indies, at Sabina Park, Jamaica. At the time, Lara, playing in the West Indies, for the first time as Test Match captain, agreed with his opposite number, Atherton, the Test Match referee, and umpires, to discontinue the game, because of a poorly prepared wicket. An astounded Michael Atherton, however, read in the Jamaica daily, *The Gleaner*, that Lara expressed surprise at the abandonment decision: if the West Indies skipper had had the chance to make a decision, he would not have discontinued the game, for cricketers have to deal with tough situations. Atherton revealed that he later inquired of Lara about his turnaround. He replied that in Jamaica he had to exercise care, because he had only just taken over the job of captaincy from local legend, Courtney Walsh, whose popularity on the island he wanted to boost.

Let me say that in offering the turnaround, Brian Lara presented a justification rather than an excuse for it. I shall state more, at a much later point in my work, about the technical distinctions between excuses and justifications. I do notice that the Lara justification did not bear a hint of what was bad or inappropriate about it.

In addition, it is one thing to boost someone's popularity. Use of routes, methods, or styles to so doing is quite another thing. What respect did Brian Lara show towards Michael Atherton with whom he had made an agreement earlier, in the presence of officials responsible for conduct of the Test Match? I pose my query in full knowledge that there was a lack of good faith in the Lara turnaround. Dare I state it is one thing to display verbal dexterity? It is quite another to maintain trust while doing so. I also fail to see the links among Lara's view about toughness of cricketers, being careful in Jamaica, and the legend, Courtney Walsh.

If Lara was attempting—albeit by implication—to justify an exclusive link with Jamaica via Courtney Walsh, then he was disrespectful to the entire West Indies region. Walsh's legendary status has never been restricted to Jamaica. I say the same about Roy Gilchrist and Lawrence Rowe (Jamaica), and will do so in regard to Learie Constantine (Trinidad and Tobago), Basil Butcher, Clive Lloyd, Alvin Kallicharran, Rohan Kanhai, Lance Gibbs, Roy Fredericks, Shivnarine Chanderpaul (Guyana), Everton Weekes, Clyde Walcott, Frank Worrell, Wes Hall, Charlie Griffith, Malcolm Marshall, Desmond Haynes, Gordon Greenidge (Barbados), Vivian Richards, Richie Richardson, Curtly Ambrose (Antigua). Herein lies a clue to the man's failure at maintaining that delicate interplay between individuality and community.

Another clue, one that can be located via the route of verbal dexterity, came to Caribbean citizens in December 2009, when Brian Lara made certain claims about West Indies cricket on the occasion of receiving the Honorary Order of Australia Medal from Mr. Kevin Rudd, Australian Prime Minister. According to a report in the *Guyana Daily, Stabroek News* (2nd December, 2009), Lara issued a stinging rebuke of the structure of West Indies cricket at the time. Some of his scathing commentary came in the form: "I say it all the time that the Australians are very good at taking mediocre young cricketers and making them into great talent." And in emphatic contrast he asserted that West Indies are good at taking great talent and transforming it into mediocrity.

While blaming what he reportedly believed is the set-up of Caribbean cricket, he added if there was a different structure geared to ensuring teenagers are categorised into one group for demonstrating they are talented both on and off the field of play, a meaningful step will have been taken. His great hope for stemming the continuing spiralling of West Indies cricket was immediate planning from the work of an astute group of persons. In very specific terms, he gave consideration to a five or ten year plan aimed at restoring a semblance to the state of West Indies cricket in the 1970s and 1980s. He called for a major reorganisation of the game and urged authorities to initiate plans for halting its slide.

Well! Well! Well! What a mouthful from the former captain who had more than five years to use his leadership craft within the field and beyond for reorganising Test Match cricket against Australia and other sides! Did Brian Lara not have enough time to show how astute a planner he was on and off the field for shepherding his flock to green cricketing pastures! Insofar as he showed he was not shy of traversing the contrastive route for highlighting talent in the 1970s, 1980s, and mediocrity in the late 1990s, as well as the early twenty-first century, what reasonable explanation has he offered for having been so instrumental to the catastrophic circumstances which engulfed West Indies Test Match cricket? What a wordy contribution to so few from a leader who had so much unlike the worthy contribution to so many from another leader, Frank Worrell, who gave so much to so many, although he had so little!

At the beginning of his article, Atherton writes about Brian Lara: "How can one man elicit such a range of contrasting opinions? Truly, Brian Lara is the Geoffrey Boycott of the Caribbean." Assuming that Atherton is reasonable, my reply to his query would be that Lara is either a dialectician's dream or a dialectician's nightmare. Further, I cannot resist the urge to compare Brian Lara and Geoffrey Boycott, Yorkshire's egocentric perfectionist (Swanton 1975, p. 138). Doing so enables me to shed some more light on the former West Indies captain.

In one of his many writings about notable Test Match cricketers of the twentieth century, John Arlott titles an article about Geoffrey Boycott "Embattled Misfit." Was captain Brian Lara embattled? Was captain Lara a misfit? My reply, in both instances, is affirmative. Was Test Match batsman, Brian Lara, a misfit? My reply is negative. Was Test Match batsman, Geoffrey Boycott, a misfit? My answer is negative. Was England Test Match captain, Geoffrey Boycott, a misfit? My reply is affirmative. Did Test Match batsman, Brian Lara, tower over Test Match batsman, Geoffrey Boycott? My answer is affirmative. What then is so significant to me about the Atherton opening?

Quite simply, it is the lure of looking at Brian Lara's selfhood and Geoffrey Boycott's selfhood. My own sociological shorthand for the term selfhood is: the identity someone constructs for him/herself within particular cultural formations where s/he has to ask who s/he is on account of his/her relations with contemporaries and predecessors. May I begin with Geoffrey Boycott through the eyes of Johnston (1989), who assesses him as a complex character, an enigma, apparently possessed of a dual personality, a feature Johnston associates with an apocryphal story.

Here is the story in exactly the way Johnston offers it:

Geoff reported to St. Peter at the Pearly Gates, who asked who he was. St. Peter looked at a list which he had, and then said: 'I'm sorry. There's no Geoff Boycott on the list. If you are not on it, you can't come into heaven. So, please go away.'

Geoff walked off very disgruntled, but after a few minutes' thought went back to St. Peter and said: 'Look, I don't think you realise who I am. Geoffrey Boycott of Yorkshire and England. 8,114 Test runs, 22 Test hundreds, 48,426 first-class runs. One of the greatest batsmen of all time. Please let me in.'

St. Peter got very annoyed. 'I repeat, if you are not on the list, you cannot come in. For the last time, please go away.'

So Geoff reluctantly left and as he did so a small old man with a long grey beard came up to St. Peter and, when asked his name, said: 'Geoffrey Boycott'.

'Oh do come in, Mr. Boycott', said St. Peter, 'we are delighted to see you. Please come straight into heaven.'

An old cricketer who was standing by said to St. Peter: 'What's going on? You turn away the real Geoff Boycott, and admit this old man with the long grey beard who pretends he is Boycott but obviously isn't!'

'Oh,' said St. Peter, 'we have to humour him. He's God and he keeps on thinking he's Geoffrey Boycott.

I think the reference to duality of personality should, in no way be construed as allusion—oblique or obvious—to what many a psychiatrist and clinical psychologist deem a version of personality disorder. My interpretation lies in the realm of what is grandly contradictory of Geoffrey Boycott's selfhood. Similarly, Brian Lara's selfhood is mired in grand contradiction.

Johnston notes that there is a great deal to be admired in attainments of the wonderfully fit Geoffrey Boycott. To me, those are attainments of Geoffrey Boycott, the Test Match batsman. Many West Indians, doubtless, admired the attainments of superb and wonderfully fit Test Match batsman Brian Lara. He, like Boycott, as seen by Johnston, was a major part of a story of complete dedication, determination, self-discipline, and importantly, single-mindedness.

Geoffrey Boycott, the Yorkshire county player, was unpopular with contemporaries, and some of the younger ones, according to Johnston, became discouraged and failed to live up to early promise as a consequence either of excuses he offered for his conduct or contradictory dispositions. Oddly, though, Johnston continues, the Yorkshire public was apparently mesmerised by his run making.

The more he scored, the more they worshipped him, and he always had a tremendous following wherever he went. Little did they realise that the more runs he made, the less likely were Yorkshire to win. He took so long about it. A perfect example was in 1971—his first year as captain of Yorkshire. He had a wonderful season—for Yorkshire alone he scored 2,197 runs and 11 hundreds and an average of

109.85. And yet Yorkshire had what Wisden describes as 'the worst season in their history.' They finished thirteenth in the County Championship, and had the longest sequence of seventeen matches without a victory which the county had ever known. They scored a lot of runs, but far too slowly, and only picked up 47 batting bonus points compared with 82 scored by Kent. Only three sides scored fewer than 47 (Johnston, 1989, pp. 156-157).

The first two sentences of the quote are clearly applicable to Brian Lara. Captain Lara did not take long periods to gather his Test Match runs. In addition, his sides, unlike the county sides led by Geoffrey Boycott, did not score a lot of runs, though. The Test Match teams captain Brian Lara led have finished close to the bottom of the international table and under him could achieve only one notable series victory against the more established Test Match teams. That sole victory took place against England, in 1998.

Another basis to close comparison between Brian Lara and Geoffrey Boycott can be seen in two separate courses of action which they justify and, simultaneously, could not help presenting as grand contradiction. What a close look at contradiction and justification reveals is the complexity of their selfhood. Once I deal with these matters, I shall begin addressing myself to understanding Brian Lara through the figurative lens of a jazz sensibility.

I have stated already that the Brian Lara turnaround, in regard to abandonment of the 1998 Jamaica Test Match, was both a justification and contradiction. Let me, again through the eyes of Johnston (1989), and telecasters Tony Greig, Geoffrey Boycott, as well as Michael Holding, start exploring the Geoffrey Boycott contradiction and justification. During the course of the second innings in the crucial fourth Test Match between England and West Indies at the Kensington Oval, Barbados, (1990), an intensely animated debate between Geoffrey Boycott and Michael Holding arose over merits of a decision rendered by umpire Lloyd Barker, against England batsman, Robert Bailey, as a result of vociferous appealing from the West Indies captain, Vivian Richards, for a catch by the wicketkeeper, Jeffrey Dujon.

Obviously perturbed, Geoffrey Boycott and Tony Greig had characterised the Richards demonstration as pressuring of the umpire. Michael Holding, on the other hand, while acknowledging the apparently dubious nature to the ruling, could see no point in being perturbed. I suppose, in an effort to inquire about umpiring decisions that do not always find favour with competing parties in Test Match cricket, Holding asked Boycott whether he had ever stood up, rather than walked to the pavilion, when given out caught behind. In a paraphrase of the query, Greig was explicit in asking Boycott whether he ever stayed at the crease when he had "nicked one." In an equally explicit manner, Boycott said he "certainly" had not.

Telecaster Geoffrey Boycott was, however, the individual, who, in his role as England Test Match batsman against Australia (1971), was involved in a run-out incident:

Geoff called for a run on the off-side but the fielder hit the stumps at the bowler's end and he was given run out. He flung his bat down on the ground and stood with his hands on his hips, before being 'steered' towards the pavilion by Greg Chappell (Johnston 1989, p. 156).

When asked by Johnston about his conduct, his reply contained the admission that he was out but only by a few inches, a margin so insignificant that any umpire should have granted the batsman the benefit of the doubt. For those who prefer a dramatic account of the Boycott run out a valuable resource can be found in the writing of Swanton (1975, pp. 130-131) who deems the Yorkshireman's conduct as thoroughly bad for cricket.

From his vantage point square with the stumps, Swanton observed an Ian Chappell throw from mid-wicket which hit the timber. Certain that Boycott, whose bat was in the air and not grounded, was out, *The Daily Telegraph* correspondent uttered 'He's out.' The umpire—perfectly positioned to observe proceedings—deliberated momentarily, before raising his index finger. Boycott, however, threw his bat on the ground and for Swanton there was the sorry spectacle of Gregg Chappell returning it to him without ceremony, whereupon he glared at the umpire.

Lest observers forget, it was Brian Lara who claimed, after defeat at the hands of an opposing side in a 2007 Super Eight World Cup game, that he did not select the team and he had to do the best with players chosen for him. Atherton has, of course, noted that he has been very integral to selection. In his own words, on 21st April, 2007, he had sat in the company of West Indies Board officials to help select the team to England and included himself.

How could a man who had just told the cricketing world, publicly, that he would not play any more international cricket, after the 2007 World Cup game against England, at the Kensington Oval, turn around and state he was not just desirous of touring England in the spring and summer of 2007, but he had also included himself as a member of the 2007 touring party! How could a man brimming with unconditional love of West Indies cricket demonstrate such affection with authenticity, not know of his horrible leadership record, but await a decision of the selectors in regard to his eligibility for the England tour! The best way in which I can deal with my astonishment is to state that he viewed his role in singularity. That is, most likely, as a Test Match batting genius.

Singularity of genius has, clearly, not been a defining feature of the selfhood possessed and displayed by the American jazz prodigy and iconic artist, trumpeter Wynton Marsalis, winner of nine Grammys and a Pulitzer Prize, whose caressing of a complex note I have heard described as trying to change a fan belt on one's car with the engine running. Marsalis, the affable, dignified, modest genius, a walking encyclopaedia of jazz, was born in the Deep South of the United States, undisputed territory of white racism. The Marsalis challenge of this evil has come largely through the splendour with which he displays his unique classical and jazz accomplishments. Wynton Marsalis has very strong ties to the extended family of African American contemporaries and predecessors.

Those are some of the important links from which he has constructed his selfhood and identity. He is a prime exemplar of connections between individuality and democratic community. When he speaks about great admiration of trumpeters, Clifford Brown and Louis Armstrong, as well as composer, Duke Ellington, he is not endeavouring to construct a selfhood dangling from pathways of personalities. He is authenticating and celebrating a collective legacy by cherishing and validating service to community through apprenticeship. He is expressing immense respect for music which he states "creates community and speaks to the human soul." In more general terms, he asserts that the arts are our "collective heritage." He adds that we are better people if we know what Shakespeare was talking about, what Louis Armstrong was actually saying through his horn, and what Beethoven struggled with, for such knowledge enables us to "speak with the wisest people who ever lived."

Clearly, Wynton Marsalis, who laments the absence among many of his countrymen of knowledge about such figures as the transcendentalist, Walt Whitman, is not pandering to some kind of narrow African-American essentialism. He is using the arts to validate community writ large. Surely, a testament to validation can be located in what was reported via the programme SIXTY MINUTES to be one of his latest projects, SWING SYMPHONY, in which classical and jazz music are combined.[8] This was supposed to be the result of collaboration between the Lincoln Centre Orchestra, which Marsalis leads, and the Berlin Philharmonic. Talk about SWING SYMPHONY was presented by SIXTY MINUTES as partly a survey of how American jazz evolved, and became reflective of accomplishments of such geniuses as Charlie Parker and Duke Ellington, the second of whom, Marsalis gives accolades: (a) the greatest American composer with the broadest variety of pieces, (b) someone possessing the greatest depth of insight into the nature of the American character, (c) a lover of America and people, generally.

Those who still do not get my point about Marsalis can turn to comments cricketing prodigy, Sachin Tendulkar, made to me in 1996. He had this message for young cricketers: "my advice is to stay away from smoking, drinking; respect your elders, be honest, be true to the game, because finally, the hard way you choose, is the right path—I feel. I mean the wrong paths are much easier to follow. But face the hard life and, definitely, you'll be successful. And that will last forever. Whereas, you choose a wrong path—there might be an overnight success, but it fades away." In the Tendulkar message there is more than authenticity, respect of authority in predecessors, a detached juxtaposition of opposites, rather than an ensnaring by their intersecting, all of which, I add, for emphasis, have deep foundation in self-sacrifice and spirituality.

I find great elements of self-sacrifice, spirituality, and juxtaposition of opposites in Marsalis. It is he who experiences no difficulty in stating: "I like pressure. I like the challenge. I don't have a problem with it, at all. I like the feeling of nervousness. I like the feeling that something counts and I like to be tested." He notes, also, that when he is caressing a note and making a tender musical statement while playing with others there is huge intensity which demands more of itself. In what I see as unmistakable reference to both spirituality and juxtaposition, he emphasises: "You have to have that edge. You have to have that sexuality. You have to have that primitive feeling and the more primitive your feeling the more refined your concept is—the more primitive you have to be." My own view of the statement above is it points to a heightened state of ecstasy whose close parallel is mysticism, the combination of intense feeling with ingenious thinking. I hope my readers can use the significance of the Tendulkar message and Marsalis immersion in music as important foundations for engaging me in my efforts to explore the Brian Lara iconic stature.

In the event that they cannot, some remarks Ian Chappell made about being a good captain.[9] might be important. Chappell noted that respect, which has to be earned in three categories, is vital to being a good captain. The categories, what I term roles, are player, human being, and leader. Respect gained within the three part set, complemented with good knowledge of cricket employed via common sense, and boldness linked to a reasonable share of luck, can move a captain to the rank of excellence. The presence of all of these features within a team of very good players makes a captain unstoppable.

No one can harbour doubts about Brian Lara's batting ingenuity. The massive reservations lie within areas of respect as a human being and leader. Brian Lara was, certainly, bold, and although he had a good knowledge of cricket, he exhibited glaring flaws in using cricketing common sense both on and off the field. He might not have enjoyed a great deal of luck as a Test Match captain, but as a three tenured skipper, he should have been, but was not, very well placed to lead teams of players who could develop into the category of very good. Thus, from my standpoint, he was neither an excellent, nor unstoppable captain.

To all of his adoring supporters who will not hesitate to bundle me along their routes of contempt, I must state what I read more than a decade ago, when Brian Lara's career was at a crucial juncture. In an article at the time, for the British publication *TOTAL SPORT*, I saw from a correspondent:

Brian Lara may not be at the crossroads of his career, but he has, certainly, reached a fork in the road. He makes no bones about his yearning to "control the show." Some believe this is the only way his talent can reach full fruition. You mean he could be even better? The chances, conversely, are that the burden of inspiring his fellow countrymen would be detrimental. England made that error with David Gower, confusing a genius for a leader. When it all comes so very easy, how can you empathise with mere mortals (Steen 1996, p. 66)?

While echoing the precautionary principle, Steen continues by arguing that Lara's position at the time he had reached the crossroads, 1996, was inopportune for appointing him to the job of West Indies captaincy: budding immortals require fresh challenges, but Brian Lara, despite the passion he declared for cricket, was "a truly free spirit at play," someone whose leadership appointment would have been unwise.

In line with the tenor of Steen's thinking, I urge Brian Lara's admirers and critics to explore my writing as a basis for determining, among other matters, three tenured captain, Brian Lara's passion for Test Match cricket, his control of the West Indies cricket show, whether his batting genius was confounded or conflated with leadership, his cricketing immortality, and free spirit.

It is only a matter of fairness for my reference to Brian Lara, the three tenured West Indies captain, to be bounded by a massive distance from Brian Lara, the jazz fighter among other Caribbean cricketing jazz fighters. It is, thus, to his placement among these other cricketers that I direct my attention now.

ENDNOTES

1 My reference to the term, sticky wicket, is derived from an article, "A Sticky Wicket, Sir," by British author, P. G. Wodehouse. The article and the exchange between Messrs. Bayliss and Crocker appeared on pp. 500-505 in the book, "Through The Covers," by Christopher Lee, Oxford University Press: Oxford (1996/1997).

2 The surname of the President of theWest Indies Cricket Board, where he replaced Mr. Teddy Griffith in 2006. After Mr. Gordon had left his post, he was replaced by Mr. Chetram Singh himself—no longer Board President.

3 I have coined the term, 'pommeland', as a result of a description ("the pommes") applied to England by the former Australian captain, Mark Taylor.

4 A term I heard former England Test Match hero, Sir Ian Botham, use to describe his Australian opponents.

5 The reference to monstrosity stems from a 2005 battle involving Digicel and Cable and Wireless, two communication giants, over team sponsorship among Mr. Teddy Griffith, Board President at the time, the President of the West Indies Players' Association, and two different West Indies player factions on team sponsorship, to one of which, Lara as unofficially connected.

6 In late October 2008, Sachin Tendulkar, the imposing Indian Test Match star, surpassed Brian Lara's total at the Test Match level, interestingly, in a series against Australia. When Tendulkar edged passed the West Indian, Shane Warne, the mysterious former Australian spinner, stated publicly that he estimated Tendulkar as a better batsman than Lara. It is not a matter of statistical triviality to note: Tendulkar, who began his Test Match career three years earlier than Lara, got his runs while playing in more games than Lara.

7 Part of Dr. Girvan's address at the University of the West Indies Seminar, "Remembering C.L.R. James" (May, 2000).

8 I heard the report from correspondent, Mr. Morley Safer, more than eight years ago, when he was interviewing the Jazz genius.

9 The Chappell remarks appeared originally in the Oxford Companion to Australian Cricket, edited by R. Cashman, W. Franks, J. Maxwell, B. Stoddart, A. Weaver, and R. Webster. The remarks appeared, also, as parts of a Chappell article, "Dogs Need Not Apply," in The Wisden Cricket Monthly Magazine, June, 1997: pp. 28-30.

10th INNINGS
CARIBBEAN
CRICKETING LINKS

Excellent Test Match batsman Brian Lara, who gave scintillating performances against some of the best Test Match bowling attacks, can be placed alongside other West Indies cricketing luminaries that have made and remade Test Match cricket. He can be positioned, with the greatest of ease, in the illustrious company of players such as Learie Constantine, who, according to Arlott, could take a hard return from the outfield with his back to the thrower, Herman Griffith, Charlie Griffith, Wes Hall, Garfield Sobers, Lance Gibbs, Roy Fredericks, Gordon Greenidge, Rohan Kanhai, Clive Lloyd, Vivian Richards, Shivnarine Chanderpaul, Richie Richardson, Everton Weekes, Clyde Walcott, Frank Worrell, and Desmond Haynes. These are all just some of the players whose performances can be seen as creative pursuits of persons that avoided being steered by Eurocentric knowledge of imperialist England (Nunn 200, pp. 430-431) and preferred to apply tacit knowing from transformative learning of an innovative Caribbean (Polanyi 1959, pp. 12-20), for the purpose of expressing themselves on cricket fields via a jazz sensibility.

Polanyi sees tacit knowing as unformulated knowing which is very different to explicit knowing. Tacit knowing is knowing persons have in the act of doing things, while explicit knowing is knowing persons have as a result of what is laid out in such things as maps, written words, or mathematical formulae. Polanyi adds that persons always know tacitly that they are holding their explicit knowing to be true. He notes that the essential logical distinction between the tacit and the explicit is that individuals can reflect on things done explicitly in ways they cannot reflect on tacit experiences. Importantly, the structure of tacit knowing is demonstrated via understanding coordinated parts of comprehensive wholes. In such manifestation, persons shift attention from apprehending particulars to the understanding of their joint meaning. Nunn lists seven matters that express Euro-centricity. They are: dichotomous reasoning, employment of hierarchies, analytical thought, objectification, abstraction, extreme rationalism, and de-sacralisation.

With a focus on dichotomous reasoning, I note that it leads to either/or conclusions and is incompatible with holistic reasoning. It is different to diunital reasoning, which leads to both/and conclusions that are incompatible with distinctions between us and them. Once phenomena have been subjected to division, dichotomies are arranged into hierarchies of greater and lesser worth. In dichotomies, one position is regarded as superior to its opposite, the inferior. Thus, the distinctions, which indicate that some things are better than others, constitute the foundation for creating relations among people based on power differentials.

In dealing with conceptualisation about a jazz sensibility and transformative education via the figurative in phantasising, I aim to locate Lara among other West Indies Test Match players who are jazz fighters. According to Davis (1992, p. 26), if people have to address themselves to the necessary means for revolution, it would be imperative to ascertain what is required for reshaping contours of political activism. Although she chooses a figurative type of phantasising, she is firmly focused on the values of inclusiveness. She reports that she sometimes daydreams about masses of black males in front of the United States Supreme Court chanting "End sexual harassment by any means necessary," "Protect women's reproductive rights, by any means necessary," in the company of women uttering "Right on!" Following Davis, my phantasy is about countless little people in front of the West Indies Cricket Board Headquarters shouting "End repression of our former Test Match cricketing heroes, by any means necessary," "Protect the cultures of resistance constructed by these heroes, by any means necessary," in the company of current players who utter "Right on!"

Those of us who are familiar with the ideas of Malcolm X would realise that Davis is referring to him. Elsewhere, Davis (1992, p. 39) provides one of the strongest instantiations of both/and, rather than either/or, dichotomous thinking in an excerpt from an interview the freedom fighter gave the Young Socialist Publication (spring 1965). For her, the excerpt points not only to critical reappraisal of his black nationalist philosophy, but also, to reassessment of male supremacist ramifications within black nationalism.

She quotes him as having stated:

I used to define Black Nationalism as the idea that the black man should control the economy of his community, the politics of his community and so forth. But when I was in Africa in May, in Ghana, I was speaking with the Algerian ambassador who is extremely militant and who is a revolutionary in the true sense of the word... When I told him that my political, social and economic philosophy was Black Nationalism, he asked me very frankly, well, where did that leave him? Because he was white. He was an African, but he was Algerian, and to all appearances he was a white man. And he said if I define my objective as the victory of Black Nationalism, where does that leave him? Where does that leave revolutionaries in Morocco, Egypt, Iraq, and Mauritania?

I note that the probative stances of Malcolm X follow his judgment about appearance. I submit that the other value of his pronouncement lies in his realisation that the efforts of separation in attempted exclusivity which has been paraded to justify distinctions among biological races lacks validity. As such, he offers observers an important glimpse of pitfalls to either/or reasoning.

While alluding to sensibility of a jazz freedom fighter, West (1992, p. 47) points, not merely to musical art form. Part of his use is figurative, in that it represents an improvisational mode of being made up of flexible or malleable stances to social reality which are inconsistent with supremacist ideologies, dogmatism, and either/or claims. The role of a jazz freedom fighter is to foster democratic sensibility through critical exchange and breadth of reflection via accountable leadership which invigorates and gives sustenance to world weary individuals.

From my standpoint, the figurative reference also means revolutionary and mellifluous. Further, the significance of this second feature should be seen through the foundation it forms for supporting a delicate cross-cultural balance between what West terms the dialectical interplay of individuality and community. Perhaps, most importantly, a jazz sensibility is indicative of vigorous totalising efforts at using non-European roots for absorbing and dissolving European imperialist and neo-imperialist imposition.

Anyone who doubts the value of my using a jazz sensibility in regard to Caribbean cricket should understand that in Brian Lara's case, the left hander was born on an island rightly regarded as the birthplace of steel band or steel pan music which has similar applicability to cricket as I have stated about jazz. Further, my use of figurative roots does parallel what I see as the very imaginative or intensely visionary. As such, there is a connection among present, past, and future. To those inclined to frown on my link with the imaginative and visionary, I react by stating: parallelism is alive and well, when one looks at the manner in which visions and imaginativeness defined the early existence of every single great West Indies Test Match cricketer who scaled massive socio-economic hurdles to become batting, bowling, and fielding luminaries in Test Match circles.

Brian Lara, was doubtless, one such luminary, but his light burned brightly solely within the spaces of batting—not leadership in the role of West Indies Test Match captain. This is a claim I am prepared to support by relaying some very significant excerpts from the Memorial address delivered by E.W. Swanton, at Westminster Abbey, on the occasion of the passing of Sir Frank Worrell, affectionately known to the imposing correspondent of *The Daily Telegraph* as Frank. Once I have supported my claim, I shall categorise Caribbean cricketers as jazz freedom fighters.

One of the many things I greatly admired in Swanton can be described as his tireless pursuit of selflessness and fair play in a sport he usually promoted as a unifier of people. It is thus important that I use his meticulously glowing and fully deserving offering at the Abbey as an indirect way of highlighting the leadership inadequacy of Brian Charles Lara.[1] While eschewing any vulgar reference to the obvious, Worrell's cricketing techniques and field accomplishments, Swanton noted the grace, dignity, and unruffled serenity that defined the late captain's persona.

He asserted, further, that under the subtle knack of Worrell's personality, colour differences and Anglo-Caribbean prejudices appeared to be obliterated. This was, to the correspondent, the type of personality inseparable from a sense of West Indian Federalism defined by a deep-rooted commitment to managing unity in diversity. Worrell, the unifier via his sincerity and friendliness, was a sporting catalyst at a time when international rivalry became far too bitter and ugly. Swanton noted that the 1960-'61 West Indies tour to Australia was triumphant within and beyond the field. This was the memorable tour which culminated in a Melbourne motorcade where half a million people lined the streets. He added that the pleasant and convivial Worrell, whose profound and candid convictions were never flaunted, transformed the English presentation of cricket and reciprocated all of England by being the ideal cricketer.

I suppose in Swanton's eyes the reciprocation was strongly encapsulated in a rendering of this tribute which prompted his rumination over the Worrell status as a paragon.

One of the opposing captains in an appreciation of him [Worrell] wrote that however the game ended 'he made you feel a little better.' (Which isn't a bad Epitaph). No doubt he made us feel a little better, from the youngsters in Boys' Town at Kingston to Sydney hoboes on the Hill.

Worrell, the unquestioned opposite of the strident and bumptious, was the supreme exemplar who contributed largely to admiration and appreciation of West Indians in England and across the Commonwealth.

I suppose one of the most interesting implications of the foregoing is not that Garfield Sobers, Rohan Kanhai, Clive Lloyd, Vivian Richards, and Richie Richardson, all of whom followed Frank Worrell in leadership posts, stepped into their predecessor's shoes and tried filling them on the field. It was, also, that they strove admirably to follow the paths he had laid for West Indies cricket beyond playing areas. I ask readers to think of Garfield Sobers—long after he had left the Test Match scene—reminiscing about two matters: (a) hard-fought contests against intensely keen opponents—tussles which were, however, followed by friendly gatherings of teams whose members left field matters where they had emerged (b) lamenting the frequent absence of such gatherings in late twentieth century Test Match settings.

Think of Rohan Kanhai batting in a Trinidad Test Match against England in 1968 when he had edged a ball caught by England captain, Colin Cowdrey, at slip and the umpire disallowing an appeal for a catch. Then consider Kanhai turning to the England captain, asking him if he had caught the ball, and walking to the pavilion once Cowdrey said he had. Think of the Kanhai, Sobers, Lloyd and Richardson unbridled simplicity expressed in inimitable ways and consider Frank Worrell. Regrettably, the other significant implication is not just that Brian Lara lacked simplicity, but that he also had no formula or scheme for traversing routes taken by leader, Frank Worrell, the man who strove, admirably, to make his charges beneficiaries of unconditional positive regard and did express unconditional love of cricket.

When I think of the Worrell leadership, I cannot avoid the enormous significance of that James contrast in regard to Matthew Bondman and Brian Lara. Like Matthew Bondman before Worrell's time, Frank Worrell—albeit as a Test Match batsman—used to play a stroke of grand elegance by going down on one knee. This was, of course, a stroke that left countless adoring West Indians far and near agog. Though of working class roots, Frank Worrell was not from the lumpen stratum within the Anglo-Caribbean. Though he was raised in Barbados as an African-Caribbean member of the working poor, he was certainly not lower working class. If I continue to follow James, I would have to conclude, however, that Frank Worrell—working class—knew how to utilise formulae for being empathetic with players whose roots were also lower working class.

Brian Lara, also of lower working class origins, was unable to locate any such formulae for Test Match cricketing success. Frank Worrell was the grand transformer, the shrewd inventor, two qualities which proved elusive to skipper, Brian Lara. It goes without saying that Matthew Bondman did not possess any of the two qualities. The big question, the workable answer to which James himself—tireless in his struggles for the West Indies working class—was unable to provide is thus: how should the working class proceed in efforts to employ Test Match cricket as the transformative avenue for regional pride, collective identity, and great international success? Worrell, clearly, had the answer and was very successful, but Brian Lara was nowhere close to replying.

Despite this great Lara shortcoming, I am compelled to use West's and Davis' claims as strong bases for formulating five groups of West Indies cricketers as jazz freedom fighters whose centrality to the greatness of Caribbean cricket has been linked inextricably to tacit knowing and non-Eurocentric thinking:

Group 1: Herman Griffith, Learie Constantine, George Headley

Group 2: Everton Weekes, Clyde Walcott Frank Worrell, Allan Rae, Robert Christiani, Alfred Valentine, Sonny Ramadhin, Roy Gilchrist, Jeff Stollmeyer

Group 3: Garfield Sobers, Lancelot Gibbs, Basil Butcher, Rohan Kanhai, Charlie Griffith, Wesley Hall, Seymour Nurse, Charlie Davis, Joe Solomon

Group 4: Clive Lloyd, Vivian Richards, Richie Richardson, Curtly Ambrose, Andy Roberts, Michael Holding, Courtney Walsh, Jeffery Dujon, Roy Fredericks, Desmond Haynes, Gordon Greenidge, Joel Garner, Colin Croft, Larry Gomes, Alvin Kallicharran, Lawrence Rowe, Malcolm Marshall, Shivnarine Chanderpaul, Ramnaresh Sarwan, Chris Gayle

Group 5: Brian Lara [the batsman—not the Test Match captain]

Lara's location in the groups, whose cricketing presence I do not associate with Eurocentric thinking, is fully deserving. I want to deal with this matter by using ideas of C.L.R. James, again. I can use, also, the example of Sobers' links to Worrell and Lara, fearlessness of Roy Fredericks, as well as Clive Lloyd's links to Lance Gibbs. My aim here is to make the case, and make it cogently, that all the cricketers named, Roy Fredericks, Gary Sobers, as well as Vivian Richards, a man steeped in socio-political consciousness about imperialism—not Brian Lara—served their apprenticeship on the field of play in the presence of greatness. With parallelism staring me squarely in the face, I note that unlike Test Match captain, Lara, President Obama could have wanted no more auspicious fields of play overflowing with greatness to serve his apprenticeship than those in Chicago where he worked as an assertive lawyer/community activist, then was elevated to the United States Senate. How can I exclude US President George Herbert Walker Bush, who passed away at 94 on 30th November, 2018! While I have made reference to him already, it is very much in order for me to do so here; I ask readers, yet again, to look for, and focus upon, DIGNITAS, PIETAS, as well as VIRTUS.

The youthful Episcopalian/Anglican, son of investment banker, Mr. Prescott Bush, whose business partner was Mr. Averell Harriman, veteran in the US domestic political and foreign policy theatres, was schooled very early on by his parents to aim for selfless service to country. This pupil at Andover, a notable private prep school comparable to the British and Australian Tonbridge, Shrewsbury, St. Peter's, Clifton, Matthew Arnold's Rugby, and Merchant Taylor's, Prince Alfred College, as well as Geelong Grammar School, began naval aviator service at eighteen, went to Yale where he became baseball captain, moved to congress and, though quite later—not until 1988—reached the highest political office, the presidency. I harbour no doubt that it was DIGNITAS, PIETAS, and VIRTUS which saturated his selfless service through which all those reflecting upon his passing state he became outstanding in the deftness with which he managed US foreign policy. No one should ever think that he did so without a lengthy apprenticeship on domestic and international fields, theatres where he was surrounded by, and immersed in, greatness. There is, quite, simply, no valid basis to making such a claim about Prince, Brian Lara, to whose links with the Gary Sobers greatness, not on, but away from, cricket fields that I turn.

THE LARA-SOBERS CONNECTION

I want to initiate exploration of this relation by doing three things: (a) offering a description of Lara's record breaking performance, when he scored an unbeaten [375] against England, at the Antigua Recreation Ground in 1994 (b) pointing to what Sobers did immediately after Brian Lara had surpassed the record breaking [365] made by the former against Pakistan, in 1958 (c) conveying Sobers' thoughts about

Lara, the batsman Sobers (1996), who holds a special affection for Lara, asserts that the latter is the greatest batsman the world has seen since the emergence of Vivian Richards. He adds that Richards himself would state that Lara is the more gifted of the two West Indians. The potent significance of the foregoing pronouncement can, perhaps, be appreciated by referring to a comparison between Lawrence Rowe, another superb West Indies player, and Brian Lara.

> *Strange to say now, there was another, more gifted West Indian batsman than Lara to emerge in recent years. Lawrence Rowe had more potential and was more graceful in his movement. He also got behind the ball better and, of course, had a far better start to his Test career than Lara, making 300 runs over two innings on his debut for the West Indies against New Zealand in 1971-'72, and following that with a triple century against England (Sobers, 1996, p. 135).*

Why then would Sobers claim that Lara is the most gifted of Caribbean batsmen since Vivian Richards? For me, the answer lies in this Sobers assessment. Lara is a special player who approaches the game with diligence, is a fine thinker, and possesses good technique. These positions are well exemplified by the observation that Brian Lara altered his approach to the game significantly during the course of the (1992-'93) tour to Australia. At the time he understood that maintenance of his position in the Test Match team and its overall progress required scoring more than a speedy [40], [50] or [60]. He had to concentrate and score massively.

Once Brian Lara had exceeded the [365], at the Antigua Recreation Ground, Sobers walked out to the centre, embraced the youthful hero, and proclaimed Lara was well aware that he, Sobers, would appear in the centre on such a great occasion. Sobers asserted further that records are made to be broken. He noted that he had frequent discourses with Lara about the latter's batting, the 1994 performance of which I describe now.

After what surely did not count as a Barbados blessing,[2] devoted disciples of West Indies cricket would have been hoping to banish all English demons from St. John's, Antigua. Their expectations were fulfilled, most admirably, by close of play on day three of the fifth Test Match, at the Antigua Recreation Ground. It was there the West Indies reminded their opponents that comfort in the region is not a commodity purchased cheaply on every Caribbean pitch.

The person largely responsible for placing his side in this position of great prominence was Brian Lara, the twenty five year old Trinidadian left hander who scored [375] runs, an accomplishment which stands above that of Sir Garfield Sobers' [365] made in March 1958 at Sabina Park, Jamaica. Lara's [375] is, of course, higher than Donald George Bradman's [334] at Headingly [1930], Len Hutton's [364] at the Kennington Oval [1938], Bob Simpson's [311] at Old Trafford [1964], Bob Cowper's [307] at Melbourne (1966), Lawrence Rowe's [302] [1974], Hanif Mohammad's [337] at the Kensington Oval [1958], as well as Graham Gooch's [333] at Lord's [1990].

It is the late John Arlott who once said since cricket is the most profound of all ball games, it is fitting that it should be the best served by literary standards. My words cannot match the intensity of Lara's illustrious performance. It was, thus, from a position of humble satisfaction that I re-presented some of the more significant paths to his progress. On the morning of the first day's play, 16th April, Lara found himself in the company of Jimmy Adams very early in the West Indies first innings and was playing the rather unusual role of restricting his aggressive inclinations: both openers, Stuart

Williams [3] and Phil Simmons [8], were back in the pavilion but fewer than [30] runs were on the board. The first [50] came only after the twenty-eighth and final over before lunch, when West Indies progress looked more like a pedestrian crawl than a race of champions.

After lunch, Lara exploded with massive bursts of brilliance and reasserted his authority by applying exquisite timing in response to England's hostile surge. Three figures were duly registered against his name, in the fourth over of the final session, when he pulled Phil Tufnell to the mid-wicket boundary. At close of play, his unbeaten [164] was an example of pure elegance that typified a flawless command performance, on a stage he had specially erected for expression of excellence.

On the second day, 17th April, he raced to an immaculate double century and strengthened his platform for launching a massive assault. West Indies were [351] for [3] at lunch; Lara's contribution was [225]. After the luncheon interval, there were four annoying interruptions from unseasonable showers, but there was no cessation of his dominance. In a style reminiscent of that displayed by Sir Garfield Sobers, Lara exuded supreme confidence to carve his name onto that exclusive register of legends. Antigua erupted in a roar of ecstasy as he cut, with infinite delicacy, to reach a triple century, the third from a West Indian at the time. When he ambled to the pavilion after the final over of the day, he had reached an unbeaten score of [320]. At St. John's, he obviously landed many leagues away from Port-of-Spain, but had piloted himself beside a dock of similar permanence to Horatio Nelson's English Harbour.

When I saw his centre stage performance of a century in a previous Test Match at Bourda, Guyana, I was moved to state: I could not think of a more breath taking experience than to be dazzled by the brilliance of a left hander's stroke play, at a ground whose beauty is heightened by very picturesque surroundings. I never thought that experience would have re-emerged through appropriateness of application in his display of fluency at St. John's.

The impact of my surprise shall remain indelible. On day three, he strode to the centre and moved his bat with the methodological precision of a senior surgeon to sever the lines of English defence. He charted his course via some delightful drives, cuts, and pulls, one of which off Chris Lewis brought him past Garfield Sobers' [365]. While I savoured the end of one glorious era of West Indies Test Match cricket, I thought about that important question posed by the Trinidadian intellectual, Cyril Lionel Robert James: what do they know of cricket who only cricket knows?

I responded by saying it is a fitting tribute to the late C.L.R. for a young cricketer from the island to have accomplished such an extraordinary feat. Through his tireless Caribbean wide campaign in the late nineteen-fifties, C.L.R. laid the initial solid foundation for removing injustice from the field of West Indies cricket. It is he who made the most persuasive case for choosing a West Indies captain on the basis of merit. It is C.L.R. who should take precedence above all others for West Indies elevated status in international cricketing circles. Had he been in St. John's when Lara sent that fateful Lewis delivery racing like a rocket to the mid-wicket boundary, he and his great friend, Learie Constantine, would have probably declared: although the boundaries of Caribbean cricket may appear to be distant, much more than the field is wide open.

The huge expanse of this field was exposed by Lara in summer 1994 while he represented Warwickshire, on the England county cricket circuit for which he scored his thousandth run in seven innings, registered more than two thousand that summer, and had won three trophies. Against Glamorgan he scored [147] in the first innings, posted two hundreds against Leicester, and got one hundred and thirty-six from ninety four deliveries against Somerset. These performances were followed by another century against Middlesex. He became much more noticeable when batting in a match against Durham from whom he extracted an unbeaten [501].

Importantly, the quintuple century was attained from four hundred and twenty-seven deliveries. Lara had also broken three notable first class batting records established in England: [345] for Australia, in fewer than four hours, by the "Governor General" A.C. MacCartney against Nottinghamshire in 1921,[424] by A.C. MacLaren for Lancashire against Somerset in 1895, and [405] by Graeme Hick for Worcestershire against Somerset in 1988. On a broader scale, internationally, he had surpassed: Don Bradman's [452] for New South Wales against Queensland [1929-1930] Bhausaheb Nimbalkar's [443] for Maharashtra against Kathiawar [1948-1949], William Ponsford's [429] for Victoria against Queensland [1927-1928], Aftab Baloch's [428] for Sind against Baluchistan [1973-1974], and Bert Sutcliffe's [385] for Otago against Canterbury [1952-1953].

On the day of that extraordinary accomplishment of [501] from Brian Lara, Hanif Mohammad, former Pakistan Test Match batsman, attributed the astonishing performance to smallness of stature. "The short heighted people like Lara and Sir Len Hutton and many other short heighted people [Test players] have got many runs."[3] Hanif, whose [499] for Karachi well over four decades ago, stood as the highest first class individual score, also noted that he, Sunil Gavaskar, who scored the majority of his Test Match runs against fearsome West Indies quick bowling quartets, and Brian Lara, were just over five feet tall. Allan Border (Australia), who had surpassed Gavaskar as the highest scorer of Test Match runs prior to retirement, can be added to the list.

I possess no expertise about the relationship between body types and cricketing craftsmanship. I do, however, want to move within and beyond the field and place Brian Lara's bat lashings within a wider context of Caribbean social life. That context can be conveyed by remembering: what C.L.R. James writes about Rohan Kanhai's batting, a unique pointer to the West Indies quest for identity, that crowded vagueness which passes for history of the Anglo-Caribbean. C.L.R. had penned his thoughts long before Caribbean cricket spectators ever dreamed of a batting sensation such as Lara. In 1994, those thoughts applied with the same force to the young Trinidadian who was, doubtless, one of the most remarkable of Test Match batsmen.

After the second Test Match of the England West Indies winter series (1994) had ended, Everton de Courcy Weekes, that distinguished doyen of Caribbean cricket, noted that Lara's timing was "fantastic," he was strong on both sides of the wicket, and was a great player who could only become greater. Like Hanif, Weekes observed that Lara is a little man, and pointed out that he could not recall "in recent times, having seen anyone bat like this young man."

Given the James, Hanif, and Weekes accounts, it is on history which I must focus, if I am going to do justice to the expanse or wider context. One of the strongest senses of history emerges as I look at the continuity established between the careers of Brian Lara and his predecessor, Garfield Sobers [G. S.]. The continuity stretches over a period that is more than half a century. The Test Match links from which Brian Lara gained had been established since 1954-1955, when Sobers played his first Test Match for the West Indies, at Sabina Park, Jamaica.

In 1995 Sobers provided me with ample confirmation of continuity. He spoke about being overwhelmed by three of his heroes, Clyde Walcott, Everton Weekes, and Frank Worrell, in 1954-1955 at Sabina.

G. S.: Well, first of all, let me say that, as a boy at the age of seventeen who had followed cricket for many years before that, as a young, up and coming player and who had always enjoyed cricket at all levels in Barbados from about the age of six and who had listened to so much cricket overseas, watched in Barbados, I've always had the great idea of, one day, playing cricket, at Barbados level and then moving on. When I was given that opportunity, particularly in my first Test, to sit in the same dressing room with those three W's (considering Everton Weekes was my idol in my early days) and to know that I had found myself among those players (sitting in the same dressing room) and as you say rubbing shoulders with them was something I don't think anyone could really explain what the thrill and circumstances were: to be able, at that age, to be sitting with those players to whom you looked up and admired, over these years, before you got into a Barbados or West Indies team. And that was, really, one of the great highlights of my cricketing career, the beginning of it. I don't think that there are many young players, at my age, who were that fortunate to have ever had that opportunity. So, that was, really, an added kind of incentive for me in the beginning of my career.

My point about continuity is that Brian Lara profited from a rich tradition of knowledge which, most certainly, did not originate with Garfield Sobers' initial presence on a Test Match ground. Sobers was a conveyor of knowledge from predecessors and what knowledge did he convey! He was the first Test Match batsman to have scored well over [8,000 runs], even though he did not enter Sabina Park as a front line batsman. Bereft, however, of profound socio-political consciousness about imperialism, not something Brian Lara ever demonstrated he could apply, as well as the vivid presence of global predecessor luminaries from which any apprenticeship of his could blossom, the Port-of-Spain Prince failed to elevate West Indies Test Match cricket.

Another West Indies Test Match batsman who had an influence on Brian Lara without any on-field vivid presence was Roy Fredericks of Guyana. Lara has stated that while growing up in Trinidad he admired the left hander's batting style so much that he wanted to be just like Fredericks. It is to the fearlessness of Roy Fredericks that I turn, fearlessness emanating from a batsman Martin-Jenkins (1996, p. 730) assesses as a small but very tough batsman of high class that hit the ball exceptionally hard. To Martin-Jenkins, he was a pocket Hercules who executed every stroke from the late cut to the leg glance with enormous gusto. What can I state about Roy Fredericks [Test Match batting average of 42.49 from 59 games]?

FEARLESSNESS OF ROY FREDERICKS

Roy Clifton Fredericks was a left handed genius from Berbice County, Guyana, for whom he scored a century in each innings against MCC [1973-74]. Remarkably, at the age of forty he opened the batting with immense pride and bravery for his country in the regional inter-territorial Caribbean Shell Shield competition to score [103] and [217] against Trinidad and Jamaica. Against Barbados, in another very crucial Shell Shield encounter [1966-67], I saw him score, in glorious fashion, two consecutive hundreds [127] and [115] against the Gary Sobers captaincy, medium fast, and spin bowling. The Fredericks performance was a brilliant and remarkable feat which, doubtless, led to his entry to, and successful presence in, the West Indies team. At the time of his two centuries, he was batting with Joe Solomon in the opening position, where he had replaced an injured Stephen Camacho. I must add that he had represented his county, Berbice, in inter-county Matches against Essequibo and Demerara, but seemed prone to being prey in the trap of fast and medium-fast away swingers.

When he was selected to replace Camacho in a meeting against a powerful Barbados side captained by Sobers, who was strongly supported by such batsmen as Sobers himself, Peter Lashley, Seymour Nurse, and Robin Bynoe, the betting boffins in Guyana were bent on confining him to a category of failure. They were seriously mistaken. He batted splendidly and superbly in the first innings on the first day of a four day contest, when he helped his side to post a sore of over four hundred. What is more is that in his medium fast and spinning capacities Sobers could not remove him early in both innings. When he batted again in the second innings, he scored another hundred.

Clyde Walcott, someone against whom Fredericks played in inter-county four day first class matches, a West Indies Test Match selector, who had watched him and given radio commentary on the Guyana-Barbados game, was so moved that he stated: he had seen Fredericks batting displays punctuated by stroke play, some of which he had not observed the great Sobers demonstrate. He was speaking on the occasion of the left hander's inclusion in the Caribbean touring side to Australia of 1968 and advised Fredericks to watch the ball moving away from his off stump. Both Walcott and Fredericks knew all too well what took place during the course of those inter-county first class matches. Here was public commentary from an expert West Indies Test Match player who would have spoken to Fredericks many times about his batting: Clyde Walcott was a very senior official, the chief social welfare adviser under auspices of the Guyana Sugar Producers Association, an arm of two British multinationals, Booker McConnell and The Demerara Company. One of his many roles was associated with assisting young Guyanese cricketers. Quite significantly, he chose to play high level cricket in Guyana among artisans and agricultural workers of these companies. Roy Fredericks was one such artisan.

I was born in and grew up in Guyana. Lest my comments about Fredericks be deemed to be founded on misappropriated nationalism, I should direct readers to comments about him that emanate from a different source:

> *Quick on his feet, a wristy cutter of deadly certainty, the perfection of his timing sends the ball flying away to the boundary with an incredible speed considering his body weight is under ten stone (Walker 1978, p. 76).*

Walker points out, also, that when asked how he felt just before going out to bat, Fredericks' invariable response would be "I think I'm going to pelt some lash at de ball man." Lash it far and wide he did.

> *Like so many Caribbean cricketers, his ability to play the game lifted him clear of a bleak financial future. But for cricket he would probably have spent his days as an insignificant filing clerk in Georgetown, Guyana, where he was born (Walker, 1978, p. 73).*

From my position, a Guyanese who is well aware of centuries of imperialist subordination, I must add that cricket also lifted Fredericks from the tedium and hard work which he had to do at one of the largest and most successful sugar estates owned by Booker McConnell. Roy Fredericks, the player I regard as the best West Indies opening Test Match batsman who emerged after his playing days to be honoured with the post of Minister of Sport in the Guyana Government, passed away in summer 2000, a time when Test Match playing successors—including batsman, Brian Lara—under captain, Jimmy Adams, failed in their battle against England. I could not help using his passing as an occasion for reflection on the depths to which West Indies cricket had sunk. It was with an interest in sharing my views with the Caribbean public—albeit painfully—that I forwarded, and was able, to publish a letter in the *Guyana Daily, Stabroek News* (September 2000).

I started by stating that the passing of Roy Clifton Fredericks, whom E. W. Swanton once described as the little man with a beard, was of no small significance, for it occurred against a foreground of Caribbean cricket fractured by the agony of capitulation and sullied by surges of delusion. Fredericks, I continued, was a proud West Indian whose cricketing mind was never trapped in a body stifled by boundaries of bowling oppression. He always stood at the door of defiance to announce that his artful, elegant, and inventive performance was a strong indication of alternate and powerful forms of self-expression by one of several creative individuals denied access to conventional routes of socio-economic development, as a consequence of official and unofficial exclusion.

In (1972-'73), when he was meeting the fury of those Ian Chappell charges in the third Test Match at Port-of-Spain (Australia vs. West Indies), commentator, Raffie Knowles, was moved to mention that if his side had won the game, a statue in gold should be made of him. In the words of that notable and insightful African-American scholar, Cornel West, Knowles was bearing witness to the Fredericks bravery and selflessness in opening batting excellence accomplished with an ebullient [76] in the West Indies second innings. It is not without enormous pride that I record all the other scores of the left hander in that series. They are: [31], [21], [98], [22], [16], [30], [6], [73], [8]. Could the Knowles pronouncement have been a cue for some of the first Brian Lara lessons in batting brilliance? Fredericks was again the standard bearer in 1996, the year of another loss to that staid assemblage of Aussies, when ex-fast bowler, Bob Massie, and Australian commentator colleagues found it necessary to consider whether a certain West Indies left hander, at the time, looked like the little man. This is the very Roy Fredericks who took the fight to the England bowlers in 1976, where he posted superb hundreds—including one at Lord's—to help his captain, Clive Lloyd, demolish England.

Some of us who are fascinated with comparison will always note Sir Donald Bradman's claims about Sir Garfield Sobers' [254] for the Rest of the World against Australia, as well as Stan McCabe's performance against England in 1938 as the best innings he has ever seen. We will also long remember Fredericks' [169] at Perth against Australian quick bowlers, Lillee, Thomson, Walker, and Gilmour [1975-1976].

We are also well aware that cricketing creativity does not spring solely from field forces and should be cognisant of the cultural transmission of which Fredericks was a prime beneficiary, but that is so obviously missing from the region. He served under Test Match captains, Sobers, Kanhai, and that "disciplined calypso" Hubert, and would have received wise counsel from Basil Butcher, that regimental Sergeant Major, Lancelot Richard Gibbs, and Clyde Walcott. The last of these, in his capacity as West Indies Board President, took Caribbean cricket to its apogee via his judicious blending of steadfastness, shrewdness, as well as incomparable insightfulness, and understood how victory should be used to transcend nationalism.

Fredericks batted in the company of I.V.A. Richards' Gordon Greenidge, to whom he was senior opening partner; Alvin Kallicharran; and Lawrence Rowe (1976) against England, whose South African born captain, Tony Greig, stated publicly that he was going to make West Indies grovel. Today, Caribbean cricket is deeply troubled by a mood of alienation. The absence of the little man with a beard means there is one fewer person to aid the process of re-subjectivisng.

One of the very significant things I am saying about Roy Fredericks is that he did have a substantial impact on Brian Lara. I am also focusing on the fact that the Fredericks cricket was more than cricket in name. It was also cricket infused with an assertive spirit that cannot be divorced from the impact of imperialism and unfairness, imperialism and unfairness that restricted the boy, Fredericks, to cruelties of life as a member of a working poor family. On the cricket field, at the highest level of the game, Test Match cricket, he surmounted those cruelties and left an indelible mark on West Indians.

GIBBS, WALCOTT, AND LLOYD

I turn now to examples of the Gibbs-Walcott- Lloyd connection and Worrell influence on Sobers who, in turn, has had considerable influence on Brian Lara. While conversing with Clive Lloyd in 1994 about the impact of Lance Gibbs on his career, he informed me that he spent his early years watching players such as Lance Gibbs, a member of the Demerara Cricket Club, which he joined later. The Demerara Cricket Club has been an organisation which attracted upwardly mobile African-Guianese professionals. Despite their achieved statuses, they were ineligible for membership of the Georgetown Cricket Club, because of their colour.[4]

What was there for Clive Lloyd, via his vivid on-field presence, to admire in his off-spinner cousin, Lance Gibbs, the man John Woodcock described as the regimental Sergeant Major, in 1976, the year of his retirement from Test Match cricket, when he was the first ever spinner to claim over three hundred wickets? I say it was the off spinner's athleticism and bowling assertiveness that have been strong bases to arousal of passionate pursuits well beyond perimeters of major Test Match cricket grounds. Lloyd indicated that he, the youthful international cricketing aspirant, was greatly influenced by Gibbs, whose early Test Match performances were excellent. He wanted to emulate Gibbs, the very keenly astute competitor that educated me about some secrets to his international success:

> I'm a dedicated type of individual. I'd be the first fellow to practice and the last to leave. I would try to bowl a length. I could put a white spot on the wicket and try to hit it as often as possible. Whatever wicket that I'm going to play on I'm going to try to impart something into the ball. And what you put in is what you're going to get out... if you look at my fingers—they are all deformed. So, it's basically what you put in. This [pointing to a knuckle region on one deformed finger] used to be eaten off. It would be raw and I would still keep going. While these fellows—they run up and bowl—if the wicket is turning, they would get a certain amount of turn. If it is not, they just try to bowl a line and length and give up.

The Walcott impact on Gibbs was no trivial accomplishment. The off-spinner helped his captain—always a keen contestant in Caribbean inter-territorial matches against former team mates such as Everton Weekes and Allan Rae—while playing the crucial role of strategic assertive slow bowler and tiger-like gully fieldsman. The bowling role of Gibbs's was particularly evident in a game against a powerful Barbadian batting side in the early nineteen-sixties at Bridgetown where the spinner, benefitting from astute Walcott captaincy, was hugely responsible for thrusting British Guiana to unexpected match victory.

At a much later time, 1990, Walcott, in his capacity as President of the West Indies Cricket Board, was participating in a discourse with telecaster, Tony Greig, of Sky Sports about the presence of a spinner in the dominant Test Match team led by Viv Richards. Greig wanted to know whether Lance Gibbs, the excellent off-spinner, would have been eligible for Test Match selection in the presence of stiff competition from "express" fast bowlers. Walcott readily responded affirmatively and pointed out that Gibbs was a great spinner who flighted the ball well.

THE WORRELL-SOBERS CONNECTION

I begin with field matters by pointing to assessment of the extraordinary Sobers. Arlott (1986, pp. 242-243) describes the "incomparable" Sobers, an honour accorded this great West Indian by friend, Trevor Bailey, as surely the greatest all round cricketer in the history of the game. While W.G. Grace set the most exalted standards, no one has done so with such immense élan or excelled so diversely as Sobers. Everything about his cricket was memorable. He scaled all the heights, and did so with a gloriously joyous athleticism. Those who watched him recognised, and still recall, that his cricket transcended records.

I am one of those who watched him for what Arlott (1970/1996, p. 237) states is an appreciable period and am in full agreement. To see him come onto the cricket field, adds England's best cricket commentator, in his long hungry stride, a feline blend of the relaxed and purposeful, is to behold a great athlete about whose giftedly versatile play most observers agree.

It was on cricket fields that I watched Garfield Sobers, in the summer of 1970 when I experienced three remarkable events which took place in three different England cities. I sat well beyond the Birmingham haze one Friday afternoon—transistor radio glued to my left ear at the Edgbaston cricket ground—to hear E.W. Swanton summarise play for the day. In one of his assessments, he informed listeners that he had been watching the best player in the world.

Swanton was bearing witness to the fluency of stroke play from a cricket captain who demonstrated the significance of ascendancy in command of a Rest of The World team competing against England. The correspondent's commentary was an integral part of his continual appreciation of what he revered as the unparalleled brilliance of a genius:

For just 20 years he decorated the Test scene in his inimitable way, an all-rounder of unparalleled versatility, completely unselfish, and with an unquenchable urge, whether batting, bowling in any of his three styles, or fielding, to attack—and, in so doing, of course, to entertain. He was always conscious of the game's obligation to give pleasure, yet was the reverse of a show-off. He allowed his cricket to speak for him. And speak it did, all over the world (Swanton 1994/1996, p. 239).

While batting alongside the great South African, Graeme Pollock, in the fifth and final game of the competition, Sobers executed an off drive against John Snow who saw a huge cloud of dust engulf the thrust of a hoisted bat as the leather it had pummelled seared the greenery along a path to the extra cover boundary of the Kennington Oval. Ardent admirer and radio commentator, John Arlott, described the shot as "a murderous stroke."

In an earlier Headingley encounter, in which his front line batsmen had succumbed to the England attack, during the course of the second innings, Sobers walked to the crease with a huge burden on his shoulders. I read the sports section in one of the Beaverbrook newspapers the next morning and saw what I deemed an extraordinary assessment. The writer claimed that at close of play Gary Sobers was left standing like Mr. Atlas with the Rest of the World on his shoulders.

Garfield Sobers is no Greek figure—mythical or otherwise. He is the Barbadian Bayland boy whose cricketing creativity blossomed well beyond Bridgetown beacons. It is within those expanses that spectators saw how his extraordinary expression of excellence was integrally linked to performances he crafted meticulously through uniqueness with which he cultivated cricketing elegance. This is a man greatly revered by numerous admirers, because they believed he embodied the principle that repetition is a resource of the reliable. In the role, preeminent West Indies Test Match cricketer, he was infused with charisma which was associated with the showering of deserving adulation.

He is the sole West Indies Test batsman to have scored unbelievably brilliant hundreds in his first and final appearances against Australia, in Australia [132, 1st innings, 1960-'61], [113, 2nd innings, [1968-'69]. He is also the first West Indies Test Match captain to have defeated mighty Australia in a series and it was largely because of this feat that his leadership presence was transformed into the margins of magnificence.

There are, doubtless, several other things I can state about him. I think he has left one of the richest legacies to Caribbean cricket. His is the gift of genius which I describe: if modesty is the supreme measure of this man's creativity, then the contradiction he derived from comparing his craft of creativity with the precision of pedestrians charmed every clever Caribbean cricketing connoisseur. I am saying that Sobers is the champion challenger. Such is the depth of this man's imagination that his unique ascendancy—even off the field he frequently transcended with immense grace—cannot be annulled.

Virtually all of the things I have stated about Sobers are linked to his relations with Frank Worrell, who was West Indies captain for Test Match series in (1960-'61, 1962, and 1963) against Australia, India, and England. While he did not win the 1960-'61 contest against Australia, his effect on teams was enormous. I want to measure the powerful presence of his leadership by looking at the (1959-'60, and 1960-'61) series against Australia and England.

In one of my discussions with Sobers, I told him the influential Australian broadcaster, Allan McGilvray, spoke about his partnership with Worrell, during the course of the first Test Match in the (1960-'61) contest. McGilvray said Worrell played an insignificant role in terms of the runs he scored "but he kept guiding Gary. You must get on top of this man [Benaud] he must not defeat us." McGilvray added that Worrell told him what was worrisome prior to the start of the Test Match series was the impact Benaud, the Australian captain and leg spin googly bowler, was having on the West Indies players. "I need a left hand and a right hand combination to defeat this man [Benaud] I must have Gary there and I must have Kanhai."

I also asked Sobers to tell me about the partnership McGilvray said indicated a Worrell victory over Benaud. Here are significant excerpts from his reply:

I think everyone was amazed at our performances. We started the tour very poorly. We didn't cut our stride. In the New South Wales game Richie Benaud had reaped havoc: he got a lot of wickets. I remember myself. I think he got me out twice and there was a rumour that I couldn't pick Richie; we were going into a Test Match with this behind me. I think Frank was expecting quite a lot from me (along with the other players). We were very fortunate that we had two captains who saw cricket in the way it should have been played, in the sense that they both played attacking cricket and neither ever intended to give up. If Sir Frank Worrell was the type of player who would give up, we would have lost the Test Match, because Australia had reached the stage where they were about two hundred and eighteen for the loss of about five wickets (only needing another twelve or thirteen runs to win).

Let me get back to the beginning. It started out that we won the toss and we elected to bat... When I went in, the situation was diabolical. Sir Frank came in and came down to talk to me: 'Things not looking too good. We're gonna have to do something about it.' There was this thing behind the Australians that I couldn't pick Richie. Richie was brought into the attack, very early. That thought [that I couldn't pick him] was soon displaced from his mind—I think—in about three or four overs. I think he looked at it differently after that, because there was one particular ball which I remember he bowled to me and this was his googly. I started to go forward. Richie started to put his hands in the air as if to say 'I've got him.' And before he could have got his hands down, he had to lift his foot. The ball hit the fence. He looked at me, applauded and said 'good shot.' I think from there the whole table turned, because Frank was quite prepared, at the other end, to stay there. He saw the mood that I was in and thought at the time, that nothing was bothering me. Frank was not the type of player that would come down and say 'you're taking chances.' He knew what was happening. He knew that the chances I was taking were calculated chances. I wasn't going beyond the ordinary and I was in full cry. I was picking the ball early. I was seeing everything and, therefore, I was able to play my shots. We went on and we batted... that was again another good partnership between Frank and me. It was at the time that we needed it; this is always important, as far as I am concerned: when they come and the circumstances under which they come are more important than when you just make runs.

While talking to me about that other partnership [1959-'60] in which he and Worrell batted for five sessions against England at Kensington Oval, Barbados, where they scored [226] and [197], Sobers had this to say:

We were in serious trouble when Frank came in. I think we were about sixty odd for five or something like it. Frank walked in. It was late in the afternoon and I was still playing a few shots. He came down to me and said 'listen son, you can't afford to get out. If you get out, we're going to lose this Test Match. You and I have got to see this thing right. We've got to put it right.' There I settled down and we batted that evening and during the next day we met in the hotel, in the evening, very late. We sat and had the odd drink together and then rolled into bed and came out the next day. We chatted about the game, how we were going to approach it and we put our heads down. From that day onward, I could see that Frank had the ability to think about the game. He knew the mood I was in and with him at the other end and me down there I think he bestowed great confidence in me. I think the confidence he bestowed in me in that match and over the years helped me in my cricketing career—batting with others. And we just went on batting until we got the team into a situation in which we knew that we could not lose the game.

Sobers (1996) is, of course, one of those who state that Worrell exploded the myth that a man of colour could not lead West Indies successfully. Worrell, the man who seemed to have the language appropriate to varied contexts (Sobers 2002), was not simply a great captain, he was also a great human that formed and solidified the glue for all that was commendable about the West Indian personality. Here is glowing tribute from the admirer who venerated his astute leader and was profoundly honoured to have taken his predecessor's baton.

Sobers revered Worrell as a charmer, a grand motivator, a leader who also corrected, and employed, a style different to the imperialist approach. That imperialist approach is best described as devoid of reason and reflection in the authoritarianism "do so, because I say so." I suppose one major impact of the Worrell strategising took the form of advising Sobers to bat, in the team's interest, at number six: this was a place from which the deft all-rounder could enhance his understanding of the game and would be crucially placed to attack or defend, in accordance with prevailing conditions. Further, Worrell took the view that Sobers was far more dependable when faced with a crisis.

Of Worrell, Johnston (1989, p. 81) writes that he exercised more influence on West Indies cricket than, possibly, any other West Indian. If Johnston is correct, it would not be inappropriate to assess the value of his association with players: in the role of a leader who needed to learn about and understand them, he was unlike white Test Match captains before him. He did not suppress player creativity and was not aloof from them.

One of Worrell's worthy successors, a successor greatly admired by Sobers, is Isaac Vivian Alexander Richards, the socio-politically conscious West Indies skipper Woodcock (1998, p. 8) assesses as the most daunting figure to have strode with a bat under his arm through a pavilion gate in modern times. Captain Richards was served by twelfth man, Brian Lara, in the 1990 Test Match series against England. The twelfth man, Lara, in 1990, who later became the three tenured West Indies Test Match captain was by no means so socio-politically conscious as Richards. This is, however, the Lara who followed Richards' batting predecessors, then Richards, via avenues of inventiveness and reshaping to become the most dominant Caribbean Test Match batsman. It is to some of that dominance at the crease that I direct my attention.

ENDNOTES

1 The written account of the Swanton Memorial address appeared in the publication: The Life of E.W. Swanton by David Ravern Allen, Aurum Press (2004), pp: 258-261.

2 The reference to absence of a Barbados blessing is my way of accounting for an unexpected 237 run West Indies loss to England, in a previous Test Match, at the Kensington Oval, Barbados, 1994.

3 I heard these Hanif statements while listening to a BBC WORLD SERVICE RADIO sports programme.

4 Some observers in Guyana claim that the Demerara Cricket Club [DCC] was formed by Portuguese citizens, largely because although they were European they were not granted membership of the Georgetown Cricket Club [GCC] that gave access only to Europeans from Britain. I have not been able to verify such a claim.

Australia supreme.

11th INNINGS
BRIAN LARA
BATTING ON THE
ROAD TO CAPTAINCY

The Caribbean intellectual genius, James (1963, p. 211), notes that cricketing observers may be able to respond to what he terms Leo Tolstoy's exasperated and exasperating inquiry: what is art? This is a query he claims is dealt with appropriately when an integrated vision of dominant Test Match batsman, Clyde Walcott, driving through the covers and the outstretched arm of Olympic Apollo, is constructed. I have never seen Clyde Walcott batting in a Test Match. I can surely think imaginatively of the man's artistry and have done so, also, in regard to Clive Lloyd's batting in Test Matches.

Although I did not see Lloyd's game-winning century against Australia at Lord's in the first ever World Cup Final (summer 1975), I do remember one stroke he played against Gilmour, the Australian fast bowler—"not the easiest problem for Lloyd to solve," according to that inimitable radio commentator, John Arlott, when he was on ninety-nine. Arlott assessed the stroke as one hit high away over mid-wicket for four, the stroke of a man knocking a thistle top off with a walking stick against a foreground of seething delight from leaping West Indies spectators. What an integrated vision following the contempt with which batting teammate, Alvin Kallicharran, had treated Australian fast bowlers, Lillee and Thomson, whose liberal resort to the short pitched stuff was ineffective!

Anyone who has seen, first hand, the Brian Lara captivation at the Test Match batting crease has, doubtless, formed his own vision. I write as one among countless viewers and do so with an interest in posing queries about his performance that clearly lies in the realm of artistry. How is belligerence beautified in bounties of the blissful! How is serenity scripted for sculptures of the shackled! How is drama distilled from dancing of the defiant! How is the best of batsmanship bathed in the bloom of boundaries! How is art anointed with the annals of ascendancy! These are meant to be questions which stir the imaginative insights of all with a very keen interest in top class Test Match batting, an indubitable fact of Brian Lara's elevated status as a world cricketer.

If you prefer to use those insights differently, consider just this assessment, in full dramatic form, of Brian Lara's presence at the crease, on the occasion of the 1999 cricket World Cup.[1]

The 1999 Cricket World Cup. Day 17, the penultimate day of the group stages. West Indies and Australia head-to-head. If Australia loses, they're out. If the West Indies lose, New Zealand is likely to seize the final Super Six place from their noses. Glen McGrath is given the new ball for the first time in the tournament. Languishing at first change for the first four games, his notorious temper is now at boiling point and the Windies are about to get scalded. Within minutes West Indies are reeling at 7-2.

Lara comes to the crease. For a few tense overs Lara and McGrath spar. Then McGrath unleashes one of the balls of the tournament. It jags back and hits Lara's off stump. 20-3. Pandemonium. Lara remains frozen in his defensive stroke. He finally turns and walks away—and out of the World Cup. The planet's most scintillating batsman has left the game's greatest stage[2] before the first act is complete, and the cricket world feels cheated.

Brian Lara was comprehensively bowled by his nemesis, Glen McGrath. What is most compelling to me about the assessment is not that Lara's batting brilliance failed to sparkle at that time. Rather, it is my ruminating over what such brilliance would have looked like had Brian Lara brought glory from the crease in battling a foe whom he had to have respected as the world's most dangerous quick bowler at the time.

I cannot resist the enthralling nature of the drama. A decade after it had unfolded, I was compelled to pen this piece of verse I title *MCGRATH'S MEDITATIONS*.

MCGRATH'S MEDITATIONS

I roam the restless reaches of steaming surfaces on verdant veldt astride the Trueman terraces of yorker titans. I scour the Lordly labours of a lamenting Lara—a javelin thrust from this teething toss for gaming grunts. I cite the snarling stealth of that righteous raider—a phantom flyer atop those cradled crevices. I hear the blameless blight of bush men's blessing writhing at the rancid torrents of tumbling ridges. I watch the missing sentry toil amidst the festering folds of promising patience. I see the artful valence of a sultry scent among the leathered lochs.

I see the Aussie oracle in praise of frugal flirting with our fabled footman—this soldier's sovereign of sulking solitudes—this seething sell of lonely labours. I smell the gravid gall of a hunter's humours—this Taino tumult of daring dreams. I feel the broker's burst for Bowral booty above the magnate mints of gilded glories. I ford the depths of stricken stardom to steal all streaming curves—their piercing passions etched on stony silence of quilted quarry. I spend the spinning spoils of Gibbs's gracious hauls to salve the sunlit searing from that sobering saint.

On this day of '99, a hundred closer to the thousandth run, a jaguar hunts the realms of ruddy radiance to rout that crossing Trinity of Tobal's murky mooring. On the seventeenth day of this sullen summer, a hawkish hell ascends from turning thread afore the Lordly Leviathans to harass those princely passions. On this day of jarring jealousies, a sacred stream of sunlit centres hails the brimming bowls for boucan bravery. On this distant day for drifting dread, a jolting gem from haunts of July Jumbies flaunts the stoic stances of a studious stumble.

My Lords! Ladies! Two fours beyond the knightly nerves and none to blend with coral blushes of Cantaro chimes. Ladies! My Lords! A rater's rant recalls the mentor's mantle. My Lords! Ladies! A tutor's tirade taunts the fielding fumbles and scars the drooping turf on grassy tears. Ladies! My Lords! A tearful torment abounds to hoard the trades of Lara's trumpet. Much more than a decade in the making, the fading forces for muted marshals slump among the humming scowls at stabled strutting.

Lara lost this battle of 1999 with the menace, McGrath. He lost quite a few other duels with the Australian terror, but it is McGrath who, I remind readers, gives him the edge over Sachin Ramesh Tendulkar, that batting genius from India authoritatively assessed:

> At Perth in Western Australia early in 1992 Sachin Tendulkar made a century for India against Australia on a lively pitch with a brilliance that no other batsman in the world could have surpassed. He was eighteen at the time—the prodigy of prodigies (Woodcock, 1998, p. 25).

Let me, therefore, look at some of the ways in which Brian Lara defeated McGrath and other bowlers on his way to becoming West Indies skipper. It was 1988 when Brian Charles Lara, the domineering Test Match batsman, first came to my notice in St. Lucia where he captained a West Indies under twenty-three side against a Pakistan team led by Wasim Akram. I remember, very clearly, that two other notables who played alongside him were Ian Bishop and Keith Arthurton. Both went on to play Test Match cricket for West Indies. In that St. Lucia game, at what was then Phillip Mindoo Park, the Pakistan bowling was spearheaded by Akram himself and Abdul Qadir, both of whom mesmerised all but one of the young Caribbean batsmen. The batsman was Keith Arthurton, the second innings centurion, who was especially severe against the complicated flippers, leg breaks, and googlies of Qadir's.

Two years elapsed before I heard about Brian Lara again. During the course of the 1990 England tour to the West Indies, his name was on the lips of many adoring regional fans that did more than ponder his entry to the Test Match side. They had to wait for two more years, a display of patience that was well justified. When he appeared on the highest cricket stage in 1992 against Australia on the island continent, he impressed the cricketing world with an exquisite batting display against Shane Warne and company, from whom he extracted a superb double hundred [277] run out in the third Test Match at Sydney. His was an eight hour innings during which he shared a [293] third wicket partnership with his captain, Richie Richardson, also a centurion.

Here was batting brilliance that signalled a taste of things to come. When I think of a very good way of setting the stage for the future, I am reminded of claims:

> At his [Lara's] best he is outrageously brilliant. He plays strokes that are surreal. Attempted by other batsmen, even those of the highest class, they could only end in disaster. He throws the bat at balls of impeccable length and sends them racing through the narrowest of gaps (Woodcock 1998, p. 28).

Upon his return to the Caribbean in 1993, Lara batted assertively against Pakistan in the company of people such as Desmond Haynes, Carl Hooper, and captain Richie Richardson. He had, doubtless, secured an important Test Match place for himself which he cemented against Mike Atherton and teammates in 1994 when England lost a series in the Caribbean. While there were excellent bowling performances from players such as Curtly Ambrose, who contributed substantially to the demolition of his opponents for [46] in the third Test Match at the Queen's Park Oval, Trinidad, it was Brian Lara whose batting in the Antigua Test Match, the final encounter, that placed him alongside Gary Sobers and Lawrence Rowe in the record books: he had surpassed Rowe's triple century against England almost twenty years earlier, and exceeded Sobers [365] against Pakistan, which was registered well before Lara was born.

I shall offer, from a rather unexpected source, an American assessment of the record breaking Antigua display, but before I do so I must issue a brief report about a satisfying prelude to that Antigua performance. I am referring here to batting in a previous Test Match, the second, at Bourda, Guyana, where centurion, Brian Lara, helped the West Indies crush a beleaguered England. That was a performance in which he operated like a driver, literally responsible for accelerating the West Indies first innings run rate, a feat which, doubtless, contributed to laying a substantial foundation for Caribbean victory. His batting, sheer disdain for bowling confinement, was punctuated by some delightful flicks, pulls, and off drives on the front foot. Nothing about his execution bore a speck of semblance to the mechanical: it was his exquisite timing on a wicket of uneven bounce which characterised the fluency of his stroke play.

With victory secured in the Bourda and Queen's Park Test Matches, West Indies arrived in Barbados for the next encounter full of confidence. The Barbados venue, Kensington Oval, known as fortress Kensington where the home side had not lost a Test Match for well over four decades, was one place where, in the mouths of locals, England could not dream of victory. Atherton and his men, who set West Indies a winning target of [446] were not, however, dreaming on day five of that Barbados encounter, for they beat Brian Lara and company, most convincingly, on the last day when what appeared to be the start of a Caribbean siege was comprehensively broken.

On that day, eight second innings West Indies batsmen, Keith Arthurton, Brian Lara, Shivnarine Chanderpaul, Curtly Ambrose, Richie Richardson [captain], Desmond Haynes, Kenneth Benjamin, and Courtney Walsh, succumbed to an England spinning surge led by Phil Tufnell, the slow left armer who was definitely on no mission of mercy. Through some painful extraction performed on well worn cracks and crevices, he rendered the Caribbean tiger toothless by antagonising opposing batsmen. Specially selected in this contest to move the ball away from them, Tufnell used every turning trick. They did not survive to blast the ball against the boundary which must have seemed as distant as the mammoth target of [446].

When the end came, only [237] of those runs were on the board. From Kingston to Kaieteur and Brighton to Birmingham, millions of West Indies cricket fans must have asked themselves how huge a roar would be required in St. John's, Antigua, to repeat the Trinidadian rout. A huge roar deafened not just St. John's, but also the rest of the Anglo-Caribbean. It reverberated all over the world, because Brian Charles Lara had posted a first innings score of [375] out of a total of [593 for 5] declared. He featured in partnerships: [179], [183], and [219] with Keith Arthurton, Jimmy Adams, and Shivnarine Chanderpaul, respectively.

Lara's [375] were noted on Ted Turner's Cable News Network [CNN], Play of the Day, and evaluated by *Time Magazine* correspondent Barry Hillenbrand. I will convey the Hillenbrand remarks in full. On 2nd May, 1994, I read this account in the American publication: For nearly two centuries cricket has been a game played by two teams of eleven players each. But the five day Test match fought out by England and the West Indies last week came down to one man's pursuit of a most illustrious record: for more than 12 hours, over three days, West Indian batsman, Brian Lara, a nimble left hander, frustrated all efforts to get him out while generating run after run in a long chase after Sir Garfield Sobers' 1958 mammoth score of 365 in a single innings. On the third day, as the Antigua sun beat down relentlessly and a crowd of 12,000 sang encouragement, Lara pivoted on his back foot and with a slashing stroke hooked the ball all the way to the fence for four runs—and a new record in international matches: 369... Lara embraced Sobers, 57, a cricket legend, who was on hand to see his record fall. 'I can't tell you how proud I am of his achievement,' said Sobers ever courtly. The record could not have been broken by a better person.' Sobers paid tribute to Lara's silken aggressive style.

APPEAL AGAINST MISTREATMENT

In late 1995, however, batsman, Brian Lara, stated that he would not appear in Australasia with the West Indies team for a series of one day games to be staged there at the beginning of 1996. His principal reason, so reported publicly in the Anglo-Caribbean media, was: dissatisfaction with the severity/injustice of disciplinary action taken against him by the West Indies Cricket Board for conduct during the course of a drawn 1995 summer series against England.

It would be true to say that Lara was accorded enormous adulation by loyal Caribbean fans who supported his decision and were not appreciative of a Board for which I had lost respect. This is a body I assessed as creating the convenient fiction and masquerading with the myth that Caribbean cricket, an ugly exhibit evident as a canker, could be cleansed. I tried to use Lara's withdrawal as a basis for sensitising the West Indies public to what I believed was the Board's injustice towards a deserving hero.

I penned a lengthy piece (December 1995) to national newspapers in Antigua, Barbados, Trinidad, and Guyana, in which I appealed to leading Caribbean cricketing luminaries whom I had hoped would hold the Board responsible for mistreating Lara. These notables were some of the very jazz fighters that had preceded Lara and influenced him. I began by appealing to Garfield Sobers. I started by reminding him of a statement he had made to Peter Walker, the British born South African sports journalist:

"I'll talk and debate cricket with anyone whose knowledge I respect, but I've no time for 'camp followers' and people who are destructive without any real understanding of the game."

I proceeded:

W.W.: *Sir Garfield, if ever there is a time at which you should talk and debate, it is now, a period when our powerful prominence is no longer paraded but has been replaced by rather painful paralysis. You are aware that the latest symbol of our suffering is Brian Charles Lara, the diminutive destroyer whose batting brilliance has sparkled in countless corners of the Commonwealth.*

I want to ask about Lara and it is with ample justification that I urge you, as well as your contemporaries and predecessors, to speak about him too. You may remember this exchange with me, on 28th November, 1995.

W.W.: *What do you think are some of the major implications of Lara's withdrawal, in view of: he is your protégé, you have been an icon and you still are an icon in the Caribbean and world cricket. Brian Lara is the most recent icon. What implications (major or minor) do you see for Caribbean cricket, as a result of his departure?*

G.S.: *Well, no man is a mountain and cricket is always going to be there. No man is Mr. Cricket or bigger than the game. But I think there will be a lot of complications for West Indies cricket team in their performances. I don't think that you can afford to lose a player of Brian Lara's calibre without feeling the pinch.*

Sir Garfield, "the little people off the street" whom you respect, are feeling the pinch and I am sure they will value additional contributions from you in a contemporary Caribbean crisis of this magnitude. Lara's greatness is rooted firmly in our history. You are eminently qualified to help plumb the depths. You can tell his tormentors that when he scored [369] in St. John's, not only did you make your way to the playing area, for the purpose of congratulating the new record holder, you also issued a bold and selfless declaration.

You spoke about the constancy of productive relations between you and him, and stated he was aware that as long as you were present, he would be congratulated by you on the field for having surpassed [365]. You also revealed that in sharing a great deal of cricketing discourse with him, you provide him with the benefits of your analytical skill.

You can refer, as well, to continuity which stretches over more than a period of forty years. Did you play your first Test Match for the West Indies, at Sabina Park, in 1954-1955? Was it in Jamaica you stated, proudly, that you were overwhelmed by the presence of your three heroes, Weekes, Worrell, and Walcott? Was the youthful Sobers impressed by the trio's performance while he watched from the pavilion? Most importantly, did you not identify, also, processes through which you acquired knowledge and skill from the three W's? How similar have Garfield Sobers' relations with Frank Worrell at Radcliffe, England, been to Brian Lara's relations with Garfield Sobers in the Caribbean?

Although Lara profited from a tradition of knowledge which did not originate with you, you conveyed that knowledge. You are, thus, well aware that the context of history within which the young Trinidadian should be located is no field matter. With Lara, Rohan Kanhai, you and many others, West Indies cricket has come of age. The rewards which spring from maturity must be savoured by those who have surmounted the obstacles of servility, systematic erection of which was a powerful stimulant to extraordinary achievement. If Lara is, today, one modern architect of ascendancy, don't you think the benefits derived from his mastery should be transformed into a collective victory for the little people off the street? Don't you also think that victory is incomplete, so long as persons such as Lara are marginalised, rather than stand aloft over pillars of emergent supremacy?

I say, too, that victory is not complete once the administrators of Caribbean cricket are not informed publicly of: in the West Indies, the game is employed as an important foreground against which several citizens have been using their inventive genius to evade climates of inequity created by the dehumanising consequences of imperialism and neo-imperialism. It is, however, with profound discomfiture that I look at the current state of our cricket in a context of twentieth century administration by the West Indies Cricket Board. This is not a context in which the continued exhibition of genius is guaranteed.

I am also deeply perturbed that some players who have contributed immensely to the West Indies triumph have hinted publicly that their treatment by the Board has been neither cordial, nor urbane. In what is, ostensibly, a post-imperialist era, the departure of leading personalities such as Desmond Haynes and Rohan Kanhai is consistent with some of the worst vices of imperialism. I must emphasise that these West Indians and others like them are powerful exemplars of successful struggle against subordination. As such, they have always stood at the forefront of the battle for human dignity and economic uplifting.

Do these individuals deserve the benefits of connections between craft and crumbs? Sir Garfield, it would not be inappropriate of you and them to let our administrators know that they should stop trading some of our best advertisements for Caribbean society construction beyond immature markets of mindlessness.

Mr. Richards, I do not know if you think current conditions in the Board are like those in Augean stables. Is it unreasonable to ask if there are profiteers from privilege and managers of mean-spiritedness who mastermind misery of the little people? Is it unreasonable to inquire whether the little people deserve paltry portions? Mr. Richards, you are not obliged to offer replies. I am, however, confident that you know some of us may be far too eager to face only what we like to see and do not like to see what we face. I call on you, the Lloyds, Kanhais, Gibbs, Sobers, Butchers, Dujons, and Greenidges, to form an ex-Caribbean Test Match Players' Association, for the purpose of protecting little people and preserving surges of significance crafted from your creativity, as well as that of your contemporaries and predecessors.

I am one of those who have stood within cramped quarters at Test Match grounds to cheer and celebrate the triumphs of those that have bypassed massive impediments. Will you remember that our battles and campaigns are not over, so long as those who have brought us great joy merely fade beyond the boundary and are not elevated to offer the benefits of their collective wisdom? I do not expect you to fade. You know: "Some people want to forget Viv Richards. Some people want him to fade into history, become a museum relic." I know full well that some people think they have killed off Viv Richards for good. Not so. "I fight on for what I believe." Continue your fight, Mr. Richards.

I want you to know that I feel compelled to ask for a comprehensive inquiry of the Board's activities to be conducted by an independent body. I am convinced that the warrants for such an investigation are well founded. I ask that those who conduct the investigation do so by exercising their responsibility via comprehension of the Caribbean public's traditional identification with efforts of our cricketers. I suggest that the little people decide who carry out the investigation. They are acutely aware of distinctions between bondage and liberation.

I supported Brian Lara in 1995 with my eyes firmly fixed on his fulfilment of enormous promise. I saw the Board as an oppressor of someone whom I believed was viewed by his predecessors as a liberator. I regarded his future endeavours as some of the main thrusts upon which the vibrancy of Caribbean cricketing dynamism in the twenty-first century could be founded. I was not, however, so naïve as to be overwhelmed by the uniqueness of his individuality. I was fully aware in 1993, well before he had scored his [375] that his presence needed to be strongly integrated with progressive West Indies sporting life.

I am speaking here of a Caribbean Institute of Cricket—as opposed to a cricket Academy—for which I had called, publicly, and written about in 1993. Five bodies would make up the Institute. They are: an ex-Players' Association, The Caribbean Community [CARICOM], the West Indies Cricket Board, the Universities of the West

Indies and Guyana, the two established universities within the Anglo-Caribbean. One of the major activities would be to examine the state of contemporary West Indies sports culture, with a particular interest in the significance of cricket, at the beginning of the twenty-first century. The focus of inquiry would not be restricted to technical details on the field of play but would encompass the socio-economic forces shaping development of the game from beachfront or backyard to Test Match level. Former players such as Garfield Sobers would be provided with opportunities to participate fully in the task of investigation. What would have been a very suitable role for him and other Caribbean leaders, Rohan Kanhai, Viv Richards, Lance Gibbs, Everton Weekes? I say the task of chairperson—albeit rotating—of rather special areas, leadership strategies which I add, would not be divorced from socio-economic matters integrally central to great respect for MOTHER EARTH. This is respect enshrined deeply in systematic development of green Caribbean economies geared to avoiding servile dependence upon fossil fuel cultures and destructive consumerism, both of which intersect with imperialist and neo-imperialist oligopoly capitalism.

What I am also asserting is that a Caribbean Institute of Cricket must always play the role of investigating the question of sporting ability in a context of regional identity formation. Fulfilment of such responsibility should be linked, among other matters, to making profound efforts in determining the value of associations between new or alternative identity formations and sporting excellence.

Apart from the role of investigator, I assigned the Institute the task of educator which would emanate from assessing the results of inquiry. This educative mission would not, however, be restricted to providing findings from examination, it should also cover vigorous regional promotion of cricket's social dimensions which exist beyond perimeters of the field. Thus, the impact of the game on everyday West Indies life would be a principal element of study at secondary and tertiary levels in areas of natural science, mathematics, ecological stewardship, economics, literature, as well as sociology and psychology.

Other significant aspects of the impact would encompass exploring: (a) the meaning in C.L.R. James's claims about Sobers as a living embodiment of centuries of a tortured history and the West Indies quest for identity in Kanhai's batting (b) links between the Richards batting genius and his understanding of Rastafarian revolutionary culture (c) the subtlety of racism in modern cricketing circles. What is so significant about exploration? Let me reply by addressing myself to the first three.

In every case, Sobers, Kanhai, and Richards, there is explicit striving for activism, a search for freedom, and productive use of what I call the embedding of knowing emanating from cricketing and non-cricketing predecessors. Every one of these matters is a rich vein to be mined via practices of recovering by the Institute. To whom is the recovering valuable? It is extremely valuable in the hands of young Caribbean citizens educated at all levels within educational organisations and should be readily available in written and audio-visual forms to members of the wider public. Further, there is more than enough of a foundational breadth for recovering and availability in the attainments of other groups of cricketers.

Although all players within the groups of cricketers I named earlier while examining the idea 'jazz fighters' cannot be associated with regular series victories, there are some who are clearly connected with impressive wins. Their achievements should certainly be examined with an aim to recovering and availability. Here, I think of certain clutches of players and their captains whose names I underline: Worrell, Sobers, Kanhai, Butcher, Solomon, Gibbs, Hall, Hunte, Griffith, Murray

(England, 1963), <u>Sobers</u>, Butcher, Gibbs, Solomon, Kanhai, Hunte, Hall, Griffith, Hendricks, Nurse (West Indies, 1965), <u>Sobers</u>, Gibbs, Hall, Hunte, Griffith, Butcher, Kanhai, Nurse (England, 1966), <u>Lloyd</u>, <u>Richards</u>, <u>Richardson</u>, Fredericks, Greenidge, Gomes, Holding, Garner, Marshall, Croft, Daniel, Roberts, Haynes, Kallicharran, Dujon, Bishop, Ambrose, Patterson, Walsh, Logie, Lara (England, Australia, West Indies, 1976-1995).[3]

To set what ought to have been stages for the value of an Institute of Cricket to Brian Lara's cricketing existence, let me point to an assessment from Garfield Sobers about Lara's ultimate greatness. On the 28th April, 1993, Sobers made the statements about Brian Lara to the BBC World Service:

> *Brian Lara's got a lot of ability and certainly a person who, in the last year, has dominated the cricket scene. He's played very well in Australia (1992) and he's played well so far in the West Indies. And he's certainly a type of player that one loves to go and watch. He's the type of player that I don't think would get carried away by what people say about him—would let things bother him. I think he's got a great future and he's got a long way to go. And I'm SURE that he's gonna finish as one of the GREAT batsmen of the world.*

Garfield Sobers is, of course, eminently qualified to offer the foregoing commentary. This is evaluation from the greatest all-rounder and a left hander who—long before Lara—had played many a great innings and contributed strongly to a West Indies presence around the world.

It was my impression, at the time of the Sobers claims, that most avid followers of West Indies Test Match cricket had been overwhelmed by the euphoria created as a consequence of Brian Lara's excellence in batting craftsmanship. I, therefore, noted that if he was not to be carried away by what people said about him and was going to finish, not merely as one of the great batsmen of the world, but a great captain also, he had to take a very important step. He needed to pay very careful attention to batting performances, collegiality, and leadership styles of his four predecessors, Frank Worrell, Garfield Sobers himself, Rohan Kanhai, Clive Lloyd, Roy Fredericks, and Alvin Kallicharran, as well as other West Indians who—though not captains to Test Match teams—were very excellent leaders and strategists both within and beyond the field. While their techniques differed, they all used their inventive genius to cultivate batting styles and Caribbean identities which were immensely productive. One of those strategists beyond the field is Mr. Bryan Davis, once a West Indies Test Match opening batsman and brother of fellow Test Match player, Charlie. Lara has noted publicly that while a Trinidad schoolboy, the Bryan Davis mentoring extended to him was crucial to his Test Match batting success.

The Lara deeply studious interest in those players' accomplishments would hardly have been ill-founded. If Alvin Kallicharran was rightly regarded by Tony Cozier as Kanhai's "carbon copy," then the artistry displayed by the former batsman—particularly modelling the forward defensive stroke of the latter Brian Johnston, England cricket commentator/writer, described as played "with the bat well angled down"—was, indeed, a strong stamp of approval he gave to the master. The meticulous nature of Kallicharran's modelling was not simply a tribute to Rohan Kanhai, it was, also a shrewd investment that produced rich dividends from which he and his West Indies contemporaries were prime beneficiaries. Ten years elapsed before I first read of ideas for creating an Institute of Caribbean Cricket. The ideas came from successor to Dr. Nigel Harris as University of the West Indies Vice-Chancellor, Hilary Beckles, who spoke at a ceremony in the Caribbean to honour the three W's, Sir Everton Weekes, Sir Clyde Walcott, and Sir Frank Worrell. To date, there has been no Institute, though.[4]

In late summer 2008, during the time of great euphoria within the Anglo-Caribbean, when Jamaican sprinter, Usain Bolt, helped himself to three gold medals in the 2008 Olympic Games, Olivia Grange, Jamaica's Minister of Sport, stated that the Island would be setting up an Institute of Sport. This promise came in the foreground of claims from her and her Prime Minister, Bruce Golding, about track and field—not cricket. Among other things, the Sport Minister asserted that Jamaica is the sprint factory of the world and Golding declared that Bolt had set the island in rapture.

He also informed the entire world of: "Usain Bolt is a super human being. The world has never seen anything like him... Not only is he physically the best in the world, but he has supreme confidence in himself and he knows how to deliver." I have to ask myself what would an Institute of Sport do to promote cricket, if Jamaica is, in fact, the sprint factory of the world? Just as importantly, I am left to wonder where the achievements of luminaries such as George Headley, Garfield Sobers, Lance Gibbs, Michael Holding, Alvin Kallicharran, Clive Lloyd, Rohan Kanhai, Courtney Walsh, Frank Worrell, Everton Weekes, and Clyde Walcott stand in relation to those of Bolt's.

Despite my criticism of Brian Lara, I do not know how his accomplishments at the crease compare to those of Jamaica's track and field hero. If you do not wish to ponder my concerns, then think of the presence of Steve Waugh, ex-Australian Test Match skipper in the presence of Australian Olympians competing in the 2008 Beijing Games. What was the significance of the presence of this resolute Aussie warrior in the land of Mao, Chou, and Deng? Waugh was there officially as a mentor to his Australian sporting compatriots. Is this not a strong indication of the precedence granted by one of the strongest cricketing societies to cricket! While Waugh was motivating other Australians in 2008 Ramnaresh Sarwan, the man named West Indies Test Match captain for the second time, and teammates were labouring at the Toronto Cricket Club for the Anglo-Caribbean against Canada and Bermuda in a low level tournament. Who knew what other perilous plunges lay in store for West Indies in this game of glorious uncertainty, cricket!

I do know that without an Institute of Caribbean Cricket, at the beginning of the twenty-first century, a West Indies captain—Ramnaresh Sarwan, Chris Gayle, Shivnarine Chanderpaul, Darren Sammy, Dinesh Ramdhin, Jason Holder, or any other who did not experience imperialism, despite the dominance of his presence at the batting crease, cannot maintain and transmit the cultures crafted by Lloyd's and Richards' leadership. In 2007, three time Test Match captain, Brian Lara, was definitely faced with such an impediment for which his Board bosses have been partially, but significantly, responsible.

My next immediate goal is to deal with what I consider Lara's fluctuating fortunes with the bat, during the period, late 1994 to late 1998, the year when he faced his first major challenge as West Indies Test Match captain. At the time he had to do battle against South Africa.

FLUCTUATING FORTUNES

Between 1994 and 1998, some of the gloss on Brian Lara's batting glory faded. In late 1994, when he toured India under Courtney Walsh, a temporary replacement of

Richie Richardson—diagnosed with acute fatigue syndrome—he did not score a century in a drawn three Test Match series which was decided late in the final game—thanks to some inspirational spells of penetrative quick bowling by Kenneth Benjamin. His Test Match average was just [33]. Brian Lara returned to the Caribbean for the 1995 series against a resolute Australian side led by Mark Taylor, who gained able assistance from, among others, Michael Slater, Glen McGrath, Paul Reiffel, David Boon, Ian Healy, and of course Shane Warne. The 1995 encounter was extremely important to the Taylor troops: no regular side from their country had beaten the West Indies since 1975-'76, and they had their sights trained on batting opponents such as Keith Arthurton, Brian Lara, as well as Jimmy Adams, who had earned the name "barnacle" Adams, because of his dogged defence against the leading Indian spinners the previous year.

The tourists were well aware of Lara's reputation, and manager/coach, Bob Simpson, "Simmo," stated publicly, before the start of the Test Matches, that he did not think his team's main opponent would be Lara. He noted the Adams prominence which was based on very high scores against the Indian bowlers. All three of these left handers were victimised by Shane Warne's strategic spin and McGrath's quick bowling genius. In the four Tests, the second of which, in Trinidad, the West Indies won, Lara never got within twenty of an even hundred. He and his West Indies teammates lost the series. In the face of such capitulation Australian cricket was ascendant once more.

Well before the series had begun, Australian player Stephen Waugh, who emerged to become the most successful captain in Test Match cricket, summed up his approach to the impending meeting by stating:

> This is obviously a big test for any batsman. It's what you're judged on, when you play the West Indies. But we're all pretty confident. I know I'm quietly confident, myself, but you don't want to go out and make any statements against these guys [West Indians]. They've probably got the best bowling attack going round. But, personally, I feel good and I think the rest of the batsmen are feeling good, too. They're feeling confident. We know we can get on top of their bowlers. It's just a matter of being patient, picking the right balls. So, if we can do that, I'm sure our bowlers can do the job, as well. We're pretty confident.[5]

Supreme confidence is what Waugh and teammates took to Sabina Park where they rightfully claimed one of the most coveted crowns, the Frank Worrell trophy.

Their possession was realised after almost four days over which Mark Taylor and others toiled ceaselessly in "one of the toughest theatres" of cricketing competition to torment their Caribbean combatants. When they made their last dismissal in the West Indies second innings, those ardent and astute members of the Australian assembly knew they had reaped one of their richest rewards. The West Indies lost the fourth and final Test Match by an innings and [53] runs. Man of the match and series was Stephen Waugh. So, after close to twenty five years, his side won a series [2-1] and took the Frank Worrell trophy to the island continent. While forces which had favoured and followed West Indies' lengthy decade and a half global assertiveness might have denied the definite discomfort, they could alter, neither the reality, nor result, of Australian resolve. Waugh and teammates must have revelled while they witnessed deterioration from poor resistance to hugely unpalatable and distasteful painful regional rout.

The 1995 encounter provided some of the strongest evidence for the reality, that glorious uncertainty of cricket, despite the panditry of reputable correspondents such as Stephen Thorpe (*Sunday Times*). Writing in the 26th March, 1995, p. 18 edition of the paper, he begins by stating:

> NO RESPITE *for the international cricketer. Barely a month after commitments in New Zealand, West Indies and Australia have already concluded a one-day joust and are set to engage in an epic four Test confrontation, starting in Barbados on Friday [21st March, 1995] for the Frank Worrell Trophy. And, lest anyone forget it the mantle of unofficial champions. The loss of [Craig] McDermott, Australia spearhead and second leading wicket taker of all time, for the first two Tests at least, will diminish the spectacle and tilt the balance inexorably in the West Indies favour.*

While noting the fever-pitch anticipation for the four Test Matches and the fiercely burning pride in every West Indian the correspondent cites what he sees as the regional Caribbean belief that West Indies invincibility is an integral part of what he deems "the natural order of things." He also notes that their Test Match supremacy is the unifying element, a source of continual regional joy, as well as a palliative to that harsh reality, everyday rum shop life.

To gauge the depth of the West Indies humiliation, I turn yet again to correspondent Thorpe, not for his panditry, but his presentation of comparative statistics: From 1980 to the 1995 encounter, the West Indies had not been defeated by any other team in 28 Test Match series. Further, no team had beaten them in the Caribbean since 1973. That I know was the year when Australia led by Ian Chappell defeated opposing captain, Rohan Kanhai. From Thorpe's standpoint, these were not figures which augured well for Australia. Struggle against West Indies in 1995 Australia most certainly did not. The constant joy and fiercely burning fires within West Indies camps had disappeared and are yet to return.

Some foreign analysts could not conceal their delight in the Caribbean debacle under Riche Richardson's leadership. In an editorial titled "Pulling Together" [June 1995 issue,: Wisden Cricket Monthly], David Frith proudly proclaimed that for those who prefer common sense to computers, Australia are champions of the world. He added:

> *The writing on the West Indian wall is now flashing in neon. Their long, long term as 'unbeatables' came to an end not merely in series defeat but in a humiliating loss that had some of their players weeping. V.J. Day took on a new meaning for younger Australians. Victory in Jamaica.*

Frith continued by stating that England's summer job (1995) was to balance some of the recent 'blackwashes' and push the West Indies further down the world league.

In another forceful blast, he asked readers for reflection on the uncertainties experienced by Richardson as rival Caribbean territories nibbled away at him in their outrage and jealousy. More importantly, he wanted the uncertainties compared to unbending and universal support given to Allan Border and Mark Taylor by the entire Australian community.

More than two decades after that Australian victory in 1995, writing on the West Indian wall still flashes in neon. Part of that writing has been stamped, quite clearly, on the leadership tenures of Brian Lara. Under his leadership, West Indies have suffered humiliating innings losses, some of which, imposed by England, have done more than balanced 'blackwashes,' and helped to push West Indies very far down the cricket standings.

Frith and other gleeful observers had to wait a while to experience humiliation and attendant relegation under his Test Match captaincy. Lara and teammates, under captain Richardson, left for England in summer of 1995 when they played a six Test Match series that ended in a draw. Lara was able to post three hundreds [145], in the fourth game, at Old Trafford, Manchester, [152] in the fifth, at Trent Bridge, Nottingham, and [179] in the sixth at Kennington Oval, London. Importantly, he did top the batting averages in Test Matches that summer and was, justifiably, named man of the series.

No keen observer of West Indies cricket, at the time, would, however, have been unaware of West Indies team troubles. So, by early spring of the following year 1996, Caribbean cricket had taken a painful exit via distasteful loss to Australia at home, and seemed stagnated before the presence of England in England where the 1991 and 1995 series were drawn. Thus, when the team—once more with Richardson at the helm—travelled to India for the [1995-'96] Cricket World Cup and was getting ready to play Kenya, in Poona, the betting money was not on the East African team. What a mistake!

Brian Lara, strongly expected by West Indies team manager, Wes Hall, to blast the cricketing novices out of the stadium, featured prominently in the mistake, and was given an early return trip to the pavilion. I offer much more than a field description and assessment of the encounter which is indelible on the minds of all West Indies supporters. Kenya, they shall all remember, beat the West Indies. Final scores in the one day game were: Kenya batting first [166] from [49 overs and 3 deliveries]. West Indies [93 from 36 overs]. Two highlights of the 73 run loss were: (a) man of the match award for Kenyan captain, Maurice Odumbe, who claimed the wickets of Jimmy Adams, Shivnarine Chanderpaul, and Roger Harper for [15 runs in 10 overs], (b) painful prelude to an embarrassing team exit exemplified by punitive parades of batsmen, Keith Arthurton, Sherwin Campbell, Richie Richardson, as well as Brian Lara back to the pavilion, well before [50] had been posted.

What a massively astounding result to manager, Wes Hall, who had featured in a 14th May, 1995, article of the British Sunday Times by the redoubtable and magisterial cricket correspondent, Robin Marlar! Marlar described as fascinating Wes Hall's progress from seventeen year old medium pacer to cabinet rank in his home island, Barbados. In so doing, the correspondent stated that Hall had emulated Alfred Lyttleton, English classical scholar and top wicket keeper, who became Colonial Secretary. More importantly, when manager Hall, quoted the poet, Horace, he was given a standing ovation at an MCC dinner to launch the 1995 West Indies summer tour to England.

It might have been of no small significance for man of letters, Wesley Winfield Hall [G.C.M., H.B.M., J.P.], previously a Barbados member of parliament and Senator in Trinidad, to be linked with Horace [Quintus Horatio Flaccus], who was both lyrical and oratorical in his poetic production. West Indies cricket, that symptom complex which Hall represented in 1995-'96, however, required less of a connection to lyricism and oratory when facing Kenya.

West Indies cricket could also have done without his bold prediction on the eve of stunning defeat to the cricketers from East Africa:

We're very confident that we will beat Kenya. I mean: everybody else has but that does not mean that we're complacent. We had a long trip from Bombay yesterday *and this morning we had a four hours practice session—going through all the rudiments and we're not taking it easy at all. We need to get that win tomorrow and we need to get it emphatically. We need to win with stuff in hand—that if the teams are tied at the end of the round we need to have a good run rate. So, if we bowl them out cheaply, we need to get what is required very quickly. And if we bat first, we need to get a big score. I think we're very focused. We need to know what we have to do and I think we're just going to do it tomorrow.*

Those who believed in the power of prediction and usually took up residence at ground level would have done well to ponder connections between cheapness and confidence on the one hand, as well as focus and failure on the other. Even such movement could not, however, have served as a suitable substitute for what I had regarded, in many a Toronto radio programme, as a rather unhealthy state: prognosis for a patient, West Indies cricket, in perpetual paralysis was very poor.

Speaking after the staggering defeat of the "calypso charmers," captain Richie Richardson's opposite number was so ecstatic about his team's unexpected elevation, that he proudly proclaimed to BBC WORLD SERVICE radio:

Well. I feel like we've won the World Cup. You know, we came here, at least to try and win one match. And the match that we wanted to win was against Zimbabwe. But to beat West Indies—it was like a DREAM come true. You know West Indies have always been our heroes. They've always been our idols. We've always looked up to them. We based our cricket on their cricket. And to come out here and beat them—I just don't have words. I don't know how to describe it.

No serious West Indies cricket lover could miss the significant implicature within captain Odumbe's pronouncement. The Kenyan admiration of Caribbean cricket, which was strongly linked to Caribbean playing styles did include admiration of Brian Charles Lara, who failed to make an impact in the game.

Lara's batting impact in a 1996-'97 encounter against Australia down under was also insignificant. In another loss to the Taylor troops, this time under Courtney Walsh, he managed to secure only one century. Early in 1997, he failed to get a hundred in any of the Test Match defeats heavily inflicted by Pakistan on the sub-continent.

Lara's fluctuating fortunes in no way outweighed his well-established batting reputation based upon his record breaking scores in 1994. Most people in the Caribbean saw his batsmanship as one of the solid foundations from which he should launch his Test Match captaincy. It would be true to say, also, that they saw Courtney Walsh as merely an interim leader playing a transition role. In 1998, captain Brian Lara was given his first placement at the helm of West Indies cricket, whose initial cause he served well. He led a team which defeated tourists from England under Michael Atherton. A much bigger challenge, however, awaited him in post-apartheid South Africa, later that year.

THE BEGINNING OF BRIAN LARA'S CAPTAINCY

It is to South Africa that I turn for the purpose of continuing my very close examination of Lara's three tenured leadership, which I deem the worst in West Indies Test Match cricket. Despite the presence of Clive Lloyd as team manager/coach, I predicted "a massive humiliating defeat" under Lara, for West Indies while I was participating in a radio programme on cricket in Toronto, Canada. West Indies lost every single duel in the five game series and managed to secure victory in merely one of five one day matches. South Africa, some would recall, shortly after its release from the racist horror of apartheid, toured West Indies, where the team played a single Test Match. The venue was Kensington Oval Barbados, where, against all odds, West Indies, led by Richie Richardson, engineered a stunning victory owed chiefly to inspirational spells of quick bowling from Courtney Walsh and Curtly Ambrose.

Cricketing memories are not so short. Hence, South African recollection of that defeat would have been fresh on the minds of both Test Match cricketers and members of a sporting public whose country's readmission to the international sports fraternity was promptly followed by victory in the Rugby World Cup before none other than new President, Nelson Mandela. Mandela was leader of a society eager to reassert its presence on the international sporting scene. When Lara, Lloyd, and fellow West Indians travelled there, I certainly did not lose sight of the facts: by 2000 the Republic of South Africa would set up a National Sports Academy, Drug Testing Institute, and Sports Information Centre. A National Sports Trust was also going to be instituted. Any company wishing to be part of it would be required to make a one million rand contribution to the organisation.

Of far greater significance to me than the organisational shift in South Africa were the words of cricket manager, Clive Lloyd, whose reflective posture signalled inability of leader Brian Lara, probably, the most important player on the 1998 tour, to grasp the transcendent features of cricket. Here is an exchange about the very 1998 disgrace only one year later between me [W. W.] and Sir. Clive Lloyd [C. L.]:

W. W.: *You were in the presence of a man [Nelson Mandela] who admired your style of play and approach to managing people, enormously, but you were, nevertheless, in a society whose cricketers were, for the most part, white, whose rugby team were, for the most part, white. I wonder if during the situation of your loss there wasn't a sense of paradox or irony in that society at the time.*

C. L.: *I think it's quite obvious that the players should have realised the importance of our tour. Our tour was to give the disadvantaged people of South Africa a chance to see that if we can do it they can do it. You know some of the disadvantaged people never had the privilege of playing in certain areas. But we let them down badly in that respect. I thought that we should have understood the importance of our trip to South Africa. And that's why the South Africans—it's not only to beat the West Indies—they had a programme for the disadvantaged people and I thought that we could have enhanced it by doing MUCH better, during that particular period. But we didn't. We failed them badly. And I have a very soft spot for South Africa and I felt that our players did not approach that tour and understood, although they were told the importance of that tour.*

Failure, disadvantage, and disappointment can certainly be juxtaposed with success, advantage, and fulfilment, which—insofar as South Africa and Namibia are concerned—are linked to resistance, resolve, and determination. How could Brian Lara, a leader noted for his views about legacy miss: (a) he was leading people of colour on a continent rightly regarded as the cradle of humanity (b) when South Africa and Namibia were trapped within the horror of apartheid, it was none other than compatriot, C.L.R. James, who wrote openly that even in the midst of such horror leading Caribbean cricketers of colour should play there. James took the position that their presence and performance would serve to greatly inspire and give hope to those burdened by the yoke of racial injustice.

What kind of a history student was Lara, who talked about inheriting a legacy? South Africa is not too distant from Mozambique and Angola, also trapped within the jaws of injustice under imperialist Portugal. Lara should have known about the hugely inspirational performances of the Jamaican reggae genius, Bob Marley, who used the words of a Haile Selassie speech to dramatise in song the plight of people of colour under Afrikaner and Portuguese strangulation. How could he, a Caribbean leader of people of colour in South Africa, someone who grew up in the West Indies, miss the significance of the maroon headgear worn by West Indies cricketers! The Maroons were Africans brought forcibly to the Caribbean for slavery which they fought courageously and successfully. Today, their descendants, proud people of colour, show the Caribbean the value of sacrifice, resistance, resolve, and determination.

Earlier, I made reference to Mr. Mandela's questioning Australian Prime Minister, Malcolm Fraser, about the great Sir Donald George Bradman. Was this just a cricket inquiry? My ready response is explicitly negative. The hallmark of Bradman's batsmanship was his refusal to be dominated, even in the face of bowling terror viciously unleashed against him and other Australian batsmen by England paceman, Harold Larwood, acting on specific instructions from his captain to employ "bodyline" bowling. The major defining feature of Mr. Mandela's lengthy imprisonment was his steadfast resolve against capitulating emergent from bedrock hewn out of principles of justice.

I must point out, also, that when Clive Lloyd was making his remarks about understanding the importance of the South African tour, he was doing so in a Toronto foreground where he, West Indies coach/manager, was saddled with an uncomfortable task of watching captain, Brian Lara, use off spinner Chris Gayle, to open the West Indies bowling against India for a one day game in the 1999 Toronto Cricket Festival where the Caribbean side suffered a humiliating defeat. Lloyd was, doubtless, fully aware that he was not the sole notable West Indies luminary in whose presence the loss eventuated, at a time, summer 1999, when Lara needed to grasp the significance of a West Indies presence to North America. Others in appearance were: Messrs. Tony Cozier, Caribbean cricket historian and commentator; Joey Carew, former West Indies opening batsman and Test Match selector; ex-West Indies express bowler and cricket commentator, Colin Croft; Sir Clyde Walcott, former famous West Indies Test Match batsman, chairman of West Indies Test Match selectors, West Indies Cricket Board President, and International Cricket Council [ICC] President.

To me the South African debacle was just a prelude to terrible trouble for Brian Lara, trouble I thought he would face when Australia, under Stephen Waugh, toured West Indies, the following year. How wrong I was! No one who saw that Test Match series in the Caribbean should ever forget the two centuries [153] and [213] he reached against the men from down under. One of the scores, the double hundred in the second game, without question, enhanced his cricketing persona, not merely in the West Indies, but also around the entire cricketing world. Here, I offer my own brief assessment of that double century achievement which will be followed by critical exploration.

In a pugnacious and purposeful display of batting before ecstatically appreciative Caribbean admirers, Brian Lara crafted an innings of sheer joy which he built from various blends of prudence in aggression and immediacy of improvisation. Both combinations enabled him to conquer Warne, MacGill, McGrath, and the rest of the Australian bowling crew. The posting of this memorable double hundred allowed him to attain four other heights. He secured yet additional placing among the batting pantheons of Caribbean cricket. He helped a hapless bunch of teammates gain a respectable draw in a series against the rampaging Australians led by the resolute Stephen Waugh. He was aided to become world cricketer of the year. Unfortunately, though, he was placed in a position from which I think he was thrust with the role 'icon of delusion.'

In late 1999, Lara led a West Indies team to New Zealand, where he and teammates were again humiliated in an overseas Test Match encounter. When he returned to the Caribbean, the following year, he relinquished his post. Thus ended his first tenure. I want to locate the core of this tenure and the other two within wider contexts which I hope will serve to highlight leadership inadequacy.

ENDNOTES

1 *The quote is the view offered by cricket correspondent, Alastair McLellan, of British television channel 4, in summer 1999. I did see that Lara McGrath confrontation and shall long remember its numbing impact on me.*

2 *The stage is indisputably accepted as the Lord's Cricket Ground, located in St. John's Wood, London.*

3 *While it is very highly probable that these and other matters are being explored by post-graduate students at the University of the West Indies, I emphasise that the University is not a Caribbean Institute of Cricket.*

4 *It remains to be seen whether intellectual work being done at the C.L.R. James Centre of the University of The West Indies—including pursuit of post-graduate studies in cricket by students—can parallel or encompass work of a Caribbean Institute of Cricket.*

5 *These statements of Waugh's were aired by BBC World Service radio.*

Courtney Walsh

Shane Warne

Inzamam-ul-Haq

Sachin Tendulkar

12th INNINGS
THE CORE OF BRIAN LARA'S CAPTAINCY

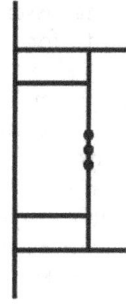

Before I get to the core of Brian Lara's captaincy, it is very important for me to lay out a template or set a frame within which I think his three tenured leadership should be examined in detail. There are, of course, several dimensions to construction of this sort. Despite its plurality, I hope to locate those which bear considerable relevance to West Indies Test Match cricket. Here, I give priority to the special place of Test Match captaincy in the Anglo-Caribbean.

In this regard, it is worth noting that numerous citizens of colour in the region have always focused upon the leadership post. They have adopted this stance, chiefly, because of comparative significance they created between fairness or lack thereof connected to the position. I am pointing to a regional gaze—with its initial intimate links to regular selection only of white Caribbean persons for the job from summer 1928, when West Indies first played Test Match cricket, right up to winter 1959-1960, when the very last such selection took place. Thus, for close to three decades, captains were chosen purely on the basis of preferred colour, rather than strategic merit and sporting skill. This posture, in its regularity, an unmistakable instantiation of prevailing shameless imperialist domination, was both depressing and annoying to the masses of cricket loving persons of colour.

Many years after Frank Worrell, one of the most talented African-Caribbean West Indies cricketers had been overlooked as a result of preference for a member of the white commercial class, George Lamming, the famous Barbadian writer, stated publicly that the Worrell mistreatment was one the most disgusting and depressing of injustices to Caribbean non-whites. George Lamming is a black Barbadian who was referring to the erroneous and harmful imperialist posture about the myth and propaganda of black inferiority which had been exposed much earlier by Miller (1960, pp. 64-73), an Australian, one of the world's most talented of Test Match cricketing geniuses. He notes that West Indies selectors are just as likely to act as peculiarly as selectors from England and Australia. He adds that they will always do so, as long as petty domestic politics and preferences are "allowed to fog cricket judgment." Where was Miller not blinded by the fog?

It is in the area of politics which he states interferes with cricket more in the Caribbean than most places. Interference, one problem in the region, "is that the captain has usually been chosen from among European stock." Just think of the most famous West Indian cricketers... Learie Constantine, George Headley, Frank Worrell, Everton Weekes, Clyde Walcott... all are coloured, but none has led his country. Yet Worrell was often skipper of a Commonwealth tour in India, and he did a fine job.

Once, however, Frank Worrell was appointed to the position of captain, he raised the expectation of Caribbean people of colour by working diligently during a period of regional agitation for independence from Britain for West Indies Test Match cricketing assertiveness. Not only did his efforts succeed, he set the exalted standards for most of his followers—all people of colour. Five of the most impressively successful of these followers were Garfield Sobers, Rohan Kanhai, Clive Lloyd, Vivian Richards, and Richie Richardson. What does such accomplishment signify to the masses of coloured West Indians? Importance lies in recognising that they look at those leaders who come after Worrell as persons who are obliged to maintain—if not surpass—achievements of predecessors. Herein resides a big part of the focus and special place of the captaincy to which I referred.

In the most general of cricketing terms, which are applicable also to West Indies Test Match cricket, the person playing the role of captain is looked upon as the individual who bears the greatest responsibility for team success. When the team is successful, he is the darling of overflowing public adulation. When, however, it loses, he has to wonder whether a lot of the vitriolic remarks spewed in his direction are any worse than calls for his hanging, drawing and quartering. Cricket captains Freddie Brown, Norman Yardley, Colin Cowdrey, and Michael Smith from England know the difference all too well. A large part of responsibility is integrally linked to how well the leader's grand strategic designs have their desired impact. This, in turn, is associated with the depth and breadth of the leader's intimate high level knowledge of the game, which he balances with repetition of consistently demonstrable ability in one or two areas of individual performance that are vital to success.

Excellent fielding, batting, and bowling come to mind immediately. All three of these pursuits serve as fine instantiations of team motivation. A few captains, notably Garfield Sobers of the West Indies, have been outstanding all-rounders. Sobers was a superb batsman, a destructively attacking bowler in more than one guise, and a menacingly brilliant fieldsman.

One can, of course, conceptualise the role of captain in non-cricketing terms and give profound consideration to what is done both by composers of opera, and conductors of classical and jazz orchestras, as well as leaders of jazz bands. In jazz, the names Ellington, Marsalis, Basie, Blakey, Gillespie, Peterson, and Goodman emerge immediately. So do the names Gergiev, Scarlatti, Bernardi, Gilbert, Cavalli, Mariner, Carissimi, Elgar, Corelli, Bach, Steffani, Tchaikovsky, Handel, Chopin, Rachmaninoff, Purcell, Abbado, Krell, Rattle, and Ormandy in opera and classical music. While some may quickly observe much more than the tenor of improvisation in jazz, I do wish to emphasise that within this area and classical music, it is the coordination of collaborative performance suffused by subtlety of play nurtured in refinement of skill that count. These were all emphases gloriously present in their alliterative, synecdochic, metaphorical, paradoxical, and ironical figurative connections to the mesmerising uniqueness of the world's greatest Test Match batsman, Donald George Bradman, a man steeped in humility, a man who at the time of his death—92 years old in 2001—was rightly deemed the greatest Australian.

When Bradman captained his Test Match side, he accomplished tremendous success against staunch rival England, by blending some of that very humility with tact in diplomacy. Significantly, he is the very first great cricketer of note whose extraordinary genius I have seen juxtaposed with that of Italian conductor, Arturo Toscanini, and German composer Johannes Brahms. Perhaps, the placement is in order, for many a time in his international playing career, he played jazz and classical music on the piano—all of this cricket and music coming from a boy who started playing what some do not disparagingly dub "bush" cricket in Bowral, Australia.

Numerous people within and outside the Anglo-Caribbean profess no understanding of what they are told is the complexity of either classical or jazz music, especially what is done by the person moving a little stick, a baton. By way of analogy, the task of captain is also complicated within Test Match cricket. Thus, the reply I got from Sachin Tendulkar in 1996, when I asked him about the special burdens captaincy brought to him, came as no surprise. While reflecting on games against Sri Lanka and Australia, he told me:

Definitely, it [the captaincy] is going to add on more responsibility to my job. I'll be very responsible taking all the decisions. When the side loses, everyone points the finger at the captain and when the side wins everyone praises the captain. So, I'm prepared to take all the criticism.

Finger pointing, that euphemism for criticism and praise in Test Match cricket, make up a dichotomy of peril, the measure of which every excellent captain shows he navigates deftly. Clive Lloyd and Viv Richards showed that they knew how to do navigating by plotting, with great skill, their moves designed to motivate players. Consequently, they steered West Indies to positions of mesmerising and unprecedented greatness. Brian Lara never came near to putting West Indies in such an elevated standing. He suffered humiliating defeats in far less than cracking contests with opponents always lurking along craggy cricketing coast lines from which they were only too eager to launch destructive raids.

I believe a reasonable first apprehension of the depth in this retrogressive descent would be to repeat what I have always stated: although boundaries of Caribbean cricket may appear to be distant, much more than the field is wide open. This is the vast terrain I shall traverse, reflectively, in the wake of Lara's first departure from the captaincy. One good way of exploring this terrain of Lara leadership would be to consider the problematic he faced, for the purpose of balancing the inventiveness and conventions governing scientific practice of leadership with the creativity and tradition in the art of leadership. Here, I must say the West Indies captain who struck the right balance was Sir Frank Worrell. Captain Brian Lara was not just hugely distant from the standard of captain Worrell, captain Brian Lara was far apart also from other captains such as Vivian Richards, Richie Richardson, Clive Lloyd, Rohan Kanhai, and Garfield Sobers.

While covering the Brian Lara leadership ground, I must also pose some pertinent queries. When the prudent "Prince" Lara, received one of his richest rewards, the Caribbean captaincy in 1998, did we not expect to hail our heroes and savour that taste of sweet success in judicious combinations of wisdom, youth, and experience from Lara? Were we not, however, forced to follow a deadly drift of Caribbean "ISLAND CRICKETERS"[1] whose searches have brought us no shores of security? Did we not wince with plaintive wailing amid torrents of trouble for a West Indies band clearly in tatters? Let me reply to these inquiries by being explicitly affirmative and add: cricket has always been a team sport in which enjoying advantages of victory depends on how well each player's talents are moulded by a leader for surmounting every complex challenge to collectivism. Dare I say Mr. Lara failed to grasp the significance of this rudimentary requirement?

My claim here is not meant to be confined to field matters. It would not be unreasonable to state that several observers/experts viewed Lara, the last non-imperialist leader of the twentieth century, as a genius and revolutionary. Despite the brevity to his first reign (1998-2000), he should be compared to his non-imperialist predecessors who were given similar assessments. When I make the comparison, I note that the predecessors were invested with authority which transcended cricket captaincy. They had been given versions of deification which they tactfully used to reduce social distance between them and regional masses.

These were leaders who occupied positions of great Caribbean revolutionaries and have given the region significance no politician was ever able to accomplish. Frank Worrell, who stood above all, was the consummate humanist, applying excellence in his inimitable empathetic skills to construct the first real West Indies cricketing society. Garfield Sobers, frequently the charismatic champion, was followed by Clive Lloyd, that astute communicator. Vivian Richards proceeded after Clive Lloyd with unbridled assertiveness that punctuated the culture of greatness from which he crafted his leadership. Regrettably, Rohan Kanhai, Alvin Kallicharran, and Richie Richardson were never granted enough time to inherit the legacies cultivated for them.

Brian Lara has had more than ample time in a leadership role: the captaincy was given to him, for a second time, in 2003, after teammate Carl Hooper, had been sacked from the leadership position. Lara promptly registered a victory against Zimbabwe, but lost, in most humiliating fashion, again to South Africa. He and teammates returned to the Caribbean in 2003 and suffered a heavy defeat at the hands of Stephen Waugh's Australians. In 2004, when he and his colleagues faced an energised England, seeking Test Match success, which the tourists had last accomplished rather narrowly in 1968 under Colin Cowdrey, Lara and his side never won a single game. Michael Vaughn's side claimed three massive consecutive victories before the final game of the series ended in a predictable draw.

Despite the huge defeats captain Lara has experienced, he and his horde of admirers had, however, been tangled in webs of collective objectification woven from a precarious perch where I have seen him as someone who was continually revered as the icon of delusion. I shall support my claim about perversity of the iconic status given to him. This position will be followed by more critical appraisal. Let me begin by stating why I think Brian Lara has been an icon.

Here are some reasonable grounds for my claim: (a) He has been a Test Match batsman associated with extraordinarily impressive performances. West Indies Test Match bowlers have, doubtless, been associated with such talents. Alfred Valentine, Sonny Ramadhin, Lance Gibbs, Michael Holding, Malcolm Marshall, Andy Roberts, Charlie Griffith, Herman Griffith, Wes Hall, Colin Croft, and Joel Garner certainly come to mind. None of them, despite his great skill, enjoyed iconic status.

(b) Lara's presence as a Test Match batsman in West Indies sides was an unorthodox one. Clive Lloyd, Rohan Kanhai, Everton Weekes, Clyde Walcott, and Vivian Richards were all domineering at the crease. It is, perhaps, only Richards and Lloyd who enjoy iconic status. Richards does because of his captaincy and batting, in the second of which he does not equal Lara's iconic elevation. I think this is so, partly on account of the fact that he was a right-handed batsman. Lloyd, of course, left-handed, was not so impressive with the bat as Lara. Importantly, Lloyd's presence among the pantheons of Caribbean cricket is linked, indelibly, to his leadership excellence which helped give his sides lengthy unprecedented supremacy.

(c) After the three W's and prior to Lara, the mesmeric feature of Caribbean Test Match batting was linked to the genius of players such as Larry Gomes, Gordon Greenidge, Richie Richardson, Desmond Haynes, Alvin Kallicharran, Vivian Richards, Roy Fredericks, Rohan Kanhai and Garfield Sobers—himself unorthodox in the left-handed category. In the public sphere, Lara was usually compared fondly to Sobers, whose dominance of bowling was not seen in left-handers such as Alvin Kallicharran, Roy Fredericks, and Bernard Julien, the last of whom was connected with a hasty exit from Test Match circuits, which left many an expectant admirer non-plussed.

(d) In the eyes of doting admirers, Lara's Test Match batting propelled him to heroic heights in the Anglo-Caribbean, where sub and non-personhood of people of colour has been linked, inextricably, to the evil in status ascription from imperialism. Lara has, thus, been standing tall with a pugnacious and triumphant stature against injustice. In addition, within a climate of poor performances from West Indies Test Match sides, Lara's extraordinary batting excellence gave his status even more force but also the dreamlike loftiness of a post-modern monarch.

(e) It is, however, not difficult for me to see Brian Lara, the persona revered, as an icon of delusion. Here are three initial replies to the query: why was the adulation heaped upon Lara in the category of delusion?

(f) The Sobers admiration of Lara has not carried a speck of significant criticism for the latter. In this regard, I ask readers to explore, for themselves, three comments, two of which are connected to leadership, from Sir Gary. Almost four years prior to Lara's first appointment as West Indies Test Match skipper (1995), Sir Gary was explicit in supporting his protégé's candidacy. He pointed out that apart from being a student of the game, Lara had very high regard for discipline. Sobers added that among all the West Indies captains—including himself and the great Sir Frank Worrell—about whom he could think Brian Lara was brimful of experience. He noted that Lara was the only "truly trained" individual to take over leadership of the West Indies. "I don't think that any of us has had the experience that Brian Lara has had. I think he was a captain when he was twelve years old."

(g) It was also in 1995—following a drawn Test Match series between England and the West Indies—that Lara announced a decision to withdraw from the Caribbean squad heading for Australasia. The withdrawal was, supposedly, connected to disciplinary action having been taken against the left-hander by the West Indies Cricket Board for his conduct during an England tour. When questioned that same year about the withdrawal, Sir Gary issued clear endorsement of the Lara decision. "I am sad to hear that that Brian Lara has withdrawn from the West Indies team to tour Australia, this year (1995). I know Brian Lara and I don't think that he would have done it without reason and very very good reason. If he feels that there is some animosity or whatever there is that is affecting him and his cricket, then I think he is right to do what he has done, because so much is expected of him, not only as a cricketer but as an ambassador. And if he is going to suffer, in any form or fashion, or his cricket, or his presence, or he himself, his person, is going to suffer, because of whatever is going on and he feels the best thing to do is to get out, well then, I would endorse what he has done."

(h) In early 2000, the immediate aftermath of Lara's first leadership resignation, the Sobers stance was: "Brian has had a lot of problems from the inside. He should have been given a freer hand at his job. And I am not surprised [at his resignation] because there have been so many things said about his captaincy which I thought was... a lot of false statements about it, because I have always believed that Brian has the knowledge and the ability to lead a team. And I think that he had come to the conclusion that he wasn't, probably, getting the support that he needed and it was time to give up the captaincy." It is my view that such comments from great admirer Garfield Sobers have constituted massive protection—if required by Brian Lara—against public disapproval. Sobers—away from the Test Match arena where his captaincy was criticised—has enjoyed official and unofficial heroic status within the Caribbean. Lara's very close association with such a luminary has been one of the best repellents to harm. Lara was also aided by the fact that no one could have questioned Sobers about the legitimacy of admiration for extraordinarily impressive batting accomplishments which Sobers had clearly and boldly predicted.

(i) Another way of expressing the Sobers-Lara link would be to state: despite the looming presence of Frank Worrell, Everton Weekes, and Clyde Walcott, Garfield Sobers was criticised heavily in the aftermath of the 1968 declaration against England. Stung by the severity of the unofficial censure, immediately after the loss following that declaration, Sobers stated publicly: when a captain wins, he is applauded. When, however, a loss eventuates, he is dubbed a fool and deserves a sacking. Twenty-two years later, 1990, when England toured the West Indies, Sky Sports telecaster, Tony Greig, secured emphatic agreement from colleague, Michael Holding, to whom he had asserted: West Indians do not have a great deal of appreciation for a captain who declares, a move he claimed Sobers made a while back. One year later, 1991, Tony Cozier, like Greig, named Sobers and described the former West Indies captain as having declared, infamously. Garfield Sobers, long retired from the Test Match scene, did not direct critical remarks to Lara's captaincy. Most of his pronouncements were about his successor's illustrious batting. Further, the Sobers link to Lara was not divorced from the uniqueness of heights to which Lara had soared as a batsman. The uniqueness has been Lara's own protector against public criticism of the captaincy. In the imagery of an admiring public, uniqueness greatly transcended the significance of the captaincy in which Lara has, of course, failed.

There is another very important reason I think Brian Lara enjoyed protection against, and was spared the impact of, systematic or incisive criticism within the Anglo-Caribbean. I think that reason was the erosion or dying of conditions in the region for serious debate about cricketing matters via the medium of Caribbean Sovereign Language. This is retrogression I attribute to saturation of the West Indies with linguistic modes of expression originating from the media culture of what Michael Holding deems "Americanisation of the West Indies." I shall be addressing myself later to this position of the ex-express bowler. At this point, I am simply referring to sophisticated electro-magnetic technology which channels audio visual messages of virtually instantaneous communication mainly from the US to the West Indies.

I do recall the time before agitation for independence of the larger territories such as British Guiana, Jamaica, Barbados, as well as Trinidad and Tobago, when Caribbean Sovereign Language was used as the preeminent medium for conducting discourse about high level international cricket involving West Indies Test Mach teams. Such discourse, which occurred also in the wake of independence, was conducted with just as much intensity, passion, and exploratory skill as that employed by dedicated post-graduate university students and their teachers. I can certainly locate one central area in imperialist ruled British Guiana where such talk was regular, and I am certain persons in other territories would not experience difficulty in locating similar places. The British Guiana location I have in mind is King Street, Georgetown. Quite apart from this type of central area, ferries, rum shops, and grocery stores were prominent discourse locales.

Allow me to offer an illuminating account about Trinidad which I heard in a broadcast from the BBC World Service radio in the early nineties. The account is a narration in a program, "TALES FROM THE CREASE," where reference is made to writing of West Indies intellectual C.L.R. James, in his best known publication *BEYOND A BOUNDARY*. After having stated that James never lost sight of cricket's social dimension, programme presenter, Michael Diamond, noted the James allusion to the bad blood often existent in colonial Trinidad between the Black farm workers and local Chinese shopkeepers.

The Chinese, in the words of Diamond, would be an immigrant who had become rich quickly, and the farm workers would be in debt to him. Quite another contrast in Trinidad ethnic relations is, however, brought to the fore by programme narrator, Leslie Gough, through words in *BEYOND A BOUNDARY*.

> *But this man, [the immigrant shopkeeper] after about fifteen years would be seized with a passion for cricket. He did not play himself but he sponsored the local village team. He would buy a matting for them and supply them with bats and balls. On the Sunday when the match was to be played he provided a feast. He helped out players who could not afford cricket gear. He godfathered very poor boys who could play. On the day of the match you could see him surrounded by locals, following every ball with a passionate intensity that he gave only to his business. All night and half the day his shop would be filled with people arguing about the match that was past or that was to come. When the team had to travel he supplied the transport. The usual taciturnity of the local Chinese remained with him, except in cricket where he would be as excited and as voluble as the rest. You could find people like him scattered all over the island. I don't believe that apart from his business and his family life, he had any contact whatever with the life around him except his sponsorship of the local cricket club (James 1963, pp. 63-64).*

Excitement, volubility, and passionate intensity within Test Match cricketing discourse saturated with Caribbean Sovereign Language abounded in the Anglo-Caribbean. Today, it is hard to find this type of interaction in a locus resembling that on King Street or the shop in Trinidad.

Trinidad is a place currently immersed or submerged in bubbling oil and exploding from more than potent pockets of huge natural gas reserves. Trinidad is a capitalist heaven where great wealth, unevenly distributed, is strongly associated with social distance among people many of whom are goaded into believing that gadgetry in consumerism of electronic communication brings them closer. This is the type of alienating consumerism helping to kill Caribbean Sovereign Language cricketing discourse in stores, rum shops, and other traditional meeting places. May I add that Guyana, with its huge reserves of oil recently discovered, is set to join—albeit, not for the better—Trinidad!

What are now powerfully evident right across the Anglo-Caribbean are such instruments and mechanisms as cell phones, the latest flat screen colour television sets, and DVD players. Test Match cricketing information from the national newspapers, then transistor radios, that were so powerful as foundational tools to discourse I have described is a rare subject for incisive discussion. Let me make my point, somewhat differently, by referring to ideas of Holt (2000, p. 85), who identifies a world where the consumer society colonises almost all of people's lives. Through colonisation, image and imagery, heightened by technological sophistication, have secured principal positions within contemporary existence where public life is played out via a breakdown of space and time.

This breakdown was patently obvious to me just a few weeks prior to the start of the 2007 cricket World Cup. At the time, I was on a visit to the Caribbean, where I was able to see young West Indian males at sports bars in places such as St. Lucia, Antigua, and Barbados watching and discussing American football, ice hockey, as well as soccer, with quite rapt attention. Here, I am referring to what correspondent Younge, of the British daily *The Guardian*, assesses as the cultural impact of television relaying the most recent performances of global superstars.

He identifies Bubba's, a sports bar in Barbados, crammed with youthful West Indians clad in Manchester United sportswear watching an all-star basketball contest emergent all the way from Las Vegas, Nevada. In addition to Bubba's basketball, British premiership soccer can be viewed at Lucky Horseshoe. So can ice hockey. Younge would, of course, know that Manchester United, a highly successful brand name, has been linked financially with the North American baseball brand, The New York Yankees.

Williams (1964, p. 183), credited by Holt (2000, p. 30) as the scholar who drew attention to credit markets and financial foundations that evolved with European trade, did point to a threat to the Caribbean in which the groundwork for heightened technological sophistication was laid. While pointing to a major danger for the region, the Caribbean historian states that what he deems the tenor of colonial independence may be replaced by an emphatic drive for restoration of the colonial system. I must stress that while the drive, these days, does not take the form of earlier brutality and dehumanisation in European conquest, it is being strongly attained through the route of oligopoly capitalism in the globalisation of discourse. This is not an inappropriate juncture for recalling the wiles of capitalism which Herbert Marcuse so brilliantly exposes. Anyone who has doubts about my claim in regard to discourse should consider:

> There is a certain paradoxical quality about social life at the turn of the twenty-first century: While there is apparently more space than ever before for individual and group differences, there seems to be at the same time a sort of 'codification' of aspects of social life which is partly a codification of discourse. What I mean by that is a narrowing down of the range of ways of using language and of the range of discourses for representing the world—the emergence of powerful dominant discourses and ways of using language, the spread of these across different domains of social life and (through the 'globalisation of discourse') across different countries. This tendency to closure is evident in different domains of social life—in work, in politics, in cultural life (Fairclough 2001, p. 207).

Observers should pay very careful attention to the use of terms such as narrowing of range, codification, dominant discourses, as well as globalisation of discourse. While Fairclough is clear that these features are not challenged, I hasten to emphasise that within the Anglo-Caribbean, the challenges are rather weak. The Caribbean is now a very receptive reservoir for globalisation of discourse, not just the homogenising of discourse globally, but also creation of an international setting where there are tendencies to shape discourse in several parts of the world.

Fairclough's example of this shaping, which doubtless has a big impact on the West Indies, takes the form of access to global and international television channels, one of which is strongly instantiated by Cable News Network (CNN), owned and operated from affluent North America. CNN is only one example of channels from regions of economic largesse that lays claim to offering a global perspective but merely presents a parochial stance on its screens where news is made up principally of Anglo-American news. Part of the narrowness includes language, constitutive mainly of North Atlantic discourse, advertising, politics, sport, and fashion. CNN is a contributor to the globalisation of the North Atlantic and United States way of life and language. Thus, many countries use the affluent world as a reference point for their own discourse practices.

Let me make my case somewhat differently by dealing with that Sobers declaration against England at Port-of-Spain, Trinidad in 1968. It was via the use of discourse in Caribbean Sovereign Language that several who had showered the skipper with deserving adulation sought to, and did, vilify him, after his declaration had been followed by a Test Match victory for England, an unexpected accomplishment that was to be the decisive and defining event of a five game Test Match series. Unlike Brian Lara, captain Garfield Sobers had taken West Indies Test Match cricket to its apogee. He had defeated Australia three years earlier, 1965, laid siege to, and crushed, England in 1966.

Sobers was not, however, spared the colourful but insightfully grounded Caribbean Sovereign Language vitriol that flowed from tongues of many a self-appointed expert/explorer, when he could not accomplish that vital Port-of-Spain win. Captain Brian Lara, whose achievements in none of his three tenures as leader, were anywhere close to those of predecessor Sobers, was not the subject of systematic and regular critical examination conducted via Caribbean Sovereign Language.

Where I ask is the discourse in the early twenty-first century? Where I ask are the conditions which facilitated such discourse? I reply readily by stating that they are absent. No one should form the impression that the electro-magnetic devices I alluded to cannot constitute bases to incisive Caribbean cricketing discourse. I must insist that their presence is conducive to vast desert-like tracks sparsely inhabited or traversed by individuals who are mostly enmeshed or cosseted by the privacy of their ties to the devices. Just as importantly, these very devices are touted by their manufacturers and advertisers as powerfully suited to the singularity of connections with persons—not the togetherness defining the group dynamics of discussion within the bell hooks, Cornel West, and Robert Nisbet community.

I have, of course, not lost sight of the fact that although the medium, Caribbean Sovereign Language, with its obvious links to West Indies cohesion and solidarity, has been so central to Test Match cricketing discourse in community, there is no effort by any political leader of the Anglo-Caribbean, at the beginning of the twenty-first century, to make a case for granting official regional status to this mode of communication. It is with equal significance that I recognise: while Test Match cricket and Anglo-Caribbean Sovereign Language have been inseparable for well over half a century, there have been no official efforts to institutionalise the links on a regional basis. This is an especially glaring and pernicious deficit.

Every one of our great cricketers who have catapulted our cricket to commanding heights of excellence is a fluent and artistic user of Caribbean Sovereign Language. Correlations among his sporting skill, oppressed existence, and language use have never been promoted systematically, though. Anyone who looks at primary and secondary school curricula within the independent Anglo-Caribbean will see that they do not include courses on understanding the origins of Caribbean Sovereign Language, as well as the inseparable links between this mode of communication and Test Match cricket.

I need to offer some other observations. CARICOM, a regional body ostensibly aiming for socio-economic integration, is supposed to be taking a very special interest in cricket at all levels. The fact that the Caribbean Sovereign Language level has been absent from its stated interests cannot bode well for any encouragement or revival of the medium as a context or setting of incisive regional cricketing discussion. Once this state of affairs continued, Brian Lara's leadership blunders could hardly have been sources of systematic public assessment and debate.

If I step away from the matter, discourse, I must note that the massive problem linked to Brian Lara's leadership can be apprehended also by examining his Test Match batting excellence as very much an art rather than science. As such, his extraordinary performance at the crease was preponderantly poetic and not prosaic. More importantly, the poetic was laced with the figurative in pathos, irony, and paradox. Thus, as the preeminent West Indies Test Match batsman, he had to infuse each batting performance with inventions and reinventions. His selfhood could then be seen as emerging from an individualism resting on constant renewal separated or truncated from the search for identity in an Anglo-Caribbean collective. Separation or truncation could—and did—not bode well for Test Match captaincy of West Indies, which had become all the more damaging in view of Lara's unprecedented three term tenure.

The keen observer can always respond by noting that like Brian Lara, ex-captains Garfield Sobers, Rohan Kanhai, Vivian Richards, and Clive Lloyd, did craft their performance upon blends of the prosaic and poetic. Although true, they were far more prosaic in their expressiveness and, crucially, were integrally linked to the search for identity and continuity of community. Outside of the Caribbean, the captain who was one of the most powerful exemplars of the prosaic was Stephen Waugh of Australia, whose leadership in the World Cup final of 1999 had completely demolished a befuddled Pakistan led by Wasim Akram. When Australia—batting last—was closing in on victory, none other than Jeremy Coney, the highly experienced New Zealand captain turned radio commentator, was moved to describe Waugh's captaincy and batting as very prosaic.

There are, of course, those who will say that captain Brian Lara was an icon full of charisma. I have absolutely no doubt that he had charisma and was an icon. When, however, I reflect on other icons who are charismatic, I detect some basic differences between them and the West Indies Test Match captain. I want to address myself to those differences as a very significant way of exposing Lara's indiscretion—if not tactlessness. Who are these other icons? They are Mohandas Karamchand Gandhi, Martin Luther King, Nelson Rohilala Mandela, and Malcolm "Omowale" X.

Like Brian Lara's, their charisma could be conceptualised by drawing from a very important source, the work of the German sociologist, Max Weber, whose view is assessed correctly by the psychoanalyst, Schiffer (1973, p. 3). He states that Weber saw charisma as an exceptional attribute within a person who appears to possess supernatural, providential, or extraordinary powers, and is capable of attracting devotees. One valuable sociological source for appreciating the Weber view of charisma can be identified:

> *Charismatic authority is that wielded by an individual who is able to show through revelation, magical power, or simply through boundless personal attraction, that he possesses charisma, a unique force of command that overrides in popular estimation all that is bequeathed by either tradition or law (Nisbet 1966, p. 143).*

Further, charismatic leadership signifies not just the eruption of individual genius, it is also dramatically incompatible with traditional or rational supervision. Its impact upon people is deeply disruptive of traditions and rules according to which those people exist.

Unlike Brian Lara's, Gandhi, King, Mandela, and Malcolm X's other attributes were simplicity, as well as the ability to juxtapose opposites from which they secured massive support of throngs of devotees, whose actions were very vital to success of causes the leaders pursued. Gandhi highlighted British advertising of rights, freedom, liberty, and pursuit of happiness enshrined in the thinking of racist philosophers such as John Locke. He also showed that what was contained in the advertising was all horrifically absent from the lives of Indian imperial subjects. King, and Mandela,[2] strongly influenced by Gandhi, highlighted the very opposites within American and South African settings. So did Malcolm X in the U. S. All four of the non-cricketers possessed another thing Brian Lara did not have. With obvious borrowing from Cornel West, I call it the quality of vibrant orality, that persuasive liveliness in speech through which throngs of followers are moved to action.

Importantly, what the non-cricketers did was combine their vibrant orality with simplicity, and throttle the combination with juxtaposition of opposites to secure their objectives. Although some observers would—rightly—not recognise vibrant orality as a cricketing quality of paramount importance, I think the close parallel to it within cricket is batting brilliance, with which Brian Lara clearly overflowed. From a West Indies cricketing standpoint, Lara's predecessors, Frank Worrell, Garfield Sobers, Clive Lloyd, and Vivian Richards, who were also charismatic, did combine their simplicity with batting brilliance, albeit not of the same quality as Brian Lara's. Crucially, they throttled the combination with juxtaposition of opposites to attain their goals of which the Test Match cricketing world knows remarkably well.

In Worrell's case, he was enmeshed in opposites. He was well aware that C.L.R. James and Norman Manley had exposed acceptance of the myth that people of colour were not fit to captain West Indies alongside the batting and leadership excellence of other non-whites like himself. Richards, of course, did openly juxtapose efforts of imperialists to devalue achievements of African people of colour the world over with the impact of capabilities emanating from the devalued. Lloyd told me he instilled in his players the principle that the time for them to fight hardest was when they were under pressure.

I state this because the youthful Clive Lloyd, in imperialist British Guiana, was intimately aware of British efforts to inferiorise non-whites and deny their personhood. He was well tutored also in how to be disciplined by parents, as well as upwardly mobile persons of colour such as his high school headmaster and officials at his cricket club, the Demerara Cricket Club [DCC], where he apprenticed with cousin, Lance Gibbs. All of the disciplinarians would have fostered in him the idea that struggle and assertiveness in the face of inferiorisation are valid strategies in the battle with pressure. In addition, all the Test Match captains, save Brian Lara, are intimately aware, via their actual experiences, of horrors from imperialist rule.

Even if I adhere to cricket, but step outside the West Indies, I still cannot locate anything redemptive about Lara's charisma to his players. No one who has heard about, and watched, the leadership of Imran Khan, the former Pakistan captain turned Prime Minister, could have any doubts about his presence at the helm and its impact on players. Consider an evaluation from Bailey (1989, pp. 108-109), who assesses Khan as the "Islamic Paladin." Imran, the ideal leader, was the greatest all-rounder for his country.

Cricket, according to Bailey, a political vehicle on the sub-continent, exemplifies how Khan's capability for success rests not merely on the quality of his players, but also upon the manner in which his specific leadership style is received by persons under his charge. Khan, whose forebears had been nurtured to rule, took decisions and delegated authority, which was routine to him and accepted by players in a similar way to that in which army privates automatically obey orders of an officer in charge. Khan was in total control and his tour manager was always at hand to accept his instructions.

The insightful observer may be inclined to claim that the Bailey reference to nurturing, routinisation, and delegating of authority are inconsistent with the explanation I provide about charisma. What is significant is that within a Test Match cricketing context of captaincy, no Pakistan leader prior to Imran Khan garnered the massive reverence he did from players. As such, the Imran leadership presence was far from routine, conventional, or traditional. That presence, rather rapturous, was constitutive of great disruption to leadership style. Remarkably, since the time of his departure, no captain, including teams led by those that inflicted heavy defeats upon Lara and his charges, has been able to emulate Imran.

During the course of 1988, the ex-West Indies Test Match player Gerry Gomez—turned expert assessor about states of play—provided a clear instance of Khan's presence among his charges, after commentator, Joseph "Reds" Perreira, had noted the Pakistan team reaction to the captain's efforts on the field late into the second day of the second Test Match against West Indies (Queen's Park Oval, Trinidad). It was the skipper whose inspirational presence had been largely responsible for West Indies having been in the position of three wickets for sixty-nine runs on that day. At that point, when Khan—bowling—had stopped a "hard" Richie Richardson drive down the wicket, Perreira observed that "just about every member of the Pakistan side" was applauding the captain.

This remark preceded the Gomez commentary: "Imran continues to plug away, there. He must be a very tired man. In fact, looking at him through the glasses [binoculars], he looks tired and he is drawing on ALL his resources. In fact, he looks tired and he is drawing on ALL his resources. In fact, I think he is working purely off the adrenaline now. Tonight, he's gonna sleep particularly well. And so he should, for he's got through: he's got three wickets under conditions which—not admirably suited to him—but just indicating to everyone what a great bowler he is." No one should ever get the impression that I am either simplistic, misguided, or illogical. Thus, I compare Brian Lara's batting to Imran Khan's medium-fast bowling.

I am referring to assessment of highly revered leadership partially but significantly instantiated by bowling and fielding. Lara's leadership, which should be partially and significantly instantiated via his batting, was not an inch close to that of Imran's leadership. It was Imran Khan who again inspired teammates to win the 1992 cricket World Cup. I add, for more than good measure, when he was sworn in as Pakistan Prime Minister, all members of that 1992 team were front row honoured invitees. The Khan inspirational leadership is the same type of inspirational leadership that saturated the successful Lance Gibbs style of captaincy for Guyana within the Caribbean where he, a highly engaging and shrewd leader, led teams against other Caribbean sides in inter-territorial games. This, I emphasise, was captaincy exhibited after years of Gibbs's apprenticeship with Clyde Walcott.

It is inspiration with which I continue by remaining within the ambit of that Queen's Park Oval second day encounter of 1988 when yet another radio commentator, Ishtihar, from Pakistan, stated: "I think it was [Javed] Miandad who went across to Imran and told his captain, 'Look, we need one more effort from you. Bring out your last reserve and just throw everything in it. You've only got ten minutes to go for close of play'. It was this remark which prompted Gerry Gomez to render "and we promise that we will carry you off."

Imran Khan, who had bowled in his medium fast mode unchanged, in very warm Caribbean conditions, since the tea interval, was also the beneficiary of more deserving glowing assessment from Ishtihar: "For those of us who watched Imran over the years, he first started as a youngster against England at Edgbaston, when he was only eighteen. He used to bowl from WIDE of the crease and all he could bowl was his in swingers. He had a swinging action. And from those days to today, he's come a long way to become one of the greatest all-rounders in the world and, clearly, one of the most inspirational captains that this game has seen."

Brian Lara's looming presence was also not associated with two other important features that marked the existence of persons such as Worrell, Sobers, and Lloyd. Those features are self-reflection and empathy, both of which are integral to communication and thought. Let me turn to the ideas of the sociologist Mead (1934) for an authoritative conceptualisation of these matters.

In the most ordinary of senses, most people regard empathy as indicative of placing oneself in the shoes of others. Sociologically speaking, placing oneself in such a position signifies taking the role of the other or expressing understanding of the other, which Mead deems the common response in one's self, as well as in another person. Mead is, of course, referring to the process of social interaction explicable by what he calls communication aimed, not just at another person, but also the individual himself or herself who initiates the communication.

Vital to successful communication is self-reflection, which gives the communicator subject and object qualities, the second of which emerge from responses of others to whom initial action of the communicator is directed. The reply to a query about how a communicator can become an object to him/herself is clear:

> The apparatus of reason would not be complete unless it swept itself into its own analysis of the field of experience; or unless the individual brought himself into the same experiential field as that of other individual selves in relation to whom he acts in any given situation (Mead, 1934, p. 138).

In captain Lara's case, teams of players came, stayed, and went. They have not, however, benefited from his use of reason in communication in any way that bears distant resemblance to the manner in which Worrell, Sobers, and Lloyd balanced their subject and object presence to secure the unswerving dedication of players under their leadership. Here, I would like observers/expositors to think incisively about the links I set up earlier between Worrell and Sobers, among Gibbs, Walcott, and Lloyd, as well as, Lloyd and his quartet of express bowlers.

My claim about communication is quite significant. I shall thus continue addressing myself to it by using Frank Worrell as the major standard bearer against whose leadership presence readers should consider Brian Lara's importance.

Let me set out the supreme, but necessary, measure of West Indies Test Match captaincy: how is role exchange through presentation of knowledge from a West Indies captain and exploration of such knowledge by the players under him managed by the skipper, so that those players might be effectively and efficiently prepared to take their places on international cricketing stages awash with the diversity of competitor strategies? My ready reply is to state that observers should begin to explore the performance of Frank Worrell through the eyes of James, who clearly demonstrates that Worrell was a brilliant communicator who allowed his players ample chances to use the route of self-reflection for the purpose of answering their own queries. More importantly, in James' own writing, a powerful glimpse of the Worrell inspirational value is brought out.

While exploring the 1960-'61 West Indies tour to Australia, James points out that he spoke with Worrell after the team had returned to the Caribbean. The captain informed him that he lectured no player about cricket. If something was wrong, he told his players what was appropriate and left them to ascertain the comparison. Here, I see the leadership value of enabling one's charges to juxtapose difference without being directive. To me, this is a crucial difference between being directive or imposing and inoffensively authoritative. The variance is aptly expressed:

> *These words [Worrell's] will always ring in my ears. They are something new, not only in West Indies cricket but in West Indies life. West Indians can always tell you what is wrong and some even what will make it right, but they don't leave it to you. Worrell did. It is the ultimate expression of a most finished personality, who knows his business, theory and practice, and knows modern men (James 1963, p. 258).*

For James, the Worrell facilitating of juxtaposition is powerfully conveyed not merely in talk from the captain, it came also in the leader's performance on the field, performance I regard as setting the example to be emulated by his players. When Sobers became captain, he too set examples of the same types to his players. Sobers did see, did benefit, and must have reflected when he and others experienced the Worrell strategies in the third Test Match of that very 1960-'61 series.

It was during the third Test Match, which West Indies won, so reports James, that some of the tactics came out. In that game, it was the eyes and ears of a noted Australian commentator, A.G. Moyes, the West Indian expert chose to use for the purpose of reporting. According to James, Moyes wrote that the Worrell second innings [82], one from the finest players—technically—on the West Indies team was lovely. He appeared to know precisely where he wanted to place the ball and exploited gaps in field placing frequently. The innings, one of superb batsmanship, reduced none other than the leading Australian quick bowler Alan Davidson, in just a few overs, to mediocrity.

With obvious admiration of the Moyes assessment, James waxes eloquent in his use of the rhetorical device many a conversation analyst terms contrast, a deliberate interactive ploy aimed at evoking respondents' rapturous approval. What was the ploy? I offer the contrast directly:

> *This is not 'playing brighter cricket for the sake of spectators who pay,' that absurd nostrum for improving cricket. Nor was it the unbuttoning that Peter May [ex-England Test Match captain] thought it was. No. It was simply the return to the batting of the Golden Age; the safest way to prevent being dominated by good bowling is to go after it yourself do the dominating. The masters of a much more deadly business than cricket lay it down that it is better to give than to take attack (James 1963, p. 259).*

Just as significantly, Worrell, in the second innings of the very next Test Match, took charge from his regular bowlers and delivered seventeen overs at a cost of three runs but secured three wickets. In the fifth game, he also got three wickets at a cost of forty-three runs, but bowled thirty-one overs. All of this came from a leader who knew what was not right, what was required to implement changes, and did so in the presence of those in charge and capable of bowling—Sobers, Hall, Gibbs, and Valentine—better than him.

Let me state, quite boldly, that the Worrell presentation could not have emerged just from cricket. It had to have emerged from social circumstances well away from the perimeters of the field. This much is clearly contained in the James view about what was new from Worrell in West Indies cricket and West Indies life. Anyone who still does not grasp the sense of circumstances outside cricket should know that James uses the Worrell persona to reflect on his own association with Leon Trotsky, Amy Garvey, wife of Marcus Garvey, and Arthur Lewis, the St. Lucian Nobel prize winner for Economics.

Without stating any detail, I must note the association was not about cricket. I want to add that Worrell had what the accomplished American jazz musician, Wynton Marsalis, describes as soul. Soul, according to Marsalis, is someone's ability to make others feel better, regardless of how well those individuals enjoy their existence. Without any reference to soul, ex-Australian skipper, Benaud (2005, pp. 124-125) states that Frank Worrell was the best he ever saw in "man management." It is Worrell whom he identifies with reasons the face of cricket in Australia and, perhaps, in the rest of the world was changed forever. Dare I repeat that Frank Worrell's managerial capability was constitutive of the best in the personae of jazz band leaders, Art Blakey, Benny Goodman, Duke Ellington, Count Basie, and Oscar Peterson?

When Sobers followed Worrell, he was a superb example to his charges whom he inspired with his incomparable all-round skill. Lloyd and Richards, brilliant batsmen in their own right, had the ability to transpose social circumstances beyond cricket fields onto arenas of play with great success. Richardson's and Kanhai's single tenures were all too short. Insofar as Brian Lara's three terms are concerned, I shall let readers use his record as the criterion for deciding what he, a successor to Frank Worrell, was able to do. I do have one proviso. The relevance of that "legacy" about which Lara spoke in New Zealand should be connected to their judgment. That "legacy" cannot be separated from the Worrell persona, which James proudly states was adorned with impressive diplomatic graciousness and defined by ease of adaptation to environment.

That is the very Worrell persona—let no Caribbean person ever forget—which was largely responsible for helping racist Australia during the early 1960s, examine its dispositions to people of colour. I make this point, because Sobers, Hall, and Kanhai,[3] were invited to, and did, play Sheffield Shield cricket in an Australia, which, though part of the Commonwealth, was a staunch ally of apartheid South Africa, and could not come to terms with its Asian surroundings, and dehumanised aborigines.

With my exploratory eye firmly focused on Brian Lara, I add that unlike the other Test Match captains, he could not use simplicity to inspire his Test Match playing colleagues. Within the context of leadership, his batting brilliance was merely a vacuous feature of West Indies Test Match cricket. In addition, owing to the fact that he grew up in, and emerged from, a post-independent Trinidad and Tobago awash in natural gas and oil riches, which first flowed in the aftermath of the very first world oil crisis during the very early 1970s, he was not in a position to juxtapose opposites of the kind his predecessors have.

I am fully aware that experience is one of the best teachers. I am in no way suggesting, however, that because Brian Lara lacked the imperialist experience, he was at a huge disadvantage. He was born among, and grew up as, a member of the Caribbean proletariat. He could certainly have used the route of self-education in a context of apprenticeship under Richardson, where he should have interpreted, very actively, creation of social circumstances outside cricket and used interpretation to make transformative links with predecessor captains. The entire West Indies cricketing world, however, knows no apprenticeship was served. Consequently, West Indies Test Match cricket is, and shall continue to be, the poorer for it.

Lara, in the eyes of numerous adoring admirers, ascended as many soaring scales as traversed by some of the most accomplished classical conductors. In all probability, he crafted countless runs out of a churning Caribbean surf—just as many as the Trinidad tidal treasures from an angry Atlantic ocean. If, however, he had no "seniority," no "power," around West Indies captaincy, he was no one in that position. I am, of course, invoking the presence of former Black Panther, Bobby Rush, who beat Barack Obama in a crucial Chicago electoral race years before Mr. Obama had ascended the presidency in 2008. According to the elegant Mr. Rush, Barack Obama had more degrees than a thermometer.

Unless Mr. Obama had some seniority and power at the Chicago grassroots level, he was no one among the constituents he sought to court. Unlike captain Lara, President Obama had acquired so much power and seniority among Chicago constituents, and even in cities within "battleground" states such as Ohio, Florida, and Wisconsin (November 2012), that he became somebody of even greater significance than the person at the time of his battle with Mr. Rush, so much so that he can look back confidently at his presidential legacy. The Obama significance is, in no small way, attributed to his bold juxtaposition of opposites during bruising campaigns and well crafted convention performances that constituted explicitly different visions for a reenergised United States.

Let me offer what I consider an example of a fine opportunity for the interpretation of social circumstances strongly defined by juxtaposition of opposites, an opportunity for use by skipper Brian Lara that went a begging. I am alluding to a second innings incident during the course of the crucial fourth Test Match between England and West Indies at Kensington Oval, Barbados, in 1990, when England were in dire straits against the searing express pace of Ian Bishop and Curtly Ambrose. England batsman, Robert Bailey was ruled out caught behind to an Ambrose delivery, after an assertive and vociferous West Indies appeal.

Barbados umpire, Lloyd Barker, appeared to hesitate in rendering a decision against Bailey in the face of what SKY telecasters, Tony Greig and Geoff Boycott, deemed extreme pressure from Viv Richards, who allegedly ran from slip down the wicket to challenge the umpire. Quite a controversy over the incident between Boycott and Holding emerged in the telecasting box, and Mr. Christopher Martin-Jenkins, a radio commentator for BBC World Service radio, made some remarks that were followed by numerous calls to Barbados radio stations requesting that he be removed from the Barbados airwaves.

I shall continue with the Richards public characterisation of the matter, his criticism of Martin-Jenkins, and the juxtaposition of opposites from Tony Cozier, whose presentation constituted a fine chance for Brian Lara to interpret the juxtaposition so that Caribbean cricket might benefit. Richards stated in a *Barbados*

Daily (April 1990) that what was characterised as his having run towards the umpire just before Bailey's dismissal was a performance of his customary ceremonial dance at the fall of a wicket. He had heard a noise and did his dance in celebration that the batsman was going to be ruled out. While he accorded great respect to commentator, Martin-Jenkins, Richards implied that as a professional commentator Martin-Jenkins did let his feeling play a part in his judgment.[4]

It is this judgment which was contained in the Martin-Jenkins statement about professionalism, gamesmanship, and cheating, the last of which, whose disparaging sense was not separated from the West Indies captain. It was the Martin-Jenkins statement which Tony Cozier claims caused an emotional furore throughout the Caribbean.

I draw readers' attention to Cozier's claims in the British daily *The Independent* on 11th April, 1990. Cozier writes that those who view the 1990 series or any Test Match series as simply a sporting contest would not understand the emotional furore caused throughout the Caribbean by the Martin-Jenkins report of Robert Bailey's dismissal. Presumably, in an effort to educate such persons, Cozier notes that the furore must be set against an historical past "dominated by British colonialism" and a cricketing presence "equally dominated by West Indian brilliance and individuality."

Cricket, he adds, has long been the pride and joy of West Indians of all races and classes. It has the badge of honour "we" can proudly wear as a sign of "our" collective excellence, and is followed with a religious fervour linked to giving the great West Indies players' deified status.

> *When therefore, the representative of an organisation [the BBC] so closely identified with the former colonial power castigates the West Indies captain and uses such a pejorative word as "cheating" to describe his tactics, it is considered a serious affront by West Indians.*

He continues by stating that those who regard cricket as an antiquated past time of merely small significance may think there has been a huge overreaction to the Bailey incident. He concludes that there might have been just such a reaction. Those who, however, cannot understand what the fuss is about, are the same people who find it impossible to follow why the Ayatollah got so worked up over Salman Rushdie, though, thankfully, no one in Barbados put a price on the head of Martin-Jenkins.

From an exploratory standpoint, Cozier directs readers to the difference between an historical past and present within the Caribbean. All of his other claims can be classified as forms of asserting in which his readers are invited to examine the veracity of his position by laying the basis to consider views different to his. It is very important to recognise also that the deified status he assigns to great West Indies cricketers is strongly linked to his insightful understanding of their extraordinary excellence. Hence, he gives these players very elevated and exalted positions, which he stamps with highly positive identity ascription consonant with distinguished personhood. This is, of course, markedly at odds with the distinctly negative identity ascription and degraded personhood or non-personhood linked to the historical past, imperialism.

I view the contrast as one significant feature of juxtaposition in opposites. The other major feature consists of opposition between the Caribbean and British understanding of the furore, as well as the Ayatollah's putting a price on Salman

Rushdie's head. Presumably, those who did not understand the fatwa are those who viewed the Ayatollah as a Muslim fundamentalist seething with vile extremism against Western democratic values. Those—including Caribbean anti-imperialists—who did understand the fatwa are persons who saw the Ayatollah issuing a robust challenge to Western inauthenticity responsible for the misery of countless people of colour around the world.

In cricketing terms, one way of dealing with the opposites would be using vigorous rejection of non or sub-personhood to: absorb and dissolve the presumptive effrontery against Richards and illuminate the highly elevated status he gave, specifically, to the West Indies captaincy and, generally, to Caribbean cricket. Let me point out, in passing, that absorption and dissolution feature prominently in the totalising display of non-Eurocentric reasoning. Did captain Brian Lara, tap absorption and dissolution? The reply is emphatically negative. Was West Indies batsman, Brian Lara, on account of having been in a position to have grasped the leadership trade under captain Richie Richardson, in a position to do any tapping? I offer another negative reply. Was captain Brian Lara, who should have inherited and used a legacy left by former West Indies skippers other than Richardson, in a position to do so? I reply negatively, yet again.

There is another approach which Lara could have adopted. John Arlott's sovereign loyalty, a loyalty the commentator associates with Richards in the 1980s, is the loyalty to which Lara could have clung while familiarising himself with the sequence of events at Kensington Oval, during the course of the 1990 encounter. This is not simply a loyalty to cricket, it is a loyalty, also, to that signifiant function which Kilburn assigns to Test Match cricket. Had Brian Lara used any meaningful insight in regard to the events and connected his insight with function and loyalty, he would, most certainly have become aware of the meaningful apprenticeship his West Indies leadership predecessors had served.

Let me deal with this matter of apprenticeship from the angle of another query: why did great West Indies Test Match batsmen who followed Frank Worrell to become single tenured skippers for over a two year period contribute significantly to West Indies prominence? Why did extraordinarily brilliant batsman, Brian Lara, who followed Richie Richardson to become a three tenured skipper for much longer than two years, fail to resuscitate West Indies cricket? My reply to the second query is that Lara, simply, was never in a position to do the things captains in the first group were able to. He played only five Test Match series under Richie Richardson. Reasoning behind my answering can be located in the response to the first question.

Here is the reply to the first question. Quite simply, the men in the former group served their apprenticeship, and Brian Lara did not serve his. This is an appropriate juncture at which I ask readers to reflect upon lives of the individuals I use while making my very early reference to leadership which I link to DIGNITAS, PIETAS, and VIRTUS: Blandina, Gnaeus Pompeius Magnus Africanus, Gaius Julius Caesar, Ms. Rosa Parks, Mr. Nelson Mandela, Dr. Martin Luther King. While I cannot state whether Blandina can be associated with apprenticeship, all the others did serve their apprenticeship. Equally important is the manner in which the cricketers other than Brian Lara who became Test Match cricket captains did their service. They benefited enormously from knowledge passed down and through a chain that stretched from Frank Worrell to Richie Richardson. What clearly did not occur was a simple rubber stamping, imitation, or regurgitation of information from predecessors. Passage from predecessors was attained through ways in which successors had to explore and interpret the value of transmissions. Thus, whatever leadership acumen was passed from Frank Worrell via the chain did carry his markings, but it was subject to practices of filtration and transformation.

While I shall shed no tears over the spilt milk of no apprenticeship served, I cannot help referring to: in the absence of apprenticeship, another reasonable arrangement would have been Brian Lara's familiarising himself with the value of juxtaposition within a Caribbean Institute of Cricket which was non-existent. How he might have been able to surmount the obstacle, lack of simplicity, is altogether an entirely different issue.

I continue my critical look at captain Brian Lara by noting that he has been a leader who conveniently distanced himself from West Indies Test Match losses, but hastily claimed credit for success. Importantly, when he set himself apart, there were no systematic or incisive attempts to have him account publicly for his tactic. Herein lies a clue to working of the man's iconic status. Let me make a bold assertion. West Indies cricket did not progress, it was stifled, when Brian Lara was team captain. This is a stance which I do not think is difficult to justify.

There is one fundamental leadership difference between Brian Lara, on the one hand, and Garfield Sobers, Clive Lloyd, and Vivian Richards, on the other. Lara was technically a highly capable batsman. Unlike the others, though, his batsmanship was not matched with great leadership skill. This is the very rare quality which Caribbean Test Match cricket sorely needed, but it had been very hard to locate in Lara's tenures.

Let me solidify my point here by paying attention to some claims from Garfield Sobers which appeared in the Barbados daily, *The Nation*, on 8th July, 2004. He is quoted as having stated:

> It has been a long time since we have been talking about the development of West Indies cricket. I have never seen a country take so long to develop. We have been doing it for the past 12 or 13 years and we are still going along the same line, talking about our young players and that it is still a new team and still developing. I think it is time we stop developing and start to produce.

Keen observers can, of course, use the conventional procedures to verify these claims, or they can attempt to assess their plausibility. They can also ask what steps captain Brian Lara had been taking to aid meaningful and productive development of young Test Match players. Regardless of the position adopted, it is quite clear that the issue of development and call for productivity could not have been separated from field leadership, whose unprecedented two term tenure in Brian Lara's case, at the time of the Sobers remarks, 2004, featured prominently as an aspect of Caribbean stagnation.

I doubt if Sobers, a leader who does know about the burden of stagnation, would assert that his great admirer, Sir Donald Bradman, Richie Benaud, and Steve Waugh (all Australian Test Match captains), as well as Learie Constantine, Clyde Walcott, and Frank Worrell (West Indies), belonged to the Brian Lara leadership class. I assume, reasonably, that he would categorise the three West Indians and three Australians in the group to which I have assigned him, Lloyd, and Richards.

One of the many occasions on which I observed stagnation under Brian Lara's leadership was September 1999, when West Indies played a series of six one day games (three against India and three against Pakistan). The venue was the Toronto

Cricket Club. Lara and his men were victorious in a single game, played against India. I offer, below, my reports about the second contest they lost, convincingly, against Pakistan. Final scores were: Pakistan [batting first] [222] for [5] from [50] overs. Yousuf Youhana [104 not out] man of the match. West Indies [180] all out from [46] overs and [2] deliveries. Hinds [65].

In a most unusual spectacle, at this picturesque park, Chris Gayle, the West Indies off spinner, opened the bowling for his side. If this was a Lara strategy to stimulate the sparse crowd, ample rewards were blown its way by a wind of change, only in the spinner's second over. He induced an aggressive—if not arrogant Anwar—to play across the line with the fatal consequence, bowled for [6]. Early excitement was not dampened in the fifteenth over as Hendy Bryan bowled Wasti comprehensively for [14] when the score was [36]. After only ten more had been added, in the very next over, Inzamam [14] suspended his good judgment, lapsed into irresponsibility, and paid the price of edging a Dillon outswinger to the keeper. He crossed paths with Youhana, the new batsman, who joined Sohail, Wasti's replacement. West Indies appeared to be ascendant, when Sohail departed for [21] with the score on [68].

It was, however, Razzaq [55] and Youhana [104] who destroyed all West Indies hope of solid elevation. Both batsmen crafted their strategic surges at the expense of poor leadership from an opposing skipper who was still incapable of motivating a mesmerised band of embattled cricketers.

When West Indies batted, it was Chanderpaul and Campbell who were charged initially with arresting possible Pakistan plunder. The two openers took the score to [21] in the eighth over, when Chanderpaul, cutting carelessly, gave a simple catch to the keeper. Hinds joined Campbell [8], who, to his detriment, was soon cutting Akram. He was caught at point off the skipper's bowling.

In came Lara, the Port-of-Spain Prince, who had to play "the innings of his life,"[5] if his Toronto image was not to be tarnished beyond restoration. In the sixteenth over, Saqlain saw that no credit was granted to him. He was trapped leg before wicket [L.B.W.] to the off spinner for [26]. What followed his departure were merely fruitless searches: Powell, [1], [L.B.W.] to Razzaq, Adams [28] caught at short leg, Jacobs, [1] bowled, Hinds [65] yorked, Walsh [1] bowled, all fell short.

I expected no great gusts from a Caribbean hurricane, when spin bowler, Gayle, bowled his first over for Brian Lara. Should torrents of trouble for a band clearly in tatters be predicted? I had posed that query, in full knowledge that tons of trouble would continue to plague Test Match captain, Brian Lara towards the beginning of the twenty-first century. Not only did Lara surrender his leadership post, thus, end his first tenure, shortly after the Toronto sojourn, but he also returned to that very position in place of a discarded Carl Hooper who had failed to take his side into the final eight of the 2003 World Cup. Upon his second coming, Lara boldly asked, rhetorically, how could he not play a role in the development of West Indies cricket? What a role he has played! He suffered humiliating Test Match losses in South Africa and in the Caribbean against Australia, within the space of a year, 2003 to 2004, but did not publicly consider terminating his tenure.

Importantly, the rhetorical remark was public expression from a man who knew that Carl Hooper, the confidant he replaced as captain, had declared, also publicly, in the aftermath of a dismal West Indies World Cup performance, that he, Hooper, wanted to continue as skipper. My point here is that Brian Lara wasted no time in leaping to the locus of leadership, when he was offered the job. I now inquire—albeit rhetorically—should Lara not have declined the offer, in view of the fact that former skipper and comrade in arms, Carl Hooper, had issued an explicit declaration about his interest in continuing as captain? Should Lara not have declined the offer and given his unswerving support to leader, Hooper? Let me say that Lara did have ample chances, in his initial captain's position, to play a part, and his performance was abysmal, under expert guidance from Clive Lloyd, Vivian Richards, as well as Malcolm Marshall. Lara has also been the beneficiary of guidance from Garfield Sobers. Did Richardson have guidance from such an illustrious group?[6]

What is, perhaps, even more important is that second tenured captain, Lara, faced his first big challenge in 2003, in a home series against Stephen Waugh's Australians for a four Test Match series. He lost the first three games in humiliating fashion. The third, the Barbados encounter, was particularly interesting, for after having won the toss, he elected to bowl. His opponents posted a daunting first innings score of well over six hundred runs. Long before the game ended in defeat for the West Indies, he was severely criticised by Caribbean cricketing experts for a lack of good judgment. There was, thus, the very strong probability that he was going to lose the fourth and final Test Match in Antigua.

Such an eventuality did not, however, emerge. Against all odds, his team posted an incredible victory, accomplished with a required second innings score of well over four hundred. His two centurions, Ramnaresh Sarwan, vice-captain, and the experienced Shivnarine Chanderpaul, were crucial to victory. He himself scored just over sixty as well.

As a consequence of the victory, some of the very correspondents who had criticised his Barbados decision were intense in their praise of a man who described the unexpected victory as the best experience of his cricketing life. One Caribbean daily even took the additional steps of conveying a report in which there were claims that Lara's leadership position was secure as a consequence of the win, and that the Australian selectors might consider replacing the very successful Stephen Waugh by Ricky Ponting. Among claims appearing, on 15th May, 2003, in *The Barbados Daily Nation*, as part of a Reuter's report about Waugh's sole loss and Lara's only gain, were: "Steve Waugh and Brian Lara face contrasting futures after West Indies extraordinary win in the fourth test over Australia."

After the declaration that Lara's leadership position appeared much more secure than that of Waugh's, there was the baseless and patently unreasonable speculation: (a) "The Australian selectors, never of afraid of making tough and controversial decisions, may decide the time has come to end Waugh's reign" (b) "Waugh earlier stated that he still believed he had several years remaining, in top class cricket. His thirty-sixth Test success as captain in the Barbados game, a feat which equalled that of former West Indies skipper, Clive Lloyd, could well be his last."

Did those people who felt secure about Brian Lara's leadership have a poor sense of history? Did they remember that when Gary Sobers beat Bobby Simpson in 1965, but lost the final Test Match in Trinidad anyone thinking about the fragility of his leadership? Were they unaware that England, under three captains in 1966, lost to the West Indies, but gained victory in the final meeting at the Kennington Oval? There was a final Test Match duck from captain Sobers then. Did he deserve to surrender his leadership post after the 1966 series?

If Caribbean people were not to be blinded by the mirage of a meaningless one Test Match victory from Lara, it was necessary for them to use basic reasoning and accept that prior to the Antigua meeting, Australia had already won a series very convincingly. The differences between the batting and bowling averages of the two teams were enormous. Ricky Ponting's batting average, the best for Australia, was well over a hundred. To be precise, it was [130.6]. His highest score was [122]. Justin Langer, whose average [69.00] the fourth highest for Australia, was clearly above that of Brian Lara's. So was Langer's highest score of [146].

It was remarkably interesting to note also that Ramnaresh Sarwan and Shivnarine Chanderpaul, West Indies batsmen occupying the third and fourth highest positions on their team's batting averages, posted averages of [47.80] and [42.80]. An average of [58.00] and highest score of [160] are, however, the records associated with Darren Lehmann, the Australian batsman whose position on his team's list was number six.

I am assuming that no statistician needs to conduct the standard parametric and non-parametric tests of differences among averages to determine that the consistently dominating Australian vice-captain and other batsmen on his team were miles ahead of Brian Lara, known in some quarters as the talisman. In the bowling department, Jason Gillespie (Australia) took [17] wickets at an average of [26.40] runs. Not only did Gillespie post a much better strike rate than Jermaine Lawson [West Indies], according to the International Cricket Council (ICC), Lawson's bowling action—suspect to Test Match umpires and referees at the time—needed to be remedied also.

Further, West Indies, under Brian Lara, could neither win, nor draw, the 2003 series, although Glen McGrath [number 6 in the Australian bowling averages: 3 wickets at an average of 52.70 runs] was out of form. Shane Warne did not participate in the series and Ricky Ponting did not play in the final Antigua Test Match because of illness. Caribbean fans would have done themselves no harm if they appreciated the fact that the immensely talented Michael Slater, was unable, shortly after the 1995 Australia tour of the West Indies, to find a place either in his country's Test Match or one day side.

Lest there are tendencies to shorten memories, it must not be forgotten that Slater was an opening batsman, the type of player all West Indians had been longing for, since Gordon Greenidge and Desmond Haynes left the scene. McGrath, Warne, and Slater did participate in the 1995 series which Richardson lost narrowly. Haynes and Greenidge did not, but leading batsman, Brian Lara, did. Captain Lara's record, which stands in the category, one of the worst, is hero of the twentieth and tenty-first centuries, while Richardson's, which, I insist, stands in the category, one of the best, has been the West Indies scapegoat.

Paradoxically, Lara heroism was enhanced in the leadership post one year later, 2004, when he scored an unbeaten quadruple Test Match century against England, surpassed his own [375], as well as [380] posted by the Australian Matthew Hayden, against Zimbabwe [2003]. I want to deal with the [400] run performance as yet another powerful foreground against which Brian Lara's leadership inadequacy and perversity of iconic status are made transparent.

When England, under Michael Vaughan, came to the West Indies in 2004 with a major mission of attaining dominance over West Indies after thirty six years in the tropical wilderness, the local cricketing panditry predicted close combat. The members of this august fraternity could not have been more inaccurate. England gave Brian Lara and his men a clobbering of catastrophic consequences in the first three matches (Jamaica, Trinidad, Barbados) of a four Test Match series, and romped to the coveted series victory which had eluded them for more than a generation. In their punitive preferences, Vaughan and his men exacted two terrible tolls in West Indies second innings scores lower than [100]. In all cases, the dutiful destroyer was a young and zestful quick bowler, Steve Harmison, who drew tears from captain Brian Lara after a three day finish in Barbados.

At St. John's Antigua, however, venue of the final game, Lara blasted an unbeaten [400] over a three day period to deny England the "whitewash" which would have served to partially annul the "blackwashes" England endured at the hands of West Indies opponents. It is the magnitude of this staggering feat whose measurement I offer with an interest in locating Brian Lara's leadership relevance to West Indies cricket. This is a stance I take as a consequence of determining the meaning of his accomplishment to the Caribbean, at the beginning of the twenty-first century. I shall do so by juxtaposing his batsmanship with leadership skill.

Let me begin my assessment by noting that on 12th April, 2004, the day he reached his [400] landmark, Lara provided a solid seal to his sense of uniqueness. No West Indies batsman had ever broken the record for the highest Test Match score twice. Not merely did Lara do so, he did it also at the same ground where he became the first person to score [400] in a single Test Match innings. This was, of course, an achievement registered shortly after he had become the player to get [9,000] Test Match runs faster than any other leading batsman. The likelihood that Brian Lara would end his Test Match career with an average close to [99.94], that achieved by Sir Donald Bradman, the Australian I call the Bowral bomber, was of course never transformed to reality.

When Bradman got his first triple century against England, he had done so against very excellent bowling. Lara has noted that when he scored his [375] in St. John's in 1994, he did so against bowling that was below the high quality with which he contended during the 2004 series. It would not be easy to dispute the claims that he is the most superb of the great modern Caribbean Test Match batsmen maybe as good as Donald Bradman. Lara, the magnificent marauder at the crease, was very different from Lara, the leader. In 2004—with the worst record as skipper of West Indies Test Match sides since 1975—he had played the leadership role twice, an unprecedented reality in Caribbean cricket. I remind readers of my claim: West Indies cricket could not improve so long as he remained at the helm. I am claiming that Brian Lara was an impediment to advancement.

I support my position by reflecting upon a radio comment from the late Learie Constantine, in 1968, when he assessed the joint presence of Rohan Kanhai and Garfield Sobers at the crease in the first innings of the final England West Indies Test Match at Georgetown, Guyana. West Indies—batting first—were in a great deal of trouble. Sobers, who was sharing the batting creases with Kanhai, decided to walk down the wicket to render advice to the audacious, liberal, and improvisational Kanhai. Constantine's reaction to the Sobers strategy was issuing a mild rebuke: Kanhai, he claimed, is a genius, and a genius cannot be told how to play.

Brian Lara was, doubtless, a Test Match batting genius, and if Learie Constantine was reasonable, how could the highly elevated record holder be amenable to guidance and direction about his terrible leadership roles! I concede the rhetorical nature of my query readily. It is just as noteworthy for me to point out that in a region, the Anglo-Caribbean, still struggling mightily to actualise the value of collectivism to its identity, Brian Lara's centrality, which was founded primarily on the uniqueness of his individuality, could hardly have been of great value to that identity. This, of course, is the very identity many Anglo-Caribbean people assume is inseparable from their Test Match cricket.

This is the same identity, the vigorous promotion of which never eluded Frank Worrell, Garfield Sobers, Clive Lloyd, Vivian Richards, as well as Richie Richardson.

Such promotion is a focus that was alien to the Brian Lara batting mystique and application of mystification in which he revelled, I dare say, with obvious arrogance.

Here are what I consider elements of his mystification and arrogance. Shortly before the beginning of the second and final Test Match in late Spring, 2004 against the weakest Test Match team then, Bangladesh, on Caribbean soil, captain Lara—second tenure—issued public statements:

> If we don't win, I don't think I would lead the team to England. If we don't beat Bangladesh in five good days of cricket in Jamaica, I think we need another leader. Some think we need one now. If we don't beat Bangladesh, who has not won a Test, have drawn three Test Matches out of 30, in this match in five good, full, days of cricket, I think we do need to try someone else.

There are several significant issues about the repetitive commitments in Lara's declaration. During the course of this second leadership tenure, his team won three out of seventeen Test Matches. He did win the second and final game against Bangladesh, thereby becoming victorious in four out of eighteen games. That performance was not, by any means, a stellar achievement. During the course of his first term as skipper, 1998-1999, he had won six of eighteen games, but lost ten.

I ask rhetorically, yet again, why would a leader of a cricketing region engaged in playing Test Match cricket since 1928 use victory against Bangladesh as a criterion of continuity in the captain's position? Why would he do so against a team, the Test Match experience of which he knew was not even a decade old? Can any astute students of the game, several of whom reside in the Anglo-Caribbean and are intimately familiar with the "legacy" of which Brian Lara spoke publicly in New Zealand, imagine England skipper, Wally Hammond, in 1939 declaring that if England did not beat West Indies, he would give up the England captaincy? Was Brian Lara suggesting that his defeat of Bangladesh should, and could, be used as a criterion of leadership against England in summer 2004? Why did captain Lara not express the undertaking that if his team did not beat England in the 2004 summer series, he would relinquish his post? England's performance would certainly have been an appropriate measure of West Indies skill and capability.

In an equally important sense, I cannot lose sight of the fact that Brian Lara's comments were public utterances. He was never put in the position of having to publicly account for what his claims implied. No serious explorer/expositor of West Indies Test Match cricket can gloss the consideration that Lara's public verbal display presupposed unquestionable rights and authority over the post of West Indies captain. There should not, however, have been any semblance of such presupposition in view of the parlous state of the team he had been leading. Rights and authority should have been in the hands of team selectors and, ultimately, the West Indies Cricket Board.

Why was Brian Lara, against a foreground of West Indies woe, not made to account for his display and what it presupposed? My simple response is that the mystification of his iconic status, though perverse, far outweighed the woe. This is mystification through which false issues are substituted for actual issues within a transformed world where persons lose control of their own intentions. In addition, agents of mystification seek to impose their own consciousness on others by giving themselves rights and powers to determine the experience of others (Laing 1965, pp. 341-342). What I am trying to do is show how a focus only or largely upon extraordinary brilliance in the excellence of cricketing individuality instantiated by batting—not captaincy—provided a mesmerising, but false, and paralysing picture of Caribbean cricket.

Mystification was not the sole feature of Brian Lara's tenure. His arrogance was hardly a concealed element of his persona. In late summer of 1999, I asked him how he, a West Indies captain, should express his responsibility to the region's sporting public, in view of the fact that its members sometimes participate in intense debate about Test Match cricketing captaincy. He justified his hasty refusal to reply by claiming that the query had nothing to do with cricket. This, I cannot help pointing out, came from the lips of a man who has experienced no difficulty in speaking proudly, confidently, and I assume, freely, but unmistakably and glibly, about the timelessness of that West Indies Test Match cricketing "legacy."

I dare say to the extent that he spoke about a "legacy" in West Indies cricket, he had not made good use of it. The warrant for this view can be found in what I term Brian Lara's failure to maintain the momentum in Caribbean unity through victory crafted so studiously by predecessors, Worrell, Sobers, Lloyd, and Richards. I begin to make my case by noting statements of Lloyd's and Manley's. Writing seven years prior to the end of lengthy West Indies Test Match dominance under Lloyd and Richards, Manley states that cricket occupies a special position within Anglo-Caribbean culture. He adds that in the West Indies more people play football but more are concerned about who the victors of cricket are. In an invocation of C.L.R. James, he adds:

> Success or failure apart, cricket has a more profound implication for the West Indies. Indeed, as C.L.R. James divined with sure instinct and unmatched descriptive flair, West Indian cricket is like a metaphor for social history (Manley 1988, p. xii).

He also notes that at a political level, cricket is the most profound regional activity undertaken by people of CARICOM member states. It is also the most successful Caribbean cooperative endeavour, and thus is a constant reminder to "a people of otherwise wayward insularity of the value of collaboration."

Manley also speaks about the profound symbolic value of the all conquering West Indies team of the 1980s to the Caribbean, and states that the team influences the mood of the region which exults it in its victories and is cast into gloom when it loses. In contrast to other institutions which struggle to survive centripetal forces of insularity, the team becomes even more West Indian. The simple reason is its success which attracts increasing regional pride. He adds that one day Caribbean people will do more than admire their cricket team, and will seek to emulate its success by discovering for themselves the unity which is its secret.[7] He notes, as well, that the team had to complete the process of professionalism before it could realise its full potential.

With obvious reference to dominant West Indies Test Match sides, Lloyd (1988, p. v) states that cricket is the ethos around which Caribbean society revolves. He points out that all our experiments in Caribbean integration either failed or maintained dubious survivability. Cricket, however, remains the instrument of Caribbean cohesion, the remover of arid insularity, and nationalistic prejudice. He adds that it is to cricket and its many spin-offs that Caribbean people owe their consideration and dignity abroad. Cricket is the musical instrument on which West Indians orchestrate their emotions from extremes of wild enthusiasm to the depths of despair.

Six years later (1994), Lloyd reiterated his position emphatically to me and lamented regional political inability at high levels to use cricket as a very strong basis of unity. He noted that cricket is the one regional cooperative practice, and "should have been the instrument that can show us the way, that if we can be involved in sport together and be successful, then we only have to take it one step further. So, I thought that we didn't use that instrument which we had over the years. We've been playing cricket for over seventy years doing quite well being the best team in the world playing in that harmony that should exist with one people, one destiny, really, one nation. There are other people now thinking of having a European nation, a community. Australia—different states but they still play as one—India—of different cultures but they still play as one. The same thing could have happened to the West Indies and I didn't think we grasped the chance when we should have, really."

Was Brian Lara put in a position, captaincy, from which he would operate to grasp the chance? I respond affirmatively and add that on the evidence of three tenures he failed to do so. Was he not expected to use cricket as that instrument for showing Caribbean people the way? I answer in the affirmative, once more, but continue by stating that he did not do so. The Test Match teams he led performed very poorly. Hence, the regional pride attracted by West Indies Test Match cricket was not associated with his team. It might well be largely linked to his batting excellence which strongly emasculated team significance that was once inseparable from the unity to which Lloyd and Manley refer. Did the Brian Lara managerial style lead to Test Match victories reflective of that ethos around which Caribbean society can revolve? I must continue with a negative response. Was Brian Lara able to use cricket as the remover of arid insularity? I reply with an emphatic NO.

One of the strongest grounds for my negativity can be located: unlike captains Worrell, Sobers, Lloyd, and Richards, Brian Lara was not the type of fighter able to use social currents beyond the field to infuse and energise field campaigns towards victory. It is clear from the bluntness in his refusal to respond to my query about public debate over West Indies captaincy that he either did not understand the significance of such currents or was unwilling to use such currents as major elements in his field strategies. Given these two states of affairs, he was in a very weak position to help Caribbean people orchestrate their emotions of great enthusiasm in the foreground of Test Match victory.

Readers can now compare his blunt refusal to the query about captains' responsibility to answers about the meaning of cricket offered by former leaders, Clive Lloyd, that amiable gentle giant, "Hubert," and Garfield Sobers, the charismatic champion, two builders of the very "legacy" Lara squandered. Comparison can certainly be used to get some flavour for the value of social currents.

From Lloyd came these words: "What cricket gave me, really, was a sense of balance. I went to different countries, saw how other people lived. Some were poor countries; some were rich countries. It gave me a broader outlook in life. The main thing about sport is not the countries that you've been to. It's the friends that you make. It broadens your outlook. Things like racism—you can't be a sportsman and be a racist. Trying to improve the lot of people, of others, those who are less fortunate than you. So you become a politician. You become a community worker. You become a better person for playing sports and I hope I've done that by playing cricket to the level I have played." Herein lies the Worrell influence via the Sobers, Walcott, Gibbs, and Kanhai routes.

From Garfield Sobers, the former captain very strongly influenced by Frank Worrell, Everton Weekes, and Clyde Walcott, the person who clearly expresses the value of the collective Caribbean identity, came this account about what he had attained as a Caribbean cricketer: the most important thing he had achieved in his career was the way in which he had conducted himself on and off the field. Sobers was referring to his role in carrying the West Indies flag as an ambassador throughout his cricketing career, which enabled people to hold Barbados and West Indies in high regard. He had always viewed that accomplishment as a highlight of his career. He added that some of the hallmarks, the great things he always admired in himself were that he had been able to respect people, live with them, understand their preferences, respect West Indies cricket and West Indies people who have always been very important to him.

I must emphasise that the Lara response to me came at a time when Caribbean cricketing confinement was not restricted to field matters. It emerged against a foreground made up of some tormenting features whose insistently powerful presence seemed immovable. Two of those features were : (a) failure to institutionalise, at all levels, the artfulness, elegance, and excellence of our international cricketing status achieved under West Indies heroes such as Everton Weekes, Frank Worrell, Clyde Walcott, Garfield Sobers, Vivian Richards, Clive Lloyd, and Rohan Kanhai. I am talking about a vibrant mode of international cricketing existence sustained by appreciation of heroism, whose expressiveness is routinely celebrated via the route of creative discourse, (b) replacement of a culture of assertiveness which captains, Lloyd and Richards, created so craftily by a culture of acceptance strewn with ravages and spoils of contemporary consumerist capitalism. These are the very destructive forces shamelessly served as benefits of globalisation where Caribbean citizenship within the "global village" has not progressed beyond serfdom. The third feature is constituted by occlusive offerings of supervisory stultification in the administration of former West Indies Cricket Board President, Pat Rousseau.

All of these forces were at work in 2001 when Carl Hooper was appointed to replace Brian Lara, who had completed an abysmal first tenure. Hooper's appointment, which Garfield Sobers and Michael Holding had criticised publicly, was not followed by improvement to West Indies fortunes. He lost Test Match series to South Africa, Pakistan, and Sri Lanka. When he failed to give West Indies what many deemed the elevation needed for the 2003 World Cup, he had to surrender the job of captain, which was conferred on Lara for a second time. That 2004 summer challenge of England which Brian Lara was not going to accept, if he had lost to Bangladesh, therefore, stared him directly in the face. In battle with quick bowler Steve Harmison, captain Michael Vaughan, and company, on the sceptr'd isle, Lara and his men capitulated in very humiliating fashion, most notably in the Lord's Test Match, which West Indies lost by a two hundred and ten run margin.

Writing in the 13th March, 2007 edition of *The British Daily*, *The Guardian* correspondent, Gary Younge, made a statement about an explicit pronouncement from Viv Richards to Brian Lara and his men shortly after the Lord's humiliation. Richards was quoted as having stated: "You guys have something serious to represent, and don't ever forget that. Because of the inspiration factor of the past, let us hope you guys understand what it is to represent the West Indies. Cricket began a long time ago. Let us not forget why you guys are here, OK?" In technical analytical terms Richards performed three actions when he spoke.

He issued an assertive ["You guys have something serious to represent"], the veracity of which hearers could examine. He performed a directive ["don't ever forget that"], whose use was connected to his authority. Rather importantly, it was the expressive laced with exhortation in his talk, his last utterance ["Let us not forget why you guys are here"] which he followed with ["OK"]. Use of expressives, according to the philosopher who first described them, J. L. Austin, can carry deep emotion, which is precisely what Richards did. When he offered a reason for his own expressive ["Because of the inspiration factor of the past..."] he was referring to the past but, I submit, offering a justification as well. Further, his ["OK"] was not just the signal to closure in his discourse, it was also his effort at getting Mr. Lara and his charges to reflect seriously. May I add, with a dramaturgical turn, that when Richards uttered his assertive, directive, and expressive, he was presenting not just his own emotional investment, his own public self image, his own face in West Indies Test Match cricket tradition to which he has been central, he was offering also the collective face of the West Indies which he never allowed to be damaged and lost. To the extent that Test Match leader, Brian Lara, failed to protect that face across the globe—including Lord's specifically—he carried huge culpability for the damage, loss, humiliation, and embarrassment connected to that loss.

What was significant also about the Lord's Test Match, after which Vivian Richards had spoken, was: prominent Caribbean commentator/historian Tony Cozier, whose eyes and ears I used to render my assessment about the debacle, was clear about his indictment of West Indies cricket. He, however, refrained from offering any evaluation of Brian Lara's decision to field after having won that Lord's toss. He merely reported the captain's choice to bowl and communication with his opposite number about not batting first. Yet, if according to Cozier, West Indies cricket was very dangerously imperilled, captain Lara could not have been immune to criticism.

His persona was, after all, the most public face involved in humiliating losses to South Africa and Australia in 2003. The very fact that Cozier was moved, in an earlier assessment, to describe the England performance at Lord's as punishment greater than that meted out to Lara's West Indies by South Africa on day one of a December 2003 Test Match and by Ricky Ponting's Australians at the start of a Trinidad game that same year was, surely, a reflective basis to critical assessment of the Caribbean Test Match captaincy.

I deem my argument, here to be quite reasonable. I am guided by consideration of interest in a sense of balance. Cozier, who never tires of heaping praise on West Indies cricketers that do well, found it necessary to pay justifiably glowing tribute to Brian Lara. At the time leading West Indies batsman, Lara was captained by Carl Hooper. Cozier credited the left hander for glorious batting in a Test Match against Sri Lanka, late in 2001, when the player performed imposingly, in the first innings of the third Test Match.

While filing one of his regular reports for the *Guyana Daily, Stabroek News* (30th November, 2001), which he titled "Lara Puts Murali [Sri Lankan spin bowler Muttiah Muralitharan] To The Sword," the correspondent began by stating: "It is on days like this, with the sun burning down from a blue sky, the pitch flawless, the outfield like a billiard table top and his mind intently focused on a particular objective that Brian Lara can elevate batting to heights reserved for a select few. It is on days like this that his mastery presents a refreshing contrast to the sordid controversies stoked by men in high places without an ounce of cricketing skill in their bones who would undermine the game for the sake of their inflated egos."

No assessment of Lara's leadership tenures would be well done if I did not pay detailed attention to Richie Richardson's achievements as skipper. This is a task on which I shall embark now and follow by an evaluation of Brian Lara from the standpoint of Clive Lloyd's pronouncements about qualities a West Indies captain should possess.

At the time of his departure, Richie Richardson had registered three consecutive victories in contests with Australia (1992-1993), Pakistan (1993), and England (1994), but lost a single series to Australia narrowly (1995). When they lost their first Test Match series, Garfield Sobers, Rohan Kanhai, and Clive Lloyd were not under pressure to relinquish the captaincy. Perhaps, the best example here is Garfield Sobers, who like Richie Richardson, won his first five Test Match series against the Australians.

The year was (1965). Like Richardson, he won his very next two series (England, 1966) India (1966-'67) Like Richardson, his first loss in a series was his fourth (England, 1967-1968) very narrowly, by a single game. At the time, there was not even a whiff that Garfield Sobers should give up his post. He lost to Australia (1968-1969), England (1969), India (1971), and played his final series, a drawn one, as captain against New Zealand (1972). It was only when he had lost to India (1971) that there were demands in some quarters for his resignation.

It is, by no means, unimportant for me to add: (a) When Gary Sobers bowed to pressure to give up the Test Match captaincy in 1972, he was pressured to surrender a post in which he ought to have continued for the crucial purpose of rebuilding West Indies into a great fighting force (b) Richie Richardson gave up the captaincy at a time, 1996, when he had been in the job for merely a four year period (1992-1996), all too short a period for him to perform the task of aiding team reconstruction (c) What is noteworthy also is that Richardson's tenure was just over half of the Sobers tenure (1965-1972).

Garfield Sobers was succeeded by Rohan Kanhai who, like Clive Lloyd, lost his very first encounter with Australia (1973). Although Kanhai beat England in the summer of that year, he had to be satisfied with a drawn series against that country in (1974) He departed from the Test Match scene about a year later. At no time during the course of Rohan Kanhai's leadership tenure were there calls for him to vacate his post. The same can be stated about his replacement, Clive Lloyd, who had won his first series (India, 1974-1975), beat Pakistan (1976-1977), but was given a (5-1) drubbing (1975-1976) by Ian Chappell, brother Greg, Jeff Thomson, Dennis Lillee, and teammates down under.

In fairness to Clive Lloyd, it can be said that that his initial loss was attributed to the important processes of rebuilding and remoulding. His immediate predecessor, Rohan Kanhai, did not have enough time to perform these tasks. While Garfield Sobers' best players in (1965) and (1966) had begun to decline, noticeably, most of their replacements did not fulfil their promise or realise their potential. Fairness to Garfield Sobers and Clive Lloyd should have been, but was not, extended to Richie Richardson with the same magnitude.

Richie Richardson was saddled with the immensely difficult tasks of rebuilding and remoulding but was never granted adequate opportunities to take the steps required for meaningful reconstruction. I am saying that Richie Richardson was never offered opportunities utilised by Clive Lloyd and Garfield Sobers. Strong criticism of his leadership and the manner of his departure belong to the category: unkind cuts of a grossly unfair nature. Lack of fairness is all the more evident given that he could not match the record of the man he had succeeded: Viv Richards never lost a series, but unlike Richie Richardson's tasks of rebuilding and remoulding, his were by no means of the same magnitude.

One of the arguments advanced against Richie Richardson is that unlike Garfield Sobers, Viv Richards, and Clive Lloyd, his batting deteriorated after he had become skipper. This argument makes no sense, in view of the fact that he was in a leadership role for only a small number of Test Matches over four series. In the captain's role, Garfield Sobers played [39] Test Matches, batted in [71] innings, got [11] centuries, [15] fifties, and [3,528] runs. His highest score was [178] runs and overall batting average [57.78]. Comparable figures for Richards are: [50] Test Matches, [74] innings, [6] centuries, [23] fifties, [3,068] runs, highest score [146], overall batting average [50.23]. What are Lloyd's? They are: [74] Test matches, [111] innings, [14] hundreds, [27] fifties, [5,233] runs, highest score [242], overall batting average [46.67].

What is also interesting about these figures is that Garfield Sobers, the captain who has lost the highest proportion of Test Match series, has registered the best overall batting average. Is this not an important indication that most of his best players had begun to decline and replacements did not realise their potential? Further, what is significant about the fact that Lloyd—with the least impressive overall batting average—was once regarded as the most successful Test Match captain? I ask, also: what is important about the fact that Richards—with the second least impressive average—never lost a series? I say, boldly, that Lloyd and Richards were not faced with the enormous task of reconstruction confronting Garfield Sobers and Richie Richardson.

Despite the tough job of steering the West Indies ship from potentially stormy seas to secure ports with which Richie Richardson was saddled, he performed admirably. His harshest critics must never forget that captains, Lloyd, Sobers, Richards, and Kanhai, dropped to lower positions in the batting order. They should—forever—ask themselves with whom captain Richardson opened the West Indies batting for two years (1994-1996), despite the fact that he did not regard himself as the best Test Match batsman of the period.

Richie Richardson's case becomes even stronger, when the leadership of Frank Worrell, the first Caribbean captain to have won all five Test Matches in a series and most successful skipper in the region, is looked at. Frank Worrell lost the keenly contested (1960-1961) series, narrowly, to Richie Benaud's Australians. In that series, however, there was a group of players who had done well against the world's best bowling attack and most powerful batsmen, Alan Davidson, Richie Benaud, Colin McDonald, Norman O'Neil, Neil Harvey, Bob Simpson, Wally Grout. The West Indies group was made up of Conrad Hunte, Rohan Kanhai, Garfield Sobers, Wes Hall, and Lance Gibbs. Not only did Lance Gibbs secure a hat trick on the tour, it was in Australia also that he began and ended a remarkable career as an off spinner who was the first to have secured the most Test Match wickets [309] in the slow bowling class.

Here are scores from the batsmen of that group: Conrad Hunte [24, 39, 1, 110, 34, 16, 79, 31, 52], Rohan Kanhai [15, 54, 84, 25, 21, 3, 117, 115, 38, 31], Garfield Sobers [132, 14, 9, 0, 168, 1, 1, 20, 64, 21]. All of these batsmen, as well as Hall and Gibbs, played at home under Frank Worrell, in (1962) against India that lost all five Test Matches. Hall's bowling figures were: [5 for 49], [9 for 128], [3 for 81], [6 for 94], [4 for 73]. Gibbs's were: [3 for 50], [5 for 113], [9 for 63], [4 for 160], [3 for 104]. In the batting department, Kanhai got [24, 138, 89, 139, 20, 44, 41]. Conrad Hunte scored [58, 10, 9, 59, 28, 30, 1, 0]. Sobers got [40, 153, 42, 19, 16, 104, and 50].

Hall, Gibbs, Sobers, Hunte, and Kanhai played with Charlie Griffith under Frank Worrell, in England where the West Indies won in 1963. Basil Butcher was also on the team. With bat and ball, they were formidable against England, from whom Charlie Griffith captured [32] wickets. Garfield Sobers beat three English captains, M.J.K. Smith, Brian Close, and Colin Cowdrey, in 1966 when Hall and Griffith, as well as Gibbs, were dominant. They were amply assisted by Kanhai, Hunte, Butcher, Seymour Nurse, and David Holford. One year earlier, the first four, leading batsmen, other batsmen, bowlers, Hall, Griffith, Gibbs, and all-rounder, Sobers were central to defeating Australia.

Hunte retired after the (1966) tour; Nurse did so three years later. With the exception of Gibbs, Sobers, and Rohan Kanhai, the others reached their peaks in 1966 after which,West Indians experienced a painful decline in their Test Match cricket. Richie Richardson, in [1995] and [1996] did not have the players Garfield Sobers had in [1965] and [1966]. Richardson—one tenure as captain—in [1995] [1995 -1996] did not have the quality of players moulded by Frank Worrell. Brian Lara—three tenures—had had more than enough time to mould players.

If the exploration above is not convincing, readers should consider Lloyd's understanding of qualities a West Indies captain should possess. These are qualities captain Brian Lara did not possess. Importantly, Frank Worrell used them and initiated what I see as a reconstruction that gave West Indies immense cricketing significance in the 1960s. Further, the success following that in the sixties was by leaders who apprenticed with those that depended on the knowledge handed down by Frank Worrell. There was, however, a break or rupture in use of that knowledge, when, as a consequence of Richie Richardson's departure in [1996] Lara, I reiterate, did not serve his Test Match apprenticeship.

While telling me, in 1994 about the qualities a West Indies captain should possess, Clive Lloyd offered: a West Indies captain, who should not be regimental, ought, nevertheless, to express his assertiveness in problematic situations, secure his players' respect in his own country and elsewhere, and have knowledge of the game. He should be trustworthy, intensely motivational, and a leader of men who is, simultaneously, an excellent ambassador for the persons he represents. All of these features, I add, were evident from the time he had made the decision to field his lightning fast pace attack Garfield Sobers told me should be described as comprising express bowlers.

Though not a West Indies captain, in 1959-'60 Frank Worrell clearly demonstrated evidence of the qualities Lloyd enunciated. He did so while batting in the company of Garfield Sobers at the Kensington Oval, Barbados. When Frank Worrell became captain, and toured Australia, in 1960-'61, he did not win the series but was immensely inspirational to his young players when they gave Benaud's Australians the fight of their lives. Worrell, lest it should be forgotten, did not have a quick bowling attack that matched the Australian attack. It is true that Wes Hall was in the side but in some cases, the captain strategically chose to be in the medium paced attack with his left arm swing, although Chester Watson of Jamaica was chosen as a quick bowler for that tour.

In the summer of 1963, while doing battle against a powerful England side whose quick bowling attack was spearheaded by Fred Trueman and Brian Statham, he used Hall and Griffith with great tactical advantage against the leading England batsmen, such as Colin Cowdrey, Ken Barrington, and Ted Dexter. Gibbs, who had done well in Australia three years earlier, was also quite destructive in the spinning department. Conrad Hunte, once a belligerent blaster of the ball from the opening position, culled his numerous aggressive preferences, and played the solidly foundational role of what many West Indies experts deemed very firm anchoring, with enormous success. He was, of course, followed by the dominant Kanhai, Sobers, as well as very productive Butcher.

Anyone who followed Worrell's career would know that although Hunte was his vice-captain, he proposed that Garfield Sobers replace him as skipper. That was a Worrell interest largely expressed on the basis of how well the outgoing captain felt his successor would be able to transmit that culture of assertiveness cultivated since the 1960-'61 tour of Australia. Not only did Sobers defeat Australia in 1965, but he also accomplished that feat by striving for, and attaining, the Worrell style.

With the sound of transistor radio commentary from Australian correspondent, Allan McGilivray, clearly audible, I remember watching, from the stand at the North Road end, almost behind the bowler's arm, one particular event in 1965 at Bourda, British Guiana. Sobers chose to open the bowling with Wes Hall in the Australian first innings, instead of throwing the ball to Charlie Griffith, Hall's partner. He bowled his first delivery to Bob Simpson, on the off stump, a delivery McGilivray described as over pitched, which Simpson drove for four through extra cover. The next Sobers delivery, a yorker to Simpson, uprooted his opponent's stumps and prompted an approving spectator roar, which would have reverberated all the way across the Atlantic ocean to Bayland, Barbados.

At the end of the day's play—thanks to his brilliant field placing—he reduced Australia to [75 for 4]. West Indies ultimately won the Test Match, another memorable highlight of which, was the Sobers "incitement" of vice-captain, Lance Gibbs, to spin the home side to premature victory. Those who are unaware of the incitement should know that bowler-vice captain Lance Gibbs, and captain Sobers, constituted an aggressive fielding partnership actualised in vicious spinning and cunning flight the captain usually rewarded by scooping some miraculous catches in the risky position of forward short leg.

Captain Sobers also commanded the unswerving respect of his players and has been described by his vice-captain as a genius. The Sobers ingenuity was put to the test in 1966 against England at Lord's where West Indies, in dire straits at the crease, needed to extricate themselves from clear danger of a humiliating loss. In the presence of cousin, David Holford, he batted with great determination, enormous purpose, and intense concentration to deny England victory.

Better justice to captain, Garfield Sobers, can be gained by placing the Lord's proceedings within the context of the entire 1966 series.

There can never have been such an all-round performance such as his in the 1966 West Indies-England series. In the first Test he scored 161, bowled 49 overs for three wickets and West Indies won: at Lord's, where he and Holford, by their long, unfinished sixth-wicket stand made a draw against all probability, he had innings of 46 and 163 not out and one wicket in 43 overs: at Trent Bridge, the second West Indian win, 3 and 94, five wickets in 80 overs: at Leeds in the match which decided the rubber, he made 174 and bowled 39 overs for eight wickets. When, at the Oval it seemed as if the side suddenly relaxed after winning the series, he scored 81 and 0 and, in England's only innings, took three wickets. His overall figures for the series: 722 runs, average 103.00, 20 wickets at 27.25 off 269.4 overs. He made ten catches, and captained the side skilfully and perceptively (Arlott 1970/1996, pp. 237-238).

Many years after his remarkable achievement (November 1995, to be precise), I had this exchange with him about his performance at St. John's Wood:

W.W.: *In 1966, at Lord's, you batted in the presence of your cousin, David Holford. And that example of excellence can be described as an indication of a sheer surge of excellence. What is it about the batting of Garfield Sobers that has enabled him to remain one of the most creative competitors at the crease?*

G.S.: *I would first of all say that the incentives and the creation of my cricket were really built around West Indies cricket and West Indies team and how West Indies performances were at the time. I have never really looked upon myself as great as people have always said. I have always looked at a man [Sobers] who has tried to do his best for his country and I have always tried to excel in certain positions, or certain circumstances like, for instance, the one... at Lord's. I think that was an area that called for the skills and the ability and the application, concentration of a player to be able to go out there under those circumstances and to be able to put all of those things into operation under those difficult circumstances particularly when you are at that stage—playing with a youngster who was probably playing his... first or second Test Match... In England it is not easy for youngsters particularly in those days when the wickets were a lot greener than they are today and the ball did a lot more than it did in the West Indies—for youngsters to be able to perform to that extent. And considering the conditions in the West Indies, you will expect players—because of the types of wickets they play on—and the circumstances that surround that at Lord's of all places which is the Mecca of cricket. It can also create a tremendous amount of pressure on a young player. And I think it is because of those circumstances in my cricket career that I have been able to develop my skills to the extent which I have done over the years and not only in that particular game but in other games where West Indies have found themselves in trouble—that I've been able to go out there and to perform under those circumstances... because the most important thing to me was the team and the position of the team—not what I've achieved or I have done but at the time that I achieved it and what I have done for the team's benefit.*

I also remember BBC cricket correspondent, Chris Florence, in a conversation twenty-four years later about that joint Sobers-Holford batting performance at Lord's. The correspondent, a high school student at the time sitting for his university entrance examinations, recalled vividly not just the Sobers hundred but, more importantly, also the manner in which he guided the youthful David Holford. With my eyes, ears, and thoughts squarely fixed along a reflective pathway, when Sobers was telling me about that Lord's performance, I recalled the mode in which he, on other occasions, relayed the Worrell guidance of him in 1959-1960 and 1960-1961.

Although he lost the 1968 series by a single Test Match to Colin Cowdrey, no one who saw that series could forget how hard he battled for victory, particularly in the final contest at Bourda, Guyana, where he scored [152] and an unbeaten [95] and delivered [68] overs which brought him [6] wickets. At Sabina Park, he had earlier rescued his side from certain defeat on a wicket crumbling with open cracks, where the late Gerry Gomez stated batting with a certain amount of luck, a certain amount of skill, and a certain amount of guts were required.

When he went to the crease, in the first innings, England fast bowler, John Snow, described by West Indies series manager, Everton Weekes, as that avalanche, trapped him [L.B.W.] for a duck. In the second innings, he stood in the centre—unfailingly meticulous and monumentally rock solid—with the immovable resolve of a seasoned general to craft an unbeaten century [113]. Shortly after that unforgettable accomplishment, he declared, late in the afternoon, took the new ball, and in the space of three overs of destructively unplayable late medium fast swing forced Cowdrey [duck, 0, L.B.W.], as well as Boycott [duck, 0, bowled] to make hasty return trips to the pavilion. This was no mean achievement, especially in view of the fact that the England skipper had batted authoritatively in the first innings for a splendid knock of [101].

Anyone who still harbours doubts in regard to the Worrell influence on the captaincy of West Indies cricket should examine the implications of what a visibly moved Wesley Hall mentioned to me about his skipper:

Now, someone needs to have chronicled our West Indian people, our attitudes, what separates us, what binds us, what sort of understanding we have of each other. And when Sir Frank Worrell said that we were a bunch of individually good cricketers thrown together on a boat going to England or Australia, he was right.

The Frank Worrell, whom James states took a special interest in players without social status that repaid him with fanatical devotion, was the leading innovator that transformed the individuality into a vibrant collectivism, which Garfield Sobers led with admirable success. The making of that success began in (1959-'60) and extended to (1967). There was, however, a void in West Indies cricket from around 1968 until 1976. Between the latter year and 1995, when Clive Lloyd, Vivian Richards, and Richie Richardson stood at the helm, West Indies Test Match cricket was second to none.

Lloyd benefited from the leadership transition of Rohan Kanhai, after Sobers had relinquished the post. Lloyd, as well as Kanhai, served under Sobers, and the entire Test Match cricketing world knows that the "disciplined calypso," "Hubert," combined the managerial styles of Worrell and Sobers to propel his region to unbelievable heights. Richards did his leadership apprenticeship alongside Lloyd. When he acceded to the captaincy, he maintained the major elevation, via the same route as Lloyd.

While there is an obvious and major time difference among Lloyd's, Richards's, Richards', Worrell's, and Lara's leadership, an examination of what Sobers (1996) states about the first three has significant implications for Brian Lara's three tenures as West Indies captain. When I take a close look at the statements I must repeat—and emphatically so—that Brian Lara did bear considerable responsibility for failure in West Indies top level cricket.

Sobers declares that Lloyd, outstanding West Indies captain, a fine leader of people, gained the respect and admiration of players through the brilliance of his performances, some of which were strongly evidenced in his batting, bowling, and fielding. As a cover point fieldsman, for instance, Lloyd was among the greatest: Colin Bland, Paul Sheehan, and Jonty Rhodes. Further, in granting fairness to Richardson, Sobers adds that unlike Worrell, he led experienced cricketers who could well have questioned his decisions, when success was not attained.

Worrell was responsible for younger cricketers following their leader without question. Had he made mistakes, there was no one to judge him. Lloyd also led a young team. His senior players, Gibbs and Kanhai, did not stay long. Importantly, he was captain at a time when large financial reward was becoming a principal feature of high level international cricket. Players unite under this feature and personal difference is marginalised in the face of tangible monetary gain.

Dare I state that in all three of Brian Lara's tenures, sizeable monetary rewards and young sides were significant features of his leadership. Perhaps, much more tellingly, there would be a good case for concluding that unlike Lloyd, Lara was unable to demonstrate the breadth of exemplary performances to be emulated by his youthful player colleagues. As such, the success Lloyd enjoyed with a young side could not be replicated by Lara. I make the point of exemplification in view of this forthright assessment:

> Let me say... that Brian has one significant factor in his favour. Whereas I was selected as a bowler and was transformed into a batsman and a genuine all-rounder as the years rolled by, Lara was selected as a batsman and will always be first and foremost a batsman. He can therefore focus all of his energies in a single-minded way on batting (Sobers, 1996, p. 130).

Once Lara had the aforementioned focus, I wonder how he could ever have dreamt of ascending the heights which the Sobers mentor, Worrell, attained. How could Brian Lara, leader of young sides reaping more financial reward, have elevated West Indies to the status Lloyd and Richards did?

I am compelled to refer to Richards, for like Lara, he was principally a batsman. How did Sobers, himself, without a young side beat Australia (1965), England (1966), and India (1966-67)? I reply by stating that it was his breadth of exemplification in performance that inspired players, rather than his position as the "best leader" of a West Indies Test Match team.

The lesson here for Brian Lara, which I think he never did grasp, was one of identifying and applying compensatory leadership skill. Some leaders can be like Clive Lloyd, who combined Sobers and Worrell. Others can be like Sobers, with a preponderance of diverse inspirational exemplary performances on the field. Still others like Worrell exhibited such preponderance within and beyond the field. Lara did, doubtless, have a tradition from which he could draw. How best could he have done so? I say via the transmission of leadership culture handed down by Worrell, but which was not appropriated from Richardson.

It was clearly Brian Lara's job to serve his leadership apprenticeship under Richie Richardson. That did not happen. Thus, a major rupture in the cultural transmission of leadership skill occurred with the departure of Richardson, whose assumption of office had received the unqualified blessing of Board President, Clyde Walcott. How much responsibility for Richardson's exit—and I am compelled to add, intrigue, as well as backstage machination surrounding the tenure of interim captain Courtney Walsh—is to be assigned to Lara himself, and the West Indies Board may never come out into the open. I know this much. Some shrewd observers of West Indies cricket note that the beginning of a Lara-Richardson friction had its origin in the West Indies tour to England in (1995). Thereafter, it did not abate.

Those who prefer not to hear my words have the option of doing more than parsing and analysing a set of claims made in the London Sunday Times:

> David Lloyd, the England coach, will fly to Rawalpindi this week on a spying mission. He plans to watch the second Test between Pakistan and West Indies as a prelude to Sharjah and the Caribbean tour which starts in January [1998]. When he arrives,

Lloyd will find a civil war that is tearing West Indian cricket apart—a dispute which puts past speculation over Mike Atherton's future into mountain and molehill territory. In opposing corners stand Courtney Walsh, the captain, and Brian Lara, his number two and would-be successor. It is a battle between one of the remaining members of the great West Indies sides of the eighties and a young man with a burning ambition to lead the team into the next century. The issue has been heightened by traditional inter-island rivalry of the Caribbean and has led to a split between the Test selectors and the West Indies Cricket Board (WICBC) (Otway 1997, p. 15).

Describing the feud as drama unfolding against a backdrop of miserable West Indies performance in Pakistan—drama that would reach an inevitable decisive flashpoint, Otway adds that "senior officials within Caribbean cricket" remained steadfast in their stance that Lara should not succeed Walsh. Further, in quite a remarkable revelation the correspondent points out that the basis to the row could be traced to the 1995 West Indies summer tour to England under captain, Richardson, and Richardson's final months in the leadership role.

During the course of the tour Lara and Hooper were fined 10% of their tour earning for unauthorised absence. Penalties were imposed also upon fast bowlers, Kenneth Benjamin and Curtly Ambrose, for attitudinal and behavioural inappropriateness. The ambitious Lara, so writes the correspondent, attempted to organise a "mutiny during the Old Trafford Test," but was unsuccessful in securing the support of senior players. Nursing a thwarted ambition, the alleged mutineer quit the tour "to lick his wounds." He returned only as a result of personal intervention from West Indies Board President, Mr. Peter Short, but excluded himself from the team taken by Richie Richardson to Austral-Asia for the World Series Cup in late 1995. There is much more from the pen and keys of correspondent, Otway.

He informs readers that for captain Richardson (summer 1995) and team manager Wes Hall, a principal matter was not Brian Lara's on field performance—he amassed 765 Test Match runs—it was "his naked ambition and his commercial interests off it [the field]." His heavy schedule of personal engagements meant frequent tardy appearances for matches and training. Quite a work ethic, I do notice! In the autumn of 1996 with Courtney Walsh at the helm, some West Indies Test Match selectors inclusive of fellow Trinidadian, Joey Carew, an architect of Brian Lara's rise to big cricket, wanted Lara to replace skipper Walsh. The West Indies Board President, Jamaican, Mr. Pat Rousseau, like Walsh and his Board, opposed Carew and colleagues, but opted as well to bypass Lara and not name a vice-captain to Walsh. Those moves, according to Otway, outraged much of the Caribbean, where Lara has been revered as a hero.

For his part, skipper Walsh handled Lara judiciously: holding consultations with him on the field, but maintaining both physical and social distance from Lara away from the playing arena. When, however, Lara voiced disapproval of the Rousseau decision and dissatisfaction with Walsh during the course of a radio interview, "it was the last straw."

Before the Pakistan tour [1997], when Trinidad went to Jamaica, Walsh, the home captain, refused to toss the coin with Lara, sending out his deputy, Robert Samuels, instead. Walsh has indicated that once Lara is handed the captaincy he will announce his retirement from Test cricket (Otway 1997, p. 15).

I cannot state with certainty that Walsh kept his promise and played under Lara in South Africa and New Zealand, where West Indies were comprehensively thrashed. I state very clearly that at the time of his retirement with a 500 wicket Test Match haul, the most for any West Indies bowler, under the captaincy of fellow Jamaican, Jimmy Adams, not too long after 1999, none other than his former skipper, Viv Richards, declared publicly that his loyal fast bowler should continue playing.

The Walsh and Richardson departures from the Test Match arena took place a long time ago. The late twentieth and continuing twenty-first disreputable performance of West Indies, at top level had nothing to do with them. It had a lot to do with Brian Lara's leadership. It is, therefore, to remarks about his captaincy against the foreground of the [2007] Cricket World Cup for which his team was hardly a meaningful competitor, that I turn. These remarks are clearly indicative of Garfinkel and Sacks's members' practices, links among biography, history, issues and troubles, and speech acts, which form the conversation analytic sociologists's socially ordered structure of talk in which Thornborrow's power play between interlocutors is at work. It is with particular attention to such power play instantiated by the speech types I identified that I ask readers to explore the talk.[8]

Let me begin with those of Viv Richards, [V.R.], "one of the greatest legends of West Indian cricket.," who gave an interview to BBC World Service Television [W.S.] during the course of the big event in the Caribbean. I urge readers to juxtapose also Otway's claims about flashpoint, naked ambition, civil war, drama, mutiny, and inter-island rivalry with the Richards claims about attempting to be very diplomatic, assessing West Indies cricket matters realistically, the circumstances under which Lara attained the captaincy, Lara's delivery with the bat, having lost his way, and from my standpoint, his face, too. This is a juncture, also, at which I see an opportunity for offering an assessment of President Obama's leadership.

[1] **W. S.:** *When West Indian cricket was in its deepest slump, you said 'one day, a MOses will come to deliver us.' Well, Moses has come and his name is Brian Lara. Hasn't quite delivered, though. Has he?*

[2] **V. R.:** *Well, maybe, with the bat. Yeah. But*

[3] **W. S.:** *As a captain.*

[4] **V. R.:** *He hasn't. No. I think that's the disappointment we have in the region. Because we all felt that he had the ammunition and the ability as a young man, early up, to become a good captain.*

[5] **W. S.:** *Lost.*

[6] **V. R.:** *Lost his way—lost his way, a little bit. I'm trying to be as diplomatic, as possible—just lost his way, just a little bit. We do, sometimes.*

[7] **W.S.:** *Let me ask you another question. Are you comfortable with the fact that he is captain for the World Cup? Is he the best man for the job?*

[8] **V. R.:** *I don't think, if you look at it, realistically, on the circumstances, the way he got the captaincy again, that you may have said he IS the best man. The jury is out there, I think.*

[9] **W. S.:** *Really!*

[10] **V. R.:** *The jury is out, in that department, because it was a common feeling, here, in the region. The jury is out there and I'll leave it at that.*

[11] **W. S.:** *Yes. It wouldn't be a very healthy state for West Indian cricket, if it approaches the World Cup—if the jury is out. Is it?*

[12] **V. R.:** *Well. The juries have always been out—with Brian's cricket. The same way I think the jury was out, when you had Flintoff and Michael Vaughan, in the same dressing room. So, you're gonna have all this talk. The juries are gonna be out, when you're faced with a situation like that: half of the people weren't too happy... It is up to Brian, NOW, to prove all these folks wrong.*

[13] **W. S.:** *Yes.*

[14] **V. R.:** *Because I think we have an excellent enough team, in my opinion, for us to take it to the next level. It depends on how well he leads. That, I think, would be most important.*

[15] **W.S.:** *What kind of hero, what kind of a man of the tournament would you like to see emerging from this World Cup? Is it gonna be a fabulous swan song, for example, for the likes of Lara—maybe—McGrath, Inzamam-ul-Haq—or would you prefer to see a BRIGHtening STARcoming through and imposing himself on the world game?*

[16] **V. R.:** *I would love—maybe—for my own sentimental reasons—to see a Brian Lara accomplish winning the World Cup for the West Indies. Because I think he would have had a very ROUGH ride, in the captaincy role. And I think it would be a bit fitting, because of what he would have been through, as an individual. And I know how much he craves winning something big for West Indies.*

[17] **W. S.:** *You'd like to see him win a reward.*

[18] **V. R.:** *I would love to see that. I'd love to see that—and not just a reWARD for Brian Lara, himself, but a reward for all the people in the Caribbean. Because it would be such a nostalgia time, again—of seventy five—seventy nine—if those days could be created. We were in a much better position, in my opinion, to negotiate, a little bit better, in the cricketing world.*

[19] **W. S.:** *I could see a DREA my look in your eyes, there, as you imagine Brian Lara holding the World Cup, after the final.*

[20] **V. R.:** *And it could happen.*

Allow me to use ideas from conversation analytic sociology for examining the first fourteen turns in talking, speaking opportunities. May I make a few observations prior to so doing? Recall my earlier distinction between speech forms: [TYPE 1]-speech forms in which use of lexico-grammatical and phonological constraints is intended to give hearers the freedom to construct their own meaning; [TYPE 2]-speech forms in which use of lexico-grammatical and phonological constraints is not intended to give hearers the freedom to construct their own meaning. Careful exploration of the fourteen turn sequence from the interviewer's standpoint indicates the order:

(a) Type 2
(b) Type 1
(c) Type 1
(d) Type 2

(e) Type 1

(f) Type 2

(g) Type 1

Many conversations of this length and more involving interviewer and interviewee consist of a mixture of the two types, regardless of whether the talk unfolds among friends, foes, constitutes parts of media conversations, is constructed by law enforcement interrogators and suspects, barristers, witnesses, and defendants in law courts, or teachers and students, at all educational levels. Speaker/interviewer choices to use the speech forms is not personal. The choices are not idiosyncratic. The choices are choices actualised as a consequence of speakers' conforming to language conventions which are revealed systematically, rather than speakers using some sort of private language. There are conversations also in which a preponderance of type 1 speech forms appears. Later, I invite readers to explore another conversational sequence in this work, specifically, that constructed by [W.S.] and notable Caribbean cricket analyst, Tony Cozier [T.C.] to locate such preponderance. Let me return directly to the twenty turn sequence constructed by [W.S.] and [V.R.].

When a speaker/hearer uses a turn to pose a question [Has he], more specifically, a question tag and a reply is offered, the questioner is provided with an opportunity to speak again. This is, precisely, what [W.S.] does at [3]. Interestingly, his [As a captain] while hearable as a question is an ambiguous utterance, the use of which, offers [V.R.] the chance to provide his own meaning. Just as interestingly, the ambiguity could have been used as an opportunity to provide agreement or disagreement, none of which [V.R.] does. Further, the question tag from [W.S.] designed to secure a specific response does not elicit such an answer. At [2] [V.R], obviously aware of his interactive obligation to respond in specific terms, chooses not to do so. While the specific response does come, emphatically at [4-He hasn't. No], it is ambiguity that brings it out. In other words, without providing any explicit or obvious signal about a question such as the signal at [1], the [W.S.] opportunity to speak again at [3] draws an explicit and obvious emphatic reply. That great emphasis is justified also in the utterance [Because we all felt that he had the ammunition and the ability as a young man, early up, to become a good captain].

Remarkably, that justification at [4] is not followed by an utterance from [W.S.] at [5] in interrogative form, but another ambiguous speech form [Lost], which [V.R.] opts not to take up as a question but as an opportunity for agreement at [6], [Lost his way—lost his way, a little bit]... followed by another justification [I'm trying to be as diplomatic, as possible—just lost his way, just a little bit...]. At [7], however, [W.S.] is very specific in laying constraints twice about how his interlocutor should speak, not granting [V.R.] the freedom to construct his own meaning. The constraints come in the utterances: [Are you comfortable with the fact that he is captain for the World Cup, Is he the best man for the job]. Although the response from [V.R.] at [8] is, at best, ambiguous, and [W.S.] could have followed the response by requesting clarification through using what conversation analytic sociologists term formulations, [W.S.] at [9] offers no hint about a formulation or other questioning strategy. Rather artfully, he opts for ambiguity in [Really] which could be hearable as a question and so treated. Just as artfully, [V.R.] evades the [W.S.] ploy and closes his turn at [10] by issuing a clear signal [The jury is out there and I'll leave it at that] that he will offer no particulars, despite the [W.S.] efforts at [7] to gain just such particulars. Despite that clear signal and closure from [V.R.] at [10], [W.S.] is persistent by ending his turn [11] with a question tag [Is it] preceded by his own utterance about West Indies cricket under Lara not being in a very healthy state if juries are out. Turn [11] is, undoubtedly, a formulation in which questioner [W.S.] looks for confirmation or disconfirmation.

A formulation is done as a check of speakers' prior unclear or opaque meaning, and is designed to seek confirmation or disconfirmation of the meaning. Crucially, it is a questioner who does formulating, the preferred response to which is a confirmation (Heritage 1985, p. 114). Thus, questioner [W.S.] was seeking, but did not secure, a confirmation.

Another way of referring to what [W.S.] did is to locate his formulation accomplishment within this conceptualisation:

A formulation is either a rewording of what has been said, by oneself or others, in one turn or a series of turns or indeed a whole episode; or it is a rewording of what may be assumed to follow from what has been said, what is implied by what has been said. Formulations are used for such purposes as checking understanding, or reaching an agreed characterisation of what has transpired in an interaction. But they are also used for purposes of control, quite extensively for instance in radio interviews, as a way of leading participants into accepting one's own version of what has transpired, and so limiting their options for future consideration (Fairclough 2001, pp. 113-114).

Very significantly, at [12] there arises a conversational conundrum for [V.R.], who is fully aware of his clear signal and turn closure at [10], as well as the formulation made up of constraints posed by [W.S.] question tag use at [11]. The conundrum is more than twofold. Does [V.R.] send another clear signal with closure about the jury being out? Does he offer any clarification after having heard the formulation—clarification in which he chooses to speak either about the not so healthy state of West Indies cricket or juries being out in regard to West Indies cricket? Does he connect that not so healthy state to juries being out and speak about the link? The [V.R.] solution is to maintain his position right up to [14] about juries and evade passing any explicit judgement about Lara's leadership.

Further observation of the [V.R.-W.S.] exchange leads me to delve deeper into the reference to MOSES, the name, according to James (1954), which means SAVED BY WATER. I consider this reference by Richards, someone fully committed to honouring his African ancestors one strong basis to ruminating over imagery encompassing linking his hopes for West Indies cricket to such ancestry: (a) The countless Africans brought forcibly to the Caribbean along the Middle Passage were certainly not saved by Atlantic Ocean and Caribbean Sea water (b) Those among them who jumped overboard, rather than face horrific bondage, would have been clearly aware of the significance to them of river spirits (c) Does the Richards' honouring his ancestry consist of reverence for those river spirits? (d) If so, in what ways was he using such reverence to express his hopes for West Indies cricket under Brian Lara's leadership? (e) To the extent that before Brian Lara Viv Richards had emerged to continue delivering West Indies cricket, how did he, Richards, use reverence for the river spirits associated with his African ancestry to deliver West Indies cricket? (f) Given the Richards reference to a Moses, deliverer of West Indies cricket, how reasonable was he in implying that such a deliverer would be someone expressing reverence for river spirits associated with African ancestry?

(g) If, however, the Richards reference to Moses was to the Judeo-Christian world, his reference implied that the cricketing Moses would save his people, fellow West Indians, not merely from horrific bondage, but provide them also with doctrines, the beneficial impact of which would stretch beyond several generations (h) It is clearly the case that in 2007 Richards knew, and knew all too well, that since the time West Indies ceased to be at the top of international cricketing circles, 1995, that Lara did not emerge as the cricketing Moses. It is because I cannot state whether he knew why such could not eventuate that I defer to the James expertise to demonstrate why. If James is reasonable about his other ideas of Moses, then I would make two conclusions about Brian Lara, the West Indies Moses: (1) it was erroneous to conceptualise Lara as the West Indies Moses (2) if Lara was the West Indies Moses, he could not have lost his way. James (1954, p. 40) sees Moses, one of the great leaders of great religions of antiquity, as an Initiate of the Egyptian Mystery System, an Egyptian Hierogrammat. Central to preparation for initiation was the keeping of ten commandments based upon principles of virtue: (a) control of thoughts (b) control of actions (c) devotion to purpose (d) maintenance of faith in masters to teach the truth (e) maintenance of faith in self to assimilate the truth (f) faith in self to demonstrate truth (g) freedom from resentment under the experience of persecution (h) freedom from resentment under experience of wrong (i) developing the ability to distinguish right from wrong (j) developing the ability to differentiate the real from the unreal (James 1954, pp. 105-106).

Using ideas from Vail and Pietschmann, James (1954, p. 27) notes that the most significant goal of the Mystery System was deification of persons via purification of body and soul. Thus, through liberation of the soul from bodily fetters, as well as the wheel of reincarnation or rebirth, persons could become Godlike, see the Gods, reach beatific vision, and commune with Immortals. Three grades of students participated in the Mystery System: Mortals, persons on probation in receipt of instruction prior to experiencing inner vision; Intelligences, those who had gained inner vision and received mind; Creators or Sons of Light, those united with Light exemplified by true spiritual consciousness.

The syllabus for the Mystery System consisted of five main areas: (1) The Seven Liberal Arts, which included grammar, arithmetic, rhetoric, music, astronomy, geometry, and dialectics; (2) the sciences of the forty-two books of Hermes, containing information about the Singer or Odus, who must know hymns of the Gods; two books pertaining to music; the Horoscopus, who must know four books about astronomy; the Hierogrammat, for whom knowledge of hieroglyphics, cosmography, geography, astronomy, as well as topography and land surveying of Egypt is essential; the Stolistes, who has to know about slaughter of animals and embalming; the Prophetes, temple President, who must gain knowledge of higher esoteric theology and complete education of priests; the Pastophori, for whom medical knowledge such as physiology, diseases, anatomy, drugs, and instruments is required (3) Sciences of Monuments, such as Pyramids, Temples, Libraries, Obelisks, Sphinxes, and Idols, as well as architecture, metallurgy, engineering, sculpture, agriculture, mining, forestry, drawing and painting (4) Secret Sciences, inclusive of the book of the Dead, myths, magic, parables, geometrical and numerical symbolism (5) Protecting the Social Order through using knowledge of the priesthood, the law, economics, census taking, civics, statistics, military science, and navigation (James 1954, pp. 135-136).

According to James, the Egyptian Mystery System, was stolen by the Greeks from Africa after Alexander the Great raided the libraries in an Egyptian city the invaders—I deduce—named Alexandria. If he is to be believed, it is this stolen Mystery System which today forms the core of what is presented by Western scholarship as Greek philosophy.[9]

> James knew that Egypt predated Greece by thousands of years. He also knew that the great teachers of Egypt, Imhotep, Sonchis, Wennofer, Amenhotep, son of Hapu, and others had not sat around doing nothing for hundreds of years. There was nothing in the ancient world to indicate that the Africans in Egypt waited in a fog until the arrival of the Greeks before they started thinking, reflecting, and acting on the basis of their cognitions. James knew that the major centres of world philosophy long before Homer's Iliad in 800 BC were the cities of On, Abydos, Mennefer, Waset, and Syene. In these sacred cities, the priests, who were also scribes, assembled to teach initiates the fundamentals of medicine, law, politics, geometry, architecture, sculpture, mathematics, and astronomy (Asante 2001, p. 2).

For Asante, the James work was a crucial blow to what he assesses as the jugular of white superiority, a matter with which Richards would find favour. What I am certain he and any other reasonable West Indian who had hoped for a Brian Lara victory in 2007 would not favour, even today, is this: Lara in 2007 could have been associated with anything similar to, or parallel with, the vast depth and breadth of knowledge, selflessness, self-sacrifice, spirituality, resolve, and asceticism James links to Moses, a Hierogrammat and Initiate/Apprentice knowledgeable about the Mystery System.

I turn straight in the direction of President Obama's leadership, after which I shall focus on Brian Lara again. No one should be mistaken into thinking that in 2008 Barack Hussein Obama was not regarded by the majority of black American voters as a Moses who would deliver them, a Moses with vast depth and breadth of knowledge, selflessness, spirituality, as well as resolve needed for dealing with US domestic socio-economic and political matters into which he was thrust. Never mind author, Toni Morrison's, figurative foray that Bill Clinton is the first black American President. I will venture to state, as well, that in regard to foreign policy, some European-American constituents saw Mr. Obama as a Moses. In using the BBC World Service Television tag query, 'Hasn't quite delivered yet. Has He?' in regard to the President I go much further than Viv Richards. My jury is not out there. He has not delivered.

Mr. Obama campaigned relentlessly in 2008 with a strident ostensible set of aims to elevate the "WRETCHED OF THE EARTH." Well into his second term and towards the end (2016), black unemployment was way ahead of the societal average, a statistic which the selfish misfit, Donald Trump, continually throws in his face by billowing and bellowing that in the America of June 2018 when the unemployment rate was the lowest in well over a decade-and-a-half, African American unemployment under Trump was way below what it was under the Obama presidency. I ask: what delivery did President Obama offer in a society wide context where there has been ever increasing militarising of police forces all across America where officers make use of tools such as assault weapons and armoured vehicles! I am well aware that it was not his administration that authorised such militarising. It was just such militarising that came down rather hard in Ferguson, Mississippi (August 2014). What did he do, however, to reduce or stop it across the US? When I consider foreign policy matters, I am led to pose other probing queries.

When he secured victory in the 2008 election he claimed that his policy direction would be one of transparency. In his first year in office, 2009, 3.4 billion dollars were spent on new headquarters for the Department of Homeland Security. This is merely a small fraction of expenditure on counter-terrorism. In addition, nobody in his administration has offered any disclosure to the American people about operations on "the dark side," integrally connected to the secret war the Bush team had begun to wage against terrorists. To be quite precise, he retained almost all the features of that secret war. He expanded the covert war in Afghanistan and Pakistan and intensified the Cofer Black and Donald Rumsfeld footprints. In fact, when Osama Bin Laden met his demise in Abbotabad, Pakistan, it was not just a Navy Seal job, the job was also done by Joint Security Operation Command [JSOC]. Is JSOC. not a creation endorsed resoundingly by Donald Rumsfeld?

According to Mr. John Rizzo, CIA Counsel during the course of the Bush administration, Mr. Obama "endorsed" the Bush team plan: "His people were signalling to us—I think—partly to try to assure us that they weren't gonna come in and dismantle the place, that they were gonna be just as tough—if not tougher—than the Bush people." I pose this to readers. Was such a stance indicative of logical embrace of that legacy left by Dr. Martin Luther King? Although I am tempted to ponder issues about the "Catch 22" situation which one African-American commentator claimed the President was in following the Michael Brown shooting, the 2014 Ebola explosion, the Darfur dilemma, and the siege on Mount Sinjar, I have no other query about embracing Dr. King's legacy.

Thus, I move straight to Viv Richards' view about captain Brian Lara having lost his way, and will do so by referring to expert ideas from that pre-eminent Nobel Prize winner, Kenyan biologist, ecological activist, and distinguished founder of the GREEN BELT MOVEMENT, as well as GREEN BELT INTERNATIONAL, Dr. Wangari Maathai, who writes about what she assesses as THE WRONG BUS SYNDROME. The goal here is enabling readers to ask themselves: (1) Can Brian Lara be associated with THE WRONG BUS SYNDROME? (2) Can Lara be linked inextricably to understanding the cultures of THE WRETCHED OF THE EARTH? (3) Is there any plausible link to be established between the Brian Lara claim about unconditional love of West Indies cricket and boarding the right bus?

While highlighting important role differences associated with her professional status, Maathai (2009, pp. 164-165) states it was in her position as a member of an exclusive Westernised elite not uncommon to several post-independence African societies that she started listening to rural Kenyan women talk about issues such as obtaining firewood for preparing nutritious meals, gaining access to clean drinking water, and fodder for their animals. It is out of such discourse that Green Belt was initiated. From a sociological standpoint, I interpret the Maathai reference to role difference between her and the rural women as a cue to cultural matters, matters which are germane to the scientist. Here, I note that her personal recognition of the significance of culture formed one basis to initiating Civic and Environmental Education seminars, integral to Green Belt Movement work, work aimed at economic and political empowerment of the poor, as well as internalisation of concepts about movement away from self-interest and fostering dedication to service for common good (Maathai 2009, p. 170). It was out of the seminars that she developed an idea she named "The Wrong Bus Syndrome," which signifies that not unlike travellers embarking on the wrong bus, numerous persons and communities are proceeding in wrong directions or on wrong pathways where they permit others, frequently leaders, to guide them well away from intended destinations (Maathai 2009, pp. 5-6).

Why do some persons board wrong buses? The reasons, often emergent from seminar participants, are many: (1) individuals fail to seek directions and do not obtain sufficient necessary information (2) informants, either unintentionally or intentionally, misinform travellers (3) travellers are incapacitated as a result of alcoholism, mental illness, drug abuse, distress or confusion (4) some possessing a misplaced sense of arrogance present themselves as omniscient (5) some cheat themselves and minimise the impact of inappropriate decision making (6) others are ignorant, harbour fear, are intimidated, are not self-confident and assured (Maathai 2009, p. 168). For Maathai these reasons/problems are not just community problems. The solutions are constitutive of efforts to grapple with poor people's issues, global issues of development which, in her words, are legion. This is the type of collective responsibility, what I characterise as something eminently sociological, she asserts is geared towards aiding people deepen their self-knowing, appreciate that to care for ecology is caring for themselves and successors, and understand that while healing planet Earth they heal themselves simultaneously.

From a dramaturgical standpoint, stage performer, West Indies Test Match captain, Brian Lara, was failing in his stage craft: his impression management, the manner in which he expressed himself, and cast impressions on his expectant West Indies audience, left a great deal to be desired. His public investment, self image emotionally invested in West Indies Test Match cricket leadership, his face in such leadership, was not just damaged severely, it was lost also. In a Marxian sense, for Lara to have lost his way, according to Viv Richards, he had become an alienated being: he could lay no valid claim to owning meaningful and productive performance. To borrow from C. Wright Mills, his glaring leadership inadequacy constituted major issues and crises for the Anglo-Caribbean. In giving further careful scrutiny to the Richards claim that he had lost his way I would state: when a person has lost his way, it is quite probable that he has done so unintentionally on a course which was charted, exclusively by him or charted by him, with assistance of capable or incapable advisers who know or do not know what are required for the purpose of avoiding any or major loss. I fail to see how Brian Lara could have lost his way intentionally. In the same breath, I state that administrators on the West Indies Cricket Board who had advised him and denied him—for whatever reasons and purposes—official counsel from wise, capable, and experienced people such as Richards, Kanhai, Sobers, and Gibbs, have contributed to his losing his way.

I am, therefore, driven to ask why—if Brian Lara, who had to have been cognisant about his loss of way—the West Indies skipper did not publicly or privately request tactful intervention from these people? They have been integral to that "legacy," the virtues of which he had extolled openly as early as the [1999-2000] West Indies tour to New Zealand, when he and teammates were trounced by New Zealand. I am also compelled to wonder what prevented him from seeking their assistance, during the course of his second and third leadership tenures, when he had not just lost his way, a bit, but had been massively off a very "ROUGH" and craggy course.

Disappointingly, Brian Lara continued way off course. At the time of the 2007 World Cup, he was nowhere close to assisting Richards and other hopefuls transform dreamy looks in their eyes from which they stretched their imaginative insights to embody "nostalgia" and "reward for all the people in the Caribbean." With a mere three weeks to the end of the competition, just at the point where the West Indies captain and his men were on the margins of elimination, Michael Holding stated: "Lara has to step aside, not necessarily as a player, but as captain." Holding was explicit about Lara's greatness as a batsman, but contrasted this greatness, quite sharply, with the captain's inability to lead, which prevented him from being a good captain, tactically. This tactical absence was reflected in the fact that West Indies not in the final-received notable drubbings underlined by large scoring margins which came from South Africa, in Grenada, Sri Lanka, in Guyana, as well as New Zealand and Australia, in Antigua.

Well before such defeats had been inflicted, March 2007, Tony Cozier [T.C.] offered a less than glowing assessment of Lara to BBC World Service Television [W.S.]. I ask readers to use the Otway claims as contexts for apprehending the initial exchange between Cozier and BBC World Service about Brian Lara's maturity.

W. S.: *Now, what about Lara and his captaincy? I mean, has he matured? I suppose, that has to be the key question.*

T. C.: *Well, he is thirty seven years of age. And if he hasn't matured at thirty seven, he's never gonna mature. I think he's a little bit better, as far as handling the players and the team and, maybe, his relationship with the administration. Although that became rather frosty, once more, during the Indian series where he criticised the selectors, criticised the ground staff for the pitches that they prepared. He got rather shirky about things, in that series. But I think he's now closer to the players. They respect him, of course. He's a treMENdous player. Tactically, I still feel that he's not the best, tactically. But, they're very few international captains who have it all sussed out, as far as tactics are concerned. I didn't feel that he was going to do any better, on the third occasion. He has done—in fact—a little better and I can—in the end—see what the Board saw, in appointing him, for the third time. The World Cup's coming up. He's a senior player, in the side. He is the fulcrum of the side. And let's have him lead the team into the World Cup. We'll see what happens, after the World Cup. He says he's not playing any more one day cricket. So, the Board has to make a decision, after the World Cup whether they will keep him on as captain, for the tour of England and then appoint a captain for the one day series and have two different captains. I think we really need to have just one captain. So, we'll see, after the World Cup which will decide a lot.*

What I notice, almost instantly, about the query to Cozier and the initiation of his reply is the strong implicature within the discussants' remarks about the Brian Lara responsibility for maturing, which has been sorely needed in West Indies Test Match cricket. Although Cozier credited him, somewhat weakly, for having matured, readers are nevertheless exposed to the captain's lifting of that frosty covering which chilled, once more, the communicative impact of his leadership style in Test Match cricket.

My examination, thus far, of Brian Lara, the three tenured West Indies captain, should not be taken to mean that he bore complete responsibility for the late twentieth and early twenty-first century disaster that is West Indies Test Match cricket. Although I insist that he bears great responsibility, I would be very unfair to him, if I failed to state that there were matters or factors over which he had no control. Readers are, of course, free to decide whether he would or would not have been an excellent leader, in the absence of these maters or factors, political activism in the United States, Latin America, and the Caribbean, parasitic blight from coaching, West Indies Cricket Board ineptitude. All three are important and can be explored at length in another publication. I must continue my focus upon captain Lara and President Obama on sticky wickets.

ENDNOTES

1 My reference to this term is a reference to a book written by former West Indies luminary, Sir Clyde Walcott.

2 While the Gandhi influence on Martin Luther King is obvious, observers should know: although Nelson Mandela's organisation, the African National Congress (ANC), advocated and used violence in its effort to end apartheid, he did not ask for the blood of racist tormentors, when he became South African President. Instead, he did not seek revenge. He formed the Truth and Reconciliation Commission, for the purpose of determining the circumstances and motivations which featured in the brutality of racist horror.

3 Charlie Griffith, one of Wes Hall's fast bowling partners, was also invited to Australia, but reveals that he declined the offer, as a consequence of sound advice from colleagues.

4 Writing ten years on in his book, Viv Richards, states: "As far as I was concerned, he [Robert Bailey] had nicked it; but when I looked at the television replay he had clearly missed it. I appealed loud and long and he was given out. It was interpreted by the media as unnecessary pressure on the umpire, Lloyd Barker. But it was up to him to maintain his composure and make a decision. It created a big row in the Caribbean as radio broadcaster Christopher Martin-Jenkins has hinted that I cheated by putting Barker under undue pressure with a prolonged appeal and forced him to change his mind. Even with hindsight I have to say that, if the same incident happened tomorrow, I would do the same thing. At the same time I am sorry for Rob Bailey as it was an appeal that might have shortened his international career."

5 A term once used by Learie Constantine in the West Indies [968] .

6 Keen observers will, of course, recognise the persons besides Lara and Richardson as former Test Match cricketers who played the roles of manager/coaches or coaches. I am, in no way, suggesting that West Indies cricket would have benefited from these roles.

7 During the time of Brian Lara's leadership tenures, that discovery had not been made and it remains elusive well after his departure.

8 These forms are: [a] forms of speech whose use of constraints is intended to allow hearers the freedom to construct their own meaning, [b] forms of speech whose use of constraints is not intended to allow hearers the freedom to construct their own meaning.

9 I am yet to read a convincing rebuttal of the James arguments.

13th INNINGS
STILL ON A
STICKY WICKET

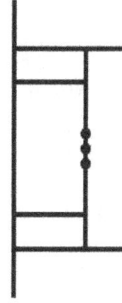

What I want to do here is ask about making links between recent and continual socio-economic and political factors outside occupational pursuits of Messrs. Obama and Lara, and those very pursuits. In so doing, I hope that readers will be encouraged to continue their focus on the captain as a way of enhancing their understanding of the Obama presidency. Within the area of socio-political matters pertinent to the United States President, Obama has always had to confront: (a) huge challenges from the race or colour problems (b) massive poverty—not, by any means insignificant—in an economic foreground of sluggish economic progress (c) rampant illicit substance abuse (d) interpersonal violence and the attendant controversial issue, gun control, across American cities and suburbs. In addition, within the foreign policy theatre, although he ended the Afghanistan and Iraq wars, he was saddled with such issues as: (a) no progress over the Israel-Palestine matter (b) failure to close the Guantanamo Prison (c) hold trials of the alleged mastermind behind the 11th September, 2001 hijackings, in the United States (d) the Libyan debacle (e) conflict in Syria over ethnic, religious, and quasi-religious matters (f) the crisis in Ukraine (g) souring of relations with President Vladimir Putin, and—certainly not least (h) roving groups of Al Qaeda malcontents within Africa, Yemen, and Iraq fronted by an organisation, Dawlat al-Islami-yah f'al-Iraq w Belaad al-Sham, Islamic State for Iraq and Syria/the Levant [ISIS], bent on establishing a Khaliphate. None of these developments, especially the movement of ISIS, could have brought any comfort to President Obama.

It is Iraq—exactly forty years after the infamous Richard Nixon resignation—that preoccupied President Barack Obama just prior to his embarking on a summer vacation (eighth August, 2014). In the immediate aftermath of US troop withdrawal, "for better or worse, President Obama—like his predecessor—was entrusting Iraq's future to Nouri Al Maliki."[1] President Obama had brought what appeared like the end to a nine year two trillion dollar war in Iraq, where over 100,000 Iraqi citizens lost their lives, 4,000 US soldiers died, and 30,000 others were wounded. American foreign policy experts and the President, I emphasise, had to have been fully aware that Maliki had embarked upon: (a) a large scale removal—if not purging of Sunni Iraqis—from his government (b) notably, attempts to arrest and carry out a death sentence on Sunni Vice President Tariq al-Hashimi, accused of handling death squads and assassinating political rivals (c) raiding offices of the Sunni Finance Minister, and detention of Sunni leaders. The US President, with his profound wisdom, could not have been unaware that one major basis to the astonishingly swift stranglehold ISIS had established over large areas of Iraq, Al-Falujah, Ramadi, Mosul, by early August 2014 was the Maliki purge. What is ISIS?

I give you replies and assessment from two of the American foreign policy experts, a Bush appointed ambassador to Iraq, Mr. Ryan Crocker, and *New York Times* correspondent, Mr. Michael Gordon. Let me refer also to a remark issued by Sir Gary Sobers, notable Lara mentor, about leadership. I do so partly but significantly with the aim of assessing the foreign policy of leader Obama as inert.[2] I shall look also at his domestic policy as inert and make similar claims, in regard to leader Brian Lara.

It is Sir Gary who once stated: "When a captain wins, he is applauded. When he loses, he is a fool and deserves to be sacked. There were many people calling for my removal after that match." The match to which he referred was the fourth encounter between England and West Indies (Port-of-Spain, Trinidad, 1968). In the West Indies second innings, he, the captain, declared at a score of 92 for 2, giving England a total of 265 runs to get in 165 minutes. Sir Wesley Hall, leading West Indies fast bowler at the time, told me that the captain's declaration was the result of a team decision resting on a belief that England could not have won. England did win that match and some of the subsequent criticism hurled at Sir Gary was vitriolic.

After two Iraq wars, President Obama wasted no time in pulling American troops out of Iraq. Although he might not know what a cricket declaration, 92 for 2, means, he would have done well to realise that unlike Sir Gary, who was given another chance to compete with England in 1969, time was not on his side, and in January 2017, when the tussle with ISIS might not end, he could have found himself in a position where he would be rather averse to coveting a legacy of war.

In the words of correspondent, Gordon, it cannot be satisfactory for President Obama to say he diminished a terrorist threat, took care of bin Laden, and dealt with the Afghanistan situation. With clear emphasis Gordon pointed to a NEW terrorist threat involving countless fighters in Western and Northern Iraq. He added: ISIS—with expansive footprints—has looted the banks in Mosul, and taken all the American arms they were capable of grabbing. They ploughed back some of the loot into Syria and also took hold of an oil rich province there. According to Ambassador Crocker, the ISIS menace "is analogous to Afghanistan—August 2001. This time it is Al Qaeda version 6.0. They make bin Laden's Al Qaeda look like boy scouts. They are far stronger, they are far more numerous, they have thousands who hold foreign passports and require no visas to get into the United States or other Western countries. They are well funded, they are battle hardened and they are well armed and they now control far more territory exclusively than bin Laden ever did." In very stark terms he claimed that as they sit in Mosul, they are figuring out how "they're gonna get at us next."

It was December 2015, just over a year after the Crocker remarks had been made, that fourteen American citizens in San Bernardino, California, were murdered, in horrific fashion, by two other American citizens, whom the Federal Bureau Of Investigation stated had established links to ISIS. Only six months later, early June 2016, fifty revellers and celebrants in Orlando, Florida, lost their lives at the hands of an ISIS inspired misanthrope. While there is no evidence that the three murderers/terrorists were battle-hardened, it is clear that they did get to the United States—not next—in Ambassador Crocker's words: only one month prior to the California horror, ISIS had struck Paris, where over sixty French citizens had been murdered.

The Crocker view is quite congruent with that expressed by Brett McGurk, US Deputy Assistant Secretary of State for Iraq and Iran. He assesses ISIS: better equipped, better trained, manned, better resourced, more effective fighting forces than Al Qaeda in Iraq. The assessment is echoed, most strongly, in remarks from, Michael Kilcullen, a former counter-insurgency advisor to General David Petraeus, and non-executive Chairman with Caerus Associates. Although Kilcullen does not regard ISIS as Al Qaeda, he concedes that their members possess the fighting skill of

Al Qaeda forces. In addition, he points to their great organisational acumen akin to the political and administrative ability of Hezbollah. In quite specific terms, they have set up hospitals, courts, schools, tax systems, land and other property holding deeds. Their expansionist territorial grasp is, de facto, rule under statehood. Rather ominously, ISIS is dramatically more dangerous than Al Qaeda."

Regardless of whether readers agree with Ambassador Crocker, Chairman Kilcullen, and Secretary McGurk, many of them know that President Barack Obama, who obviously did not want his legacy to be tainted by Iraq, went further than posting military advisers to Al Maliki's Shia dominated Iraq. With ISIS poised to pounce on Erbil, where American non-military personnel were located, and stories of the malcontents' unspeakable brutality, as well as their imminent threat to Christians, Yazidis, Kurds, and other Iraqi ethnic groups, The US President ordered air strikes against Al Qaeda 6.0. in early August 2014, and vowed that the strikes would continue as long as they are necessary. He also dispatched United States Special Forces to Mount Sinjar—apparently with the aim of mounting a rescue mission on behalf of Yazidi Iraqis driven from their homes by rampaging ISIS forces.[3]

Interestingly, Britain with which the US has a special relationship, did not join the robust early August US military effort, but was reported to be poised towards aiding the US rescue mission. France was also supposed to be intent on arming Peshmerga fighters. Prime Minister David Cameron, who claimed "we [British] are a peaceful people," and stated that he always welcomes good partners on the cricket pitch when fellow Oxford toff, London Mayor, Boris Johnson, announced he would become a parliamentary candidate during the 2015 British general election, made no statement of official British intentions.

It was not until late September 2014—with parliamentary approval behind him—that David Cameron sent jets to Iraq. Conservative Stephen Harper of Canada, another very close and trusted American ally, did not step up to the frontline military plate: in early September 2014 under a NATO umbrella Canada's contribution amounted to military advisers in Iraq. By month end, however, amidst robust questioning from the Federal opposition leader in Parliament, Mr. Tom Mulcair, the Canadian Government had become evasive about whether the Canadian presence against ISIS would become assertive. In early October, however, the Canadian Government was getting ready to dispatch jets to the combat zone. Conservative, Tony Abbot of Australia, did step up to the frontline military plate. It is fair to state that despite assistance, President Barack Hussein Obama was left very much to do the literal and figurative heavy lifting on his own, even though bombing runs had been conducted by friendly allies in the region such as Saudi Arabia and Jordan.

I have already stated that Mr. Obama has used every opportunity he could find for the purpose of invoking the names of Mr. Nelson Mandela, "the last great liberator of the twentieth century" to Mr. Obama [Madiba], Dr. King, and President Kennedy. One thing I have never heard him do is invoke the names of Mr. Mandela, Mr. Malcolm X, along with Dr. King's as a way of coming to grips with the imposing domestic issues he has had to confront. Even more importantly, Mr. Obama has never made any efforts—in dealing with the domestic issues—to use collectively the insights of writer, Mr. James Baldwin, Mr. Malcolm X, Dr. King, Presidents, Lincoln, and Johnson, the second of whom did implement Head Start, a war on poverty, and wanted to build a Great Society. I do not suppose anyone had to educate him about the fact that when Dr. King made his Washington speech in 1963, the forceful presentation of its introduction carried more than strong echoes of Mr. Lincoln's Gettysburg address.

I suppose, also, that no one had to educate him that when Dr. King gave his very last speech in April 1968, about having been to the mountain top, the Civil Rights leader was honouring his African ancestors via the route of selflessness and self-sacrifice. No one, I suspect, had to educate him that like Dr. King and Mr. Malcolm X, Mr. Baldwin honoured his African ancestry. Does anyone have to remind the President that the Mandela idea of reconciliation is not something which emerged within the cramped confines of a prison cell on Robben Island? Does he need to be reminded that the idea has some of its very deepest roots in the Mandela education about democracy acquired from his childhood days within the Xhosa extended family?

Dr. King's ancestry, which the Civil Rights leader honoured in 1968, is right out of Africa. So is Mr. Obama's. Did the President—while tackling the thorny foreign policy issues he had to confront—make any attempts to look for intersections between validity in the combined significance from the legacies of Mr. Mandela, Mr. Baldwin, Mr. Malcolm X, Presidents Kennedy, and Johnson, and that from some of his African fathers: consciencism [Kwame Nkrumah-Osagyefo], harambee [Jomo Kenyatta-Mzee], The Arusha Declaration [Julius Nyerere-Mwalimu]? My reply is negative. Similar claims and questions about the Lara leadership on regional Caribbean domestic matters can be made. I am not hinting that President Obama had to be a "Tanzophiliac," nor am I implying that he had to be an ardent student of the ancestor, intellectuals Ali, Mazrui and Wangari Maathai. Can he lay any valid claims to combining their significance with that of other African ancestors I have noted, as well as the American ones, to deal with American domestic socio-economic and political issues? I do not regard these as fanciful or farfetched queries: notable American politicians of European ancestry, both within and outside government, never flinch to extol the virtues emanating from the impact of European thinkers such as theologians, historians, economists, jurists, scientists, and philosophers.

The Anglo-Caribbean in which Brian Lara became West Indies captain has been, and still is, bedevilled by a race/colour problem, intense poverty in an oppressive foreground of economic retrogression, the destructive impact from rampant illegal substance abuse, as well as interpersonal violence. Like Mr. Obama captain Lara used to speak effusively about a great West Indies tradition. This is a tradition outside of cricket which has been shaped by liberators such as one of the very first to introduce the idea of Pan Africanism, the Trinidadian, George Padmore/Malcolm Nurse, Kwame Nkrumah's mentor-in-chief, Haitians Toussaint L' Ouverture, Christophe, Alexandre Petion, Jean-Jaques Dessalines, the Cuban Dr. Fidel Castro, the Trinidad intellectuals Mr. C.L.R. James, Dr. Eric Williams, the Guyanese intellectual, Dr. Walter Rodney, the St. Lucian Nobel Laureates, Sir. Arthur Lewis and Mr. Derek Walcott, the reggae doyen Mr. Bob Marley, and Prime Minister Mr. Michael Manley, both from Jamaica. Within Lara's own theatre, cricket, there has always been the tradition created by Sir Frank Worrell, Sir Clyde Walcott, Mr. Gerry Gomez, Mr. Allan Rae, Mr. Learie Constantine/Baron of Maraval and Nelson, and Mr. Herman Griffith. I ask: did captain Lara make any meaningful efforts to use the combined validity of ideas from predecessors for the purpose of developing his leadership and motivating the Test Match teams he led? My explicit reply is NO.

When the issue of foreign policy leadership in the face of hostility from competitors/enemies is considered in regard to President Obama coming to the end of his eight year tenure, and captain Lara coming to the end of his tenure, very different pictures appear to emerge at first sight. In captain Lara's case, his two illustrious predecessors, Clive Lloyd and Vivian Richards, had the immensely awesome might of quick bowling fire power in their express bowling attacks, as well as the imperious force from assertive and artistic batting geniuses. No one should, however, ever make the mistake of claiming that Lloyd's and Richards' leadership was gifted with such immense advantage. They worked very closely with ideas from some of the Caribbean people named above to place West Indies teams they led on the lofty perches so grandly admired by compatriots. When Lara assumed the post of captain, he did not have the immense advantage Lloyd and Richards had. No one should overlook the fact that like Lloyd and Richards, he did have several opportunities to draw from ideas of predecessors both within and outside cricketing theatres. As such, he did have opportunities to lay foundations for, and building, that advantage for the teams he led, and in turn, helping to set a stage from which plans could be made to help tackle issues outside the cricketing theatre.

The Obama leadership issues on foreign policy, insofar as they pertain to resources and use of the resources, have been of a hugely different nature to those of captain Lara's. Unlike captain Lara, the President was a leader who had massive military might from which he could draw. No society today can match that American might. That is the very might which Mr. Obama's predecessor, President G.W. Bush, unleashed in Afghanistan and Iraq (2001 and 2003), and President Obama unleashed in early August (2014). The world knows, however, that Senator Obama, unlike Senator Clinton,[4] who became Mr. Obama's Secretary of State, and on whose watch the Benghazi terrorist attack was accomplished, cast his senate vote against the Iraq war and ended that war. Further, although some old neo-conservative hawks—both civilian and military—and some of Mr. Obama's staunch congressional opponents were chomping at the bit over using massive force in the forms of "boots on the ground" against the Assad regime in Syria and in response to advancing ISIS malcontents within Iraq, Mr. Obama, along with his new Secretary of State, Mr. John Kerry, and I presume, his erudite National Security Chief Susan Rice, eschewed, studiously, any temptation to send military forces to fight on Iraqi soil.

My point here is a simple one. To the extent that Mr. Obama had to know there could have been no validity to the farcical—if not embarrassing—Iraq invasion—never mind the frightful might of American military power—he did not want to misuse that might. Mr. Obama, a shrewd thinker and insightful student of history, cannot be unaware of what West (2004, pp. 5-6) assesses as aggressive militarism, a mode of existence glorified in the name of flags of invasion, conquest, and domination, which doom victims to bondage, cultural, and physical death. What is aggressive militarism? Here are some of its elements, which would not be easy to detach from the ideology of neo-conservatives such as Dick Cheney: (a) military might is salvific in a world where the mightiest with the biggest weapons is the most masculine and moral (b) aggressive militarism is practised as unilateral intervention, colonial incursion, and armed occupation (c) aggressive militarism, hewn from a buccaneering mythology of a lone ranger strategy, a frontier phantasy, resorts to perpetration of cowardly terrorism it lays claim to containing and abolishing.

As with the bully on the block, one's own interests and aims define what is moral and one's own anxieties and insecurities dictate what is masculine. Yet the use of naked force to resolve conflict often backfires. The arrogant hubris that usually accompanies this use of force tends to lead toward instability—and even destruction—in the regions where we have sought to impose our will. Violence is readily deployed by those who cloak themselves in innocence—those unwilling to examine themselves and uninterested in counting the number of innocent victims they kill (West, 2004, p. 6).

Readers can judge for themselves whether the Obama judiciousness in regard to use of aggressive militarism against ISIS was, indeed, an effort to avoid going down the Lyndon road to full presence within Vietnam, a road dramatically and vividly exposed during the course of that riveting September 2017 PBS documentary THE VIETNAM WAR, made by filmmakers, Ken Burns and Lyn Novick. What was at stake here "for better or worse" for President Obama's legacy is something far more significant than the Vietnam debacle. It was deeply rooted in how he negotiated very difficult terrain, as a leader whose place in the political annals of American life can be made secure and unsullied. It is to placement that I turn now.

President G.W. Bush's eight year tenure came to be defined by the huge foreign policy mess over the American invasion of Iraq. President Kennedy's all too brief presence at the White House will, forever, be remembered for the manner in which he confronted Secretary Khrushchev of the Soviet Union. Although Watergate kept saturating the Nixon years, the steadfast anti-communist will not be forgotten for his China overtures and eventual success.[5] In each instance, as well as the Johnson Presidency, the leaders were operating within a set of wider political contexts: the war against communism and jihadist terror. For better or worse, those contexts emanated directly from the American hegemonic necessity to perpetuate the expansionist aims of imperialist forbears. Just as importantly, all the American Presidents I identify have regarded themselves as heirs to, and empathisers with, the aims noted.

They are inheritors—if not descendants—of a European tradition which they cultivated and broadcast with enormous pride. This is not a tradition to which President Barack Hussein Obama belongs, even if he broadcast it in assertive or strident fashion during the course of his tenure. In the role of President, he always had the foreign policy choices to replace the hegemonic necessity or sidestep it. In my view, he has made neither choice. As such, he has been trapped within two poles. Even if he drew a highly persuasive semantic tableau in that soaring rhetoric for which he became very well known, and made a very cogent case for ISIS threats to the American "homeland," and defeated them, he would still be entrapped.

On the one hand, hawkish neo-conservatives, mainly men of minute muster always willing to set fires of fury to their own fictive forests, self-appointed heirs to the imperialistic hegemonic necessity, continued being censorious in their strident claims that he was wrong to disengage from Iraq so early as 2011. These are the very men who gave their blessing to "torture" techniques more sickeningly revulsive than those used by British slave owner, Thomas Thistlewood, in Jamaica. These are the very men who sugared their syllabic stench with glib distinctions between morality and immorality, condemned what they deemed to be "heinous crimes" and "moral obscenity" from others, trumpeted distinctions between justice and injustice, tyranny and democracy, and stated, quite calmly, that "bad things happen in war." These are the social amnesiacs who bleated belatedly about genocide. These are the men who must be greatly relieved that that the Leon Panetta Report connected to what the CIA did at "black sites" remains at the Agency Headquarters and was never released to the American public. How different are they to the grand American citizens indicted so rightfully by Mr. Frederick Douglass!

By late September 2014, these brooding barbarians, none of whom could have ever stood a strategic chance against the brilliance of Gaius Julius Caesar[6] or placed himself within the shoes of Marcus Aemelius Lepidus, Caesar's second Master Of The Horse, crowded before some of the grandest gates they had erected and were baying for Barack Obama's blood. To them he had squandered American world leadership.

One of them, Mr. Newt Gingrich, trumpeted that two former Defence Secretaries, Robert Gates and Leon Panetta, who served the President, were very critical of his foreign policy in their tomes.

Gates and Gingrich are not just examples of heirs I noted: they are also persons who do not come from the tradition to which Barack Obama knows he belongs. To the duo I add Senators Ted Cruz, Marco Rubio, Governors Jeb Bush, John Kasich, and Scott Walker, party contenders for President in 2016. How could I forget that MAAFA MUZUNGU MONSTROSITY and phantom fascist flaunt, Donald Trump, riding roughshod with his raucous racism which he used to remove every semblance of a Presbyterian pulpit from his polarising prognoses? Here, it is not out of place for me to recall that the Reverend Wright made a statement in which he claimed 2008 presidential candidate, Barack Hussein Obama, knew about the white power structure. Quite contrastively to the men of minute muster, the grand citizenry, remnants of the US anti-war movement, especially those on the organisational frontlines against American presence in Afghanistan and Iraq, were, perhaps, discomfited and would not have minded discrediting Mr. Obama.

While I am ready, willing, and able to entertain challenges to my claims, I would request that any and all challengers perform some basic exercises. They should juxtapose President Obama's implementation of foreign policy with his two inauguration speeches, his great eagerness to embrace the validity of Dr. Martin Luther King's ideas, and his address at West Point where he enunciated and reiterated his foreign policy strategies. These are all issues of historical recency, but they matter a great deal. So do the implications of one of the claims made by Iraqi President, Sadaam Hussein, just before he faced the might of a superior military force marshalled so strategically in 1991 by Generals, Colin Powell and Norman Schwarzkopf, in the Desert Storm Campaign under the Bush senior presidency.

It was President Sadaam Hussein who declared that his battle with the impending American storm/invasion was going to be "the mother of all battles." Although Bush junior launched an assault on Iraq in 2003, and strode onto an American aircraft carrier not very long after when he was greeted to rapturous applause from US forces under a banner "MISSION ACCOMPLISHED," no reasonable foreign policy expert would justify the banner claim. President Obama, who - more than most - was uncomfortably cognisant of nightmarish prospects for the US handling of Iraq, might not have been willing to ponder what was far greater than the figurative significance of the Hussein declaration. Be that as it may, it is precisely a connotation similar to that very significance which I heard one US military analyst assess publicly in summer 2014 as enactment of Shakespearean tragedy he likened to developments in *HAMLET* or *MACBETH*.

What did he say? Here are his own words: "What's going on in Iraq is NOT eight hundred Syrian militants running into Iraq. It's the Sunnis—TRIBES—probably twenty percent of the country have lost patience with the government in Bhagdad led by Prime Minister, Maliki, and encouraged by the Syrian war and in part armed by the Syrian war. I keep on thinking in terms of a Shakespearean tragedy and I think we're probably only in Act IV right now—Act V, the bloody conclusion of *Hamlet* or *Macbeth* STILL has not happened." I am no ardent student of Shakespearean works. I, nevertheless, do appreciate the importance of the figurative to everyday living, especially as it applies to the realms of cricket. I did state earlier that world leader, President Obama, would need far more than that cricket bat he displayed with high back lift and offered as preparation for the forward defence in the presence of Brian Lara while dealing with tortuous global issues and concerns.

Such was the case in regard to Iraq (August 2014), when he needed to play what Lara compatriot/Test Match cricketer/activist/university administrator/diplomat, Learie Constantine, would have described as "the innings of his life." Dare I state that no matter how excellent a political player President Barack Hussein Obama was, not unlike every superb Test Match cricketer, he needed more than David Cameron's good partners on the pitch. Even with their support, his movements on both the back and front foot, I reiterate, did not guarantee him success: he was not batting on something like the mother of all sticky wickets, Iraq. He had to bat on a devil of a wicket. That is the very wicket on which a confident, assertive, and strident eleven led by skipper, G.W. Bush, chose to bat, after they had told a world audience they won the coin toss and were going to take first strike on a wicket very far from admirably suited to their batsmanship.

It is worth informing readers that the Bush eleven, the number needed for a Test Match, consisted of G. W. Bush (captain and attacking fast bowler, first slip), Dick Cheney (vice-captain and all-rounder, gulley), Condoleezza Rice (silly mid-on), Donald Rumsfeld (attacking fast bowler, gulley), George Tenet, (silly mid-off),[7] Paul Wolfowitz second slip), Michael Hayden (third slip and leg spinner), Colin Powell (short point), John Ashcroft (third slip), Cofer Black (short cover), Paul Bremer (wicket keeper-standing back, rather than up close behind the stumps), Carl Rove (manager). It is a good idea also to make readers aware of what Woodcock (1998) states about the Australian Test Match captaincy of Ian Chappell, that tough, but straight, dinkum Aussie (Martin-Jenkins, 1996: p. 21) in England. For Woodcock, the Australian on field presence, a highly intimidating presence of green capped Australians fronted by the quick bowling menace of Dennis Lillee and Jeff Thompson, with the captain himself, a man as allergic to ambivalence as he was contemptuous of compromise, brother Greg, Ian Redpath, and Ashley Mallet in the slip and gulley cordon, as well as Rod Marsh behind the stumps, struck fear in the hearts of England spectators and players.

To keen students of cricket, perhaps, the impact of a sharper juxtaposition can be attained by recalling the destruction emanating from West Indies use of lightning fast, fearsome fast bowling strike forces unleashed by captains Clive Lloyd and Vivian Richards, with "shock and awe" on world Test Match cricket pitches in Australia, England, New Zealand, India, and Pakistan, where Caribbean invasion was followed by major conquest. Years later—I repeat—one member of those forces informed me that whatever captain, Clive Lloyd, wanted from his top bosses at the West Indies Cricket Board Lloyd got. He added "Lloyd ran the Board." It has never been a secret that after a catastrophically humiliating West Indies defeat by Australia in Australia, Lloyd told his bosses he wanted a powerful strike force which he got.

This is as good a juncture as any other at which I can offer an expert source of conceptually incisive statements about the type of strike force Lloyd had at his disposal. Writing about fast bowling, Kilburn (1950, p. 7) claims that ten years constitute the approximate span of fast bowling mastery. A decade, he adds, is the foundation for inspiration of greatness to nurture counter-greatness, time for the bowling pendulum to swing through its arc. A decade is the foundation for rise, zenith, and waning of fast bowling mastery. With a specific focus upon England and Australia, he observes that Frank Tyson and Brian Statham succeeded Keith Miller and Ray Lindwall, while Harold Larwood and William Voce succeeded Jack Gregory and Edgar McDonald.

In Australia particularly, but also to a great extent in England, fast bowling wins the Test match rubbers. It may not strike the single blow that turns a match, it may not provide the outstanding averages, but it is the overall oppressive force. It shapes the conquering character of a side. Test matches and even Test rubbers have been won without fast bowling, but only rarely and never easily, except in special circumstances of weather and wicket. A touring team without strong fast bowling is always a struggling team (Kilburn 1950, p. 7).

Astute observers may well quibble with Kilburn about the validity of his claims, especially that contained in the last sentence of the quote. If they so choose, they will be able to make use of an almost seven decade span since the time of his writing across which they could lay their challenges. In so doing they would be compelled to highlight, very significantly, the accomplishment in England and Australia of West Indies fast bowlers under the Viv Richards and Clive Lloyd leadership.

If there is any comparison between the Lloyd leadership impact and the captain Bush impact, such can be made by looking at the speed with which the Afghanistan Taliban Government collapsed, largely as a result of CIA direction under Mr. Cofer Black. While it would be highly unreasonable to claim that Mr. Black "ran" the US Presidency, it would be very prudent to claim that whatever Mr. Black wanted from the Bush administration for the Afghanistan campaign, he got and unleashed with lightning fast fearsome force through a set of astonishingly strategic ploys. With my comparative lens closely trained upon the Black success in Afghanistan, allow me to peer at one expert view offered to explain the Lloyd devastation:

The non-stop blitzkrieg by the West Indies quickies softened up the opposition in a way which was not unreminiscent of 'bodyline' and judging by the number of casualties—despite far more protective clothing, including helmets—far more dangerous (Bailey, 1989, p. 41).

Bailey observes that danger is always associated with batting against extremely fast bowling, particularly when bowlers are permitted to deliver bouncers excessively and bowl short of a length with great frequency. He adds, rather insistently, that the Lloyd West Indies quick bowlers were not prevented by umpires from violating Law 42:8, painfully instanced when England batsmen, John Edrich and Brian Close, were subjected to a torrent of bouncers in failing light at Old Trafford, Manchester.

The Bailey reference to contravention is instructive for me. Here, I am drawn to thinking about the imagery of late afternoon Manchester dull light and the imagery from vice-President Dick Cheney's view of the US operating under "the dark side" after the attack on 11th September, 2001. Quite apart from the creation of "black sites," highly secret locations around the world where terrorists such as the Khadr brothers,[8] Canadian citizens, and Khalid Sheik Mohammed were held, the Bush administration was using waterboarding. If a PBS report is to be believed, waterboarding, unquestionably torture, and illegal under the US constitution, as well as the Geneva Convention, was employed against Mohammed on more than one hundred and eighty occasions.

While the cricketing positions I assigned to captain G.W. Bush and teammates are merely figurative, any cricketing aficionado insightful enough to conjure imagery of the Bush players on a cricket field can picture the very offensive postures of those players. Better still, a good political cartoonist in the employ of one of the British dailies such as the *Mirror* and *Guardian*, or weeklies such as *The New Statesman* and *Punch*, can have a fine field day in sketching the presence of the Bush team on a cricket field. What a sight that would be! With or without sketching, every position I assign to the Bush players—perhaps, not the wicket keeper—is one of forceful attack: there is not a hint of defence. While skippers Chappell's and Lloyd's intentions materialised in wondrously victorious ways for Australia and West Indies, no such eventuality, however, emerged for the Bush team in the long run.

None of them was a member of captain Obama's eleven in August 2014. That eleven—obviously, in my view—consisted of: Dick Durbin (wicketkeeper)), President Obama (captain, first slip, medium fast, leg spinner and back-of-the arm bowler), Vice President Joseph Biden (second slip, all-rounder), John Kerry (gulley), Charles Hagel[9] (short cover), Eric Holder (off spinner and third slip), Susan Rice (gulley), Brett McGurk (cover-orthodox), John Brennan (mid-off—orthodox), Charles Schumer (mid-on-orthodox), Jeh Johnson (mid-wicket, orthodox), Dianne Feinstein (manager). To be fair, if the Bush team can be subjected to the cartoonist's keys/pen/pencil, the Obama team should be subjected also. While I cannot, however, use my own imagination to state what the captions for the respective teams would be, this is an appropriate juncture at which I can remind readers about: one of my main exploratory tools is C. Wright Mills' SOCIOLOGICAL IMAGINATION, which I think is certainly relevant here.

In an effort to make such relevance obvious, I ask readers to juxtapose my remarks about the US cricket team led by Mr. Obama with those from leader writer(s) for the ECONOMIST (16th August, 2014) and remember the significance of: structures of societies, biographies of persons, who are losing power, who are becoming powerful, and the positions of societies in history, as well as distinctions between issues and troubles.

According to the ECONOMIST, Mr. Obama's "gamble," withholding all but minimal military support to the Iraqi government for the purpose of forcing political change in Baghdad, has been associated with costs. Nevertheless, so claims the weekly, he should be credited for learning from mistakes of predecessors. With an obvious eye on history and—dare I state—the biographies of three Obama predecessors, the ECONOMIST claims:

> AMERICA'S last two presidents have got things wrong in Iraq in opposite ways. George W. Bush went into the country in 2003 guns blazing, with 148,000 soldiers and too little thought of how to stabilise it after Saddam Hussein had been defeated. The consequences were disastrous. Barack Obama took a different approach. Americans, he reckoned, were not capable of bringing peace to this complex, violent and distant place. He allowed the troops' mandate in the country to run out with insufficient attention to what might follow, and then applied the same logic in Syria where he did little to support moderate opponents of Bashar Assad. His policy aided the rise of the Islamic state (IS), a Sunni terrorist group, that has taken territory in Syria and Iraq... Now the prospect of a caliphate run by extremists bent on attacking the West has persuaded a reluctant Mr. Obama that he cannot walk away from the Mesopotamian mess, and he is trying a new tack—combining modest military force with hard-nosed political brinkmanship. Given conditions in the region, the chances of success are limited. But they are better than those offered by any other approach.[10]

The Mesopotamian mess which was largely created by ardent unapologetic imperialists such as predecessors to Mr. Winston Churchill, someone about whom Mr. Obama spoke effusively on one of his official visits to Britain, and those long before him, was tossed onto the President's turf. It is he in 2014 who was left, however, to bat on a horrible wicket trampled all over by captain Bush, his running mates, imperialist predecessors, as well as ruthless invading forces on fielding sides playing for nothing less than total annihilation of the enemy. Although captain Obama and teammates possessed the capability to do much more than merely survive, he—not unlike quite a few cricket captains, in the eyes of onlookers/spectators including ex-players—was required to have tons of luck, guts, and skill. Those he doubtless possessed, but could not use advantageously in a "lame duck" presidency, where some of the most sparkling of political luminaries just fade away. This, I emphasise, is not a dimming which is alien to some of the most deserving of cricket captains within the Test Match realm where they once appeared to be destined for greatness.

Whether President Obama attained greatness insofar as his handling of what his fellow Americans regard as the thuggery from barbarous brutes comprising the ISIS ranks is clearly a matter for the judgement of history. He was well on his way to setting the wheels in motion for just such judgement on 5th September, 2014. Amidst tabular transactions evocative of a bowling bluster at the Kennington Oval, the President offered foundations to a NATO coalition which would degrade and defeat ISIS. Only a few days earlier his vice President, Mr. Joe Biden, declared "they [ISIS] should know that we shall follow them to the gates of hell." Much is left to the cricketing imagination here, and those who remember Jim Laker's nineteen wicket haul in that Ashes-To-Ashes Dust-To-Dust 1956 Oval Test Match between Australia and England, might well wonder about the Biden statement.

Insofar as NATO unanimity is concerned, some of the principal players in the duel with ISIS were: Obama, Cameron, who can perhaps recite line by line Sir Henry Newbolt's poem, Kerry, Harper, Hagel, Hammond—no relation to the legendary Walter Reginald (England) or Geoff Hammond (Australia), who tore through the columns of a Kanhai led cluster one very humid afternoon from the North Road end at the Bourda Ground. The Bourda billiard table surface is fundamentally different to the rough and rugged terrain in Iraq and Syria, literally and figuratively. Sticky wickets the latter two have never been. Dangerous pastures they shall always be, especially to cultural outsiders whose imperialist impositions and lineage can never be erased. So, that Mesopotamia mess to which the Economist refers, that I think Colonel Bacevich, Boston University Professor Emeritus, would describe as part of the "residue of European colonialism," and in which the US under President Obama became mired, is without question, very much a product of naked British Empire ambitiousness—never mind the David Cameron claim about the British being a peaceful people.

Those who wish to challenge me are free to do so. While taking this route they should explore, also, the meticulous thousand page inquiry of Robert Fisk's, who warned America in 1990 about perils of treading upon ground in those dangerous pastures where the man with more degrees than a thermometer,[11] the very deliberative President Obama found himself in late summer 2014. It was there, hypothetically, "between a rock and a hard place," that he pondered options—not for Dr. King's non-violence, a position he praises so effusively, but choices for using deadly force daily and nightly. Deadly force is deadly force, regardless of whether it is used on the ground or from the air. Deadly force, I repeat, is deadly force, regardless of whether it emanates from what Secretary of State, John Kerry, describes as a heightened counter-terrorism effort geared to bending the arc of history in the right direction[12] and not a war. Such is a very far rallying cry in an Obama led administration from Dr. King's message.

Some measure of the distance can be gauged by looking at an analysis in the British daily, *The Guardian*, about a much awaited Obama prime time speech to fellow Americans on the eve of the thirteenth anniversary of the 11th September attacks (10th September, 2014). *The Guardian* assesses the speech as one filled with euphemisms, questionable claims, omissions, and caveats. While I am not pleading a case for the paper, I could not help noticing: (1) What Obama said: "And in two weeks, I will chair a meeting of the UN Security Council[13] to *further mobilise the international community.*" What it really means: Obama didn't commit to seeking a United Nations resolution to bless Iraq War III itself (2) What Obama said: "This strategy of taking out terrorists who threaten us, while supporting partners on the front lines, is one we have consistently and successfully pursued in Yemen and Somalia for years." What it really means: Very few people who are not part of the administration consider either of those cases a success. Less subjectively, neither has finished, years later, and it is unclear what success in Yemen and Somalia even is (3) "May God bless our troops, and may God bless the United States of America." And with those fourteen words, Obama inaugurated the Third Iraq War, after winning the presidency on a pledge to end the second.

Allow me to state immediately that when Dr. King sought God's blessing, he did so with the intent of advancing peace and justice. President Obama's speech is one in which he asks for God's blessing to advance the use of force. It never did escape me that this erudite legal scholar had given no hint that although he would be in the Chair's seat at the Security Council, he might well need the authority of the Security Council to do what America and NATO partners intended.

It is, therefore, by no means out of place for me to recall that when his predecessor, G.W. Bush, declared war on Iraq in 2003, he knew he had done so without Security Council authority. The UN Secretary General at the time, Mr. Kofi Anan, stated explicitly that the 2003 war was illegal. I also heard the eminent Canadian scholar, Dr. Gwynne Dyer, say very much the same thing. His compatriot, Monsieur. Jean Chretien, Canadian Prime Minister in 2003, and leader of another significant NATO partner, refused to back President Bush, because of no UN mandate. So, the Nobel Peace Prize recipient who had to have known about the illegality and lack of justice associated with the 2003 war and voted in Congress, also, against the use of violence, as well as injustice at the time, found himself appealing to the very Congress for authority and funding to use violence.

Just as significantly, in that speech to fellow Americans, the President was very explicit about <u>taking out and hunting down</u> America's terrorist enemies. I thought there were utterances in the speech that sounded as if they were made by President G.W. Bush or his Secretary of Defence, Mr. Donald Rumsfeld. <u>HUNTING DOWN</u>, Mr. President, is part of street language, the ungrammatical argot, right out of the gutter similar to what the evil slave masters did to capture their "runaway" slave "property."

It was President Obama who authorised hunting down, which led to the deaths on the Pakistan-Afghanistan border of an Italian citizen and three Americans in January 2015. It was not until late April that year when he stated publicly in an apology that the deaths of one of the Americans and the Italian citizen were accidental. It was early 2015, also, during which American men in California, North Carolina, Maryland, and Oklahoma were brutalised and killed by the hands and feet of police. The officer in Oklahoma who shot and killed his fellow American claimed he was reaching for his taser and used his gun with deadly force by accident. Although he apologised, he faced criminal charges. Given the unintended deaths in

January 2015, did President Obama have any ethical validity in denouncing the brutality and killing within the United States? The Obama speech on 10th September, 2014, in which he alluded to hunting down, was delivered shortly after the time of very assertive demonstrations in Ferguson, Missouri, over the police shooting of black teenager, Michael Brown, and almost simultaneously with the strident condemnation of football player Ray Rice's dehumanising treatment of his fiancée, later wife. All across the American audio-visual media came strident condemnation of the Rice conduct and police shooting. Notable black personalities, Reverends, Jesse Jackson, Al Sharpton, Congressman, Mr. John Lewis, and Attorney General, Mr. Eric Holder, among them, either travelled to Ferguson and, or, spoke there. What is equally significant is that President Obama had something to say about the Ferguson shooting and Ray Rice conduct.

All of them, Susan Rice, and President Obama himself, have benefited immeasurably from the incalculable sacrifices made by Dr. King. Was it not revulsive in 2014 to learn that these people had neither sought to remind themselves about standing on the lofts of ALL versions of violence nor have spoken openly against it, comprehensively in the name of Dr. King? On more than one occasion President Obama has called publicly for his fellow Americans to initiate conversations about what I term the fiction about RACE CLASSIFICATION and the ever present realistic dangers from RACISM. I wonder if it is necessary to state that no such conversation should be devoid of all forms of violence—including American violence perpetrated abroad and at home, where the so-called grid iron thrusts and tumbles, especially in the Sunday, Monday, and Thursday night versions of American televisised football matches, are received by raucous witnesses, most of whom are not outraged in knowing about chronic traumatic encephalopathy (C.T.E.) discovered many years ago by American coroner and medical researcher, Dr. Bennet Omalu, who had performed a post-mortem on the body of "IRON MIKE," Mr. Michael Webster, once a leading Pittsburgh NFL player.[14]

Is it not imperative also to state that such conversations should encompass the links among domestic violence today, brutally dehumanising European imperialist thrusts through Africa for slaves, and the continuation of just such brutality—if not more intense cruelty against the captured slaves and their descendants. Has it not been imperative also for you, Barack Hussein Obama, son of an African from the cradle of humanity, to name the Atlantic slave trade and its attendant plantation slavery, precursors to contemporary capitalism, genocide? Were you not offered just such an opportunity when you spoke, late September 2016, on the occasion to open the African-American Museum in Washington DC? I hope these questions serve as reminders, not merely about the Colin Kaepernick choices linked to giving the knee, but also moving well beyond the physical action to the core of oligopoly capitalist degradation.

The Atlantic slave trade to the West Indies and the seaboard colonies, the most cruel in the names of Church, State, and Flag in Britain, was in no way tangential to the implementation of British foreign policy superiority. That its impact is alive and well in America's tussle with ISIS, I harbour no doubts. I am firm in my view, also, that the Ferguson killing of teenager Mike Brown emanates from the cultures of violence during slavery and so does the Ray Rice conduct—albeit for different reasons. So, any conversation about race has to be an exchange in which slavery, violence, and the foreign imperative expansion of European ancestors linked to that violence and slavery are explored incisively.

Insofar as no efforts have been made by the President, some of the notables I identify, and those clutching Dr. King's legacy, I ask: are they affiliated with, or in the same religious institution as was Dr. King? If they are, are they sitting in the same pew, using the same song book, singing the same songs and praises as Dr. King? Are these people alien apostles craving a corrupt creed? History is the best judge here. Perhaps, some implications from President Obama's words can be used to aid an understanding of this history.

It is he who has asserted, boldly: "<u>America will always be America</u>." I want to juxtapose his directive for air strikes in Syria with a claim from Professor/Colonel Bacevich then make an observation. When asked about the bombing campaign on 13th September, 2014, Colonel/Professor Bacevich regarded it as "whack-a-mole,[15] frankly silly." He stated also, "our [American] efforts have fostered greater instability." Not quite one year later, Professor Bacevich emphasised his stance by stating: "History shows, pretty emphatically, history of the last thirty or forty years, that our efforts to police the Middle East haven't worked; and we talk about moral obligations. There is also a moral obligation, it seems to me, to take history seriously, to LEARN from one's mistakes, rather than simply to insist that if we try harder next time we will get a better outcome." I am certainly not implying that readers take one or other side, that of the President's or that of the Professor's.

It is, however, the President who was concluding his European visit for the 2015 G7 Summit who told the entire world his anti-ISIS campaign had not been well-crafted. Those with a keen eye for the figurative minutiae within international cricket might recall that I refer to Tony Cozier's claim in 2007, when the Cricket World Cup was staged in Brian Lara's backyard, about very few cricket captains having sussed out the leadership roles required of them: "they're very few international captains who have it all sussed out, as far as tactics are concerned." Both the cricketing and politically insightful with much more than keen eyes for history can wrestle with the question of the President's ability to suss out an effective anti-ISIS strategy. It is he and, perhaps, he alone who had to use the rest of his tenure to do what many observers say he is very good at doing, pondering profoundly implications from claims attributed to him: "The President said we should not do stupid shit... In a horrible bleak world, of this conflict, civil war in Syria that's not a bad motto. You know, you need to realise the limits of your ability."[16] May I add that to the extent that America will always be America, I am well aware that America was America when it made interventions with very disastrous consequences—even today—in: Cuba, Nicaragua, Panama, El Salvador, Viet Nam, Libya, Lebanon, Pakistan, Afghanistan, Grenada, Haiti, Philippines, Brazil, Bolivia, Chile, British Guiana, the Dominican Republic, Congo.

I suppose the President was showing the world that America will always be America when he stood in the General Assembly chamber and spoke assertively about the evils of extremism. I want to remind him that it was in America that Senator Barry Goldwater stood up and stated loudly and proudly: "<u>EXTREMISM IN THE DEFENCE OF LIBERTY IS NO VICE. MODERATION IN THE PURSUIT OF JUSTICE IS NO VIRTUE.</u>" The Goldwater claim was issued at the time he was challenging Lyndon Johnson in 1964 for the Presidency. Years after the Arizona Senator's passing notable American conservatives, among them vice President, Mr. Dan Quayle, stated that although Goldwater was roundly defeated by Mr. Johnson, he had lain the foundations for emergence of none other than Ronald Reagan.

It is President Reagan who let the world know that after the government of Nicaragua had secured an International Court verdict against the US for mining the harbours outside Managua, America would ignore, for two years, the Court's decisions. It was, of course, President elect Ronald Reagan, who declared that he would not negotiate with "barbarians" when questioned about holding talks with Iran in regard to the American hostages whom President Carter had tried to "rescue." This is the very President Reagan whose administration had become embroiled in what was described as the Iran-Contra Affair, a sordid tale, part of which involved representatives of the US government travelling to, and holding discussions with, Iranian officials.[17]

President Obama was, therefore, fully in order on 24th September, 2014, when he told his fellow world leaders: "Too often, we have failed to enforce international norms when it's inconvenient to do so. And we have not confronted forcefully enough the intolerance, sectarianism, and hopelessness that feeds violent extremism in too many parts of the globe." Dare I state that in quite different, but even more eloquently persuasive language and tone, Dr. King had delivered this very message to America. America—always being America—ignored him.

No one should assume I am suggesting President Obama was influenced by Senator Goldwater or President Reagan. I am making the point expressed by the Iranian government, which refused to cooperate, openly or explicitly, with the US over the ISIS threat on grounds that America's hands are dirty hands. Interestingly, one feature in the soiling of those palms can be seen in the work of President Kennedy, whom Mr. Obama quoted in the 24th September General Assembly address: "Of course, terrorism is not new." Speaking before this Assembly, President Kennedy put it well: "terrorism is not a new weapon," he said. "Throughout history it has been used by those who could not prevail, either by persuasion or example."

Is this not the same Kennedy who authorised the Bay Of Pigs invasion of Cuba, a plot conceived during the Eisenhower presidency? Is this not the same Kennedy who unleashed terror against the Cuban people in a disastrous effort to destroy the glory of the Cuban revolution? President Obama had the chance from his very first day in office to use Dr. King's ideas and begin removing the soil from America's dirty palms. Five years into his presidency, he stood in the General Assembly, where he confined the profundity in the core of Dr. King's legacy to the book end of a delivery in which he glossed the atrocity in the killing of Mike Brown within the racist terror reaches of Ferguson, Missouri.

Many who are better positioned can add to the list of societies where America was playing roles of America and a soiling on palms was taking place. If some of them are steeped in cricket, they may well understand a spectator pronouncement about West Indies quick bowler, Courtney Walsh, to telecaster, Ian Chappell, during the course of a one day match between Australia and the West Indies (Bourda Ground, 1991). In full Caribbean speak the spectator stated: "Walsh like a washa woman: he hangin outside di line steady." My equivalent statement in English is: Walsh is like a washer woman: he is hanging outside the line steadily. Expressed alternatively, a bowler who is repeatedly outside the line has few chances of attaining his objective, getting opposing batsmen out. Worse, he can, and does, concede vital runs in the form of wide deliveries to the other team.

Dare I state: Obama, Rice, Holder, Sharpton, and Co., like washa woman: deh hangin outside Dr. King line steady. In English, they were hanging outside Dr. King's line steadily and were way off course. President Obama, specifically, had very little chance of attaining his objectives. In what ways did he give very serious thought to: the bases upon which young citizens in Western democracies join their brethren in far off locations and are motivated to dislike and harm America and the rest of the capitalist heartland? Are there any peaceful measures his administration took to remove such bases?

Let me make my case somewhat differently. During the 1980s and early nineties America battled what was called Muslim Fundamentalism. Violence did not work. In the nineties, after a much vaunted victory against communism, America funded and abetted the violent battles against the Afghanistan government of Dr. Najibullah. Osama bin Laden and the Taliban were central to those battles. In the immediate aftermath of the 11th September events, events I stated elsewhere severed the soul and bruised the body politic of America, Osama bin Laden, Al Qaeda, and the Taliban became highly prominent foes to be fought with violence. Even before his second term had begun, President Obama claimed he had Al Qaeda and the Taliban on the run.

In late September 2014, however, after having let out a significant and highly suggestive sigh, he was telling Mr. Steve Kroft, a host of the acclaimed CBS television programme *SIXTY MINUTES*, his Intelligence Chief, Mr. James Clapper, had underestimated ISIS. This kind of talk from Mr. Obama should not be unfamiliar: He acted in similar fashion in the immediate aftermath of the unsuccessful effort from the "underwear" bomber to destroy an American aircraft. This is the same distancing conduct which I have shown characterised Brian Lara's leadership. Very importantly, in Mr. Obama's case, the reference to intelligence failure is not just an instance of analytic, rather than synthetic reasoning, it is an example also of rationalisation and explicit, rather than focal awareness. Just as relevant here is: in every case he and his predecessor Presidents have been beholden to violence. Like them, he has not stepped away from the line of violence. He was supposed to have given America a fresh start with his message about HUGE CHANGE.

History knows change and has not seen it from Mr. Obama's politicking. History, which is not alien to cricket, especially within the spotlight of leadership circles, knows change all too well. By now readers should be well aware that Brian Lara, West Indies Test Match captain, West Indies leader, specifically, was in a worse position than a washer woman hanging outside the line he so boldly asserted he was following. It is, partially, but significantly, to his locus outside that line that I make my final turn.

ENDNOTES

1 *Remarks from New York Times correspondent, Mr. Michael Gordon, to Mr. Charlie Rose, host of the PBS programme, CHARLIE ROSE, in August 2014.*

2 *In so far as this policy can be connected to Iraq- never mind the official US government line from Secretary McGurk, General David Petraeus, Mr. David Kilcullen, his ex-adviser on counter-terrorism, and correspondent, Gordon, speak in unison when they refer either to a vacuum left by the United States in Iraq or the mess it created in Iraq. Despite the Petraeus counsel to President Obama that he should not announce publicly the date of official US withdrawal from Iraq, the President nevertheless, did. According to the General, the architect of the Bush surge in Iraq, when he returned to Iraq-not as general Petraeus—but as CIA Director, he noticed the telling absence of US four star military presence in Iraq. Under President Obama the US had also downgraded its diplomatic footprint. In the eyes of correspondent, Gordon, the speedily dramatic ISIS move in Iraq was a*

surprise to the Obama administration, simply because no military advisers were left in Iraq as part of the act of withdrawal.

• *Here are the words of Kilcullen responding to a Charlie Rose query:*

C.R.: *Where is Iran and what is it doing as we speak—both in Iraq and in Syria?*

D.K.: *I think that the critical factor here is the relationship between the Iranian government and the new Iraqi government and I would just make the point that if we could succeed in destroying ISIS., but if we don't also break the nexus between the Iranian government and the Iraqi government, who are cooperating very closely under Maliki, the result of that—quote - success could be Iranian controlled territory all the way from western Afghanistan to the Golan heights and it would be very hard to spin that as a success in a strategic sense. So, I think that the Russians and the Iranians are in a very very strong strategic position now, largely because of the rise of ISIS. I actually don't see a US strategy. What I see is an immediate crisis response to the situation in Iraq that's largely driven by baggage related to our own conflict there between 2003 and 2011. That's one way to look at it as a successful conflict to the war in Iraq. I think the more important way to think about it is a geographical spillover of the civil war in Syria. And that's where our policy is really lacking coherence.*

• *When Charlie Rose posed a query about making US policy more coherent, Kilcullen replied: Well. I think it`s a matter of sequencing. I don`t think that we should back Assad against ISIS. We should deal with ISIS first and then we should think about what comes next with respect to Assad.*

3 *Another remarkable exchange between Brett McGurk and Charlie Rose is relevant, at this juncture:*

C.R.: *I read a story today and you MAY not want to comment on this but I hope you will in which Maliki was in—ah—some kind of signing of and agreement and was supposed to be signing with the President and—and moved his hand over the paper and did not sign it. And you were in the room and you went over to an aide and you said 'Do NOT screw around with the American President.'*

B.Mc.: *No. I was in the room when that happened and—ah I'll—I'll leave the—the anecdotes for—ah—somebody's books. But I was there when that happened.*

C.R.: *Ah—I assume—I assume—that's a confirming YES but I'll go to another question, finally. The President calls you into the Oval Office. Ah—you know more of the players than anybody around and they're people no longer in government like Petraeus and Ryan Crocker who know a lot of the players. But you in today's government with the experience you have had and the President says to you: TELL me what is the risk here for the United States and what is the threat to our national security. What do you tell him?*

B.Mc.: *Excellent question, Charlie and we have that conversation at the highest levels. What—what are US interests? Are our interests in ah—the territorial integrity of Iraq? Is that something that is fundamental to our interests and ah? The answer is NO. We're looking at-US interests and in IRAQ in particular a viTAL US interest at stake. If you look at OIL. You know—OIL—ah—particularly our strategy vis-a-vis Iran—to take a million barrels of oil off the international markets—Iranian oil off the markets. That had to be replaced somewhere and it was actually replaced with a million barrels of Iraqi oil that have—has gone on to the international markets—the increase from about 2009 until now. That is number one. Al QAEda—ISIS is Al Qaeda. It is a GLObal expansionist—global jihadist organisation. It is swollen with foreign fighters and suicide bombers. In Iraq in any given month there can be twenty, thirty, sometimes up to fifty suicide bombers a month. These are ALL—we assess foreign fighters who come into Syria to join the global jihad and they are directed to Iraq—ah—to KILL themselves and to commit mass murder. That funnel of suicide bombers—AH—you know—they don't say I'm going to go and do my jihad and—ahm—ahm—I'm gonna commit mass murder in Iraq. They will go wherever the organisation tells them to go. And that could be very easily capitals in the region. It could be capitals in Europe and God forbid, it could be here. So, Al Qaeda—and ahm—also—you know—the expansionist tendencies of IRAN—ahm—IRAN—ah—is definitely has a huge interest in Iraq. All you have to do is look at a map—and you can see why. But—we also have some mutual interests with the Iranians when it comes to Iraq and we have to be very mindful of that and pragmatic. Ah—but it—it affects our global—our own domestic economy and the global economy, given the need for Iraqi oil onto international markets, the threat of Al Qaeda to our—ah—friends in the region, to Europe, and, potentially, here and getting a handle on this very dangerous—ah—expansionist organisation of ISIS—ah—of course the expansion in some of the more nefarious tendencies of Iran. Everything comes to a head in IRAQ. If Iraq were to imPLODE—ah—into a real—ah—civil war or state of anarchy, the effects will not only be ah—the expansion—ah—of global jihadists—ah—Al Qaeda groups which which—can—threaten us but also REAL—ah—real—economic impact here on—on our own G.D.P. at home. So, for ALL of these reasons we have to be foCUSED on it. The PREsident IS focused on it ah- eh—from top to bottom in the US government. This has daily attention and—ah—you know as we speak when we leave here today [13th August, 2014], I'll be going for meetings about what to do in the North to try to—roll back—roll back some of the ISIS gains.*

4 *At one point, during the course of the PBS television programme, host, Mr. Charlie Rose, who was conversing with Mr. Dexter Filkins, analyst on Iraqi affairs, posed the question: "Where is the opposition to what the President is doing?" Dexter Filkins replied by stating: "I don't see it." Not too long after the programme airing, the President's former Secretary of State, Mrs. Hilary Clinton, presumed White House aspirant (2016) had a great deal to say while being interviewed by the Atlantic Magazine. Here is part of the great mouthful she delivered: Great nations need organising principles, and [quoting the President], "Don't do stupid stuff is not an organising principle. In assessing what she saw as the President attempting to communicate to Americans that he was not going to do something "crazy"over Iraq, she claimed he offered a political message, rather than the President's world view. Her reasoning behind the claim was presented in what I see as an oblique reference to his administrative judiciousness when she pointedly conveyed: "I've sat in too many rooms with the President. He's thoughtful, he's incredibly smart, and able to analyse a lot of different factors that are all moving at the same time. I think he is cautious, because he knows what he has inherited." Further, in her book, HARD CHOICES, about which she conversed with Charlie Rose well before the August 2014 mess, she writes about the President's decision not to arm the Syrian rebels: "Risks of both action and inaction were high. Both choices would bring unintended consequences. The President's inclination was to stay the present course and not take the significant further step of arming the rebels. No one likes to lose a debate including me. But this was the President's call and I respected his deliberations and decisions." I certainly do not miss the force of the implicature in the statement about losing a debate. What is not opaque is her view about failure: "The failure to build up a credible fighting force of the people who were the originators of the protest against Assad there were Islamists, there were secularists, there was everything in the middle—the failure to do that left a big vacuum which the jihadists have now filled."*

It is equally important for me to record part of an exchange Brett McGurk had with Charlie Rose (13th August, 2014).

C.R.: Do you have an opinion on the idea that if—in fact—that if there had been more support for Syrian rebels several years ago that ISIS would never be where it is today?

B.Mc.: Charlie, I know they're different views on that and I—just—ah—you know—leave it to historians to look at that. We're dealing right now with this situation we have and—ahm—as I said, it is—it is—in Iraq, in particular, trying to help the Iraqis control their sovereign territory. And that means harnessing the resources of the state, with federal security structures and the local populations being able to—ah—to protect their people—and make sure that ISIS can't come in and establish a governing zone of authority.

5 *Towards the end of his tenure, the same steadfast anti-communist who became a highly successful and often quoted American writer on US foreign policy was invited by none other than steadfast communist, Leonid Breshnev, Mr. Khrushchev's replacement, to visit the Soviet port of Vladivostok. To this day, Richard Nixon is the sole Western leader to have ever visited Vladivostok.*

6 It is, of course, William Shakespeare who describes Caesar:
> He doth bestride the narrow world
> Like a Colossus, and we petty men
> Walk under his huge legs and peep about
> To find ourselves dishonourable graves

While I do not miss the Shakespearean figurative significance, I will hasten to add that the brooding barbarians are worse than petty men totally unfit to walk even beside the shadows from the Colossus.

7 I do recall that when it had become very obvious to the rest of the world that there were no "weapons of mass destruction" in Iraq, and leading members of the G.W. Bush eleven were seeking to justify or find excuses for the 2003 invasion, the basketball term, "SLAM DUNK" came to be connected with George Tenet. I trust that my placement of President, G. W. Bush and his team within a cricketing ambit is, thus, not lost to readers. In staying within the cricketing world I add: it was Australian Test Match Captain, Ian Chappell, who stated assertively that his England opponent, Ian Botham, was no great cricketer. Chappell deemed Botham "a bully." Some very harsh Bush critics do not regard the President as a great President. While I cannot be sure that it was either Archbishop, Desmond Tutu, or President, Nelson Mandela, who described President Bush as a schoolyard bully, cricketing aficionados with a strong political bent may find some value in contrastive exploration of the claims I attribute to captain, Ian Chappell, and either the South African President or Archbishop.

I am aware, also, that Mr. Richard Clarke, former counter-terrorism expert in the White House, stated publicly that when he left the White House, on the night of the 11th September attack, he had the feeling—not unlike that in hockey games—that the other team had scored a winning goal. It is also Ms. Frances Townsend, another counter-terrorism expert, who spoke about an FBI decision in 1998 not to send agent, Mr. John O'Neil, to Kenya and Tanzania for the purpose of investigating the Al Qaeda bombing in those countries. Referring to the O'Neil absence, she states "It's the World Series and he's [Mr. O'Neil] gotten benched." Although he stated he does not like to use analogies from sport, President Clinton stated: "It's [the war/battle/fight against ISIS], an away game and we [Americans] need to back the home team."

How can I exclude Mr. Cofer Black's words to a Congressional Committee, when he spoke about OPERATION GREYSTONE, a Bush administration plan drawn up the very night of the attack for the purpose of waging a 'secret war'against terrorists.' Mr. Black, a senior CIA official, was one principal strategist behind OPERATION GREYSTONE, which was given the necessary legal mandate, as a result of a presidential FINDING. I offer his own words about the new ball game, kicking ass, getting past defences, as well as rocking and rolling, terminology quite familiar to followers of popular outdoor sports in the USA. In a foreground of official US anger and resolve Cofer Black declared to Committee members: "When I speak, I think the American people need to look into my face. And I wanna look the American people in the eye. My name is Cofer Black. This is a very highly classified area. All you need to know is that there was a beFORE 9/11 and there was an AFter 9/11. After 9/11 the GLOVES COME off."

In an interview, Mr. Black asserted: "This one [the 11th September 2001 attack] has finally got past ALL of our defences. We had plans that had been... developed in the past, that... had reached their due date with 9/11. Where everybody else [presumably, Defence Secretary Mr. Donald Rumsfeld and colleagues] was looking for their maps on Afghanistan, we were ready to ROCK. We were ready to ROLL. I mean we were waiting for the bureaucracy to catch up. NOW, basically in a nano-second we were going from where we were staked to the ground like a junk yard dog: you can report but you can't DO anything TO—do—authorities—the rules of engagement, lots of funding to supPORT this. This is a WHOLE NEW ball game. The action was planned to be classic CIA It was gonna be a multi-pronged thread attack where we worked with locals, minimise the American footprint. We like the survivors of 9/11 to know that those of us in the business... consider this the CIA's finest hour. We went into Afghanistan to KICK ass and we DID."

8 *The younger of the Khadr brothers, Omar, captured during the course of a firefight with US forces in Afghanistan when he was only fifteen, spent a long time imprisoned at Guantanamo, Cuba, as a terrorist accused of having killed a United States soldier. As a result of a very lengthy legal tussle involving his lawyers, lawyers for the US Government, and lawyers for the Canadian government, Mr. Khadr, who pleaded guilty in military court, was taken to Canada. There, he was committed to spend the rest of a prison sentence. On 24th April, 2015, his Canadian legal team convinced an Alberta Judge that Khadr posed no threat to the Canadian public and should be released on bail. His father, a confidant of Osama bin Laden's and terrorist accused by the United States, was killed in Pakistan.*

9 *Defence Secretary, Hagel, whose confirmation hearing was very rocky for the former Senator, and someone who was strongly supported by President Obama, during the course of that hearing, resigned from his post in late 2014. In the immediate aftermath, there was huge speculation and theorising about whether he departed as a result of fundamental policy differences with the President. A few months prior to the Hagel move, Eric Holder announced his resignation, a decision which gave major relief to conservative and neo-conservative thinkers.*

10 *A story in Washington news circles was: in an interview President Obama described the terrorists in Syria and Iraq as members of what some call a JV [Junior Varsity] team. He claimed that putting on the Los Angeles Lakers Basketball Jerseys do not make those who do so Kobe Bryant. I must say that claim is quite an imaginative stretch on the President's part. When asked by Chuck Todd of NBC about whether the JV remark was referable specifically to ISIS, the President emphasised to him that it was not. The person to whom he is supposed to have made the JV claim stated that for the President not to have confirmed that he had made a specific reference to ISIS was disingenuous. That person added, also, that the President's foreign policy performance was subpar. What Mr. Obama did admit of was that his continuation of summer golfing at around the time an American hostage was beheaded by ISIS made for bad optics to his fellow Americans.*

11 *The reference to more degrees than a thermometer are, of course, those of Mr. Bobby Rush, who used them while engaged in a successful political campaign against Mr. Obama in Chicago before Obama had become President.*

12 *The Kerry assertive uttered in regard to bending the arc of history, quite an exaggerated super stretch, was made when he journeyed to the Middle East shorty after the NATO summit in Wales. It is presidential candidate, Mr. Kerry, I recall, who once likened a President G.W. Bush's policy initiative to decision-making from Mr. Tony Soprano, patriarch in the popular American television series, THE SOPRANOS.*

13 *I have been keenly interested in UN affairs since I was eleven years old. I cannot recall, either from news reports or my own presence in the public gallery on First Avenue, a US President chairing Security Council meetings. From the time of the cold war" to the present. I have paid rapt attention to the debates involving ambassadors such as Fedorenko, Zorin, Stevenson, Bush, Moynihan, Young, and Kirkpatrick. I know of no occasion on which an American President travels to New York for the purpose of chairing a Security Council meeting. Taken together, perhaps just perhaps the 2014 Obama chamber presence and General Assembly talk are part of the legacy plan. I awaited, with great eagerness, the result of the Obama presence and looked forward to hearing about what Security Council Resolution emerged from the 2014 American presidential chairing. Much as I had thought, there was no resolution authorising the use of force over Syrian territory. There was a resolution unanimously adopted—against extremism and terrorism. None of this, however, could have been used to deal with the issue of an American military presence in Syria, which the U. S. Ambassador to the UN, Samantha Power, claimed is consistent, if not justified by Article 51 of the UN Charter: Nothing in the present Charter shall impair the inherent right of individual or collective self-defence if an armed attack occurs against a Member of the United Nations, until the Security Council has taken measures necessary to maintain international peace and security. Measures taken*

by Members in the exercise of this right of self-defence shall be immediately reported to the Security Council and shall not in any way affect the authority and responsibility of the Security Council under the present Charter to take at any time such action as it deems necessary in order to maintain or restore international peace and security.

14 How sad it is to know that Mr. Aaron Hernandez, once a leading player with the New England Patriots, convicted of murder charges, jailed with no possibility of freedom, committed suicide! Sometime after his horrible death behind bars it was revealed, via the televisual media, that he too had been a victim of C.T.E. Who care about just another casualty of oligopoly media capitalism!

15 In early November 2014, while reading the Canadian daily, THE GLOBE AND MAIL, I was quite surprised to have seen the very term used by Colonel Bacevich. The Newspaper Correspondent did not write in reference to the Iraq problem. His topic was the continuing debacle in Zimbabwe led by ninety year old, Mr. Robert Mugabe. According to the correspondent, Mr. Mugabe's former typing pool secretary/mistress later wife—Grace Mugabe, was employing whack-a-mole tactics against her husband's heiress apparent, Joice Mujuru. Politics, everywhere, I suppose, overflows with endless intrigue.

16 A remark made by a foreign policy expert, during the course of a telecast of the PBS programme, FRONTLINE.

17 Some of these matters were revealed during the course of the Iran-Contra hearings when Colonel North indicated, partially, his role in that affair. When questioned about the role of CIA Director, William Casey, President Reagan's former campaign manager, the Colonel refused to provide answers. He chose not to divulge any information. Subsequent to the hearing, when the Colonel was interviewed by BBC correspondent, Gavin Hewitt, in regard to his probable misleading of Mr. Terry Waite, the Archbishop of Canterbury's personal envoy, who assumed it was largely his negotiating efforts which led to release of American hostages held in Lebanon, the Colonel chose not to reply. In the view from one of the American officials who had travelled to Iran in secret, "Waite was duped." Quite significantly, when Admiral, John Poindexter, the President's National Security Director, appeared at the inquiry, he became even more well known for his remark about plausible deniability, apparently a move some observers interpreted as the Admiral's elegant preference to shield his Commander-in-Chief. Mr. Reagan did, of course, plead total ignorance about any arms to Iran for hostage release, a deft but illegal arrangement about which Waite knew nothing, at the time the scheme was being implemented. Many years later, shortly after Donald Trump had secured 2016 presidential success, North assumed the role of National Rifle Association [NRA] President. From the great heights of his new perch he and other members roared approvingly when Trump addressed them in 2019. Soon after North was, however, thumped from his perch amidst claims about a swirling sea of administrative mismanagement within the Association. It is this mismanagement which formed part of the core to a New York State examination of the Association, a matter over which the state legal authorities remained tight lipped.

Clyde Walcott

14th INNINGS
WELL OUTSIDE
THE LINE

In the immediate aftermath of the Indian Test Match victory against West Indies in 2006, Brian Lara stated publicly that he could reconsider his decision to lead the Caribbean side. The public presentation was strongly linked to his views about the pain he claimed existed during the course of not just the Test Match series, but also the one day competition. He even left keen observers steeped in their exploratory pursuits when he declared that he did have West Indies cricket at heart, but opted not to finish his statement about what would happen or what he would do if his reputation was being degraded. What can, however, be assessed as a major Lara change of orientation did not take long to materialise. With an eye to the summer of 2007, he identified a Test Match series in England that year as a principal motivational force.

While expressing a bold desire to play in what he termed the home of cricket, he noted the great significance of the cricketing competitiveness in which he had been engaged there. He took the additional step of erasing the pain to which he had referred, and identified a good period of cricket against India in which his team only lost the decisive fourth and final Test Match, but defeated the tourists [4-1] in the one day competition. Speaking as a leader obviously proud of his players he claimed were maturing, improving, and reciprocating the faith shown by West Indies selectors in them, he exuded optimism about their future.

Notably absent from his pronouncements, though, was any allusion to his doing the job of captain, after the 2007 World Cup. Captaincy against a foreground of 100% performance from all involved—including selectors, the public, and administrators—he emphasised was insignificant. His main interest after the impending big event in England was that of being integral to resurgence of West Indies cricket in the position of world leaders.

The interesting thing about the Lara turnaround is not simply that it took place, but also the task of traversing—if not, uncovering—grounds to the shift. Such a job may be too onerous with its heavy burdens of speculation. I opt to do something else. I want to be transparently fair to Lara, and hope that I can tread exploratory routes usually taken by leading diplomatic correspondents of major news organisations and make a strong case for the captain laying a solid basis to winning a "power struggle" identified by correspondent, Thornhill, against the West Indies Cricket Board. I begin by looking at the meaning in what seemed to be his future position as merely a brilliant world class Test Match batsman, after the 2007 World Cup.

Let me state that if Brian Lara, brilliant West Indies batsman in a successful Test Match team captained by someone else did well in the future, and continued to demonstrate unparalleled excellence at the crease, he would have become a huge winner. He would, doubtless, have been regarded as someone his team needed. If the same batsman as performed well found himself in a team failing to perform, he would have won massively, too. He would have stood out as unique or unusual among huge mediocrity. If he was in the position of a captain who batted excellently in a victorious team, he would have been able to claim credit for doing something towards fostering continuity of improvement and maturity which he had begun to develop.

If in the role of captain, he had batted well, but his team failed to perform, he could not have lost the power struggle. His batting prowess, a very attractive feature to throngs of adoring Caribbean admirers, would have served to insulate him from criticism. Whose authoritative discourse had been his biggest protector? From whom has that talk emanated? It has come from his most adoring admirer, Sir Garfield Sobers, the luminary whose words have given him the greatest insulation.

This is the very predecessor that said Brian Lara is the type of player people love to go and watch. These people should not be seen merely as belonging to the Anglo-Caribbean, they came also from Test Match playing countries that have been highly motivated to, and have been, defeating West Indies sides. Some of these persons were broadcasters, telecasters, and pandits of varied exploratory bent. Lara's stage has been far grander than the tiny Caribbean region. It was a world cricketing stage. Which West Indies Board and selectors would have been able to deny him a place in the team if he had done well with a bat?

My reply is none. I add: captain Lara's team did lose in the Tri-Nations competition and the Champions Trophy in a 2006 final to a domineering Australia he and his men had beaten convincingly in an earlier game. Though on the losing side, Lara did very well with the bat. Later in the year, West Indies played a one day series against Pakistan, won a single game, lost the Test Match series to their opponents from Asia without winning any game, but one of the memorable highlights of the Asian campaign was Lara's breath taking Test Match double hundred, a performance which elicited effusive praise from his opposite number, Inzamam-ul-Haq.

It was Pakistan where Brian Lara chose to state publicly that after the conclusion of the 2007 World Cup, he would stop playing the shorter version of the game. One of his explanations was that he wanted to concentrate on Test Match cricket. Was he looking to England in 2007 and beyond? Part of the answer came early in March that year, just before the start of the World Cup. At the time, Lara made a public announcement that he would continue to play Test Match cricket into his forties. Let me say that in the announcement, Lara used the elevated status of his captaincy to issue what is technically regarded as a declarative.

He knew, most certainly, that there were people of high status on the West Indies Cricket Board where officials can, and do, also issue declaratives. His own declarative, just from a field cricketing standpoint, might well not have been compatible with those from Board officials. Thus, not only do I think he was looking to England and beyond, he must have been fully aware that part of the significant work towards achieving his goal was waging that "power struggle" and, of course, winning it. Apart from having been aware of doing well at the crease, he knew that one way of gaining the advantage in his "power struggle" with the West Indies Board was appealing to a public whose members shower him with adulation.

More significantly, the West Indies Test Match captain, Brian Lara, with sights on England, in all likelihood, never bothered to find out whether those who followed Roman General, Fabius Maximus Verrucosus,, also known as the Cunctator, ever got close to, or on, any of the sites where England Test Match grounds are located. He might not even have tried to familiarise himself with the strategies of the military tactician and statesman. One thing is certain. The Lara leadership strategy was one of gradualism at its best, but only up to nineteenth April, 2007, the day he announced, publicly, that after the World Cup he would retire from all forms of international cricket.

The announcement, of course, meant that the world should not be paying attention to a highly enthusiastic Brian Lara brimming with boundless energy ready to be unleashed in blistering bat lashes within England and beyond. No one would, thus, have known whether he had trained his eye on breaking the 400 barrier in England. I have little doubt that those enthralled by his grandeur would have dearly loved to watch him help orchestrate part of a "blackwash" at the St. John's Wood location, where Tony Cozier claims his decisions in 2004 were associated with his team having been in a black hole twice.

What dramatic relief in liberation to behold at a place brimful of records, some of the most important of which have been set by West Indies titans!

It is a wonderful arena—the theatre, as such, for actors, really. I mean it is our grand stage to display your talent. And I think that if there is one place a cricketer would like to make a hundred of any sort, it would be at Lord's. It has that aura. It has a greatness about it. It excites people and I think I have been fortunate to have done well there. So, I have some great memories of Lord's.

The comments above were made to BBC World Service radio by Clive Lloyd, in 1988, the bicentenary of Lord's, the place where West Indies under the "disciplined calypso" won the very first Cricket World Cup (1975) and, against all odds, beat England, most convincingly, in a 1984 Test Match.

Such are the greatness, aura, and excitement of the Lord's location that I could not resist the captivating nature of four segments of radio commentary connected to that very World Cup and England West Indies Test Match duels (1950, 1963). When West Indies—through the admirable achievements of players such as Weekes, Worrell, Walcott, Ramadhin, and Valentine, "those little pals of mine," won a Test Match series against England in England for the very first time (1950), the touring side's victory in the second game at Lord's was, and is still, hailed as one of the most memorable of attainments at the crease for the Anglo-Caribbean region.

Through the eyes of an English commentator I offer an account of what took place just prior to, and after dismissal of, the last England second innings wicket: "Worrell bowls! And an almighty sweep. And he's out L.B.W. Wardle is L.B.W. He snatches a stump. And the players are running off the field. There're one or two West Indian characters running out on the field waving their hats as the West Indies players walk quietly off the field. Yes. There are several West Indian players running from the far end and they're going to escort their players off the field. The score is two hundred and seventy four—Goddard [West Indies captain] running in with his stumps being chased harum-scarum by lots of West Indian players. Such a sight never been seen before, at Lord's."[1]

On the last day of the 1963 encounter, in which West Indies skipper Frank Worrell, had fast bowlers Wes Hall and Charlie Griffith, produce very long quick bowling spells, I heard, against a background of loud cheering from eager spectators, BBC commentator, Alan Gibson, say: "So, it is a gripping hat trick. There are two balls to go. England needing two hundred and thirty four to win are two hundred and twenty eight for nine with Cowdrey—his left forearm in plaster—coming out to join Allen. And the crowd now swarming out of the stands coming up—the West Indians, particularly coming up eagerly right round the boundary ropes waiting to charge onto the field as soon as this dramatic and gripping Test Match has ended."

In 1984, against most English expectations, West Indies amassed three hundred and forty four runs in their second innings and romped to a hugely shattering nine wicket victory over England from whom opening batsman, Desmond Haynes's partner, Gordon Greenidge, exacted an unbeaten two hundred and fourteen. Hilary Gomes, the elegant left hander from Trinidad, batting at number three for West Indies, crafted a breath taking unbeaten ninety-two.

Which West Indies supporter unable to attend for the conclusion of the 1975 World Cup would not have been gripped by the boundless excitement of BBC radio commentator, Brian Johnston,'s description of events surrounding the last ball of the Australian innings at two hundred and seventy four for nine wickets, an Australian total that fell seventeen runs short of the victory target? Johnston began by observing the score and, rather solemnly, noted that the restless Lord's crowd, in standing position behind rings of focused police, was poised to surge onto the ground. Almost in an instant, the commentator began to describe the confrontation between West Indies fast bowler, Vanburn Holder, and fellow Australian quick bowler, Jeff Thomson, batting at the time.

A wild hit at the delivery from Holder brought the batsman no contact, no runs—only a position out of his precious ground. Deryck Murray, the West Indies wicketkeeper, keen to punish the hapless adventurer, gathered the ball, and threw it at the stumps, whereupon the uncontrollable commentator erupted, "He's out! Stumped! He IS out! Murray threw the ball down, I think!" No such drama unfolded at Lord's via the sight and voice in the commentary box many years earlier, when description awash with serenity to match an occasion of batting excellence was used for conveying the genius of Walter Reginald Hammond—blue silk handkerchief flowing gently from the reaches of his right trouser pocket—striding to a superbly crafted hundred. Hammond was obviously starting to revel in his batting, after an earlier dormant period, and launched into stroking some "typical fours," one of which, a cover drive, brought him to the century from a short ball pitched outside the off stump.

There was no "blackwash," no dramatic sight to behold, and no Brian Lara at Lord's in summer 2007 to invoke the spirit of predecessor play. The irony—if not paradox—about Lara is that if he had been using half the energy, intellectual insight, and presentation skill he applied in his turnabout, just over one year earlier, after the 2006 series against India, selectors, public, administrators, and cricketers might have been able to enjoy the resurgent ride—including historic Lord's—he so desperately craved well before his April 2007 decision to leave international cricket. I trust that my remark is not imponderable to a reflective Brian Lara. He is a member of a rather special class of Test Match captains who broke the 300 batting barrier: Walter Hammond, Graham Gooch, Garfield Sobers, Len Hutton, Donald Bradman, Bob Simpson.

Mere batsmanship in no way, however, meant that he had come close to their leadership achievements. In 1965, Sobers was the first ever West Indies captain to defeat Australia. At the age of forty, Bradman returned to England in 1948, ten years after 1938, to score two big Test Match hundreds in a five game series: [138: Trent Bridge, Nottingham] and [173: Headingley, Leeds]. His place was third in the Australian batting averages [72.57], behind opening batsmen, Arthur Morris [87.00] and Syd Barnes [82.25].

Captain Bradman imposed a heavy [4-0] defeat on Norman Yardley, his Yorkshire colleague, Len Hutton, and other England notables such as Alec Bedser, Cyril Washbrook, Denis Compton, as well as Bill Edrich. It was, however, the same Hutton who reclaimed the ashes from Australia, down under in the 1954-'55 series. It is, doubtless, true that Sobers in 1965 was ably supported by players such as Conrad Hunte, Rohan Kanhai, Basil Butcher, Joe Solomon, Jackie Hendricks, Lance Gibbs, Wes Hall, and Charlie Griffith. In the summer of 1948, Bradman got the backing of stalwarts like Syd Barnes, Arthur Morris, Lindsay Hasset, Keith Miller, Don Tallon, Ray Lindwall, Ian Johnston, and Neil Harvey.

When Hutton regained the ashes, he depended on the reliability of men such as Denis Compton, Trevor Bailey, Alec Bedser, Peter May, Colin Cowdrey, and that very destructive duo, Brian Statham and Frank Tyson. It was Frank Tyson who humiliated Australia with a blistering [7 for 27] from just twelve and a half overs in the crucial second innings of the third Test Match, at Melbourne, described by Swanton (1975) as a dog fight all the way. Several years later, I heard Bradman assess "the typhoon" as the fastest bowler he ever saw.

In that series, Tyson—just behind Appleyard in the England bowling averages—got 28 wickets at an average of [20.82] runs. What would thus have been very useful to Lara, had he prepared himself fully for the summer 2007 England challenge, was granting consideration to how leadership styles of the other skippers and their colleagues were linked to the energy, insight, and presentational skill they employed to motivate the Test Match cricketers on teams they steered to victory.

On the sceptr'd isle, he would have done himself no harm by focusing on achievements of Bradman, Hutton, and opening partner, Cyril Washbrook, whose cricket went way beyond perimeters of the field, well before the time of his birth. All of these men played memorable cricket in the spring and summer of 1948. My resource here is the work of Arlott (1948), who makes links among the craft of cricket, tact, selflessness, adaptability, and batting genius; in so doing, he points, very clearly, to what would have been valuable lessons for the ageing Lara.

I want to begin with Bradman. Arlott states that in 1948 Bradman played cricket, performed the role of captain, delivered speeches, extended courtesy to bores, evaded spite from those who carried grudges against him, maintained his equanimity, and solidified the greatness of a public reputation. Here is an account about a man who was definitely excellent in using his tact, shrewdness, and equanimity to do what has come to be known as versatile task performance. All of these, I must say, are qualities badly needed in West Indies Test Match captaincy, but sorely missed at that level. I add, very significantly, that for Arlott, the Bradman of 1948 whom watchers had not observed prior to that year was a cricketer expressing batting greatness. To those lookers in 1948 who had seen him at the crease between 1930 and 1938, he showed new greatness derived largely from exploratory thinking.

Both greatness and new greatness enabled him to score brilliant centuries which—even if he had stage managed them—could hardly have been more suitably attained. At forty, the maturing Bradman, not unlike John Berry Hobbs, abolished strokes of youth requiring intensity in speed of footwork and keenness of sight.

Because he was an older man, eighteen years older, than the Bradman of 1930, he was less hungry for records. He was concerned to make runs for his side, no doubt he found it pleasant still to make a century. He could still annihilate almost any bowling on a friendly wicket. But some of the old fierce single-mindedness which urged him to go on breaking record after record was gone. The quality of his single-mindedness had not weakened but the will to that particular single-mindedness was blunted by maturity and a wider consciousness, a different general aim (Arlott 1948, p. 304).

The age of forty was not, however, a barrier to Bradman stroke making beyond the possibilities of other cricketers in the world. He did start his batting with great uncertainty. He could, nevertheless, alter a perfectly immobile position at the crease to one of mercurial speed for attack. He was able to evade packed off-side fields by pulling deliveries with precision outside off-stump beyond the reach of wide mid-on. He did not lose the ability to beat mid-off unable to bend for the drive and moved with the grace of a swooping bird to hit via the covers. He could also play incredibly late in defence.

Here are some other Bradman features to which I think a well prepared and committed Lara could have attended. Bradman was much more than the person I term the Cootamundra conqueror. He was a champion who evaded flirtation with the fanciful. Importantly, he was also a genius among giants in a game where few, today, are immune to the pettiness of parochialism in its myriad forms. Between the years of his first and last tours to England, Donald Bradman was a superb example to teammates. Perry (2001, p. 416) observes that his central goal was retention of the Ashes, always a challenging task. His cricket ambitions took precedence above all else.

As a batsman and thinking captain he had no peer. It is no disrespect to his fellow players to suggest that in 1936-'37, 1938 and 1946-'47, Australia could have fielded its second eleven and still done as well. Given an ordinary side like that of 1938, when the bowling options were more limited than ever in Australia's history, or a young, good team as in 1946-'47, Bradman refused to cut the cloth accordingly. He always found creative ways to improve a side from ordinary to fair, or from good to very good (Perry 2001, p. 494).

Those with a keen eye on cricket history may wish to know that when Bradman and his team set foot in England during the spring of 1938, the team was regarded as the weakest to tour in the twentieth century thus far.

There was no Clarence Grimmet, the great leg spin bowler. Bradman and fellow selectors thought that at age forty-six he had passed his best. The core of experience came from Bradman himself, Stan McCabe, and 'Tiger' O'Reilly. They were ably assisted by Leslie Fleetwood-Smith, Benjamin Barnett, Charles Walker, Arthur Chipperfield, and William Brown. The newcomers were Lindsay Hasset, John Fingleton, Francis Ward, Sid Barnes, Clayvel Badcock, Ernest McCormick, the sole quick bowler, and all-rounders, Edward White and Mervyn Waite (Perry 2001, p. 416). Among the reputable England opponents the Australians had to face there were Bill Edrich, Les Ames, the promising Denis Compton, and Len Hutton, as well as the dangerous skipper, Wally Hammond, known all too well by Bradman. Australia did very well to retain the Ashes in 1938, but crucially, the Bradman batting leadership brought him an average of [108.50].

I observe that Arlott stated nothing in regard to craftsmanship and Bradman. When I look at the link he establishes between professionalism and craftsmanship of the analytically inseparable England openers, Cyril Washbrook and Len Hutton, I am fully convinced about those Brian Lara lessons which the West Indies captain should have connected to a leadership apprenticeship, the value of which was forfeited. Arlott observes that the growth of the professional game in England has been a history consisting of crises just as basic within cricket as the phases of English social history, itself, a reflection of cricket.

If Arlott is reasonable, then no reader can ignore the assertiveness in struggles—at times heroic—of the English working classes during the industrial revolution when a pernicious form of capitalism aided Britain's global socio-economic domination. Some of those struggles did bring triumph to the working classes. To the extent that professional cricketers, Hutton and Washbrook, emerged in Lancashire and Yorkshire, two principal cores of the revolution, and did not come from the upper class of old capitalism, but did convey the essence of craftsmanship as Test Match stalwarts, their success does have implications for Brian Lara, who came from one major theatre of British imperialist and racist exploitation to become a batting genius.

No one should ever get the impression from me about Brian Lara as a batting craftsman that had not served an apprenticeship at the crease. Captain Lara had not, by any means, been in a position of a craftsman who served his leadership apprenticeship. There would, however, have been useful lessons via the Hutton and Washbrook routes for leader, Lara, in England in the summer of 2007. In or out of the role of captain then, lessons would still not have been useless. It is thus to Arlott that I turn once more.

He points out: under the assumption that cricket as entertainment is not insolvent, English professional cricketers survived till 1948 as craftsmen because of two things. They are desire to engage in practising a craft which is the route to a romantic adventure and irreplaceability by machinery. I believe the importance of irreplaceability is best conceptualised by recognising the enduring and unchangeable qualities of humanness which transcend then replace absence of fluency in growing precision of automation.

Its additional significance lies in apprehending the inseparable connections between unfailing commitment to excellence and fervency of hope for success. No less important is the reference to romantic adventure, for it connotes triumph of will and spirit nurtured by insightfulness, passion, and steadfastness. Arlott goes on to state that two of the best exemplars of craftsmen cricketers in 1948 were Len Hutton, "all scholarly as he bent over his work," and Cyril Washbrook, "cap a-cock, patrolling the covers as threatening as he was jaunty," fully immersed in their cricket. Beyond the field, they preferred cricketing discourse to any other subject.

Within the field, they applied their craftsman skills for solving the difficulty of adjusting to the Australian opening attack. Their surmounting the challenge of Australian pace was vindication of English professional cricket. The Washbrook approach to bowling short of the very quickest was one of gathering runs a plenty between slips and cover. He flicked rising deliveries outside off-stump with elegance in his timing, drove imperiously, especially past mid-on, and hooked without mercy.

Hutton, like Australian all-rounder Keith Miller, and England batsman, Denis Compton, one of the most handsome stroke-makers of his time, was at his best accepting the challenge of spin against which his intensely deep knowledge about cricket was brought to bear. His clever footwork enabled him to be perfectly poised for playing close to the pads and in negotiating any delivery his head was absolutely over the line of the ball. His deflection skill employed late against turners was sheer mastery. He was imaginative to spin, thereby displaying perfection in dealing with the spin-sensitive stroke.

Regardless of the merits in my disposition about plumbing depths of Brian Lara's Test Match cricketing captaincy against England (summer 2007), which many adoring admirers would have dearly loved to experience while he stood and performed on his batting stage with a commanding persona, they must deal with a daunting reality. It is twenty-first century management of a demoralised West Indies band which replaced a fearsome and highly respected unit guided by leadership talent cherished and envied for using sporting transcendence to re-position every boundary of cricketing excellence.

Ramnaresh Sarwan, the man who was first designated West Indies Test Match captain in place of Lara, after the 2007 World Cup in the Caribbean, did not have an easy job. He lost his very first series to England, in summer 2007. During the course of that very series, he sustained a painful injury which prevented him from taking up his position against South Africa for the 2007-2008 Test Matches. West Indies—albeit narrowly—were beaten yet again by South Africa, and some Caribbean cricketing experts began to do far more than whisper about the excellent motivational capability of his leadership successor, Chris Gayle.

Quite apart from field matters, the captain, Chris Gayle, had to contend with factors well beyond playing area perimeters. I begin closure to my work by considering some of those very factors.

Writing in the July 1993 edition of the now defunct monthly regional publication CARIBBEAN CONTACT about CARICOM, West Indian academic, Dr. Ikael Tafari, observed that regional politics was not a healthy practice, political parties had been devising manifestoes but failing miserably to translate their most progressive ideals in these documents to programmes of genuine development. Consequently, isolation of parliaments and politicians had been growing, and there had been a marked trend for parties to be victorious at national elections with significantly reduced sections of the voter population. Let me add that the Tafari assessment is applicable today. Keen observers should not, therefore, miss the opportunity to recognise that the troughs into which West Indies Test Match cricket reclines currently parallels the definite disarray which now bedevils regional socio-economic life.

Apart from politics, Dr. Tafari had his eye firmly planted on what he termed lessons for politics to be learnt from West Indies superlative performance in world cricket at the time. My point here is that regional Caribbean political arrangements, which could have been well served by lessons from unsurpassed excellence in West Indies Test Match cricket prior to 1995, cannot be so served currently. Education, politics, economics, as well as cricket, do not currently serve interests of West Indies people satisfactorily. I must stress this point, for in writing about politics and economics, Williams (1942, pp. 104-105) emphasises political Federation of territories as one of the paths to Caribbean statesmanship. From an economic standpoint, Federation would provide strength to bargain on the world market. Further, viable Caribbean economic structure—of necessity—dependent on diversification, rested upon a federation of democratic government.

A significant part of the Williams justification for Federation lay in an understanding that Caribbean territories have a common heritage in slavery, a common labour base. They have all been oppressed by an identical curse, sugar, and careful attention ought to be granted to fundamental identities, rather than incidental differences. For Williams, the alternative to Federation was economic collapse.

Williams, no doubt, espoused Federation most passionately, I think, largely because of his great aversion to imperialism. His dream, however, seems to have evaporated.

Imagine nineteen scattered units, each with its own complicated governmental structure, customs service, medical system, police, etc., run at enormous expense. No one need argue today the value of one single expert agricultural service for all the islands. It is not the sea which has stood in the way of Federation, but the opposition of local potentates, big bosses over small areas (Williams 1942, p. 103).

Having moved from imagination to reality, I am well aware that West Indies Test Match cricket is being administered in a region where separation still exists, potentates still dominate, and I wonder how close the region is either to economic collapse or ruin.

Further, it is well known that independent countries operate with the Westminster parliamentary model and are incapable of using the diverse experiences of the poor who suffered under imperialism as a basis to identifying: the groundwork for societal and regional progress in educational and economic contexts. Anyone who has doubts about this claim of inability needs to examine the views of Mr. Michael Manley, aired in a conversation to which I shall refer later. Manley, who always thought that socialism was about using social action to create social justice, asserted: a politician who succumbs to a largely theoretical view of political process insufficiently grounded in understanding of his/her own culture can make tremendous errors. While reflecting on his major Prime Ministerial missteps during the course of the 1970s in Jamaica, he also observes what he had erroneously done as theoretical conceptualising.

Regardless of whether an observer agrees with Mr. Manley, it is a fact that ranks of the economically and politically dominant within the West Indies have not been filled by members of the Caribbean masses. The economically powerful were once selected from absentee minority European and American groups, whose members meticulously preserved the interests of overseas capitalists. In so doing, these very capitalists secured active cooperation of local European, African, Indian, and mulatto bourgeoisie sources usually proud of their socio-economic dominance over non-whites.

Those non-European locals who played and continue to play roles of the politically and economically dominant pose no threats to international capitalist control. Their administrative activities are accommodating of all the appropriate conditions which protect and promote economic operations of global cities[2] and globalisation, in New York, Washington DC, and London, integral sectors of what the late, Julius Nyerere, of Tanzania once assessed as "the heartland of capitalism." More importantly, locals are at the mercy of aid and rescue programmes whose terms of application are generally[3] determined by political, economic, and military elites operative in Western governments, oligopolies, as well as agencies such as the International Monetary Fund. This last, I insist, is not an organisation instituted for the purpose of rendering assistance to developing societies.

How could I avoid reference to the excruciatingly devastating consequences for the Caribbean of the world-wide economic crash that allegedly began within the housing sector of the USA? In a foreground of technical discourse from Western financiers, politicians, and economists, such as Henry Paulson, United States Treasury Secretary to President, G.W. Bush; Timothy Geithner, once New York City Financial Regulator, then US Treasury Secretary to President Obama; and Ben Bernanke, Federal Reserve Board Chair to Presidents, Bush and Obama, about toxic assets, dubious financial instruments such as "over-the counter-derivatives," moral hazard, systemic risk, as well as ordinary talk about financial meltdown, trillion dollar debt, bankruptcy, and bailout, everyday life in the Anglo-Caribbean for the working poor has become nightmarishly miserable. The foundation for this figuratively earth-shattering catastrophe is, to my mind, deeply embedded within the bedrock of inherent contradictions of capitalistic practices (Yunus 2017), which powerful people such as Mr. Paulson, who served Goldman Sachs, then G.W. Bush as Treasury Secretary, once touted with brazen pride.

Let me offer one instance of brazenness. It took place on 13th August, 2002, in Waco Texas, against a foreground of stock market volatility, uncertainty and confusion about corporate integrity, as well as weak consumer demand, especially within the airline industry. It was against this troubling foreground that President, G.W. Bush presided over an "economic forum," some of whose principal participants were chief executive officers of large American corporations. Among the important things Mr. Bush told the gathering were: (a) he expressed confidence in the US economy (b) he identified a main purpose of the participants as providing a report on "the front lines of the [American] economy" of which he was "incredibly optimistic." President Bush added that he wanted to encourage an "ownership economy."

Mr. Bush's remarks preceded those of his Commerce Secretary, Donald Evans, who saw the American economy as fundamentally strong. The Secretary also characterised capitalism as a system which is the hope for the world, a planet of more than six billion, the vast majority of whom earn less than $2 (US) per day. He viewed chief executive officers as some of the stewards of capitalism. I wonder if Mr. Evans ever foresaw the days in 2008 when Mr. Paulson, a staunchly committed capitalist, summoned chief executive officers of the American banking system to New York or Washington, and twisted their arms to accept what more than a few American observers have assessed as "socialism," US government takeover of commanding heights of the American banking sector.

Mr. Paulson's basic premise was that government control was essential to preventing destruction of the American economy. This dramatic turn of events took place early in 2008, under the watchful eyes of Professor Ben Bernanke, the Princeton intellectual turned Chairman of the U. S. Federal Reserve Board, and of course, President Bush, who had refused to acknowledge that the economy of his country was in free fall. When Senator Barack Obama, also a committed capitalist, acceded to the presidency, his government spent billions to rescue dying auto titans, Chrysler and General Motors. So much for the freedom of markets to which the United States is wedded and hope for the poor in underdeveloped societies such as those in the West Indies.

I am, of course, expressing my position in a manner I see fit. Those who do not wish to traverse the courses I have outlined can, however, consider just one facet of the burden to which I am alluding. I ask that that they consider a stance adopted in 1989 by notable British intellectual and broadcaster, Geoffrey Stern.

Prior to the conversation, one aired on the BBC World Service, with Mr. Manley, admittedly an uncompromising socialist, full of "idealistic purpose," and a political leader employing a social activist interpretation of Christianity, Stern prefaced his interview with remarks:

Since the end of the Second World War, the number of states has more than trebled.
But many of the newly independent countries have been unable to attain economic,

as well as political freedom. Often, they are at the mercy of adverse trends in the world economy and when their leaders try to wrest greater national control, as did Jamaica's Michael Manley, in the nineteen-seventies, they find the cards heavily stacked against them. In Jamaica's case, the attempt at national self-assertion was to upset Washington and the international corporations. And their active hostility compounded a national economic crisis bringing violent strife and, for Manley, a humiliating electoral defeat.

Which leader of the Anglo-Caribbean at the beginning of the second decade of the twenty-first century, a turbulent time of that nightmare for the masses within the region, had been offering servings of national self-assertion? Who among them dared upset Washington and the international corporations?

In 2009, for instance, both the Commonwealth and Organisation of American States [OAS] summits were held in oil and natural gas rich Trinidad. President Barack Obama, a staunch believer in that sham of free market corporate capitalism and globalisation, was on the Caribbean island for the OAS meeting. So were heads of Latin American and independent West Indies territories. While the heads of state were all charging and raising glasses and silverware at the Hilton, millions of their compatriots could only dream about the fringes of socio-economic comfort.

Further, when I refer to globalisation, I use the term to convey the meaning signified by views of Winant (2004, p. 131) and Fairclough (2001, p. 205). Fairclough sees globalisation, to which unfettered free trade is central, as primarily an economic practice infused with neo-liberal principles. Free trade, the concept, means the unimpeded movement of goods, finance, and people on an international scale. In reality, it operates as modification in links between market mechanisms and states geared to loosening state regulation, thus emasculating the ability of states to offer social welfare and changing their roles to those of advocates and agents of free markets.

Those who tout globalisation, which I note is driven principally by American and European transnational companies, claim that it is a major creator of wealth from which everyone shall benefit. Those who are not in favour argue that loosening of state administration serves to widen the gulf between rich and poor domestically, as well as internationally, and contributes to tremendous environmental destruction (Fairclough 2001, p. 204).

I am certainly opposed. I, therefore, agree with Winant, who views globalisation as a version of imperialism which re-racialises the world in which international socio-economic stratification is shaped by transnational companies and national governments in the affluent North to the great disadvantage of the impoverished South. Some of the leading mechanisms behind the difference emanate from actions of transnational corporations and the IMF, the very international organisation I have named above. Winant notes that imperialism was supposed to end in the decades subsequent to the Second World War. He asks whether the age of empire has been replaced. His reply is negative: socio-economic discrepancies between the world's wealthy white of the North and the Southern poor dark skinned are unmistakably racial.

Transnational activity is strongly exemplified within a poor Anglo-Caribbean region of dark skinned people from separate territories whose governments have been unable to integrate socio-economically. Activity takes place mainly via workings of corporate America in a worldwide foreground of ever increasing diversity of cultural formations. Significantly, the leaders of corporate America have successfully staked out spectra of consumer indulgence in commodity estheticisation. My reference points for the foregoing claim about the esthetic can be located in ideas from Schneider (1975, pp. 214-215). His position is that tendencies toward the esthetic packaging of commodities is a necessary consequence of incompatibility between exchange value and use value. On the one hand, commodities have real value to consumers. On the other hand, sellers view commodities as means towards accomplishing exchange value in the form of money. To sellers, use value is bait.

From a cricketing standpoint, the Schneider stance is echoed, strongly, in remarks by Tony Cozier, who pointed to some obvious indications of American prevalence within an economically sluggish Caribbean around the mid 1990s. In the summer of 1996, Cozier made this claim to BBC World Service Radio:

> *There is a great deal of interest in American basketball... on television sets and also through things like clothing—fashion—so that the Chicago Bulls you see on—Denver Nuggets—you see on the shirts of people in the Caribbean who don't even know what they're wearing. Cricket does not promote itself in that way and, really, has only just started to do so.*

Was Cozier telling the world about trade routes along which Caribbean citizens have been racing to position perils that serve as platforms of their ruin? I am sure readers have their own responses. Mine is emphatically in the affirmative.

I must add that 1996, the year of the correspondent's observation, was part of a juncture at which the globalisation imperative had begun to gain great momentum. That was a time when efforts were being made to form huge free trade blocks, from which flow today many of the very consumerables and services in the forms of televisual entertainment pivotal to fetishisation of free market fundamentalism (West, 2004), a matter to which I shall give attention along with depuertoricanisation, as well as what some describe as McDonaldisation.

Only one year earlier, 1995, an animated Michael Holding [M. H.] had an exchange with Curtly Ambrose [C.A.], in which the former West Indies express bowler insisted on the negativity of televisual entertainment via the vehicle of "Americanisation," about which he had made an assertion to former England captain and cricket telecaster, Tony Lewis [T. L.], when England toured the West Indies (1990). This is, of course, the very Holding whom former frontline West Indies Test Match batsman, Alvin Kallicharran, [A.K.], told me in 1992 spoke with him about Americanisation. I shall offer readers information from conversations during all three years.

I start with 1990 and the Holding-Lewis conversation in the Caribbean.

> **T. L.:** *Great American influence on the sport out here, we read, these days. Great threat of cricket being in decline as softball becomes very big and television—you can see American basketball and baseball. One or two people feel that cricket gets too expensive and exposed to these American sports, the game might decline here.*

> **M. H.:** *The Americanisation of the West Indies. That's what taking place.*

Holding would, of course, not—in any way—be surprised to learn about versions of thinking that parallel his own about Americanisation. More than five decades earlier, Concepcion [1943/2004, p. 49] issued some dire commentary about Puerto Rico. These are remarks that are clearly applicable to the Anglo-Caribbean.

Concepcion's position is that Americanisation would, unavoidably, signify what he terms depuertoricanisation, the sad presence of gradual disintegration and a sentencing of Puerto Ricans to barren adaptation. Further, the creative energy of islanders would be damaged, their culture corrupted, their collective soul would fail to reach maturity of expression, they would experience emptiness while drifting without an apprehension of their history and ties to their destiny.

Those who follow Concepcion's lead would not be surprised to learn about what Bhattacharyya, Gabriel, and Small (2002, p. 154) assess as McDonaldisation, the dominance of Western cultures—particularly U. S. culture—its harmful consequences on local cultures, its advancement of capitalist consumerist values, and its contribution to ways in which global culture revolves around the primacy of US norms, rather than advancement of respect for diversity. The idea of McDonaldisation is not inconsistent with what Jacoby (1999, 2002) endorses as the truth and attractiveness of diversity. Jacoby is—among other insights—criticising one of several calls from President G.W. Bush for consumer indulgence in shopping, action that can be identified with the fetish of pluralism which undermines a serious interrogation of reality through its flirtation with cultural homogenisation.

I submit that this type of indulgence intersects with what West describes as one of the anti-democratic dogmas, free market fundamentalism, from which emanates ideas of fetishising and idolising unregulated and unfettered markets. Such ideas serve to designify focus on public interest, but glamorise materialistic gain, narcissistic pleasure and pursuit—particularly by youths—of individualistic preoccupations. Recall my earlier reference to use of hand held electronic gadgetry in the Anglo-Caribbean, use which I have stated serves to replace valuable unmediated and intense socio-linguistic interaction about Test Match cricket.

The fundamentalism of the market puts a premium on the activities of buying and selling, consuming and taking, promoting and advertising, and devalues community, compassionate charity, and improvement of the general quality of life (West 2004, p. 5).

There is no doubt in my mind that West, Concepcion, Jacoby, as well as Bhattacharyya et al., are laying blame at the feet of the US. According to Williams (1942, p. 109), the USA is obliged to accept responsibility for a region, the West Indies, to whose protection it committed itself and for whose woes it is partly to blame. The alternative is the twin burden of Yankee imperialism and the Almighty dollar.

I am under no illusion that Yankee imperialism has ruined the Anglo-Caribbean, and the massive greenback is a rather powerful vehicle of cultural doom within the region. More importantly, Williams was warning of what he had accepted in the expert words of another intellectual as the real "yankee peril," the act of Americanising the Western hemisphere. This was the danger that West Indians might take prosperity American-style and abandon posterity constituted by labouring hordes making sugar to be poured in coffee cups of the Temperate Zone.

Today, the Williams assessment reverberates and carries with it a pungent aroma far beyond significance of coffee cups and sugar in a region he describes as governed by and for sugar forming part of many ailments in a Pandora Box of foreign domination. Commodity production—industrial and agricultural—is still controlled by Western capitalists. The very valuable Caribbean tourist industry is—I add—virtually in the hands of foreigners, who extract millions of almighty dollars, annually, from the islands and help to impose cultural forms alien to Caribbean cultures. This is the very tourist industry responsible, via layoffs, for economic hardship in the region during one of the harshest periods of economic meltdown that became publicly transparent in 2008, when Lehmann Bros., American International Group [AIG], and Merrill Lynch were clearly on economic precipices.

More than thirty years after Williams has passed on, other claims of his are so powerfully relevant that it would not be easy to reject them, given socio-economic developments in the Anglo-Caribbean of the twenty-first century. He notes that the fate of the West Indies are intertwined with the fate of the global market. The region, he adds, has paid expensively for its monoculture and industrial backwardness, alternating among prosperity, misery, and bankruptcy. The way out is not simply diversification in production which brings independence of food importation, it is also what he terms, rational economic organisation in a world where commodities are produced within locations where they are most appropriate and where nature will not be "flouted by man's ersatz and sacrificed to political considerations of autarchy." (Williams,1942, p. 106).

He contends that until such conditions are met, the strategic situation of the West Indies will demand economic movement in the direction of the West. Anyone who doubts the scale of such movement should pay attention to American televisual presentation of sporting events, such as soccer, The Africa Cup of Nations, COPA America, Women's World Cup, NBA championship basketball, and the cricket World Cup during the spring and summer of 2019, as well as advertising artefacts to the Anglo-Caribbean.

Basketball was very much a feature of this 1995 Michael Holding [M. H.] Curtly Ambrose [C.A.] discourse:

M. H.: *There is a lot of talk around the entire Caribbean about effects of the same thing you were watching—American basketball—is having on our youngsters—pulling them away from cricket. How do you view THAT?*

C. A.: *I'm not so sure. With the cable TV, we get a lot of live programmes from America. I still think that cricket is our number one sport. It doesn't matter what people are gonna say. Cricket, you know, is still our number one sport and it is the only thing in the Caribbean that we favour.*

M. H.: *But don't you think the Board needs to do something more than what they are doing now to make sure that the youngsters ARE attracted to the game, because as you have said, they have seen these stars earning too much money in America? Don't you think the Board can do something to—sort of—atTRACT the youngsters BACK to CRIcket?*

C. A.: *Yeah. I honestly believe so—try and develop youth cricket, a bit more, try and get as many youths as possible in cricket involved. I don't think there is enough, REALly, to market our cricket and stuff like that. I mean there is a lot of talent around here but they need someone to guide them. You know, in the Caribbean, kids need someone to push them forward. They are not going to do it on their own. They need help but I think the Board should do a lot .*

What I find most analytically interesting about the foregoing exchange is the Holding conversational ploy, a formulation beginning with "But don't you think the

<u>Board needs to do something?</u>" While I cannot be certain about whether Holding secured confirmation from former Test Match teammate, Alvin Kallicharran, in regard to Americanisation, I do know that, according to Kallicharran, the duo exchanged ideas pertinent to this very matter.

When I told the assertive West Indies left hander in 1992 about the 1990 Holding assertion to fellow telecaster Tony Lewis, and asked him if Americanisation was affecting Caribbean cricket, he told me:

> *Yes. Michael and I have spoken along that line before and there is a definite truth in that. You find parents migrating to different parts of the western world and kids are being born there. So, they pick up different sports. And apart from that, places like Jamaica are very close to America. They have American television programmes. Kids see the games... They pick up the games, because the future looks rosy, financially.*

Readers should be aware, also, that when the West Indies were losing to the men down under (1996), its manager/coach, Clive Lloyd, gave a radio interview to the Australian Broadcasting Corporation [ABC]. Lloyd did acknowledge that cricket was still significant to the Anglo-Caribbean. Youthful West Indians, he however conceded, were being drawn to activities such as track and field events, and he saw no reasons they should be criticised for expressing such interests. I dare say that in view of expressing such ideas, his high profile presence in West Indies cricket would have demanded some extremely delicate balancing.

He should, therefore, know that other observers have identified the very platforms of ruin to which I alluded above, platforms that seem to be partial but substantial foundations to contemporary Caribbean Test Match cricketing problems. One of those observers is Mr. Michael Manley [M. M.], who also had this exchange in his discourse with Geoffrey Stern [G.S.]:

> **G. S.:** *What are the special problems that a Jamaican Prime Minister has?*
>
> **M. M.:** *Well. He has the enormous problem of the highest per capita debt in the world. Let's start with that. We're paying fifty one-cents out of everything we earn to service debt. So, we're running a forty-nine cents country. You ought to try that some time. It's quite a trick. So, we start with that problem. And there are all sorts of other interesting problems in our part of the world. You know one of the things you have to wrestle with is the treMENdous effect of the cultural penetration of the canned TV show with the Dallas and the Falconcrest which—all the time—in some way it's positive, perhaps—but promote an idea of what the society can achieve that has no relationship to your economic realities and so on and so forth and tends—I think—to divert people from a concern with savings and investment and sacrifice to make the economy grow. So I think you have serious social-psychological problems of that sort. But you have to wrestle with them.*

Mr. Manley's figurative reference to a trick does deserve some exploratory attention in the twenty-first century. Let me state that in the foreground of the massive financial meltdown, the United States national debt ran into trillions of dollars. Although it continued to borrow on a huge scale, its economic predicament was, in no way, parallel to some of the Caribbean territories such as Jamaica or Guyana. The West Indies societies have never had access to the same types of creditors as the US. Further, their terms of borrowing have never, by any means, been so favourable as those extended to the US.

In 2002, more than a decade after the Manley conversation had taken place, the Caribbean News Agency [CANA] announced that it would cease operations because of financial trouble. Tony Cozier's own publication, *Red Stripe Cricket Quarterly*, was also no longer going to be published because of insufficient advertisers. Whenever Test Match cricket is being played in the Caribbean, one sees and hears about television coverage from Rupert Murdoch's Sky Television, part of a massive media organisation News Corp, and Trans World International [TWI]. The second is a subsidiary of the worldwide North American owned International Management Group [IMG]. In 2002, there was no Caribbean film industry from which the glorious history of West Indies Test Match cricket can be presented. Since 1988, though, Jamaica, where there was never a semblance of freezing rain, sleet, or snow, has been participating in the Winter Olympic Games. A very popular film, *Cool Runnings*, about the island's first presence in the winter competition has been made by the North American film industry. Which films for worldwide distribution have been made by a Caribbean film industry in the Caribbean about the grand accomplishments of excellent West Indies Test Match cricketers?

There is no doubt in my mind that a critical reference was made to Americanisation in a *Stabroek News* report of seventeenth January1996. Caribbean media experts were quoted as having "knocked" regional providers for the "one way flow" of communication signals into the region from the United States. Carl Moore, Chairperson, Barbados Broadcasting Authority, one of the experts at the time, stated that the Caribbean was sitting on its laurels while information had been flowing in from the USA. Moore added that no situation where there was a one way flow of information could be a good one. Recipients have something to say, as well.

Further, Aggrey Brown, Director of the Caribbean Institute of Mass Communications, issued a strong criticism of regional TV providers for heavy reliance on overseas programming:

> It is obvious if you have an opportunity to get material transmitted around the region and globally on a daily basis and when you don't take advantage of that you have nothing to say.

Brown and Moore expressed their positions to the Caribbean News Agency [CANA], in view of concerns from local providers about the proposed impact at the time of Direct TV [Digital Telecasting by Satellite from the USA] on Caribbean households. Direct television is well established in the Caribbean today. Brown and Moore were concerned that Caribbean subscribers would have access to nearly 200 television channels, films, pay per view programming, and other entertainment specials via the Hughes Galaxy 111-R satellite launched in Florida.

At the beginning of the 1980s, well before Brown and Moore had made their remarks, the United States was hard at work ensuring that it lay the groundwork for dominance over the spread of information, internationally Given the proximity of the Caribbean to mighty America, expressing great concern about the spread of communism in the Western hemisphere, it comes as no surprise to me when I look at an assessment from the notable American historian, Franklin (2005) about his view of American preparation for the twenty-first general conference of UNESCO convened in socialist, Yugoslavia, during the autumn of 1980.

While writing about the US State Department briefing for the gathering in Washington and Belgrade, he is clear about his observation that the principal American issue was control over information dissemination within other societies, especially the third world and Soviet bloc. Information control was pivotal to influencing political developments, as well as manipulating scientific and cultural knowledge. Franklin adds that the Belgrade discourse centred on The New World Information Order, which Irish foreign Minister, Sean McBride,[4] and colleagues saw as correcting a perceived imbalance in communication and information resources favouring industrialised societies. According to Franklin, the official stance of the US to the New Information Order was a sense of wariness of any suggestions that appeared to put communication and information beyond its reach.

Of course, I do not forget that as part of their mean-spirited reaction to the New Information Order, governments of Prime Minister, Margaret Thatcher, and President Ronald Reagan, ceased to make financial contributions to UNESCO, and withdrew from the organisation in 1983 as well. Is there any coincidence between that American reaction and the illegal occupancy by that country of Grenada led by Maurice Bishop? You may not find an answer immediately. If you need some guidance, it would not be unhelpful if you turned to this assessment about the actual UNESCO Belgrade conference:

> I could not resist the thought that, perhaps, as the countries of the world evolved, becoming more modern and sophisticated, the United States still persisted in the notion that it could take them lightly, as though neither they nor the times had changed. The acrimony and suspicion with which some of them viewed us and the persistence of our attitude of condescension toward them indicated to me that we were not aware of the profound transformations taking place in many parts of the world. If these changes did not always indicate the acquisition of power, they marked an alteration in the attitude of nations toward power. America, I sadly concluded, had not adjusted to these new realities (Franklin 2005, pp. 298-299).

You might also be tempted to ask yourself if American electronic dominance and control over the media and information within the Anglo-Caribbean is an indication of adjustment to new realities of the twenty-first century. So much for that 1941 Atlantic Charter announced in the names of Prime Minister Churchill and President Roosevelt, both of whom urged, and secured assistance from, people of colour to fight Nazi terror and racism, but did very little to contend with the racist evil in their own backyards.

Thus, 2019, more than two decades since Brown and Moore's comments came to light, is a time in which many more than 200 channels are available to the Anglo-Caribbean, via digital telecasting, along with google glasses, Samsung and Apple watches, high definition television, high speed internet, IPods, IPads, MP3, satellite radio, and mobile phones of ever increasing technical complexity and sophistication, which facilitate instant photographic mechanisms linked to internet messaging, Twitter, Facebook, Snapchat, aimed at youths. I must not forget Blackberries, I-Phones, PlayStation, and X-Box. All of this gadgetry in the Caribbean is being used against a foreground where governments are plagued by uncontrollable problems of illegal drug trafficking and use, at a time when Europe via the European Union, against whose British membership Sir Ian Botham campaigned successfully, because he wants to give Caribbean farmers better prices for their exports to Britain, has chosen to abandon Caribbean sugar and bananas.

So "totally devastating" is the nature of abandonment, in the eyes of former Guyana Trade Minister, Mr. Clement Rohee, that he has warned of Caribbean residents resorting to cultivation of illicit drugs. I am creating a juxtaposition within which young Caribbean men who are supposed to be aspiring Test Match cricketers are very likely to be trapped. The development of such a state, I dare say, does not bode well for West Indies cricket, which is today hugely problem bound, partially, but significantly, in the wake of Prince Lara's leadership.

This is an appropriate juncture at which I should offer my concluding remarks. Let me state it is by no means far-fetched on my part to invoke the fervently persuasive presence of a slave by the American writer, Mr. James Baldwin, for posing questions: will the invaders who come in the night take us, all, in the morning?[5] Will West Indies cricket ever achieve the grandest reaches of Holding Heights from which it thrives in Declaration for <u>Victory Tomorrow</u>? Will West Indies cricket see the fire next time[6] in Alexander's arousal? Will West Indies cricket be able to soar like the <u>Birdmen of Bourda</u>? Will West Indies cricket rekindle itself with Wes Hall's[7] "Pace Like Fire" to stoke its furnaces while avoiding <u>Darien's Dread</u> and flow with Rohan Kanhai's "Blasting For Runs"? Will West Indies cricket ever evade the lure from luckless loafers snared below a crush of <u>Citadel Cordons</u> and make a tremendous turn to <u>Opal Orders</u>?

If West Indians—Brian Charles Lara included—are uncertain of their replies, they can be sure to drown in <u>Watery Whispers</u> of dying <u>Bondmen</u> while they writhe in <u>Turning Tosses</u> to <u>The Art Of The Spinner</u>. If West Indians are uncertain of their replies, they can be sure to lose their <u>Reins Over Sabina</u> and soil their <u>Sacred Silence</u>. If West Indians are uncertain of their replies, they can be sure to court the haunts of ruthless rivals <u>Passing Hispaniola</u> while they fill their <u>Plebeian Purse</u> with sales adrift beyond the Gilchrist charges. If West Indians are uncertain of their replies, they can be sure to live with their <u>Alien's Apostle</u> of <u>Tobal's Terrors</u> haunting trails of that <u>Adelaide Abyss</u> beside what many of them know are only <u>Fuss Ball</u> ducks.[8]

OPAL ORDERS

An Oval oracle emerges beyond the guilder green. He pens a pulsar promise pure with pacer purchase for wholesome hooking. This soul mate skipper serenely suited for the trekker tussle, his partner poised with purpose, they streamed the squares of sundrenched divots with runs of razor red and heap a core of sober sentries outside the questing covers. Their bounties bloom beyond the clueless cordons while bowlers blame their blinding bats. Solar shimmer from both blades spans the doom for misplaced muddle. Fielding fissures and scuttled searching salute five score in feasting figures stamped upon the sovereign stages. Their styles secure along an ageless axis, metrics mull each medial merit free of flasher fiction edged through silly slippage, and cutter comforts parade a pitch for pandit postures.

No hail or Snow to snare those stars of that seventy sojourn. No frugal flakes from the Sabina sixties. No angry avalanche from the vicar's vintage. No sextant sounding for the Sunday service. No appealing parson for a Sussex sermon. No Browning bustle for a Worcester wonder. Just the thrall encamped above cervical spaces linking circuit clusters for greying geniuses. No missing maidens from the scorers' columns. No lordly lieutenants sporting scowls inside the bowlers' benchmarks. No bearded beacons from pointless pathways. No Frindall favours from futile fixtures. Just the cloudburst brilliance atop that vacant velvet soothed with sensual showers from the boldest bloomers. No riveting returns from the Swanton seasons. No Grimmett judgement against the Warner whispers. Just silken stairwells along the sweeping sunsets.

No Herman hustle for the Hammond hundred. No Ponsford pulleys with their fulsome flavours. No Hylton hunger against the kingdom craft. No Griffith gemstones looping with the lift. No lifeline lustre from a Roman Rector. No patient pondering from the plaintiff patrons. No deafening drama from the Dockyard denizens. Just the joy in glorious glancing flush with footwork favours leaping with the lumber. No steadfast surging from the seamless sparkles. No guttural gibberish from that restive roamer, the Lancelot lightning in Richard's radiance. No island extras from the Garrison gifted. No tamarind testers from the scaffold seamers. No partial Procter preening patience upon that verdant veldt. Just the Bacher boundaries from Ali's emblem to a Tayfield tilting.

No gloating grudges against the journal, George. No keeper chances for wayward watchmen. No poacher pardons for careless covers. No blistering burdens from laneway leaders. No grateful gullies for straying spinners. No captain consent to bumper barrages. No skipper standards from cornered chieftains. No dropper dragnet from fractious frontlines. Just the tedious travails from a Tennyson torment. No daunting distance for titan travellers. No boot mark bounce from roughened ridges. No awkward angle from the Bishan barter. No doorsa drayage from a Saqlain saunter. No Gupte goading from a Qadir quantum. No Yorker yardage from an Elconn eyelid. No balata beloved from the Vauxhall valiant. No beamer blessing from a muted marshal. No Afridi attainments from the partnership pedigrees. No googly gospel from a crofter chairman. Just the Arlott anthem from Opal Orders.

No Withsun wonders from the cresting canals. No Regent rival from the polder plosive. No Confessor coding from the Cathedral chimeras. No abandoned icons stooping square beyond the circle craters. No transcribing Taverner sensing music from the soaring section. Just a West Indies wind rush to the teeming tidal. No wind wood wave length from a scorching silence. No riveting rescue from the returning rivals. No rousing rallies from frontline futures. No willow welcome from impish elders. No fielding fortunes from the Conduit cluster. No maple mid-wicket from the labouring long-on. No fraternal fiefdom from the blighted blazers. No redemptive rhythms from the flustered factions. Just the sweetest sounds along each radial route to Graeme's genius capped for hopeful history.

No cricketing signals from sustainable storage. No de Courcy drubbing from the casebook chameleons. No studious sequel from the provost presence, a Frankish flame to the Hobbesian hearth. No Clyde side quilting from the feline femurs. No papyrus penman from the Evertonian insignia. No eucalyptus indemnity from the wielding woodcutters. No sequoia shunting from the laneway litter. No Demerara dossier from the Hubert history. No Vengsarkar victories from a mindful mentor. Just a tundra tumult staring at the strident steppes. No belated baptism from a commanding Sonny. No tapered tossing from a cordial Conrad. No code breaker concepts from comedic custodians. No blizzard bundles from batting beacons. No pilot portals from wicker wonders. No cradle converts from the courier chariots. Just a Cyclops seizure sifting stench atop the bovine bootstraps.

No panther parlours from baronial bliss. No saluting shaman from the subtle Herbert, that Summerbridge sage with notches notable too numerous to name. No sweltering sessions from the Ganguly glory. No stroke making stalwarts among the snivelling subordinates. No crafty challenge from a bolting Bishop. No tracer taunting from the Trueman traffic. Just a telephoto fiction soiling caring centurions across the pigment pathways. No statesman service from that bustling Brian. No raiment rosters from that Arsenal ensign. No Pudsey prince from the baseball bunting. No threaded tangle from the Bristol blossom. No showering Statham from the Harrogate high ground. No magnolia mascots from the Marylebone motifs. Just an escalator egregious prostrate upon the bullion bluster.

No steaming stealth from a leaping Lindwall. No songbook survival from a Russell rondeau. No magnificent mergers from the Lindsay ledger. No coronation cantor from the Hutton highlands. No gargantuan Gentlemen from the Mailey marking. No Victorian vintage from the Trumper terraces. No Moravian mantle from the Pudsey placement. Just the Fazal flavour cresting matted murmurs. No Kingston quartile from the Leyland lumbering. No celestial shallows from the headmaster hero, a helmsman, Hassett. No cresting claims from a Kanhai cosmos. No Bowral busking from the bleating bidders dancing dreadfully upon the Cootamundra conquest. No Langian insights from that border barker, the Annandale orca, Mumbai menace, a demon Douglas, bane to Bradman for Woodfull woe. No Geelong garland from the genial governor. Just the regal routes to a Rohan rapture.

No arithmetic assumptions from the scarlet secretary. No policing proctors from the gamesman jobber. No Player patricians from the Wisden worldly. No prolific pantheons from the premier prudence. No algebraic arousal from the protean prefecture. No appellate honour from the O'Reilly assessment. Just the principled posture to a theatrical torment. No newspaper nabobs hidden from the Kippax calculus. No Boolean bilingual from the Taunton tribunal. No algorithmic ascendance from the doting diarists. No headmaster humility from the rustic road builders. No fulsome formation from the Percy parabolas. No frontier promoters from the gadfly gullies. Just the martial madness mocking Vivian's valence.

No centennial summers from the savoury spells. No rampart runners from the batsmen believers. No stellar subjects from the constellation charters. No Antillean advancement from the Aussie equation. No breadfruit breeders from the boyhood bravado. No orchard owners from the grounds men green. Just the abusing antiquity inside autumnal enclosures. No curator croppers from the Winfield waxing. No harvester haulage from the Hendren hoisting. No electrifying alternates from the dreary dozers. No sapodilla solutions from the St. Barnabas sustainers. No prodigious plantations from the Leonard leaseholders. No foreboding fieldsmen from the Newtonian nightmares. No Big Bird beckoning from the bedrock behemoths. Just a ruddy recessive aloft the obtrusive archways.

No Atkinsonian exemplars from the assertive airman. No colossal clarity from the seafarer sovereigns. No enquiring earful from the Johnston juries. No

Himatial hundreds from the Manohar muster. No conformist collaboration from the Burgundian bookbinders. No redeye resurgence from the threadbare triumvirate. Just the grapefruit gushers pricking fractile faith. No bullish bidders from the Sang-Hue sermons. No Miandad missives from the Turner tracker. No solstice cipher from the gendered grateful flush with flannel flagrance. No Octavian editor from the pantheon pages with triumphal tenures. Just the parchment poachers stealing stylish script for blotter bondmen.

No Melbourne mischief from the Tyson traffic. No Bourda bargains from the market mystery. No Basin blasting from the typhoon tenders. No Mohali missions from the tossing target. No Trafford thicket from a thumping trader. No Sydney surface from a genteel grazier. Just a trio of palatial pantheons pleased about their precious prospects. No Headingley hunting from a muted mascot. No Hambledon herald from the noble neighbours. No Harrow history from the Byron blemish. No Pickwick pardons from the pavilion pathos. No Adelaide imprint from a stellar signal. No Eden expressive from a Brabourne baron. No Hobart hoisting from the colonel claimant. No Trent Bridge bidders from the catcher cordons. No Christchurch choosing from a Sheppard statement. Just a Menzies missive in solemn service to the maestro McCabe.

ADELAIDE ABYSS

From three of the kindest quarters cricketers came to rage and roar, to blight the boldest blasters and lay the curse of Kensington. They blew their Wagga Wagga winds, and swelled their soaring spirits across our silly seasons. This staid assemblage of Aussies that banished our baying brethren beyond the Bridgetown beacons claim a victor's vintage. Beyond the breakers Botany stands a flightless fancy, that colossal cramping of weary warriors, their cruel currencies parade on priceless pathways.

Here! We bottled our purest brew, in recipes of ruin amidst that dreadful daze. Here! We spurned symphonic surges for boisterous buoyancy, and seized the heights of Hubert's horror.

There? We cured all claimants' crises with patient purges, and scaled the tallest tales to raid those rival roots for future fortunes. There? Within our wonders of that weighty womb reside the doleful deputies. They dare their dreams to dance among our suffocating soles. There? We charm a cheated crucible, and freeze the course of excellence. Here! We aid abrupt arousals of tactile turns to invite a touring torment. There! We fault the fleeing edifice we forge on fading forests. There! We frame that futile frowning on Clive's crafty Caribbean beyond a fiery maze for moulding maddening fixtures.

You may have absolutely no interest in cricketing verse. If such is the case, then you might wish to stretch your insightfulness through pondering a few expert claims, as well as the questions which follow them: Restoration of English cricket emanated from resolution and development of the few: while the 1950 West Indian conquest and Australian success in 1946-'47 and 1948 were bitter, they served as purges to some poisoning complacency and created room for healthy growth.

There need be no denying the greatness of the great ones and no withholding of gratitude for it. From the very thin line of flaming glory must come the culture, the inspiration, the framework of cricket to be. That cricket will require continuity, co-operation and understanding: continuity to maintain pride and appreciate possibilities, co-operation to make history a servant and education acceptable, understanding to find privilege, the responsibility and the pleasure in the game (Kilburn 1960, p. 170).

To such wisdom I add the Woodcock (1998, p. xv) claim that the manners of cricket have always reflected society in general. Such reflection means that the game is becoming increasingly more regimented, ever more materialistic, and audibly more aggressive. It still enriches the moment, nevertheless, gilds the memory, and its roots continue to spread. Expressing great certainty that those who attain contemporary cricketing excellence would have done so at any time, Woodcock ponders what he considers as much a sociological as a cricketing question: whether their predecessors of long ago would have excelled at the modern game, or would have wanted to. He answers that he is not so sure. Given what I have written and I know about that cricketing <u>SPIRIT</u>, unlike Woodcock, I choose to avoid ambiguity and claim that they, most certainly, would not have wanted to. Emphatic that my reply is neither a sociological, nor a cricketing reply, nor for that matter, a combination of the two, I state it lies at the confluence of the two. As such, I hope I have set the stage for vigorous debate, the subject of which, via written prosaic and poetic offering, could well constitute much more than what I offer about the Prince and the President.

What I have tried to do, as faithfully as I could, is go beyond the periphery of sociological and cricketing matters. I have endeavoured to situate President, Barack Hussein Obama's, as well as captain, Brian Charles Lara's, greatness or lack thereof within the context of political, socio-economic, and sporting life, that is, without question, increasingly more materialistic, regimented, and aggressive on one side of an ever increasing thin line. This is the thin line I think is straddled by inspiration within cultures of flaming glory where history is rapidly ceasing to be servant and possibilities of understanding via education are being detached from responsibility.

Whether and how Brian Lara's West Indies cricketing presence from 1998 to 2007, a period of almost two decades, has enriched and adorned the moment are questions I leave you, the readers, to ponder. Whether and how Barack Obama's two term presidential presence has adorned the moment are queries you can ponder also. While you ponder, grant no small exploratory measure to the difference between promise and performance, as well as yearning for impressive legacy. These are important matters of the Obama two term tenure, especially his second term, not unlike a second term from which many a predecessor has shaped his legacy, even though the Obama second effort, despite the President's popularity, came to be dubbed 'lame duck' by some observers who claim that the MAAFA MUZUNGU MONSTROSITY and fascist flaunt, Donald J. Trump, would undo Mr. Obama's good work for America. Thus, I offer two verses about this *MONSTROSITY.*

MAAFA MUZUNGU MONSTROSITY[9]

You: despicable wretch. You: utter moron. You: utter lunatic. You: bum. He said he a'int going. So, there a'int no invite. Everything was all right until you showed up. I am fixated! I am the crater of my Kremlin conspiracy! I AM God! No collusion and no obstruction: total exoneration. Make America great again: no corrosive and no occlusion: total exoneration. Make America great again through the Barrman's befuddling. No chastising and no colliding: total distrust and total delusion. I am the carousing convfefe sealing the startled Seine with my choking carbon. I am the tweeting taxpayer priming the pristine Pantanal with my toxic tar. I am the convivial collector calming cyclone showers with my celebrity cascading. I am the grotesque gargantuan stealing solar stewardship from Haida history with my tarnished tenure. I am the rose garden rabble mauling magnolia memories with my teething terror. I am the conniving custodian scorching Sahara sand dunes with my coal oil caravans. I am the koala curtailer banding buffalo bullies on an aching Atlantic with my sordid soul mates. Make America great again with pittance through prisms for the poor. Make Africa great again! Make Africans grovel again for grub. You could see there was blood coming out of her eyes. You could see there was blood coming out of her ears, blood coming out of her WHEREVER, because that makes me as smart as a dragon jousting triffid. You could see wherever you want. But where are my Africans? You can tell them to go fool themselves with what I don't know. Oh! I don't remember. Oh! I don't remember. Oh! I don't remember. Oh! I don't remember. I grope to grab anything I want with my fingers five. So, I'll show my furnished fixture from flaccid fortunes. That's just boy talk. That's just boy talk. That's just boy talk. That's just boy talk! Look at me. Look at me. Look at me. Look at me. You tell me I don't think so. You tell me I don't think so. You tell me I don't think so. You tell me I don't think so. I like muscle, minstrels, mongrels: they do a good turn for toads, newts, and nasty nabobs. They don't fool around on woman wisdom. I know more than the generals. More than the fascist, Franco! More than the monster, Mussolini! More than the Chilean culprit, the panzer patron! Who! Rudolf! The restless rodent! No: he's a clotting corpuscle. He hauls housewives beside hellish hovels. Who! Hess! No. He's a tribal traitor—plus, he wasn't captured. The alpine ogre, Adolf, that lance corporal! No: he's a corpuscle. I don't like corpuscles. They capture sentries. A corpuscle! A corpuscle! A corpuscle! A corpuscle! A land grabber! A land grabber! A land grabber! A land grabber! No. I don't care for lance corporals—plus, he didn't win. I won the wall. I won the wall. I won the wall. I won the wall. I declare a total shutdown on all Museums, Murals, and Media, because that makes me as smart as a dragon jousting triffid. You: despicable wretch. You: utter moron. You: utter lunatic. You: bum. He said he a'int going. So, there a'int no invite. Everything was all right until you showed up. I am fixated! I am the crater of my Kremlin conspiracy! I AM God! No collusion and no obstruction: total exoneration. Make America great again: no corrosive and no occlusion: total exoneration. Make America great again through the Barrman's befuddling. No chastising and no colliding: total distrust and total delusion.

You: despicable wretch. You: utter moron. You: utter lunatic. You: bum. He said he a'int going. So, there a'int no invite. Everything was all right until you showed up. Weekee Leaks! Weekee Leaks! Weekee Leaks! Weekee Leaks. I love Weekee Leaks. I hate Whitehouse leeks. I love loathsome leakers. I love lodestone leakers. Do I still love Weekee Leaks! I know nothing about Weekee Leaks. It's not my thing. My thing is flagrant FISA fording against my towering triumph. I love the General's journals spread across his gaols of justice sealed securely by that shameless sergeant. My thing is the matador mistrustful impounding muted mazes for migrant matrons shielding soulful suns from braying bidders. I love blameless bullfighters borrowing blood soaked benchmarks from the Barrman's bemoaning. My thing is codebreaker cartographers conniving cheerily against that Roget rendition. I love that bullfrog bombast from the rudest remnant on my dockland drool thick with despot drudgery. My thing is prodigious pestilence marred by scholarly certitude against my regressive revival. I love the predicate primers on beaming Bill boards standing high above that gaming groundswell from my guardian judgment. Do I still love the HIV-HPV lessons! I know everything about HIPS. It is my thing. I am the judge, jury, and Janus jobber for bearded bliss on that marauding munificence fronted by a Kipling calendar. I am worsted wondrous waiving woollen wisdom far across the sun drenched seasons for my Julian Godfather. I am that steadfast centurion fanning flaming fortunes on the Adrian ascent way above my Kremlin quandaries. I am that Philby fancy roaming randomly beside those chafing clusters atop my rustbelt remission on behalf of commissar chieftains. I am the leadership line items from wicket waders pained by Aussie ashes spread for spymaster stalwarts shunting statesman sutures round quaestor confidants. My thing is blistering babble for that silkworm solicitor. I love turncoat traders steaming secrets to mainstream missives. My thing is sanctuary sustainers on chafing citizens screened by sledgehammer sovereignty. I love the shoreline seminarian spying studiously on behalf of lawmen languor. Weekee Leaks! Weekee Leaks! Weekee Leaks! Weekee Leaks! I love Weekee Leaks. I hate Whitehouse leeks. I love loathsome leakers. I love lodestone leakers. Do I still love Weekee Leaks! I know nothing about Weekee Leaks. It's not my thing. Do I still love the HIV-HPV lessons! I know everything about HIPS. It is my thing. I love ageless idiocy from my imploding intellect on that crumpled cabinet lamed outside my phantom foundries. You: despicable wretch. You: utter moron. You: utter lunatic. You: bum. He said he a'int going. So, there a'int no invite.

ENDNOTES

1 These remarks were aired by BBC World Service radio, during the course of a broadcast about Lord's hosted by Christopher Martin Jenkins in 1988.

2 My use of the term, 'global cities' is taken from the work of Saskia Sassen: Global Networks: Inked Cities. London: Routledge: (2002.)

3 These are the terms notably present in many a standard and non-standard economics textbook.

4 I do remember the courageous and excellent work of a Mr. McBride against apartheid in South Africa and Afrikaner illegality—with its attendant blatant racism in South West Africa, which later became Namibia.

5 I remind readers that Mr. Baldwin's exact words in part of an open letter to an embattled Angela Davis, who was facing serious criminal charges, were: "The enormous revolution in Black consciousness which has occurred in our generation, my dear sister, means the beginning or the end of America. Some of us, white and Black, know how great a price has already been paid to bring into existence a new consciousness, a new people, an unprecedented nation. If we know, and do nothing, we are worse than the murderers hired in our name.

If we know, then we must fight for your life as though it were our own—which it is—and render impassable with our bodies the corridor to the gas chamber. For if they take you in the morning, they will be coming for us that night."

6 Mr. Baldwin's final words in his book, "THE FIRE NEXT TIME" are "God gave Noah the rainbow sign, No more water, the fire next time." He reports that these words constitute a re-creation from the Bible in song by a slave.

7 The names in quotation marks are those of books from two Test Match notables.

8 All terms underlined are titles of cricketing verse, two of which, I offer for contrast.

9 The first three sentences in this verse are taken from the second Philippic, invective/deliberative speech delivered by Marcus Tullius Cicero, the uniquely talented Roman oratorical genius whom expert, D.H. Berry, states was assessed by Gaius Julius Caesar Octavianus, Caesar's great nephew, adopted son, and Roman Emperor in the aftermath of Caesar's assassination as a patriot and master of words. Cicero was murdered and his head and hands were displayed on the rostra, as a result of the invective against Marcus Antonius, consul, fraudster, and former Master Of The Horse to Gaius Julius Caesar, Dictator Perpetuo, assassinated on 15th March, 44, B.C. Marcus Antonius, who had formed Rome's second triumvirate with Marcus Aemilius Lepidus, Caesar's Master Of The Horse at the time of the Dictator's death, and Octavianus, made himself an enemy of the Emperor. That enmity led, of course, to what British historian, H.A.L. Fisher, describes as a sea fight at Actium between Octavianius and Antonius in which the latter was defeated. I obtained almost all of this information from the D.H. Berry publication, CICERO, POLITICAL SPEECHES, (2011: p. 224), Oxford University Press. It is, of course, Antonius who remains unforgettable in Shakespeare's play, JULIUS CAESAR, but merits no more than two or three sentences in an account from Gaius Suetonius Tranquillus.

Berry, however, writes: "Caesar's funeral took place on c. 20th March. Antony gave the oration, but his words so stirred up the crowd (whether intentionally or not) that they burned the body themselves on an improvised pyre that had been prepared in the Campus Martius. There was considerable violence and attacks were made on the houses of the conspirators [about sixty three men, according to Gaius Suetonius Tranquillus] The chaotic scenes must have recalled those which had accompanied the impromptu cremation of Publius Clodius Pulcher in the senate-house in 52. Antony brought the situation under control, however, and soon afterwards won the approval of Cicero and other republicans by proposing that the office of dictator be abolished. But it was no longer safe for the conspirators to remain in Rome. Brutus [I presume, Marcus Junius] and Cassius [Longinus] withdrew from the city on c. 12th April (in Brutus' case, special permission was required, since he was a city praetor), and others left to take up the provincial governorships assigned to them by Caesar. Brutus's cousin, Decimus Junius Brutus Albinus, went to Cisalpine Gaul. Cicero himself, although he had not been a conspirator, left Rome on 7th April to visit his country estates." In the very publication, pp. xxiii-xxiv, Berry states that Caesar's autocracy led to his assassination. Adding that Cicero had offered discreet encouragement to the assassins or liberators (a Cicero term) Berry notes that the orator was actually present at the time of the murder. "Brutus [I presume, Marcus Junius] raised his dagger and congratulated him on the recovery of their freedom. As the last of the senior republicans still surviving, Cicero had a symbolic value: he had become a token of the republic. And ... we do have evidence for his joy at the death of his enemy." If readers do not find the foregoing intriguing, they should consider a claim from Suetonius Tranquillus that many of the conspirators, including Marcus Junius Brutus, committed suicide by using the very daggers they had plunged into the body of Caesar.

The statements about declining an invitation which follow my reference to Cicero's 'epideictic' oratory are attributed to the exceptionally ingenious National Basketball Association (NBA) player, Mr.Lebron James, of the Cleveland Cavaliers and Los Angeles Lakers who gave his public assessment, via twitter, of Donald Trump. It is Mr. Curry, who made it clear that he would not be in attendance at the White House after Trump's invitation to him and teammates for having won the 2016 National Basketball Association championship. In his own turgid twitter terminology Trump claimed that after it had appeared that Mr. Curry was uncertain about visiting the White House he (Trump) withdrew his invitation to the player. In a clear dismissal of the Trump stupidity Mr. James offered his own assessment. Rather remarkably, as well, all of Mr. Curry's teammates made an explicit decision not to visit the White House but chose, instead, to visit Washington DC where they planned to use their presence in the capital to highlight the great significance of diversity within the United States, a matter very alien to the Trump schema.

BIBLIOGRAPHY

Achebe, C. "An Image Of Africa: Racism In Conrad's Heart Of Darkness," Second Chancellor's Lecture. Amherst: University Of Massachusetts. February (1975): 12pp.

Allen D.R., Arlott. The Authorised Biography. London: Harper Collins (1994).

Arlott, J. The Oxford Companion To Sports And Games. Oxford: Oxford University Press (1976).

_____. Two Summers At The Tests: England vs. South Africa 1947, England vs. Australia 1948. London: The Pavilion Library (1948).

_____. One Hundred Greatest Batsmen. London: McDonald/Queen Anne Press (1986).

_____. "Garfield Sobers," in C. Lee. (ed.), Through The Covers: An Anthology Of Cricket Writing. Oxford: Oxford University Press (1970/1996), pp. 237-238.

Asante, M.K. "Preface: Stolen Legacy," in G.G.M. James. Stolen Legacy. African American Images (1954/2001).

Atkinson, M. Our Masters' Voices: The Language And Body Language of Politics. London: Methuen (1984a).

_____. "Public Speaking And Audience Response: Some Techniques For Inviting Applause" in M. Atkinson & J. Heritage (eds.), Structures Of Social Action: Studies In Conversation Analysis. Cambridge: Cambridge University Press (1984b), pp. 370-409.

Atkinson, M. & Drew, P. Order In Court: The Organisation Of Verbal Interaction In Judicial Settings. London: Macmillan (1979).

Austin. J.L. "A Plea For Excuses," in V. C. Chappell. (ed.), Ordinary Language. New York: Dover Publications (1964), pp. 41-63.

_____. How To Do Things With Words. Cambridge: Harvard University Press (1962).

Bailey, T. The Greatest Since My Time. London: Hodder and Stoughton (1989).

Baldwin, J. The Fire Next Time. New York: Vintage Books (1962).

_____. "An Open Letter To My Sister, Angela Y. Davis," in A. Davis, If They Come In The Morning. New York: Signet Books (1971), pp. 19-23.

Bhattacharyya, G., Gabriel, G., and Small, S. Race And Power. London: Routledge (2002).

Becker, H.S. The Outsiders. New York: The Free Press (1963).

Belafonte, H. My Song. A Memoir Of Art, Race, And Defiance. New York: Vintage (2012).

Benaud, R. My Spin on Cricket. London: Hodder and Stoughton (2005).

Berger, P. and Pullberg, S. "Reification and The Sociological Critique of Consciousness," History and Theory. Vol. 4. (1965), pp. 196-211.

Berger, P. and Luckmann, T. The Social Construction of Reality.New York: Doubleday (1966).

Berry, D.H. Cicero: Political Speeches. Oxford: Oxford University Press (2011).

Blackshire Belay, C.A. "Linguistic Dimension of Global Africa: Ebonics As International Languages of African Peoples,"in C. Crawford. (ed.), Ebonics And Language Education Of African Ancestry Students. London: Sankofa World Publishers (2001), pp. 164-189.

Bolinger, D. "Interrogative Structures Of American English (The Direct Question)." American Dialect Society No. 28. University Of Alabama Press (1957).

Brathwaite, E. K. History Of The Voice. London: New Beacon Press (1984).

Brown, A. A Pictorial History of Cricket. London: Bison Books (1988).

Brown, D. "Ethnicity, Nationalism & Democracy In South-East Asia," in J. Hutchinson & A.D. Smith (eds.), Ethnicity. Oxford. Oxford University Press (1996), pp. 305-311.

Brown, P. & Levinson. S. "Universals In Language Usage: Politeness Phenomena," in E. Goody (ed.), Questions And Politeness. London: Cambridge University Press (1978), pp. 56-288.

Bundock, M. The Fortunes of Francis Barber: The True Story Of The Jamaican Slave Who Became Samuel Johnson's Heir. New Haven: Yale University Press (2015).

Churchill, L. Questioning Strategies In Sociolinguistics. Rowley: Newbury House (1978).

Chomsky, N. Problems Of Knowledge And Freedom: The Russell Memorial Lectures. New York: Fontana (1972).

_____. "The Ideas Of Chomsky," in B. Magee, Men Of Ideas. Oxford: Oxford University Press (1982), pp. 73-193.

Concepcion, G. "The Future Of Colonialism In The Caribbean: Puerto Rico," in E.F. Frazier and E. U. Williams (eds.) Dover: The Majority Press (1943/2004), pp. 41-54.

Connor, W. "Beyond Reason: The Nature Of The Ethnonational Bond, in J. Hutchinson & A.D. Smith (eds.), Ethnicity. Oxford: Oxford University Press (1996), pp. 69-75.

Conrad. J. "Heart Of Darkness," in J. Conrad. Tales Of The Sea. New Jersey: Castle Books (1984/2002), pp. 445-500.

Cutteridge, J. O. Nelson's WEST INDIAN READERS BOOK IV. London: THOMAS NELSON AND SONS LTD (1957).

Davis, A. Y. "Meditations On The Legacy Of Malcolm X." in J. Wood. (ed.), Malcolm X In Our Own Image. New York: St. Martin's Press (1992), pp. 36-47.

De Witte, L. The Assassination Of Lumumba. London: Verso (2001).

Douglass, F. Narrative Of The Life Of Frederick Douglass, An American Slave. New York: Penguin Books (1852/2014).

Du Bois, W.E. The Souls Of Black Folk. Chicago: A.C. McClurg & Co. (1903).

Dyson, F. Maker Of Patterns. New York: Liveright Publishing Corporation (2018).

Eastaway, R. Cricket Explained. New York: St. Martin's Press (1992).

Elliot, J.H. Imperial Spain: 1496-1716. London: Penguin (1963).

Elliot, J.L., & Fleras, A. Unequal Relations. Scarborough: Prentice Hall (1992).

Espinoza, L., & Harris. A. "Embracing The Tar-Baby: LatCrit Theory And The Sticky Mess Of Race," in R. Delgado & J. Stefanic (eds.), Critical Race Theory. Philadelphia: Temple University Press (2000), pp. 440-444.

Esterson, A. The Leaves Of Spring: A Study In The Dialectics Of Madness. London: Pelican (1972).

Fairclough, N. Language And Power. London: Pearson (2001).

Farley, J.E. Majority Minority Relations. New Jersey: Prentice Hall (1988).

Frith, D. "Edwardian Cricket," in C. Lee. (ed.), Through The Covers: An Anthology Of Cricket Writing. Oxford: Oxford University Press (1978/1996), pp. 111-124.

Fisher. H.A.L. A History Of Europe. London: Edward Arnold (1949).

Fleras, A. Immigration Canada: Evolving Realities And Emerging Challenges In A Postnational World. Vancouver: U.B.C. Press (2015).

Fleras, A., & Kunz, J.L. Media And Minorities. Representing Diversity In A Multicultural Canada. Toronto: Thompson Educational Publishing (2001).

Franklin, J. H. Mirror To America. New York: Farrar, Strauss, and Giroux (2005).

Garfinkel, H. Studies In Ethnomethodology. New Jersey: Prentice Hall (1967).

Garfinkel, H., & Sacks. H. "On Formal Structures Of Practical Actions," in J.C. McKinney & A. Tiryakian (eds.), Theoretical Sociology: Perspectives & Developments. New York: Appleton Century Crofts (1970), pp: 337-366.

Gillespie, J.B. Dizzy. Petaluma: Pomegranate Art Books (1991).

Goffman, E. The Presentation Of Self In Everyday Life. New York: Anchor Books (1959).

_____. Asylums: Essays On The Social Situation Of Mental Patients And Other Inmates. Harmondsworth: Penguin Books (1961).

Goldsworthy, A. Caesar: The Life Of A Colossus. London: Weidenfeld & Nicholson (2007).

Grant, Greatest Moments In Cricket. London: Bison Books (1991).

Gregg, P. A Social And Economic History Of Britain. London: George G. Harrap & CO. LTD (1965).

Green, S. Lords: The Cathedral Of. Cricket. London: Tempus Books (2003).

Haney Lopez, I. "The Social Construction Of Race," in R. Delgado & J. Stefanic (eds.), Critical Race Theory. Philadelphia: Temple University Press (2000), pp. 445-447.

Hawking, S. W. A Brief History Of Time: From The Big Bang To Black Holes. London: Bantam Books (1988).

Heap, J.L. "On Recollecting The Possible: A Critique of The Repair System In Conversation Analysis," Paper Prepared For Presentation At The Annual Meetings Of the Society For Phenomenology And Existential Philosophy, West Lafayette, Indiana (1979): 13pp.

Heritage, J. Analysing News Interviews: Aspects Of The Production Of Talk For An Overhearing Audience, in T. van Dijk. (ed.), Handbook Of Discourse Analysis. Vol. 3. Discourse And Dialogue. London: Academic Press (1985).

Hill, D. "Books, Banks, & Bullets: Controlling Our Minds-The Global Project Of Imperialistic and Militaristic Neo-Liberalism & Its Effect On Education Policy," Policy Futures In Education. Nos., 3 & 4 (2004): pp. 504-522.

Hirschfeld, F. George Washington And Slavery: A Documentary Portrayal. Columbia: University Of Missouri Press (1997).

Hochschild, A.R. The Commercialization Of Intimate Life. Berkeley: University Of California Press (2003).

Holt, T.C. The Problem Of Race In The Twenty-first Century.Cambridge: Harvard University Press (2000).

hooks, b. Teaching Community. New York: Routledge (2003).

Hurston, Zora Neale. Barracoon: The Story Of The Last Black Cargo. New York: Amistad (2018).

Hutchby, I., & Woofitt, R. Conversation Analysis. Cambridge: Polity Press (2002).

Ichheiter, G. "Misunderstandings In Human Relations," Supplement To The American Journal Of Sociology. Vol. LV. September 1949, pp. 6-7.

Jackson, G. "Towards The United Front," in A.Y. Davis, If They Come In The Morning. New York: Signet Books (1971), pp. 156-162.

Jacoby, R. The End Of Utopia: Politics And Culture In An Age of Apathy. New York: Basic Books (1999).

_____. "The Death Of Political Ideology," Royal Society Of Arts Journal. Vol., 3 (2002), pp. 42-45.

James, G.G.M. Stolen Legacy. African American Images (1954).

James, C.L.R. Beyond A Boundary. London: Stanley Paul (1963).

_____. "Exciting Cricket Depends Upon Exciting Personalities," in C.L.R. James, Cricket. London: Allison And Busby (1937/1986), pp. 53-55.

_____. "Gilchrist Before And Gilchrist After (1959)"in C.L.R. James, Cricket. London: Allison And Busby (1986), pp. 92-94.

_____. "Kanhai: A Study In Confidence (1966)," in C.L.R. James, Cricket. London: Allison And Busby (1986), pp. 165-171.

_____. "Garfield Sobers" in C.L.R. James, Cricket. London: Allison And Busby (1969/1986), pp. 218-232.

Johnson, W. The Challenge Of Diversity. Montreal: Black Rose Books (2006).

Johnston, B. It's Been A Piece Of Cake. London: Methuen (1989).

Kay, J. "Hedley Verity" in J. Kay (ed.), Cricket Heroes. London: The Sportsman's Book Club (1960), pp. 111-118.

Laing, R.D. The Divided Self. London: Pelican (1965a).

_____. "Mystification, Confusion And Conflict," in I. Bosor Menyi-Nagy and J. L. Framo. (eds.), Intensive Family Therapy. New York: Harper and Row (1965b).

Lane, A. Hack Work. New York: The New Yorker Magazine (2011), pp. 24-30.

Lee, C. Through The Covers: An Anthology Of Cricket Writing.Oxford: Oxford University Press (1996).

Lloyd, C.H. "Introduction," in M. Manley, A History Of West Indies Cricket. London: Andre Deutsch and Pan Books (1988), pp. v-vi.

Lucas, E.V. "The Lure Of Cricket" in C. Lee. (ed.), Through The Covers: An Anthology Of Cricket Writing. Oxford: Oxford University Press (1933/1996), pp.1-3.

Maathai, W. The Challenge For Africa. New York: Pantheon Books (2009).

Majumdar, B. "Cricket In Colonial India: The Bombay Pentangular, 1892-1946," International Journal Of The History Of Sport. Vol. 19 (2002), pp. 157-188.

Mandela, N. Notes To The Future. New York: Atria Books (2012).

Manley, M. A History Of West Indies Cricket. London: Andre Deutsch and Pan Books (1988).

Marcuse, H. Eros And Civilization: A Philosophical Inquiry Into Freud. Boston: Beacon Press (1955).

_____. Negations: Essays In Critical Theory. Boston: Beacon Press (1969).

_____. "Marcuse And The Frankfurt School," in B. Magee, Men Of Ideas. Oxford: Oxford University Press (1982), pp. 43-55.

Martin-Jenkins, C. World Cricketers. Oxford: Oxford University Press (1996).

McDonald, T. Viv Richards: The Authorised Biography. London: Pelham Books (1984).

Mead, G.H. Mind, Self, And Society. Chicago: University Of Chicago Press (1934).

Miller, K. Cricket From The Grandstand. London: The Sportsman's Book Club (1960).

Mills, C.W. The Power Elite. Oxford: Oxford University Press (1956).

_____. The Sociological Imagination. Harmondsworth: Pelican Books (1959).

_____. The Racial Contract. London: Cornell University Press (1997).

_____. Blackness Visible. London: Cornell University Press (1998).

Morrison, T. Playing In The Dark: Whiteness And The Literary Imagination. London: Harvard University Press (1992).

Nehushi, K.S.K. "From Medew Netjer To Ebonics," in C. Crawford. (ed.), Ebonics And Language Education. London: Sankofa World Publishers (2001), pp. 56- 122.

Nisbet, R.A. The Sociological Tradition. London: Heinemann (1966).

Nunn, K.B. "Law As A Eurocentric Enterprise," in R. Delgado And J. Stefancic (eds.), Critical Race Theory: The Cutting Edge. Philadelphia: Temple University Press (2000), pp. 429-436.

Olusoga, D. Black And British. London: Pan Books (2017).

Omrani, B. Caesar's Footprints. London: Head of Zeus Press (2017).

Otway, G. "West Indies In Disarray As Captaincy Row Rages." Sunday Times. London (1997), p. 15.

Painter, N.I. The History Of White People. New York: W.W. Norton (2010).

Perry, R. The Don. London: Virgin Publishing (2001).

Plant, D.G. "Afterword, to Zora Neale Hurston." Barracoon: The Story Of The Last Black Cargo. New York: Amistad (2018), pp. 117-137.

Polanyi, M. The Study Of Man. Chicago: University of Chicago Press (1959).

Pullan, B. In Focus: Frank Worrell (1924-1967) Manchester. This Week Next Week: pp. 10-11.

Roberts, W.A. "The Future Of Colonialism In The Caribbean: The British West Indies," in E.F. Frazier and E. U. Williams. (eds.), The Economic Future Of The Caribbean. Dover: The Majority Press (2004), pp. 37-39.

Roebuck, P. The Colossus Leaves. London: Sunday Times (1993): 10pp.

Rogers, C. "The Carl Rogers Reader," in I. Kutash & A. Wolf (eds.), Psychotherapist's Casebook. New York: Jossey-Bass (1986), pp. 197-208.

Ryle, G. The Concept Of Mind. New York: Harper And Row (1949).

Sacks, H., & Schegloff, E. "Opening Up Closings," in R. Turner (ed.), Ethnomethodology. Harmondsworth: Penguin Books (1975): 233-264.

Sacks, H., Schegloff, E., & Jefferson., G. "A Simplest Systematics For The Organisation Of Turn Taking For Conversation," Language. Vol. L. (1974), pp. 696-734.

Sacks, H., Schegloff, E., & Jefferson. G., "The Preference For Self-Correction In The Organisation Of Repair In Conversation," Language. Vol. LIII (1977), pp. 361-382.

Schegloff, E. Sequencing In Conversational Openings," in J. Gumperz & D. Hymes (eds.), The Ethnography Of Communication.New York: Holt, Reinhart, & Winston (1972), pp. 349-380.

Schiffer, I. Charisma: A Psychoanalytic Look At Mass Society.Toronto: University of Toronto Press (1973).

Schneider. Neurosis And Civilisation. New York: Seabury Press (1975).

Schutz, A. On Phenomenology And Social Relations. Chicago: University of Chicago Press (1970).

Searle, J.R. Speech Acts. London: Cambridge University Press (1969).

_____. The Philosophy Of Language. Oxford: Oxford University Press (1971).

_____. "Chomsky's Revolution In Linguistics," in G. Harman (ed.), On Noam Chomsky: Critical Essays. New York: Doubleday (1974).

_____. "What Is An Intentional State?" Mind. LXXXVIII (1979a).

_____. Expressions And Meaning. London: Cambridge University Press (1979b).

_____. "The Background To Meaning," in J. R. Searle, F. Kefer, and M. Berwisch (eds.), Speech Act Theory Pragmatics.Dordrecht: Reidel Publishing Company (1980).

_____. "The Philosophy Of Language: Dialogue With John Searle," in B. Magee, Men Of Ideas. Oxford: Oxford University Press (1982), pp.153-172.

_____. Mind, Language, And Society. New York: Basic Books (1999).

Smith, R. The Judge: More Than Just A Game. London: Yellow Jersey Press (2019).

Snow, P. "Bula," in J. Kay (ed.), Cricket Heroes.London: The Sportsman's Book Club (1960), pp. 72-82.

Sobers, G.S. The Changing Face Of Cricket. London: Ebury Press (1996).

_____. Garfield Sobers: My Autobiography. London: Headline Books (2002).

Standal, S. The Need For Positive Regard: A Contribution To Client-Centered Therapy. Unpublished Ph.D. Dissertation: University Of Chicago (1954).

Steen, R. "Brian Lara: A Day In The Life Of The Best Cricketer In The World," London: Total Sport. July (1996), pp. 62-66.

Strachey, J. Civilisation And Its Discontents. London: W.W. Norton & Company (1961).

Suzuki, D. "The Challenge of The Twenty-first Century: Setting The Real Bottom Line," Lecture To the Commonwealth Foundation. London:(2008).

Suzuki, D., And Hanington I. Just Cool It! The Climate Crisis And What We Can Do. Vancouver: Greystone Books (2017).

Swanton, E.W. Swanton In Australia With M.C.C. 1946-1975.London: Collins (1975).

_____. "Sobers," in C. Lee. (ed.), Through The Covers: An Anthology Of Cricket Writing. Oxford: Oxford University Press (1994/1996), pp. 238-241.

Turner, R. "Words, Utterances, & Activities," in R. Turner (ed.), Ethnomethodology. Harmondsworth: Penguin Books (1975), pp. 197-214.

_____. "Utterance Positioning As An Interactional Resource," Semiotica. Vol. XVII (1976), pp. 233-254.

Thornborrow, J. Power Talk: Language And Interaction In Institutional Discourse. London: London (2002).

Tranquillus, G.S. Lives Of The Caesars: Translation by C. Edwards. Oxford: Oxford University Press (2008).

Trevelyan. G.M. "A Game For All Classes," in C. Lee (ed.), Through The Covers. Oxford: Oxford University Press (1996), p. 4.

Van den Berghe, P. South Africa: A Study In Conflict.Westport: Greenwood Press (1980).

Van Sertima, I. They Came Before Columbus. New York: Random House (1976).

Walcott, C.L. "Foreword," in G.S. Sobers. Garfield Sobers:My Autobiography. London: Headline Books (2002), pp. vi-viii.

Walcott, W.H. "Deconstructing Racism: Analysing The Coolie Bully Slur In Sport." Indo-Caribbean Review. Vol. 1 (1994), pp. 83-96.

_____. Competence And Communication: Chomsky, Friere, Searle And The Communicative Movement. Montreal: Black Rose Books (2007).

Walker, C. "Beyond Reason: The Nature Of The Ethnonational Bond," in J. Hutchinson & A.D. Smith (eds.) Ethnicity. Oxford: Oxford University Press (1996), pp. 69-75.

Walker, P. Cricket Conversations. London: Pelham Books (1978).

Weber, M. The Theory Of Social And Economic Action. New York: The Free Press (1964).

West, C. "Malcolm X And Black Rage," in J. Wood (ed.), Malcolm X In Our Own Image. New York: St. Martin's Press (1992), pp. 48-58.

_____. Race Matters. New York: Vintage Books (1994).

_____. The Cornel West Reader. New York: Civitas Books (1999).

_____. Democracy Matters. New York: Penguin Books (2004).

Williams, E.U. The Negro In The Caribbean. New York: A & B Books (1942).

_____. British Historians And The West Indies. New York: A & B Book Publishers (1964/1994).

_____. "The Economic Development Of the Caribbean Up To The Present," in E. F. Frazier and E. U. Williams (eds.), The Economic Future of The Caribbean. Dover: The Majority Press (2004), pp. 19-24.

Winant, H. The New Politics Of Race. Minneapolis: University of Minnesota Press (2004).

Woodcock, J. One Hundred Great Cricketers. London: Macmillan (1998).

Yunus, M. A World Of Three Zeroes: The New Economics Of Zero Poverty, Zero Unemployment, And Zero Net Carbon Emissions. New York: Public Affairs/Perseus Books (2017).

GLOSSARY

All out: The end of one team innings when ten wickets have fallen and no other person has to bat.

All-rounder: A cricketer who is an excellent batsman, bowler, and fieldsman.

Appeal: A person or persons on the fielding team who ask(s) the umpire if a batsman is out. A typical appeal takes the shouting forms, 'How's that?' 'How is that?' When an appeal to an umpire is successful a batsman is, of course, out, and to signal his demise the umpire raises one hand just above head height and usually points an index finger skywards.

Arm ball: A ball from a slow bowler that appears as if it is an off-break but moves straight.

Ashes: A Test Match series between England and Australia in which there is very keen competition for a trophy containing real ashes of a burnt bail. The Ashes go all the way back to 1882, the year of England defeat at the hands of Australia. At the time, THE SPORTING TIMES, an English publication printed the obituary: "In affectionate remembrance of English Cricket which died at the Oval 29thAugust, 1882 deeply lamented by a large circle of sorrowing friends and acquaintances. RIP. NB The body will be cremated and the Ashes taken to Australia." Only a year later, Australia beat England on the island continent, and some Australian female cricket fans burned a bail which they placed in a small urn they gave to the England captain, Ivor Bligh. The urn was kept by his family up to 1927 when it was sent to Lord's.

Back foot: The foot of a batsman nearer the wicket keeper. The back foot of a right hand batsman is his right foot. That of a left hand batsman is his left foot.

Bad light: Natural light which the two umpires in a cricket match determine is too dull for continual playing of the game.

Bails: Four small pieces of wood which sit at the very top of a set of three stumps positioned at both ends of the cricket pitch, the wicket [the 22 yard long strip in the middle of the cricket field].

Batting crease: The painted white lines on and within which batsmen face bowlers.

Batting wicket: A pitch [the 22 yard strip in the middle of the cricket field] on which leading batsmen should be able to score many runs.

Beamer: A very fast ball which does not touch the ground that is bowled to a batsman at just above chest height.

Beaten: A state in which a batsman plays to hit a ball bowled either fast or slowly but fails to make any contact or, if s/he makes contact, does so unconvincingly.

Beaten in flight: A state in which a slow bowler deceives a batsman who, although he makes contact with the ball bowled, fails to judge correctly its speed and trajectory. On some occasions when a batsman is beaten in flight, his mis-judgment leads to him being caught by the bowler, after he mistimes his stroke or he fails to make any contact with the ball, is out of his crease or ground, only to discover that the ball eluding his bat is taken by the wicket keeper, who dislodges the bails, and the batsman is ruled by the umpire to be out STUMPED.

Behind the bowler's arm: A spectator's position almost directly behind the three stumps on the pitch beside which the bowler delivers the ball [bowls] to batsmen.

Bodyline: A term first used to describe a fast bowing ploy employed in the infamous (1932-'33) Test Match series between England and Australia, where England captain Douglas Jardine instructed his two fast bowlers, Larwood and Voce, to deliver the ball on the batsman's leg side on the pitch, wicket, so that it might bounce and become very difficult to negotiate. Bodyline bowling is very dangerous to batsmen. Bodyline bowling is sometimes referred to as leg theory. Upon observing it for the first time, an English cricketer is supposed to have assessed it as head, neck, and chest theory, rather than leg theory.

Bouncer: A ball which is usually delivered almost half way on the pitch, so that it might bounce at chest or head height at batsmen. Bouncers, though less dangerous than beamers, have felled batsmen on some occasions. Sometimes batsmen duck in anticipation that the bouncer will pass over their crouched bodies, but discover that the ball does not rise much. Some aggressive and highly skilled batsmen do not duck but position themselves and play what is known as the hook shot which earns then six or four runs. On other occasions, they are not successful, and although they strike the ball, it is hit off one of the edges of the bat from which it falls into the hands of a fielder.

Boundary: The edge of the field where a ball is hit by a batsman on any part of the playing area without being stopped by a fieldsman. Such a stroke will usually earn the batsman a score of four runs. If the batsman hits the ball and it goes over any part of the boundary without touching the ground, the batsman earns six runs. Umpires signal four runs by raising one arm just around waist height and waving it at the scorer. They signal six runs by raising both arms over their shoulders crossing them in formation of an X and waving the shape to the scorer.

Bowl: The manner in which a bowler either trots or runs in and delivers a ball at speed or slowly—not by throwing or pitching it. At the point of delivery his arm cannot be bent. A bent arm for delivering the ball is a serious violation of the Laws of cricket. Such action, termed throwing, or "chucking," in most cases, leads to the permanent removal of such bowlers from the game.

Bowled: One of the many different ways in which a batsman is out to a bowler. Someone is bowled or clean bowled when the ball that is bowled hits the stumps, which are sometimes knocked from their positions and the bails are seen in the air.

Bowler: Anyone of ten cricketers who is asked by his captain to bowl. The wicket keeper, an eleventh fielder, is usually not asked to bowl.

Bowler's end: The end of the pitch towards which a player runs or trots in until he reaches beside the three stumps and bowls the ball to a batsman.

Bye: A run or runs awarded to the batting side—not to a batsman—when a ball that is bowled is not hit with the batsman's bat, is not stopped by the wicket keeper, and a batsman and his batting partner at the bowler's end run from one end of the pitch to the other. If the ball that is not stopped by the wicket keeper rolls to the boundary, four byes are earned by the batting side.

Caught: One way in which any batsman can be out when the ball that is bowled touches his bat or any part of his hands up to his elbow and is caught by a fieldsman before it touches the ground.

Caught behind: A batsman who is caught by the wicket keeper when a ball is bowled.

Century: An important landmark for a batsman who reaches a hundred or more. Excellent batsmen at the Test Match level are expected to, and do score, double centuries, and in very rare cases triple and quadruple centuries.

Chance: A state in which any fielder fails to grasp a catch, even if the ball hit to him merely touches the tips of his finger or fingers, or a wicket keeper fails to collect a ball that beats a batsman who is out of his crease.

Chinaman: A type of ball so named in a fit of racial prejudice from an England Test Match captain, Robins, in 1932, after he had been bowled by a left arm West Indies leg spin bowler, Edgar Ellis Achong. While Robins was walking back to the pavilion, he is supposed to have conveyed his astonishment to Learie Constantine, a West Indies fieldsman, about being bowled by a "Chinaman." One description of the Chinaman is: any left arm spin bowler who bowls a leg break bowls this ball.

Cover or cover point: One of several fielding positions taken by the fielding team. It is the captain who tells players where they have to field. Captains change the positions of fielders with great frequency, especially after each ball is bowled when a left and right hand batsman are batting. I shall designate all fielding positions: think of a large round clock face. Clearly visible is an inner circle made up tiny strokes depicting minutes. Just beyond this inner circle an imaginary outer circle can be visualised. Every fielding position on the rim of this imaginary outer circle is part of the boundary. The central point from which the two hands originate lies where the middle stump is placed at the end where a batsman receives a bowler's deliveries. From the position where the batsman faces the deliveries, cover point lies at a spot on the field where the two hands meet between the numbers 3 and 4 on the rim of the inner circle. Extra cover lies approximately at the twenty-minutes-to-eight position approximately midway between inner and outer circles.

Crease [batting and bowling]: The horizontal and vertical painted lines on the pitch or wicket.

Cut: A stroke played by batsmen usually placing their body weight on the back foot and hitting the ball so that it slides off the full face of their bat. Variants of the cut are the square cut and late cut, strokes of enormous elegance. A square cut is a stroke which a batsman accomplishes by striking the ball in the eight forty five position, while the late cut is accomplished by playing the stroke approximately in the nine fifty position. Importantly, it is the late cut that is executed by a batsman who relies on timing and precision, just when the ball is about to pass him, rather than when it is in front of him.

Dead bat: A defensive stroke played by placing the body weight either on the back or front foot and holding the bat firmly to block the ball bowled to him.

Declaration: A decision taken by the captain of the batting side before all the batsmen on his team have had a chance to bat. Batsmen at the wicket can anticipate a captain's declaration decision as a result of the runs their team has scored. A declaration, merely a hand signal from the captain on the pavilion steps or balcony, is usually made when a team has scored many runs.

Dismiss/dismissal: One of several ways in which a batsman can be out. He can be out if he hits the ball and a fielder catches it before it touches the ground. Some other frequent ways in which batsmen can be out are: (a) bowled—if he fails to hit the ball bowled and it hits the stumps (b) played-on—if he hits it and it touches the stumps (b) stumped—if he fails to hit it, the wicket keeper catches it and hits the stumps when he is out of his crease (c) run-out—if in running after he hits a ball, he fails to get back to his crease before a fielder throws the ball to the wicket keeper, who hits the stumps, or the fielder himself throws the ball and hits the stumps directly or after it bounces on the turf (d) if he treads accidentally backwards and hits the stumps, although he makes no contact with the ball bowled or his bat touches the ball (e) he is also out if his cap hits the stumps accidentally (f) he is out Leg Before Wicket [L.B.W.] if the ball hits him on the right or left pad, but does not touch his bat, and in the view of the umpire, whose prime consideration must be the angle from which the ball is bowled, the ball would hit the stumps. Before the introduction of high technology to the game it was the ruling umpire and he only who rendered [L.B.W.] decisions—out or not out—as a result of appeals from fielders. These days it is the technology that is applied often for the purpose of rendering [L.B.W.] decisions, although umpires described as "neutral" or "independent", have rendered their decisions.

Double century/double hundred: A batsman's score of between two hundred and two hundred and ninety nine runs.

Draw [drawn game/match]: A state in which play has ended but no team has won the game. Drawn games can result from rain, or insufficient time for each team to complete two innings while batting, although a game at the highest level, Test Match cricket, is played for five days and there are three two hour sessions, pre-lunch, the session between lunch and tea, and the session after tea, each day. Prior to 1938, Test Matches ran well beyond five days and draws still resulted. Under the current cricket Laws, a total of ninety overs are supposed to be bowled in one day. Such is seldom attained in a six hour day, and if daylight permits umpires extend the playing time and sometimes impose financial penalties on fielding sides for not completing ninety overs.

Drop a catch/dropped: A state in which any fielder fails to hold on to a catch.

Dropped: A decision not to select a player for a game/match, which usually results from a previous poor performance or a run of previous poor performances.

Duck: A state in which a batsman is out before he makes any runs in one or both innings in which he is eligible to bat. A batsman out for a duck has the score [0] beside his name on the scoreboard. A batsman who scores two ducks in one game is said to be out for a "pair." If he is out to the very first deliveries he faces in both innings, he is said to be out for a "king pair."

Edge: An involuntary stroke occurring when a ball just touches the outermost sections of a batsman's bat. Bowlers who send down very fast deliveries, fast/quick/pace bowlers, with a ball that is hard and shiny usually bowl for their deliveries to bounce and deviate off the pitch/wicket and to make it difficult for batsmen to strike the ball in the middle of their bats, thus enabling the wicket keeper to catch the ball off the edge. Many times one of four fielders, standing in an arc next to the wicket keeper, the "slips" and "gulley" are able to hold some spectacular catches diving either to their right or left. Very very speedy pace bowlers usually ask their captains for, and get, an "attacking" or "umbrella" field in which—along with the wicket keeper—there are three or four slips and a gulley or three slips and two gullies. The arc can be pictured by placing the minute hand at approximately three minutes to the hour and the hour hand at a point equidistant from nine and ten. An edge is either a thick, thin, inside or outside edge. The inside edge is the edge of the bat nearer to the batsman. The outside edge is the edge nearer to the slip area. A thin edge is a condition in which the ball touches the edge extremely lightly or faintly while a thick edge is a state in which it touches the edge quite noticeably.

Fine leg: A fielder's position for a right hand batsman well behind the stumps at the position approximately two minutes after twelve o'clock on the rim to the imaginary outer circle .

For a left hand batsman, fine leg is just about three minutes to eleven o'clock. Deep fine leg is a field placing for either position of the hands but close to the boundary.

Follow on / enforce the follow on: When a team that bats first compiles a large score, the captain of that team assumes he has a huge tactical advantage over his opponents batting second. He assumes that he can get all ten wickets on the opposing team without that team attaining a certain fraction/proportion [at one time under the Laws, about two thirds] of the score his players have made. If that fraction is not reached, he has the right to enforce what is known as the follow on. The other team has to bat a second time with the aim of erasing the deficit. If in batting a second time, the opposing team does not erase the deficit and all of its ten wickets are lost, that team loses the match by an innings and the run difference between the scores it makes batting twice. Such a loss is, of course very humiliating. Even if the deficit is erased and a total above the score made by the team batting first is reached, but all wickets are lost and the team enforcing the follow on bats again and surpasses what is above, it still wins the match. If the score surpassed is overtaken, and no wickets are lost, the winning team is adjudged to have won by ten wickets. If two wickets are lost, the win is attained by eight wickets.

Follow through: A term used to describe the momentum created as a result of a bowler's effort [chiefly from fast bowlers] to deliver the ball to batsmen. It is the momentum that propels most fast bowlers almost half way down the pitch/wicket after they have delivered the ball to batsmen. Under the Laws of cricket no bowler, fast, medium fast, or spin, can run straight down the pitch in his follow through. Such movement contributes to a roughening of surfaces close to the areas where batsmen have to negotiate balls bowled to them. Such roughening is especially helpful to spin bowlers on a team that is bowling. When a bowler runs straight down the pitch in his follow through, he is warned initially by the umpire. If he continues the action, his captain is notified by the umpire. The maintenance of such action leads to the umpire disallowing that bowler from bowling for the remainder of the innings.

Forward defensive stroke: A stroke employed by a batsman on his front foot to prevent the ball delivered by a bowler from hitting his stumps. This stroke is played by carefully positioning the bat in direct line behind the outstretched front foot.

Front foot: A batsman's foot which is closer to the bowler.

Googly: A ball delivered by a right arm leg spin bowler which is used to deceive batsmen into thinking that it will deviate away from them towards the area where the slips are positioned. A googly, which is delivered from the back of the arm, turns into batsmen.

Green pitch/wicket: A pitch prepared by curators/grounds men and their staff with some grass on the surface. Green pitches are usually prepared to suit fast/pace/quick bowlers.

Gulley: For a right handed batsman a position just after the number, 10, within the inner circle. With the wicketkeeper directly in line with the number, 12, gully—occasionally two gullies - to this keeper's right completes an arc within which three and, sometimes, four slips, of course, to the batsman's right, can be seen between 10 and 12. Leg gully can be seen within the inner circle between the numbers, 2 and 3. Leg slip can ne located immediately after the number, 12. Not too far from gully very close to the batsman is the position, silly point, on a line that can be drawn directly between the number, 9, and the centre spot where the two clock hands intersect. On that same direct line just beyond the rim of the inner circle the fielder at point is located. Many commentators use the terms, point, and a man square of the wicket on the off side, interchangeably. On the batsman's leg side short leg and square leg are opposites of silly point and point. Without intending to complicate the cricketing initiate I note deep point and deep square leg in opposite locations on the rim of the outer circle (boundary) directly in line with the numbers, 9 and 3, respectively. I add, for more than good measure, that all of these opposites, variations, and combinations do mean that no more than eleven fielders - including the bowler and wicketkeeper—are allowed on a Test Match playing area.

Hat trick: A state in which a bowler who gets three batsmen out in three consecutive deliveries he bowls either in a single over six deliveries everywhere except Australia, where an over for many years consisted of eight deliveries. A hat trick can be accomplished, also, via three consecutive deliveries in two separate overs. According to the Laws of Test Match cricket today, each team fielding must bowl ninety overs in a single day. If that does not happen, the team must pay a fine. Hat tricks are rare feats in high level cricket. Helmet tricks, taking four wickets in four consecutive deliveries, are even rarer.

Hitting/playing across the line: A stroke played by a batsman on his leg side to a straight ball, a ball which does not deviate.

Hook shot: A stroke played on the leg side by a batsman usually to a bouncer.

In form/in good nick: When a leading batsman is batting well and makes a large score in one or more games, he is said to be in form. He is said to be out of form when his batting performance in one or more games is poor and he struggles to make even a low score. It is not unusual for team selectors to drop batsmen who are out of form.

In swing/in swinger: A delivery—usually from a fast/pace/quick bowler—which deviates away from a batsman in a direction to the left of the slips and the wicket keeper. The out swing/out swinger is bowled to deviate in the opposite direction. In and out swingers are bowled to get an edge from batsmen. Bowlers who do not bowl with great speed, medium paced bowlers, send down variants of the in and out swingers. These deliveries from medium pacers are described sometimes as off and leg cutters.

Leg stump: The closest of the three stumps behind a right handed batsman to his left t leg, or in the case of a left handed batsman the leg stump is closest to his right leg. This stump is on the same side as a fine leg fielder. The off stump is the stump closest to the position of the slips.

Leg spin bowler: An integral part of spinning the ball through movement of the wrist. A leg spin bowler, who bowls slowly, usually aims to make the ball deviate from the area of the batsman's leg stump towards the position of the slips and does possess the capability to bowl the googly, also.

Long-off: For a right handed batsman this is fielding position close to the boundary in the position between the numbers, 6 and 7 on the clock face.

Long-on: For a right handed batsman long on is also close to the boundary but in the position between the numbers, 5 and 6.

Maiden/Maiden over: An over from which a batsman does not score any runs. A wicket maiden is a maiden over in which a bowler is credited with having taken batsmen's wickets through having them bowled, caught, stumped, or L.B.W.

Mid-off: A fielding position for a right handed batsman on the rim of the inner circle in approximately the point where the number, 7, can be seen. Mid-on is the opposite. The fielder is approximately in the spot where the number, 5, can be seen. Variants of mid-off and mid on are wide mid-off and wide mid-on.

Mid-wicket: On the rim of the inner circle a fielding position which can be located by placing both hands between the numbers between three and four.

New ball: A brand new, shiny, and well-polished leather cricket ball around which there is a single seam. According to Australian Test Match captain, Mr. Ian Chappell, the size of a cricket ball is roughly the same size as a baseball,.The new ball used in Test Matches is also about the size and weight of a baseball. The exterior is brown in colour. The interior is made of hard cork. It is used by the fielding side at the beginning of each innings. A second new ball can be used and is used frequently in all Test Match playing countries, except the West Indies, after eighty five overs [510 deliveries] have been bowled in one innings. In the West Indies, it has usually been taken after seventy five overs [450 deliveries] have been bowled. It is the umpire who has possession of the new ball before the start, and during the course of an innings. When play begins, he tosses the ball to the captain of the fielding side. The umpire also has possession of the second or third new ball, if necessary. When the captain of the fielding side is eligible to take it, the ruling umpire, who is positioned at the end of the pitch/wicket from which bowlers deliver their overs, removes it from one of his coat pockets and holds it aloft in a signal to the scorers who note the number of overs bowled at the point it is taken.

Nick: Another term for an edge.

Night Watchman: A batsman who is not selected for his batting capability and someone who does not usually get a chance to bat in the early part of an innings. The Night Watchman is, however, sent to bat in place of one of the regular leading batsmen, if one such player is out, at a time very close to the end of play for a day. According to Mr. Trevor Bailey, England Test Match cricketer and expert commentator, it is the job of the Night Watchman to guard or protect the team from losing any wickets during the crucial short period before the close.

No ball: An illegitimate delivery from a bowler who—in the judgement of the "ruling umpire," the umpire standing at the stumps closer to the bowler—drags his front foot over the crease. The Law about no balls was at one time used if the bowler's back foot was over the crease. When a no ball is bowled, one run is added to the total of the batting side under the category EXTRAS. The run is not given to the batsman. Because a no ball is an illegitimate delivery, the bowler must bowl one more ball. Thus, in a six ball and eight ball over he bowls seven and eight times respectively. The umpire at square leg, a position when both hands of the clock are on the number three, can also call "no ball," if in his judgement a bowler throws "chucks" or bowls a ball with a bent arm.

Not out: A batsman who has either faced an over or overs or has not but has not lost his wicket at the end of an innings through being caught, bowled, stumped or in any other way. Some leading batsmen who are not out [unbeaten] frequently as a result of a declaration have scored many runs.

Opening batsmen/openers: Two of the very capable batsmen who walk out immediately behind the fielding team and take their positions at one of the ends of the pitch/wicket where the stumps are located. The batsman who has to face the first over from a bowler is regarded as the person who takes the strike.

Off break bowler/off spinner: A slow bowler who uses his fingers to move the ball from a position just outside the off stump into batsmen.

Opening bowlers: These are usually bowlers who bowl either very fast, the pace/quick bowlers, or medium paced bowlers, with the new ball.

Over the wicket: A bowler whose bowling arm is closer to the stumps. When a bowler bowls around the wicket his bowling arm is away from the stumps.

Overthrow(s): After a batsman plays a stroke and he and his partner run from one end of the pitch to the other fielders can do one of: throw the ball to the bowler, throw the ball to the wicket keeper, throw the ball directly at the stumps with the hope that they make contact and the batsman is not back in one of the creases. If the bowler fails to grasp the thrown ball and it runs away from him, if the same things happen to the wicket keeper, the batsmen run again. Every time they run after the ball escapes the person to whom it is thrown [overthrows], runs are added to the score of the batsman who hit the ball. If the ball thrown directly at the stumps hits them, continues to travel away from any fielder, but a batsman close to those stumps is not out of his crease, then that batsman usually calls on his partner to run again. Once again, the batsman who hit the ball is credited with more runs. If the thrown ball travels all the way to the boundary then the batsman is credited with four runs.

Rabbit: A term used to describe some tail-enders. The term, rabbit, is used often with negatives to indicate that a few tail-enders can, at times, produce decent scores—perhaps [30], [50], or even between [60] and [75] runs. Some tail-enders have scored centuries in Test Matches.

Return catch: When a batsman strikes a ball delivered by a bowler and he hits it in the direction of the bowler without the ball touching the ground and the bowler catches that ball, a return catch is taken.

Run out: One way in which a batsman can be out. He is said to be out in this fashion if in trying to complete a run to the other side of the pitch he fails to reach his crease before a fielder throws the ball hit by him or his partner and it hits the stumps. He is run out also under conditions: if a fielder throws the ball to the bowler or wicket keeper and one of them hits the stumps before he reaches his crease, if the bowler gets the ball that is hit before he or his partner reaches the crease at the bowler's end of the pitch. Batsmen—even the best—are run out many times as a result of misunderstanding their partner's call for a run. On some occasions, the best of batsmen are left stranded at quite some distance down the pitch. When this happens, or at any time a run out decision is made by an umpire, only one batsman's innings [time at the crease] has ended. In the Laws of cricket, two batsmen cannot be out run out at the same time. Some run outs are very obvious. In other cases batsmen are out of their crease by just a few inches. The umpires, who are in the best positions to see and judge where a batsman is positioned when close to the crease, render their decisions in response to appeals from fielders. If, in their view, the batsman is run out, the index finger is raised.

Short leg: A fielding position very close to the batsman on strike in the position where both hands of the clock are between the numbers one and two. Short leg, not unlike silly mid-off and silly mid-on, is a "bat-pad" fielding position.

Sightscreens: Two huge white screens positioned at northern and southern ends of cricket grounds on boundaries directly behind the pitch. Bowlers are seen by batsmen running from the position of these screens towards them. The principal purpose for the erection of sightscreens when Test Matches are played is to enable batsmen to see, without difficulty, the brown or dark beet red ball which is being delivered, especially by very fast bowlers. Whenever a bowler—especially a quick bowler—is bowling to a batsman, no spectator is supposed to be moving in any position in front of the sight screen. Such does however happen, and the batsman's concentration is disrupted. When it does, batsmen are quick to spot it, they raise a hand upright which an umpire, and, sometimes, a bowler notices. The umpire stops the bowler, and the process of bowling begins again. Under the Laws of cricket, no fielder can be placed directly behind the bowler. Such a placement also disrupts the concentration of batsmen. Pitches on cricket grounds are, of course, laid so that umpires, batsmen, bowlers, and wicketkeepers face north and south to avoid the setting late afternoon sun impeding their vision.

Silly mid-off: For a right handed batsman another position very close to the batsman on strike located well within the inner rim of the circle just after the number, 8. on the clock. Silly mid-on is the opposite. The fielder is again very close, well within the inner circle just after the number, 4.

Single: When batsmen run once from one end of the pitch to the other, one run or a single is earned by the batsman who hit the ball bowled. When they run twice, two runs—not a double—are earned. Running on three occasions will bring three runs—not a triple. When batsmen hit the ball to far corners of the cricket ground and fielders have to run considerable distances to get it, some quick runners run four times. There are, of course, occasions on which batsmen are not quick enough, and even before they can run to the other side of the pitch some excellent fielders pick up the balls they hit and return them to either the bowler or wicket keeper in a flash and batsmen are not in their crease. Such batsmen are adjudged by umpires on appeal to be run out.

Square leg: A fielding position just next to the square leg umpire.

Tail, tail end batsmen, tailenders: Batsmen who are not selected for their batting and are not expected to score many runs. They are usually positioned to bat at numbers eight, nine, ten, and eleven. The tail in a batting side is usually made up of players selected for their bowling. Such batsmen are not usually described as rabbits.

The toss: Before every Test Match begins, the two captains walk out to the pitch in full view of the spectators and commentators to spin a coin for the purpose of determining which team shall bat first. A captain who wins the toss does not, necessarily, bat first. He who wins the toss has the choice of batting first or using his right to ask the losing captain to bat first. Captains who win the toss usually bat first if they reason that the pitch/wicket is very good for batting, the weather conditions are not overcast, or there is no moisture in the pitch/wicket. In overcast conditions, many astute captains reckon that the ball, especially from quick/fast bowlers, will move laterally in the air, and such movement will contribute to the doom of batsmen. If there are grounds for a captain who wins the toss to reason that there is moisture in the pitch, although it is protected from rain that has fallen the night before the beginning of a game, he usually asks the loser of the toss to bat. It is also the case that a captain who has at his disposal four terrifyingly quick fast bowlers will ask the opposing captain to bat when he wins the toss, even if conditions are not overcast and there is no assumption and reasoning that the pitch contains moisture. Such a disposition, which has been implemented repeatedly by West Indies captains who spearheaded ferocious quick bowling quartets, has led to the ignominious defeats of opponents. It is, of course, the case that a captain who reasons correctly that a pitch is very good for batting, a placid pitch, a wicket full of runs, a batsman's paradise, will bat first with the aim of his team making a huge first innings total and in a strong position to enforce the follow-on.

Twelfth man: In a Test Match each team is made up of eleven players and a twelfth man. The twelfth man is not allowed to bat or bowl, but is usually called upon by his captain to field if one of the eleven is hurt or leaves the field for other reasons. Through their excellent fielding, some cricketers in the position of twelfth man have contributed to the dismissal of batsmen by having them caught or assisting in running them out.

Umbrella Field: This is a term that was once used quite frequently to describe attacking fields which were often set for very fast bowlers, such as Lindwall, Miller, Trueman, Statham,

Tyson, Hall, Griffith, Lillee, Thompson, Daniel, Holding, Marshall, Croft, Roberts, and Garner. While looking at an umbrella field, an observer can connect the various fielding positions by using a set of lines which when drawn appear to be umbrella shaped. Thus, when the captain of a fielding side uses three slips, two gullies, a silly-mid off and mid-on, point (short), and leg slip, he has set an umbrella field. A straight line from the wicket keeper's position to the bowler's end completes the umbrella shape.

Wicket keeper: One of the eleven players on the fielding team. His position is behind the three stumps and batsmen who have to face balls/deliveries bowled by bowlers. He crouches or stoops to "gather" or "collect" balls which batsmen either do not try to hit or try to hit but do not make contact. He stands at the very end of the minute hand on the clock where the time is six o'clock. If a very speedy fast bowler is bowling, the wicket keeper has to stand at considerable distance behind the stumps to gather or collect the ball without it dropping or slipping out of his hands onto the ground. If a spin bowler is operating, he crouches or stoops very close to the stumps ["stands up"] mainly to take advantage of a batman being out of his crease and getting him out stumped or waiting for a catch from an edge. In some instances, when there is a thick edge, the ball cannons into the bat on a batsman's front foot and pops up rather gently. Agile wicket keepers run from behind and take such catches regularly. So do fielders at silly mid-off or silly mid-on/the "bat-pad" positions. Virtually all Test Match wicketkeepers, who clearly know how their team bowlers want the ball to deviate, position themselves slightly to their left or right according to the expected deviation and usually do not place themselves in a straight line behind the stumps.

Wide: A delivery bowled that a batsman with his outstretched bat and moving feet cannot reach. The umpire who signals a wide to the scorer raises both arms and extends them in full horizontal positions. A wide is signalled, and one run is added to the EXTRAS—not the batsman's score—even if the wicket keeper gathers/collects the ball. If the wicket keeper does not gather/collect the ball and it reaches the boundary, four EXTRAS/WIDES are added to the score.

Yorker: A ball delivered by a pace/quick/fast bowler or a medium paced bowler to a batsman which is pitched in a position almost under the very bottom of his bat. The bowler who bowls a yorker aims to pitch the ball so that when the batsman lifts his bat to play a stroke the ball passes in the tiny space between the turf and the hoisted bat then hits the stumps to the doom of the batsman. Yorkers are bowled to swing into or away from batsmen. They are also bowled without deviating. Sometimes they do hit the stumps, but batsmen survive, because bowlers bowl no balls in their extra effort to deliver the balls strategically. Fred Trueman, the great England pace bowler, was a yorker expert. When he bowled his yorkers very few of the best batsmen survived.

ALSO AVAILABLE FROM BLACK ROSE BOOKS

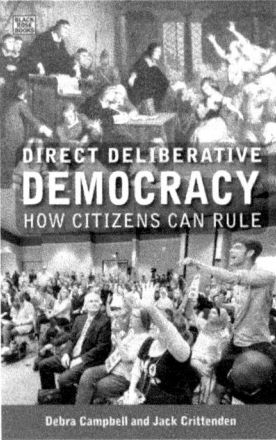

Direct Deliberative Democracy:
How Citizens Can Rule
Debra Campbell and Jack Crittenden
Paperback: 9781551646695
Hardcover: 9781551646718
Ebook: 9781551646732

Militarism and Anti-Militarism
Karl Liebknecht
Paperback: 9781551643403
Hardcover: 9781551643410

Friendly Fascism:
The New Face of Power in America
Bertram Gross
Paperback: 9780920057230
Hardcover: 9780920057223

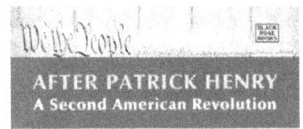

After Patrick Henry:
A Second American Revolution
Neal Herrick
Paperback: 9781551643205
Hardcover: 9781551643212

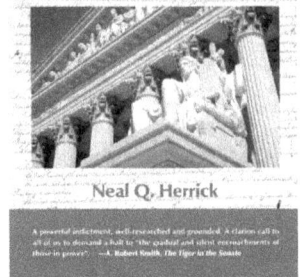

www.ingramcontent.com/pod-product-compliance
Lightning Source LLC
Chambersburg PA
CBHW070549270326
41926CB00013B/2255